Library of
Davidson College

THE DEFENSE OF THE WEST

Also of Interest

†*Defense Facts of Life: The Plans/Reality Mismatch*, Franklin C. Spinney, edited and with commentary by James Clay Thompson

Military Strategy in Transition: Defense and Deterrence in the 1980s, edited by Keith A. Dunn and William O. Staudenmaier

†*Arms Control and International Security*, edited by Roman Kolkowicz and Neil Joeck

†*Thinking About National Security: Defense and Foreign Policy in a Dangerous World*, Harold Brown

†*Military Power and the Advance of Technology: General Purpose Military Forces for the 1980s and Beyond*, Seymour J. Deitchman

U.S. Military Power and Rapid Deployment Requirements in the 1980s, Sherwood S. Cordier

The Politics of Resource Allocation in the U.S. Department of Defense, Alex Mintz

The Half War: Planning U.S. Rapid Deployment Forces to Meet a Limited Contingency, 1960–1983, Robert P. Haffa, Jr.

Soviet Nuclear Weapons Policy: A Research Guide, William C. Green

†*The Soviet Art of War: Doctrine, Strategy, and Tactics*, edited by Harriet Fast Scott and William F. Scott

†*U.S. Defense Planning: A Critique*, John M. Collins

†Available in hardcover and paperback.

A Westview Special Study

The Defense of the West: Strategic and European Security Issues Reappraised
edited by Robert Kennedy and John M. Weinstein

Drawing on their daily involvement with defense issues and their interactions with the military and political elements of the national security community, civilian and military defense analysts in the U.S. Army War College's Strategic Studies Institute offer a lucid analysis of the complex mosaic of strategic and European defense issues. Their contributions are probing, balanced, and provocative, designed for students of foreign and defense affairs, as well as for policymakers.

In the first section of the book, the offensive and defensive aspects of the strategic balance between the United States and the Soviet Union are examined. Going beyond sterile, static weapons counts, the authors address the relationship between the overall disposition of military forces and deterrence and are attentive to possible future developments, including the impact of new technologies and changing Sino-Soviet relations that are likely to affect the U.S.–USSR relationship.

The second section of the book focuses on crucial East-West defense issues within Europe: the balance of conventional and theater nuclear forces, prospects for European arms control, the impact of chemical weapons on deterrence and defense, and the fashioning of an effective nonnuclear NATO defense. The book concludes with a chapter that illuminates U.S.–West European historical and cultural divergences, explaining in a new way the political strains that frequently plague the alliance.

Dr. Robert Kennedy has published articles on national security issues in a variety of professional journals. He is professor of military strategy in the Department of National Security at the U.S. Army War College, where formerly he was a senior researcher at the Strategic Studies Institute. **Dr. John M. Weinstein,** author of numerous articles on Soviet and U.S. strategic matters, is a strategic nuclear forces analyst on the Army General Staff. He has taught at several colleges and universities and served as a visiting research professor at the U.S. Army War College's Strategic Studies Institute.

THE DEFENSE OF THE WEST

Strategic and European Security Issues Reappraised

edited by Robert Kennedy
and John M. Weinstein

Westview Press / Boulder and London

355.03
D3133

A Westview Special Study

All rights reserved. No part of this publication may be reproduced or transmitted in any form or by any means, electronic or mechanical, including photocopy, recording, or any information storage and retrieval system, without permission in writing from the publisher.

Copyright © 1984 by Westview Press, Inc.

Published in 1984 in the United States of America by Westview Press, Inc., 5500 Central Avenue, Boulder, Colorado 80301; Frederick A. Praeger, Publisher

Library of Congress Catalog Card Number 84-51278
ISBN 0-86531-612-0
ISBN 0-86531-613-9 (pbk.)

86-215

Composition for this book was provided by the editors
Printed and bound in the United States of America

10   9   8   7   6   5   4   3   2   1

CONTENTS

List of Tables and Figures ix
Preface xi

PART 1 — STRATEGIC ISSUES 1

1 THE CHANGING STRATEGIC BALANCE
  AND US DEFENSE PLANNING
     by Robert Kennedy 5

2 ALL FEATURES GRATE AND STALL:
  SOVIET STRATEGIC VULNERABILITIES
  AND THE FUTURE OF DETERRENCE
     by John M. Weinstein 39

3 THE STRATEGIC IMPLICATIONS OF
  CIVIL DEFENSE
     by John M. Weinstein 77

4 CHINA AND THE GREAT POWER BALANCE
     by Todd R. Starbuck 117

5 BALLISTIC MISSILE DEFENSE, SPACE-
  BASED WEAPONS, AND THE DEFENSE
  OF THE WEST
     by Daniel S. Papp 157

6 START: PROBLEMS AND PROSPECTS
     by Robert Kennedy 185

PART 2 — EUROPEAN SECURITY ISSUES ... 223

7 SOVIET THEATER NUCLEAR CAPABILITIES: THE EUROPEAN NUCLEAR BALANCE IN TRANSITION
by Robert Kennedy ... 225

8 THE SOVIET THREAT TO EUROPE: PROSPECTS FOR THE 1980's
by Otto P. Chaney ... 259

9 CHEMICAL WEAPONS REARMAMENT AND THE SECURITY OF EUROPE: CAN SUPPORT BE MUSTERED?
by John M. Weinstein and Henry G. Gole ... 299

10 IMPROVING EUROPE'S CONVENTIONAL DEFENSES
by Edward A. Corcoran ... 349

11 THE ONCE AND FUTURE QUEST: EUROPEAN ARMS CONTROL — ISSUES AND PROSPECTS
by William P. Boyd ... 375

12 NATO DEFENSE THROUGH EUROPEAN EYES
by Henry G. Gole ... 413

EPILOGUE
by Keith A. Barlow ... 439

Contributors ... 443
Index ... 445

TABLES AND FIGURES

TABLES

Chapter 2
Decrease in Growth of Soviet Gross Domestic
    Product (GDP) 44
Soviet Production Shortfalls 45
Russians versus Central Asians: Age Comparison 53

Chapter 7
Short Range Nuclear Systems 232
Shorter Range Intermediate Nuclear Forces (SR/INF) 234
Longer Range Intermediate Nuclear Forces (LR/INF) 236

Chapter 8
Non-Soviet Warsaw Pact Divisional Strength 262
Ground Forces Available in Peacetime 262
Comparative Divisional Compositions 264
The Central European Balance 264

Chapter 9
Actual and Projected US Expenditures
    for Chemical Weapons 314
World War I Chemical Warfare Casualties/Fatalities 318
Estimated Potencies of Selected CW Agents 340
Persistency of Selected Liquid CW Agents 340

Chapter 11
Summary of MBFR Proposals, 1973-1983 390

FIGURES

Chapter 3
USSR Map: Concentration of Soviet Industry 87
USSR Map: Concentration of Great Russian
  Population, Industry and Strategic Forces 91

Chapter 5
BMD and ASAT Expenditures from Fiscal 1982
  to Fiscal 1985, in Millions of Dollars 163
Number of Space-Based Lasers Required
  to Provide Constant Launch Site Coverage,
  According to Different ICBM Hardness 172

Chapter 8
Likely Warsaw Pact Axes of Advance in an
  Attack Against NATO 270

PREFACE

No two issues have dominated the postwar defense debate more than the Soviet-American strategic nuclear competition and the defense of Western Europe. And no two defense issues have been more interrelated.

World War II confirmed for the United States a lesson that had been resisted since Washington's Farewell Address—namely, the fact that US security was intimately linked to that of Europe. This postwar transatlantic security perspective provided the rationale for the formation of the North Atlantic Treaty Organization as a bulwark against the threat of Soviet expansionism. The West, unprepared to match the conventional might of the Soviet Union on the Continent, embraced America's dominance in atomic power as a relatively inexpensive guarantor of Western security. However, the Soviet Union's August 29, 1949 detonation of an atomic weapon challenged America's security at the most fundamental level while shattering the illusion that Western European security could be assured by an American nuclear monopoly. Henceforth, it was inevitable that the perceived balance of US-Soviet strategic nuclear might and Western European defense would be inextricably linked.

The Soviet Union's attainment of strategic parity with the United States heightened the importance of this strategic-theater linkage while making its maintenance more difficult. This difficulty is now manifest in the increasing debate on both sides of the Atlantic on US strategic force modernization, NATO initiatives to redress nuclear and conventional force imbalances, and the role of arms control in the East-West security equation.

The Defense of the West examines these crucial issues with analyses that go beyond static and sterile weapons counts and reflects a philosophy that "strategic" issues dealing exclusively with military force levels are defined too narrowly. The authors, all former or current analysts at the US Army War College's Strategic Studies Institute, combine their professional experience and daily interactions with the national security community to provide insightful analyses of these momentous issues. The views, opinions, and/or findings contained in this volume, however, are those of the individual authors and should not be construed as an official Department of the Army or Department of Defense position, policy, or decision unless so designated by other official documentation.

Our grateful appreciation for assisting in preparing this volume is extended to the staff of the Strategic Studies Institute and its director, Col. Keith A. Barlow. We also thank the faculty of the Institute and of the US Army War College, and others in Washington and abroad who, through their thoughtful suggestions, have contributed significantly to this undertaking. In addition, special thanks are due to Mrs. Marianne P. Cowling and Mr. Charles W. Taylor, the Institute's publications editors.

ROBERT KENNEDY Carlisle, PA	JOHN M. WEINSTEIN Washington, DC

PART 1
STRATEGIC ISSUES

The unrelenting growth of Soviet strategic nuclear power over the past two decades and concurrent perceptions of a decline in the ability of the United States to exercise the degree of influence on world affairs it did in the immediate postwar era have created serious concerns over the changing US-Soviet strategic relationship. Today, defense specialists are divided over the nature of the change which has taken place as well as the efforts that must be undertaken if security and stability are to characterize the US-Soviet relationship and if Western interests are not to be placed in jeopardy.

In this first section, the authors address the many aspects of the newly developing American-Soviet strategic relationship. In the section's opening essay, Robert Kennedy examines the nature of and objectives behind the continuing buildup of Soviet strategic nuclear forces. He concludes that while the Soviet Union *may* be seeking some "margin of superiority," deterrence of nuclear war remains a preeminent Soviet objective. Kennedy further contends that while US land-based strategic retaliatory forces have become more vulnerable to a Soviet preemptive attack, the Soviet Union does not yet have the capability to execute a disarming "first-strike." In short, Kennedy maintains that the strategic balance is rather robust. Nevertheless, he believes that the United States must begin now to revamp completely its strategic forces while simultaneously engaging the USSR in serious arms control efforts if future strategic instabilities are to be avoided.

John Weinstein examines Soviet strategic weaknesses and vulnerabilities. According to Weinstein, there is no doubt that the massive Soviet military buildup undermines deterrence and stability. However, it is important to recognize that deterrence is a state of mind that incorporates more than quantitative force balances and asymmetries. He concludes that while it would be imprudent and potentially cataclysmic to overemphasize Moscow's political, economic, and military weaknesses, recognition of those weaknesses is crucial to the fashioning of sensible and effective policies for dealing with our principal adversary.

In the next essay, Weinstein builds on his understanding of Soviet vulnerabilities and explores the relationship between civil defense and deterrence, and strategic stability. He analyzes the problems and potential effectiveness of Soviet, as well as US, civil defense programs and concludes that while civil defense measures are likely to reduce the number of casualties suffered in a nuclear war, they would not contribute much to making nuclear war a feasible policy option. Central to his thesis is that one must not confuse biological survival with national survival. Nevertheless, Weinstein holds that since Americans *will* evacuate high risk areas in the event of a nuclear crisis, it remains the responsibility of the government to minimize the chaos and deleterious effects with prior planning. Thus, the United States should undertake a modest population evacuation civil defense program.

No collection of essays on the US-Soviet strategic relationship would be complete without an exploration of the role China plays in the superpower balance. In this regard, Todd Starbuck identifies the relevant national interests and security objectives of the United States, the Soviet Union, and China. He then analyzes the near-term implications of China's increasingly independent international strategy for Sino-Soviet relations, US-China relations, and the US-Soviet military balance. Finally, he examines China's potential as a world power in the year 2000 and concludes that its emergence on the global stage may create a tripolar balance of power by the end of this century.

Daniel Papp explores the technical feasibility and future deterrent utility of strategic defense. He believes that strategic defensive measures present American and Western security planning with a staggering number of possibilities. According to Papp, however, the uncertainties pertaining to future ballistic missile defense technologies, the unknown deployment constraints, and potential costs make acquisition decisions highly problematic. Indeed, except in the improbable circumstance in which the United States and the Soviet Union deploy strategic defensive systems simultaneously, the deployment of such systems is likely to lead to instability. Thus, Papp concludes, a major effort to deploy strategic defensive systems is clearly a double-edged sword. Consequently, the United States would do well to reexamine the merits of current strategic defensive initiatives as well as to explore the potential for effective arms limitations in this area.

In the closing essay Robert Kennedy examines the problems associated with attempts to limit strategic armaments. Despite the myriad difficulties, however, strategic arms limitations are as much a political act as they are a function of overcoming technical complexities. And while the political environments in Moscow and Washington suggest that the superpowers may be impelled toward agreement in the near future, Kennedy finds little evidence that the goals set in Washington or the Kremlin have been framed as part of a long-term strategy to secure balance and stability at the strategic level. Thus, although an agreement may be reached, the United States and the Soviet Union will continue to be disappointed with the results.

1

THE CHANGING STRATEGIC BALANCE AND US DEFENSE PLANNING

Robert Kennedy

On March 31, 1982 President Reagan, addressing the US-Soviet strategic nuclear relationship, asserted that the Soviet Union had achieved a "definite margin of superiority."[1] Previous presidents had been concerned about the growth of the Soviet strategic arsenal. Indeed, President Reagan had warned earlier that the United States was entering a period known as the "window of vulnerability,"[2] in which its land-based missile forces would be increasingly vulnerable to a Soviet preemptive first strike. This was, however, the first time an American president had suggested that the United States had actually fallen behind the Soviet Union in strategic might.

The President's assessment was quickly challenged.[3] James R. Schlesinger, Secretary of Defense during the Ford Administration, and Zbigniew Brzezinski, National Security Advisor to President Carter, felt that the President had overstated the case. Dr. Schlesinger, noting the differences in the strategic arsenals of the two superpowers, said that these differences made it virtually impossible to determine which side was stronger. He said, "Neither side has superiority. It is a standoff."[4] Similarly, Dr. Brzezinski stated that "the situation is one of ambiguous equivalence."[5] Even Senator Henry Jackson, known for his tough stance toward the Soviet Union and strong support for defense, criticized the

President, arguing that US quantitative advantages in bombers and nuclear [weapons aboard] missile carry submarines balanced Soviet advantages in heavy intercontinental ballistic missiles (ICBMs).[6] Despite such criticisms, the President's remark seemed to lend credibility to those who had warned that, as a result of the inadequate defense policies of previous administrations, the United States was rapidly becoming the inferior superpower.

The United States, indeed the entire Western world, had watched apprehensively the development of Soviet nuclear capabilities ever since the USSR exploded its first atomic weapon in 1949. From the mid- to late 1960's, however, the unrelenting building of Soviet strategic power has been viewed with increasing alarm. Indeed, in the latter years of the Carter presidency, while the administration maintained that US and Soviet strategic forces were roughly equal in strategic capability, official statements reflected a mounting uneasiness over Soviet intentions and strategic capabilities and emphasized the need to modernize US strategic forces in order to reduce the vulnerability of these forces to preemptive attack.[7] Thus, President Reagan's assessment brought to sharp focus more than a decade and a half of increasing concern over the implications of the growing Soviet strategic arsenal.

SOVIET INTENTIONS

The current debate over Soviet strategic objectives can be traced to the findings of the so-called Team B, a team of "outsiders" which was asked to assist in the preparation of the 1976 National Intelligence Estimate (NIE) on the Soviet Union.[8] According to the newspaper reports, the 1976 NIE stated flatly that, in the majority's view, the Soviet Union was seeking strategic superiority. This judgment ran counter to all previous national estimates of Soviet intentions since 1950, which had apparently concluded the Soviet Union was seeking rough parity.[9] It also appeared to contradict those who had argued that the Soviet Union had accepted some variant of MAD with its emphasis on deterrence and stability.

The NIE reflected, in part, a number of concerns increasingly voiced by Major General George J. Keegan, Jr., Paul Nitze and others in and outside of government. General Keegan, then Chief of Air Force Intelligence, intrigued by the findings of Albert

Wohlstetter in his "Legends of the Strategic Arms Race"[10] and reflecting on the evidence that Air Force Intelligence had assembled, had been arguing that a formal audit be conducted of every NIE produced since the first. He believed that such an audit would reveal that the intelligence community not only had consistently underestimated Soviet strategic nuclear capabilities (as Wohlstetter had contended), but that such an audit would reveal that the Soviet Union was pursuing superiority.[11]

Like Keegan, Paul Nitze was also becoming concerned over growing Soviet strategic power. Nitze, who had served as a member of the US SALT delegation from 1969 to 1974 and as Deputy Secretary of Defense for two years before that, had been skeptical of Soviet intentions since the days of NSC-68.[12] As Soviet strategic power continued to grow so did Nitze's concern over the US inability to understand and meet the challenge. In March 1976 Nitze and others of similar mind formed the Committee on the Present Danger. Nitze was designated chairman of the Committee's policy studies and in its first statement the Committee made clear its view of Soviet intentions. The Committee warned that the principal threat to world peace was the Soviet drive for dominance based on an unparalleled military buildup.[13] Nitze believed that the SALT II Agreement then being fashioned was an inadequate constraint on the Soviet Union's strategic nuclear capabilities. He also believed that the Soviet Union was pursuing a war-winning capability designed to give them a strategic advantage they would be "duty bound" to exploit.[14]

In the wake of his participation on Team B, Professor Richard Pipes offered further support for such views. In a seminal piece in *Commentary* in 1977, Pipes suggested that differences between American and Soviet strategies are traceable to different conceptions of the role of conflict and its inevitable concomitant, violence in human relations; and secondly to different functions which the military establishment performs in the two societies.[15] He contended that

> The Soviet ruling elite regards conflict and violence as natural regulators of all human affairs: wars between nations, in its view, represent only a variant of wars between classes....[16]

The strategic implications of such a view of conflict, according to Pipes, is a rejection by Soviet leadership of the Western view that nuclear war is unthinkable and that the application of force is *prima facie* evidence of failure of rational analysis and patient negotiations. Rather, according to Pipes, the Soviet Union views war, even nuclear warfare, according to Clausewitz's classic dictum—that war is politics pursued by other means.

Pipes further argued that support within the Soviet Union for large offensive forces and the rejection of the theory of mutual deterrence is driven by a combination of political, institutional, and technical factors. Lacking a tradition and a popular mandate, the Soviet elite needs and wants a large armed forces which serve as the mainstay of the regime's authority. At a time when its ideology is declining in appeal and its goods are noncompetitive in world markets, the Soviet Union sees large forces as the principal instrument of its external policies.[17] For this reason alone, Pipes argued

> ...the Soviet leadership could not accept the theory of mutual deterrence. After all, this theory, pushed to its logical conclusion, means that a country can rely for its security on a finite number of nuclear warheads and on an appropriate quantity of delivery vehicles; so that, apart perhaps from some small mobile forces needed for local actions, the large and costly traditional military establishments can be disbanded.[18]

Pipes also identified other reasons that compel Soviet strategists to reject Western notions of mutual deterrence. First, mutual deterrence does not acknowledge the potential instability resulting from technological breakthroughs which may undermine a deterrent. Second, mutual deterrence is "passive." It only threatens punishment to an aggressor after he has struck. The preferable objective of physically negating an attack requires an "active defense," i.e., damage limitation through nuclear preemption. Third, the threat of a second strike may prove ineffectual. The side subject to a first strike may be deterred from retaliation by the threat of the enemy's third strike. Therefore, Pipes opined that Soviet strategists "make no secret of the fact that they regard US doctrine...as second rate." Soviet doctrine, in Pipes' view, calls for victory, not deterrence; superiority, not sufficiency in weapons; and offensive action, not retaliation.[19]

SOVIET INTENTIONS: AN ALTERNATE VIEW

Must one interpret current Soviet force postures and strategic weapons programs in the manner of Pipes and others? Must one conclude, as has Colin Gray, that the Soviet Union does not seem to believe in "crisis stability?"[20] Indeed, the weight of evidence in open Soviet literature suggests the contrary.

Soviet thinking on war has undergone evolutionary development. Following the emergence of the Soviet socialist state, Communist dogma generally held that war between rival social systems was inevitable. Lenin underscored this point.

> We are living not merely in a state, but *in a system of states,* and it is inconceivable for the Soviet Republic to exist alongside of the imperialist states for any length of time. One or the other must triumph in the end. And before the end comes there will have to be a series of frightful collisions between the Soviet Republic and the bourgeois states.[21]

Lenin further embraced the Clausewitzian dictum that war is a continuation of politics by other measures. War was viewed as a catalyst for the inevitable advance of socialism throughout the world.

The advent of the nuclear weapon, however, had a substantial impact on Soviet thinking. By the mid-1950's, concern was being expressed over the implications of the "inevitable conflict" in the nuclear age. In 1954, Soviet Premier Georgiy Malenkov wrote that nuclear warfare could result in the mutual destruction of both the capitalist and communist societies[22] and therefore warranted a serious reconsideration of the Leninist conception of war as precursor of world revolution. While Nikita Khrushchev initially opposed Malenkov's unorthodox views, by 1961, he warned that "within 60 days of an atomic attack 500 million to 750 million people could perish." Krushchev concluded that a "sober calculation of the inevitable consequence of nuclear war is an indispensible requirement for pursuing a consistent policy of preventing war."[23]

Since then, the avoidance of strategic nuclear conflict has become a central theme of Soviet public policy.[24] War no longer is considered an inevitable consequence of the struggle between diverging social systems.[25] Rather than believing that nuclear war is a "feasible instrument" of policy, Soviet civilian and military analysts have come to view strategic nuclear conflict as an enormously dangerous endeavor with a high potential for unprecedented disaster.[26] Fritz Ermarth has noted that

> For a generation, the relevant elites of both the United States and the Soviet Union have agreed that an unlimited strategic nuclear war would be a sociopolitical disaster of immense proportions.[27]

The Soviet delegation, in its prepared statement presented at the first business meeting of the two SALT delegations in Helsinki in November 1969, expressed the then official Soviet view, one strikingly similar to the US assured destruction precept:

> ...even in the event that one of the sides were the first subjected to attack, it would undoubtedly retain the ability to inflict a retaliatory strike of crushing power. Thus, evidently, we all agree that war between our two countries would be disastrous for both sides. And it would be tantamount to suicide for the ones who decided to start such a war.[28]

Since then, senior Soviet leadership has expressed similar views.[29] What then is it that accounts for the seemingly different American and Soviet force postures and strategic doctrine?[30] Dennis Ross has offered one answer:

> ...the fact that there is a general distinctiveness between Soviet strategic nuclear doctrine and American deterrence perspectives...should not be taken to mean that deterrence is not the Soviet military's primary mission.[31]

Ross argued that while the United States has adopted an approach to deterrence based on the promise of punishing an aggressor should deterrence fail, the Soviet Union has opted for deterrence through denying the enemy any possibility of a military success.[32] John Erickson and Robert Legvold hold similar although not identical views. Erickson writes that for the Soviet Union, defense and deterrence go hand in hand. Military power is seen by Soviet leadership as a major instrument for impressing the "imperialist camp" that military means cannot solve the historical struggle between the two opposing social systems. Erickson concludes that in the context of deterrent theory, the United States has embraced a concept of "deterrence by punishment," while the Soviet position is one of "deterrence by denial."[33] Similarly, Legvold has written that deterrence, "For the Soviet Union is a residual concept, an effect produced by performing other primary tasks as well, tasks involving a deft foreign policy and a carefully prepared defense."[34]

Indeed, rather than signaling a rejection of deterrence as Pipes has suggested, current Soviet force postures and strategic doctrine reflect a different approach to a deterrence and strategic planning.

Soviet theoreticians view complex American concepts of deterrence, extended deterrence, limited nuclear options, intrawar deterrence, and deescalation as attempts to impose those rules of crises and conflict behavior that maximize the advantages enjoyed by the United States, while minimizing Soviet capabilities.[35] Moreover, they consider such concepts to be dangerously destabilizing. Instead of controlling escalation during crisis or conflict, Soviet leaders view Western concepts of deterrence as making more likely the use of nuclear weapons, and thus as contributing to the potential for that very devastating nuclear exchange which both they and the United States wish to avoid.

In other words, the Soviet elites have rejected specific American conceptualizations of deterrence. Instead they have concluded that deterrence of nuclear conflict is best served by strategic doctrines and carefully prepared strategic forces which promise to deny a potential aggressor any hope of success. Such a deterrent demands not only an active capacity to attack the enemy's war-fighting capability, but also an ability to blunt the enemy's attack through home defense measures. On this, highly regarded Rand analyst, Benjamin Lambeth, who specializes in Soviet political and military affairs, has written:

> ...although Soviet forces and concepts reflect an undeniable combat orientation, their principal purpose remains deterrence rather than war. The fact that, through tradition and preference the Soviets have sought security in hedges against failures of deterrence...in no way bespeaks any underlying predisposition to put those hedges to the test.[36]

Such an approach to deterrence would be consistent with Soviet ideological predispositions. The Soviet Union believes nuclear war is possible so long as "imperialism" exists. While Soviet leaders have discarded Lenin's and Stalin's views concerning the inevitability of conflict, they believe that inevitable Socialist successes may make the "imperialists" desperate enough to unleash a nuclear war, believing they can reverse the course of history.

Deterrence through denial also would be congruent with Soviet political and institutional pressures for large armed forces and conceptually consistent with traditional military approaches to potential conflicts. On the first point, the forces required to insure deterrence through punishment can be empirically determined, and thus be limited to those necessary to inflict a specific degree of punishment. But the forces required for a denial strategy are likely to be more open-ended, as they always require a greater quantity than foreseen in the most pessimistic estimates of the adversary's future capabilities. On the second point, a deterrent posture that calls for war-winning and damage-limiting capabilities is consistent with traditional views of the military missions of insuring success in warfare and protecting populations and government structures.

Finally, such a Soviet approach to deterrence is reminiscent of the one so often advocated in the United States during the 1950's and early 1960's.[37] Indeed, it is not unlike the approach taken by those who have argued the case for the further development of US counterforce capabilities since then.[38] Nor is it unlike the rationale that has driven US strategic targeting doctrine as reflected in the US Single Integrated Operational Plan (SIOP) for over two decades. On this point, Harold Brown noted in his Annual Report for fiscal year 1981:

> It has never been US policy to limit ourselves to massive counter-city options in retaliation, nor have our plans been so circumscribed. For nearly 20 years, we have explicitly included a range of employment options—against military as well as non-military targets—in our strategic nuclear employment planning.[39]

He went on to note that there was no contradiction between such an attention to militarily effective war-fighting capabilities and our "primary and overriding policy of deterrence." According to Brown:

> Deterrence, by definition, depends on shaping an adversary's prediction of the likely outcome of a war. Our surest deterrent is our capability to deny gain from aggression (by any measure of gain)....[40]

To argue that Soviet leaders reject nuclear warfare as a "feasible" instrument of policy and consider deterrence of nuclear conflict a paramount political and military objective is not to suggest that they reject the notion that strategic superiority, or at least the appearance of superiority, may yield tangible political benefits. Nor is it to suggest that the Soviet Union does not view military power as *a*, if not *the*, central instrument in its plans to shape the world in its own image. Soviet leaders may not be seeking active strategic superiority to execute a comprehenive preemptive first strike. Indeed some Soviet theorists contend that such a capability is unattainable, given the diversity of forces available to the United States.[41] However, the Kremlin does believe the United States enjoyed a measure of political leverage during the period of its unquestioned strategic superiority. Soviet leaders also believe military advantage creates political opportunity in what is surely a continuing long-term struggle to preserve their interests and extend their influence throughout the world.[42]

Furthermore, to argue that the Soviets emphasize deterrence is not to suggest that a deterrence which relies on damage limitation and an active capacity to attack the enemy's war-fighting capabilities is nonthreatening. Unchecked, such a deterrent capability may lead Soviet leaders to believe that the Soviets could successfully eliminate a large portion of America's retaliatory capability before it was launched and could further reduce damage to the Soviet Union to acceptable levels through civil and air defense measures. As a result, Soviet leadership may be emboldened as the Soviets come to believe that they possess some measure of "escalation dominance." More importantly, however, during a severe crisis, when confronted with what they may perceive as an imminent strategic exchange, Soviet leaders might be tempted to initiate a strategic nuclear exchange that otherwise might have been avoided.

Any Soviet decision to resort to the use of nuclear weapons, however, would depend on the capabilities of their strategic forces as well as on relative US and Soviet vulnerabilities. Therefore, let us now turn our attention to Soviet strategic capabilities and the uncertainties that would confront Soviet leaders in a strategic crisis.

SOVIET CAPABILITIES

To even the casual observer, it is patently clear that the relative balance of strategic nuclear power has changed drastically over the last twenty years. In November 1963, the International Institute for Strategic Studies (IISS) reported in its annual tabulations of the American and Soviet military balance that the USSR had about 100 single warhead ICBMs, about 190 Bear and Bison strategic aircraft, and 30 or so missile carrying submarines. The in-service rate of their ICBMs was low. Many of their ICBMs did not have storable liquid fuel and thus had to be fueled before they could be launched. Their missile carrying submarine fleet was of questionable capability. Their boats were noisy and subject to detection and tracking; many had to surface to fire the two or three missiles they carried. In contrast, the United States had 234 Atlas and Titan missiles with 800 solid-fueled Minuteman ICBMs due to be in place in hardened underground silos by the middle of 1965. It also had about 1300 strategic bombers and ten nuclear submarines (SSBNs) each carrying 16 Polaris submarine launched ballistic missiles (SLBMs) capable of being fired from submerged locations, with eight more Polaris submarines scheduled to enter service before mid-1964. The balance of strategic striking power, which clearly favored the United States, led the IISS to conclude unequivocally that US strategic retaliatory forces were expected to deter war with the Soviet Union by an ability to destroy Soviet war-making potential, including nuclear strike forces, military installations, and urban society.[43]

Over the past two decades, such a clear relative quantitative and qualitative advantage has disappeared. Today, the Soviet Union has 1398 ICBM launchers, over half of which are newer generation SS-17s, SS-18s, and SS-19s. These new missiles, at the forefront of ICBM technology, have a high in-service rate, can be held on alert for lengthy periods of time, are highly accurate, and are housed in hardened missile silos. Moreover, many of these new missiles have been equipped with multiple independently targetable reentry vehicles (MIRVs) and are thus capable of delivering, in some cases, as many as ten warheads on separate targets.

The USSR ballistic missile carrying submarine fleet also has been vastly improved. In the 1970's the Soviet Union first deployed its long-range (7800 Km) SS-N-8 SLBM and later the MIRVed SS-N-18 SLBM on nuclear powered Delta-class submarines. In 1979, the Soviets tested the new MIRVed SS-NX-20 SLBM which will be deployed on the new Typhoon-class SSBN.[44]

The Soviet Union also has deployed over 70 BACKFIRE bombers and is producing 30 more each year. While the BACKFIRE appears to have been given primarily theater and maritime missions, it could have a strategic capability for intercontinental attack.[45] By way of comparison, today the USSR fields 1398 ICBM and 950 SLBM launchers, and about 150 bombers, not including the BACKFIRE. The United States has about 1045 ICBM and 576 SLBM launchers, and about 300 bombers. Admittedly, the United States still maintains a slim lead in the total number of strategic warheads, but this lead is quickly disappearing.

Such static measures of US-Soviet strategic capabilities, while of concern, have not been so troubling as Soviet technological improvements in missile accuracy and the MIRVing of Soviet heavy throw-weight missiles. Such capabilities have focused attention once again on the potential for a successful Soviet "first-strike" on US retaliatory forces.

Concern over the growing vulnerabilities of US strategic forces led the United States to harden its missile forces and place some of its bombers on airborne alert in the early 1960's. Before the era of MIRV and high accuracy ICBMs, however, conventional wisdom held that the Russians would have to fire two or three missiles in order to have a high confidence of destroying one US ICBM in its silo. Thus, the Soviet Union would have had to expend its entire strategic missile force to destroy only a portion of the US land-based deterrent. Today, however, with the MIRVing and increased accuracy of Soviet missiles, some defense specialists argue that the Kremlin now can or soon will be able to destroy preemptively all but a few US ICBMs, as well as a large portion of our bombers on the ground and submarines in port.[46]

One scenario which has become fashionable is a sequence in which the Soviet Union first explodes a number of nuclear weapons 300 miles above the continental United States. These warheads would create an electromagnetic pulse (EMP) capable of destroying unprotected electrical and electronic equipment, disrupting communications over the entire continent and potentially preventing or interrupting communications between the US National Command Authority (NCA) and US retaliatory forces. If Soviet SLBMs stationed on the east coast were used, the United States would have about seven minutes from the time of launch before communications were interrupted. Next, in an effort to pin down US missile forces, the Soviet Union would detonate a series of weapons 100 miles above US ICBM fields to generate x-rays capable of damaging or destroying US missiles during their early phases of flight. Finally, highly accurate Soviet ICBMs would arrive at US ICBM sites, bomber bases and possible dispersal locations and nuclear submarine bases.[47] In the aftermath of such an attack, it is argued, given Soviet air defenses, a possible limited antiballistic missile (ABM) capability, and Soviet civil defenses, the

United States would have an insufficient number of surviving retaliatory forces capable of attacking meaningful military targets and would be discouraged from pursuing an irrational and futile counter-city exchange. Under such circumstances, the Soviet Union would have escalation dominance and an American president would surely seek political accommodation rather than a further extension of the war. Perhaps of equal concern, in a severe crisis a rational American president would be forced to choose between concession or destruction.

Such pessimistic conclusions, however, are deserving of further scrutiny. Calculations concerning the vulnerability of US retaliatory forces usually are based on theoretical mathematical models which consider missile accuracy, available warheads, warhead yields (usually expressed in megatons or kilotons of TNT), and target hardness (i.e., missile and silo resistance to blast, heat, radiation, and EMP). A number of intervening factors, however, seriously complicate the task of transforming *theoretical* capability into *operational* reality.

First, concerning missile reentry vehicle reliability, calculations concerning the overall performance of ICBMs and SLBMs under actual combat conditions must be projected from data on test firings under conditions unrepresentative of a wartime operational environment. As far as can be determined from the public record, the Soviet Union has never fired a strategic missile on short notice from an operational land-based silo or sea-based platform, has never fired an ICBM on a full polar trajectory, nor has it fired more than a few missiles simultaneously or in close coordination.[48] Generally speaking, greater care is taken to insure that systems function as designed and even then the record of Soviet as well as American missile tests is marked with some failures. While it is generally assumed that Soviet missile reliability is good, a fifteen percent failure rate would seriously complicate Soviet targeting. Of course, it would be possible, through the use of sophisticated surveillance techniques, to monitor the missile force during its boost, post-boost, and reentry phases so that back-up missiles could be programmed to replace those that failed. However, the strict requirements of attack timing, as we shall see below, raise serious questions about the effectiveness of such reprogramming as a method of compensating for missile malfunctions under wartime operational conditions.

Second, a variety of factors will affect the operational accuracy of missiles fired over intercontinental ranges. Accuracy is usually measured in terms of circular error probable (CEP) or the radius of a circle in which 50 percent of the warheads can be expected to land. Today's strategic missiles rely on inertial guidance systems to maintain their trajectory along an intended track to the target. Inherent imperfections in the gyroscopes and accelerometers, positioning and alignment errors, or errors induced by vibration and shock can result in inaccuracies which although individually small can be constant and accumulating with time, as well as random. Inertial systems also rely on a mathematical model of the earth's gravity field in order to take into account the earth's gravitational pull on the missile.[49] The earth's nonuniform sphericity, however, produces gravitational variations that could have an uncertain effect on the ballistic trajectories of warheads fired over untested polar routes. Also, thrust termination errors, upper atmospheric winds, variations in atmospheric density, anomalies in the burning rate of the reentry vehicle's ablative shield, and target positioning errors all can contribute to the uncertainties associated with missile accuracy.[50] Much has been done by the United States, and undoubtedly by the Soviet Union, to minimize the effects of such factors. Nevertheless, a degree of uncertainty remains and will continue to remain in the absence of extensive ICBM testing over polar routes at intercontinental ranges. Unlike firings on test ranges, there is no ability to "tweek" over time the guidance packages of operational ICBMs to compensate for missile guidance biases or other errors revealed as ICBM traverse untraveled courses to attack US targets.

Third, although perhaps of less consequence, there is a degree of uncertainty associated with warhead yields as well as silo hardness. Limitations on the peacetime testing of nuclear weapons have created uncertainties not only as to the precise effects of warheads of a given yield, but also on estimates of the yield of a given class of warheads. Actual warhead yield may vary from the given yield depending the extent of testing and the accuracy of scale model interpolations. Perhaps even more uncertain have been estimates of silo hardness. Such estimates are based entirely on theoretical models and scale model testing with nonnuclear explosives. Actual hardness may vary from such theoretical calculations depending on individual silo construction anomalies and characteristics of the surrounding soil and rock. Indeed, from an attacker's point of view, silo hardness may be one of the more predominant uncertainties.[51] Even if, for example, the Soviets had access to classified US estimates of the hardness of American Minuteman silos, they more than likely would be aware of the limitations of those estimates. It is also likely that they would assume that the American estimates reflected US worst-case thinking and thus represented the low end of the spectrum of uncertainty of US silo hardness. The real point here, however, is that an unfavorable variation in Soviet warhead yield such that the actual yield at detonation were 10 percent less than expected, coupled with an unfavorable variation in US silo hardness such that actual hardness were 20 percent greater than expected, might well reduce the effectiveness of a hypothetical attack by between 10 and 15 percent.

Finally, a disarming first-strike would require monumental feats of timing. While US ICBMs indeed have become more vulnerable to a Soviet first-strike, the Scowcroft Commission noted that the diversity of land, sea, and air forces comprising the US strategic Triad renders a fully disarming simultaneous strike a virtual impossibility. US submarines at sea are esssentially invulnerable to attack and are likely to remain so for a long time. They operate virtually undetected by Soviet antisubmarine warfare (ASW) forces. While in theory it may be possible some day to track nuclear submarines by satellite, that technology does not yet appear promising. Moreover, any Soviet attempt to strike US ICBM silos and bomber and submarine bases simultaneously, by delaying missile launches from close-in submarines so that such missiles would arrive at US bomber bases at the same time as Soviet ICBM warheads (with their longer time of flight) would arrive at US silos, would permit a high portion of US bombers on alert to escape their bases. On the other hand, if the Soviet Union chose to launch their ICBM and SLBM forces simultaneously in an attempt to catch US bombers before they could be launched, there would be a period of over 15 minutes between the time Soviet short time-of-flight SLBMs arrived at US bomber bases and the first Soviet ICBM warheads arrived at US ICBM silos. Under such circumstances, Soviet leadership would have no confidence that the United States would refrain from launching its entire ICBM force during the interval after US bomber bases had been struck.[52]

The problem of timing, however, extends beyond that created by America's diversity of forces. Even an attack with the limited objective of eliminating a large portion of the US ICBM silos would be highly uncertain. Within the first millisecond after detonation of a nuclear warhead at or in close proximity to the ground, temperatures at the earth's surface raise to several hundred thousand degrees Celsius, overpressures may exceed 100,000 pounds per square inch, and radiation that can destroy a nuclear warhead extends outward hundreds of meters. Vertical winds caused by such high temperatures and an outwardly expanding fireball and shock front reach speeds of several hundred kilometers per hour. Dust and other debris from the ground are sucked upward, rising rapidly into the upper atmosphere. As a result, where more than one warhead is required to achieve a high degree of confidence that a missile silo has been destroyed (invariably the case with today's CEPs) or where missile silos are in close proximity to one another, nuclear or thermal radiation, violent upper atmosphere winds, and debris from previous blasts may pose or may be perceived by the Soviets as posing insurmountable targeting problems.[53]

This phenomenon is known as "fratricide." Incoming RVs might either be destroyed, neutralized, or their accuracy degraded by the effects of previous blasts. In an effort to avoid the effects of fratricide, it is usually assumed that the Soviet Union would attack southern most US silos first. Through split-second timing and a system of cross-targeting in which the RVs of each Soviet ICBM simultaneously are targeted on different US silos and every silo is covered by at least two Soviet RVs, it may be theoretically possible to minimize the impact of fratricide. However, neither superpower has much test experience with this phenomenon. Even where simultaneous detonations are planned in order to avoid fratricide, a few millisecond's delay in the arrival of an RV caused either by minor differences in warhead reentry characteristics or by the developing effects of previous downwind detonations, or even by minor variations in silo departure during launch, or guidance corrections during flight, could be enough to subject the RV to the potentially neutralizing effects of nuclear radiation and EMP. Under such circumstances, even a well-planned attack is not without its uncertainties. Moreover, follow-on attacks, including those by missiles reprogrammed to replaced previous ICBMs that had malfunctioned, are highly problematical.

Such uncertainties as these seriously compound the problem of achieving the high kill probabilities that would be necessary for the

Soviet Union to achieve a disarming first-strike. Even a successful attack on the US land-based forces is not nearly as certain as some pessimists suggest. Today, given perfect reliability and a successful two-on-one attack, a strike by Russian SS-19 MOD 3 missiles, which carry 6 warheads each with an estimated yield of 550 kilotons (kt) and a CEP of about 250 meters, would have a mathematically derived probability of destroying a US Minuteman silo hardened to 2000psi of about 86 percent. A two-on-one attack by Soviet SS-18 MOD 4 missiles which have accuracies and yields which are similar to the SS-19 but carry 10 warheads, would have a similar probability of kill.[54] However, such kill probabilities are only theoretical. When all potential compounding operational factors are considered, kill probabilities are likely to diminish substantially. Indeed, it would appear that such a conclusion contributed, in part, to the Scowcroft Commission's recommendation to deploy the MX missile in US Minuteman silos.

Civil defense preparations also often have been cited to indicate a distinct Soviet advantage in event of nuclear exchange.[55] Some note that in the wake of a Soviet counterforce first strike, US retaliatory forces could kill as few as 10 million people or about one-half the number of Soviet citizens lost during World War II. As a result of such calculation, it is argued, the ability of the United States to deter a Soviet first-strike is deteriorating rapidly. Indeed, some pundits contend that under such conditions in which forecasted Soviet losses might be less than those experienced from 1941 to 1945, Soviet leadership might be willing to threaten or initiate nuclear war. As a minimum, the Soviet Union might be able to exercise a degree of coercive diplomacy in a severe crisis.

However, is it really likely that Soviet leaders would initiate a conflict in which they are assured of 10 million prompt fatalities? It is one matter to find oneself engaged in a defensive conflict, not of one's choosing, which produces 20 million casualties over the course of 5 years. It is quite another matter to deliberately start a war in which 10 million fatalities, at the very least, can be expected within the first few hours of conflict and all major cities are likely to be destroyed along with, perhaps, the fabric of society. The point is that those analysts who posit Soviet victory due to such "low" losses erroneously assume that biological survival and national survival are one and the same. Indeed, the 10 million deaths suggested would not be a cross-section of Soviet society.

Because of the nature of the Soviet target array, the ethnic Great Russians would suffer most.[56] The postulated 10 million deaths also fail to account for those additional fatalities likely to result through military action should war continue beyond the first day. Nor do they include the millions of fatalities, casualties, or losses likely to result from fallout, disease, starvation, societal chaos or the effects of a "nuclear winter" which would certainly follow a strategic nuclear exchange. Indeed, as Carl Sagan has suggested "Except for fools and madmen, everyone knows that nuclear war would be an unprecedented human catastrophe."[57] Moreover, it is probable that the Soviets recognize that their own civil defense efforts are not likely to alter that truth in any appreciable way. In fact, Soviet calculations concerning the impact of nuclear war on world climatic conditions produced even more pessimistic results than did those of American scientists such as Sagan and Richard Turco. According to Soviet scientists, 40 days after a nuclear exchange of 5000 megatons the clouds of dust and soot created would cause temperatures to fall as much as 100 degrees with a devastating impact on human existence.[58]

The notion that the Kremlin could exercise a degree of coercive diplomacy knowing that it might sustain as few as 10 million casualties is also misleading. Any attempt at coercion through the threat of nuclear war would provide the United States an important measure of warning for its strategic and forward-based forces. Warning would enhance force survivability, increase the military effectiveness of the US strike, and significantly increase the casualties likely to be suffered by the Soviet Union should a conflict occur. Bomber forces might be placed on airborne alert or laterally dispersed to numerous airfields. On airborne alert, they would remain essentially invulnerable to preemptive attack, while lateral dispersal would add to Soviet targeting difficulties. Ballistic missile submarines in port could be put to sea. Forward-based forces, particularly aircraft, might be vertically or laterally dispersed. The President might even consider authorizing the launch "under attack" of the ICBM force. Under such circumstances, the apparently conservative nature of Soviet defense planning is likely to induce Soviet defense specialists to make force exchange calculations that are not likely to be outweighed by the benefits of threatening to or initiating a strategic nuclear conflict.

This analysis indicates that US and Soviet strategic forces are not in delicate balance over sharp fulcrum. Instead they are counterpoised on a broad base of uncertainties that will permit a number of force alterations on either side without cataclysmic results. While increases in accuracy will make Soviet missiles theoretically more lethal, such technical improvements are not easily translatable into operational and political advantages that can be exploited readily by the Soviet Union in the near term. Such a comparatively comforting conclusion, however, is not likely to remain valid indefinitely.[59] American ICBMs are becoming more vulnerable to preemptive attack. Moreover, this will increasingly be the case should the Soviet Union incorporate terminal guidance capabilities on its next generation ICBMs and SLBMs. Technologies are already under study to overcome the effects of dust clouds and EMP on reentry vehicles. Indeed, much already has been done by the United States, and presumedly by the Soviet Union, to harden its strategic forces to the effects of EMP. There is always the possibility of break-through in antisubmarine warfare, especially if the United States abandons the ICBM leg, thereby allowing the Soviet Union to concentrate its resources on ASW. The question confronting the United States today is how to respond to the increasing vulnerabilities of its forces, while avoiding a further escalation of the arms race and a potentially destabilizing US-Soviet force balance. Should the United State abandon the land-based missile leg of the strategic Triad? Or should it adopt a less vulnerable form of land-based basing? What is the future role of the manned bomber? Should the United States shift its strategic investment to sea-based components which are currently clearly less vulnerable?

STRATEGIC PLANNING FOR THE DECADES AHEAD

As the United States looks to the 1990's and beyond, three objectives will continue to dominate American strategic force planning: US strategic forces must continue to serve as a credible deterrent to Soviet aggression against the United States and its allies; the forces chosen must contribute to crisis stability; and, however incredible or unthinkable it may be, should deterrence fail, US forces must be structured in such a way that they contribute to conflict termination short of Armageddon. To accomplish these tasks the United States must reduce the vulnerabilities of its strategic retaliatory arsenal; maintain a capacity of limited nuclear options; and engage the Soviet Union in the vigorous pursuit of stability through arms control.

Reducing Vulnerabilities. America's strategic arsenal must remain capable of absorbing a Soviet first-strike and retaliating decisively. This has been a clear requirement for deterrence and stability since President Kennedy's administration formulated the first SIOP. In the past, America has relied on a combination of ICBMs, bombers, and SLBMs to accomplish these tasks. There is, however, nothing sacrosanct about the Triad. Some defense specialists have suggested that the growing vulnerabilities of certain strategic systems eventually may force the United States to abandon the Triad concept in favor of a dyad (bombers and SLBMs), or perhaps even a monad (SLBMs alone). Nevertheless, the abandonment of the ICBM or the bomber legs of the Triad would not come without cost.

The current diversity of strategic forces (land, sea, and air) serves several purposes. First, diversity provides a hedge against a technical surprise that might render one or even two legs vulnerable to preemptive attack. Force diversity also poses attack timing problems, as noted earlier, which make it difficult for the Soviets to coordinate simultaneous strikes on all three legs of the Triad. Thus, while one leg may be technically vulnerable, its elimination from the force mix would heighten the vulnerability of the remaining legs. Third, diversity provides a hedge against tactical surprise—bombers can be placed on airborne alert where they are virtually invulnerable to a preemptive attack, nuclear submarines can stay submerged and hidden for months, and the high alert rates of ICBMs allow them to be launched quickly from under attack. Finally, force diversity dilutes the ability of the Soviets to defend themselves successfully against retaliatory strikes. Hence, a balance of forces would appear to offer greater promise than a move to a dyad or monad in meeting the twin goals of deterrence and stability. What then should be done to reduce vulnerabilities?

First, the land-based component must be completely revamped. This need not be done in a panic nor in complete disregard of long-term arms control objectives. Nor should the United States sacrifice the modernization of its other military capabilities, which are likely to be called upon to protect US interests in a world plagued by numerous conventional and unconventional conflicts. However, planning for the eventual replacement of the entire Minuteman missile force must begin now. The prospect of reducing the vulnerability of the current Minuteman missile force through the superhardening of silos exists. The potential for a promising payoff, however, is very uncertain. As terminal guidance technologies permit missile accuracies to approach zero CEP, the probability of destroying even super-hardened silos through either a systems kill resulting from ground shock or the cataclysmic destruction of the silo will approach unity. Like other precision-guided weapons, however, precision-guided ICBMs still demand that the attacker acquire the target before killing it. Under such circumstances mobile missiles offer the most promising prospect for reducing the vulnerability of the US strategic ICBM force.

Mobility was one of the desired features of the MX program as originally conceived. The size of the MX system, however, precluded real mobility. The most promising and at the same time technologically feasible option for the land-basing of MX involved the shuttling of the MX between a number of protected shelters. The multiple protective shelter (MPS) system, however, required a limit on the development of the Soviet missile force. Otherwise the USSR would be able to increase the number of RVs in its striking force to compensate for the increase on the number of targets to be struck. Furthermore, deploying MX in multiple protective shelters over large tracts of land proved politically infeasible. As a result and in light of the Scowcroft Commission's realistic assessment of Soviet hard-target kill capabilities, a decision to deploy 100 MXs in existing Minuteman silos was made.

This decision has been criticized widely. The principal concern of MX critics, however, is that the ten highly accurate MX warheads threaten strategic stability. From a Soviet perspective, placing MX in vulnerable fixed silos suggests that the United States intends to close the "window of vulnerability" by acquiring its own disarming counterforce first-strike capability. In a severe crisis, concerned about a potential US first-strike, Soviet leaders might opt for preemption in an effort to eliminate this American threat. While it is beyond the scope of this paper to recreate the MX debate, at least two points are in order. First, the Soviet Union *is* likely to harbor a greater degree of apprehension over America's capability for a strike on Soviet missiles resulting from MX deployments.

However, given the diversity of US strategic forces and the current uncertainties associated with a preemptive attack on those forces, the deployment of 100 MX missiles is not likely to alter Soviet calculations as to the potential benefits of preemption. Second, the MX missile will be no more vulnerable than the current Minuteman force, but each surviving MX will have over three times as many warheads as a surviving Minuteman III missile and many times the destructive power.

As a follow-on to the MX, the United States is developing a small, single-warhead ICBM. Nicknamed the "Midgetman," this new small ICBM (SICBM) would weigh about 15 tons rather than the nearly 100 tons of the MX and offer greater flexibility for mobile deployment. The Midgetman is not only an attempt to reduce vulnerability through mobility, but also an attempt to disinvent the MIRV which has been a principal culprit in the creation of strategic force vulnerabilities. It is inherently more costly, however, to build additional missiles than it is to build additional warheads. Thus, whether the follow-on to MX and Minuteman has a single warhead may well depend on whether the Soviets can be convinced of the inherent stability of single-warhead systems,[60] whether they are willing to spend the money in a major alteration of their strategic force arsenal, and whether adequate arms control verification procedures can be negotiated to preclude cheating. What is essential for genuine stability, however, is that US and Soviet land-based missile systems be truly mobile.

Second, the United States must also continue to modernize its SLBM force. The ballistic missile submarine force when at sea is the most survivable leg of the Triad and is likely to remain so in the foreseeable future. The new Ohio-class Trident submarines are significantly quieter than America's Poseidon SSBNs which were constructed in the 1960's. With the planned addition of the longer-ranged Trident II (D-5) missile, the United States will be capable of retaliating from greater ranges than was previously the case with the Polaris or Poseidon fleet or with the Trident I (C-4) missile. This will permit the US SSBN fleet to use the protection of a vaster expanse of the world's seas to increase its survivability. The planned deployment of the D-5 missile, however, has not been without criticism. Like the MX the principal criticism has been that the planned accuracy of the D-5 missile will permit it to destroy hardened Soviet targets. Again, like the MX such a capability is seen as dangerously destabilizing. Indeed, New York Representative Thomas J. Downey is reported to have complained that the D-5 is "the most destabilizing 'first-strike' weapon ever built."[61]

Strategic instability, however, is more a function of one's vulnerability than of the accuracy of one's missile forces. While the Soviet Union may be concerned over a growing US SLBM hard-target kill potential, there is nothing against which to preempt if US submarines cannot be located. Perhaps, the real concern is less the near-term implications for crisis stability and more the potentially destabilizing arms race at sea which might ensue as the USSR searches for ways of locating US SSBNs and the long-term implications should the seas become less opaque.

Two factors should guide future developments in the US sea-based force if such instabilities are to be avoided: the United States must avoid putting too many eggs in a single basket; and, the invulnerability of SSBNs must be preserved.

Today, a high percentage of US striking power resides in slightly more than 30 SSBNs. This will be even more the case as Ohio-class submarines with their D-5 missiles replace Poseidon submarines. Thus, while there is a high probability that the Ohio-class Trident fleet will remain invulnerable to preemptive attack into the next century, it is important that we continue to guard against future vulnerabilities and the instabilities they will beget. In this regard, the United States must look to a future nuclear submarine fleet which includes smaller boats which are hopefully less costly, but more numerous. Employing a logic similar to Midgetman, the development of a small single-warhead SLBM would make such a fleet feasible. To increase stability the Soviet Union should be encouraged to do the same. The United States should also engage the Soviet Union in a variety of discussions designed to reduce the threatening nature of SLBM deployments and to preserve, perhaps enhance, the invulnerability of SLBM forces.

Third, the United States must modernize its strategic bomber forces. Bombers are the most flexible leg of the Triad. They can be used to demonstrate US interest, concern, and determination during severe crisis situations. They can be placed on ground and airborne alert as well as launched on warning and recalled. They can make use of electronic countermeasures (ECM), evasive action, low altitude penetration tactics and standoff missiles to mitigate enemy air defenses. Bombers are capable of striking hardened targets such as residual or reuseable Soviet ICBM silos. They can provide post-strike reconnaissance for attack assessments. They can be moved to a theater of operations to augment theater nuclear capabilities in a severe crisis and they can be reconstituted for follow-on uses.

Bombers are also the Triad's most stabilizing element. Their long flight times preclude their use in first-strike counterforce attacks. Moreover, because airborne bombers are virtually invulnerable to a preemptive first-strike and because a large percentage of America's megatonage is carried by bombers, an airborne alert called during a critical confrontation with the USSR might deter all forms of direct hostilities between the United States and the Soviet Union.

Nevertheless, it is frequently argued that as Soviet air defenses continue to improve and look-down/shoot-down air defense interceptors are developed, bombers no longer will be capable of penetrating to their targets. B-52s, however, successfully penetrated some of the heaviest air defenses ever assembled in the December 1972 air campaign against Hanoi; suffering less than a three percent attrition rate.[62] While Soviet surface-to-air missile technologies have improved since then, so have the tactics and ECM capabilities of the US bomber force. Even these considerations may be moot in a nuclear war, however, inasmuch as Soviet SAMs and interceptor airfields would be logical candidates for early ICBM and SLBM suppression strikes. Moreover, the task of locating and subsequently attacking with interceptor aircraft bombers which are deliberately attempting to conceal their locations would not be easy. Frequently, there is a very narrow window in which to attack a penetrating aircraft and a successful reattack may not be possible following a missed intercept. This problem has been demonstrated by the Soviets in the past as they often have been unable to track and quickly intercept civilian aircraft flying obtrusive routes at high altitudes. Such problems would be severely compounded in a nuclear war. US bombers would arrive in Soviet airspace some nine hours or so after a nuclear exchange. They would be equipped with nuclear short-range attack missiles and ECM capable of destroying or disrupting remaining Soviet SAM sites and interceptor airfields. Air-launched cruise missiles would be used to attack highly defended targets. Furthermore, the communications necessary for the effective positioning of interceptor aircraft would be severely disrupted by the effects of nuclear weapons. The task of locating penetrating aircraft would be compounded by the presence of clouds of dust and debris from previous nuclear detonations. Under such circumstances, the probability of the USSR successfully intercepting US bombers enroute to their targets is likely to be very low.

Hence, the critical question is not whether the bomber should be retained as part of the Triad. Rather, it is whether the United States should replace a portion of its B-52 fleet with the B-1 now or wait until the so-called Advanced Technology Bomber (ATB) incorporating stealth technologies is developed. The current B-52 force is a product of 1950's technology. The last B-52 rolled off the assembly line in the early 1960's. While many recent modifications have been made to the fleet to increase its ability to penetrate enemy defenses, a number of deficiencies remain. The B-1 is capable of a quick start, a short takeoff run, and rapid acceleration to escape an airbase under attack. The B-52 is not. The B-1 is hardened to survive many of the effects of nuclear blast and radiation which might be encountered as it attempts to escape a Soviet attack on US air bases. The B-52 was not designed to counter such effects. The B-1 has a smaller "footprint"[63] and shorter takeoff roll and thus can be dispersed to a greater number of airfields than can the B-52. The B-1 incorporates the latest ECM technologies. Moreover, the B-1 is available now and the B-52 is a rapidly aging airframe.

A convincing argument can always be made to postpone modernization and its associated costs for some technologically promising furture development. However, there are hazards to this. The technology may not develop at a pace fast enough to be available when replacement becomes the only real option for an aging force. Then the United States might well be left with a stealth bomber fleet which is not only invisible to the adversary, but also not visible on America's bomber bases. Moreover, the technology may not come cheaply nor represent the significant breakthrough anticipated. On the other hand, the ATB indeed may represent a significant breakthrough in stealth technology; however, the B-1 already has a radar cross-section many times smaller than the B-52. Thus, the decision to procure the B-1, to a certain degree, is a judgment call which is designed to insure that the United States has an effective bomber leg of the Triad well into the 1990's.

Fourth, the United States must place great emphasis on insuring the survivability of its strategic command, control, and communications (C^3) nets. Perhaps the most vulnerable components of our strategic retaliatory forces are the communication links that make timely retaliation possible. Soviet doctrine and nuclear warfare exercise scenarios, their emphasis on communications disruption through the use of electronic warfare, and their preoccupation with the survivability of their own command and control links suggest that the Soviet Union would devote a significant portion of attacking forces to attempts to sever the links between the President and US strategic nuclear forces in an effort to delay or disrupt a US strategic retaliatory response.

While the United States is well advised to pursue in a deliberate fashion the force modernizations identified above, certain programs on the horizon merit reconsideration. For instance, the United States should move with great caution on the development and deployment of land-attack sea-launched cruise missiles (SLCMs). The United States has been deploying Tomahawk cruise missiles to improve the striking power of its surface naval units. Although, in a strict sense, Tomahawk is not a strategic system, there is no doubt that systems such as a land-attack SLCM could play a vital strategic role, especially if deployed by the Soviet Union on ships near the American coast line. Under such circumstances there is some serious question as to whether the United States would be the net beneficiary of further deployments of modern cruise missiles. The Soviet Union has a greater number of submarines than has the United States. The USSR also has a large surface fleet upon which to deploy SLCMs. The United States has virtually no air defense capability against a large-scale cruise missile attack. It also has more targets which are close to the coastline. Thus it is potentially more vulnerable to current and near future generations of SLCMs. Moreover, once deployed it will be difficult to determine how many nuclear SLCMs the Soviet Union actually has. This would further complicate the arms control verification problem, if an agreement to monitor production closely could not be reached. Indeed, failure to seek limits on sea-launched cruise missiles may be an error of the same magnitude as the failure to limit the deployment of the MIRV.

The United States should also move cautiously in the area of strategic defense. The Scowcroft Commission recommended a "vigorous research and development program" on antiballistic missile (ABM) technologies to avoid technological surprise. However, the commission concluded that no ABM technologies appeared to combine "practicality, survivability, low cost, and technical sufficiency to justify proceeding beyond the stage of technology development."[64] Indeed, there is no certainty that the United States would be the net beneficiary of deployments of strategic defensive systems.[65] Thus, while such deployments may eventually be necessary, arms control efforts should be exploited to avoid a future arms race of strategic defensive systems.

Maintaining a Capability for Limited Options. One of the principal difficulties of developing a strategic arsenal which not only is a credible deterrent to aggression against the United States and its allies and enhances the prospects for an early conflict termination should deterrence fail, but also contributes to crisis stability is that the forces necessary for the former frequently appear to be at odds with the requirements of the latter. For example, deterrence of Soviet aggression against America's European allies requires the Kremlin to believe that any aggression in Europe might ultimately result in a strategic exchange with the United States. This is known as the linkage concept that presents the Soviet leadership with potential costs of aggression in Europe that overwhemingly outweigh any conceivable gains. In an age when the United States possessed an overwhelming superiority, it was reasonable for Soviet leaders to believe that the United States might deliberately initiate a nuclear war to protect Western Europe. Thus, threats of massive attacks on Soviet urban and industrial centers seemed credible enough to deter a potential Soviet aggression. Linkage, although less certain, still seemed somewhat assured even after the Soviet Union began developing a substantial nuclear capability, as long as the United States had a clear relative advantage and was perceived to have a measure of "escalation dominance." However, today, in an age of nuclear parity, or as some have suggested, increasing quantitative if not qualitative inferiority, linkage and thus deterrence depends not so much on the notion that the United States would deliberately initiate a massive nuclear war with the Soviet Union as it depends on the Soviet Union believing that the United States might use lesser options to keep Western Europe from being overrun. Deterrence further depends upon the USSR believing that despite any American attempts to limit or terminate conflict through such options, the force of events would lead eventually to a massive US-Soviet strategic nuclear conflagration. Similarly, should a conflict occur, the President must not be limited to all or nothing strategic options. Such options would force the President to choose between annihilation or surrender. A flexible and robust force of modern strategic weapons contributes significantly to both these objectives. By offering the President the capability for limited strikes on militarily significant targets, deterrence is strengthened and the potential for conflict limitation and eventual termination is preserved should deterrence fail.

Arms Control. The arsenals of the superpowers have reached levels in which genuine security increasingly will depend not just on force planning, but on arms control. While it will be theoretically feasible to plan and build strategic forces in the absence of arms control, such efforts are likely to result in higher levels of insecurity at increased cost. Whether the militaries of either superpower can be convinced of it or not, both the United States and the Soviet Union are highly dependent on each other for their future security. Indeed, future strategic programs designed by one side to increase strategic stability may well require the cooperation of the other if stability is to be assured. This was the case with the MX MPS system—only through an agreement which limited the number of warheads available to the Soviet Union would a multiplication of the number of targets which would have to be struck to destroy US MX missiles provide an increased measure of stability. This is likely to be the case with future systems. Arms control can contribute to crisis stability in such an environment. Arms control can also reduce pressures which if unrestrained might lead to an upwardly spiraling arms race. In this regard, a truly stable environment is likely to require: (1) a movement away from MIRVed ICBM and SLBM systems; (2) a reduction in time-urgent hard-target kill capability and perhaps a reemphasis on non-time urgent systems such as bombers; (3) a ban on terminal-homing ICBM and SLBM warheads; (4) a reduction in the total warheads deployed by each side; (5) the establishment of "safe zones" for each side's nuclear ballistic missile submarines; (6) a limitation on the future deployments of SLCMs;[66] and (7) the avoidance of an upwardly spiraling race of antisatellite, and space and land-based strategic defense systems.

A FINAL NOTE

There is no question that the West is interested in avoiding nuclear war and the strategic instabilities that might set events in motion that could lead to a cataclysmic confrontation with the Soviet Union. There is ample evidence to suggest that despite hopes of using military power to underwrite their superpower status, the Soviet Union is also interested in stability and the avoidance of nuclear war. This is where there is convergence between the United States and the Soviet Union. Our societies are not similar nor are they becoming so. We do not share similar values and that is not likely to change in the foreseeable future. The Soviet Union has not given up on its struggle with the West nor should we expect this to happen. Nevertheless, we both share a paramount interest in avoiding nuclear war. It is upon this base that cooperative efforts to reduce strategic instabilities and the potential for war can and must be built. Such efforts, of course, should include a continuation of discussions on future limits of strategic forces. Perhaps, more importantly, they must include discussions aimed at sorting out differences in strategic doctrine and force structure and identifying those factors which threaten stability. Only then can we have some confidence that bilateral as well as unilateral actions are contributing to a long-term strategic design that will reduce the probability of nuclear war.

What is required now is reason not rhetoric, prudence not paranoia, objectivity not emotion, and above all a strategy for dealing with the Soviet Union, not a litany with its ritualistic incantations which has so far obscured rather than clarified those factors which separate the superpowers from real progress toward a stable strategic environment.

ENDNOTES

1. "President's News Conference on Foreign and Domestic Matters," *The New York Times,* April 1, 1982, p. A-22.

2. The so-called "window of vulnerability" has been described as that period of time in the 1980's when, because of the increasing accuracy of the Soviet strategic missile force, US land-based ICBMs would be vulnerable to a disarming preemptive Soviet attack. The Soviet Union, at least in theory, so the argument goes, would be able to destroy all but a few US ICBMs with a small percentage of their own ICBM force. The remaining forces would be held in reserve to deter a US retaliatory attack. Thus, the US president confronted with the loss of his highly accurate ICBM force (potentially capable of attacking residual Soviet nuclear forces) and with highly effective Soviet air defense capability against US bombers (also potentially capable of striking residual Soviet nuclear forces) would be forced to either accede to Soviet demands or engage in a virtually suicidal counter-city exchange.

3. See for example, Robert G. Kaiser, "Critics Dispute Reagan, Say Soviets Not Superior: 'Voodoo Arms Control' Assailed by Kennedy," *The Washington Post,* April 2, 1982, p. A-1.

4. Hedrick Smith, "The Strategic Balance," *The New York Times,* April 5, 1982, p. A-7.

5. *Ibid.,* p. A-1.

6. Adam Clymer, "2 Senators Deny Soviet Arms Lead," *The New York Times,* April 5, 1982, p. A-7.

7. For example, see Harold Brown, Secretary of Defense, *Department of Defense Annual Report Fiscal Year 1981,* Washington: US Government Printing Office, January 16, 1981, pp. iv & 14.

8. The so-called "Team B" members included Richard Pipes, Professor of Russian History at Harvard; Thomas W. Wolfe of the RAND Corporation; LTG Daniel O. Graham, retired former head of the Defense Intelligence Agency; Paul D. Wolfowitz of the Arms Control and Disarmament Agency; Paul H. Nitze, former Deputy Secretary of Defense; GEN John Vogt, USAF, Retired; and Professor William Van Cleve of the University of Southern California.

9. See David Binder, "New CIA Estimate Finds Soviet Seeks Superiority in Arms," *The New York Times,* December 26, 1976, p. 1.

10. Albert Wohlsletter, "Legends of the Strategic Arms Race, Part 1: The Driving Engine," *Strategic Review,* Fall 1974, pp. 67-92.

11. While no formal audit was conducted, President Ford accepted the suggestion of his Foreign Intelligence Advisory Board which, having taken note of the concerns of Keegan and others, recommended that the views of outsiders be considered in the preparation of the NIE. It was this suggestion which led to the formation of the so-called "Team B" for the 1976 NIE. For a summary of some of the concerns voiced by Keegan, see MG George J. Keegan, Jr., "New Assessment Put on Soviet Threat," *Aviation Week and Space Technology,* March 28, 1977, pp. 38-48; and David Binder, "U.S. General Fears Soviet Has Won Military Superiority," *The New York Times,* January 3, 1977, p. 3.

12. Nitze had been a principal author of NSC-68, the 1950 joint report by the Secretary of State and Defense on US Objectives and Programs for National Security. NSC-68 had been requested by President Truman, after the Soviet nuclear explosion of August 1949. The report underscored the aggressive nature of the

Soviet Union and its "design for world domination" and served to provide a basis for a reversal of the US postwar policy of accommodation with the Soviet Union to a policy of confrontation and rearmament. Nitze also served as a principal author of the Gaither Report in 1957 which again pointed to the "expansionist" nature of the Soviet state and warned of the impending "missile gap." For NSC-68 and the Gaither Report, see "NSC-68, A Report to the National Security Council," republished in the *Naval War College Review,* May-June 1975, pp. 51-108; and US Congress, Joint Committee on Defense Production, *Deterrence and Survival in the Nuclear Age (The 'Gaither Report' of 1957),* 94th Cong., 2d sess., Washington: US Government Printing Office, 1976.

13. *Common Sense and the Common Danger,* Washington: The Committee on the Present Danger, November 11, 1976, pp. 1-3.

14. Paul H. Nitze, "Assuring Strategic Stability in an Era of Detente," *Foreign Affairs,* January 1976, pp. 207, 216-217.

15. Richard Pipes, "The Soviet Strategy for Nuclear Victory," *Commentary,* July 1977, p. 25.

16. *Ibid.,* p. 26.

17. *Ibid.,* p. 29.

18. *Ibid.*

19. *Ibid.,* pp. 30-31.

20. Colin S. Gray, "Force Postures, Arms Races, and the Future of Salt," Address before the University of Southern California/US Army Russian Institute Symposium, Garmisch, West Germany, December 1978.

21. V. I. Lenin, *Collected Works,* Vol. 29, Moscow: Progress Publishers, 1965, p. 153.

22. *Pravda,* March 13, 1954.

23. *Pravda,* January 25, 1961, cited in William D. Jackson, "The Soviets and Strategic Arms: Toward an Evaluation of the Record," *Political Science Quarterly,* Summer 1979, p. 247.

24. For example, see Michael MccGwire, "Soviet Strategic Weapons Policy, 1955-70," in *Soviet Naval Policy: Objectives and Constraints,* edited by Michael MccGwire, Ken Booth and John McDonnell, New York: Praeger Publishers, 1975, p. 488. See also Robert Legvold, "Strategic 'Doctrine' and SALT: Soviet and American Views," *Survival,* January/February 1979, pp. 8-13.

25. See Thomas W. Wolfe, "The Communist Theory of War," *Marxism, Communism and Western Society,* Vol. 8, ed. by C. O. Kernig, New York: Herder & Herder, 1973, pp. 316-317.

26. For a sketch of the Soviet debate since the early sixties on the utility of nuclear warfare as an instrument of policy, see Raymond Garthoff, "Mutual Deterrence and Strategic Arms Limitations in Soviet Policy," *International Security,* Summer 1978, pp. 113-125. Also see John Erickson, "The Soviet View of Deterrence: A General Survey," *Survival,* November/December 1982, pp. 242-251, esp. p. 244.

27. Fritz W. Ermarth, "Contrasts in American and Soviet Strategic Thought," *International Security,* 3, Fall 1978, p. 143.

28. See Garthoff, p. 126.

29. For a survey of Brezhnev's views see Mark E. Miller, *Soviet Strategic Power and Doctrine: The Quest for Superiority,* Washington: Advanced International Studies Institute, 1982, pp. 188-189. Also see Erickson, p. 244.

30. It could be argued that there is little difference in the force postures and doctrine of the two superpowers other than what has been fundamentally a product

of differing levels of technological development. Both have highly accurate missile systems. Both are capable of striking each other's strategic systems (although estimates vary on how successful the United States would be in striking hardened Soviet missile silos). However, Soviet declaratory policy emphasizes surprise and attacks on meaningful military targets thus suggesting a war-fighting capability, while American declaratory policy suggests an emphasis on deterrence rather than war-fighting. Nevertheless, US targeting doctrine has always included attacks on Soviet military power. Thus, perhaps the real difference lies in whether Moscow is more predisposed to a preemptive first strike than is Washington. On this point Ben Lambeth contends that Soviet military doctrine scarcely offers a hard prediction of how the Soviets would actually respond in a crisis. See Benjamin S. Lambeth, "Uncertainties for the Soviet War Planner," *International Security,* Winter 1982/1983, p. 142. Also see James McConnell, "Soviet and American Strategies Doctrines: One More Time," *Professional Paper 271,* Alexandria: Center for Naval Analysis, January 1980.

31. Dennis Ross, "Rethinking Soviet Strategic Policy: Inputs and Implications," *The Journal of Strategic Studies,* May 1978, p. 6.

32. *Ibid.,* p. 9. For a detailed discussion of the concepts of deterrence through denial or punishment, see Glen H. Snyder, *Deterrence by Denial and Punishment,* Princeton: Princeton University Press, 1959.

33. Erickson, pp. 244-245.

34. Legvold, p. 8.

35. For example, see Henry Trofimenko, "The 'Theology' of Strategy," *Orbis,* Fall 1977, pp. 498-500.

36. Lambeth, "Uncertainties for the Soviet War Planner," p. 140.

37. In the immediate postwar period through the 1950's, the American defense community's approach to deterrence often focused on ways to maintain US strategic nuclear superiority. For many defense specialists, deterrence and stability were functions of power. The nation that possessed superior strategic nuclear capabilities had the power to deter. Moreover, the power to deter born of strategic superiority extended beyond deterrence of strategic nuclear conflict to lesser conflicts. Strategic nuclear superiority was considered a useful political tool in securing US interests and objectives elsewhere in the world.

This approach to deterrence was epitomized by John Foster Dulles in his famous speech before the Council on Foreign Relations in January 1954. Referring to America's strategic superiority, Dulles informed the world that the United States would base deterrence on its great capacity to retaliate instantly and massively anywhere in the world. He also detailed the extended nature of America's deterrent capability when he stated that, "the way to deter aggression is for the free community to be willing and able to respond vigorously at places and with means of its own choosing." He contended that there was no local defense which alone could contain the mighty land power of the Communist world; local defenses must be reinforced by the threat of massive strategic nuclear retaliation.

By the late 1950's and early 1960's, however, the Soviet Union's growing strategic capability increased concern over the credibility of a deterrence based on a massive nuclear response and heightened awareness of the potential perils should deterrence fail. In the debate which ensued, some defense specialists continued to believe that deterrence could only be achieved through superiority. They concluded that the United States had to redouble its efforts to maintain a sufficient margin of superiority. Others openly discussed the potential need for preventive or preemptive war. See John Foster Dulles, "The evolution of Foreign Policy," *Department of State Bulletin,* XXX January 25, 1954, p. 108. For an excellent but brief survey of this period of US nuclear policy, see Herbert Y. Schandler, *U.S. Policy on the Use of Nuclear Weapons, 1954-1975,* Washington: Congressional Research Service, Library of Congress, August 14, 1975, revised November 14, 1975, pp. CRS 7-10. For a survey of the preventive/preemptive war debates of the early 1960's, see George E. Lowe, *The Age of Deterrence,* Boston: Little, Brown & Co., 1964, pp. 201-203.

38. Counterforce options are those designed to attack an adversary's military forces, especially his strategic nuclear capabilities. Countervalue options are those designed to attack population centers, industries, resources, and other such things of "value" to the fabric of society. For a review of the justification used by Secretary of Defense James R. Schlesinger for the further development of US counterforce capabilities, see his *Annual Report to the Congress, Fiscal Year 1975,* Washington: US Government Printing Office, March 4, 1974, pp. 3-6, 32-42.

39. Harold Brown, Secretary of Defense, *Annual Report to the Congress, Fiscal Year 1981,* Washington: US Government Printing Office, January 29, 1980, p. 66.

40. *Ibid.,* p. 67.

41. For example, see Trofimenko, "The 'Theology' of Strategy," p. 499.

42. For thought provoking view of the role military power plays in Soviet strategy, see Phillip A. Petersen and John G. Hines, "Military Power in Soviet Strategy Against NATO," *RUSI,* December 1983, pp. 50-57.

43. *The Military Balance 1963-1964,* London: The International Institute for Strategic Studies, November 1963, pp. 3-11.

44. *Soviet Military Power,* Washington: US Government Printing Office, 1982, p. 54. Also pp. 21-24 of the 1983 version of the booklet.

45. *Ibid.*

46. For example, see R. J. Rummel, "Will the Soviet Union Soon Have a First-Strike Capability?" *Orbis,* Fall 1976, p. 582 and Colin S. Gray, "The Strategic Forces Triad: End of the Road?," *Foreign Affairs,* July 1978, pp. 775-778.

47. See John Steinbruner, "Launch Under Attack," *Scientific American,* January 1984, pp. 37-47.

48. See John D. Steinbruner and Thomas M. Garwin, "Strategic Vulnerability: The Balance Between Prudence and Paranoia," *International Security,* Summer 1976, p. 141.

49. Matthew Bunn and Kosta Tsipis, "The Uncertainties of a Preemptive Nuclear Attack," *Scientific American,* November 1983, p. 39.

50. *Ibid.*

51. For a further discussion of these two factors, see *Ibid.*

52. *Report of the President's Commission on Strategic Forces,* Washington: April 6, 1983, pp. 7-90.

53. See Bunn and Tsipis, pp. 40-41.

54. *Ibid.,* p. 40.

55. For a thorough treatment of the civil defense issue, see John M. Weinstein, "The Strategic Implications of Civil Defense," in *The Defense of the West: Strategic and European Security Issues Reappraised,* ed. by Robert Kennedy and John M. Weinstein, Boulder: Westview Press, 1984.

56. Gary L. Guertner, "Strategic Vulnerability of a Multinational State: Deterring the Soviet Union," *Political Science Quarterly,* Summer 1981, pp. 209-223.

57. Dr. Carl Sagan, "The Nuclear Winter," *Parade Magazine,* October 30, 1983, p. 4.

58. See Philip J. Hilts, "Nuclear Winter: Catastrophe Confirmed by Soviet Scientists," *The Washington Post,* November 2, 1983, p. A8.

59. Bunn and Tsipis, p. 47.

60. There is some evidence that the USSR is currently testing a mobile single RV ICBM. See *The Military Balance 1983-1984,* London: The International Institute for Strategic Studies, Autumn 1983, p. l2.

61. Robert C. Toth, "U.S. Reliance on Nuclear Subs Being Debated," *The Los Angeles Times,* May 22, 1983, p. l.

62. See US Congress, House, Committee on Appropriations, *Department of Defense Appropriations,* Hearings Before a Subcommittee of the Committee on Appropriations, 93d Cong., lst sess., 1973, p. 18.

63. Footprint refers to the amount of stress placed on a runway because of the relationship between aircraft weight and the pattern of weight distribution on a runway through the landing gear. The weight/pattern of weight distribution of the B-1 places much less stress on runways, thus it can be deployed to a greater number of dispersal bases.

64. *Report of the President's Commission on Strategic Forces,* p. 12.

65. For a thorough examination of the issues, see Daniel S. Papp, "Ballistic Missile Defense, Space-Based Weapons, and the Defense of the West," in *The Defense of the West.* Also see Donald M. Snow, *The Nuclear Future: Toward a Strategy of Uncertainty,* Tuscaloosa: University of Alabama Press, 1983; Daniel Kaplan, "Lasers for Missile Defense," *Bulletin of the Atomic Scientists,* May 1983, pp. 509; and US Congress, Senate, *Department of Defense: Authorizations for Appropriations for Fiscal Year 1983,* Hearings Before the Committee on Armed Services, 97th Cong., 2d sess., pp. 4884-4904.

66. For a further discussion of this and other alternatives, see Thomas J. Downey, "How to Avoid Monad—and Disaster," *Foreign Policy,* Fall 1976, pp. 193-201.

2

ALL FEATURES GRATE AND STALL: SOVIET STRATEGIC VULNERABILITIES AND THE FUTURE OF DETERRENCE

John M. Weinstein

INTRODUCTION

The last decade has not been a happy time for US defense planners. During these years, they have witnessed a profound and ominous expansion and modernization of Soviet nuclear and conventional military capabilities. At the nuclear level, the Soviet Union has deployed the SS-17, -18, and -19 intercontinental ballistic missiles (ICBMs) with multiple, independent reentry vehicles (MIRVs) which rival the accuracy of the most modern US Minuteman III. Moreover, the larger yields of the Soviet warheads have led many planners to fear that the Soviet Union is rapidly approaching and, indeed, may now possess the ability to deliver a debilitating strike against the land-based leg of the US strategic Triad—which has been instrumental in the postwar period in preserving peace by deterring nuclear conflict.

The deployment of more than 350 mobile SS-20 (with MIRVs) intermediate range ballistic missiles (IRBMs), more than two-thirds of which are targeted against NATO Europe defenses;[1] the ability of the Soviet Union to threaten the Middle East, Northern Africa, Southwest Asia, Japan, South Korea, the People's Republic of China, and even Alaska with these weapons (as well as the Backfire bomber); and the persistent augmentation and modernization of Soviet conventional land, air and naval forces in Europe and around the world have had several unsettling consequences that threaten the security of the United States and its allies. In Europe, NATO nuclear superiority, which for years has countered Warsaw Pact conventional superiority, has disappeared. Consequently, we observe (1) a reemergence of the doubts first voiced by Charles DeGaulle more than 25 years ago about the credibility of the US nuclear guarantee of Europe's security,[2] (2) a broad-based nuclear freeze movement on both sides of the Atlantic, (3) calls by some to abandon America's continental military strategy in favor of one which puts more emphasis on maritime assets,[3] and (4) an increase in anxiety and ambivalence among the NATO allies across a broad range of military issues. The emotional debate in Europe about the December 1983 initiation of deployment of the 572 US intermediate-range nuclear missiles most vividly illustrates these concerns.[4]

The distressing, massive Soviet military expansion of the last two decades shows few signs of abatement. In fact, some have argued that in spite of the economic dilemmas currently confronting the Soviet economy, the Soviet Union conceivably, *cannot* reduce the militarization of its economy.[5] Such a transition might cause serious personnel, bureaucratic and economic dislocations and deprive the Soviet Union of one of its most lucrative sources of capital: the foreign military sales which brought the equivalent of $63.4 billion in 1982 dollars into Soviet coffers from 1975 to 1982.[6]

It is not surprising that these developments have caused great alarm in the West, especially when they are viewed in conjunction with a Soviet military doctrine which stresses speed, shock and surprise in offensive operations[7] and the active Soviet civil defense program which is designed to minimize the destruction of nuclear war and allow rapid postattack recovery[8]. While one need not conclude that the Soviet leadership views war with the United States as desirable or imminent, it is likely, however, that heightened Soviet military power may cancel many prior US advantages, reduce US policy flexibility and allow the more active and ambitious pursuit of Soviet foreign policy objectives.[9] Indeed, it is very likely that the continuing Soviet intervention in Afghanistan; Soviet support for the aggressive policies of Vietnam; and Soviet collaboration with its Cuban proxy to exploit instability in Africa and Latin America led President Reagan to conclude that:

> Soviet military power has spread around the globe threatening our access to vital resources and our sea lines of communication, undermining our forward line of defense in Europe and Korea and challenging us even at home here in our own hemisphere.[10]

The following may well be considered as significant trends which present crucial domestic and international military and political challenges to the United States and its allies: (1) relentless increasing of Soviet military power across all functional and geographic fronts; (2) current destabilizing contentions in the NATO alliance; (3) expanding US, Western European and Japanese reliance on continued access to scarce and critical strategic resources (e.g., petroleum, chromium, uranium);[11] (4) proliferating opposition in the United States and Western Europe to the growth of defense spending at a time of global recession and economic stagnation; and (5) an expanding "peace movement" in Europe and the United States which has helped to undermine the prodefense consensus that helped Ronald Reagan in his quest for the US presidency.

Undoubtedly, the Soviet Union is—and will continue to be into the foreseeable future—the principal threat to and adversary of the United States. As such, the student of national security wisely wonders whether, in light of the expansion of Soviet military power and the shifting correlation of forces it generates, the Soviet Union will be deterred from starting a war with the United States.[12] To evaluate the present state of deterrence, it is important to understand that deterrence is a state of mind which incorporates far more than the quantitative or even qualitative balance of weapons and military forces. Richard Betts has argued that:

> Much of what passes for net assessment, however, is a narrow focus on static orders of battle—the observable and quantifiable constituents such as manpower and equipment—or dynamic simulations of combat engagement. The numerous subjective or intangible factors such as campaign strategy, operational doctrine, training, morale, or command competence receive shorter shrift, yet these factors (unless material imbalance is overwhelming) almost always do more to determine the outcome of battle than the numbers of troops and distribution of weapons. This point is illustrated by the

German campaigns of World War II, the Israelis in 1956 and especially 1967, and, more recently, the South Atlantic War, in which a numerically inferior force of British Marines with little fire support quickly rolled up the well-entrenched Argentinian garrison on the Falkland/Malvinas Islands.[13]

Moreover, the military doctrines which govern the use of these forces and relate their capabilities to the political objectives they support depend on far more than static ratios. Deterrence also depends on numerous and, often, indeterminate nonquantitative considerations—the domestic and international political, economic and military vulnerabilities of the actors, and the uncertainties about one's own capabilities as well as those of an adversary. Former Army Chief of Staff (1955-59) and Chairman of the Joint Chiefs of Staff (1962-64) Maxwell D. Taylor in March 1983 noted the deterrent contributions of the:

> ... uncertainties that plague [Soviet leaders] ... such as 1) the unpredictable performance of their strategic weapons, which, like our own are of necessity incompletely tested; 2) the way an American president may react to a nuclear attack; and 3) the likely behavior of the Soviet people and unfriendly neighboring states under such circumstances....[14]

From this he concluded that "non-military adjustments of deterrence are [equally] important and add substantially to the improbability of deliberate Soviet nuclear aggression."[15] Historical experiences and national culture which color the prisms through which states view international events, together with the national will of the various key actors, are final elements that contribute to the often arcane and, generally, ambiguous interpretation of deterrence at any time. Without these views, a state's ability to pursue its national interests may be paralyzed irrespective of its aggregate raw military power.

The thesis of this essay is that when one views the potent military capability of the United States, its allies, and the PRC, and incorporates the nonquantitative factors noted above into the strategic equation, one may concur with General Taylor's assessment that the vulnerabilities and uncertainties confronting Soviet leaders and military planners will continue to provide powerful incentives to the Soviet Union to avoid war with the West.[16] Rather, the best interests of the Soviet Union would be to maintain an atmosphere of peaceful (albeit, politically competitive) coexistence with its political and military rivals. In reviewing the arguments below that support this conclusion, the reader is reminded that while serious domestic and international problems may face the Soviet Union, it remains a dangerous foe which is best deterred by Western vigilence and maintenance of a strong military posture. However, the reader also should acknowledge that the position of the United States and its allies is not nearly so precarious as some contend.

SOVIET DOMESTIC VULNERABILITIES

Except perhaps in the view of the most brazen martinet, national power is not an end in itself. Rather, it is a means to an end, or set of ends, which usually include such goals as the survival of the nation-state, its culture and its way of life; the improvement in the quality of life of its citizens; and the state's continued ability to increase its influence with other states in the pursuit of these goals. From this broader perspective, the national security of the Soviet Union is vulnerable to serious structural and systemic problems facing its industrial and agricultural bases as well as demographic trends which some believe threaten to interact to tear apart from within the last of the world's great multinational empires. The systemic roots of these problems, the bankruptcy of ideological exhortation, and political/bureaucratic constraints in dealing with these problems must make Soviet leaders far from sanguine in their evaluation of their future prospects.

Soviet Economic and Agricultural Vulnerabilities. The December 1982 Central Intelligence Agency (CIA) study of the Soviet economy came as a surprise to some who learned that between 1950-80, the standard of living in the Soviet Union tripled, and overall economic growth, evaluated at 4.8 percent, was not very different from the growth rates of the United States and the Western democracies.[17] Nevertheless, these aggregate figures obscure the fact that the Soviet Union is facing unprecedented economic problems which have worsened since that time and show little prospect of improvement in the near future.

Numerous factors contribute to the recent and rather precipitous drop in the growth of the Soviet Gross Domestic Product (GDP) found below.[18]

Year	1978	1979	1980	1981	1982
GDP growth rate (in percent)	3.4	2.0	1.5	1.2	1.0

The Soviet Union's relentless military expansion has imposed a mammoth burden upon industrial production, investment and modernization. Military spending, which grew more rapidly than the growth of the Gross National Product (GNP) during the 1970's,[19] retarded the development of the productive capital base. For instance, Soviet investment priorities during the 1970's decade favored heavy machine building needed for application in military production.[20] The expenditure of funds in this area came at the expense of investment in transportation, agriculture (which remains labor intensive, accounting for 23 percent of the Soviet workforce, as opposed to about 3 percent in the United States)[21] and food processing, to name only a few critical areas whose deficiencies ripple through the Soviet economy. Furthermore, Soviet maintenance of a large military force robs the economy of manpower which, as we shall see, is becoming increasingly scarce and costly. Finally, the diversion of a large portion of that society's best minds from the civilian economy into the uniformed services along with the massive industrial efforts that support military research, development and acquisition are bound to result in an economy that functions at low levels of efficiency.

The deleterious effects of the Soviet military burden are only one of numerous *systemic deficiencies* that retard the economy and defy easy or rapid resolution. In short, many of the problems currently plaguing the Soviet economy result from the very nature of the over-centralized political and planning systems themselves. Hence, the calls by Andropov for general proletarian discipline, less corruption, more rapid mechanization and the linkage of wages to increased productivity are expected to bring little significant or long-lasting improvement.[22]

At the heart of the Soviet economic malaise is what, at times, amounts to a deep hostility between the state planners who determine production goals and the managers charged with goal fulfillment. The excessive demands of the planners, once described as extortive by Nikita Khrushchev, were cited recently by Secretary Andropov as a significant contributing factor to the waste, black market activities, and the hoarding of resources required for production of scarce goods, and the theft, poor quality control and the falsification of production records prevalent in the Soviet economy.[23] These reactions to unrealistic production goals, in turn, contribute to Soviet production shortfalls. The 34 percent underfulfillment of the transportation plan during the tenth Five Year Plan is the rule rather than the exception in the Soviet production process as illustrated in the table below.[24]

	Planned (1976-80)	Actual	Achieved
		Millions of Tons	
Steel	250	148	59.2
Oil	690-710	603	87.4
Natural Gas	680-720	435	64.0
Coal	1180-1200	716	60.7
Cement	233-235	124	53.0
Synthetic Fibers	3.1-3.2	1.17	37.7
Leather Shoes	900-1000	744	82.7
		Billions of Kilowatt Hours	
Electric Energy	2700-3000	1296	48.0

The rigidly centralized Soviet economic planning production and distribution systems are a second structural vulnerability. This centralization, an artifact of the requirements from the rapid industrialization of 1920-30 and the alleged ideological imperatives, now interferes with the flexibility, incentives and innovation crucial to maximizing productivity. Such centralization is characterized by differentiated responsibility which, for instance, does not make those who transport raw materials responsible to those who produce the finished product. In a country encompassing 11 time zones and lacking an efficient transportation infrastructure, it is not surprising that many production plants often lack critical resources while others have more resources than they can use effectively. Consequently, the Soviet economy is characterized by frequent and serious bottlenecks which undermine planning and coordination efforts as well as sabotage cost control efforts. A second problem associated with rigid oversight is the discouragement of innovation. Apart from the low funding of nonmilitary research and development (R&D) and the geographical and administrative separation of those who seek and develop new ideas from those charged with their implementation, experimentation and innovation usually are viewed as counterproductive because they divert resources from the plan's fulfillment and often result in immediate production shortfalls. Consequently, the short-term prospects of innovation threaten the careers of industrial managers whose advancement depends upon obedience and productivity rather than experimentation. Among the many shortcomings of this inflexible system are the production of shoddy merchandise which is not competitive in international markets (military goods and energy exports are the notable exceptions) and the subsequent limitation of foreign exchange earnings.[25] Furthermore, the rigid system is hard pressed to anticipate or to control wild production fluctuations resulting from various factors (such as an extraordinarily harsh climate)[26] which lie outside of the planning system. Hence, the Soviet economy is notorious for the frequent *post hoc* revision of its plans.

A third systemic problem, which greatly affects the Soviet economy, is the lack of investment in the neglected and woefully inadequate transportation system. The few paved roads[27] in the Soviet Union mostly are rendered impassible by rain, mud and snow three seasons each year. This "roadlessness," known as *rasputitsa,* hampers distribution of materials and goods and largely limits the ability to coordinate and to integrate the vast national wealth and efforts of the Soviet Union's far-flung citizenry.

Problems of motor transport place a premium upon water and rail transport. Many Soviet waterways, however, are frozen during 8 months of the year, thus precluding commercial transport. Soviet transportation shortfalls are hardly ameliorated by the railroads, which are underutilized. Vast regions of the Soviet Union, including many areas rich in critical natural resources such as petroleum, remain unserved by rail transport. Moreover, the concentration of population in the European portions of the Soviet Union causes the inefficient use of many rail cars travelling toward the east. Fully loaded cars travelling in the opposite direction face severe delays at all six transshipment points that handle 80 percent of all Soviet rail freight.[28] This condition, in part, explains why as much as 30 percent of all agricultural production is lost in transit[29] and why the completion of the Baikal-Amur Mainline railroad will alleviate, but hardly resolve, the serious transport problems faced by the Soviet Union.

Extant demographic trends, which will not be overcome by planning, ideological exhortation or marginal adjustment, present additional problems for Soviet decisionmakers. These trends, which will be examined at length below, will affect the Soviet economy in numerous ways. Among the most salient trends in this regard are the aging of the entire population and the population flow away from the economically crucial but underpopulated eastern territory. The aging of the population increases the social welfare strain of monumental pension payments as well as slows down the expansion of the workforce.[30] Workforce expansion is particularly crucial to the Soviet Union, as its increasing allocation of national resources to the military obliges it to rely more upon increased labor assets than increased productivity for economic growth. Soviet labor shortages will not be reduced as long as the military continues to receive so large a percentage of the youth cohort and labor productivity of individual workers (who are given to alcoholism, sloth, and absenteesm) is not increased. These problems, which will become more serious toward the end of the decade, will continue to trouble the Soviet Union which already relies upon workers imported from allies to meet the annual demand for 700,000 new workers.[31] A second demographic trend, the flow of people from the resource rich but inhospitable eastern regions to the urban centers, has not been reversed despite the Soviet establishment of salary and educational inducements for those working in these harsh regions.[32]

Finally, the continuing problems of Soviet agriculture, which has not yet recovered from the brutal, forced collectivization and inefficient management of Stalin, place the Soviet Union in the unenviable position of many Third World countries. Despite their intensive efforts, Soviet leaders are embarrassed that the country cannot feed itself. Having suffered its fourth consecutive poor harvest in 1982, the USSR is compelled to import vast quantities of grain from the very economies whose demise has been predicted by every Soviet leader since Lenin.[33]

The facts that only 10 percent of the Soviet Union is arable, that 90 percent of its land mass lies north of the parallel demarcating the US-Canada border, and that the weather is harsh are not adequate to dismiss the system's inefficiency or low per capita output which is only 5-10 percent of that of the US farmer.[34] Among the many systemic obstacles to agricultural self-sufficiency are, specifically: (1) the absence of adequate and stable agricultural and transportation investments owing to the military spending burdens; (2) ruthless exploitation of the land which is not offset due to problems with the production, packaging and distribution of fertilizers; (3) insufficient incentives to the individual farmer; and (4) the flight of rural manual and skilled laborers to the cities causing labor shortages and larger percentages of female and older farm workers.[35] In an amazingly frank condemnation of his country's economy, I. N. Buzdalov, an economist with the Soviet Academy of Sciences, lamented that ". . . profitability, efficiency and quality play virtually no role in the work of state and collective farms."[36] The absence of faith of Soviet workers in the agricultural system's validity is demonstrated vividly by the vast differences between state and collective farm productivity on one hand and that of the workers' private plots on the other. The appallingly low output of state farms is well known and a direct cause of the Soviet Union's dependence upon Western grain imports. Less well known is the fact that the workers' one to several-acre plots, constituting only 1.4 percent of the available farmland, produce 61 percent of the country's potatoes, 54 percent of the fruit, 34 percent of the eggs, 30 percent of the vegetables and 29 percent of meat and milk![37] These figures suggest that Soviet deficiencies in agricultural organization and incentives, rather than the abilities of the workers themselves, account most readily for the deplorable food shortages throughout the country. Such figures also lead one to conclude that in the absence of a ". . . judicious (re)orientation and state investment policy" that improves rural housing, child care, educational opportunities and consumer services[38]—in short, an unlikely and revolutionary political, bureaucratic and economic transformation that redirects military expenditures to the consumer and rural economies—the debilitating burdens of agricultural backwardness will continue unabated. Since many of the popular demonstrations have been related to food shortages, the concern of Soviet leaders with the continuing agricultural ossification is easily understood.

The Soviet Union has been forced to rely increasingly on hard currency earning enterprises because of: (1) the need to import vast amounts of agricultural goods; (2) the low level of industrial innovation and the need for Western technological "transfusions"; and (3) the need to subsidize the Eastern European allies (whose economies, like that of the USSR, are similarly plagued and suffer dislocations due to the collapse of the Polish economy as well).[39] While foreign military sales are an important source of such income, energy sales constitute the lion's share (72 percent) of their export earnings.[40] However, the Soviet Union's ability to resolve its economic and political problems will be constrained by:

- rapidly falling commodity prices for petroleum and increased Soviet and East European energy consumption;
- growing exhaustion of easily recoverable assets and the inadequate infrastructure to exploit Siberian and the Eastern territorial riches (where 85 percent of the petroleum potential lies);[41] and
- reduced access to and increased cost of Western technology.

Although the quality of life for the average Soviet citizen is the best ever, its current stagnation comes at a dangerous time according to Crane Brinton, author of *Anatomy of Revolution,* when continued material improvement is expected.[42] It also comes at a time of (1) calls in the Soviet Union for a redistribution of wealth to the rapidly growing number of Muslims and Central Asians who reside east and south of the Urals, a development vigorously opposed by the Great Russians, Slavs and Balts living in European Russia; (2) a rapidly declining hard currency accounts balance[43] and a growing debt service burden,[44] and (3) heightened financial obligations and political deterioration throughout much of Eastern Europe. The Soviet Union could solve many of these problems by reducing its level of military spending and by rectifying the numerous systemic problems discussed above. Such prospects, however, short of a radical transformation of the Soviet politico-economic edifice, are highly unlikely.

Soviet Demographic Vulnerabilities. In the previous section, we observed the profound impacts of current demographic trends in the Soviet Union upon the availability of an adequate supply of labor manpower. Indeed, the impact of numerous demographic trends will ripple through every aspect of society and will cause unprecedented problems for Soviet leaders. These trends, analyzed perceptively by Murray Feshbach, the foremost US authority on Soviet demographics, so alarm the Soviet elite that they have refused to publish the details of the country's 1979 census.[45] Their silence is a striking departure from their publication of the 16 volume results of the 1959 census and the seven of 1970.

To understand the significance of these trends as well as the Kremlin's sensitivity to them, one must recognize the Soviet Union as the last of the great multinational empires. The Great Russians, the dominant ethnic group which comprises approximately 52 percent of the total population, control either directly or indirectly every aspect of national power: the Communist Party of the Soviet Union (CPSU), the national and republic governments, the military, the economy, education, the national academies, and the like.[46] The Great Russians have maintained their primacy through difficult times including internal instability, global war and intense postwar competition with the United States; however, their primacy has not gone unchallenged. Many of the more than 100 nationalities, speaking more than 150 languages and dialects, have revolted against Great Russian control; collaborated and fought with the Nazis against their masters during World War II; and stubbornly resisted and continue to resist linguistic and cultural Russification—which would establish national integration and homogeneity at the expense of the national identities of these groups.

The Russians (henceforth referring to the ethnic/cultural group) have repeatedly maintained that the nationality issue is artificial—a result of foreign intervention that would reverse the growing fraternal solidarity among all Soviet citizens. Because nationalism, according to Leninist doctrine, is a remnant and tool of reactionary capitalism, "bourgeois propaganda channelling nationalism into anti-Sovietism" is identified as the culprit.[47] While the Russians are alarmed by the nationalism and enmity of their Ukranian Slavic brothers and European countrymen (e.g., ethnic Poles and Germans, Latvians, Lithuanians and others), they are most sensitive to the ferment in the Central Asian republics. They have stressed that:

> ... in their propaganda for the Soviet Central Asian republics, including the Turkmen republic, the imperialist centres of lies and disinformation pay particular attention to the preaching of Pan-Islam and Pan-Turkism, bourgeois nationalism and religious prejudice.[48]

Apparently, as a result of these "great efforts to introduce 'the flame of Islamic rebirth' into the Soviet Union and thus destabilize ... the republics of Central Asia,"[49] great interest in Islam, a system which offers a competing value system to official Marxism-Leninism has been maintained and according to some is growing rapidly. Indeed, Soviet leaders lament that:

> ... many misguided men and women, accompanied by their children, have paid homage to various graves and burial grounds ... they make sacrificial offerings, pay homage to graves, ... beseech the saints to grant one plea or another ... and perform their prayers five times a day.[50]

The four demographic trends identified below are vital to the interests of those who would retain their political *status quo* because the shifting patterns of population growth and distribution threaten to undermine the dominance of the Great Russians while imposing upon them unsavory economic and political dilemmas. And such vulnerability was acknowledged in September 1981 by the vice-president of the Academy of Sciences when he noted that "neither we nor our friends are immune to harmful influences and a certain revival of various prejudices.[51]

The most ominous demographic trend is the differential rates of population growth among the various nationality groups. As a result of higher fertility rates of the Central Asians and the higher Great Russia mortality rates (which have climbed 40 percent since 1964) due to alcoholism, increasing suicides, and so forth, the 1970-79 rate of increase of the Russians and other Slavs (+.7 percent) is substantially below the average Muslim rate (+2.7 percent), in general, and the Uzbek (+3.7 percent), and Tadzhik (+3.5 percent) rates, in particular.[52] In short, these rates explain why the Russians, who comprised 54.6 percent of the total population in 1959, are expected to contribute only 46-48 percent of the population by the year 2000.[53]

Second, males in the Soviet Union have failed to regain their pre-World War II and normal share of the population, usually estimated to be approximately 48.5 percent.

The current male percentage of the population is 46.7. The situation is substantially worse, however, for the Great Russians (46.0 percent) than it is for the Central Asians such as the Uzbeks (49 percent).[54] Furthermore, Soviet males, who live a full 10 years less than females, have the singular and dubious distinction among citizens of the world's developed states of a life expectancy rate which plummeted from 66 to 62-63 years between 1966-80.[55] Once again, alcoholism, suicides and inadequate health care, especially among the 20-44 year-old Russians, are the major causes.

The uneven geographical distribution of the youngest population cohorts is the third demographic trend of import to the Russians. Specifically, the percentage of Russian 0-9 year olds (14.8 percent of the population) is less than the national average (16.8 percent) and far less than the Uzbeks (29.2 percent) and their Central Asian brothers.[56] Numerous reasons account for the decline of Russian youths in the Russian Soviet Federated Socialist Republic (RSFSR): (1) high levels of female alcoholism; (2) abortion as the principal form of birth control (the average number of abortions for Russian women is six, more than 12 times the rate for US women);[57] (3) the widespread use of artificial milk and crowded nurseries where the babies are placed when Russian women return to work; and (4) the trend of the European Slavs to have fewer babies than mothers in rural Central Asia. The result is a steep rise in Russian infant mortality and a drop in Russian youths relative to the Central Asian increases. Hence, by the year 2000, approximately 85 percent of all Soviet citizens below 9 years of age will be Moslems.[58] The long-term prospects for continued Russian primacy in the Soviet Union become highly uncertain in such a scenario.

Finally, as noted in the previous section, the Soviet population is aging. However, the phenomenon, which is tied to declining Russian birth rates and declining Central Asian mortality rates, is most notable once again among the Russians. Moreover, the figures in the table below demonstrate that the Russians' position relative to the Central Asians will continue to deteriorate.[59]

Average Age by Year

Grouping	ALL USSR	RSFSR	UZBEKISTAN
1975	28.7	31.1	17.8
2000	33.1	37.1	21.7

Clearly, the Muslim population is increasing at a more rapid rate than other populations of the USSR. Between 1979 and 2000, the percent of the entire Soviet population made up by Central Asians will rise from 16.5 to 30 percent, while the percent of Great Russians will fall from 52.4 percent to 46-48 percent.[60]

Some of the implications of these trends have been identified already: (1) increased pension costs which will divert money from needed investment; (2) increased adherence to Islam which will challenge the primacy of Marxism-Leninism; (3) demands from the Asian republics for a reorientation of investment and redistribution of wealth; and (4) severe manpower shortages in European Russia which will occur (despite the origination of 60 percent of the Soviet GNP in the RSFSR)[61] because few Central Asians are inclined to move to the region where they do not speak the language, find the culture alien, and themselves the butt of racial antagonism. Such shortages will be exacerbated if the military continues to call up approximately 700,000 18 year-olds to maintain the 4.8 million man Red Army.[62] In addition to these problems, military reliability and effectiveness are likely to decline, and serious constraints upon Soviet foreign policy may become evident.[63] Moreover, the Russians take little comfort from the knowledge that their traditional efforts to resolve the nationalities problem have been disappointingly slow and ineffective.[64]

Political and Ideological Vulnerabilities. The economic, agricultural and demographic vulnerabilities described above confront the leaders of the Soviet Union with a particularly acute dilemma. The physical separation of resources from the bulk of the population, labor shortages west of the Urals and an inadequate transportation infrastructure to connect resources and capital assets with the future labor supply will force Soviet leaders to consider two basic options.[65] The first entails relocating existing industrial assets and building future industrial installations in Central Asia to exploit the abundance of labor, reduce transportation costs and, ultimately, to lower production costs. The problem with this strategy has been understood by the Soviet leadership for decades. It will amount to a massive redistribution of wealth and probably would require a substantial redirection of investment monies from the military; no doubt a policy fraught with danger for its proponents. An "eastern" investment strategy would certainly incur Great Russian and Slavic resentment given these peoples' racial and religious hostility toward their countrymen as well as the increasingly resource-constrained environment.[66] Increasing investments in areas closer to contested and vulnerable border areas with the PRC complicate the Soviet Eastern strategy.

As another possibility, the Politburo could encourage its Muslim and Asiatic population to resettle west of the Urals. Such a labor relocation, however, would be unlikely for a number of reasons: the delay that would be imposed upon the access to and development of eastern natural resources; further reduced eastern agricultural production due to the heightened immigration of male farm workers; the unattractiveness of European Russia's religious and cultural environments to the eastern peoples; and the racial animosity toward and economic threat posed by the easterners to their western countrymen who traditionally have been *primus inter pares* in every institution of influence in Soviet life.[67] Moreover, the Soviet Union's decisions regarding this dilemma will be made within a context of (1) Great Russian chauvinism toward all other Soviet nationalities; (2) a debate among the Russians about whether future Soviet greatness is to be found within a western or a Slavophile context which extols the historical and cultural uniqueness of the country's Slavic elements; and (3) an apparent widespread sense throughout the Soviet Union that the ideology has lost its relevance and the government its efficiency and effectiveness in the increasingly complex and interdependent national and global environments.[68] This third context would be manifested by increased numerical and vociferous levels of the dissidents,[69] growing political apathy and a resurgence of interest in religion which is challenging Marxism-Leninism as the society's primary guiding force.[70]

The difficult determination of the most economically efficient yet politically feasible manner of dealing with these problems will require innovative and flexible thinking by CPSU and government leaders along with popular confidence in the correctness of their decisions. As noted above, it is unlikely that any government decision will meet with uncritical acclaim because of the country's political apathy and heterogeneity. Even if popular acceptance could be assured, the chances of an actual decision being made is uncertain.

In effect, the decisions to identify priorities and to redistribute wealth require some flexibility and decentralization. Yet this is hardly the first time that such needs have been prescribed. Lenin's New Economic Policy, Leibermanism in the 1960's, and the management by objective approach adopted by Alexei Kosygin in the early 1970's are the precursors of Yuri Andropov's current initiatives.[71] The unhappy condition in the Soviet Union is that broad-based social change either is not implemented at all or it is done haltingly and inefficiently, at best.

There are several straightforward explanations of the Soviet Union's limited ability to reform. A major cause is the country's massive and rigid party and government bureaucracies. Their size and fragmentation contribute to inertia. Furthermore, the myth of the CPSU as the sole repository of truth and its status as the only party needed in a classless society to function as the vanguard of the proletariat places every national decision and development—no matter how trivial—under its aegis. Consequently, the CPSU must meddle in every matter, often imposing inappropriate "solutions" from the top and causing delay when questions are debated upwards through the hierarchy in accordance with the principles of democratic centralism.[72]

Second, even a stultified and obstructed bureaucracy can be motivated to act by a strong leader. However, Soviet leaders no longer enjoy the omnipotence of Stalin. The acceptance by Khrushchev of a concensus-based Politburo, designed to prevent Stalinist abuses in the future, has been strengthened over the years. Consequently, the power of each successive first secretary and plenipotentiary has been reduced. Within this general trend, numerous reasons and hints indicate that Mr. Andropov, though powerful, has yet to consolidate his power and remains limited in the scope and depth of reformation he can pursue.[73] Furthermore, at 68 years of age and in frail health, his longevity at the pinnacle of the Soviet state, will be rather limited.   Third, is the problematic nature of the data available to the decisionmakers. In the Soviet

Union, high-level party functionaries still remember Stalin's legacy to kill the messenger bearing bad news. Although no longer fearing for their lives in the event of mission failure, CPSU functionaries recognize that their own advancement depends on their mission success. Naturally, such pressures in the face of adverse economic, societal and cultural obstacles result in sycophancy and generate falsification of information by commission or omission throughout the chain of command. Furthermore, as one would expect in a garrison state with Russian cultural antecedents, every issue affects national security and, therefore, is shrouded in secrecy. The resulting compartmentalization of information means that in the Soviet Union, the left hand often is unaware of what is being done by the right. Moreover, the absence of a genuine loyal opposition precludes the attenuation of the distorted information problem.

Ideological considerations provide an additional set of constraints to flexibility in dealing with extant economic and social problems. Because Marxism-Leninism is viewed as a set of prescriptions, in addition to an explanation of current and past social developments, the Soviet Union is limited in the degree to which it can pursue certain palliatives such as greater economic decentralization. Also, due to the ideology's revolutionary ethos, Soviet leaders find it difficult to abandon obligations such as its $9 million per day subsidation of the Cuban economy at a time when Soviet hard currency reserves are dangerously low.[74] Hence, the ideological gurus find difficulty in maneuvering since their orthodox interpretation of ideology justifies their own primacy within the CPSU, the primacy of the CPSU within the Soviet Union, and the primacy of the Soviet Union in the "progressive" world. In short, to acknowledge the limitations of the ideology would undermine the very *raison d'etre* and legitimacy of the Soviet hierarchy, Party and State.

Related to the above is the implication of change for Soviet dissidents and the Warsaw Pact allies. The Kremlin has long resisted substantial departures at home and within its alliance from its own mandated policies. To the extent that the Soviets permit reform at home or in East Europe, they acknowledge limits to the universality of their ideology, open the door to demands for more change and ultimately risk losing control of the Party, the State and the Empire. Interestingly, while Soviet leaders are obligated to limit reform at home and abroad due to ideological imperatives, their endorsement of Basket 4 of the Helsinki Final Act of the Conference on Security and Cooperation in Europe (as well as greater interaction with the West) not only commits them to the observance of fundamental human rights but also gives the United States and its allies the formal right to critique Soviet performance in this regard. Once again, those in the Kremlin find it difficult to move in either direction.

Thus, the Soviet Union is beset with difficult domestic problems but lacks many of the means necessary to deal with them. Inasmuch as the traditional "muddling through" response is likely to prove unsatisfactory[75] in the absence of major structural, ideological and military reforms (all of which are highly unlikely), one well understands why, at least with regard to the domestic situation, one analyst has concluded that from the crest, all directions are down for the Soviet Union.[76] In any event, the combined effect of the domestic problems described above is likely to make the Soviet Union less, rather than more, interested in confrontation with the United States.

SOVIET MILITARY VULNERABILITIES AND UNCERTAINTIES

The disturbing military developments cited in the opening paragraphs of this essay and the 1981 and 1983 publications of *Soviet Military Power* leave little room to doubt the massive strength and potential of the Soviet military. The development of a strategic nuclear arsenal that is at least as powerful as that of the United States and the continuing modernization and augmentation of Soviet conventional forces in Europe, its blue-water navy and long-range power projection assets are troubling. When one views these developments through the prism of Soviet military doctrine that is characterized by an offensive orientation and an emphasis upon seizing the initiative with an overabundance of forces, the concerns of US national security planners appear well-founded. Specifically, some fear that in certain crisis scenarios, US decisionmakers may be forced to acquiesce to Soviet demands or be less capable of pursuing US interests with confidence. At worst, it is feared that Soviet leaders might be tempted to seize the initiative and exploit their military potential in a decapitating preemptive strike against the United States.[77] Estimates in various nuclear exchange scenarios that the United States would suffer more than twice the number of casualties than the Soviet Union, lend a frightening plausibility to these speculations and help to explain why the adequacy of the US defense posture is increasingly questioned by many.[78] On a less stark but equally important level is the concern in the United States that the Soviet Union, in an effort to exploit its only influential foreign policy instrument, will increasingly use its intimidating military capability to pursue its principal foreign policy objective: the estrangement of the United States from its allies. Such an objective would be achieved, in large part, by demonstrating that the correlation of forces increasingly favors the Soviet Union and by raising questions in the minds of American leaders and their allies about the ability and willingness of the United States to defend crucial US and Western interests.

Strategic Military Uncertainties. The military capability of the Soviet Union to threaten the United States and its allies with strategic and theater nuclear and conventional weapons has been analyzed in many fora. Without denying the potency and genuine threat emanating from the Soviet military arsenal, a growing body of literature has focused on the vulnerabilities of Soviet military power and the uncertainties which surely complicate the assessments of national security planners in the Kremlin.[79] With regard to Soviet strategic capabilities, Robert Kennedy of the US Army War College, and Benjamin Lambeth, a noted student of Soviet military strategy, have concluded, independently, that Soviet strategic planners who are better aware of their own vulnerabilities than American worst-case force planners (who must emphasize all plausible capabilities of their adversary), can hardly afford to feel sanguine about the prospects of a successful Soviet preemptive strike. Kennedy and Lambeth argue that the Soviet Union (1) has never fired a strategic missile at random or on short notice, many misiles at once or exploded a nuclear warhead at the end of a test flight; (2) maintains lower ICBM alert and reliability rates than the comparable US missiles; (3) has derived its missile data from unrepresentative tests (such as east to west test flights rather than the north to south trajectory required of an actual attack against the United States); (4) remains uncertain about its ability to coordinate the timing of the hundreds of warheads that would constitute a preemptive strike as well as the effects of electromagnetic pulse (EMP) and fratricide; and (5) confronts numerous additional complicating variables and imprecise doctrinal questions about the initiation, duration, dynamics and controllability of nuclear war. Further, to support their position, Kennedy and Lambeth assert that the risks of miscalculation provide ample discouragement to the normally cautious Soviets. Indeed, they ask why should the Soviet elite—whose ideology has preordained their victory, who draw sharp distinctions between the desirable and the necessary, and who recognize that nuclear war might undo their advances toward the Communist millenium—contemplate such cataclysmic initiatives when patience is certain to deliver the millenium into their hands?[80]

In addition to questions about Soviet strategic capabilities and doctrinal uncertainties, Soviet planners cannot be sure of the US response in a preemptive scenario. They know that the United States is undertaking numerous initiatives, partially in response to the Soviet Union's massive military expansion of the last two decades, to assure the command and control, survivability, and, therefore, assured retaliatory lethality of its strategic arsenal.[81] They also know that even if a preemptive strike against US ICBMs were successful, they might have to contend with the two remaining legs of the Triad:

- (with the deployment of the Trident D-5 missile) the mobile, relatively invulnerable and counter-silo capable SLBM fleet—which contains much of America's strategic nuclear arsenal; and
- the intercontinental bomber fleet—which, although currently capable of penetrating Soviet anti-air defense in great numbers, will become even deadlier with the deployment of air-launched cruise missiles and the stealth technology. Whether US ICBMs would be launched on warning; whether an American President would be driven by fear, desperation or vindictiveness to order a counter-value strike; and whether the potent US forward-based systems in Europe and other locations on the USSR's periphery, as well as the nuclear arsenals of the United Kingdom, France, and the People's Republic of China would be unleashed against Soviet military, other counterforce and key industrial targets are questions that are certain to bedevil Soviet strategists and urge them toward caution.[82]

What the military and political leaders in the Kremlin do know is that the relatively low number of high-value Soviet military targets; the excessive concentration of Soviet industry (50 percent of the Soviet industrial output comes from less than 200 plants) and transportation assets which could not be easily protected against a US bottlenecking strategy;[83] and, most importantly, the potential fragility of Great Russian control over the political, economic, social, military and cultural institutions of their vast multinational empire would be threatened by a retaliatory strike of even a small portion of US strategic warheads.[84] Despite the resources directed toward civil defense, Soviet planners cannot be certain that such efforts would allow them to escape the effects of US retaliation, maintain the integrity of the Soviet Union and continue to play a dominant role in the Communist world.[85] In the calculus of Clausewitz, the Prussian military theorist often cited by Lenin, Soviet military operations are not undertaken out of concert with political realities. From this perspective, a preemptive strike against the United States would violate the most elementary dictum of war.

Conventional Military Uncertainties. While not denying that the Soviet Union possesses the most frightening conventional military force ever assembled, it is important to acknowledge that the Red Army faces numerous problems and uncertainties that are bound to impose moderation even upon its most optimistic advocates.

Soviet military theory extols the virtues of speed, shock and surprise to achieve a quick victory. Nevertheless, John Mearsheimer has argued persuasively that the need to reinforce Soviet units comprising the Group of Soviet Forces-Germany (GSFG) precludes the USSR from achieving strategic surprise. He also maintains that the most gross Warsaw Pact advantages disappear when the static quantitative ratios comparing NATO and Warsaw Pact inventories—manpower, tank, artillery, and so forth—are translated into the more realistic armor division equivalents (which take mobility, firepower and survivability into account). Mearsheimer argues that ratios based on divisional equivalents do not give the Pact the necessary wherewithal to punch quickly through NATO forward defenses and rush to the Rhine, especially when the capabilities of the sizable French army are factored into the equation. Furthermore, force-to-space ratios created by urban sprawl, natural geographic features and prepared NATO defenses will force critical Warsaw Pact follow-on echelons and formations to mass, thereby becoming highly vulnerable to long-range conventional and nuclear weapons as envisioned by NATO strategy and the US military's new AirLand Battle concept.

These arguments are among those Mearsheimer marshals to conclude that, in the absence of delayed NATO mobilization, the Soviet Union cannot win quickly in Central Europe.[86] Because of a Soviet need to win quickly, Mearsheimer's conclusion supports the view of Lambeth, who argues below, that in light of certain advantages that occur to a defender, the denial of quick victory may be adequate to deter the Soviet Union.

> . . . the chances of success are heavily bound up with the correctness of planning assumptions and opportunities for regrouping are likely to be few and far between. Countries on the receiving end that are politically bound to defensive and reactive strategies have options for flexibility generally denied to those who would start a war. In many cases, the defender might need only be capable of disrupting the attacker's designs to forestall defeat.[87]

Additional problems and vulnerabilities confront Soviet military leaders (who also are likely to base their plans upon worst-case scenarios) which are likely to cause them to ponder their own assessments of the combat capabilities of their forces. Many of these problems are qualitative in nature and, therefore, not easily integrated into a force-level calculus. Their importance, nevertheless, was not lost to Stalin who identified the quality of commanders, stability in the rear, morale of the Army and the quality of divisions as four of the five permanently operating factors which affect the outcome of war.[88] Nor has the need for more frequent and realistic training, the abolition of alcoholism in the armed forces, better troop discipline and less rigid command and control been lost on current Soviet military officials—who recently have been allocating increased space to these concerns in *Krasnaya Zvezda (Red Star)*, the offical newspaper of the Soviet military.[89]

Otto P. Chaney, Richard Clayberg, and Edward Corcoran, analysts of the Strategic Studies Institute and experts on Soviet and Eastern European militaries, have identified numerous nonquantitative considerations that bedevil Soviet and Warsaw Pact military planners.[90] In the area of training, they have identified the following as sources of problems: (1) the absence of troop initiative caused by over-supervision, rote learning and training exercises which rely heavily on simulators at the expense of real-time exercises;[91] (2) little attention to map reading and basic land navigation skills that would be required in an unfamiliar and fast-moving battlefield environment;[92] (3) the absence since World War II of any combat experience against a sophistcated adversary; and (4) the dearth of combat training (and ammunition) given to Muslim and other nationality group troops who are considered unreliable.[93]

The personnel area provides additional vulnerabilities that surely concern Soviet political and military leaders. Examples are high turnover rates, physical beatings of new conscriptees by senior troops, inedible food, absence of a professional NCO corps, and racially generated violence between Great Russians and various minorities. These characteristics of the Soviet Army are unlikely to inspire *espirit de corps* or confidence in the coordination of military operations among Soviet force planners and technicians.[94]

Additionally, Soviet leaders probably anticipate problems involving command, control, communications and intelligence (C^3I) which could well result from (1) the excessive concentration of authority at the top of the command structure;[95] (2) the inability of increasing numbers of recruits to communicate effectively in Russian (the sole language of command and control);[96] (3) the discipline of troops who have been beaten and abused;[97] (4) epidemic levels of drunkeness at all levels of rank;[98] and (5) the mutual distrust and, on occasion, antagonism between Soviet Army troops and their "fraternal" Eastern allies whose homelands stand to be destroyed in any future European conflict.[99] Such problems could well stifle the initiative and timeliness of Soviet responses; reduce Pact ability to exploit tactical advantages on the fast-moving and confused future battlefield; and leave Soviet C^3I networks vulnerable to information deception and denial.

Finally, serious problems and vulnerabilities imposed by geography (e.g., the absence of natural borders; the threat of a two-front war; easily interdictable naval choke points), maintenance and resupply (e.g., lines of communication passing through Poland, Czechoslovakia and East Germany and the vulnerability of the Friendship Pipeline System and rail transshipment points to NATO interdiction), and logistics cannot be viewed with equanimity by Soviet leaders.[100] Evidence of concern with these and other problems is abundant in the pages of *Red Star* which suggests that Soviet military planners may concur with a conclusion of London's prestigious International Institute for Strategic Studies:

The overall balance continues to be such as to make military aggression a highly risky undertaking. Though tactical redeployments could provide a local advantage in numbers sufficient to allow an attacker to believe that he might achieve tactical success, there would still appear to be insufficient overall strength on either side to guarantee victory. The consequences for an attacker would be unpredictable, and the risks, particularly of nuclear escalation, incalculable.[101]

IMPLICATIONS AND CONCLUSIONS

A prominent student of Soviet affairs and military doctrine lamented recently that:

> Most assessments of Soviet capability emphasize elements that contribute to Soviet strength. By contrast, vulnerability analysis remains undeveloped in strategic research.[102]

There are good reasons for this state of affairs. US national security planners' concern with the capabilities of our adversaries to deny the basic national interests of and to bring physical damage to the United States is well founded. An overemphasis on Soviet vulnerabilities could well lead to an erroneous assessment that the Soviet Union is not strong or dangerous enough to constitute a serious threat to critical US interests, and thus does not justify the expenditure of American defense dollars to maintain a secure and credible deterrent force.

In evaluating the domestic and military problems and vulnerabilities of the Soviet Union, various analysts have seized upon these shortcomings over the last 65 years to predict the demise of the Soviet state.[103] Yet, the speculation of Soviet dissident Andrei Amalrik about whether the Soviet Union will survive until 1984 can now be answered in the affirmative.[104] Corroboration is furnished by the CIA's recent analysis of the Soviet Union, which concludes that while problems certainly exist, they neither presage the "Decline of an Empire," nor attenuate the Soviet threat.[105] Those who would argue to the contrary would do well to reflect on the Russian proverb: "All that trembles does not fall." Indeed, rather than causing the Soviet leaders to abandon their military expenditures, forsake their national objectives, and decentralize the Soviet state with all its attendant revolutionary implications, these problems may have an opposite effect. They may encourage the "hounded bear" to pursue its objectives more recklessly while it still possesses the initiative and most military requisites.[106] In short, American complacency stemming from an overemphasis on Soviet vulnerabilities would be imprudent and, potentially, cataclysmic.

Vulnerability analysis, however, is an important part of the strategic calculus. The recognition of Soviet weaknesses is crucial to the fashioning of sensible and realistic policies to deal with that superpower. Soviet economic and agricultural deficiencies must be considered in the determination of trade policy, and military weaknesses can guide the development of military operations and doctrine designed to deter a Soviet resort to force in a crisis situation. Simultaneously, vulnerability analysis may assure that the United States does not overreact to the threat.

Hence, the ultimate goals of US security policy must remain the maintenance of a military capability that deters the Soviet Union from using military force, directly or indirectly, in pursuit of its political objectives, and the development of stable and mutually beneficial bilateral US-Soviet relations.

As noted recently by Under Secretary of State Lawrence Eagleburger, the maintenance of deterrence is the country's most essential goal.[107] To this end, the continued vigilance of the Soviet threat as well as a number of current US initiatives to assure a military balance between the superpowers is necessary and well-advised. Improvements in the survivability and connectivity of the nation's nuclear arsenal and command structure; the deployment of mobile, survivable, and highly accurate strategic missiles such as the Trident D-5 SLBM; the creation of a rapidly deployable force to defend global US interests; the modernization of NATO's nuclear arsenal; and the continued modernization of the strategic bomber fleet will do much to ensure the potency of the US retaliatory force. Furthermore, these initiatives will discourage the Soviet Union from believing that the threat of military operations against the United States or its allies or a preemptive strike against the United States can ever result in anything but failure imposed with unacceptable costs. Such a realization would not be lost to the Soviet leadership which has a supreme appreciation for the roles of its military as a symbol and an element of national power.

Many of the initiatives described by Secretary Weinberger in his *Annual Report to Congress*[108] are designed to exploit many of the Soviet Union's vulnerabilities described above. For instance, the development of weapons capable of destroying Soviet C^3I facilities in a conventional war can capitalize upon vulnerabilities stemming from its rigid command and control structure and reduce the Soviet ability to execute planned operations. The development of the AirLand deep-strike concept also is designed to exploit Soviet vulnerabilities in the event of war by neutralizing the massed follow-on echelons crucial to Warsaw Pact military operations while bringing the battle to Pact territory. This latter thrust will impose a real cost upon the East European Pact allies and reduce their solidarity with the Soviet Union. To the extent that this new strategy can increase the divergence of interests between the Soviets and their allies and reduce Soviet confidence in the reliability of those allies, deterrence in Europe is strengthened.

At the strategic level, a targeting plan that aimed at the relatively few critical nodes of the Soviet Union's industrial, communications and transportation infrastructures and the elements of political and social control by the Communist Party, in general, and the Great Russians, in particular, might allow, in the words of Colin Gray:

> . . . the centrifugal forces within the Soviet empire to begin to bring that system down from within.[109]

Surely, the threat of the disintegration of their empire and the knowledge that the major upheavals in the USSR in this century occurred in the midst of wartime failures (Russo-Japanese War and World War I) would constitute powerful deterrents to those in the Kremlin who might contemplate the utility of military operations in pursuit of their interests.[110] In the same vein, deterrence could be strengthened by occasional and oblique allusions to a launch on warning in the event of a Soviet first-strike[111] along with constant reminders by US political and military officials that, while the United States recognizes the necessity to assure its ability to respond in the long as well as short-time frames to aggression at all levels of the conventional and nuclear continuum, war may not be controllable but instead could escalate to total and horrific proportions. Such statements will (1) demonstrate US resolve to protect its interests in all scenarios; (2) dispel any Soviet perceptions that they could achieve a victory worth having; and thus, (3) induce moderation and circumspection rather than boldness in military initiatives that could have disasterous consequences in the event of miscalculation. Indeed, the Soviet Union is sensitive to the uncertainties and risks stemming from miscalculations and war, as Ye. Rybkin acknowledged:

> In setting for oneself definite and concrete goals of defeating the enemy and preserving one's forces and placing society in a special situation with the beginning of military action, the opposing sides are frequently and unexpectedly faced with the fact that they have put into action processes which were undesirable. As a result, *war has a powerful reverse effect on the social processes long before victory or defeat, frequently counter to the design and plans of the instigator which unleashed the war.* [emphasis added].[112]

The Soviet vulnerabilities described above as well as the current political climates in the United States and Europe make the present a propitious time to pursue arms control with the Soviet Union. The increasingly certain prospects of the deployment of 108 Pershing II and 464 ground launched cruise missiles on NATO territory[113] as well as the Soviet Union's expressed concern over the French, British and Chinese nuclear arsenals[114] provide real incentives to negotiate nonstrategic, nuclear arms control agreements.[115] Furthermore, projected demographic trends, especially those indicating manpower shortages, are certain to create great tension between the Soviet Army's manning requirements (qualitative and quantitative) and the labor needs of Soviet agriculture and industry.[116] The Soviet Union is likely to find the manpower reductions proposed in MBFR talks conveniently attractive.[117] Relaxation of border tensions with the PRC would further accommodate a Soviet manpower shortage, perhaps permitting a reduction in the number of 6 tank and 41 motorized rifle divisions deployed on the border area.[118]

Finally, the fact that Soviet leaders have demonstrated the willingness and the ability to spend whatever is necessary to develop and maintain a frightening strategic arsenal[119] does not preclude the possibility that they will become more amenable to genuine and verifiable strategic arms control initiatives as Soviet economic and agricultural problems become more severe, the costs of maintaining their internal and external empires escalate, and the United States begins to deploy many improved weapons systems in its own strategic arsenal.[120]

The Soviet Union appears to be faltering at the international, political and economic levels, thereby facilitating competition by the United States and its allies with the Soviet Union in these settings. Throughout the Third World, Soviet ideology as a moral force and model of development increasingly is becoming impotent.[121] Also, Great Russian chauvinism and repression of their own Muslim populations are well known in many Third World countries. The Soviet Union could well find the pursuit of "national liberation" abroad increasingly difficult, especially when internal deprivations are so evident in the Soviet state. Although the USSR has been a willing supplier of arms to Third World clients[122] and an eager exploiter of local instability, the absence of Soviet economic aid as well as internal racism and political heavy-handedness have prevented the Soviet leaders from consolidating their advantages and fulfilling the Leninist anti-imperial destiny Khrushchev so smugly anticipated in the 1950's. Quite simply, many states in the Third World are loathe to buy what the Soviet Union is selling and when they do buy, they carefully guard the prerogatives of their hard-won national sovereignty.[123]

In Europe, detente with the West has contributed to the increasing disunity within the Eastern bloc. While Soviet trade with Europe does provide the former with potential leverage, it also opens the Soviet leadership to certain problems including the drain on Soviet hard currency assets,[124] the reliance upon Western technology (at the expense of the further postponement of Soviet nonmilitary R & D developments), and the example viewed by increasing numbers of Soviet citizens that Westerners are neither evil nor made destitute by an allegedly-doomed economic system that cannot meet their most elementary needs.[125] Hence, with appropriate controls over the transfer of sensitive technology, it is in the West's and US interests to continue to compete with the Soviet Union in the politcal and economic arenas where the West holds most, if not all, of the advantages.

To this end, improvements in and augmentation of the training of US civilian and military personnel in the Russian language, as well as in Soviet political, economic and cultural subjects are critical though neglected US national security initiatives. Similarly, the continuation of cultural exchanges that allow Americans to develop a realistic understanding of Soviet weaknesses (as well as strengths) and which demonstrate American strengths (as well as weaknesses) will do much to stabilize Soviet-US relations in ways entirely amenable to US interests and those of the West.

Of course, these recommendations do not mean that the United States should abandon its scrutiny and criticisms of Soviet human rights abuses or cease to demand that the Soviet Union observe certain basic standards of national behavior.[126] After all, the Soviet Union represents the antithesis of many fundamental Western values and objectives. However, the Soviet Union is not without serious weaknesses and vulnerabilities which provide the United States the opportunity and ability to deter aggression while as Under Secretary of State Lawrence Eagleburger has argued: "We . . . work on our own and with our friends to build a world order compatible with our values and our interests."[127]

ENDNOTES

1. Caspar Weinberger, *Soviet Military Power,* Washington: US Government Printing Office, 1983, pp. 36-37. There are also more than 200 older INF missiles (SS-4, SS-5) based opposite NATO Europe. Counting *only* warheads on launchers, there are *over 1000* warheads unquestionably in range of NATO Europe backed up with over 750 additional SS-20 warheads on their "reload" or "spare" missiles. Counting the Eastern USSR (from which *Alaska* can unquestionably be reached), there are altogether over *2000* INF warheads available to the USSR *all* within range of NATO. The *only* NATO country the USSR's INF missiles cannot reach from present bases is *Canada.*

2. Henry Kissinger, "The Future of NATO," *The Washington Quarterly,* Vol. 2, Autumn 1979, pp. 6-7.

3. Robert Komer, "Maritime Strategy vs. Coalition Defense," in *Foreign Affairs,* Summer 1982, pp. 1124-1144, provides an excellent analysis of the maritime-coalition debate. Also see Jeffrey Record and Robert Hanks, *US Strategy at the Crossroads: Two Views,* Foreign Policy Report, July 1982, Cambridge, Massachusetts: Institute for Foreign Policy Analysis.

4. Atlantic Council, "The Credibility of the NATO Deterrent: Bringing the NATO Deterrent Up To Date," Washington: May 1981. On December 12, 1979, the NATO ministers decided that the US INF missiles would be deployed in the absence of progress in INF arms control.

5. Josef Adamek, "Centrally Planned Economics of Europe," *Economic Overview 1982,* Amsterdam: The Conference Board Inc., June 25, 1982, pp. 31-37.

6. This figure, based on a Congressional Research Service study, was derived from data in Brad Knickerbocher's "US Overtakes Soviets in Arms Sales to Third World," *Christian Science Monitor,* April 19, 1983. The figures cited by Knickerbocher are consistent with those presented by the US Arms Control and Disarmament Agency, *World Military Expenditures and Arms Transfers, 1975-1979,* Washington: US Government Printing Office, 1982, p. 118. During the 1970's, ACDA data indicates that arms represented about 15 percent of total Soviet exports.

7. See Otto Chaney, "The Soviet Threat to Europe: Prospect for the 1980's," in *The Defense of the West: Strategic and European Security Issues Reappraised,* ed. by Robert Kennedy and John Weinstein, Boulder, Colorado: Westview Press, 1984. Also, see Joseph D. Douglas, *The Soviet Theater Nuclear Offensive,* Washington: US Government Printing Office, 1976; John M. Weinstein, "Soviet Civil Defense and the US Deterrent," *Parameters,* March 1982, pp. 70-83.

8. John Weinstein, "The Strategic Implications of Civil Defense" in *The Defense of the West,* 1983.

9. Lawrence S. Eagleburger, "Review of U.S. Relations With the Soviet Union," *Current Policy No. 450,* US Department of State, Washington, February 1, 1983.

10. John Williams, "Soviets Endanger US 'Forward Line of Defense' Reagan Says," *The Washington Post,* February 20, 1983, p. 1.

11. Alwyn H. King, *The United States Strategic Minerals Position in the 1980's and Beyond,* Futures/Long-Range Planning Group Report, Carlisle Barracks, Pennsylvania: Strategic Studies Institute, US Army War College, 1981.

12. Eagleburger, p. 2.

13. Richard Betts, "Conventional Strategy: New Critics, Old Choices," *International Security*, Spring 1983, p. 142. For other arguments supporting this thesis, see William Kincade, "Repeating History: The Civil Defense Debate Renewed," *International Security*, Winter 1978, pp. 99-120; and Arthur M. Katz, *Life After Nuclear War: The Economic and Social Impacts of Nuclear Attacks on the United States*, Cambridge, Massachusetts: Ballinger Publishing Company, 1982.

14. Maxwell D. Taylor, "Build Up the Forces We Really Need," *The Washington Post*, March 6, 1983.

15. *Ibid*.

16. Kincade; also see Gary Guertner, "Strategic Vulnerabilities of a Multinational State: Deterring the Soviet Union," *Political Science Quarterly*, Vol. 96, Summer 1981, pp. 209-223; Benjamin S. Lambeth, "Uncertainties for the Soviet War Planner," *International Security*, Winter 1982/1983, pp. 139-166; and Keith A. Dunn, *Soviet Military Weaknesses and Vulnerabilities: A Critique of the Short War Advocates*, Strategic Issues Research Memorandum, Carlisle Barracks, Pennsylvania: Strategic Studies Institute, July 31, 1978, p. 12.

17. US Congress Joint Economic Committee, 97th Congress, 2d session, *USSR: Measures of Economic Growth and Development, 1950-1980*, Washington: US Government Printing Office, December 8, 1982.

18. Adamek, p. 33.

19. *Ibid*. On the other hand, Daniel Bond and Herbert Levine ("The Soviet Economy to the Year 2000: An Overview," Paper #12 of the Soviet Economy to the Year 2000 Symposium, sponsored by the National Council for Soviet and East European Research, Washington, May 19, 1982, p. 32) argue that modifications in the Soviet rate of military spending will not have a determinate ripple effect upon the Soviet economy.

20. Adamek, p. 34. Also, see the "Summary" of the National Council on Soviet and East European Research Symposium on the Soviet Economy to the Year 2000 (hereafter known as the *National Council Summary*), 1982, p. i.

21. Adamek, p. 34.

22. John F. Burns, "The Emergence of Andropov," *The New York Times Magazine*, February 27, 1983, pp. 24-29. Also, see note 71 (this paper) and *National Council Summary*, p. i.

23. Edward Crankshaw, *Khrushchev Remembers*, Boston: Little Brown, 1970, p. 232; James Ellis, "NATO Colloquium Sheds New Life on Economics of Eastern Europe and the USSR," in *NATO Review*, No. 3, 1982, pp. 20-24. Soviet industries are rewarded lately for fulfilling or over-fulfilling goals. However, such rewards are understated to the market and the bottlenecking tendencies of centralized economies are not mitigated by such payments.

24. Adamek, p. 32.

25. Of course, this argument could also be directed at the United States.

26. Ninety percent of the Soviet land mass lies north of the latitude bordering the continental 48 states of the United States.

27. See Dunn. In 1977, there was only one automobile for every 52 citizens and numerous factors impinge against the proliferation of automobiles in Soviet society. See M. Elizabeth Denton, "Soviet Consumer Policy: Trends and Prospects" in *The Soviet Economy: Continuity and Change*, ed. by M. Bornstein, Boulder, Colorado: Westview Press, 1981, pp. 172, 180. There were 109 million automobiles in use in 1976 in the United States, almost one for every two citizens. *The World Almanac and Book of Facts, 1982*, New York: Newspaper Enterprises Association, Inc.

28. T. Powers, "Choosing a Strategy for World War III," *The Atlantic Monthly,* November 1982, p. 109.

29. Thomas Land, "The Trouble with Soviet Agriculture," *International Perspectives,* Ottawa, Canada: September/October 1982, pp. 29-30; also Adamek, p. 32.

30. Murray Feshbach, "The Soviet Future: A Different Crisis," *Military Review,* June 1981, pp. 34-40; also *National Council Summary,* p. ii.

31. Dusko Doder, "Soviets Turning to Allies to Boost Their Workforce," *The Washington Post,* June 3, 1982, p 1. Since so many women work full time and so many students work during holidays, the Soviet Union will be unable to increase its workforce by tapping these already employed assets.

32. "Soviet Asia," *Asia 1983 Yearbook,* Hong Kong: FEER, Ltd., 1983, pp. 246-251. Also, see John Burns, "Siberian Treasure Hunt Hits a Vein of Skepticism," *The New York Times,* April 5, 1983, p. 2. Burns notes that annual labor turnover runs at 30 percent despite salaries that are two to three times higher than those paid for similar jobs in the more temperate regions of the USSR.

33. Adamek, p. 33.

34. Land, p. 29.

35. *Ibid; National Council Summary,* p. ii.

36. Land, p. 30.

37. *The New York Times,* May 24, 1982, p. A3. Of course, part of the explanation for the large percentages of these crops grown on peasant plots is their suitability. Grain, for instance, is most amenable to production on large and mechanized farms in the Soviet Union as well as the United States. Potatoes and eggs, on the other hand, are amenable to "postage stamp" agriculture.

38. Land, p. 30.

39. John Kifner, "Warsaw Outlines Three-Year Plan," *The New York Times,* March 23, 1983, p. 3; David Binder "Czechoslovakia, The East's New Economic Disaster," *The New York Times,* November 8, 1981; Paul Pannkuk "Eastern European and Soviet Economic Outlook," *Weekly Economic Package,* Chemical Bank, New York, February 15, 1983, pp. 8-12.

40. Paul Pannkuk, "Soviet Union's 1982 Economic Prospects," *Weekly Economic Package,* Chemical Bank, New York, May 11, 1982, pp. 15-16.

41. *Ibid.*

42. Crane Brinton, *The Anatomy of Revolution,* rev. and exp. ed., New York: Vintage Books, 1965. The possibility of economic crisis for the Soviet Union is discussed in the *National Council Summary,* p. iii.

43. In 1981-82, the Soviet Union's debt service obligations to the West equalled 12 percent of its total trade with hard currency countries. Furthermore, its hard currency reserves in Western banks dropped from $8.6 billion in 1980 to $3.6 billion in 1981. See Adamek, p. 35. The Soviet trade deficit increased from -$.8 billion in 1980 to -$5.1 billion in 1981 (and -$6.5 billion in 1982) despite gold sales of $2.5 billion and $7 billion in arms sales. See Pannkuk, p. 16.

44. *Ibid..*

45. Murray Feshbach, "Between the Lines of the 1979 Census," *Problems of Communism,* January-February, 1982, pp. 27-37.

46. Helene Carrere d'Encausse, *Decline of an Empire: The Soviet Socialist Republics in Revolt,* New York: Harper Colophon Books, 1981.

47. Cited in "Soviet Asia," *Asia 1983 Yearbook,* p. 246.

48. *Ibid.*, p. 247.
49. *Ibid.*, p. 246.
50. *Ibid.*
51. *Ibid.*
52. Feshbach, "Between the Lines of the 1979 Census," p. 29.
53. *Ibid.*, p. 35.
54. *Ibid.*, p. 30.
55. *Ibid.*, p. 31.
56. *Ibid.*, p. 33.
57. Feshbach, "The Soviet Future," 1981, p. 36.
58. Feshbach, "Between the Lines of the 1979 Census," p. 33.
59. *Ibid.*, p. 34.
60. *Ibid.*, p. 35.
61. Feshbach, "The Soviet Future," 1981, p. 38.
62. *Ibid.* Feshbach notes "The Kremlin annually calls up about 1.7 million 18 year olds to replenish the 4.8 million men in its armed forces. But if it takes its usual quota, the army will conscript enough manpower in 1986 to equal six times that year's net increase in the labor force." For a different point of view of the (limited) impact of Soviet demographic trends upon military manpower requirements, see Ellen Jones, "Soviet Military Manpower: Prospects for the 1980's," *Strategic Review,* Fall, 1981, p. 65.
63. d'Encausse, pp. 266-277.
64. *Ibid.*, pp. 13-46.
65. Jeffrey Hahn, "Soviet Demographic Dilemmas," *Problems of Communism,* September-October, 1981, pp. 56-61.
66. To date, the Soviet Union has not undertaken a program of geographical dispersal and it is unlikely that such a program will materialize within the foreseeable future. See Weinstein, 1982.
67. See d'Encausse, Chapters I, III-VI; Guertner, "Strategic Vulnerabilities;" and Hugh Seton-Watson, "The Last of the Empires," *The Washington Quarterly,* Spring 1980, pp. 41-46.
68. Daniel S. Papp, "From the Crest All Directions are Down: The Soviet Union Views the 1980's," *Naval War College Review,* July-August 1982, pp. 50-68 (especially pp. 61-62); Burns, "The Emergence of Andropov," p. 27.
69. d'Encausse, pp. 165-190, 210-213.
70. Within the Muslim religion, powerful value systems and codes of behavior (such as provided by the Sufi brotherhood) increasingly challenge Marxism-Leninism. See d'Encausse, pp. 237, 261-262, 270.
71. See R. W. Davies, "Economic Planning in the USSR," pp. 7-28, in *The Soviet Economy: Continuity and Change,* Morris Bornstein, ed., Boulder, Colorado: Westview Press, 1981. See pp. 30-32 for an excellent discussion of reforms within the Soviet economic system. Also, see Burns "The Emergence of Andropov."
72. Democratic centralism is, in theory, analogous to decisionmaking in the US military. Decisions may be debated freely up the chain of command. When a decision is made, however, subordinates implement it obediently.
73. John F. Burns, "Rumblings in the Kremlin," *The New York Times,* December 13, 1982, p. 8.; Hedrick Smith, "Though Andropov is Back on Job, US Officials See Health Problems," *The New York Times,* March 31, 1983, p. A4; also see Burns, "The Emergence of Andropov."

74. See note 43. Of course, the Soviet Union can "bend" the ideology to fit reality, as it has done often in the past. Such ideological gymnastics undermine the myth of the universal applicability and scientism of Marxism-Leninism and undermine the Soviet claim to primacy in the "progressive" world.

75. See Burns, "The Emergence of Andropov."

76. Papp.

77. For instance, see Richard Pipes, "The Soviet Strategy for Nuclear Victory," *Commentary*, Vol. 64, July 1977, pp. 21-34; Leon Goure, *War Survival in Soviet Strategy*, Coral Gables: Center for Advanced International Studies, University of Miami, 1976. For an excellent counterargument that maintains that US deterrent forces are still secure, see Jack H. Nunn, "A Soviet Disarming First Strike: How Real is the Threat?," *Parameters*, March 1983, pp. 69-79.

78. See Joseph Kraft, "Russia's Winning Streak," *The Washington Post*, May 4, 1978; Richard Pipes, "Why the Soviet Union Thinks It Could Fight and Win a Nuclear War," *Commentary*, July 1977.

79. For an excellent analysis of the Soviets' military vulnerabilities, see Richard P. Clayberg, *The Problem of Soviet Vulnerabilities*, Special Report, Carlisle Barracks, Pennsylvania: Strategic Studies Institute, December 30, 1977.

80. See Lambeth; Robert Kennedy, "The Strategic Balance in Transition," in *Soviet Armed Forces Review Annual*, ed. by David Jones, Gulf Breeze, Florida: Academic International Press, 1980.

81. For a discussion of US initiatives to improve its arsenal, see Ermma Rothschild, "The Delusions of Deterrence," *The New York Review of Books*, April 14, 1983, pp. 40-50. Also see Caspar Weinberger, *Annual Report to Congess, Fiscal Year 1984*, Washington: US Government Printing Office, February 1, 1983. It is interesting to note that the conclusions of the President's Commission on Strategic Forces repealed "six years of dogma about the growing vulnerability of fixed land-based missiles to a Soviet attack and the consequent doubts about American nuclear deterrent power." See Leslie H. Gelb, "Vulnerability and the MX," *The New York Times*, April 12, 1983, p. Al.

82. Henry Trofimenko, *Changing Attitudes Towards Deterrence*, University of California ACIS Working Paper No. 25, July 1980, p. 54. Trofimenko defines the major threats facing the USSR as: (1) from NATO, including British and French nuclear forces and US forward based systems (FBS); (2) from the US strategic arsenal; (3) from China; and (4) from large US naval units in forward deployment.

83. T. Powers, "Choosing a Strategy for World War III," *The Atlantic Monthly*, November 1982, pp. 82-110 (esp. p. 109).

> The Soviets have 1,398 missiles in twenty-eight missile fields (including the test centers at Tyura Tam and Pletetsk with 300 command-and-control centers, 500 airfields with runways longer than 4,000 feet (suitable for intercontinental bombers), three submarine bases (Murmansk, Petropavlosk, Vladivostok), 167 infantry and armored divisions, sixteen headquaraters of PVO Strany (the Soviet air-defense command), and five naval fleet headquarters. Fifty percent of key Soviet industry is contained in 200 complexes. Only six Soviet rail trans-shipment yards load 80 percent of all empty railcars. There are twenty-six low-frequency radio transmitting stations that broadcast military traffic, and thirty-six stations of one type or another that handle communications with satellites. This comes to a total of 3,543 'targets.'

Moreover, in the Soviet Union, there are only 15 integrated iron and steel mills; 34 sizeable petroleum reserves; 8 copper refineries; 6 lead-zinc refineries; 17 meat-packing plants; 8 major shipbuilding works; 5 factories processing 5 percent of the USSR's aluminum, and so forth.

84. Nunn, "A Soviet Disarming Strike," p. 76.

85. Weinstein, "Soviet Civil Defense," 1982.

86. John Meersheimer, "Why the Soviets Can't Win Quickly in Central Europe," *International Security,* Summer 1982, pp. 3-39.

87. Lambeth, "Uncertainties," p. 155.

88. A fifth factor identified by Stalin was the quantity of divisions and their armament. See *Ibid.,* p. 156.

89. The amount of space critical of Soviet military morale and discipline increased 15 percent over the 1981 figure. See Table 7 in monthly editions of *Red Star,* translated by the Special Operations Division of the Office of the Joint Chiefs of Staff. This document can be obtained through the Defense Technical Information Center.

90. Otto P. Chaney, "The Soviet Threat to Europe," and Edward Corcoran, "Building a NATO Conventional Defense," both in *The Defense of the West* and also Clayberg, *The Problem of Soviet Vulnerabilities.*

91. Lambeth, *Uncertainties,* pp. 147-149; 157-158. See also Chaney, *Soviet Threat to Europe,* and Clayberg, *The Problems of Soviet Vulnerabilities.*

92. *Ibid.*

93. Viktor Suvorov, *The Liberators: Inside the Soviet Army,* London: Hamish Hamilton, 1981. Also, see Edmund Brunner, Jr., *Soviet Demographic Trends and the Ethnic Composition of Draft Age Males, 1980-1985,* Santa Monica: Rand Corporation, February 1981; S. Enders Wimbush and A. Alexiev, *The Ethnic Factor in the Soviet Armed Forces,* Santa Monica: Rand Corporation, March 1982; and Wimbush and Alexiev, *Soviet Central Asian Soldiers in Afghanistan,* Santa Monica: Rand Corporation, January 1981.

94. Wimbush and Alexiev, *The Ethnic Factor.* Also see Nathan Leites, *What Soviet Commanders Fear from Their Own Forces,* Santa Monica: Rand Corporation, May 1978; Kiril Podrabinek, "An Inside Look at Life in the Soviet Army," *Russia,* No. 3, 1981, p. 11; Alexiev Myagkov, *Inside the KGB,* New Rochelle, New York: Arlington House Publishers, 1976, pp. 86-112; and Richard Gabriel, *The New Red Legions: An Attitude Portrait of the Soviet Soldier,* Westport, Connecticut: Greenwood Press, 1980, pp. 151-182.

95. Lambeth, p. 158.

96. Wimbush and Alexiev, *The Ethnic Factor;* d'Encausse, *Decline of an Empire,* p. 155-164; Marshal of the Soviet Union N. V. Ogarkov, *Vseyda v. Gofovnostik Zashchite Otechestva,* Moscow: Military Press of the Ministry of Defense of the USSR, 1982, p. 64.

97. Wimbush and Alexiev, *The Ethnic Factor,* pp. v, vi, 23; Myagkov. See note 94.

98. *Ibid.*

99. John Tagliabue, "4000 East Germans Dispute Official Defense Policy," *The New York Times,* February 15, 1982, p. A3. For a lengthy discussion of the reliability of the Soviet Eastern European allies, see Dale R. Herspring and Ivan Volgyes, "Political Reliability in The East European Warsaw Pact Armies," *Armed Forces in Society,* Winter, 1980, pp. 279-296.

100. Papp, pp. 52-55.

101. For instance, see *Red Star,* Vol. 2, No. 3, 1983, pp. 32-34; "The East-West Conventional Balance in Europe," *The Military Balance 1982/1983,* London: International Institute for Strategic Studies, 1982, p. 131.

102. Lambeth, p. 140.

103. For instance, see Max Eastman, *Stalin's Russia and the Crisis of Socialism,* New York: W. W. Norton, 1940; *Reflections on the Failure of Socialism,* New York: Devin-Adair, 1955.

104. Andrei Amalrik, *Will the Soviet Union Survive Until 1984?* (expanded and revised edition), New York: Harper Colophon Books, 1981. See Bond and Levine for a more positive assessment of the Soviet Union's future prospects.

105. d'Encausse; Eagleburger, p. 1-4.

106. Papp, p. 67. Also, see Myron Rush, "Guns Over Growth in Soviet Policy," *International Security,* Winter 1982/1983, pp. 167-179. Especially see p. 178; Lambeth, p. 165. However, one must also acknowledge that the problems described herein are likely to interact to present the Kremlin with dilemmas which may be the most serious yet.

107. Eagleburger, p. 2.

108. Weinberger.

109. Colin Gray, "Soviet Strategic Vulnerabilities," *Air Force Magazine,* March 1979, p. 64.

110. Weinstein, p. 83; Guertner; Kincade.

111. "How MX Will Transform Nuclear Strategy," *US News and World Report,* April 25, 1983. Also see Hedrick Smith, "Colonel Stirs Questions on MX-Firing Doctrine," *The New York Times,* April 8, 1983, p. D15; Lambeth, p. 153-154.

112. Ye. Rybkin, "The Leninist Concept of War and the Present" (*Kommunist Voorzhennykh Sil,* trans. by US Joint Publications Research Service, JPRS, No. 60667, November 30, 1973, *Translations on US Military Affairs,* No. 987). Also see Lambeth, p. 151.

113. W. Perry Boyd, "The Once and Future Quest: European Arms Control--Issues and Prospects," in *The Defense of the West.*

114. See note 82.

115. Boyd.

116. Freshbach, 1981, p. 38.

117. Boyd. Also see Todd Starbuck, "China and the Superpower Balance," in *The Defense of the West.*

118. *The Military Balance,* 1982-1983, London: International Institute for Strategic Studies, p. 14.

119. Rush.

120. See Richard Halloran, "CIA Analysts Now Said to Find US Overstated Soviet Arms Rise," *The New York Times,* March 5, 1983.

121. Robert Kennedy, "The Problems and Prospects of START," in *The Defense of the West.*

122. Michael Kaufman, "Soviet Groups Losing Ground at Third World Conference," *The New York Times,* March 11, 1983, p. 1.; Robert J. Lilley, "Constraints on Superpower Intervention in Sub-Saharan Africa," in *Parameters,* September 1982, pp. 63-75.

123. In "Who Will Determine Africa's Destiny," *AEI Foreign Policy and Defense Review*, Vol. 1, No. 1, 1979, Gen. Olusegun Obasanjo, former Nigerian head of state noted, pp. 72-73:

> In the context of foreign intervention in Africa, there are three parties involved. There are the Soviets and other socialist countries, the Western powers, and we the Africans. If the interests of Africa are to be safeguarded, there are certain considerations which each of the parties must constantly bear in mind. To the Soviets and their friends, I should like to say that . . . they should not overstay their welcome. Africa is not about to throw off one colonial yoke for another. Rather, they should hasten the political, economic, and military capability of their African friends to stand on their own. . . .

124. The Soviets expect to reduce their hard currency outflow with the sale of natural gas to Western Europe. The extent of their earnings will depend upon the stability of the price of natural gas and the Europeans' renegotiation rights in the event of a substantial price change, a change in consumption levels, and so forth.

125. Drusilla Brown, "Psychological Operations (PSYOP): United States-Soviet Union," *Military Intelligence,* October-December 1982, p. 46-49.

126. Eagleburger, p. 2.

127. *Ibid.,* p. 4.

3

THE STRATEGIC IMPLICATIONS OF CIVIL DEFENSE

John M. Weinstein

INTRODUCTION

The cumulative effect of the massive expansion and modernization of the strategic and conventional forces of the Soviet Union has caused many to reevaluate the strategic balance between the superpowers. Specifically, there has been substantial concern about the Soviet development of a potent first-strike capability. This assessment, arrived at by the last two US administrations, reflects a number of technological improvements in the Soviet Strategic Rocket Forces (SRF) which appear ominous in light of Soviet strategic operational employment plans which stress seizing the strategic initiative through preemptive attacks against American ICBM launch silos, launch control facilities, support and maintenance facilities, strategic bomber bases, submarine berths and loading facilities, and nuclear storage and production facilities.[1] Secretary of Defense Caspar Weinberger outlined the principal cause of the Reagan administration's concern in *Soviet Military Power* when he observed:

The 1970's modernizations, which only now are reaching a conclusion, were largely technological in nature. More than half of the 1,398 Soviet ICBM launchers have been rebuilt to house the SS-17, SS-18 and SS-19 ICBM in vastly more survivable, hardened silos. These ICBMs, all of which are MIRVed, are in the forefront of ICBM technology. Certain versions of the SS-18 and SS-19 are among the most accurate ICBMs operational anywhere. Together, these systems have the capability to destroy a large percentage of the more than 1,000 US ICBM launchers, using only part of their total numbers.[2]

The SS-17, SS-18 and SS-19 ICBMs, which are the focus of the Secretary's most urgent concern, incorporate a cold-launch capability for the SS-17 and SS-18, allowing their silos to be reloaded for subsequent salvos. Furthermore, these recently deployed missiles have impressive accuracies which rival and yields which surpass those of the most accurate US Minuteman III ICBM with the Mk-12A warhead.[3] Most worrisome to Secretary Weinberger is, despite the overall balance in total numbers of US and Soviet ICBM and SLBM warheads (approximately 6,920 [US] v. 7,000 [USSR]), the Soviet Union leads the United States in the number of the highly accurate and hard-target capable warheads by approximately 4,600 (sum of warheads on SS-17, SS-18 and SS-19) to 1,650 (Minuteman III).[4] Secretary Weinberger warns that:

> As the accuracy of future Soviet missiles increases, it will be feasible for the Soviets to reduce the size of individual RVs and thereby to increase the number of MIRVs carried on each missile, assuming no external constraints such as that imposed by arms limitations.[5]

When viewed through the prism of Soviet strategic doctrine, the ongoing improvements to the Soviet SRF, as well as those realized in their submarine and long-range aviation, there is indeed room for genuine concern. Clearly, these trends portend potentially dangerous consequences in a superpower crisis in which the Soviet Union believed war was about to erupt.

Within this context, a number of civilian and military analysts take a particular ominous view of the Soviet Union's long-standing attention to civil defense.[6] In light of America's inattention to civil defense since the aftermath of the Cuban missile crisis, numerous implications have been drawn from alleged Soviet plans and capabilites to undertake crisis relocation of urban populations, to disperse and harden industry, and to achieve rapid postattack recovery. Most serious among these implications is the potential effect of Soviet civil defense capabilities upon the real or perceived stability of deterrence.[7] Specifically, some contend that the Soviet civil defense program threatens deterrence by upsetting the balance of mutual population vulnerability if, under certain conditions, Soviet civil defense measures might limit their fatalities to the low "tens of millions."[8] According to 1979 projections by the Congressional Office of Technology Assessment and 1982 Congressional testimony, significant asymmetries exist in the number of US and Soviet fatalities that would occur in several nuclear warfighting scenarios.[9] In most scenarios, the percentage of American casualties is double that of the Soviet Union and in an all-out Soviet attack upon the US population and its counterforce, military and economic targets, American fatalities might range as high as 88 percent of the population.[10]

Furthermore, it is frequently argued that Soviet civil defense capabilities could threaten deterrence stability to the degree that they protect that country's economic power and recovery prospects relative to those of the United States. Such projected asymmetries are destabilizing because they suggest that under certain circumstances, the Soviet Union might emerge from a nuclear war in a better position than that of the United States. If the Soviet Union were to perceive nuclear war as potentially less costly and, thus, less frightening, they might feel more inclined in a crisis to launch a preemptive strike against the United States.

Those who are concerned about Soviet civil defense improvements are also frequently among those concerned over the comparative lack of US civil defense measures. Often these critics contend that there are several additional implications that result from the inability of the United States to protect its citizens or production base from nuclear assaults.[11] First, America's allies would naturally have less confidence in the US nuclear umbrella if they could envision a situation in which the United States were facing a choice between sacrificing New York or assenting to Soviet coercion or occupation of Oslo or Bonn.[12] Second, tactical nuclear weapons, whose use might escalate to a strategic exchange, might "no longer substitute for conventional strength as credibly as they did in the past."[13] Any resulting loosening of the bonds between the United States and its NATO allies might contribute ultimately to the disintegration of NATO and other US alliance systems. Such developments would constitute a major blow to US security and realize one of the principal Soviet postwar objectives. Finally, defensive inferiority might subject the United States to Soviet coercion with few alternatives to acquiescence, irrespective of raw, destructive power.

Such commentary has not fallen upon deaf ears in the executive branch. Recently, numerous analysts in government and academe have argued that the United States must improve the readiness and capabilities of its own civil defense program. They maintain that the United States might protect itself from any attempted Soviet intimidation by evacuating its urban positions during a crisis and accordingly reducing American fatalities, and facilitating economic recovery should deterrence fail.[14]

Presidential Directive 41 (PD 41), issued on September 29, 1978, streamlined America's civil defense goals and committed the country to crisis relocation planning.[15] Recent declarations of the Reagan Administration, including a commitment to double federal allocations for civil defense, provided additional evidence that the subject is being taken even more seriously in the United States.[16]

This paper will (1) examine the effectiveness of the Soviet civil defense program, selected Soviet strategic vulnerabilities, and Soviet views of deterrence, and (2) evaluate the direction and scope of the current US civil defense program. These assessments will explore the relationship between US civil defense and national security and provide a basis for policy recommendations that attempt to identify civil defense goals and initiatives which are desirable and feasible.

SOVIET CIVIL DEFENSE: PLANS AND PROBLEMS

Population Protection. Protection of leadership is considered of paramount importance to Soviet civil defense planners. The CIA notes that sufficient blast-resistant shelter space exists to protect approximately 110,000 Soviet government and Party officials at all levels.[17] A second priority is the protection of workers at essential industrial installations. By current estimates, the Soviet Union has shelter space for 24-48 percent of the essential work force or 12 to 24 percent of the total work force that would be left behind in the event of crisis evacuation.[18] Those most concerned about the estimated Soviet ability to protect much of their critical political and industrial populace point to several disquieting ramifications. First, while conceding the US ability to destroy shelters which are targetted directly, these shelters must first be identified; hardly an easy or assured task for intelligence. Second, the destruction of these shelters would require continued survival and connectivity of US strategic communications and missile installations as well as the expenditure of a disproportionately large percentage of land-based, hard target-killing warheads on these targets.[19] Third, the survival of the Soviet political and military command and control systems might provide a capability to fight a protracted nuclear war designed to outlast the US adversary.[20] Finally, the survival of key political and industrial cadres would facilitate rapid economic reconstruction vis-a-vis the United States.

Those who question the potential adverse impact of Soviet shelter capabilities counter with several points. First, a first-strike capability that exists on paper does not guarantee that it will exist under uncertain and confusing actual attack conditions.[21] Second, the estimates of available Soviet shelter space are open to question. The CIA estimates that the space available for each person in a shelter would be only one-half to one square meter. This space allotment is inadequate according to most analyses of long-term survival requirements.[22] In addition, the Oak Ridge Laboratories maintain that the shelters' ventilation systems are their most vulnerable aspect and that, even if a shelter were not destroyed by a nuclear blast, its inhabitants would risk suffocation and death from asphyxiation or heat exposure.[23] Starvation also would prove to be a severe problem if shelter were required for more than a few days. Chronic Soviet food shortages make it unlikely that the Soviet Union would prestock shelters for more than a few days during peacetime. Furthermore, normal food distribution snarls, and the fact that Soviet citizens buy their food from day to day, are likely to prevent many from bringing additional supplies of food and water to the shelter. Even current Deputy Under Secretary of Defense for Strategic and Theater Nuclear Forces, T. K. Jones, an analyst who has written extensively on the dangerous implications of Soviet civil defense capabilities, concedes that inplace urban shelters "could not help much against a US attack designed to destroy populations."[24] Thus, it is argued that the Soviet Union is likely to harbor few illusions about the potential success of its civil defense programs in a nuclear war with the United States. Furthermore, since urban shelters are not in place to protect the average Soviet citizen (assigned the lowest priority in the Soviet civil defense program), such citizens would be forced to build expedient shelters using "handy" materials and tools such as bricks, timber, boards, and shovels.[25] Their plight would be compounded at night; during autumn when the ground is muddy, or winter when the ground is frozen, or during spring and summer when foodstuffs are depleted.

Finally, Leon Goure, author of numerous articles and studies of Soviet civil defense, described elaborate Soviet evacuation plans that are to be carried out by the urban populace within 72 hours after an evacuation order is issued.[26] However, those who question the potential value of such an evacuation point out that the Soviet Union has never practiced full-scale evacuation of a major city; used more than one mode of transportation in their limited practice; conducted a drill without a long period of preparation; or carried out several evacuation exercises simultaneously.[27]

The Soviet road network is one of the country's major strategic vulnerabilities. Because it has been constructed to accommodate travel within that country's cities, it would be hard pressed to support mass exoduses by motor transport or by foot from these cities. One report states that:

> [The Soviet Union] lacks a developed highway system to connect the outlying regions to its industrial hub. Less than 250,000 miles of paved roads exist in the entire nation. No two Soviet cities are connected by a divided highway . . . . In addition, Soviet severe weather conditions hamper what possible road travel exists. During the winter, spring thaw periods, and autumn rainy seasons, Soviet roads are virtually impassable. The Soviets describe their situation as *Rasputitsa* or roadlessness during those months.[28]

In addition to motor transport, Soviet evacuation plans depend heavily on railroads. Most railroads in the Soviet Union, however, are single track. To evacuate large cities by rail transportation, the Soviet Union would have to arrange that the trains were in their assigned evacuation locations and that they were not loaded with freight or allocated to carry troops or supplies to Eastern Europe. That so many logistical problems would be handled by a country whose transportation system is inefficient, at best, during calm and peaceful times is questionable.

Moreover, since most Soviet citizens do not have automobiles,[29] Soviet evacuation plans also call for some 17 million urban residents to walk 30 miles (1.5 mph for 20 hours) and then, build expedient protection.[30] How the very young, the very old, and the sick are to make such formidable progress (while carrying two weeks' worth of food, water, and supplies), is not clear. Furthermore, how evacuees in expedient shelters would survive the higher levels of radioactive fallout that would result if the US retaliatory strike included ground bursts, is unclear and is seldom addressed by those who assert the effectiveness of Soviet civil defense.

The Soviet urban population, largely an apartment society, is more highly concentrated than the American urban population.[31] This heavy concentration of urban citizens results in certain obstacles to successful evacuation. For instance, Moscow is surrounded on all sides by satellite industrial centers, and Leningrad is similarly bordered on three sides and by water on the fourth. Citizens from these population centers would face major problems evacuating to rural reception centers or areas suitable for the construction of expedient shelters.

Even if one disregards the logistical problems that would attend a decision to evacuate Soviet cities and assumes that such a momentous exodus could be executed, the Soviet Union would still face a major strategic dilemma. The declaratory policy of the United States, as well as employment policies which have resulted in increasing accurate guidance systems, such as the NS-20, eschew the targeting of Soviet population *per se*.[32] Within this context, one may wonder what impact from a Soviet perspective the evacuation of its citizens would have on deterring an American retaliatory strike. Civilian evacuation serves certain humanitarian goals, but it has little effect upon the US ability to destroy critical Soviet military, industrial, and economic targets.[33] The destruction of Soviet civilians would be an unintended effect of US plans to destroy Soviet military and economic infrastructures under certain retaliation scenarios.[34] In some ways, the Soviet Union may see evacuation as potentially counterproductive. In the event of a Soviet evacuation, the United States would undoubtedly undertake a variety of measures (e.g., disperse its bombers and put them on a runway or airborne alert, send its subs in port to sea, and upgrade the readiness of its missile installations) to reduce the effectiveness of a Soviet first strike and increase the destructiveness of a US retaliatory strike. Thus, it could even be argued that the successful evacuation and survival of the Soviet Union's civilian population might prove detrimental to the country's long-term prospects for recovery. In the aftermath of a US retaliatory strike, one may wonder how the Soviet leadership plans to care for two hundred million survivors with the devastation of its economic, agricultural, medical, and transportation infrastructures.

With "strangelovian" logic, one could argue that rapid recovery indeed might be more expeditious and effective with fewer rather than more survivors to drain scarce recovery materiel. The crucial element of civil defense revolves, then, around the ability of the Soviet Union to protect its economy and sustain survivors of a nuclear war.

The Protection of Soviet Industry. Traditionally, Soviet leadership has sought to protect their industry by two means: geographical dispersal and hardening against nuclear attack. Little is debated about the effectiveness of Soviet programs to protect their industry from the primary and collateral effects of a nuclear attack by means of the former. More recent analytical efforts[35] concur with the 1978 CIA conclusion that the Soviet program for geographical dispersal of industry is not being implemented to a significant extent. The CIA concludes further that:

> . . . new plants have often been built adjacent to major existing plants; existing plants and complexes have been expanded in place; no effort has been made to expand the distance between buildings or to locate additions in such a way as to minimize fire and other hazards in the event of a nuclear attack; [and] previously open spaces at fuel storage sites have been filled in with new storage tanks and processing units.[36]

In fact, because of economic exigencies, the value of productive capacity added to existing areas is increasing more rapidly than in new areas. This trend heightens rather than diminishes the vulnerability of Soviet industry. More debate has concerned the effectiveness and implications of Soviet efforts to harden their industrial installations. Although the Soviet leaders themselves point out that:

> It is impossible to make buildings less vulnerable to a shock wave without radical structural changes that involve considerable difficulty and cost. . . . It is impossible to guarantee building survival in a damage area even by somewhat increasing the strength of individual structures and their components . . . ;[37]

they probably recognize that vulnerability and even massive impairment do not amount to permanent devastation.[38] Consequently, the Soviet leadership has opted for low-cost means of protecting vital equipment from secondary damage of nuclear explosives. These "engineering-technical" measures include rapid shutdown of equipment for protection against electromagnetic impulse; the use of expedient protective devices (e.g., wooden and metal bracing, covering equipment with sandbags, and the like), acknowledged by the Arms Control and Disarmament Agency (ACDA) as effective in areas on the periphery of a nuclear blast;[39] contamination protection, and the protection of raw material supplies through underground storage. In a two-year study of the effectiveness of Soviet expedient measures, T. K. Jones concluded:

> ... Russian methods could protect machinery within the three-day warning that would be provided by a Soviet evacuation. A full scale attack could be absorbed and production could renew in four to twelve weeks.[40]

Such projections take on chilling importance if one posits that a Soviet preemptive strike knocked out as much as 90 percent of the accurate land-based US missiles, leaving the United States with less accurate SLBMs and its aging bomber fleet (which would have to penetrate increasingly sophisticated air defenses) to deliver the retaliatory strike. In such a scenario, the relatively limited destructiveness of the US response might seem tolerable to Soviet military planners.[41]

Critics of this line of argumentation respond that a substantial gap exists between the theoretical and actual abilities to mount a successful first-strike. They maintain that the Soviet leaders, who are normally cautious in military operations, would be loathe to gamble the survival of their state on the many unknown parameters relating to the coordination, timing, effects and consequences of so precipitous an action as a nuclear strike against the United States.[42]

These same critics also point to the inability of the Soviet Union to harden many of the critical industries upon which their fragile economy and continued superpower status depend. These vulnerable industries include oil refineries; power plants; chemical storage plants; steel mills; pharmaceutical laboratories; component assembly factories; major truck, tractor, and rolling-stock plants; railheads and marshaling yards; major surface transshipment points and highway intersections; and pipelines.[43] Because these targets cannot be hardened and their destruction does not require the pinpoint accuracy of ICBMs, they remain vulnerable to a US retaliatory strike. With respect to industries that the Soviet Union might attempt to harden, the critics cite the ACDA conclusion that "any attempt to harden [industrial installations in targetted areas] can be easily overcome by detonating weapons at lower altitude with only a minor reduction in the 10 psi destruction capability."[44] The 10 psi figure is significant because it represents the nuclear blast overpressure that collapses most factories and commercial buildings and destroys and scatters all lesser structures as debris within a 4 to 5 kilometer radius of ground zero.[45] The ACDA study also stated that even the expedient threefold hardening of Soviet equipment in peripheral areas could be offset by greater accuracies and yields of future US weapons.[46]

Third, these critics focus upon the observation of T. K. Jones that after absorbing a first strike, the United States would be able to hit only a "few thousand aim points," precluding the infliction of unacceptable damage on the Soviet Union.[47] Critics committed to an assured destruction philosophy contend that Soviet industry (50 percent of which is contained in 200 complexes[48]) and the transportation and power infrastructure that support it are so concentrated in a narrow crescent stretching from Leningrad through Moscow, Sverdlovsk, Omsk, Novosibirsk and to Irkutsk that the United States would not require many weapons to achieve its Soviet industrial damage requirements.[49] (See Figure 1.) Geoffrey Kemp[50] and Richard Garwin,[51] both prominent students of strategic studies, maintain respectively that as few as seven Poseidon submarines (one-third of the number normally on station at sea) could destroy 61 percent of the Soviet industrial base and that, even if only 10 percent of US ICBMs survived a Soviet preemptive strike, those 100-110 missiles could be retargetted (assuming the survival of American C^3 facilities) to deliver unacceptable damage to the Soviet Union. An ACDA estimate that recognizes the need for no more than 1300 warheads to destroy 70 percent of Soviet industry is consistent with these estimates.[52]

Finally, and most crucial, is that even if one accepts the argument that the Soviet Union can protect individual pieces of industrial equipment from proximate nuclear detonations, it does not follow that the resumption of industrial production will be a

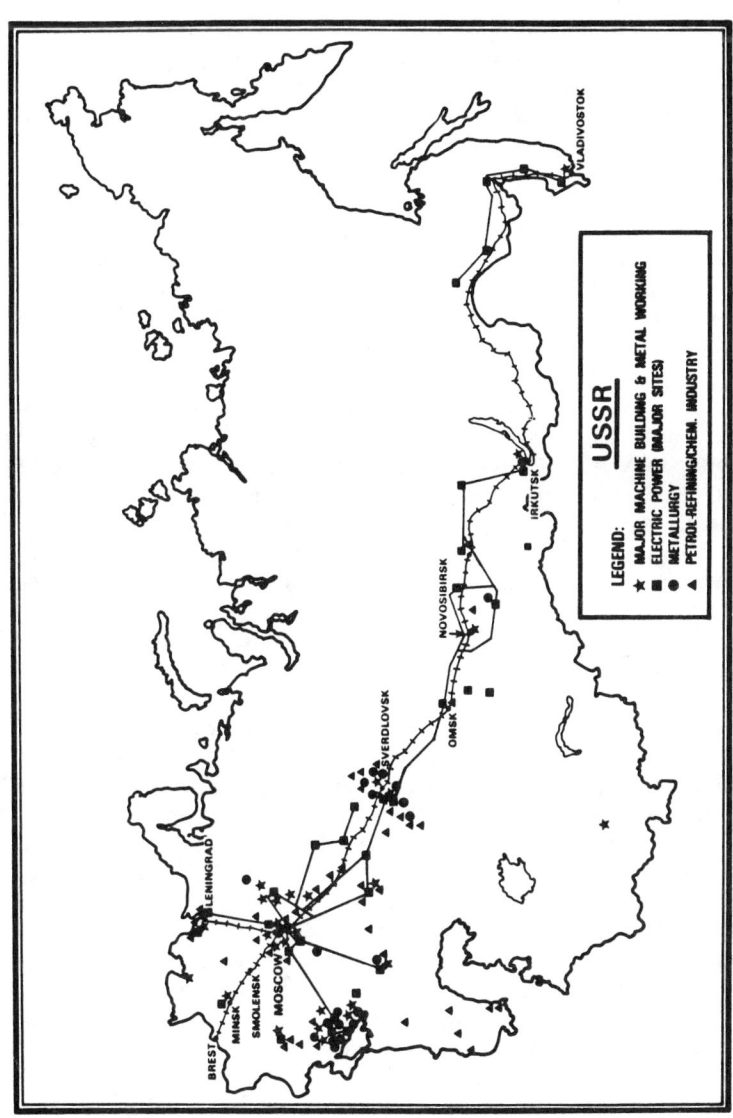

Source: Central Intelligence Agency, USSR Summary Map

Figure 1

near-term proposition. Industrial reconstitution and recovery will be hampered by a number of factors. For instance, how will production be resumed if the electrical infrastructure and available supplies of and transmission lines for diesel fuel, gasoline and petroleum are destroyed? How will industrial activity and recovery be realized if stocks of raw materials and the six rail transshipment points which load 80 percent of all empty railcars[53] and are critical to the Soviet industrial supply and distribution are destroyed also? How will workers deal with residual radiation in targetted areas, especially in the absence of easy access to medical personnel and supplies? And who will feed, clothe and shelter workers and protect their equipment during the recovery phase?

Postattack Recovery. Absent effective protection measures, the significant and vulnerable concentration of Soviet industry cited above makes T. K. Jones' prediction that the Soviet Union could recover "within no more than 2 to 4 years from a US nuclear retaliatory attack"[54] appear optimistic at best.

The psychological condition of the survivors is critically important for postattack recovery. Yet those who examine nuclear attack/recovery scenarios say little about this variable, implicitly assuming that as a result of their civil defense training, (1) the survivors of Armageddon would calmly set about postattack reconstruction in a disciplined and effective manner; and (2) that the termination of the nuclear crisis and threat of continued exchanges would be unambiguous and evacuees would willingly return to their homes to aid their fellow citizens and begin reconstruction.

Such discipline and cooperative effort may not occur in the aftermath of nuclear war. The reactions of the survivors of Hiroshima and Nagasaki offer a limited, though imperfect, insight into what might be expected in the aftermath of a Soviet-American nuclear exchange.[55] They expected that they were about to die. As a means of protection from the grotesque scenes around them, they closed their minds to the ubiquitous horror. This psychic numbing, causing profound blandness and insensitivity to the surrounding suffering, was temporary and dissipated as the outside world responded with aid to the victims of the disaster. A nuclear war, however, would result in unprecedented destruction and limit the amount of aid available from the "outside," especially if the war were massive in nature. Robert J. Lifton, a noted psychiatrist who has written extensively on the subject, concludes that the devastation that would attend a nuclear exchange would probably give rise to such extreme psychic numbing as described above that its effects would be irreversible.[56] Lifton stated that:

> The suddenness and the sheer ferocity of such a scene would not give survivors any chance to mobilize the usual forms of psychological defense. The normal human response to mass death and profound horror is not rage or depression or panic or mourning or even fear; it is a kind of mental anesthetization that interferes with both judgment and compassion for other people.[57]

In such circumstances, the mind may become desensitized to the degree that it is "no longer connected to its own past" and is, therefore, cut off "from the social forms from which it drew strength and a sense of humanity. The mind would, then, be shut down altogether."[58] According to Lifton, a major consequence of psychic shock could be the inability of the survivors to gather food, to bury their own dead, and perform other basic social rituals. Their behavior could be characterized by extreme suspiciousness and primitive forms of thought. Furthermore, Lifton argues that those from unscathed regions may not be willing to aid the survivors and share their horror. In light of these considerations, the prospects for the assured and disciplined recovery posited by Jones and others appear less certain.

Recovery from a nuclear attack depends heavily on the capability to rescue, feed, and care for the survivors and on the capability to provide repair parts and energy for capital reconstruction. Under certain strategic exchange scenarios described by the National Academy of Sciences, Soviet recovery efforts would be hampered severely by numerous obstacles. Massive urban areas could be too "hot"—too radioactive—to enter for several months. Depending upon the profile and scale of a US retaliatory strike, radiation sickness could be widespread, with 80 percent of the Soviet population, including the evacuees, having been exposed to at least 100 roentgens of radioactivity. In light of the coincidence of Soviet major food producing regions and its ICBM fields which would surely be targetted in a counterforce scenario, food would be in short supply. Half of the country's grazing livestock would be dead and, if the attack occurred during the growing season, 30 percent of all crops would be destroyed. Attempts to distribute surviving foodstuffs from farms and emergency storage sites could be delayed for several months, and this estimate is probably optimistic since the Soviet Union's 28 ICBM installations are interspersed throughout the heart of the rail network (See Figure 2). The ozone layer might be so depleted that outdoor activity beyond 30 minutes in duration would be hazardous for several years.[59] As much as 80 percent of all medical personnel, supplies, and hospitals are likely to be destroyed. And, of course, a host of social and psychological problems would ensue. Additional problems would result from the low horsepower design and disrepair of Soviet heavy equipment[60] as well as the destruction of the chemical fertilizer industry, upon which an already woefully deficit Soviet agriculture is heavily dependent.

The most critical obstacle that would hamper Soviet efforts to achieve postwar recovery, however, relates to command and control (C^2). The pace and extent of recovery will depend heavily upon the ability of the national and regional political and party leaders to establish a concensus on national priorities, communicate their directives, and coordinate materiel supply and human effort. These recovery requisites, however, are likely to be affected adversely by the multinational nature of the Soviet society and the potential fragility of the various infrastructures of control. While many analysts have described (l) the polyglot composition of the Soviet Union; (2) the declining percentage of Great Russians and ethnic Slavs in the population relative to the rapidly increasing numbers of Moslems and Central Asians (who traditionally have resisted incorporation into the Russian empire); and (3) the ominous economic and political consequences of these developments for the Soviet policy,[61] relatively few have recognized the Soviet state as multinational when the discussion turns to the matter of strategic deterrence and the requisites of postattack recovery. Indeed this consideration is paramount in Soviet strategic calculations.[62] Recognizing the geographical coincidence of the majority of ICBM fields, key industrial installations and rail lines, and Great Russian population concentrations in a narrow Leningrad to Irkutsk crescent (See Figure 2), Gary Guertner of the US Army War College observed that even a limited American counterforce strike against the Soviet Union's missile and C^3 installations would affect most seriously the Great Russians[63] who

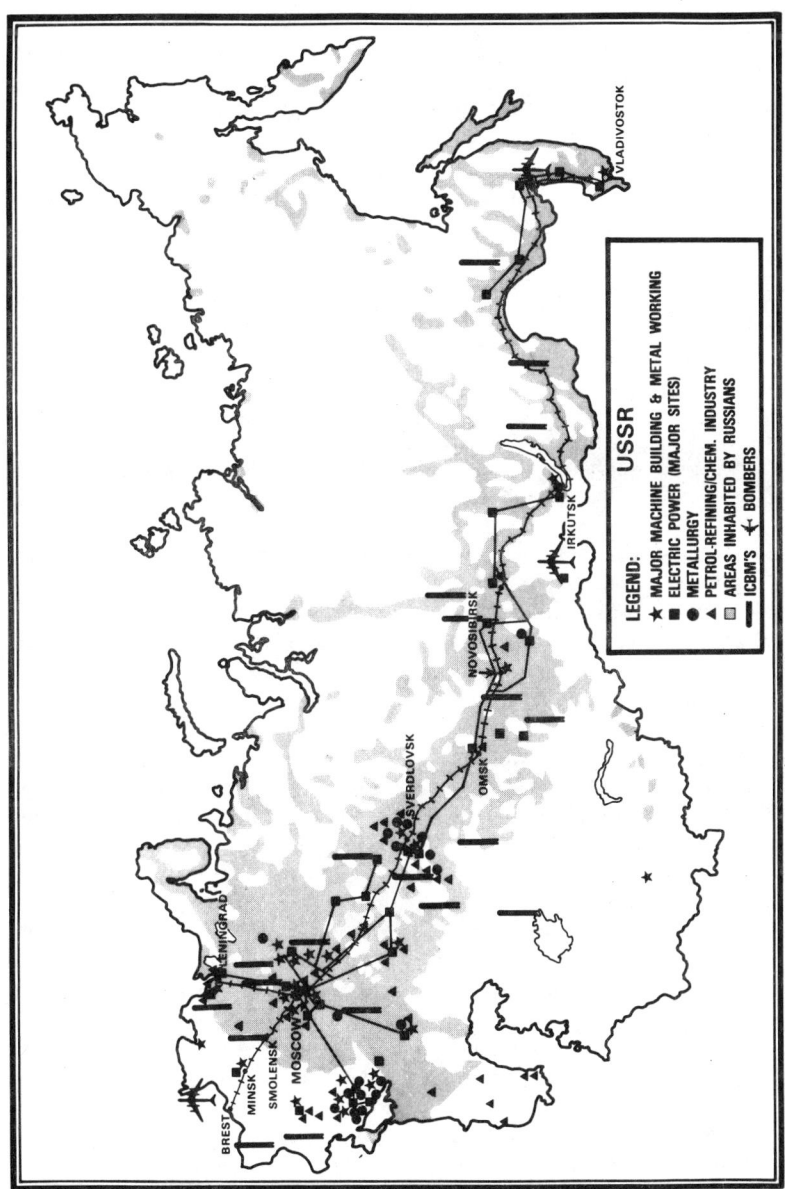

Sources: CIA, "USSR Summary Map;" DOD, *Soviet Military Power*, 1983.

Figure 2

would perish in numbers disproportionately higher than their rapidly declining percentage (52 percent) of the total population. Whether they would be able to maintain control of the vast governmental, Communist Party, educational, and military hierarchies is questionable. Nuclear war might well usher in the decline of the Soviet empire in light of the current American interest in retaliatory targeting of the Russian dominated infrastructures of political and ethnic control, communication, and transportation in various escalation scenarios.[64] Adam Ulam recognized this possibility (and implicitly explained the Soviet emphasis upon the protection of its leadership) even in the event of a "small" nuclear war when he asked:

> As to the possibility of a 'small' nuclear war, the USSR has to think in political terms: against a small nuclear power she would undoubtedly emerge victorious; but could a Communist regime survive such a war? What would be the consequences of even one nuclear missile falling on Moscow and destroying the top leadership of the Party and state?[65]

Even if one assumes that the Soviet infrastructure of political control remained intact in the aftermath of a nuclear strike, it would still have to confront the problem of economic recovery. In the previous section, the hypothesized 2- to 4-year economic recovery period was criticized as overly optimistic. Four years is hardly enough time for economic recovery assuming the large-scale physical destruction that many believe the United States could inflict upon the Soviet Union. Moreover, 2 to 4 years may be an eternity in the political dimension. During this period of incapacitation, could the Soviet leaders be confident that they could maintain the integrity of the Soviet Union? Is it likely that the Soviet-Moslem population might reaffirm religious and territorial ties to a Pan-Moslem movement? Would the nationalists in the Ukraine or the Baltic republics attempt to secede? And would the Russians have the wherewithal to prevent such centrifugal forces? Finally, would the East Europeans be inclined to maintain their political and economic ties to the Soviet Union? Assumptions and the role of uncertainty play heavily on the calculas of deterrence and one cannot be certain of the way leaders in the Kremlin arrive at their strategic estimates.

It is quite possible that, given the priority placed upon leadership survival in Soviet civil defense plans, the Russian leadership may view its own survival as a sufficient objective in its own right. If, however, the Russian leaders entertain uncertainties such as those described above, and in my opinion they do, and if they view civil defense as having a limited mitigating effect upon the problems outlined above, nuclear war necessarily would be viewed as counterproductive to their most basic national interests: the survival and integrity of the Soviet state, its rapid reconstitution and continuation of superpower status.

SOVIET CIVIL DEFENSE: IN SEARCH OF A BOTTOM LINE

The essential debate surrounding the Soviet civil defense program is the extent to which Soviet plans and goals could be translated into damage-limiting benefits in an actual nuclear exchange with the United States. In brief, those who fear the Soviet civil defense capabilities point to the prestige of Soviet General A. Altunin who directs civil defense efforts and the continuing massive monies and attention his programs receive. They also argue that the myriad programs described in Soviet civil defense manuals are designed expressly to mitigate the very obstacles and war consequences identified by those who view said programs with skepticism. Furthermore, while acknowledging the unprecedented destruction that would attend a massive and spasmodic nuclear exchange between the superpowers, those who view Soviet civil defense as threatening contend that if escalation control is feasible, then defensive preparations, indeed, may serve the USSR well in a limited war scenario. Civil defense, though admittedly imperfect, takes on substantial weight when viewed as a component of a Soviet warfighting strategy that also emphasizes other damage-limiting expedients such as a first strike against US warmaking capabilities and active (e.g., air and antisatellite) defense against actual US retaliatory strikes. If not, why would the Soviet leaders continue to spend increasingly scarce defense rubles on a civil defense program they consider ineffective? Jones and others fear that the synergistic effects of these components might lead the Soviet Union under certain crisis scenarios to perceive an exploitable strategic advantage which, through miscalculation, could lead to a nuclear conflict of disasterous proportions. While few Americans can accommodate themselves to the plausibility of such grave calculations, the Soviet (and Russian before them) history of invasions, revolution and civil war, purges, and suffering imposed by a harsh and unforgiving climate and land are cited by Richard Pipes to demonstrate that the memories and attitudes of the Soviet leaders have hardened them so that losses in the "low tens of millions" in a nuclear war might seem acceptable.[66]

Skeptics of the Soviet civil defense program make several counterarguments. Civil defense spending, they argue, continues due to a number of extraneous factors, such as bureaucratic inertia, legitimizing the continuation of the garrison state, Leninist ideological imperatives, and so forth.[67] Also, to the skeptics, either the devastation of limited war is so great as to render it indistinguishable from unlimited war or there is little chance that a limited war would remain limited.[68] Therefore, they liken Soviet (and US) civil defense efforts to the uneasy whistling of a frightened stroller in a cemetery at midnight. Surely, they argue, the normally cautious Soviet leaders recognize (1) the numerous, uncontrollable and uncertain nature of nuclear war, (2) the likelihood that the US deterrent will remain credible into the 1990's[69] and (3) that nuclear war between the superpowers will be an unprecedented disaster for each combatant—his civil defense preparations notwithstanding. They refute Pipes' contention, noting that the 10-20 million deaths suffered over a period of 5 years during World War II is hardly analogous to a self-initiated holocaust that results at a minimum in the same number of deaths and widespread economic destruction within a matter of hours or days.[70] Indeed, Soviet political and military leaders have consistently acknowledged the fact that the disruption, destruction and suffering of the Second World War would pale to insignificance against even a limited nuclear war.[71] And, finally, critics explain the asymmetry of war casualties by pointing out that the higher US estimates are predicted on a Soviet first strike designed to reduce the destructiveness of a US retaliatory strike.[72]

What can be concluded from the point-counterpoint discussions of civil defense and deterrence? It is evident that the Soviet civil defense programs are imperfect and are beset most certainly with herculean problems. However, such programs are firmly in place and would probably reduce the number of deaths and contribute to economic recovery in the aftermath of a strategic exchange with the United States. The exact contributions of Soviet civil defense to their warfighting and war-survival capabilities as well as their perceptions of security are impossible to determine. The ambiguity of such speculation is illustrated in the "bottom line" of the CIA's 1978 study which, while stating that civil defense capabilities will not alter the Soviet leadership's evaluation of their efficacy, offers no insight into the actual level of those perceived capabilities. A conclusion of the CIA study was that:

> Present evidence does not suggest that in the foreseeable future there will be any significant change in the Soviet leaders' judgment that civil defense contributes to warfighting and war-survival capablities, nor that their uncertainties about its effectiveness would be lessened. Thus we have no reason to believe that the Soviet leaders' perception of the contribution of civil defense to their capabilities for strategic nuclear conflict will change significantly.[73]

CIVIL DEFENSE PLANNING IN THE UNITED STATES

The Recent Initiatives. The increasing lethality of the Soviet nuclear threat, as well as asymmetries in the projected numbers of Soviet and American citizens that would survive a hypothetical major nuclear exchange in the mid-1980's, were major factors in the renewed emphasis upon civil defense in the United States.

This emphasis was made explicit in 1978 by the Carter Administration with the promulgation of Presidential Directive 41 (PD 41). Concerned that the absence of a credible civil defense program in the United States might destabilize deterrence if the Soviet leaders perceived nuclear war as less devastating to their own population and industry than to those of the United States, PD 41 committed the United States to a program of crisis relocation planning. The proponents of PD 41 argued that the planned ability to evacuate over 140 million Americans from more than 400 military and industrial high-risk areas would redress the asymmetry of superpower population vulnerability. Such an initiative would discourage the Soviet leaders from concluding that they enjoyed a decisive strategic advantage that could support attempts at coercion or greater risk-taking in a nuclear crisis. Moreover, it was argued that an increased civil defense capability would bolster the credibility of the US commitment to the nuclear defense of NATO. It should be pointed out that the renewed US interest in civil defense was not, simply, a knee-jerk reaction which concluded that such a US program was needed simply because the USSR had one.

In other words, there were and are other humanitarian, political and economic factors unrelated to deterrence that generated renewed interest in an American civil defense effort.

The Reagan Program. Early in 1982, President Reagan built upon President Carter's foundation with the signing of National Security Decision Directive Number 26 (NSDD 26). In this document, the President identified civil defense as "an essential ingredient of our nuclear forces." Noting that while the United States would continue to rely upon its strategic nuclear offensive forces (rather than civil defense) as the preponderant factor in maintaining deterrence, he observed that US civil defense efforts must contribute to "an improved basis for dealing with crises and carrying out eventual national recovery" in the event of the failure of deterrence. Specifically, he established the following goals for a revitalized civil defense program:

- Enhance deterrence and stability in conjunction with our strategic offensive and other strategic defensive forces. Civil defense, as an element of the strategic balance, should assist in maintaining perceptions that this balance is favorable to the US.
- Reduce the possibility that the US could be coerced in time of crisis.
- Provide for survival of a substantial portion of the US population in the event of nuclear attack preceded by strategic warning and for continuity of government, should deterrence and escalation control fail.
- Provide an improved ability to deal with natural disasters and other large-scale domestic emergencies.[74]

The Federal Emergency Management Agency (FEMA), which had replaced the Defense Civil Preparedness Agency, was given overall operational supervision of a program that was to include the following elements:

- *Population Protection.* By the end of 1989, the development of plans and deployment of supporting operational systems will be completed. Primary reliance will be placed upon relocating the population of US metropolitan and other potential high-risk areas to surrounding areas of lower risk during a period of international crisis, taking advantage of extensive US transportation resources.
- *Industrial Protection.* Analyses and preparation will be completed which will allow a funding decision to be made on a program to protect key defense and population relocation support industries.
- *Blast Sheltering.* Analyses and preparation will be completed which will allow a funding decision on blast shelters for key industrial workers in defense and population relocation support industries.[75]

The most significant and immediate thrust of the President's civil defense program emphasizes population evacuation and protection. This emphasis distinguishes the population protection program (which requests $4.2 billion over a 7-year period)[76] from the Soviet program which assigns to population protection the lowest priority of importance after the protection of the leadership and industry.

An analysis of the recent and current spending allocations demonstrates the high priority assigned by the President's civil defense initiatives to the identification and restoration of existing civil defense facilities, public education, improvement in the warning and communication infrastructure, and the management and support of an evacuation program. Currently, relatively meager funds are allocated to industrial hardening and onsite protection of key workers pending the results of feasibility studies beginninig in FY 1983.[77]

The Administration has argued that the scope of its civil defense program is modest compared to that of the Soviet Union as well as to costly US offensive and defensive systems such as the MX, Trident and BMD. The scope, as Assistant Secretary of Defense Richard Perle noted in his March 1983 statement to the Senate Foreign Relations Committee, is consistent with the US view that modest civil defense expenditures "represent little more than insurance—insurance that in circumstances short of a central strategic exchange—some lives might be saved that would otherwise be lost."[78] Mr. Perle observed in his testimony that such a program would not lead the Administration to a false sense of security inasmuch as:

> We do not seek, nor do we believe that it is possible to obtain, levels of protection from the effects of all out nuclear war that would reduce significantly the unspeakable horror of such an event.[79]

He went on to argue that the horror which would surely attend any nuclear exchange would not absolve any political administration from its responsibility to strive for the protection of the populace, however problematic such plans might appear;

> But neither do we believe that we can, in good conscience, make a deliberate decision to refrain from even those minimal plans for expedient measures that might diminish the loss of life that a nuclear war would entail.[80]

CIVIL DEFENSE AND CRISIS STABILITY

Two principal goals for civil defense planning by NSDD-26 were established: (1) to contribute together with strategic nuclear offensive forces to the deterrence of nuclear war between the superpowers and (2) to limit the number of casualties and amount of destruction should deterrence fail. While listed as separate objectives in NSDD-26, the contributions of civil defense to deterrence and to mitigating the effects of nuclear war cannot, in fact, be separated. Obviously, the effectiveness of civil defense plans and consequences as well as the credibility of the adversary's deterrent are important variables in the cost/benefit strategic calculus that leaders will assess in a crisis as they ponder the initiation of nuclear war.

In the absence of precise and unambiguous determinations of the damage-limiting effectiveness of civil defense plans or a clear understanding of an adversary's intent if civil defense plans are implemented during a crisis, it is impossible to ascertain the ultimate impact of these plans on the minds of Soviet and American strategic planners as they perceived their respective capabilities. Therefore, much debate has surrounded the issue of whether civil defense planning and the implementation of such plans would stabilize or destabilize superpower deterrence. To American proponents of civil defense who seek to redress the asymmetries of Soviet-American programs, the Soviet Union's unique possession of a defensive capability—assessed by its American evaluators as effective—destabilizes deterrence because it suggests to the Soviet leadership that nuclear war will be less destructive to the USSR than it will be to the United States. Such an assessment might make the Soviet leaders more, rather than less, inclined to institute a preemptive strike during a severe crisis in an attempt to limit further potential damage to the Soviet Union. Likewise, if the United States lacks an effective evacuation program and its leaders observe the initiation of a massive Soviet evacuation during a crisis (real or perceived by Soviet leaders but consistent with US interpretations of Soviet warfighting doctrine and capabilities), pressure might motivate an early, damage-limiting American strike. In either case, civil defense might be viewed as destabilizing.

Civil defense planning and implementation, however, during crises must not be viewed in a vacuum. Under almost any conceivable scenario the implementation of civil defense plans would take place in conjunction with a wide variety of other events, many of which would be observed by Soviet leaders and some of which would be specifically communicated to them in Moscow. For example, if the United States implemented its civil defense plans while simultaneously placing its forces on full alert and communicating to Moscow a desire to defuse the crisis along with a warning that any premature strike would fall on vacant US silos and vacated runways, would the Soviet leadership be inclined to execute a preemptive first strike for fear of a simultaneous US strike? Or, would Moscow believe any preemption now might more clearly result in risks which outweigh benefits? If such American events took place during an ongoing conflict in Europe, would the Soviet leaders believe that strategic nuclear war was inevitable and be inclined to preempt? Or, might they believe that further risks associated with war in Europe were not warranted and, thus, seek to de-escalate the conflict in Europe? Likewise, if the Soviet Union implemented its civil defense plans and commenced an evacuation, would the United States be inclined toward a preemptive nuclear strike? In short, much would depend upon who evacuated first, upon the relative abilities of each side to evacuate, and a number of complex and uncertain calculations made by US and Soviet decisionmakers relative to their independent perceptions of the intent of the other.

It would appear that civil defense plans and implementation during a crisis are likely to have less of an effect on the question of crises stability than a host of other factors and signals during a crisis. Furthermore, there is reason to believe that their impact is not inalterably and unambiguously in the direction of instability.

CIVIL DEFENSE PLANNING IN AN UNCERTAIN ENVIRONMENT

The expression by Mr. Perle that civil defense "might diminish" the loss of life in the place of a more definitive prognostication illustrates the uncertainties that must attend all models, scenarios and plans for nuclear war contingencies. Whether, as examined above, civil defense planning is a benign instrument of strategic policy or a provocative and destabilizing gesture which might result in the very war it seeks to avoid is, at present, an unanswerable question that has generated much debate.[81] Furthermore, whether, and the extent to which, one can draw lessons from the strategic bombing survey of World War II or the 1979 evacuation of Three Mile Island which underlie certain assumptions about the effects of nuclear war and the consequences of relocation are questions similarly shrouded in uncertainty.[82]

Nevertheless, even the casual observer of the nuclear war/civil defense issue can be fairly certain in at least one speculation: that in the event of a severe crisis between the United States and the Soviet Union, millions of Americans who perceive themselves to be in high-risk areas will evacuate to areas they believe to be safer.[83] Moreover, in such a situation, one can expect them to look to their government for assistance. To the extent that such anticipations are valid, and short of an ability to guarantee the nonoccurrence of such crises, it becomes incumbent upon the government to identify safe host areas, designate appropriate travel routes, provide for the support of the evacuees, and plan for the aftermath of the crisis.

This is the essential thrust of the current civil defense program being directed by FEMA. Indeed, the ACDA has concluded that the United States is in a much superior position relative to the Soviet Union to mount such an ambitious and difficult program and at far less cost. This optimism is due to the following factors that favor the United States: (1) the US population is more dispersed than that of the USSR; (2) the United States has developed a superior rural infrastructure, an extensive highway system, plentiful food reserves, efficient distribution system, and a high degree of industrial redundance; and (3) the uniform belief of all Americans that the political integrity of the United States as currently constituted should continue to exist in the aftermath of a nuclear war.[84]

It is imperative to note, however, that the importance and desirability of such planning and even the advantages the United States may enjoy in its pursuit reduce neither the uncertainties that attend such planning nor the obstacles that would impede the effective execution of civil defense plans in time of crisis or war. Certainly, many of the difficulties that bedevil the Soviet programs are also applicable to the United States. Let us consider some of the uncertainties and economic, social and political obstacles that might occur in a crisis scenario where the United States implemented the evacuation of its population from the more than

400 high-risk areas identified by FEMA. While such estimations are inherently open to conjecture, they illustrate the complexity of the task facing FEMA planners.

Evacuation/No War. Laurino, Trinkl, Miller, and Harker, authors of several computer simulations of the effects of crisis relocation (CR), have estimated that in a crisis, 13-26 million Americans would evacuate before any directions to do so were issued.[85] As a result of these evacuations, there would be a doubling of unemployment, and absenteeism would reduce industrial productivity by about 10 percent.[86] Furthermore, individuals with reduced incomes and access to savings would engage in savings withdrawals, hoarding and panic buying. These effects on individuals in the pre-CR phase would ripple through the economy, greatly affecting businesses and banks and other financial institutions.

Upon the initation of a preplanned CR, many of the problems noted above would be amplified and new ones would develop. For many individuals, income would cease, their checks and credit cards would be less acceptable in host areas and cash shortages would be experienced, all at a time when emergency costs would soar. Businesses would be confronted by general shutdowns (resulting in the unemployment of 60-70 percent of all nongovernment workers),[87] freezes on assets and payment, unprecedented security problems, and distribution stoppages resulting in the need to find alternate supplies. This latter need would be difficult to satisfy due to the evacuation of central management and corporation headquarters,[88] as well as to problems associated with rerouting goods in transit. Banks in high-risk areas, already forced to balance large withdrawals from domestic and foreign accounts with greatly reduced and delayed accounts receivable, deposits and interbank loans, would shut down and would face increased security problems. Meanwhile, banks in host areas would undergo extraordinarily high service demands, all at a time of reduced interbank transfers and the closing of financial exchanges.

As the CR's duration increased, the evacuees in the host areas would find it increasingly difficult to pay for services. Businesses in risk areas would remain shut down and would experience reduced accounts receivable, and businesses in host areas would face distribution problems and low support from essential industries. Banks would (1) receive reduced debt payments from individuals, businesses, and governments in high-risk areas and (2) be confronted by continued withdrawals, resulting in lower profitability and increases in their net borrowers' reserves. Local and state governments would continue to face greatly increased emergency costs; although restricted access to liquid credits, reduced revenue from intergovernment transfers, and reduced tax revenues would impede the discharge of their financial obligations.

Economic problems would not disappear with the end of the CR and the return of the evacuees to the high risk areas.[89] Citizens and businesses, with greatly reduced assets, would likely face overdue financial obligations. Businesses would need time to sort out their debts and financial situations (inadequate working credit, loss of asset values, and reduced access to credit) and reconcile their depleted inventories and resource imbalances with their production obligations. Hence, the buildup of production would be slow, and unemployment would be prolonged. The collapse of businesses which were marginal before the CR would aggravate an already bad situation. Banks would be required to undertake massive records updating and the clearing of backlogged checks. The maintenance of bank liquidity would be endangered by recent outflows, delayed revenues, a lowered savings rate and excessive credit demands. The developments might reduce further the prospects of numerous marginal economic concerns with effects that would ripple through the economy for some time.[90]

Many of the economic consequences of an evacuation can be expressed in quantitative terms and, as such, are calculable. The social and political effects of an evacuation are more speculative. Nevertheless, the maintenance of social and political concerns is equally critical to the country's well-being.

> Without the political and social consensus that binds disparate groups into a nation, the organization necessary to guide and focus recovery effort, and the individual's ability to confront and overcome disruptive personal emotional demands, all the surviving economic and military capability will be of little concern.[91]

Particularly serious social problems would arise from a temporary or permanent evacuation as a result of the differences between urban and rural racial compositions[92] and lifestyles. It may be optimistic to expect that in a moment of peril and uncertainty, host area residents will welcome a massive influx of these urban individuals. In addition, latent racial, cultural and religious prejudices may mitigate against the effective relocation of the evacuees in the host areas, especially if the evacuees are viewed by their hosts as interlopers, burdens and competitors for scarce provisions. Moreover, the tremendous overcrowding in many of the Eastern states[93] would further intensify these hostilities and prejudices.

Ironically, even a decision *not* to evacuate the largest, high-risk metropolitan areas would be socially disruptive and politically dangerous since the urban poor and minorities would surmise that, at best, they were not welcome by their rural compatriots and, at worst, they were expendable. The social and political consequences of these perceptions would undermine the country's social cohesion and erode the legitimacy and support for future initiatives of the political leadership.

The sick, the very young and the very old—those groups requiring the most attention and care in society—would also suffer severely in the evacuation. These individuals would face numerous physical rigors in an evacuation, reduced attention and support services in the relocation centers and, possibly, death in many circumstances.[94] Given all this suffering, the anger, remorse and recriminations among the host area individuals and the evacuees would be heightened at the end of a crisis in which a war did not occur

Essential workers assigned to remain at their posts, yet who desire not to be separated from their families in time of crisis, will face incredible psychological strains. Since "the powerful need to remain with community and family was . . . the reality that undermined the British evacuation plans,"[95] one may expect that many essential workers will evacuate the risk areas with their families, irrespective of official procedures and pleas. It is uncertain that those who design CR plans can calculate accurately the effects of these pulls both into and away from the high-risk areas.

Hence, a CR could have numerous and severe social effects upon the young and the old, the sick, the poor, and the minority individual. Many of these effects could be translated into unprecedented political developments. Even if war did not occur, the government's assertion that it was the evacuation that helped to avoid Armageddon would be difficult to prove. While the nonoccurrence of war would be attributed by some as testimony to the government's efficient CR planning, others might view a return to the risk areas as an admission of error in the government's estimation of the crisis' seriousness and its ability to plan adequately for the welfare of the citizenry. The government's assertions to the contrary would probably be belied by internal allegations and recriminations of faulty analysis.

> The experience of evacuation and its anxiety-producing sense of vulnerability may traumatize the evacuees into losing faith in the government in power. Implicity, this may be translated into a sense that stability and continuity has been lost; that the government has failed in its most basic function, which is to act as a protector, a surrogate parent, in providing security. A loss of this implicit trust cannot help but injure the government's prestige, and thus, its ability to lead.[96]

NUCLEAR WAR AND POSTATTACK RECOVERY.

This analysis suggests that even a logistically "successful" evacuation would have numerous and long-lasting deleterious economic, social, and political ramifications. Hence, the cumulative effects of the evacuation experience might well mitigate against *future* successful evacuations, irrespective of the prior evacuation's logistical success.

These effects of CR, however, would pale to insignificance if a nuclear exchange actually did ensue between the United States and the Soviet Union. Mr. Perle underscored the Administration's position when he noted that while the magnitude of death, physical destruction, social disruption, and psychological distress would vary with the size, timing and target selection of the attack, one should not believe that some proper mix of strategic retaliation against the Soviet Union and US civil defense preparation would make nuclear war anything less than a nightmare surpassing all comprehension.[97] When one considers (l) the existence of scores of industrial and military targets in the United States;[98] (2) the Soviet denigration of limited warfighting scenarios;[99] (3) the easterly direction of the prevailing winds across the United States which will carry radioactive fallout to major population centers;[100] (4) the location of many strategic targets in the country's breadbasket[101]

Many of the problems for economic recovery that would confront the Soviet Union also would apply for the United States. According to the Stanford Research Institute's (SRI) input-output study of the United States, economic recovery from even a less than all-out nuclear attack would be most problematic, especially if the Soviet Union complemented its counterforce strikes with an economic "bottlenecking" target strategy.[103] For instance, a Soviet attack of 750 warheads against the 15 major sectors of the US economy would require more than 9 years to engage fully the amount of initially surviving industrial capacity (67 percent). In other words, a substantial part of the surviving industrial capacity would not be used in the early years following an attack due, in part, to the loss of producers and consumers as well as capital investment and supporting infrastructures. Moreover, reflecting the sensitivity of econometric models to their assumed parameters and the difficulties involved in predicting far into the future, the SRI estimates depict nothing of how much time would be required to return to preattack GNP levels. SRI estimated that the GNP would remain only two-thirds to three-fourths of the preattack levels 9 years after Soviet attacks using 750-1250 warheads against US economic targets. During these years, one would expect that the experiences of infrastructural reconstitution would override investments in consumer goods. The result would be slow recovery of the quality of life at a time when the war's survivors would require much support and be least able and willing to make sacrifices.

One must bring caution to the interpretation of these figures since their aggregate nature may obscure the actual vulnerability of key industries. In *Economic and Social Consequences of Nuclear Attack on the United States,* Arthur Katz examines the percent of surviving industrial capacity that would remain if the Soviet Union attacked critical industrial targets in the 71 largest standard metropolitan areas (SMSA).[104] He then computes the additional numbers of weapons that would be required to reduce the remaining capacity to 10 percent and then to 2-3 percent. According to Katz's calculations, only 481 additional warheads (beyond those used to attack the 71 SMSA) would be required to reduce these eight critical industries to 2-3 percent of their prewar levels. In light of the interdependent nature of the input-output US economy, these few warheads, which constitute far less than 10 percent of the Soviet Union's strategic arsenal, would be quite well invested from the Soviet Union's perspective.

Political and Social Problems. Many of the economic, political and social problems associated with a CR are germane to postattack scenarios because for many, a CR becomes permanent after a nuclear exchange. Those local, state and federal officials who survived would face a host of difficult problems. They would have to begin economic reconstruction without a once mighty industrial/financial infrastructure and thousands of skilled workers and consumers, along with massive regional imbalances, few prospects of international trade or aid and the threat of continued occasional nuclear attacks. Competing with economic reconstruction for scarce government resources would be incredible demands for social services and government intervention required by the millions of dead and injured. Certainly, the destruction of many hospitals, medical supplies, and trained personnel, along with the psychological trauma and numbing induced by the shock of war, would mitigate against the provision of orderly, rapid, and effective aid to the survivors. Whether the government chooses to emphasize the country's economic or social needs, it can expect significant opposition. When one considers that this decision would be made within the context of (1) the disruption of social, especally racial, stability due to the forced interaction of the country's rural and urban residents, (2) the government's allocation of the greatest recovery resources to some areas ahead of others; (3) confusion about jurisdictional authority among local, state and federal governments; and (4) the possibility that the government may be obligated to wage protracted war, thereby postponing any kind of reconstruction although not obviating the possibility of future destruction, it is quite possible the authority of past leaders would not be acknowledged and that the country's federal structure would disappear, being replaced by a confederated patchwork of quasi-feudal areas of association.

CONCLUSIONS

The relationship between Soviet offensive and defensive capabilities and the intentions of the Soviet Communist regime is speculative at best. In fact, the extent of Soviet civil defense effectiveness is a matter still debated with vigor by strategic analysts. The entire issue of civil defense and deterrence is arcane and necessarily dependent upon various assumptions, uncertainties and scenarios. Hence, it is unlikely that facile solutions or an unshakeable consensus will attend efforts to develop a civil defense policy that is militarily prudent and feasible politically as well as economically.

In this paper, I have examined the arguments of those who fear and those who dismiss as ineffective the efforts of Soviet civil defense planners. The actual effectiveness of their programs probably lies somewhere in between. Those who criticize the Soviet program are likely correct in noting that such initiatives would not spare the Soviet Union from massive and unprecedented destruction. Their conclusion that these efforts would not contribute much to making nuclear war a more feasible policy option to the Soviet leadership is persuasive to this author. However, it is also probable that these, albeit imperfect, programs would reduce significantly the number of casualties in a nuclear war with the United States and contribute to postwar recovery. Hence, former Secretary of Defense Donald H. Rumsfeld was correct in his observation that:

> . . . while the Soviets may not preserve or succeed in this admittedly complex and difficult task, their growing capabilities must play a major role in U.S. force planning.[105]

The attention directed to civil defense by the Carter and Reagan Administrations has been consistent and justified in light of even the limited capabilities ascribed to civil defense. Since one can only speculate about the extent to which Soviet civil defense capabilities destabilize deterrence, the contributions of an American program of population evacuation as initiated in PD-41 and expanded upon in NSDD-26 must also remain within the realm of conjecture.

Current US initiatives in civil defense planning are most accurately viewed as humanitarian and contributing little to a warfighting capability. In the first place, as is also the case with the Soviet Union, industry cannot be moved quickly or easily and, therefore, remains vulnerable to the increasingly accurate and destructive warheads found in the strategic arsenals of both superpowers. Moreover, it is not a particularly difficult objective for one superpower to destroy its adversary's industrial infrastructure, its civil defense efforts notwithstanding. Each superpower recognizes that the destruction of its adversary's population as an end in itself is neither desirable nor necessary to guarantee deterrence. Second, as John Troxall observed in his assessment of the US civil defense program:

> ... there is no claim being made concerning the efficacy of such a program that would cause any leader to disregard the disasterous consequences of a nuclear exchange and thus lead to a greater willingness to initiate such an exchange.[106]

Nevertheless, it remains an obligation of any government responsible to its citizens to plan for the preservation of life in the event of a nuclear war. The horror that would attend a strategic exchange and the imperfections of the civil defense plans do not relieve the government of this responsibility. Furthermore, if we assume that people will evacuate what they perceive as high-risk areas in a nuclear crisis, well coordinated plans identifying safe areas and assisting the populace in their efforts to relocate are prudent and necessary. While no amount of planning can ever mitigate the tragedy of nuclear war, there is no reason why efforts directed at reducing some of the economic and social dislocations described above should not be made.

As to the question of how much civil defense is enough, it appears to this author that the $4.2 billion which would be allocated over 7 years would be money well spent if, as argued, it is not inherently destabilizing and is able to increase to even a modest degree the percentage of Americans who would survive a medium to heavy Soviet strike. Relative to other high cost research, development and acquisition programs such as the MX-ICBM and Trident submarine,[107] the costs of an American crisis relocation capability are rather modest.

However, it may be a mistake for future US administrations to pursue a major blast-shelter program for essential industrial workers for several reasons. First, the proliferation of highly accurate warheads in the Soviet strategic aresenal makes it likely that the Soviet Union could target these installations more rapidly and at a lower relative cost than the United States could build them. In fact, the initiation of an American shelter program might provide the incentive for the Soviet Union to expand its already massive arsenal, further thwarting efforts to slow down the arms race. Second, the cost of such a program would be quite high and could place major strains upon the US economy.[108] Related to this question of economic feasibility is the impact upon the development and acquisition of other weapons systems and defense initiatives which are crucial to the maintenance of stable deterrence. At a time when defense spending is coming under increasing public criticism and heightened congressional scrutiny and control, it is quite possible that efforts to secure billions for a shelter program of questionable effectiveness will jeopardize funding for more necessary and urgent defense priorities identified by the Reagan Administration—such as increasing the survivability of the country's command, control, communications and intelligence (C^3) facilities; deploying a new manned bomber fleet, cruise missiles, and the Trident D-5 SLBM; and strengthening America's conventional forces and improving their mobility. Finally, the development of a shelter program may generate various cultural, political and social issues that would be a consequence of and problematic for this country's democratic institutions.[109]

ENDNOTES

1. Caspar Weinberger, *Soviet Military Power*, Washington: US Government Printing Office, 1981, p. 54.
2. *Ibid.*
3. International Institute of Strategic Studies (IISS), *Military Balance, 1982-83*, London, 1982, p. 140.
4. *Ibid.*
5. Weinberger, p. 54.
6. For studies citing the effectiveness of Soviet civil defense programs, see Leon Goure, "Another Interpretation," *Bulletin of the Atomic Scientists,* Vol. 34, April 1978, pp. 48-51; *Shelter and Soviet War Survival Strategy,* Coral Gables, Florida: University of Miami, 1978, and numerous other studies cited herein. See also T. K. Jones, *Effect of Evacuation and Sheltering on Potential Fatalities from a Nuclear Exchange,* Seattle: The Boeing Aerospace Co., 1977; and *Defense Industrial Base: Industrial Preparedness and Nuclear War Survival,* testimony before Joint Committee on Defense Production, Part I, November 17, 1976; and John Troxall, "Soviet Civil Defense and the American Response," *Military Review,* January 1983, pp. 36-46. Studies and essays that are skeptical of the effectiveness of the Soviet civil defense program include US Arms Control and Disarmament Agency, *An Analysis of Civil Defense in Nuclear War,* Washington: ACDA, December 1978, (hereinafter referred to as ACDA study); Central Intelligence Agency, *Soviet Civil Defense,* NI-78-1000 3, July 1978 (hereinafter referred to as CIA study); Oak Ridge National Laboratory, trans. *Grazhdanskaya Oborona,* Civil Defense, 1974; Fred Kaplan, "The Soviet Civil Defense Myth," (in two parts), *Bulletin of the Atomic Scientists,* Vol. 34, March 1978, pp. 14-20 and April 1978, pp. 41-48; Robert Kennedy, "The Strategic Balance in Transition," in *Soviet Armed Forces Review Annual,* ed. David Jones, Gulf Breeze, Florida: Academic International Press, 1980: Ed Zuckerman, "Hiding from the Bomb Again," *Harper's,* Vol. 259, August 1979, pp. 33-40, 90; William Kincade, "Repeating History: The Civil Defense Debate Renewed," *International Security,* Winter 1978, pp. 99-120; and National Academy of Sciences, *Long Term Worldwide Effects of Multiple Nuclear Weapons Detonation,* Washington: 1975; Arthur M. Katz, *Life After Nuclear War: The Economic and Social Impacts of Nuclear Attacks on the United States,* Cambridge, Massachusetts: Ballinger Publishing Company, 1982; and John Weinstein, "Soviet Civil Defense and the US Deterrent,"*Parameters,* March 1982, pp. 70-83.
7. See Richard Pipes, "The Soviet Strategy for Nuclear Victory," *Commentary,* Vol. 64, July 1977, pp. 21-34; Leon Goure, *War Survival in Soviet Strategy,* Coral Gables: Center for Advanced International Studies, University of Miami, 1976; T. K. Jones, *Industrial Survival and Recovery After a Nuclear Attack: A Report to the Joint Committee on Defense Production, US Congress,* Seattle: The Boeing Aerospace Co., November 1976, p. 84; Leon Goure, F. D. Kohler, and M. L. Harvey, eds., *The Role of Nuclear Forces in Current Soviet Strategy,* Coral Gables: University of Miami, 1974, p. 60.
8. CIA study, p. 4.
9. See US Congress, Office of Technology Assessment, (OTA), *The Effects of Nuclear War,* 1979, p. 140 (hereinafter referred to as OTA). Also see *Military Posture and H.R. 3519. DOD Authorization for Appropriations for FY 1982,* Hearings, House Committee on Armed Services, 97th Cong., 1st Sess., February 26-27, 1981, p. 862.

10. OTA, p. 140.

11. John Collins, *US-Soviet Military Balance,* New York: McGraw-Hill, 1980, pp. 174-175.

12. America's commitment to risk annihilation in the defense of Europe has long been a matter of concern and debate. DeGaulle questioned it two decades ago. More recently, former Secretary of State Kissinger's acknowledgment of certain scenario-dependent divergencies between European and American security interests ("The Future of NATO," *The Washington Quarterly,* Vol. 2, Autumn 1979, pp. 6-7) shocked NATO members.

> It is absurd to base the strategy of the West on the credibility of the threat of mutual suicide. [NATO should not rely too strongly on] strategic assurances that [America] cannot possibly mean, or if we do mean, we shouldn't want to execute, because if we do execute them we risk the destruction of our civlization.

13. *Ibid.,* Collins, p. 175.

14. House Record 3519, p. 862; Troxall, pp. 45-46. Also, see United States, *Military Posture for FY 1983,* prepared by the Organization of the Joint Chiefs of Staff, pp. 25, 77-78. For a complete statement of the Administration's civil defense plans and objectives, see "Civil Defense Program Overview," March 12, 1982, distributed by the Federal Emergency Management Agency.

15. PD-41, issued on September 29, 1978, seeks to improve deterrence by increasing the number of Americans who would survive a nuclear attack (through crisis relocation planning from more than 400 high-risk areas) and insuring greater continuity of government.

16. "US Official Supports Civil Defense Proposal," *The New York Times,* April 1, 1982, p. 17.

17. CIA study, pp. 1-3.

18. *Ibid.,* p. 9.

19. *Military Balance 1982-1983,* p. 140.

20. Weinberger, *Soviet Military Power,* p. 56. Also, see T. Powers, "Choosing a Strategy for World War III," *The Atlantic Monthly,* November 1982, pp. 82-110 (esp. p. 103-107).

21. Kennedy, pp. 366-367.

22. *Ibid.,* and ACDA study, Kaplan, and Oak Ridge.

23. Oak Ridge Laboratory, p. vii.

24. Jones, 1976, pp. 7, 10.

25. Goure, 1976, pp. 3, 125, 177.

26. *Ibid.,* pp. 3, 11, 77-119.

27. Kaplan, Goure, 1976, pp. 114, 118.

28. Keith A. Dunn, *Soviet Military Weaknesses and Vulnerabilities: A Critique of the Short War Advocates,* Strategic Issues Research Memorandum, Strategic Studies Institute, July 31, 1978, p. 12.

29. In 1977, there was only one automobile for every 52 citizens. See M. Elizabeth Denton, "Soviet Consumer Policy: Trends and Prospects" in M. Bornstein, ed. *The Soviet Economy: Continuity and Change,* Boulder, Colorado: Westview Press, 1981, pp. 172, 180. There were 109 million automobiles in use in 1976 in the United States, almost one for every two citizens. *The World Almanac and Fact Book, 1982,* New York: Newspaper Enterprises Assoc.

30. Jones, 1976. T. K. Jones is currently Deputy Under Secretary of Defense for Strategic and Theater Nuclear Weapons.

31. ACDA study, p. 3. Approximately 49 percent of the Soviet urban population is located within less than 5000 nautical square miles. Sixty-one percent of the US urban populace lives within a 13,000 nmi^2 area.

32. Powers, pp. 90-91, 104-110. In National Security Decision Memorandum, No. 242, developed by Secretary of Defense James Schlesinger and signed by President Nixon in January 1974, the United States adopted a nuclear policy characterized by a) counterforce targetting, b) escalation control, and c) the specification of "nontargets" and "withholds." Among the counterforce targets was the Soviet economic infrastructure, 70 percent of which was to be destroyed according to US plans (Policy Guidance for the Employment of Nuclear Weapons). See Desmond Ball, "Counterforce Targetting: How New? How Viable?," *Arms Control Today,* Vol. ll, No. 2, February 1981.

33. *Ibid.*

34. Moreover, if war occurred and a US retaliatory strike arrived before the Soviet evacuation could be completed, the number of civilian casualties could be very high indeed.

35. Weinberger, p. 69; Troxall, p. 43.

36. CIA study, p. 10.

37. Oak Ridge, pp. 50-54.

38. Troxall, p. 43.

39. CIA study, p. 10.

40. T. K. Jones and W. Scott Thompson, "Central War and Civil Defense," *Orbis,* Fall 1978, p. 699.

41. Troxall, pp. 37-38.

42. Kennedy, pp. 366-367. More recently, the President's Commission on Strategic Forces reversed what had become conventional wisdom in their affirmation that the vulnerability of the United States' ICBM force will remain within tolerable limits until the 1990's. Also, see Benjamin Lambeth's "Uncertainties for the Soviet War Planner," *International Security,* Winter 1982/1983, pp. 139-166.

43. US Joint Committee on Defense Production, *Civil Preparedness Review, Part II: Industrial Defense and Nuclear Attack,* April 1977, pp. 20, 68.

44. ACDA study, p. ll.

45. OTA, p. 18 (A 1 megaton airburst at 8000 feet produces a 10 psi. radius of 4.8 km and a wind velocity of 290 mph.

46. ACDA study, p. ll.

47. Jones, 1976, p. 7.

48. ACDA study, p. 5. In the Soviet Union, there are only 15 integrated iron and steel mills; 34 sizeable petroleum reserves; 8 copper refineries; 6 lead-zinc refineries; 17 meat-packing plants; 8 major shipbuilding works; 5 factories processing 65 percent of the USSR's aluminum, and so forth.

49. Kincade and Kaplan. See Gary Guertner, "Strategic Vulnerabilities of a Multinational State: Deterring the Soviet Union," *Political Science Quarterly,* Vol. 96, Summer 1981, pp. 209-223. Also, see Powers, p. 109, who also discusses the high level of concentration of Soviet military targets:

> The Soviets have 1,398 missiles in twenty-eight missile fields (including the test centers at Tyura Tam and Pletetsk with 300 command-and-control

centers, 500 airfields with runways longer than 4,000 feet (suitable for intercontinental bombers), three submarine bases (Murmansk, Petropavlosk, Vladivostok), 167 infantry and armored divisions, sixteen headquarters of PVO Strany (the Soviet air-defense command), and five naval fleet headquarters. Fifty percent of key Soviet industry is contained in 200 complexes. Only six Soviet rail transshipment yards load 80 percent of all empty railcars. There are twenty-six low-frequency radio transmitting stations that broadcast military traffic, and thirty-six stations of one type or another that handle communications with satellites. This comes to a total of 3,543 'targets.'

50. See Geoffrey Kemp, *Nuclear Forces for Medium Powers,* Part II, Adelphi Paper No. 107, International Institute for Strategic Studies, 1974, pp. 5,9.

51. Richard Garwin, Testimony Before Joint Committee on Defense Production, *Civil Preparedness and Limited Nuclear War,* April 28, 1976, p. 55.

52. ACDA study, p. 5.

53. Powers, p. 109.

54. Jones, 1976, p. 84.

55. Robert J. Lifton and Kai Erikson, "Nuclear War's Effect on the Mind," *The New York Times,* March 15, 1982, p. A17. Dr. Lifton's other publications which examine the psychiatric effects of nuclear war include *Death in Life: Survivors of Hiroshima* and a coedited volume, *Last Aid: The Medical Dimensions of Nuclear War,* Freeman: San Francisco, 1982.

56. Lifton and Erikson, p. 17.

57. *Ibid.*

58. *Ibid.*

59. E. J. Sternglass and W. T. Land, Letter to the Editor, *The New York Times,* May 28, 1982, p. A26. The authors, professors of radiological physics and geology, respectively, note:

> . . . the real amount of sunlight-reflecting stratospheric particles would be 20 to 40 times greater per megaton detonated than estimated earlier, so that a 10,000 megaton nuclear war would produce a cooling effect . . . equivalent to some 10,000 Mt. St. Helen eruptions.
>
> Since a 10-degree reduction in the average temperature of the earth would be able to trigger another ice age, even a limited nuclear [war], using some 2,000 to 3,000 megatons for an attack on purely military targets is likely to result in an irreversible lowering of the earth's climate, accompanied by a reduction in rainfall in the mid-latitudes.
>
> That would destroy the wheat-producing areas of North and South America, Europe, Russia and China, areas on which the world's population depends for survival. And what followed would be another advance of the polar ice sheets . . . .

60. Earl Rubenking, "The Soviet Tractor Industry: Progress and Problems," *Soviet Economy in a New Perspective,* US Congress Joint Economic Committee, October 14, 1976, p. 55.

61. Murray Feshbach, "Population and Manpower Trends in the USSR," *The USSR and the Sources of Soviet Policy,* Washington: The Council on Foreign Relations and the Kennan Institute, 1978; and Hugh Seton-Watson, "The Last of the Empires," *The Washington Quarterly,* Vol. 3, No. 2, Spring, 1980, pp. 41-46.

62. See Guertner, 1981, and Desmond Ball, "Soviet ICBM Deployment," *Survival,* Vol. 22, July-August 1980, pp. 167-170. The Great Russian percentage of the Soviet population will drop below 50 percent by the year 2000. See Murray Feshbach, "Between the Lines of the 1979 Census," *Problems of Communism,* January-February 1982, pp. 27-37.

63. Guertner.

64. Helene Carrere d'Encausse, *Decline of an Empire,* New York: Newsweek Books,1979, Chapter IV.

65. Adam Ulam, *Expansion and Coexistence: Soviet Foreign Policy 1917-1973,*(2d ed.), New York: Praeger, 1974, pp. 663-664. Also, see Colin Gray "Targeting Problems for Central War," *Naval War College Review,* January-February, 1980, pp 3-21, for a persuasive discussion of the deterrent value of prospects of the demise of the Soviet state.

66. Pipes, pp. 21-34.

67. Weinstein, pp. 77-79.

68. Louis R. Beres, *Myths and Realities: US Nuclear Strategy,* Occasional Paper 32 of the Stanley Foundation, Muscatine, Iowa, 1982, pp. 6-7. Also, see Collins, p. 118; Pipes, p. 30, and S. Drell and F. von Hippel, "Limited Nuclear War," *Scientific American,* November 1976, pp.27-37. In his confirmation hearings for the Directorship of the ACDA, Kenneth L. Adelman noted: "If nuclear weapons are ever used, there can be no guarantee that their use would remain limited. In fact, I believe the chances of escalation would be dangerously high." See "US Arms-Control Nominee Asserts He Backs Reductions," *The New York Times,* February 4, 1983, p. 8.

69. Congressional Budget Office, *Retaliatory Issues for the US Strategic Nuclear Forces,* Congress of the United States, June 1978. Also, see Arthur M. Katz, *Life After Nuclear War,* Chapter 10, 1982.

A Carnegie Endowment Panel of high ranking defense experts also has maintained that the credibility of the US deterrent would remain secure in the 1990's. See *Challenges for U.S. National Security: Defense Spending and the Economy/The Strategic Balance and Strategic Arms Limitation.* The Carnegie Panel on US Security and the Future of Arms Control, Washington: The Carnegie Endowment for International Peace, 1981, see pp. 7-10 and Chapter 1; another report by the same panel entitled *Nuclear Strategy Issues of the 1980's,* 1982, supports this view, see pp. 3-13 and Chapter 1.

70. Kennedy, pp. 367-368.

71. See Kennedy, pp. 356-357. Also, see Fritz Ermarth, "Contrasts in American and Soviet Strategic Thought," *International Security,* Fall, 1978; Robert Legvold, "Strategic 'Doctrine' and SALT: Soviet and American Views," *Survival,* January-February 1979, pp. 8-13; and Raymond Garthoff, "Mutual Deterrence and Strategic Arms Limitations in Soviet Policy," *International Security,* Summer, 1978, pp. 113-125.

72. CIA study, p. 12. Asymmetric albeit artificial casualty estimates favoring the United States could be achieved if the scenario were reversed.

73. *Ibid.* p. 13.

74. An unclassified version of NSDD-26 was released by the White House on March 16, 1982. Also see S. Norris "President Reagan's Civil Defense Program," *The Defense Monitor XI,* Vol. 5, 1982, pp. l-8, for a critique of US defense planning.

75. *Ibid.*

76. *The New York Times,* April 1, 1982, p. 17.

77. Office of the Secretary of Defense, "OSD Assessment: The FY 1983 Federal Emergency Management Agency Civil Defense Program" transmitted February 8, 1982, by Frank Carlucci to Senator John Tower and Representative Melvin Price, Washington, p. 16.

78. Richard Perle, "Statement to Subcommittee on Arms Control, Senate Foreign Relations Committee," Washington, March 31, 1982, p. 5.

79. *Ibid.,* p. 4.

80. *Ibid.,* p. 4-5.

81. See Perle and Norris for arguments debating the nonprovocative nature of civil defense. For instance, a great deal of anger was focused on the federal government in connection with the Three Mile Island evacuation. See *Report of the President's Commission on the Accident at Three Mile Island,* October 1979, p. 7.

82. Also, see Cynthia B. Flynn and J. A. Chalmers, *The Social and Economic Effects of the Accident at Three Mile Island: Findings to Date,* NUREG-CR-1215, Washington, January 1980, also see Katz, pp. 197-200 for a discussion of the applicability of lessons learned from the study of conventional bombing in WWII to planning for nuclear war.

83. This was the case during the Cuban missile crisis. R. H. Laurino, *et. al.,* estimate that 13-26 million Americans will evacuate in a crisis before any order is given, also see note 85, below *(Impacts of Crisis Relocation).*

84. ACDA study, p. 3.

85. R. K. Laurino, F. Trinkl, C. F. Miller and R. A. Harker, *Economic and Industrial Aspects of Crisis Relocation: An Overview,* DCPA 01-75-c-0279, Palo Alto: Center for Planning and Research, May 1977; and R. K. Laurino, F. Trinkl, R. Berry, R. Schnider, W MacDougell, *Impacts of Crisis Relocation on U.S. Economic and Industrial Activity,* DCPA 01-76-c-0331, Palo Alto: Center for Planning and Research, October 1978, pp. 5-ll, also Katz, pp. 291-308.

86. Laurino, *et. al.,* 1977, p. 33.

87. *Ibid.*

88. Ninety and 95 percent, respectively, of central management and corporate headquarters are in high-risk metropolitan areas.

89. This scenario assumes that the end of the crisis will be unambiguous and that people will return to the high-risk areas without fear of future attack.

90. See Laurino, *Impacts,* pp. 5-ll. The cost of a CR is estimated at $100 million during the following two years. There would be numerous severe and long-lived effects of a CR on the international economy as well. The needs of Third World states requiring food and economic aid would go unfilled. International businesses would confront reduced and delayed demands from US consumers and delayed deliveries from American producers. The international monetary system would probably require restructuring due to the reduced value of OPEC holdings and myriad related problems. The interdependence of the global economy in general and western economies in particular assure that the serious effects of a CR in the United States would be widespread.

91. Katz, p. 193.
92. *Ibid.*, p. 73. Approximately 25 percent of the central city populations in the 157 largest metropolitan areas is nonwhite compared to only 6 percent of the country's rural populations.
93. A relocation housing factor of three in the event of a full evacuation is considered normal. However, 18 states east of the Mississippi River have relocation factors equal to four (8 states), five (1 state, Florida) or six (9 states, including Massachusetts, New Jersey, New York and Pennsylvania). See C. M. Hoaland, C. V. Chester and E. P. Wigner, *Survival of the Relocated Population of the US After a Nuclear Attack,* ORNL-5401, Oak Ridge Laboratory, June 1976, p. 28.
94. For a discussion of British experiences with evacuated populations during World War II, see R. Mitmus, *Problems of Social Policy,* London: His Majesty's Stationary Office and Longmans, Green and Co., 1950, p. 334.
95. Katz, p. 30l; Ronald Perry, Michael Lindell, and Marjorie Greene, *The Implications of Natural Hazard Evacuation Warning Studies for Crisis Location Planning,* Final Report, Seattle, Washington: Battelle Human Affairs Research Center, February 1980, p. 24.
96. Katz, p. 74.
97. Perle, pp. 3-5.
98. Center for Defense Information, *The Defense Monitor,* July 1982, pp. 4-5. The CDI is a private research institute with no official ties to the US Government.
99. Collins, p. 118. Also John Erickson, *Soviet Military Power,* London: Royal United States Institute for Defense Studies, 1971, p. 35.
100. US Congress, Committee on Foreign Relations, Subcommittee on Arms Control, International Organizations and Security Agreements, *Analyses of Effects of Limited Nuclear War,* Committee on Foreign Relations, United States Senate, Washington: September 1975, p. 52; also, see Drell and von Hippel, p. 34.
101. See Stephen L. Brown and Ulrich F. Pilz, "U.S. Agriculture: Potential Vulnerabilities," Menlo Park, California: Stanford Research Institute, 1969, p. 60; also, see Katz, pp. 50-62 for an analysis of the coincidence of the major food-producing areas of the United States with ICBM installations.
102. Perle, p. 3.
103. F. W. Dresch and S. Baum, *Analysis of the U.S. and USSR Potential for Economic Recovery Following a Nuclear Attack,* Menlo Park: Stanford Research Institute, Strategic Studies Center, January 1983, p. II-7.
104. Arthur Katz, US Congress, Committee on Banking, Housing, and Urban Affairs, *Economic and Social Consequences of Nuclear Attacks on the United States,* Washington: 1979.
105. *Civil Preparedness Review-Part II: Industrial Defense and Nuclear Attack,* Joint Committee of Defense Production, 95th Cong., 1st Sess., Washington: April 1977, p. 75.
106. Troxall, p. 45.
107. The costs (in billions), according to Secretary Weinberger, FY 1983, *Annual Report to Congress,* Washington: 1982, p. III-58-60, of the MX program are $4.256 and $5.844 in FYs 1983 and 1984. For Trident, these years' costs are $3.132 and $3.152, respectively. These prices include the development and procurement costs of the MX and the costs of the Trident sub and missiles.
108. The cost of a shelter program envisaged by NSDD-26 could run to $10 billion; also see Norris, p. 1-2.
109. Arthur Washow, "The Shelter-Centered Society," *Scientific American,* Vol. 201, No. 6, May 1962, pp. 44-51.

4

CHINA AND THE GREAT POWER BALANCE

Todd R. Starbuck

Strategists and statesmen in the West recognize intuitively that China is, to some as yet unspecified extent, a factor in the global balance of power. Far too large and distinct, both culturally and geographically, to be absorbed into the Soviet security system as another satellite, China has emerged as a major regional and global competitor of the Soviet Union.

The existing pattern of US-China-USSR triangular relations is not merely the product of developments since the 1969 Sino-Soviet border clashes, or President Nixon's visit to China, or the Soviet invasion of Afghanistan. Rather, it is part of a long and distinctive history of great power involvement in China's affairs predating the establishment of the People's Republic.

The scramble among the Western powers and Japan for political and economic advantage had brought China to the brink of dissolution by the beginning of this century. World War I weakened the sway of the imperialists, however, and awakened a spirit of intense nationalism in many Chinese intellectuals. This spirit spread to the masses during the period between the wars, when China attempted painful and ultimately unsuccessful transition to republican government. The victorious Communists proclaimed an end to a century of humiliation and foreign domination in 1949, but immediately turned to the Soviet Union for economic assistance and international support. The United States, meanwhile, was castigated as a capitalist and imperialist warmonger, and the principal threat to the new Chinese Communist state.

From a historical perspective, the period of Sino-Soviet alliance was remarkably short. Personality conflicts, ideological disputes, and unfulfilled expectations on both sides contributed to a rapid deterioration of the relationship after 1954, prompting Mao Zedong to adopt a "dual adversary" strategy in the early 1960's. Emerging from its self-destructive binge during the Cultural Revolution, China found itself more isolated in the world than at any time since the early 19th century. The process of Sino-American rapprochement, initiated in 1969-70 primarily to alleviate this isolation, accelerated in the late 1970's as a result of the growing perception in both Washington and Beijing of unrelenting Soviet expansionism. However, the US-China strategic relationship, up to now based almost exclusively on mutual antipathy toward the Soviet Union, is only one part of a much more complex set of interrelationships. Recent developments in Sino-US and Sino-Soviet relations have reconfirmed this complexity and underscore the need for a fuller understanding in the West of the dynamics of the triangular relationship.

US-China relations cooled considerably in 1981 with China's growing criticism of US global policy, its generally more independent and assertive stance, and a strong reaffirmation of its solidarity with the Third World. The first phase of a reformulation of Chinese foreign policy along lines more closely resembling the "classical" conceptualization of Mao's Theory of the Three Worlds was underway.

During 1982, three major interrelated trends were discernible in China's foreign relations. First was the persistence of an acrimonious relationship with the United States, centering on the issue of continued US arms sales to Taiwan. Solutions proved maddeningly elusive and despite a series of US conciliatory gestures throughout the year, Sino-American relations had dropped to a postnormalization low by year's end. The second major trend was an apparent breakthrough in the Sino-Soviet dispute, most noticeably after the death of Soviet President Leonid Brezhnev in

November, which raised the possibility of at least a marginal reduction in bilateral tensions. The third trend, China's deepening involvement in and identification with the Third World, was also a carry-over from 1981, but by the end of 1982, it appeared to have supplanted the earlier "united front against hegemony" formulation which explicitly incorporated the United States into the "antihegemony front."

Although events through the first several months of 1983 tended to confirm these trends, by midsummer the first two were clearly less pronounced. Despite continuing strains over Taiwan, US-China relations warmed somewhat as a result of progress on longstanding trade and technology transfer issues, coupled with increasing economic payoffs for China from its "opening to the outside world." Meanwhile, prospects for significant improvements in Sino-Soviet ties dimmed noticeably as the first blush of reconciliation gave way to inconclusive bargaining on substantive differences.

This ebb and flow in bilateral relations is likely to remain a consistent feature of the triangular relationship in the future, and should not be permitted to obscure the fundamental, underlying interests of the principals. The discussion which follows will attempt to identify these interests, and will assess the nature and extent of China's impact on the US-Soviet balance of power.

US INTERESTS AND SECURITY OBJECTIVES

The identification of broad, fundamental *interests* is an essential first step in formulating a national strategy, but the interests themselves have little or no operational utility until they are translated into concrete national security *objectives*. Moreover, interests represent only part of the equation in strategic planning; *perceived threats* to national security are the second principal ingredient. As defined here, interests are more or less immutable, and include (1) survival; (2) sovereignty (independence, unity, and territorial integrity); (3) a favorable world order; and (4) economic well-being. An ideological component, the promotion of national values abroad, can also be added.[1] Because these interests are closely interrelated, each one shapes national security policy to some extent. Over time, changes in the content of these fundamental interests and perceived threats to them produce changes in objectives, i.e., the supporting goals and aims of national strategy or policy.

Any assessment of the impact of China on US interests and objectives is complicated by the nature of international relations. In this instance, the United States and China interact simultaneously on three distinct but interrelated levels: global, regional, and bilateral. Ideally, the objectives established on the bilateral level would be fully compatible with those on the global and regional levels. Of course, in reality, they seldom are. Ordering priorities and developing policies in such a complex environment is an extremely difficult task, and one which no nation has been able to accomplish with complete success. In the case of China and the United States, for example, both parties perceive the Soviet Union as the principal threat to their crucial interests. Because the Reagan Administration has generally adopted a more forceful stance toward the Soviet Union than did the Carter Administration, the Reagan stance should be more appealing to China than that of its predecessor. In practice, the opposite has proved true, because incompatible views on several important *bilateral* issues have tended to attenuate the Sino-American strategic consensus.

The global dimension of US national security policy focuses primarily on the Soviet Union and the threat it poses to US national interests. This is prudent since the Soviet Union is the only country which is capable of independently threatening either the survival or sovereignty of the United States. President Reagan's national security strategy, which became clear in 1982-83 through the statements of administration spokesmen, emphasizes some traditional themes, such as deterrence, strategic force modernization, improved conventional capabilities, support for allies, and forward deployment of US forces.[2] Greater emphasis has been placed on a coalition strategy, designed to exploit the capabilities of allies and friends and to augment these capabilities by means of an expanded security assistance program. The overarching objective of US national security policy is to "prevail with pride" by forcing the Soviet Union to "bear the brunt of its economic shortcomings" and by convincing its leadership "to turn their attention inward, to seek the legitimacy that only comes from the consent of the governed, and thus to address the hopes and dreams of their own people."[3]

US objectives in the Asia-Pacific region complement, and in some instances directly implement, global security objectives. However, factors of geography, demography, and politics are such that presently no nation in the region, aside from the Soviet Union, constitutes a direct threat to the survival or sovereignty of the United States. US interests thus focus on economic well-being, a favorable world order, and an environment conducive to the promotion of American values. While political and ideological interests are longstanding, the economic dimension has grown in importance in recent years. Since 1976, total annual US trade wth East and South Asia and Pacific Oceania has equalled or exceeded US trade with Western Europe.[4]

Regional security objectives are influenced by economic and political considerations, but are primarily determined by US world order interests.[5] In a March 1982 speech to the Japan National Press Club, in which he identified the "six pillars of America's Asian policy," Secretary of Defense Caspar Weinberger provided the definitive statement of the administration's approach to the security of the region. The six pillars are (1) the intent of the United States to remain a Pacific power; (2) the primacy of the political, economic, and security relationship with Japan; (3) the principle of freedom and independence for the Korean peninsula; (4) the strategic rapprochement with China; (5) support for the Association of Southeast Asian Nations (ASEAN); and (6) an expanding US presence in Southwest Asia.[6]

In a manner reminiscent of earlier statements by Carter Administration officials, Secretary Weinberger outlined the US rationale for a cooperative Sino-American relationship on all three levels: global, regional, and bilateral.

> Our policies toward China are predicated on the belief that a strong, secure and progressing China is in our national interest and that of our allies. We are prepared to contribute in a responsible way to China's modernization, both for the benefit of China and of the United States, and we want to do so in ways which enhance our own security and that of our allies and friends . . . . We seek to build an enduring relationship with China that recognizes our common interests and our differences and which permits us to take complementary actions when our common interests are challenged.[7]

A brief review of each of the other components of US regional security policy, as defined by the Secretary of Defense, underscores both the potentialities and the limitations of the US-China security relationship he envisioned. So long as the Soviet Union remains the principal threat to Chinese interests and China itself remains relatively weak militarily—both long-term propositions—the determination of the United States to maintain a forceful presence in the Pacific will be welcomed by China. The growing prodefense consensus in Japan has likewise been encouraged by China in recent years as a positive contribution to the latter's anti-Soviet united front strategy. This sentiment has practical limits, however, as the controversy in mid-1982 over Japanese textbook revisions demonstrated. China is not likely to favor a significant expansion of Japanese military capabilities which appear (1) to be well beyond those required purely for self-defense or (2) to justify a reduced US military commitment to East Asia.[8]

The situation on the Korean peninsula also offers both challenges and opportunities to the US-China relationship. Clearly the interests of all the major outside powers, including the Soviet Union, are best served by continued peace on the peninsula. China maintains close political, economic, and ideological relations with the North Korean regime of Kim Il-sung. These ties, which have been expanding recently at Soviet expense, place Beijing in a position to discourage any ill-conceived reunification moves by P'yongyang. While US security interests are served as a result, these interrelationships are precarious at present, and US-China ties could be severely strained by a resumption of fighting on the peninsula or even a serious crisis.

In Southeast and Southwest Asia, the last two "pillars," the prospects for productive US-China strategic cooperation are similarly ambivalent. Southeast Asia remains polarized into two groups: Communist Indochina, dominated by Vietnam, and the non-Communist developing countries which compose ASEAN. Since its split with Hanoi in the late 1970's, China has vigorously supported ASEAN in its anti-Vietnam campaign over Kampuchea. US and Chinese objectives *vis-a-vis* ASEAN and Vietnam are thus compatible in some respects, even though their motives differ. China has been particularly vocal in its support for Thailand, the ASEAN "frontline state," but remains a controversial partner.[9] Malaysia and Indonesia, in particular, are suspicious of Beijing's regional aspirations and tend to view China, rather than the Soviet Union, as the more serious long-term threat to their security interests. In an attempt to improve its image with the ASEAN countries, China has reduced its ties with indigenous Communist insurgent groups to relatively inconsequential levels. Although the non-Communist countries of Southeast Asia welcomed the Sino-American rapprochement, lingering distrust of China would predispose them against an expanded US-China security relationship.[10]

The short-term compatibility of US and Chinese objectives is more apparent, and less controversial, in Southwest Asia. The Soviet invasion of Afghanistan abruptly halted the tentative warming of Sino-Soviet relations in late 1979 and added fuel to their simmering dispute. Pakistan, the recent recipient of a $3.2 billion military sales and economic aid package from the United States, is a longstanding regional ally of China as well. Together, these three countries have spearheaded the international reaction to the Soviet occupation. Even Indira Gandhi, whose initial criticism of the invasion hardly qualified as a condemnation, has recently sought to establish a more balanced relationship with Washington, while simultaneously improving India's bilateral relations with Pakistan.

Bilateral relations constitute the third and final level on which the evolving US-China cooperative relationship is played out. Economic well-being is the principal, but not the only, US interest served; the impact on world order and ideological interests is clearly evident as well. The formalization of trade and investment procedures since 1979 has greatly facilitated the expansion of commercial ties. Two-way trade between the two countries totaled less than $400 million in 1977, but more than doubled each of the next three years to reach $4.9 billion by 1980. Volume began to level off in 1981, climbing to $5.5 billion with the balance less heavily in favor of the United States. This trend continued in 1982; in fact, US-China trade dropped slightly to $5.2 billion. Despite this burgeoning trade, the total volume in 1981—when China ranked 14th among US trading partners—was still slightly less than half that between the United States and Taiwan.[11]

Exploration and development of China's vast oil reserves, which a recent Chinese estimate optimistically placed at 219 billion barrels, may eventually prove to be the most lucrative area for Sino-American economic cooperation.[12] China cannot begin to reach its full energy potential, particularly in offshore production, without substantial inputs of Western drilling technology and investment capital. US corporations are well-positioned to meet China's needs. In September 1982, the Atlantic Richfield Company became the first American oil company to sign an offshore drilling contract with its official Chinese counterpart. It will be joined in the South China Sea by the Occidental Petroleum Corporation and the Exxon Corporation, both of which won major drilling contracts in August 1983 after a year-long round of competitive bidding.[13]

China's opening to the West has another important dimension as well: advanced schooling and technical training. Over 8,000 Chinese students, the largest single group from any foreign country, are studying in the United States.[14] Several hundred Americans are studying in China, although reciprocity in scholarly exchanges has not yet been achieved. On the other hand, tens of thousands of Americans visit China annually as tourists, and cultural exchanges and exhibits—such as the one at the recent Knoxville World's Fair—have provided a glimpse of China to millions more. While bilateral educational and cultural contacts may have little impact on US-China security relations, they are crucial ingredients in building a stable, positive, and durable relationship between the two nations.

Taiwan is by far the most divisive issue in US-China bilateral relations and its implications pervade the global and regional dimensions of the relationship as well. This is a complex and emotional problem, deeply rooted in the political cultures of both nations and devoid of quick or easy solutions. Recent efforts to ameliorate the increasing strains caused by Taiwan have been only partially successful. If unresolved, and they may well be unresolvable for the present, these strains will inevitably limit the nature and scope of future Sino-American strategic cooperation.[15]

In order to analyze critically the strategic rationale which underlies US-China relations in general and US-China security relations in particular, an attempt must be made to go beyond generalities and to define more precisely the operational components of this rationale.[16] However, if generalities are excluded from the discussion, then surprisingly little of substance remains. In a broad global sense, the United States views China as a "strategic counterweight" to the Soviet Union.[17] Implicit here are nonhostile relations between China and the United States which now allow each party essentially to ignore the other as a serious military threat and concentrate its attention and resources on the Soviet Union instead. This in turn poses a more credible two-front threat to the Soviet Union and leads, hopefully, to improved deterrence on both fronts.

In a more concrete sense, only one operational objective of a US-China strategic alignment has ever been publicly articulated from the US perspective. That objective—which presupposes continued Sino-Soviet enmity—is for China to pose a credible threat to Soviet territory or interests sufficient to preclude or at least discourage the shifting of Soviet forces to another theater, either in peacetime or during an undefined East-West conflict. This objective is usually expressed in terms of "tying down" the estimated 500,000 Soviet troops stationed on or near the Chinese border.[18] Other objectives are either too narrowly focused, such as the shared intelligence sites reportedly in Western China,[19] or are too problematic to serve as realistic planning factors. In the latter category are hypothetical scenarios which postulate substantive military cooperation between the United States and China if either or both become involved in a conflict with the Soviet Union.

Despite the modest scope and content of the current strategic relationship, it is not insignificant—particularly if one assumes that Soviet forces no longer required on the Chinese border could be redeployed against NATO, or be repositioned to reinforce more easily the NATO front.

SOVIET INTERESTS AND SECURITY OBJECTIVES

As one of the world's two superpowers, the fundamental national interests of the Soviet Union are similar to those of the United States. Survival and sovereignty naturally assume the highest priority and only the opposing superpower poses a credible immediate threat. The late President Brezhnev, in one of his last major speeches, described the nature of that threat as it was viewed from Moscow. "The ruling circles of the United States of America have launched a political, ideological and economic offensive on socialism and have raised the intensity of their military preparations to an unprecedented level."[20] The centrality of the United States is evident in every aspect of the Soviet strategic calculus at the global level, including economic, ideological, and world order interests.

The underlying attitudes and assumptions of Soviet decisionmakers regarding the United States are necessarily a matter of conjecture among Western analysts, but the cumulative record of Soviet behavior is sufficient to afford some useful insights. Harry Gelman of the Rand Corporation has identified a set of postulates and objectives which could be considered the essence of the Soviet leadership's contemporary world view. He sees Soviet strategy toward the United States as both defensive and coercive; it seeks to free the Soviet Union from US-imposed isolation and, in turn, isolate the United States from its allies and friends. Soviet leaders perceive that trends in the correlation of forces—"an amorphous amalgam of political, social, economic, and military factors"—have been favorable to the Soviet Union over the past decade. While the US advantage has dwindled and the "enervating effects" of American pluralism represent a serious US weakness, the Soviet Union must be continually prepared to safeguard its authority within its own bloc; to further its aspirations for global preeminence; and to preserve the favorable military asymmetries which it now enjoys. "The common element in this family of defensive-offensive concerns is the assumption that if the Politburo does not continue to press for advantage, it may fall back." Differences between the United States and its allies are deep, perhaps even fundamental, and offer opportunities to split the anti-Soviet coalition. Finally, the Soviet leadership is determined to insulate its external ambitions from its serious economic weaknesses and internal difficulties.[21] If successful in this regard, the Politburo would neutralize the ultimate objective of the Reagan national security strategy outlined earlier: to compel the Soviet Union to redirect its energies and resources from expansionism to domestic priorities.

By virtue of geography, the Soviet Union is not only a global power, but a regional power in both Europe and Asia. And as a continental power, its global and regional interests are closely intertwined. Indeed, the Soviet geostrategic position is considerably more precarious than that of the United States, which is blessed with wide oceans on two sides and nonthreatening nations on the other two. The vastness of the Soviet Union is both an asset and a liability; although it dominates the Eurasian landmass, it is not unassailable. The proximity of Soviet territory to competing power centers, combined with centrifugal tendencies within the Soviet empire, creates a sense of vulnerability in the minds of the leadership. Whether such external threats are plausible any longer in light of the USSR's impressive nuclear arsenal is irrelevant; conditioned by centuries of violent history, Soviet leaders *accept* this vulnerability as the basic assumption underlying their national security strategy.[22]

Its claims to be an Asian power notwithstanding, the Soviet Union is a relative latecomer to East Asia and the Northwest Pacific. Nonetheless, it is the only European colonial power which has been able to retain—and even expand—its empire in Asia. Despite a strong residual interest in Siberia and the Far Eastern territories, the Soviet Union's understandable preoccupation with the security of its western flanks meant that initially its eastern domain would be accorded a much lower strategic priority.[23] Moreover, threats from the east tended to be more manageable— during World War II, for example, a conflict with Japan was postponed until the very end of the war. Finally, the low order of political and economic power which the Soviet Union was able to wield in Asia, as compared to Europe, contributed to a lower level of interest in the Far East.[24]

This situation began to change after the defeat of Japan, and in the postwar period Soviet diplomatic and security objectives in the region were gradually upgraded. This trend accelerated after 1965 due to (1) the deterioration and then complete collapse of the Sino-Soviet alliance in the late 1950's and early 1960's;[25] (2) the continuation of the cold war and the US-Soviet competition in Asia; (3) the increasing availability of resources for strengthening security on the less sensitive eastern flank; (4) the new demographics of the Soviet Union and the need to disperse populations and industries for both strategic and economic reasons; and most importantly, (5) the deepening Sino-American rapprochement which emerged after 1970. This linkage between the Soviet Union's two most dangerous adversaries—tentative and conditional though it was—established a pattern of triangular politics which was to persist into the next decade and necessitate a fundamental and far-reaching reassessment of the threat to Soviet national interests. The most salient characteristic of this triangular relationship was the more or less chronic disadvantage at which the Soviet Union found itself *vis-a-vis* the powers at the other two corners of the triangle. This condition reinforced Moscow's tendency to turn to the only means of leverage at its disposal: a gradual but ultimately substantial increase in Soviet military power, both globally and regionally.[26]

Soviet survival, sovereignty, and world order interests in Asia are now being complemented by crucial domestic economic interests in Siberia and the Far East, an area of tremendous untapped natural resources. Despite the region's harsh environment and sparse population, Soviet leaders are proceeding with the intensive development of Siberia's vast energy (oil, gas, coal) and mineral resources, and the construction of an indigenous industrial base and a transportation infrastructure to move raw materials and manufactured goods immense distances to foreign and domestic markets. Although handicapped by a shortage of investment capital and inadequate extractive technology, the Soviet Union has no alternative if it is to maintain resource self-sufficiency and begin to balance its massive foreign exchange shortfalls. As sources of energy and minerals in the western USSR are exhausted or seriously depleted, Soviet planners will be forced to draw increasingly from the east in order to propel their stagnating economy into the next century.[27] Nevertheless, numerous intractable obstacles remain.[28]

Given the long-term economic importance of the eastern USSR, the strategic vulnerability of the region (especially Eastern Siberia and the Far East) is a source of major concern. And if the eastern anchor of the Soviet empire is vulnerable, then Western Siberia and the central heartland of the USSR are threatened as well. Over two-thirds of Siberia's population of 30 million are concentrated in the south, near the border with China. In the Far East, much of the population lives adjacent to the Chinese border, along the double-track Trans-Siberian Railroad which parallels the course of the Amur River to Khabarovsk, and then turns south to Vladisvostok and the Pacific coast. The Trans-Siberian is the lifeline of East Siberia and the Far East (60 percent of the region's food requirements must be shipped in), and lies within a few miles of Chinese territory at several points. The vulnerability of this link will be partially alleviated if construction of the oft-delayed Baikal-Amur Mainline (BAM), roughly paralleling the Trans-Siberian, is completed as planned by 1985. Although it lies 150 to 300 miles north of the Chinese border, the BAM would also be subject to interdiction in wartime, and, in any event, will extend no farther east than Komsomol'sk and the connecting line south to

Khabarovsk. The significance of the BAM thus appears to be at least as much economic as it is strategic.[29]

Soviet policy in Asia is multifaceted and derives from both global and regional interests of the USSR. Among these, economic well-being ranks low. Although Siberia is crucially important to long-range development, Soviet attempts to elicit foreign investment and technological assistance have yielded poor results overall. Economic relations with the countries of Asia, other than Japan, are very limited.[30] Ideological, economic, and even world order interests thus defer to the primacy of fundamental security interests which transcend expansionist ambitions in Soviet Far Eastern policy. Vulnerabilities inherent in the Soviet geostrategic emplacement in Asia pose serious challenges to Moscow, while constraining opportunities to exercise power and influence.

Aside from the United States and China, potentially the most important Asian relationship for the Soviet Union is that with Japan. Nevertheless, Soviet-Japanese relations deteriorated during the past decade and show no sign of imminent improvement. The singular lack of flexibility in Soviet diplomacy toward Japan, as demonstrated by the uncompromising position in the disputed Northern Territories adjacent to Hokkaido, appears rooted in the traditional Russian conviction that the only way to deal effectively with the Japanese is by employing threats and coercion. The signing of the Sino-Japanese Treaty of Peace and Friendship in 1978 was partially responsible for the hardening of Soviet attitudes. The ongoing reinforcement and upgrading of its military garrison in the Northern Territories—the three large islands and one small island group at the southern end of the Kuril Island chain—was one Soviet response. The rapprochement between Japan and China was also a factor in the buildup of the Soviet Pacific Fleet after 1978, but the consequences were counterproductive in both instances. The Soviet Union made few political gains in Tokyo and succeeded only in sharpening the Japanese perception of threat, which until then had been unfocused at best (and indeed nonexistent in some quarters).[31] Soviet economic interests did not suffer appreciably, however, until Japan joined in the economic sanctions imposed in the wake of the Afghan invasion and the crisis in Poland. As a result, extensive Japanese participation in the development of Siberian resources—long sought by the Soviet Union—was deferred indefinitely.[32]

Elsewhere in Asia, the Soviet Union pursues complementary policies designed to reduce, contain, or eliminate the power and influence of both China and the United States. The main features of its strategy are expansionism and opportunism on the one hand, balanced by patience and a desire to avoid a direct military confrontation with either rival on the other. Although afflicted with a deep sense of insecurity as well as serious social ills, the Soviet Union nonetheless seems confident in the ultimate triumph of its system.

On the Korean peninsula, the Soviet Union formally supports Kim Il-sung's reunification demands, but not to the point of a North Korean attack on the South. Kim's delicate balancing act between Moscow and Beijing has resulted in a succession of "tilts" over the past five years. These shifting alignments are largely due to a fundamental ambivalence on the part of both the Soviet Union and China: neither sees any advantage in an attack by North Korea which could lead to a confrontation with the United States, nor is willing to exchange the *status quo* for a unified Korea in which it might lose what influence it presently enjoys.[33]

The interests of the Soviet Union in Southeast Asia are corollaries of its global and regional interests, but its policies are bifurcated along ideological lines. Soviet diplomatic initiatives, such as Brezhnev's ill-fated collective security proposal, have been consistently rebuffed by the non-Communist nations of the region. Indeed, the Soviet Union is even less attractive now than it was in 1969, when Brezhnev first floated his proposal. The five non-Communist countries (Thailand, Malaysia, Singapore, Indonesia, and the Philippines) composing ASEAN have experienced unprecedented economic growth and rising standards of living, while the Soviet (as well as the Chinese) social and developmental model is badly tarnished. Moreover, the growth and projection of Soviet naval capabilities, coupled with the Soviet Union's continuing $3 million a day subsidy of the Vietnamese[34] and their occupation of Kampuchea, have alarmed everyone. As a result, the ASEAN countries are upgrading their individual defenses against external aggression and are moving slowly in the direction of collective security.[35] Given its estrangement from the non-Communist countries of Southeast Asia, Moscow has little choice except to capitalize on Vietnam's dependence to further Soviet influence in the region.[36]

Although confined to flexing its military might for the time being, the access afforded the USSR to naval and air facilities in Vietnam has direct implications for Soviet national security interests. The southern sea route via the Indian Ocean represents an important alternate link to the Soviet Far East, supplementing the Trans-Siberian Railroad. The Malacca-Singapore Straits and the Indonesian Straits of Sunda, Lombok-Makassar, and Ombai-Wetar constitute the principal links between the Pacific and Indian Oceans for both the US and Soviet navies.[37] These straits are also chokepoints along Japan's vital sea lines of communication, through which two-thirds of its crude oil imports must transit. Another 15 percent of Japanese oil imports originate in Indonesia.[38] Soviet forward bases at Cam Ranh Bay, Danang, and elsewhere permit peacetime surveillance of the region and could be used to stage combat operations in wartime.[39]

Southeast Asia also provides a connecting link to South Asia and the Indian Ocean, where Soviet objectives are similar but the prospects for success are marginally brighter. This region leaped into the consciousness of the West in the late 1970's as a result of the successive crises in Iran and the Soviet invasion of Afghanistan. During the preceding decade the Soviet Union had assiduously courted India, establishing a firm bilateral alignment which proved highly profitable for both partners. Meanwhile, China had refurbished its *entente cordiale* with Pakistan as the United States tended, for a time, toward noninvolvement in South Asian regional affairs. But as noted earlier, Mrs. Gandhi has sought since mid-1982 to place some distance between herself and Moscow by simultaneously seeking to improve relations with Pakistan, China, and the United States. As a result, the prospects for wider Soviet political influence have received at least a temporary setback, providing still another incentive to resolve the Afghan problem quickly.

It is clear that Soviet interests in bilateral relations with China are inextricably bound up with its global and regional interests. Despite a visceral fear of China which sometimes borders on paranoia, China—as an independent actor—is presently a lower order security threat than the United States and its NATO allies. Thus the Soviet Union will seek to decouple China from any substantive alignment with other major powers, especially a US-Japan-China coalition with transregional linkages to NATO. Soviet leaders have been waiting patiently since the death of Mao to improve relations with China and recent initiatives reflect their measured, incremental approach. China now appears favorably disposed to a lessening of bilateral tensions for reasons of its own. Progress on at least one of the three preconditions it has set for the "normalization" of relations—reduction of forces on the Chinese border, withdrawal of Soviet troops from Afghanistan, and termination of support for Vietnam's occupation of Kampuchea—is a possibility which cannot be discounted. In any event, the Soviet leadership views a reduction of tensions with China not only as a short-term gain, but as an essential first step in the process of splitting the anti-Soviet coalition and eventually isolating both the United States and China.

Other bilateral issues once prominent in the Sino-Soviet dispute contributed to the initial split but have now faded into the background or been overtaken by actuarial inevitabilities. Ideological purity is hardly a matter for serious contention; both sides are sufficiently "deviationist" or "revisionist" that neither sees any advantage in berating the other over a point upon which they are themselves vulnerable. The border dispute could be quickly removed to the negotiating table, if the Soviet leaders were agreeable, and the Chinese have set aside the larger territorial question, at least for the time being. In past negotiations with other neighbors, the Chinese have demonstrated a willingness to compromise on the specifics of a border agreement so long as a political settlement was reached.[40] Finally, the personality conflicts which poisoned the atmosphere 20 years ago died with Khrushchev and Mao. The rancor and emotional rhetoric of personal diplomacy have been replaced with formal diplomacy conducted largely by ministers of state and professional bureaucrats.

Nationalism and pragmatic self-interest are the fundamental issues which will separate China and the Soviet Union in the future as the latter seeks to preserve a decisive advantage over its less powerful geostrategic rival.

CHINA IN TRANSITION

China exists today on an economic level which is not only far below that of the superpowers and the other developed countries, but which threatens to consign China permanently to a position of global inferiority and consequent strategic vulnerability. This prospect is totally incompatible with the aspirations of China's leaders, who are committed to the eventual "restoration" of their country to the first rank of world powers. In order to fulfill this vision in the next century, China has embarked since 1978 on a massive, highly ambitious program of economic and technological development. While economic well-being will not (and indeed cannot) supplant survival and sovereignty interests as first priority, the developmental program is so closely linked to China's contemporary security concerns that it deserves a brief review.

China's leaders began to revise their collective assessment of the world situation following the Czechoslovakian invasion of 1968 and the Sino-Soviet border clashes of 1969. As a result, the Soviet Union replaced the United States as the principal threat to Chinese security interests. These and other concerns prompted the Chinese to seek rapprochement with the United States, now only the "second major enemy" in their revised formulation, shortly thereafter. At some point during the five year period from 1968 to 1973—precisely when depends upon one's interpretation of the limited information available[41]—a separate, but interrelated, decision was made to give economic development the top domestic priority. During the Fourth National People's Congress in January 1975, an ailing Premier Zhou Enlai proposed the bare outline of a modernization program, calling for modernization in four key sectors: agriculture, industry, national defense, and science and technology.[42]

Following the deaths in 1976 of first Zhou and then Mao, Hua Guofeng, a moderate Maoist, emerged from the ensuing tumult as both premier and Party chairman. Hua developed the basic outline of the "Four Modernizations" program in early 1978, but his misguided preference for heavy industry over agriculture—compounded by unrealistic growth and production targets—contributed to his subsequent political demise. Deng Xiaoping, China's leading pragmatic reformer, had been "rehabilitated" for a second time in 1977 and over a three year period he was able to wrest control of the Party and state bureaucracies from Hua and his associates. By 1981, Deng's developmental program was firmly in place and proteges Hu Yaobang and Zhao Ziyang had replaced Hua as Party chairman and premier, respectively.

The 12th National Party Congress in September 1982 marked the culmination of Deng's drive for political supremacy. In his report to the Congress, Chairman Hu Yaobang established the "general objective" of China's economic construction: to quadruple the gross annual value of industrial and agricultural production between 1981 and the year 2000.

> This will place China in the front ranks of the countries of the world in terms of gross national income and the output of major industrial and agricultural products; it will represent an important advance in the modernization of her entire national economy; it will increase the income of her urban and rural population several times over; and the Chinese people will be comparatively well-off both materially and culturally. Although China's national income per capita will even then be relatively low, her economic strength *and national defense capabilities* will have grown considerably, compared with what they are today.[43] (Italics added.)

The vehicle for implementing this policy in the near term was provided a few months later, at the Fifth Session of the Fifth National People's Congress, when Premier Zhao Ziyang outlined the major provisions of the long-awaited Sixth Five-Year Plan. The new plan, covering the period 1981-85 and therefore two years retroactive, calls for a continuation of the policy of slow but solid economic growth followed by the Dengists since late 1978. Annual growth of industrial and agricultural output is set at a modest, and probably achievable, 4 percent. The present leadership appears determined to avoid past mistakes, particularly unrealistic, overly ambitious production targets.[44]

CHINA'S INTERNATIONAL STRATEGY AND FOREIGN RELATIONS

While economic development remains a major long-term objective of China's modernization program, it is not just an end in itself. Rather, it is viewed as an essential prerequisite for attaining other national objectives of comparable importance. In his opening address to the 12th National Party Congress, Deng Xiaoping reaffirmed the three major tasks for the coming decade and succinctly defined the role that modernization would play.

> To intensify socialist modernization, to strive for reunification and particularly for the return of Taiwan to the motherland, and to combat hegemonism and safeguard world peace—these are the three major tasks of our people in the 1980s. Economic construction is at the core of these tasks as it is the basis for the solution of China's external and domestic problems.[45]

China clearly believes that its interests cannot be satisfied or its future security assured unless it is able to achieve its developmental goals. "Socialist construction" is a long-term process, and China presumably requires an extended period of international peace and domestic stability. This view partially explains China's abandonment of Mao Zedong's attempts in the 1960's to radicalize and destabilize not only the non-Communist nations of the world, but his own country as well.

Whatever the vicissitudes of its relationship with the United States and the Soviet Union, a common thread which runs through all the various phases of China's foreign policy is identification with the interests and problems of the developing countries, the Third World in Mao's conceptualization of the international system. A self-proclaimed developing country, with recent memories of foreign subjugation and no natural geographic allies, China naturally aspires to a leadership role among these nations.

Mao's "Theory of the Three Worlds" evolved gradually from his earlier, more simplistic notion of a world divided into two camps, socialist and capitalist. By the early 1970's, Mao saw the world divided into three groups: the First World, consisting only of the two superpowers, both struggling for hegemony; the Second World, consisting of the other developed countries of Europe, North America, and Japan; and the Third World, composed of the weak, the poor, and the exploited. In a major speech at the United Nations in April 1974, Deng Xiaoping expounded the theory in detail, castigating both the superpowers—especially the Soviet Union—for "vainly seeking world hegemony," and calling on the Third World countries to "strengthen their unity" and "struggle against colonialism, imperialism and hegemony."[46] Subsequent refinements to the theory in the late 1970's included an expanded role for the developed countries of the Second World as allies of the Third World in the battle against superpower hegemonism. The hegemonic nature of the United States was downplayed even more in the aftermath of unabated improvements in Soviet military capabilities in the Far East and the accelerated deterioration in Chinese relations with pro-Soviet Vietnam. By 1978, the dominant theme in the Chinese formulation was the "united front against hegemony," which incorporated the United States as a full partner in the struggle to defeat Soviet hegemony.[47]

Despite emphasis on political and economic solidarity with the Third World, China's survival, sovereignty, and world order interests are primarily dependent upon its relations with the two superpowers. Historically, these relationships have been driven by Beijing's perception of the relative threat posed by each—perceptions which have fluctuated widely over the years. For several years post-Mao Chinese commentaries expressed alarm over the apparently insatiable expansionist appetite of the Soviet Union while stressing the largely defensive nature of the United States. This assessment underwent a subtle alteration in 1981-82, however, as US-China relations became increasingly strained over a number of issues, the principal one being Taiwan.[48] The term "hegemonist," reserved almost exclusively for the USSR after the normalization of Sino-American relations, began to appear with increasing frequency in Chinese media characterizations of the United States as direct references to the united front were dropped. By late 1982, in a paean to the Third World—now "the main force in the antihegemonist struggle"—*Guangming Ribao* concluded that:

> Since the start of the 1980's, the global contest between the Soviet and U.S. hegemonist powers has become ever more fierce . . . . The two superpowers—the Soviet Union and the United States—are the biggest international exploiters and oppressors and the main causes of instability and upheaval in the world.[49]

Aside from the anti-US rhetoric, which is still quite mild compared to the vitriolic denunciations of the United States in the 1960's, the fact remains that the Soviet Union is the only superpower which presently poses a credible immediate threat to China's security. Interestingly, the Chinese seldom acknowledge this threat directly; rather the Soviet Union is identified as the "major threat to *world* peace."[50] The reasons for downplaying the Soviet threat to China while emphasizing that Europe is the USSR's primary objective—"feinting in the East while attacking in the

West"—are characteristically complex. Four distinct audiences are involved: the Soviet Union, the United States, Western Europe, and the People's Liberation Army (PLA). First, China hopes to divert Soviet attention away from itself and toward Europe, while simultaneously complicating the Soviet Union's European detente strategy. Second, China hopes to alert both the United States and NATO Europe to the urgent need to bolster the Atlantic Alliance in the face of a growing Soviet military threat. If successful, NATO will be preserved as a credible potential threat to the Soviet western flank and the USSR will be unable to turn its full military might against China.[51] Third, the Chinese fear that if they appear too seriously threatened by the Soviet Union, it will reinforce Washington's "China Syndrome," the perception that "the Chinese need us more than we need them." Finally, the pragmatic ruling faction is attempting to convince the PLA, reputedly one of the last Maoist strongholds, that the Soviet security threat to China is long-term rather than immediate. Consequently, the central government can afford "temporarily" to divert scarce resources from defense modernization—the lowest in priority of the Four Modernizations—into development of a sound, broad-based economy which will provide substantially improved military capabilities in the more distant future.

If China is adjusting and perhaps compartmentalizing its strategic alignment with the United States, the current leadership clearly does not intend that cooler relations will extend to trade, investment, and technology transfer. The "opening to the West" has been seriously questioned by domestic critics of Deng Xiaoping not only because of the failure of the security relationship to blossom forth, but because widespread exposure to "pernicious influences" such as crime, corruption, and "bourgeois liberalism" are inevitable if contacts with the West are developed and expanded. Nevertheless, at the 12th National Party Congress, Deng declared that:

> We will unswervingly follow a policy of opening to the outside world and actively increase exchanges with foreign countries on the basis of equality and mutual benefit. At the same time, we will keep a clear head, firmly resist corrosion by decadent ideas from abroad and never permit the bourgeosis way of life to spread in our country.[52]

As a realist, Deng is aware that he is taking a calculated risk with this policy. Severe strains will be placed on the collective psyche of the Chinese people in the coming decades, as the transformation of social and political values accelerates in the drive for economic development. The creation of technical, managerial, and intellectual elites will supplant Maoist China's relative egalitarianism—and may, in fact, already have done so. The opening to the West will exacerbate these tendencies, but Deng has little choice if he expects China ever to become truly competitive with the rest of the world. The obvious alternative, which can never be discounted if his policies fail, is a return to a more orthodox Marxist-Leninist developmental strategy, accompanied by the reimposition of stringent control measures on all aspects of Chinese life.

One final dimension of China's global impact must be briefly addressed. As an element of national power, China's present military capabilities seriously constrain its influence. The low overall level of economic development, the longstanding tradition of self-reliance in all endeavors, and the vicissitudes of Chinese politics and economic policy over the past 30 years, have all perpetuated China's military inferiority and consequent strategic vulnerability. This is painfully apparent when comparing Chinese military capabilities to those of the Soviet Union, easily the most serious threat to China's security. Although China's huge armed forces—totaling over three million in the active ground components alone—outnumber those in the eastern military districts of the Soviet Union by at least six to one, the Soviet forces hold heavy quantitative and qualitative advantages in virtually every category of modern land, sea, and air weapons systems, whether conventional, theater nuclear, or strategic.[53] China is acutely aware of its vulnerability, and this realization is a driving imperative in the formulation of its foreign policies and national security strategies.

As a practical matter Chinese military weakness dictates strategy. To discourage a Soviet nuclear strike, the Chinese rely on their small strategic missile force—a modest assortment of medium and intermediate range ballistic missiles (MRBM and IRBM), and a handful of intercontinental ballistic missiles (ICBM)—as a minimum deterrent. China's strategic capabilities approached a new level in October 1982, with the successful test launch of its first sea-launched ballistic missile (SLBM), reportedly from a nuclear submarine.[54] Conventionally, China is saddled with "people's war under modern conditions," an updated version of Mao's classic strategic doctrine. Defensive in nature, the Chinese strategy presumes multiple penetrations of Chinese territory by mobile, well-equipped enemy forces enjoying air and firepower superiority. With a strategy similar to that employed by the Russians against Swedish, French, and Nazi invaders, the Chinese intend to "lure the enemy deep," resisting all the way, until he is overextended and the momentum of his attack has been dissipated. Massive counterattacks would then be launched by a combination of regular forces, militia, and guerrillas. Despite a great deal of critical discussion in the West about the relative merits of this strategy, the PLA has no realistic alternative to a "people's war" at present, even though it is not pleased by the situation.[55]

As noted earlier, the modernization of national defense has been accorded the lowest priority among the Four Modernizations; however, this may be more out of necessity than an accurate reflection of national priorities. Given the magnitude of the task, the deficiencies in the PLA can only be corrected if China possesses a sound economy and a modern, efficient industrial base. Until China has laid the foundation for domestic armaments production, the full-scale modernization of national defense cannot proceed. Meanwhile, the Chinese cannot entertain any hope of purchasing outright enough weapons to make a real difference.[56]

This brief review has touched on only a few of the more important issues which will determine China's impact on the global balance.[57] Due to its sheer mass, its growing international activism, and its distinctive world view, China is already an important, integral factor in world power calculations. Nonetheless, the full weight of its global impact will not be felt until well into the next century, and even then will be contingent upon China's success in controlling its population, increasing agricultural and industrial productivity, and providing an environment which satisfies both the material and the psychological needs of its vast citizenry.

A CONCLUDING ASSESSMENT

The synergistic nature of triangular and extra-triangular relations makes it impossible to organize conclusions under neat headings, but several broad areas need to be considered. These are the prospects for Sino-Soviet rapprochement, the future of US-China relations, and the implications for the US-Soviet military balance.

The Prospects for Sino-Soviet Rapprochement. As the warming trend in Sino-Soviet relations began to unfold in 1982-83, concern mounted in the United States, Japan, Western Europe, and elsewhere that this trend might adversely affect the security of the West. Discussion tended to be unfocused and often unproductive, however, and one major reason was the failure to make conceptual distinctions among the various terms used to describe the potential outcomes of this trend. In an attempt to overcome this handicap, an arbitrary continuum is suggested here which at least recognizes the not-too-subtle differences in these outcomes, and lends a bit more precision to our analysis. At least six separate outcomes can be used to establish a representative range; these are detente, normalization (China's stated goal), accommodation, rapprochement, entente, and alliance.[58]

Based on developments through mid-1983, a token Soviet troop withdrawal was still possible, and perhaps even likely, although the second round of bilateral talks concluded in March without visible progress.[59] The Chinese demand for a withdrawal of some forces from the border as proof of the Soviet Union's goodwill is the one precondition which Soviet leaders could meet fairly easily. Some Chinese sources have demanded troop reductions back to the levels of the Khrushchev era, but this appears out of the question, inasmuch as the Soviet Union maintained only 17 divisions in the Far East in 1964, compared to 51 today. The other two preconditions—movement on the Afghanistan and Kampuchea issues—will be much more difficult to satisfy, should China choose to press the point, because the Soviet Union cannot act unilaterally to resolve differences. The possibility of a stalemate cannot be discounted, considering the longstanding animosity on both sides. In fact, the few relatively stress-free years in Sino-Soviet relations during the early 1950's can be viewed as an aberration in an otherwise well-established pattern of bilateral contention dating back to the 17th century.

While an indeterminate period of Sino-Soviet detente or limited accommodation may well be in the offing, Soviet leaders will have to make substantial concessions if the current thaw is to carry the relationship much beyond that point. This assessment is based on several factors. First, China and the Soviet Union are, in a geostrategic sense, inevitable, long-term rivals. They are both large and ambitious; they have the world's longest land border between them (4,150 miles, plus 2,700 miles of Sino-Mongolian border); and they have a lingering territorial and boundary dispute which almost sparked a war in 1969. Second, both countries are already major regional powers in Asia, and China's ascendancy to the global stage adds still another dimension of competition and potential conflict. Third, prospects for diminishing tensions will be further dampened by Soviet plans for Siberian development and the likely proliferation of its political, economic, and security interests in Northeast Asia and the Northwest Pacific. The vulnerability of the Soviet strategic emplacement in the Far East is a serious long-term security concern for Kremlin planners and China is a major potential threat. Fourth, while less salient than in the 1960's, China and its socialist system represent an implicit threat to the legitimacy of the rival Soviet system. Should recent Chinese structural reforms actually succeed in building a more competitive socialist state in China, Soviet prestige and self-assurance would be diminished accordingly. Finally, the eventual modernization of China, even if 20 or 30 years off, carries elements of both promise and threat for much of the world, but few countries stand to be more directly affected than the Soviet Union. In the near term, the Soviet Union would be capable and perhaps willing to provide valuable economic and technological assistance to the Chinese; after all, most of China's heavy industry was either provided by the Soviet Union during the 1950's or subsequently derived from Soviet designs. In the long term, however, the Soviet leadership would be very reluctant to contribute in a meaningful way to a modernization drive which included among its ultimate objectives the development of the full range of modern military capabilities.

Before the three preconditions for better relations were specifically identified, Chinese sources spoke in terms of only one: the Soviet Union must stop trying to achieve hegemony. This declaration implied that since the Soviet Union would probably never do that, Sino-Soviet rapprochement was virtually impossible. Nothing in the recent statements of Chinese leaders indicates that their basic assessment of the Soviet Union as a hegemonist power has been altered in the least. Given the circumstances that exist now, and which will likely exist in the future, the possibility of an even more cooperative Sino-Soviet relationship—entente or alliance on our continuum—is so remote that it hardly needs to be seriously considered. This could happen only if China, both as a state and as a nation, allowed itself to be absorbed as a *de facto* Soviet satellite, *or* if another nation (presumably the United States) somehow supplanted the Soviet Union as the principal enemy in China's strategic calculus. Since the former is inconceivable and the latter highly unlikely, movement along the continuum will be confined to tactical adjustments and perhaps a limited accommodation.

As noted earlier, the Soviet defensive situation in the Far East is very unfavorable. In addition to severe geographic limitations, the Soviet Union must confront two major adversaries simultaneously in the East—China and the United States—while contending with NATO in the West. Despite its military buildup in the Far East since 1978, particularly in air and naval assets, the Soviet Union faces the imminent prospect of further intensification of its military competition with the United States, Japan, and China. The Soviet Union improved its position when it obtained access to bases in Indochina, but still finds itself seriously constrained. Moreover, Soviet leaders cannot entertain any thought of reducing aid to Vietnam in order to mollify China; if they do, their access to the badly needed Vietnamese facilities could be jeopardized.

The Future of US-China Relations. While the potential for significant improvement in Sino-Soviet relations appears constrained beyond the level of detente or, at the most, accommodation, prospects for a complete reversal of unfavorable trends in US-China relations are not encouraging. The deterioration of ties from 1980 to early 1983 can be attributed to many factors. In one respect, the overriding imperative for a united front with the United States no longer exists: the United States has been alerted to the serious threat posed by Soviet expansionism and is taking strong measures to rebuild its defenses and revitalize its alliances. In addition, the Soviet Union's prospects in Afghanistan, Kampuchea, Eastern Europe, and much of the Third World have soured, thereby lowering China's threat perception. Under the circumstances, China can afford to stake out a more independent international position while making a bid for Third World leadership. Perception of threat is the key motivation behind any strategic alignment, and the Soviet threat is now considered less imminent. Moreover, the post-Brezhnev leadership in the Kremlin may be more inclined to make concessions to the Chinese than was its predecessor, and this possibility is worth exploring. Finally, China may well be able, for the first time, to occupy the coveted position of "pivot power" in the triangular relationship; i.e., that power having the best relations with the other two.

Chinese critics of the alignment with the United States have also pointed to the disappointing failure of the Sino-American relationship to "pay off" in terms of substantial trade and technology transfer despite the preferential treatment accorded China over all other Communist countries. Moreover, increased arms sales by the United States, promised by former Secretary of State Haig, have not materialized due to the sensitivity of the technology, bureaucratic inertia, and the Taiwan issue. The frustration felt by the Chinese was summarized by former Foreign Minister Huang Hua in an address to the Council on Foreign Relations in late 1982.

> . . . I once said that the U.S. authorities had made many nice remarks about developing our bilateral relations. Yet, what has happened can be described by a Chinese saying, 'loud thunder, little rain.' . . . In view of recent developments, one cannot but help asking: Does the U.S. government regard China as a friend or an adversary?[60]

The insoluble problem of Taiwan persists as the main impediment to a near-term improvement in US-China relations. It is a dilemma that both parties would have preferred to avoid, but which was to some degree inevitable given the prominent place Taiwan occupies in the political cultures of both the People's Republic and the United States. Although each side wants and needs to build a positive, durable bilateral relationship, when it comes to Taiwan neither is willing or, perhaps more accurately, able to pay the price which would be required to reach a full settlement.

Given the nature of the impasse over Taiwan, the most sensible short-term course for the United States to follow with China may simply be to deemphasize the strategic relationship for the time being, turn to other areas where interests are more compatible, and attempt to work around the Taiwan issue on the basis of the Joint Communique of August 17, 1982. By concentrating on trade, investment, and such cooperative ventures as development of offshore oil deposits, the United States and China may be able to construct a more durable relationship.[61] These ties, which have always been important, can be supplemented by contacts over the full range of nonsensitive mutual interests, including management training, professional education, scientific and technical exchanges, and cultural affairs.

This approach does not mean that the strategic alignment would be ignored or abandoned, but both sides are already well aware of where their parallel strategic interests lie. It does imply, however, that cooperation will be stressed in those areas where interests are most compatible, and least sensitive, and that strengthening the strategic alignment must follow an improvement in the overall political dimension of the relationship. The recent warming trend in Sino-American relations noted earlier has been based largely on this modest blueprint and may eventually lead to revived substantive contacts in the security realm.[62] The events of 1981-82 proved conclusively that insofar as US-China relations are concerned, pure anti-Sovietism is an insufficient basis for international cooperation unless the perception of threat is so strong and immediate that survival interests appear to be in jeopardy.

Implications for the US-Soviet Military Balance. China's impact on the global balance is both perceptual and substantive, and in each instance finds its widest expression within the framework of the US-USSR-China triangular relationship. At least for the present, the perceptual role of China clearly outweighs its substantive role. As a large country with a massive population and huge agricultural and industrial output in aggregate terms, China is perceived to "count" in important ways. In addition, it possesses a great deal of long-term potential in some areas, and this reinforces the perception of Chinese power. When China's current capabilities—political, economic, and military—are objectively analyzed, its rather serious inadequacies quickly become evident. Nevertheless, the original perception persists and makes China's position relative to the two superpowers an important factor in the security calculations of the West.

The revival of Sino-Soviet bilateral negotiations underscores the tendency to focus on perception at the expense of reality. As noted earlier, the prospects are dim for anything more than a limited accommodation between China and the Soviet Union, even over the long term. Both China and the Soviet Union are playing as much to the gallery, especially the United States, as they are to each other. The Soviet leaders intend to show Washington that they have a "China card" of their own and that China is not a reliable partner in any neocontainment strategy directed at the Soviet Union. For their part, the Chinese wish to prove to the United States that their cooperation and goodwill cannot be taken for granted, while perhaps obtaining some incremental reductions in the Soviet threat arrayed against them.

Perceptual factors can also operate to the advantage of the United States and the West, however. The two explicit US security objectives identified earlier—to use China as a strategic counterweight to the USSR and to tie down Soviet forces on the border with China—have been achieved in the past largely by virtue of Soviet perceptions. The same factors which contributed to the *perception* of Chinese power in the West are mirrored, and indeed magnified, in the eyes of the Soviet Union due to inherent security imperatives (military-strategic factors) and inordinate fears of Chinese expansionism (psychological factors). Soviet leaders know that they cannot regain the dominant position over China which they enjoyed in the 1950's, and can only hope to drive a wedge between their adversaries, deal with each one independently, and play off one against the other. Therefore, China should remain a strategic counterweight to the Soviet Union despite tactical shifts in its relations with the United States and other Western nations. Of course, China's value as a counterweight can be substantially increased by strong bilateral ties with the West in all areas, and this should be the overarching US policy objective *vis-a-vis* China.

The second objective, tying down Soviet forces in the east to prevent their redeployment against NATO, is somewhat more complex, but it has also been achieved in the past largely due to Soviet perceptions of a residual Chinese threat. First of all, the purpose of Soviet air and naval forces stationed in the Far East must be clearly understood.[63] China has never been a significant naval power in modern times and is unlikely to become one in this century. The presence of the Soviet Pacific Fleet, and the recent quantitative and qualitative improvements it has undergone, is primarily a function of the air and maritime threat to Soviet territory, population centers, and base facilities posed by the forward deployed forces of the United States and, presumably, allies such as Japan and South Korea.[64] Moreover, the bulk of the Soviet fleet could not redeploy outside the Northwest Pacific in either peacetime or wartime without leaving crucial areas in the Soviet Far East exposed. Finally, a wartime redeployment would face the added complications of a long, contested transit—perhaps halfway around the world—with little or no fleet air cover. Thus the Soviet Pacific Fleet will remain tied to the Far East so long as the US Seventh Fleet or any other credible naval threat remains in the area.

Much the same logic applies to the Soviet Far East air forces, although long-range and frontal aviation assets can be employed against either a US or a Chinese threat. However, the bulk of these air resources, and in particular the most modern aircraft, are committed either to the defense of key Far Eastern cities and military installations, which could not be seriously threatened by the PLA air force,[65] or are configured for antiship strikes against the US fleet. Few of the aircraft committed specifically against China would likely be available for release to the West, and even if they were, their additive contribution against NATO would be marginal inasmuch as they tend to be among the oldest models in the Soviet inventory. Once again, the presence of substantial forward deployed US and allied forces is the principal threat tying down Soviet air forces in the Far East.

The bulk of Soviet ground force deployments, on the other hand, is clearly oriented against China. Soviet forces deployed opposite China and elsewhere in the Far East are variously estimated at between 47 and 52 divisions with a total manpower of 460,000.[66] According to a 1981 US Departmnt of Defense estimate, however, only 15 percent of these divisions are at a high (greater than 75 percent) level of readiness.[67] Whether any of these forces could be shifted to the west in wartime, a distance of up to 6,000 miles over the highly vulnerable Trans-Siberian Railroad, is debatable. The Soviet Union is prepared to fight a two-front war, as the formation of a Soviet Far East High Command in 1979 demonstrates. Even if a nonaggression pact was somehow concluded with China, substantial Soviet forces would still be required in the Far East to protect against US and allied initiatives and/or possible Chinese treachery.[68]

The Soviet Union, as a concession to China, could easily make a token withdrawal of up to several of its least capable divisions without seriously degrading its capabilities in the theater. Moreover, the equipment for these divisions, usually of the oldest types, would probably remain in the east even if the troops were withdrawn. In conclusion, a reduction of tensions on the Sino-Soviet border, even if it includes the withdrawal of a few Soviet divisions, is not likely to have serious *substantive* impact on US or allied security interests elsewhere. The *perceptual* impact, on the other hand, would probably be more significant. It need not be serious, however, so long as Western leaders understand the actual military implications. Such an eventuality should be treated with the concern which it warrants, but without excessive alarm.

CHINA AND THE GLOBAL BALANCE: TOWARD THE YEAR 2000

Overall, the economic constraint on Chinese power emerges as clearly the most crucial and it appears highly improbable that China will be able to build an economy which could challenge those of the United States or the Soviet Union by the end of this century. China may possess the requisite territory, population, natural resources, political skill, social cohesion, and national will to become a superpower, but it will take more time than the brief span of two decades. The tremendous disparities in current levels of economic development are simply too great a handicap to overcome that quickly.

If China is not on the verge of superpower status, is a future of static or even reduced relative power a likely possibility? In order to fulfill such a prophecy, it would seem that China would have to experience either a disastrous war or prolonged upheaval akin to the Cultural Revolution. At present, the latter does not seem likely. The self-destructiveness of the past has been a bitter lesson, one which no one in China is eager to repeat. Whether "reformers" or "conservatives" rule in Beijing, progress is the measure by which their performance will be judged. Progress may be "two steps forward, one step back," but regression is not a tolerable policy option.

It appears that China, 20 years in the future, is likely to fall somewhere between the two extremes. While the variables are too numerous to allow any specific forecast, growth and development in some form appear most probable. While China will not be a superpower in the year 2000, it could conceivably join the first rank of world powers, no small achievement in itself. Spared war and catastrophic internal upheaval, China is probably the most prominent among a small handful of countries possessing the potential to develop into superpowers in the next century.

Problems in forecasting China's power are compounded by the dynamics of the international system. The power of China can only be assessed relative to the power of the other major players in the system, but the system itself is constantly in flux. For example, the future relationship between the United States and the Soviet Union is extremely important to China. Over the next two decades, both superpowers will continue to share crucial interests in raising standards of living in their respective countries; managing shortages in military manpower; reducing somewhat the burgeoning economic costs inherent in uncontrolled arms races; resolving crises short of war; and maintaining a stable deterrent balance. Bilateral negotiations will remain a prominent feature of US-Soviet relations,[69] but are not likely to resolve conclusively the divergent interests which underlie their global competition. Soviet foreign policy will continue to reflect the basic dualism of expansion and coexistence, and the United States will be compelled to respond accordingly.

If this projection of US-Soviet relations materializes, what would be China's impact on the global strategic balance 20 years hence? The growth in national power which can be expected to accompany a moderately successful modernization and development program should reduce China's strategic vulnerability. This would most notably affect the Soviet Union, but extends to the United States and any other nation with the capacity to threaten seriously China or its crucial interests. To the extent that China overcomes its military deficiencies, gradual shifts in its foreign policy should become evident. As Chinese power grows, the "united front" aspect of its international strategy will likely be retained, but the operational importance attached to it progressively diminished. At present, other "antihegemonists"—the United States, the Third World, or whomever—play a critical role in redressing the strategic imbalance between China and the Soviet Union. If the upgrading of its own capabilities begins to close this gap of vulnerability, China will be afforded greater flexibility in its foreign policy to pursue exclusive Chinese interests.

The single most potent element of China's expanded power and influence will likely be the growth of its strategic nuclear forces. Despite the economic setbacks and political turmoil of the past 25 years, China has carefully nurtured a modest, independent nuclear weapons development program, producing both warheads and delivery systems. From a fission device in 1964, through a thermonuclear detonation in 1967, to the successful test of a full-range ICBM in 1980 and an SLBM in 1982, the Chinese effort has been characterized by steady, if unspectacular, progress. The current emphasis on scientific advancement, industrial modernization, and the acquisition of advanced foreign technology can provide an unprecedented boost to China's strategic programs. The operational deployment of nuclear missile submarines sometime in this decade will further extend China's global reach.

As ICBM and nuclear missile submarine deployments expand the limits of Chinese power, it would not be surprising if China's global interests proliferate accordingly. The ability to project power well beyond its own borders could make China more inclined to identify crucial economic and world order interests in affairs previously beyond its capability to influence. As a practical matter, greater involvement in affairs once considered within the exclusive domain of the two superpowers is not only possible, but probable. At the same time, Chinese claims to regional predominance in Asia would be largely realized, Japan's economic power notwithstanding. Finally, China cannot hope to match fully the strategic capabilities of either the United States or the Soviet Union, at least by the year 2000. But the Chinese need not duplicate the arsenals of the two superpowers in order to create the perception of a fairly high order of usable power. As an independent player possessing a modest range of nuclear capabilities, China could seek to more directly influence the course of global events if it felt its crucial interests were being threatened.

In conclusion, even if China's modernization efforts are only moderately successful, the long-term impact on international relations may well be dramatic. Should China continue to develop independently and improve its nuclear capabilities, and there is no reason to expect otherwise, the implications for the strategic balance are especially significant. After decades of managing a bipolar balance, the superpowers, by the year 2000, may have to acknowledge the existence of a triangular balance. Strategic considerations may align China with one superpower or the other for a time, but in the long term it is, and consciously seeks to be, an independent power center. Assuring global stability in an environment which features continued East-West competition, growing North-South tensions, global energy crises, and a precarious world economy could be seriously complicated by China's emergence. The arms limitation process, for example, is already threatened by the proliferation of participants—among them China—and the increasing complexity of the issues. Finally, China aspires to be the major power in Asia, and here, perhaps more than anywhere else, Chinese, Soviet, and American interests are likely to conflict in future decades.

ENDNOTES

1. For one approach to national interests, see Donald E. Nuechterlein, "National Interests and National Strategy," a paper prepared for the Ninth National Security Affairs Conference, National Defense University, October 8-9, 1982. See also Nuechterlein, *National Interests and Presidential Leadership: The Setting of Priorities,* Boulder: Westview Press, 1978, Chapter 1.

2. Among the most definitive statements of US national security strategy under the Reagan Administration was the address by the President's national security advisor, William P. Clark, to the Center for Strategic and International Studies, Georgetown University, May 21, 1982. See also the address of the Presidential special assistant, Thomas C. Reed in *Vital Speeches of the Day,* Vol. XLVIII, No. 21, August 15, 1982.

3. Clark, *ibid.*

4. US Department of Commerce, Bureau of the Census, *Statistical Abstract of the United States 1982-83,* Washington: US Government Printing Office, 1982, pp. 836-839. Japan is now second only to Canada as the largest trading partner of the United States; South Korea, Taiwan, Hong Kong, Australia, and China are also important partners. Indonesia provides 6 percent of the petroleum consumed annually in the United States, and other Asian countries supply scarce strategic minerals. US trade with South Asia is relatively insignificant; in 1981 it accounted for only 2.5 percent of the total trade with Asia.

5. The range of security issues and problems, with particular emphasis on Southeast Asia and the Southwest Pacific, is explored in William T. Tow and William R. Feeney, eds., *U.S. Foreign Policy and Asian-Pacific Security: A Transregional Approach,* Boulder: Westview Press, 1982.

6. Address by Secretary of Defense Caspar W. Weinberger to the Japan National Press Club, Tokyo, Japan, March 26, 1982.

7. *Ibid.*

8. David Jenkins, "Measuring the Response," *Far Eastern Economic Review,* Vol. 118, No. 43, October 22, 1982, pp. 25-28. See also the interview with Chinese Foreign Minister Wu Xueqian in *Far Eastern Economic Review,* Vol. 119, No. 13, March 31, 1983, p. 26.

9. In November 1982 Premier Zhao Ziyang informed Thai Prime Minister Prem Tinsulanonda that "Should the Vietnamese authorities dare to invade Thailand by force, the Chinese Government and people will stand firmly by the side of Thailand and give all support to the Thai people in their just stand of opposing aggression." *Beijing Review,* Vol. 25, No. 48, November 29, 1982, p. 7.

10. For an introduction to China's relations with Southeast Asia, see Takashi Tajima, "China and South-East Asia: Strategic Interests and Policy Prospects," *Adelphi Papers No. 172,* London: International Institute for Strategic Studies, 1981.

11. *Statistical Abstract of the United States 1982-83,* p. 838, and Christopher S. Wren, "US-China Trade Down 5.5%," *The New York Times,* February 3, 1983, p. D11.

12. "China Says Oil Reserves Total 219 Billion Barrels," *The Wall Street Journal,* November 9, 1982, p. 39. Western experts now estimate China's offshore reserves to range between 30 and 100 billion barrels. Thomas J. Lueck, "Plumbing China Oil Reserves," *The New York Times,* August 18, 1983, p. D1.

13. Dinah Lee, "Exxon, China Said to Agree on Oil Accord," *The Washington Post*, August 17, 1983, p. A1.

14. "Peking Says 15,000 Students Will Be Sent Abroad for Study," *The New York Times*, December 13, 1982, p. A8.

15. For background and an up-to-date summary of the Taiwan issue in Sino-American relations, see "U.S.-China Joint Communique," *Department of State Bulletin*, Vol. 82, No. 2067, October 1982, pp. 19-22, and Michel Oksenberg, "A Decade of Sino-American Relations," *Foreign Affairs*, Vol. 61, No. 1, Fall 1982, pp. 175-195.

16. See, for example, Michel Oksenberg, "The Dynamics of the Sino-American Relationship" and Strobe Talbott, "The Strategic Dimension of the Sino-American Relationship," in Richard H. Solomon, ed., *The China Factor: Sino-American Relations and the Global Scene*, Englewood Cliffs: Prentice-Hall, Inc., 1981, pp. 48-80 and 81-113, respectively.

17. Statement of Admiral Robert L. J. Long, Commander in Chief, US Forces, Pacific, before the Committee on Armed Services, US House of Representatives, March 16, 1982. *Hearings on Military Posture and H.R. 5968 (H.R. 6030) Department of Defense Authorization for Appropriations for Fiscal Year 1983*, Part 1, Military Posture, Washington: US Government Printing Office, 1982, pp. 1003-1004.

18. Statement of Walter J. Stoessel, Jr., Deputy Secretary of State, before the Senate Foreign Relations Committee, June 10, 1982, in "Allied Responses to the Soviet Challenge in East Asia and the Pacific," US Department of State, Current Policy No. 403.

19. Philip Taubman, "U.S., Peking Jointly Monitor Russian Missiles," *The New York Times*, June 18, 1981, p. A1.

20. Address by Leonid I. Brezhnev to a conference of Soviet Army and Navy command personnel, Moscow, October 27, 1982, in *Vital Speeches of the Day*, Vol. XLIX, No. 3, November 15, 1982.

21. Harry Gelman, *The Politburo's Management of Its America Problem*, Rand Report R-2707-NA, Santa Monica: The Rand Corporation, April 1981.

22. The origins of Soviet security policy are not all functions of US-USSR global competition or simple reactions to perceived vulnerability; elements of historic imperialism, nationalism, and militarism, are often cited as well. See Rebecca V. Strode and Colin S. Gray, "The Imperial Dimension of Soviet Military Power," *Problems of Communism*, Vol. XXX, No. 6, November-December 1981, pp. 1-15. Also see John Weinstein, "All Features Grate and Stall: Soviet Vulnerabilities and the Future of Deterrence" in Robert Kennedy and John Weinstein, eds., *The Defense of the West: Strategic and European Issues Reappraised*, Boulder: Westview Press, 1984.

23. For an example of the growing interest of Western Sovietologists in the importance of Asia in Soviet strategic calculations, see Donald S. Zagoria, ed., *Soviet Policy in East Asia*, New Haven: Yale University Press, 1982, and Allen S. Whiting, *Siberian Development and East Asia: Threat or Promise?*, Stanford: Stanford University Press, 1981.

24. Sidney Bearman, "Soviet Power and Policies in the Third World: East Asia," in Christoph Bertram, ed., *Prospects of Soviet Power in the 1980s*, London: Archon Books, 1980.

25. Thomas W. Robinson, *The Sino-Soviet Border Dispute: Background, Development, and the March 1969 Clashes,* Rand Research Memorandum RM-6171-PR, Santa Monica: The Rand Corporation, August 1970, pp. 1-32, and especially pp. 29-32.

26. For a detailed examination of the origins of the strategic triangle, focusing on the Sino-Soviet dynamic, see Thomas M. Gottlieb, *Chinese Foreign Policy Factionalism and the Origins of the Strategic Triangle,* Rand Report R-1902-NA, Santa Monica: The Rand Corporation, November 1977, and Kenneth G. Lieberthal, *Sino-Soviet Conflict in the 1970s: Its Evolution and Implications for the Strategic Triangle,* Rand Report R-2342-NA, July 1978.

27. Robert W. Campbell, "Prospects for Siberian Economic Development," in Zagoria, ed., *Soviet Policy in East Asia,* pp. 229-254; Theodore Shabad, "Siberian Development and Soviet Policies in East Asia," *Asian Perspective,* Vol. 6, No. 2, Fall-Winter 1982, pp. 195-208; and Whiting, Chapter 2.

28. Weinstein, "All Features Grate and Stall."

29. Shabad, pp. 202-208. See also *Asian Security 1979,* Tokyo: Research Institute for Peace and Security, 1979, pp. 55-56.

30. Edward A. Hewett and Herbert S. Levine, "The Soviet Union's Economic Relations in Asia," in Zagoria, ed., *Soviet Policy in East Asia,* pp. 201-228; see also Stuart Kirby, "Siberia and East Asia: Economic and General Relations Between Siberia and Its Far Eastern Neighbors," *Asian Perspective,* Vol. 6, No. 2, Fall-Winter 1982, pp. 151-194.

31. For an evaluation of Japanese threat perceptions see Hiroshi Kimura, "The Soviet Threat and the Security of Japan," in Roger E. Kanet, ed., *Soviet Foreign Policy in the 1980s,* New York: Praeger Publishers, 1982, pp. 231-246.

32. *Asian Security 1981,* pp. 43-47; and *Asian Security 1982,* pp. 39-43.

33. Statement of Admiral Long, p. 1000. Other sources give estimates ranging up to $6 million a day; see *Asian Security 1982,* p. 36.

34. For a discussion of the impact of the great powers on Korea, see Robert G. Sutter, "U.S.-Soviet-PRC Relations and Their Implications for Korea," *Korea & World Affairs,* Vol. 7, No. 1, Spring 1983, pp. 5-20.

35. Michael Richardson, "ASEAN Extends Its Military Ties," *Pacific Defence Reporter,* Vol. IX, No. 5, November 1982, pp. 55-58.

36. *Asian Security 1981,* pp. 47-64, and *Asian Security 1982,* pp. 35-38 and 117-122.

37. For additional data on the Southeast Asian straits, see US Central Intelligence Agency, *Indian Ocean Atlas,* August 1976, p. 31, and Michael Richardson, "Missile Maneuvers," *Far Eastern Economic Review,* Vol. 116, No. 18, April 30, 1982, pp. 32-33.

38. The Arab oil exporting countries plus Iran accounted for 68 percent of total Japanese crude oil imports in 1982. US Central Intelligence Agency, *International Energy Statistical Review,* July 26, 1983, p. 5.

39. John McBeth, "To Moscow the Spoils," *Far Eastern Economic Review,* Vol. 117, No. 37, September 10, 1982, pp. 27-28.

40. For a somewhat more pessimistic assessment of the border issue, see David Rees, *Soviet Border Problems: China and Japan,* Conflict Studies No. 139, London: Institute for the Study of Conflict, 1982. The dispute flared again publicly in early 1983; Serge Schmemann, "China is Assailed in Soviet Journal," *The New York Times,* January 15, 1983, p. 1.

41. See, for example, Samuel S. Kim, "Mao Zedong and China's Changing Worldview," in *China in the Global Community,* James C. Hsiung and Kim, eds., New York: Praeger Publishers, 1980, p. 32, and Thomas Fingar, "Introduction: The Quest for Independence," in Fingar, ed., *China's Quest for Independence: Policy Evolution in the 1970s,* Boulder: Westview Press, 1980, pp. 2-5.

42. Zhou Enlai, "Report on the Work of the Government" to the Fourth National People's Congress, *Peking Review,* Vol. 18, No. 4, January 24, 1975, p. 23.

43. Hu Yaobang, "Create a New Situation in All Fields of Socialist Modernization," (Report to the 12th National Party Congress), *Beijing Review,* Vol. 25, No. 37, September 13, 1982, p. 15.

44. Robert Delfs, "Laying the Foundations," *Far Eastern Economic Review,* Vol. 118, No. 50, December 10, 1982, pp. 58-60, and Zhao Ziyang, "Report on the Sixth Five-Year Plan," *Beijing Review,* Vol. 25, No. 51, December 20, 1982, pp. 10-35. China's developmental strategy was further refined in Zhao's "Report on the Work of the Government" delivered at the First Session of the Sixth National People's Congress, *Beijing Review,* Vol. 26, No. 27, July 4, 1983, pp. I-XXIV.

45. *Beijing Review,* Vol. 25, No. 36, September 6, 1982, p. 5. For the full text of Deng's opening speech, see *The Twelfth National Congress of the CPC (September 1982),* Beijing: Foreign Language Press, 1982, pp. 1-6.

46. Deng Xiaoping's address to a special session of the United Nations, as reported in *Peking Review,* Vol. 17, No. 16, April 19, 1974, pp. 6-11.

47. William R. Heaton, Jr., *A United Front Against Hegemony: Chinese Foreign Policy Into the 1980's,* Monograph Series No. 80-3, Washington: National Defense University Press, March 1980, pp. 8-9.

48. Hu Yaobang, "Create a New Situation in All Fields of Socialist Modernization," pp. 16-17. Other instances of alleged US hegemonism frequently cited include US Middle East policy in general and continued support for Israel in particular, cooperation with South Africa, and (largely for Kim Il-sung's benefit) the continued US military presence in South Korea.

49. Zhou Jirong, *et. al.,* "Stick Together Through Thick and Thin, Join Forces in Fighting Hegemonism," Foreign Broadcast Information Service (FBIS), *China Daily Report,* October 26, 1982, p. A3.

50. See, for example, Mu Youlin, "Opposing Hegemonism," *Beijing Review,* Vol. 25, No. 32, August 9, 1982, p. 3, emphasis added.

51. For detailed assessments of the European dimension of the Sino-Soviet dispute, see Trond Gilberg, "The Impact of the Sino-Soviet Dispute in Eastern Europe," and Joan Barth Urban, "The Impact of the Sino-Soviet Dispute in Western Europe," in Herbert J. Ellison, ed., *The Sino-Soviet Conflict: A Global Perspective,* pp. 268-294 and 295-324, respectively.

52. *The Twelfth National Congress of the CPC,* p. 4.

53. *The Military Balance 1982-1983,* London: International Institute for Strategic Studies, 1982, pp. 78-81.

54. "Peking Fires Its First Submarine-Launched Missile," *The New York Times,* October 17, 1982, p. 15. See also Agatha S. Y. Wong-Fraser, "China's Nuclear Deterrent," *Current History,* Vol. 80, No. 467, September 1981, pp. 245-249ff.

55. For a detailed discussion of Chinese military doctrine, see William R. Heaton, Jr., "The Defense Policy of the People's Republic of China," in Douglas J. Murray and Paul R. Viotti, eds., *The Defense Policies of Nations: A*

Comparative Study, Baltimore: The Johns Hopkins University Press, 1982, pp. 419-440.

56. Douglas T. Stuart and William T. Tow, "Chinese Military Modernization: The Western Arms Connection," *China Quarterly,* Vol. 90, June 1982, pp. 253-270.

57. For further discussion of China's impact on the global balance, with particular attention to Europe, see the essays in Gerald Segal, ed., *The China Factor,* New York: Holmes & Meier, 1982.

58. The following definitions apply to these terms: detente - *relaxation, easing, or reduction of tensions;* normalization - *establishment of "normal" state-to-state relations;* accommodation - *adjustment of differences, reconciliation;* rapprochement - *reestablishment of harmonious relations;* entente - *a friendly understanding (to cooperate for mutual benefit);* and alliance - *a formal agreement to cooperate for specific purposes.*

59. Mary Wisniewski, "All Talk, No Action," *Far Eastern Economic Review,* Vol. 119, No. 12, March 24, 1983, p. 12. For a detailed analysis of the post-Brezhnev thaw in Sino-Soviet relations, see Donald S. Zagoria, "The Moscow-Beijing Detente," *Foreign Affairs,* Vol. 61, No. 4, Spring 1983, pp. 853-873.

60. Richard M. Weintraub, "State Dept. Wary on Sino-Soviet Initiative," *The Washington Post,* October 19, 1982, p. A11.

61. The Deputy Assistant Secretary of Commerce for East Asia, Eugene Lawson, may have been exaggerating only slightly when he stated that "offshore oil is the cutting edge of Sino-U.S. relations for the rest of this century." Christopher S. Wren, "China Energy: Chance for U.S.," *The New York Times,* October 14, 1982, p. D1.

62. Richard Nations, "Raising the Barriers" and "Turning the Other Cheek," *Far Eastern Economic Review,* Vol. 120, No. 24, June 16, 1983, pp. 16-18, and Vol. 121, No. 30, July 28, 1983, pp. 14-15, respectively.

63. For an extensive analysis, see Harry Gelman, *The Soviet Far East Buildup and Soviet Risk-Taking Against China,* Rand Report R-2943-AF, Santa Monica: The Rand Corporation, August 1982.

64. For a thorough analysis of the dynamic interaction of weapons systems, geographic constraints, and opposing forces in Asia (especially the Northeast Asia/Northwest Pacific area), see *Asian Security 1981,* Tokyo: Research Institute for Peace and Security, 1981, pp. 73-85.

65. An analysis of PLA Air Force operations during the 1979 border war with Vietnam concluded that PLAAF activities were "largely cosmetic" and that it "could hardly be an effective instrument for any *offensive* actions." James B. Linder and A. James Gregor, "The Chinese Communist Air Force in the 'Punitive' War Against Vietnam," *Air University Review,* Vol. XXXII, No. 6, September/October 1981, pp. 73 and 74, respectively.

66. *The Military Balance 1982-1983,* London: International Institute of Strategic Studies, 1982, p. 15, and US Department of Defense, *Soviet Military Power,* 2d ed., Washington: US Government Printing Office, March 1983, p. 9.

67. US Department of Defense, *Soviet Military Power,* Washington: US Government Printing Office, September 1981, p. 7. Soviet ground force readiness levels are classified by category levels: I (75-100 percent strength with complete equipment), II (50-75 percent strength complete with fighting vehicles), and III (less than 50 percent strength—typically 25 percent—with some fighting vehicles). Approximately 35 percent and 50 percent of the Soviet divisions in the Far East are

at Category II and III levels respectively. However, the USSR's current peacetime military deployments are more than ample to deal with any thrust by the Chinese PLA, which is severely constrained by outdated weaponry, poor communications, a lack of battlefield mobility, and limited power projection capabilities. Moreover, the Chinese military doctrine, still essentially that of "people's war," is suited only for strategic defense.

68. Michael Sadykiewicz, "Soviet Far East High Command: A New Developmental Factor in the USSR Military Strategy Toward East Asia," *Asian Perspective*, Vol. 6, No. 2, Fall-Winter 1982, pp. 29-71, and Gelman, *The Soviet Far East Buildup*, pp. 108-112.

69. Robert Kennedy, "The Problems and Prospects of START" in Kennedy and Weinstein, eds., *The Defense of the West*.

5

BALLISTIC MISSILE DEFENSE, SPACE-BASED WEAPONS, AND THE DEFENSE OF THE WEST

Daniel S. Papp

In his March 23, 1983 address on military spending, President Ronald Reagan presented his vision of a future in which American defenses could "intercept and destroy strategic ballistic missiles before they reached our own soil or that of our allies." To achieve this objective, Reagan directed that a "comprehensive and intensive effort" be undertaken to define a long-term research and development program designed to "achieve our ultimate goal of eliminating the threat posed by strategic nuclear missiles."[1] Although Reagan's address itself contained no references to specific strategic ballistic missile defense (BMD) technologies, it was apparent to many that his vision of a future free of the terror of nuclear weapons was based on the development and deployment of beam technology weapons such as lasers, particle beams, and microwaves.

Public reactions to Reagan's proposal were rapid and diverse. Critics reviled strategic defense as a dangerous delusion, and claimed that it was technically unfeasible, economically too costly, strategically destabilizing, and militarily unsound. Proponents of the concept argued that existing technical difficulties could be overcome; that costs were a minor constraint when ultimate security was at stake; and that space-based defenses were a solution to the apparent weakness of the current offensive, force dominant deterrence posture.[2] Whatever the actual merits of his proposal, Reagan had undeniably generated more public debate on a high technology defense issue than had been heard for years.

Reagan's address, however, did more than generate public debate over the wisdom of strategic defense. Since the early 1960's, US nuclear deterrence policies had been based at least in part on the assumption that no effective defense against nuclear attack existed. Reagan's speech challenged that assumption and forced strategic analysts to reexamine questions they believed had been satisfactorily answered.[3] Could strategic defense with little or no leakage (i.e., no penetration by enemy warheads) be achieved? Would it be stabilizing or destabilizing in a crisis? Would it lead to a defensive arms race and would it accelerate the offensive arms race? What would be the implications for the strategic balance and for the future of deterrence if one side achieved a low-leakage or no-leakage strategic defense before the other? What if both sides achieved such a defense simultaneously, or if one or both sides achieved only a high-leakage defense? How would any strategic defense affect the allies of each superpower, and how would arms control be affected? This paper will examine these and other related questions.

First, however, a clarification of terminology used throughout this paper is appropriate. Although President Reagan's so-called Star Wars proposal referred primarily to beam weapons (also known as directed energy transfer (DET) weapons), other defensive technologies do exist. Some are nearer operational status than DET weapons. Certain types of antiballistic missiles (ABMs) may be operationally tested by 1985—this form of BMD uses missiles to destroy incoming ICBMs. Thus, both DET and ABM technologies are subsets of BMD,[4] and both can be either space-based or land-based.

Indeed, according to some strategists, a layered BMD system employing, for example, space-based DET weapons and ground-based ABM capabilities, could reduce or eliminate any leakage problem that an exclusively space-based DET system may have. More ambitious layered BMD systems project space-based defense systems coupled with both a ground-based non-nuclear exoatmospheric (i.e., above the atmosphere) ABM capability.[5]

Conversely, development of effective antisatellite (ASAT) capabilities may negate the utility of DET or conventional space-based defenses. Therefore, it is appropriate that this effort also investigate the potential impacts that other technologies such as ABMs and ASATs may have on the calculus of strategic deterrence if and when DET weapons become operational. First, however, it may be helpful to present an overview of the American BMD and military space programs.

AN OVERVIEW

To those familiar with the Reagan administration's record in the areas of ballistic missile defense (BMD) and space, the President's March 23 address on strategic defense offered few surprises. It had been evident for some time that the Reagan administration was intensely interested in BMD and active military uses of space.

BMD Technologies. American BMD efforts were substantially deemphasized following the signing of the 1972 ABM Treaty and the 1974 ABM Protocol.[6] During the late 1960's, US ABM expenditures averaged approximately $1 billion per year (in FY 1980 dollars). By 1980, expenditures on strategic defense had fallen to $100 million.[7]

Shortly thereafter, however, American interest in BMD and active space-based military systems increased as technical advances, the collapse of detente, and changes in political leadership altered the prevailing strategic environment. Technical breakthroughs in radar, high-speed computers, boost technologies, command, control and communications (C^3) abilities, and laser capabilities increased the feasibility of both ABM and DET BMD. The recent successful destruction of five 2,000-miles-per-hour Sidewinder missiles by an airborne high energy laser clearly indicated that DET technologies had progressed substantially. Meanwhile, traditional ABM technologies also showed promise, perhaps most notably with the US Army's small radar homing interceptor (SR Hit) program, currently being developed by Vought and scheduled to be flight tested in 1985.[8]

Active Military Technologies in Space. As with BMD capabilities, significant studies had been undertaken during the 1970's in technologies designed for military use in space. Space, of course, had been used in a largely passive manner by both the United States and the Soviet Union for military purposes almost since the beginning of the space age. By the early 1980's, the military establishments of several countries, but especially the

United States, had become highly dependent on orbiting space systems for strategic and tactical communications, navigation, surveillance, reconnaissance, early warning, and weather reporting purposes. One measure of the importance that space communications had attained in the American military was revealed during the abortive raid to rescue American hostages in Iran during 1980. Then-President Jimmy Carter was in direct contact from Washington via satellite with American forces on the ground in Iran, and personally aborted the raid. A second example is more mundane but perhaps more illustrative: each month a single US Navy carrier battle group sends or receives over forty thousand satellite-carried messages.[9]

One reason that space has rarely been used for active military purposes was the 1967 "Treaty on Principles Governing the Activities of States in the Exploration and Use of Outer Space, Including the Moon and Other Celestial Bodies," also known more conveniently as the "Outer Space Treaty." This multilateral international agreement prohibited placing "nuclear weapons or any other kinds of weapons of mass destruction" into space. Other treaty provisions included agreements to explore and use space "in the interest of maintaining international peace and security" and denial of all claims of sovereignty over outer space, the moon, and other celestial bodies.[10] Other factors have also led to a limited active military presence in space. These factors included a generally prevailing public sentiment that space should be recognized as a zone of peace, and recognition that technical limitations of available space hardware permitted few active space-based military undertakings.

Nevertheless, some active military uses of space have been explored. One area that was under investigation during the 1960's and 1970's was antisatellite (ASAT) weaponry. Put simply, an ASAT is any weapon that can destroy or degrade the operation of a satellite. An early US ASAT program sought to develop the capability to destroy an enemy satellite by launching an explosive satellite into an orbit identical with the target. This coorbital approach, also favored by the USSR, was abandoned by the United States in favor of a direct ascent system called the "Air Launched Miniature Vehicle" (ALMV). The ALMV is launched by a high-flying F-15 at a satellite passing overhead in low earth orbit. The purpose of the ALMV is to "intercept Soviet satellite systems and to deter Soviet first use of their antisatellite weapon."[11] The Soviet

Union, meanwhile, had developed a rudimentary coorbital ASAT system, and was working on DET weapons including lasers and particle beams.

When viewed from a Soviet perspective, the US space shuttle also has ASAT and BMD potential. During the US-USSR ASAT negotiations, terminated in December 1979 by the United States in response to the Soviet invasion of Afghanistan, the USSR regularly insisted that the United States suspend development of the space shuttle because of its potential use in antisatellite operations.[12] Other analysts have observed that the space shuttle itself as well as follow-on technology could be used to deploy, maintain, and service orbital BMD systems. Beyond whatever potential ASAT and BMD utilities the shuttle may have, it does have clear reconnaissance, surveillance, communications and satellite-launching operations. The military potential of the shuttle is perhaps best indicated by the number of military space shuttle launches, which although in fiscal year 1983 was zero, is projected to increase in fiscal year 1987, with six launches completely dedicated to military purposes and seven launches each of one-fourth military dedication.[13]

To date, no space-based BMD has been developed or tested. As emphasis on BMD grows, however, research and development will almost inevitably follow. Indeed, the Reagan administration itself had already undertaken a number of organizational changes, doctrinal pronouncements, and policy initiatives on BMD and related space-based military activity throughout its tenure.[14] These changes, pronouncements, and initiatives when viewed in conjunction with the President's March 23 address are clear indications of the Reagan administration's interest in BMD and the military utility of space.

Reagan, BMD, and the Military Utility of Space. The Reagan administration's interest in BMD and space appeared as early as spring of 1981 when the Department of the Air Force formed a new Space Laser Office. In September 1981, the Deputy Chief of Staff for Plans and Operations of the Air Force created the Directorate for Space. The following month, President Reagan himself verbally supported the development of technologies needed for space-based defense. Secretary of Defense Caspar Weinberger agreed with Reagan in the 1982 Defense Guidance issued in March and subsequently "leaked to the press, declaring that the United States should "exploit opportunities through the use of space for increasing deterrence at all levels of conflict." He also directly addressed space-based weapons, calling for development of prototypes "so that we will be prepared to deploy fully developed and operationally ready systems should their use prove to be in our national interest."[15] Shortly thereafter, in April 1982, the General Accounting Office (GAO) issued a report that added momentum to the push to develop laser, particle beam, and microwave weaponry, observing that such technologies could "revolutionize military strategy, tactics, and doctrine." The GAO report urged the Pentagon to accelerate its laser research and development.[16]

In June, the Department of Defense finalized its own space policy statement, and following the successful July 4th landing of the fourth space shuttle mission, Ronald Reagan issued his own national space policy statement. According to press released reports, Reagan's space policy contained several phrases that clearly pointed to accelerated American military activity in space; for example:

> Purposeful interference with space systems shall be viewed as an infringement upon sovereign rights. . . .
>
> The US space program will comprise two separate, distinct, and strongly interacting programs. . . .
>
> The US will pursue activities in space in support of its right of self-defense. . . .[17]

Within a few months, the US Air Force created its Space Technology Center at Kirtland Air Force Base and operationalized its Space Command on September 1st of the same year. The Space Command's responsibilities included operating military space shuttle flights; maintaining surveillance, warning, and weather satellites; developing US ASAT capabilities; and conducting research on DET weapons. Also in September 1982, according to reports, Caspar Weinberger met with Alan Pike, the Acting Director of the Directed Energy Office of the Defense Advanced Research Projects Administration, and was informed that within 5 years the United States could deploy a rugged and survivable space-based laser that would be capable of defending itself. The following month, the Air Force finalized its space doctrine manual.[18]

Discussions of BMD and space-based defense continued within the Reagan administration, with BMD, reportedly, being a major issue of discussion at a February 1983 meeting of the Joint Chiefs of Staff.[19] Weinberger released *The 1983 Defense Guidance* in March which, according to accounts, stressed the military's role in space. As reported by Richard Hallovan of *The New York Times*, the guidance for US systems had to:

. . . assure robust support to nuclear and conventional forces.

. . . negate enemy use of space systems to support forces hostile to the United States.

. . . provide a credible defense of United States space assets.

. . . protect associated terrestial functions from hostile space supported actions.[20]

Increased American emphasis on BMD and military uses of space under the Reagan administration may be tracked by budgetary analysis as well. The Department of Defense's requests for space appropriations climbed from about $3.9 billion in fiscal year 1980 to $4.7 billion in 1981, $5.8 billion in 1982, and $8.5 billion in 1983 (all in current dollars).[21] Space-based laser funding grew from $57.8 million in fiscal year 1981 to $139.4 million in 1983.[22] The growth in Department of Defense funding emphasis for both BMD and ASATs (shown below as "space defense") is amply demonstrated in Figure 1.

	Actual FY 82	Planned FY 83	Proposed FY 84	Proposed for FY 85
BMD:				
Development	462.1	519.0	709.3	1,564.0
Procurement	--	--	--	--
Space Defense:				
Development	200.9	209.5	205.6	108.3
Procurement	--	--	19.4	196.9

Source: <u>Department of Defense Authorization for Appropriations for Fiscal Year 1984, Hearings Before the Committee on Armed Services</u>, US Senate, 98th Cong., 1st Sess., p. 337.

Figure 1. BMD and ASAT Expenditures from Fiscal 1982 to Fiscal 1985, in Millions of Dollars

Even more strikingly, the Department of Defense is seeking additional funds through 1988 for BMD and military uses of space, excluding communications, navigation, and weather satellites. According to Hallovan, a 1983 Pentagon memorandum indicated that the Department of Defense would take $10 billion over the next 5 years (1984-89) for research on defensive arms, including lasers, particle beams, microwave beams, and traditional missile-oriented defensive technologies. Of this $10 billion, $8 billion would be spent on land-based BMD, with $2 billion allocated to space-based BMD. An additional $6.3 billion would be requested for military uses of space, including funds for shuttle missions, space defense, surveillance and reconnaissance, and other active and passive uses of space, excluding communications, navigation, and weather satellites.[23] Since this memorandum was not identified as being for planning purposes or for final decision, and since the listed budget categories were sufficiently detailed to identify precise programs, far-reaching conclusions are uncertain. Nevertheless, one may safely conclude that the Department of Defense clearly intends to continue its BMD and space-related military activities.

Hence, rather than being viewed merely as a simple initiative, the strategic defense section of President Reagan's March 23d speech should be viewed as a clear indication of a growing emphasis in the American defense establishment on BMD and related space-based activity.[24] Beyond his March 23d address, Reagan's own interest and the country's commitment to BMD were institutionalized by the creation of an executive committee chaired by Secretary of Defense Caspar Weinberger to study BMD-related issues. By October 1983, Weinberger and the Defense Technologies Study Team had urged the President to support a 5-year, $18 to $27 billion program to develop space-based and land-based BMD capabilities for the defense of the United States and its allies.[25]

SETTING THE STAGE: CATEGORIES OF BMD

BMD may be divided into two broad categories: passive and active. Passive defenses, which may be further divided into absorptive and evasive techniques, attempt to reduce the effects of a weapon on its target by increasing the target's ability to absorb punishment (absorptive defense) or by increasing the target's ability to avoid punishment (evasive defense). Neither method of passive defense will be addressed in this article.[26]

Active defenses may also be subdivided into two categories, prelaunch defense and postlaunch defense. Prelaunch defense is synonymous with a damage-limiting preemptive attack against an enemy's strategic offensive forces. Preemptive attacks as a category of BMD also fall beyond the purview of this article. Here, we will deal only with postlaunch BMD, that is, the effort to prevent ballistic missiles already in flight from striking their intended targets.[27] Thus, only one of several possible BMD categories will be examined.

Postlaunch active BMD may itself be further subdivided according to technologies and basing modes. Land-based BMD includes exoatmospheric ABM and endoatmosphere ABM of both nuclear and nonnuclear varieties, as well as DET weaponry, most prominently (because of technical reasons), particle beams. Space-based BMD includes DET weapons and homing vehicles.[28] Sea-based and air-based BMD are also possible, but appear to present no significant advantages over space-based and land-based systems.

Despite the different technologies involved in each system, the problems that each must overcome are similar. All must identify the target, track it and verify its trajectory, overcome the target's countermeasures, attack the target, and finally, destroy, disable, or misdirect it. These are formidable tasks, and depending on which technical source one uses, the possibility of any BMD system accomplishing all of these tasks with a high degree of reliability ranges from "no way" pessimism to "can't miss" optimism.

Even the most optimistic proponents of BMD admit that a highly reliable system with low or no leakage will not be possible before the 21st century. President Reagan recognized this in his March 23d speech. Nevertheless, considerable optimism exists about the feasibility of designing a moderately to highly reliable system, even one where technologies have yet to be developed. Most BMD advocates maintain that the most effective BMD system would be a "layered" system consisting of several distinct components. In one such system, the first component would be a space-based system, probably a high energy laser, capable of engaging ascending international ballistic missiles (ICBMs) still in their boost phases before warhead separation occurs.[29] Thus, in the case of ICBMs with multiple independently targetable reentry vehicles (MIRVs), several warheads would be destroyed by intercepting a single missile, and the threat presented by MIRVs would be correspondingly lessened.

Any ICBMs that were not destroyed by the space-based system would be confronted by a second layer of defense, most probably a nonnuclear exoatmospheric ABM. Depending on the capabilities and design of the ABM, it could attack incoming targets either before or after warhead separation. Boost phase attacks, however, would be preferable, since the number of targets would be fewer.

The final component of a layered BMD system would be a low altitude nonnuclear endoatmospheric ABM (some scientists believe that land-based DET weapons eventually may be developed for close-in defense as well). Any warheads that penetrated the first two components of the system, proponents of BMD argue, would be intercepted and destroyed by a terminal defense system. Thus, it is argued, a sophisticated layered BMD system would have the same advantages of redundancy that add to the reliability of the American strategic retaliatory triad and might also be so structured to permit an overall leakage of about .1 percent.[30]

Although a layered system would seemingly provide BMD with the least leakages, any single BMD component could be deployed by itself. Thus, a layered system is only the most sophisticated variant of several BMD alternatives.

BMD ISSUES AND IMPLICATIONS

Discussion following President Reagan's March 23d address raised a number of significant issues and implications related to BMD. The issues raised may usefully be divided into six major and interdependent areas: 1) technical feasibility; 2) cost-effectiveness; 3) the impact of BMD on arms race and crisis stability; 4) the implications of BMD for arms control agreements; 5) the effect of BMD on deterrence theory and strategic thought; and 6) the impact of BMD on the Western alliance.

Technical Feasibility. Even within the technical community, disagreement exists over whether a no-leakage or low-leakage BMD will ever be technically feasible. Most authorities, however, agree that a high-leakage or moderate leakage system could be developed. While this is not an appropriate forum to discuss the merits of the arguments that lead different authorities to different conclusions on the technical feasibility question, we can analyze some of the implications that follow from each level of reliability.

Thus, for example, some BMD critics often argue that only a perfectly reliable no-leakage system can guarantee safety of civilian population centers, and therefore BMD should be deployed only if such a system can be perfected. Even a single warhead would cause unprecedented death and destruction, they correctly argue, and therefore, unless a no-leakage BMD is perfected, no BMD makes sense.

This line of logic overlooks two points. First, even in the event of an attack on cities, a BMD that successfully intercepted all but a single warhead targeted against a major metropolitan area, such as New York City, would, in fact, significantly limit the damage the city suffered. The more porous (i.e., the easier the penetration) a BMD is, of course, the less this observation holds true. A BMD that failed to intercept five or six warheads targeted against diverse locations in New York City would, in fact, be virtually valueless. Nevertheless, the point to be made is simple: a low-leakage BMD system could be of some value in the defense of cities, or so-called countervalue targets.

Second, even a high-leakage BMD may be useful in the defense of America's retaliatory missile force (counterforce defense). In the event that future BMD technologies permit the destruction of only one of every two ICBMs in the boost phase and one of every two reentry vehicles (RVs) after warhead separation, a hypothetical attack against defended counterforce sites must employ twice as many ICBMs and RVs as in an attack on an undefended site to achieve the same level of target destruction. Since the purpose of a large-scale counterforce attack would be to disarm an enemy, it is reasonable to assume that even a high-leakage counterforce defense would have one of two effects. First, it may goad the potential attacker into increasing the size of his strategic offensive forces, thereby creating an offensive-defensive arms race and thereby raising questions of cost-effectiveness examined below. Second, it may increase the uncertainty of a potential attacker about the possibility of a successful disarming first strike, thereby influencing him not to strike. Assuming one places credence in the possibility of a disarming first strike, under certain crisis scenarios, deterrence would therefore be enhanced by even a high-leakage BMD.[31]

Additionally, a high-leakage or even a no-leakage BMD deployed for counterforce defense would provide little incentive to the side that had it to initiate a disarming first strike, if simply because its BMD defended targets would themselves be gone in the event that it launched a first strike. In this scenario, BMD would be meaningless.

This logic runs into difficulty, however, if a low- or no-leakage BMD could be used to defend counterforce *or* countervalue targets. Space-based BMD may well be such a system. With such a capability, a scenario could be foreseen in which a national command authority would gamble that were it to launch a highly successful disarming first strike, its space-based BMD could cope with the degraded countervalue retaliatory strike. In this situation, both sides would have an incentive to strike first. Conversely, if space-based BMD had a moderate leakage or high-leakage rate, such logic would not be possible. Counterforce BMD would be somewhat improved, and countervalue BMD would be of low quality. Thus, a moderate leakage or high-leakage space-based BMD may be preferable to a low- or no-leakage BMD, at least from the viewpoint of crisis stability.

Inherent technical factors also have a significant impact on the effectiveness of BMD defense systems. For land-based BMD, the responsiveness of the system, the number of interceptors available, and the ability of ABM radars, C^3, and other associated hardware and software to withstand detonation shocks, electromagnetic pulse (EMP), and other effects of an attack are critical. A space-based system also must be able to withstand these effects, in addition to other challenges. A space-based system would be in a position where an opponent could use its ASAT capabilities to destroy or degrade it. Hence, space-based BMD must itself be defended, which most suitably would be by built-in technical defensive capabilities.

Proponents of space-based BMD assert that such a system could defend itself just as it defends against missiles. However, this argument overlooks three points. First, if an enemy were to develop DET weapons, space-based BMD would itself be subject to both land-based and space-based DET attack. Such an attack would not necessarily have to destroy the BMD's orbital platform, but would merely have to degrade the ability of the space-based unit to identify, track, or perform any of the tasks necessary in the BMD process. Indeed, the US Department of Defense fears that the USSR may already have developed and tested a rudimentary DET anti-satellite capability.[32] Laser versus laser battles in space may be the stuff of science fiction literature, but advocates of space-based BMD must also recognize the utility of an adversaries' DET weapons against US space-based assets. Even a space-based laser would have great difficulty in defending itself against a DET weapon that attacked it first.

A second obstacle to effective defense of space-based BMD is direct ascent ASAT technology. Direct ascent ASAT has a smaller boost phase signature than that of an ICBM in boost phase; it is in this phase for a shorter period of time; and it may also accelerate more rapidly than an ascending ICBM. Space-based BMD systems must, therefore, be more sensitive and more responsive than their anti-ICBM tasks require if they are to successfully defend themselves against direct ascent ASAT weapons.

A third obstacle to defense of space-based BMD is space mine technology. As most commonly envisioned, space mines would be lofted into a coorbital position near space-based BMD platforms where they would then passively remain until an opponent's national command authority decided to detonate them to destroy the BMD platform.[33] Two solutions to this problem appear plausible. First, space-based BMDs could be programmed to destroy anything that came within a given distance. Such actions, of course, could lead to war. A second option could be to negotiate an international agreement in which all sides agreed not to introduce other satellites to or near positions in space that are already occupied.

The problem presented by the need to defend space-based BMD is somewhat reduced by the fact that any large-scale attack on the system would provide strategic warning time to the nation whose space assets had been attacked. The strategic warning time afforded by such an attack, however, might be compressed into meaninglessness if one's adversary simultaneously initiated an ASAT attack and launched a counterforce first-strike with his strategic offensive forces. Smaller attacks, moreover, would be more difficult to read, and would, therefore, present less unambiguous warning.

Would BMD be effective against depressed trajectory submarine-launched ballistic missiles (SLBMs) and other strategic offensive systems? Depressed trajectory SLBMs and other shorter range missiles such as the SS-20[34] present special difficulties to BMD because of their shorter flight times. System responsiveness would, therefore, have to be more rapid to cope with such offensive systems. BMD systems would not, of course, be designed to cope with other strategic offensive systems such as cruise missiles and intercontinental bombers, although it is possible that space-based BMD may have some utility against them as well.[35]

What one concludes about the technical feasibility of BMD at the present time is essentially a function of what one hopes BMD will accomplish. Only a leak-proof system could provide a perfectly reliable defense against all forms of strategic offensive delivery vehicles, and such a system will be difficult to develop, deploy, maintain, and operate. If one hopes for a perfect defense, then, one is likely to be disappointed. Below perfection, however, different levels of leakage carry with them different arguments for and against deployment. Barring development of a perfectly reliable BMD, then, this analysis of the implications of technical feasibility drives one to ambiguous conclusions. Given certain capabilities and certain deployment patterns, BMD could improve American and Western security. Given other capabilities and deployments, it would not.

Cost-Effectiveness. BMD cost-effectiveness has been criticized from two different perspectives. The first argues that an effective BMD will cost hundreds of billions of dollars, and therefore, even if BMD is technically feasible, it will be too costly to deploy, operate, and maintain. Much of the cost that would accompany space-based BMD results from the necessity to orbit a sizeable number of BMD platforms. Such platforms, it is generally conceded, must be in low earth orbit to be effective. This fact stems from the propensity of beams to disperse over distance, and from the need for relatively "slow" ABM weapons to be near their intended targets. Therefore, space-based BMD platforms will not be in geosynchrous orbit, and, consequently a large number of BMD platforms would need to be orbited to achieve constant coverage of ICBM, much less SLBM, launch sites. According to one analysis of a space-based laser defense system, as many as 700 satellites with 5-megawatt lasers would have to be orbited to produce effective constant coverage of the current generation of Soviet missiles.[36] Even as ardent an advocate of space-based defense as retired Army Lieutenant General Daniel O. Graham sees a necessity to have 432 operational satellites, each armed with 50 miniature homing vehicles to provide effective constant coverage of

Soviet launch sites.[37] While Graham projects the cost of deploying his satellites as only $10 to $15 billion, most other estimates are several times his total. Indeed, given the uncertainties of the technologies involved in space-based missile defense, any cost projection is highly speculative. However, the initial deployment costs of a space-based missile defense would very likely require tens of billions of dollars at a minimum. Operation and maintenance would add billions of dollars more to the total cost.

A land-based BMD would probably cost less than space-based BMD, but would not by itself have the latter's advantages of boost-phase interception. Thus, unless intercept took place before warhead separation occurred, the number of targets would have multiplied, and the likelihood would increase that at least some warheads would penetrate the defenses to reach their targets. A BMD without space-based components would, therefore, probably be more porous than one with space-based components.

A second criticism of the cost-effectiveness of BMD argues that offensive efforts to penetrate a deployed BMD system would be less costly than efforts to upgrade the deployed BMD system's ability to counter the offense's penetration aids. Thus, it is argued, the defense would always have to spend more to overcome offensive advances than the offense would have to spend to overcome improved defensive capabilities. If this is true, it clearly places any BMD at a distinct cost effectiveness disadvantage in an offensive-defensive cost spiral.

Types of potential penetration aids vary. Hardening the skins of ICBMs is one penetration enhancement option. If ICBMs were hardened, DET weapons would either have to dwell longer on a target to destroy it, or increase the energy of the beam they project. The effect of an ICBM hardening program on a space-based laser defensive system is well illustrated by Figure 2. Assumptions include that constant coverage of launch sites is desired; that the number of ICBMs deployed remains constant at about 1500; and that only missile hardness is used as a penetration enhancement device. Would it cost more to deploy, operate, and maintain the requisite number of space-based lasers than it would cost one's opponent to harden his ICBM arsenal? Again, only speculation is possible.

While hardening may be a cost-effective method of overcoming DET BMD, hardening would provide little penetration

Laser Type	Missile Hardness (in Joules/cm^2)	Space-Based Lasers Required
5 Megawatts	Soft (300)	700
	Medium (2,000)	4,700
	Hard (20,000)	
10 Megawatts	Soft (300)	55
	Medium (2,000)	400
	Hard (20,000)	4,000

Source: Derived from Daniel Kaplan, "Lasers for Missile Defense."

Figure 2. Number of Space-Based Lasers Required to Provide Constant Launch Site Coverage, According to Different ICBM Hardness.

enhancement against ABMs. Even so, penetration aids such as maneuverable reentry vehicles (MaRVs) could present difficulties for ABMs. MaRVs hope to overcome ABMs by altering the ballistic trajectory of the incoming reentry vehicle (RV). An ABM's task of arriving at a predetermined point on a ballistic trajectory at the same instant as the incoming RV is, therefore, rendered impossible for the simple reason that the RV is no longer on that trajectory. Once again, the race would be on between the cost of adding MaRVs to MIRVs and the cost of upgrading ABM capabilities to cope with maneuverability, with the cost-effectiveness winner uncertain at this time.

Even the simplistic penetration enhancement option of overloading a space-based, land-based, or layered BMD system does not present as clear a picture of offensive advantage as is sometimes imagined. To a great extent, the ability to overload a BMD system is determined by the capabilities of the system. Thus, a low-leakage BMD would force a potential attacker to deploy significantly greater numbers of ICBMs than a high-leakage system. Whether or not a potential attacker could derive a cost-effective advantage by seeking to penetrate a BMD by overloading it is determined, therefore, by the BMD capabilities.

In the event that a low-leakage BMD is deployed, a national command authority may opt to enhance its strategic offensive forces' abilities to penetrate a BMD by increasingly deploying air-breathing delivery vehicles such as cruise missiles. At the present time, how effective BMD, in general, would be against such targets is uncertain. Nevertheless, such a change in offensive force structure would have significant implications for crisis stability and deterrence and will be explored below.

Unfortunately, this discussion of cost-effectiveness, like the discussion of technical feasibility, offers no definitive conclusions about the wisdom of future BMD deployment. Costs will be unknown but great, and an expenditure spiral of offensive penetration and countering defensive improvements appears probable. However, which side would enjoy a cost-effectiveness advantage or even whether such calculations have meaning on such an environment is far from certain at this time.

Crisis Stability and Arms Race Stability. The concept of crisis stability refers to a condition in which during a crisis situation neither side perceives a necessity for the immediate employment of its weapons for fear of a preemptive strike by its adversary. In simpler terms, crisis stability exists when a national command authority does not feel pressured to "use 'em or lose 'em," with " 'em" referring to its strategic offensive delivery vehicles. By comparison, arms race stability is the condition that exists when neither side considers it necessary to introduce new channels to the arms race or to increase significantly its present rates of military expenditure. BMD deployment has major implications for both crisis and arms race stability.

The implications that BMD deployment would have for crisis stability are functions of the timing, location, and effectiveness of BMD deployment. In many scenarios, BMD deployment would reduce the first-strike incentive of the side that first deployed BMD. This would be particularly true if a low-leakage BMD system were deployed in defense of strategic retaliatory forces because the possibility of an attempted disarming first strike being successful will decrease as the degree of leakage of the BMD system decreases. Thus, a national command authority's belief in its ability to launch an assured second strike would be improved if it had a low-leakage BMD system defending its retaliatory forces. Additionally, as previously discussed, BMD deployed in defense of counterforce assets would not influence the deploying side to launch a first strike because its countervalue assets—cities—would remain unprotected. BMD deployed in defense of strategic delivery vehicles should then contribute to crisis stability to the extent that it adds uncertainty to the ability of an attacker to successfully carry out a disarming first strike.[38]

Two caveats are necessry. First, BMD deployed in defense of countervalue assets would probably be destabilizing in a crisis scenario. If a low-leakage BMD were deployed to protect countervalue targets, the deploying sides' national command authority may initiate a first strike if it had confidence in the combination of its strategic offensive forces' abilities to destroy a significant percentage of an enemy's nuclear capabilities and of its BMD's abilities to defeat those forces that survived. In this scenario, a low-leakage BMD deployed in defense of countervalue assets would undermine crisis stability. Indeed, both sides may well perceive a necessity to strike first.

The second caveat relates directly to space-based BMD. By its nature, space-based BMD provides protection to both counterforce and countervalue assets. Thus, inevitably, its impact on crisis stability would be ambiguous. On the one hand, a national command authority with confidence in its space-based BMD would not feel pressured to launch its missiles in a crisis, for they would be protected. On the other hand, a national command authority with confidence in its space-based BMD may feel confident enough to initiate a disarming first strike, with its BMD to be used to destroy surviving retaliatory forces. Here, crisis stability would be undermined.

Two other aspects of the implications of BMD for crisis stability deserve comment. First, assuming that deployment of a large-scale BMD system could not proceed in secrecy, the national command authority of a country that trailed in a "BMD race" could be placed in a position of "use 'em or leave 'em useless" with reference to its ICBM or SLBM forces. Would a national leadership placed in such a situation, in fact, sit meekly by and watch construction of a BMD system that rendered its nuclear forces impotent? Or would it seek to frustrate the deployment of its rivals' BMD? Failing that and fearing a "win now, lose later" situation, would it even consider using its missiles before they become useless? Care should be taken not to overstate the case, however, that the deployment of a BMD system has a potential for generating a major crisis in and of itself.

Interestingly, President Reagan suggested one way to avoid the crisis that might almost inevitably result from a unilateral BMD deployment. In a late March 1983 interview with selected newspaper columnists at the White House, Reagan speculated on the possibility that a president:

> . . . could offer to give . . . defensive weapons to (the Soviets) to prove to them that there was no longer any need for keeping these missiles.[39]

Whether such an offer would ever be feasible in the context of American politics is, of course, an open question. Nevertheless, shortly after Reagan's interview was published, the Soviet government proposed that US and Soviet scientists meet to discuss "possible implications of establishing a large-scale ABM system." The United States responded affirmatively to the Soviet suggestion in mid-July 1983.[40]

The course of such talks, if and when they fruitfully conclude, will largely determine the impact that BMD will have on arms race stability. As pointed out earlier, the United States is increasingly committing itself to BMD development, and there is every reason to believe the USSR is doing the same. Thus, in the event of failure of the proposed BMD talks, arms race instability in ballistic missile defense systems appears guaranteed. Moreover, there is some probability that an offensive-defensive expenditure spiral will be forthcoming as well.

The second aspect that deserves comment is the effect that a highly capable space-based BMD with limited endoatmospheric abilities could have on crisis stability. If such a system were developed and deployed, current generations of ICBMs and SLBMs would have reduced utility, and national authorities may opt to restructure their strategic delivery forces to emphasize bombers and air- and sea-launched cruise missiles. The current major threat to crisis stability is the great speed of highly accurate ICBMs and SLBMs. Restructuring toward less time-urgent systems, brought about by space-based BMD, would, in fact, add to crisis stability. Again, however, a renewed arms race in antiaircraft and anticruise capabilities may be the result.

BMD and International Treaties. Three treaties—the 1967 multilateral "Outer Space" Treaty, the 1972 "US-Soviet ABM" Treaty, and the 1974 "US-Soviet ABM" Protocol—could conceivably be affected by a newly deployed BMD system. Specifically, the Outer Space Treaty prohibits the stationing of nuclear weapons and other "weapons of mass destruction" in space; the ABM Treaty prohibits the development, testing, and deployment of space-based ABM systems or components, and, in an agreed statement, notes that BMD systems "based on other physical principles" "would be subject to discussion" by the Standing Consultative Commission established by the treaty; and the 1984 Protocol limits the United States and the Soviet Union, each, to one ABM site located either at its national capital or at a single ICBM launch site.

There is little disagreement that deployment of a large-scale BMD system will necessitate revision of some aspects of the ABM Treaty and, depending on the technologies deployed, possibly the Outer Space Treaty. While some may question whether DET weapons should be defined as weapons of mass destruction, even Caspar Weinberger has recognized that large-scale BMD deployment "may necessitate" an update of the ABM Treaty.[41] Even with this recognition, however, the United States assured the Soviet Union shortly after Reagan's March speech that the speech "in no way" should be interpreted as reducing the US commitment to the ABM Treaty.[42]

Short of a withdrawal from the treaty by either of the parties, revision of the treaty would probably take place under the auspices of the Standing Consultative Commission. Negotiations would occur either in a special session or during one of the review periods mandated at five-year intervals by the Treaty. Indeed, when the United States indicated its willingness to begin scientific discussions with the USSR over the implications of BMD, the United States insisted that those discussions be held either in the context of the Standing Consultative Commission or of the ongoing Strategic Arms Reduction Talks. Whether mutually satisfactory BMD agreements could be negotiated or ratified is a tendentious question.

Strategic Thought and Deterrence Theory. An operational BMD system would have a major impact on strategic thought in general and deterrence theory in particular. Throughout most of the nuclear age, deterrence theory has been based on the certainty of retaliation. Ultimately, this meant that if the Soviet Union launched a first strike on the United States, the United States would retain enough of its strategic forces to render the USSR inoperative as a functioning modern society. In recent years, however, the expansion of Soviet nuclear capabilities and the development of highly accurate MIRVs have undermined the certainty of deterrence as some strategic theorists calculated that disarming first strikes may now be possible.

However, if BMD were deployed, new elements of attack uncertainty would be interjected into such calculations.[43] While highly accurate MIRVs introduced a level of certainty into counterforce strike planning, BMD could reduce this destabilizing level of certainty. Even with a high-leakage BMD, planners contemplating a disarming first strike would have to ask the question: "What if the BMD is more effective than we project?" Thus, uncertainty again could play a larger role in deterrence.

BMD would also have a major impact on the attractiveness of theories of nuclear war-fighting. If one or both sides were increasingly uncertain about whether its warheads would reach their targets, the likelihood that strategic forces would be used to achieve a particular military objective would probably be reduced. The growth of uncertainty brought about by deploying a BMD may, therefore, negate the feasibility of war-fighting strategies made possible by MIRVs and great accuracy.

It must be reemphasized that the key factor in determining the impact of BMD on deterrence is whether a potential opponent would view BMD as a threat to the utility of his retaliatory forces. If any BMD were deployed so that all counterforce assets were protected, no opponent could realistically view his ability to deliver a successful retaliatory attack as being jeopardized. Conversely, if a moderate-, low-, or no-leakage BMD were deployed to defend countervalue assets, a potential enemy might conclude that the deploying side was seeking to attain a retaliation-free first strike capability. Such a perception could be disastrous for deterrence. This differentiation has serious implications for space-based defense. A potential enemy could not discriminate between space-based BMD intended for counterforce defense and space-based BMD intended for countervalue defense. In this sense, land-based BMD appears clearly preferable to its space-based counterpart. The tradeoff, however, is that a low- or no-leakage land-based BMD is likely to be more difficult and more costly to achieve.

BMD and the Western Alliance. What effect would BMD have on our NATO and Japanese allies? The answer depends on the type and capability of the system deployed. If a BMD were deployed that provided the same level of protection to alliance countervalue targets (cities) as it did for American countervalue targets, little reason exists to imagine that alliance views of BMD would be different from American views. However, if less BMD protection were afforded to foreign cities than to those of the United States, the impact on the Western alliance could be immense.

Throughout the nuclear era, the defense of Europe and Japan has been coupled directly to the American strategic nuclear arsenal. Any Soviet aggression in either theater invited, as a last resort, American nuclear response. As the USSR developed its own nuclear delivery capabilities, thereby holding the United States at greater risk, American willingness to use nuclear weapons in defense of its allies became less credible. American allies responded to this new situation in various ways. Some ignored the implications of US vulnerability and continued to rely upon collective security; some sought their own nuclear deterrent; others emphasized indigenous conventional forces; and still others stressed the necessity for peaceful relations with the Soviet Union.

BMD deployment would lead inevitably to readjustments of policy. While the elimination of American vulnerability to nuclear attack could, on the one hand, renew allied faith in the credibility of the American deterrent, it could also point out to United States allies that they remained vulnerable, while the United States pursued the destabilized and dangerous goal of military superiority. Given the vagaries of international politics, such a perception might lead to one of two distressing possibilities: neutralization in Europe and Japan or the upgrading or creation of European and Japanese nuclear retaliatory forces. Here, it should be remembered that Great Britain, in particular, strongly opposed large-scale BMD deployment during US-Soviet SALT I negotiations because BMD threatened to degrade the credibility of Great Britain's nuclear deterrent.[44]

Conversely, if BMD deployment were undertaken around US ICBM sites, a Japanese and European response may be more muted. Currently, the United States believes there is a higher potential for a Soviet disarming first strike during an intense crisis than do the American allies. Any American defense of its own strategic forces would probably be seen as simply a US effort to meet a peculiarly American fear, but an effort which, nevertheless, would have only limited implications for its allies. One would expect similar perceptions within the Warsaw Pact if the USSR were to deploy BMD to protect its ICBM forces.

However, in the event that the USSR were to deploy unilaterally a low-leakage or no-leakage BMD, protecting countervalue sites, the Western alliance undoubtedly would be shaken. Europeans and Japanese, already feeling vulnerable in the current strategic environment, would become even more so. America's strategic deterrent, then, would have even less credibility. In this scenario, "Finlandization" would become increasingly attractive to Europeans and Japanese.

CONCLUSIONS

Ballistic Missile Defense clearly presents American and Western security planners with a staggering number of possibilities. The uncertainties pertaining to future BMD technologies as well as the unknown constraints of deployment and operational costs make acquisition decisions highly problematic. As a result, neither the proponents nor opponents of BMD in space-based, land-based, or layered deployment modes present evidence that drives one to an unambiguous set of final conclusions.

But some observations are in order. First, all American assessments of BMD must proceed not only from the vantage point of American intentions, but also from the outlook of Soviet perceptions. Soviet security planners cannot and will not accept United States assurances that the development of BMD was intended to protect the United States against a Soviet first strike, rather than providing the United States the means to launch its own first strike against the USSR. To the Soviet planner, American efforts to develop BMD carry with them all of the implied dangers of an American drive for strategic superiority; these, of course, are the same dangers that American planners perceive in corresponding Soviet efforts. The second observation relates specifically to the fact that space-based BMD could be used for either counterforce or countervalue defense. Since no planner can verify that an opponent would limit his space-based BMD to counterforce defense, all planners must view an opponent's space-based BMD as an adjunct to his offensive forces. Thus, unless both sides can arrive at a space-based BMD regime simultaneously, space-based BMD inevitably must appear destabilizing to the side that trails in its deployment. With the dangers that instability presents, either simultaneous deployment or nondeployment of space-based BMD appears preferable to any nonsymmetrical deployment.[45]

Beyond prevention of increased strategic instability, what advantages would accrue to simultaneous deployment or nondeployment? Assuming that either a low-leakage or no-leakage system can be developed, simultaneous deployment could lead to a reduction of the nuclear threat facing the superpowers. From the perspectives of both the United States and the Soviet Union, this would of course be desirable. (Third countries such as China may be expected to have a significantly different perspective, however.) However, if only a moderate- or high-leakage system becomes technically feasible, no additional advantages become apparent. The second option, a decision to forego space-based BMD, clearly carries with it a considerable cost savings as well as the advantage that neither side could attempt to punch holes in the other's space-based BMD system with a surprise coordinated DET and ICBM attack in an effort to gain strategic superiority. These are both considerable advantages, but they can only be attained through a negotiated decision not to deploy such defensive systems.

Indeed, the single most persuasive argument for space-based BMD is that it provides the opportunity to intercept and destroy an opponent's ICBMs which incorporate MIRVs in the boost phase before warhead separation occurs. However, if the United States and the Soviet Union were to build and deploy the small, single RV ICBMs advocated by the President's Commission on Strategic Forces (the so-called Scowcroft Commission),[46] one of the strongest rationales for space-based BMD would be removed.

A third observation relates specifically to land-based BMD deployed for counterforce defense. The preceding analysis suggests that under most conditions, possession by both sides of a counterforce or "point" BMD enhances stability since it increases the uncertainties that a first strike could be disarming. Conversely, land-based BMD deployed for countervalue defense suggests that instability would increase because of the linkage that could occur in an opponent's eyes between an offensive first strike and a countervalue defensive effort.

As usual, however, the choices the United States is likely to face are not limited to the relatively easy ones of space-based defense versus land-based defense, or of countervalue defense versus counterforce defense. Given the emphasis that both the United States and the Soviet Union are placing on space- and land-based systems using both conventional and DET technologies, the most likely future choices, undoubtedly, will include mixes of both technologies and both basing modes. It is imperative, then, as the capabilities and costs of BMD and space-based defense become clearer, that strategy be developed along with technology. To do what is technologically feasible while giving only limited thought to the implications that technologies carry with them is to repeat what has been done too often in the past. Deploying military technologies without careful consideration of the implications of their deployment too often has led not to an increase in security, but to an increase in threat. BMD and space-based defenses, then, are the same two-edged swords that H-bombs and MIRVs have become.

ENDNOTES

1. Transcript of President Ronald Reagan's March 23 speech on military spending, *The New York Times*, March 24, 1983, p. 20.

2. For a sampling of reaction to Reagan's speech, see Patrick Callahan, "The Delusion of Defense Once Again," *America*, April 30, 1983, pp. 340-41; Thomas H. Karas, "The Star Wars Scenario," *The Nation*, April 9, 1983, pp. 444-445; Daniel Kaplan, "Lasers for Missile Defense," *Bulletin of the Atomic Scientists*, May 1983, pp. 5-9; and Charles Mohr, "Scientists Dubious Over Missile Plan," *The New York Times*, March 25, 1983, p. A8.

3. See, for example, Abram Chayes and Jerome B. Weisner, eds., *ABM: An Evaluation of the Decision to Deploy an Antiballistic Missile System*, New York: Harper and Row, 1969.

4. Donald M. Snow, *The Nuclear Future: Toward a Strategy of Uncertainty*, University, Alabama: University of Alabama, 1983, p. 86.

5. For one detailed discussion of a layered BMD system that combines space-based DET and conventional weapons with land-based ABM capabilities, see the Heritage Foundation's "High Frontiers" study, contained in *Department of Defense Authorization for Appropriations for Fiscal Year 1983: Hearings before the Committee on Armed Services*, US Senate, 97th Cong. 2d sess., pp. 4884-4904.

6. For texts of both, see US Arms Control and Disarmament Agency (ACDA), *Arms Control and Disarmament Agreements*, Washington: 1982, pp. 139-142, and pp. 162-163, respectively.

7. E. C. Aldridge, Jr., and Robert L. Maust, Jr., "SALT Implications of BMD Options," in Michelle Marcouiller, ed., *US Arms Control Objectives and the Implications for Ballistic Missile Defense: Proceedings of a Symposium Held at the Center for Science and International Affairs, Harvard University, November 1-2, 1979*, Cambridge: Center for Science and International Affairs, 1980, pp. 55-56.

8. "Airborne Laser Disables Missiles in Air Force Test," *The Washington Post*, July 26, 1983, p. A5; and "Army to Flight Test Non-nuclear ABM," *Aviation Week and Space Technology*, January 24, 1983, pp. 30-31.

9. Richard Halloran, "Military Divided Over Space Policy," *The New York Times*, July 5, 1983, p. 11.

10. For the complete text of the Outer Space Treaty, see ACDA, pp. 510-555.

11. *Department of Defense Authorization for Appropriation for Fiscal Year 1984, Hearings before the Committee on Armed Services*, US Senate, 98th Cong., 1st sess., p. 488.

12. The Soviet Union, it should be noted, is developing its own version of the space shuttle, although it is several years behind the United States.

13. *Department of Defense Appropriations for Fiscal Year 1983: Hearing before the Committee on Appropriations*, US Senate 97th Cong., 2d sess., p. 558.

14. Governmental space and BMD activity was paralleled by expanded private research and publishing in the fields. From 1981 to early 1983 alone, at least six books were published on the military uses of space. The books of differing quality and ideological outlook, are David Baker, *The Shape of Wars to Come*, New York: Stein and Day, 1982; Blupendra Jasani, ed., *Outer Space—A New Dimension of the Arms Race*, Cambridge: Taylor and Frances, 1982; Thomas Karas, *The New High Ground*, New York: Simon and Schuster, 1983; David Ritchie, *Spacewar*, New York: Atheneum, 1982; and G. Harry Stine, *Confrontation in Space*, Englewood Cliffs: Prentice Hall, 1981.

15. Richard Halloran, "US Military Operations in Space to be Expanded Under Air Force," *The New York Times*, June 22, 1982, p. A19.

16. Brad Knickerbocker, "Space Race Takes Military Turn," *Christian Science Monitor*, May 26, 1982, p. 1.

17. "Reagan Policy Expected to Aid Space Station Definition Work," *Aviation Week and Space Technology*, July 12, 1982, See also "Air Force Space Plan to Orr This Week," *Defense Week*, July 5, 1983, pp. 1, 19d.

18. These events are detailed in "Air Force to Orr This Week," *Defense Week*, July 5, 1983, pp. 1, 19; Halloran, "US Military Operations in Space to be Expanded under Air Force;" and Clarence A. Robinson, "Defense Department Backs Space-Based Missile Defense," *Aviation Week and Space Technology*, September 27, 1982, pp. 14-16.

19. Gelb, *The New York Times*, March 25, 1983, p. A1.

20. Halloran, "Air Force Seeking Joint Space Unit," *The New York Times*, June 19, 1983, p. A17.

21. *Department of Defense Authorization for Appropriations, for Fiscal Year 1983*, US Senate, 97th Cong., 2d sess., p. 4854.

22. *Department of Defense Appropriations for Fiscal Year 1983*, p. 601.

23. Halloran, "Pentagon Seeking More in Research," *The New York Times*, April 14, 1983, p. A13.

24. None of the preceding discussion should be interpreted to imply that previous administrations completely ignore BMD and the military implications of space. Jimmy Carter's space policy, for example, was set forth in Presidential Decision 37. See "Space Policy Directive Broadens Civil Programs," *Aviation Week and Space Technology*, May 29, 1978, p. 23; Richard D. Lyons, "Administration Discloses Plans for Use of Space Technology," *The New York Times*, June 20, 1978, p. 84; "Space Policy Bills Prepared for Introduction," *Aviation Week and Space Technology*, September 25, 1978, p. 14; and Robert Hotz, "Space Policy Debate," *Aviation Week and Space Technology*, December 4, 1978, p. 11.

25. "Panel on Missile Defense," *The New York Times*, April 2, 1983, p. A38; and Clarence A. Robinson, Jr., "Panel Urges Defense Technology Advances," *Aviation Week and Space Technology*, October 17, 1983, pp. 16-18.

26. These differentiations may be found in Snow, pp. 68-69, 86-88.

27. *Ibid*.

28. For a discussion of the latter, see the Heritage Foundation's "High Frontier" study.

29. Warhead separation refers to the separation of MIRVs from the MIRV-ejection platform, or "bus."

30. See Robinson, Jr., "Panel Urges Defense Technology," p. 16.

31. BMD success rates can be leveraged beyond the leakage rate of the system if BMD is combined with deceptive basing. For example, a single LoADS unit deployed to defend the single shelter where an ICBM was housed in a multiple protective shelter (MPS) basing system would force multiple targeting of every protective shelter. For a discussion of the cumulative effects of LoADS and MPS, see Raymond E. Starsman, *Ballistic Missile Defense and Deceptive Basing: A New Calculus for the Defense of ICBMs*," *The National Defense University Monograph Series* 81-1, Washington: NDU Press, 1981.

32. Richard Burt, "US Says Russians Develop Satellite-Killing Laser," *The New York Times*, May 22, 1980, p. A9.

33. For references to space mines see John Noble Wilford, "Despite 1967 US-Soviet Treaty, Drive for Space Weapons Goes On," *The New York Times*, March 27, 1983, pp. A1, A14.

34. From a Soviet perspective, this would be true of the US Pershing II.

35. US Air Force Chief of Research and Development, Lieutenant General Kelley Burke, raised this possibility shortly after President Reagan's March 23d address, when he noted that the USSR could orbit an antiaircraft satellite weapon by the end of the 1980's. See "Soviet Speed, US Outlook, in Laser Weapons Reported," *Christian Science Monitor*, April 23, 1982, p. 2.

36. See Daniel Kaplan, "Lasers for Missile Defense," *Bulletin of the Atomic Scientists*, May 1983, pp. 5-9.

37. See the "High Frontiers" study.

38. For more detailed discussion of what has been termed "a strategy of uncertainty," see Snow, pp. 122-167.

39. "Transcript of Group Interview with President at White House," *The New York Times*, March 30, 1983, p. A14.

40. Charles W. Corrdry, "Soviets Seek Talks on 'Star Wars' Plan," *Baltimore Sun*, June 18, 1983, p. 1; and Walter Pincus, "Soviets Told US Ready for Space-Arms Talks," *The Washington Post*, July 14, 1983, p. A18.

41. John Darnton, "Weinberger Says ABM Pact May Ultimately Need Amending," *The New York Times*, March 25, 1983, p. A9.

42. Bernard Gwertzman, "Soviet Told by US ABM Pact Stand," *The New York Times*, March 27, 1983, p. A1.

43. Snow, pp. 122-167.

44. Christopher Makins, "Bring in the Allies," *Foreign Policy*, Summer 1979, p. 97.

45. This observation raises a difficult question that extends beyond the scope of this paper, but which nevertheless must be raised here. Put simply, the question is, how, in the event of simultaneous deployment, should BMD systems be structured so that they provide equal security to nonsymmetrical strategic nuclear forces?

46. See "Report of the President's Commission on Strategic Forces," Washington: US Government Printing Office, 1983.

6

START: PROBLEMS AND PROSPECTS

Robert Kennedy

Arms control has been a means of achieving US foreign policy objectives since the earliest days of the Republic. In 1817, the United States and Great Britain signed the Rush-Bagot agreement regulating naval forces on the Great Lakes. That agreement was one of the first freely negotiated arms control agreements and it is one of the oldest still in existence. Since that time, the United States, responding to an increasingly complex and interdependent world, has been actively engaged in seeking the regulation of armaments.

The advent of the nuclear weapon, however, has added a new dimension to modern warfare and has increased the urgency of efforts designed to regulate and control armaments. Total war no longer simply represents a threat to the survival of a particular state. Rather, the existence of civilization as we know it is now threatened by an awesome capacity for mass destruction which is now in the hands of mankind. In recognition of this fundamental truth, the United States has undertaken a series of international negotiations aimed at limiting the further expansion and profileration of nuclear capabilities.

The most visible and perhaps most important arms control efforts, however, have been aimed at stabilizing the strategic military relationships between those nations most capable of mass destruction, the superpowers. To this end, the United States and the Soviet Union have engaged in Strategic Arms Limitation Talks (SALT) I and II, and are now engaged in a new round of strategic arms reduction talks (START).

THE BEGINNINGS

The origins of SALT can be traced to increasing concerns in Washington during the mid-1960's over growing Soviet strategic might.[1] Two impulses were set in motion by the expansion of Soviet strategic offensive and defensive power which followed in the wake of the Cuban missile crisis. One was to hedge against future Soviet and Chinese strategic nuclear capabilities by expanding US capabilities. The other was to seek to limit the further expansion of the strategic forces of the superpowers. Both impulses existed simultaneously and, indeed, the implicatons of the first impulse may have increased interest in the second in both Washington and Moscow.

In 1964, the United States took its first hesitant steps toward controlling strategic arms by formally proposing that an equal number of Soviet and American long-range bombers be removed from operational inventories. Later that same year, in what has often been considered a rhetorical effort, Washington proposed a "freeze" on the number and characteristics of nuclear offensive and defensive vehicles. The proposal, which also called for on-site inspection as a means of verifying compliance, was rejected by Moscow. Nevertheless, by late 1966 and early 1967 many in the defense community were becoming involved, in one way or another, in crafting or responding to initiatives designed to seek limits on strategic forces.

After a series of interchanges between Washington and Moscow in direct response to US initiatives by President Johnson during his 1967 Glassboro meeting with Alexei Kosygin, First Deputy Foreign Minister V. V. Kuznetsov announced at the United Nations on May 20, 1968, that the Soviet Union was "ready to reach an agreement on practical steps for the limitation and subsequent reduction of the strategic means for delivering nuclear weapons."[2] The Soviet invasion of Czechoslovakia in August 1968 and the change of US administrations in 1969 resulted in a postponement of the actual negotiations until late 1969. The SALT process, nonetheless, had been set in motion.

WHY SALT?

The answer to the question: Why did the Soviet Union and the United States engage in SALT? remains yet incomplete. John Newhouse in *Cold Dawn* noted that SALT I was a political process concerned with finding an equilibrium in which the great powers felt secure.[3] One might go further and argue that the Soviet-American strategic arms control process, in an abstract sense, was the natural outgrowth of an attempt by the superpowers not only to stabilize their potentially threatening nuclear relationship, but also to orchestrate their continued dominance over the other countries in the international system. In this sense, SALT could be viewed as (1) a means of achieving strategic stability at weapons levels sufficiently high to mark clearly the superpower status of both the Soviet Union and the United States; and (2) a process by which both powers maintained that status through mutually agreed upon increases in their capabilities during the successive stages of SALT. Certain other arms control initiatives, then, could be viewed as part of a complementary pattern. While the task of SALT might be seen as regulating the upper limits of superpower strategic nuclear capabilities (always insuring a safe margin of superiority over lesser nuclear powers), the nonproliferation treaty, the Latin American nuclear free zone, and other such agreements could be viewed as an attempt by the superpowers to prohibit others from entering the nuclear competition.

However, to argue that SALT was simply the result of a Machiavellian attempt by the superpowers to orchestrate their continued dominance over the internatonal system is, of course, an oversimplification of the complex factors which drew Washington and Moscow to the conference table. Such an approach can also be faulted in that it attributes to the superpowers a greater degree of long-range thinking and planning than the historical record would support. Indeed, evidence suggests that SALT was founded on more concrete objectives sought by the leadership elites in both the United States and the Soviet Union. To be sure, bureaucratic, institutional, economic, as well as strategic factors played a role in propelling both Washington and Moscow to the conference table.

In Washington, bureaucratic and institutional factors surrounding the debate over whether the United States should deploy an antiballistic missile (ABM) system served as an immediate impetus to negotiation.[4] In a larger sense, however, the nagging fear of nuclear holocaust coupled with the continued expansion of Soviet nuclear capabilities and prospects of a two-sided nuclear exchange provided ample impetus for negotiations aimed at controlling and restricting the growth of strategic forces, especially at a time when increasing demands were being placed on the federal dollar and competition for funds was tight within the Department of Defense itself.

By 1967, the growth in US intercontinental ballistic missile (ICBM) and submarine-launched ballistic missile (SLBM) forces had reached its peak, while the number of US strategic bombers continued to decline. In the winter of 1967 and in 1968, the intelligence community was reporting that the Soviet Union was nearing parity with the United States in land-based ICBMs and was believed to be deploying its first solid fueled missiles. In his January 1968 defense posture statement, Secretary of Defense McNamara told Congress that the Soviet Union had more than doubled its ICBM force—from 340 to 720—in the space of a year.[5] To many in the Washington community, negotiations with the Soviet Union on limiting strategic armaments suggested a means of capping the growth of Soviet strategic capabilities. To be sure, a few saw SALT as a process through which the United States might preserve a margin of strategic superiority while avoiding the costs of a full-scale strategic arms race with the Soviet Union. However, many proponents of arms negotiations believed that Moscow had come to share Washington's concern over the dangers of nuclear war and that with an impending, if not extant, parity at the strategic level, the time was ripe for an agreement limiting US and Soviet strategic arsenals. Thus, through SALT the Soviet strategic threat might be fixed. US strategic weapons procurement planning could then take place against a more predictable backdrop of SALT-constrained Soviet capabilities. The invulnerability of the US strategic retaliatory forces could be preserved. The general strategic relationship between the United States and the Soviet Union might be stabilized. Mechanisms for crisis management and conflict avoidance needed to prevent the occurrence of accidental or unintended wars might be developed; tensions might be reduced;

and, a costly arms race might be avoided. As a result, defense planning might come to be dominated by a measure of rationality as the need to hedge against the "greater-than-expected" threat receded.[6]

In February 1970, three months after the opening of the SALT talks in Helsinki, President Nixon emphasized the importance of the SALT process. Underscoring the precarious nature of the military balance between the United States and the Soviet Union and the potential for violence and devastation should deterrence fail, he stated:

> There is no area in which we and the Soviet Union . . . have a greater common interest than in reaching agreement with regard to arms control.[7]

Like Washington, Moscow was driven to the conference table in response to a number of strategic and domestic economic, bureaucratic and institutional factors. While it remains impossible to determine with any degree of certainty the specific factors that led to the final decision of the leadership in Moscow to travel the SALT path, several concerns probably affected Moscow's decision to enter into negotiations.

First, by the late 1960's the Soviet Union had deployed a sizeable strategic arsenal. Nevertheless, the USSR still fell short of the United States in overall strategic nuclear capabilities and, indeed, in most other measures of national power. From a Soviet point of view, the initiation of SALT and the existence of strategic nuclear parity suggested by the talks themselves were likely to have a favorable impact on third party perceptions of the position of the Soviet Union in the world community of nations. Thus, Soviet leaders could reason that SALT confirmed the great power status of the USSR and promised to be psychologically advantageous to Moscow in the Soviet-American competition for world influence.

Second, despite its improved strategic nuclear capabilities, Soviet leadership remained concerned over the strategic military position of the USSR vis-a-vis the United States. The Kremlin had invested heavily in the early and mid-1960's to improve its strategic position. Soviet leaders were clearly concerned over the implications of US developments in the field of missile warheads, specifically the multiple independently targetable reentry vehicle (MIRV), and in the field of ABM defense. MIRV threatened to multiply US capabilities many fold while ABM represented a potential for limiting the effectiveness of Soviet strategic forces. In combination, such developments might, once again, yield psychological advantage to the West at Soviet expense. Soviet leaders were also concerned that when President Johnson left office in January of 1969, he might be replaced by someone less committed to arms control.[8]

Third, Soviet domestic economic pressures, no doubt, played a role in the Kremlin's move toward SALT. Lawrence Caldwell, a prominent observer of the Soviet system, writing in 1971, noted that those in the Soviet bureaucracy who were concerned with modernizaton had "sensed that the Soviet economy had entered a qualitatively new stage of its development—one dictated by the elevation of science and technology to the status of direct productive forces."[9] This new stage of development demanded that the bureaucracy provide additional resources if further development was to be expected not only in heavy industry, but especially in lighter technologically intensive electronics and chemical industries, and in the consumer sectors, all of which had become more capital-intensive. To secure these resources, the so-called modernists, according to Caldwell, favored a tighter reign on military spending.[10]

Finally, by the 1950's, some Soviet leaders had come to share a more generalized concern over the effects of nuclear war. In 1954, Malenkov wrote that nuclear warfare could result in the mutual destruction of both capitalist and communist societies.[11] For Malenkov, the awesome destructive potential of a cataclysmic conflict between communist and capitalist camps had apparently warranted serious reconsideraton of the Leninist conception of war as a precursor of world revolution. Khrushchev, initially opposed to Malenkov's unorthodox views, came to hold similar views concerning the dangers of nuclear conflict. By the mid-1950's, Khrushchev was espousing the idea of "peaceful coexistence" as the safest and most reliable form of class warfare in the international arena. In 1961, Khrushchev warned that "within 60 days of an atomic attack 500 million to 750 million people could perish" and concluded that "sober calculation of the inevitable consequence of nuclear war is an indispensable requirement for pursuing a consistent policy of preventing war."[12] Since then, a number of Soviet civilian and military analysts have spoken of nuclear war between the superpowers as "a great danger for all mankind," the "extreme catastrophic threat" which would be "suicidal for both" and would bring "unprecedented calamities to all mankind."[13] Similarly, Leonid Brezhnev cautioned that nuclear war could result in "hundreds of millions of deaths," in the "mass annihilation of peoples," and spoke of the need to eliminate "the threat of thermonuclear catastrophy."[14] Such themes were reiterated in the prepared statement presented at the first business meeting of the two SALT delegations in Helsinki in November 1969.[15]

In sum, for the Soviet leadership, the idea of limiting or controlling nuclear arsenals through strategic arms control negotiations was consonant not only with their desire to project and maintain an image of strategic parity with the United States, their interests in precluding threatening weapons developments by the United States, and their attempts to secure resources for economic development and expansion, but also with their general concerns over nuclear war. Moreover, SALT had an appeal within the context of detente or "peaceful coexistence." At a time when Soviet leadership had become increasingly concerned with the decided anti-Soviet character of an emerging China, the idea of pursuing detente and arms negotiations with the West, no doubt, was considered a promising means of avoiding hostile confrontation on all fronts.

REACHING AGREEMENT

Despite, however, an apparent Washington-Moscow harmony of interests—forged of imperatives which mandate that each seek to reduce the other's incentives and capability to initiate a strategic nuclear exchange—negotiations on limiting strategic armaments have been difficult and at times strained, and a mutually acceptable follow-on agreement to the SALT I accord remains elusive. Like SALT I, SALT II was criticized in the United States from both the left and the right. Some liberal critics registered their disapproval over the failure of SALT II to restrain the arms race. Even before the signing of SALT II at Vienna, Senators Mark Hatfield, George McGovern, and William Proxmire, in a letter to President Carter, announced that they found the SALT II treaty "very difficult, if not impossible" to support. They criticized the treaty for not being "a true step toward arms reductions."[16] According to Senator Proxmire what was needed were "real reductions in the land-based missiles on both sides."[17]

On the other hand, in testimony before the Senate Committee on Foreign Relations, Paul Nitze, a leading opponent of SALT II argued:

> Despite the superficial appearance of equality, the agreements are unequal . . . they put no effective limit on Soviet offensive capabilities. Rather than forcing a reduction, there will be a continuous and large increase in Soviet capabilities during the term of the treaty . . . [and] in net terms, the strategic balance will move from a position not far from parity to one of Soviet strategic superiority.[18]

Similarly, Lieutenant General Edward Rowny, after serving as the Joint Chiefs of Staff representative to the SALT II negotiations, testified that SALT II:

> . . . is not in our interest since it is inequitable, unverifiable, undermines deterrence, contributes to instability and could adversely affect NATO security and allied coherence.[19]

One critic even suggested that SALT II was "Devoid of merit," that "the West needs the MX ICBM, and it needs cruise missiles . . . , and that SALT II and particularly the future negotiations on a SALT III can only hinder rational Western defense planning . . . ."[20] While the reasons offered by critics of both SALT I and SALT II have been many and varied, their objections have underscored the complexities of achieving a strategic arms limitations agreement perceived as equitable by both sides.

Like the three presidents before him, President Reagan has committed his administration to a continued dialogue with the Soviet Union on nuclear weapons reductions. Early in February 1981, shortly after taking office, President Reagan indicated his willingness to meet with the Soviet leadership to discuss legitimate reductions in nuclear weapons.[21] Mindful of the criticisms of both SALT I and II, however, he ordered an in-depth review of US arms control policy. The objectives of the review were to examine the lessons of previous SALT negotiations and to explore alternative solutions to the problem of reducing strategic nuclear forces. On May 9, 1982, at Eureka College, the President announced his intent to depart from what he considered the past course of events. According to Richard Burt, Assistant Secretary of State for European Affairs, instead of seeking an agreement which would do no more than codify and marginally restrict the growth of strategic forces, the President was determined to seek an equitable and verifiable arms agreement that would actually reduce the levels of nuclear weapons on both sides and make a meaningful contribution to securing a stable nuclear balance.[22]

Despite the President's interest in achieving a stable US-Soviet nuclear balance, differing strategic perspectives, strategies, and doctrine; different approaches to deterrence; dissimilar force structures, weapon systems characteristics and capabilities; and different historical, geographical, and political/bureaucratic factors impede the establishment of an equitable balance of nuclear capabilities through strategic arms control negotiations.

THE PROBLEMS OF START

Threat Comparability. The first major difficulty confronting Soviet and American negotiators is the problem resulting from dissimilar perceptions of threat. The problem of threat comparability focuses on the question of *whose* forces should be counted in threat calculations and why. It addresses the questions of who are the potential adversaries and what is an equitable arms control solution. Thus, the problem of threat comparability adds to a two-sided negotiation, a multidimensional aspect which further complicates equitability calculations.

The principal threat to US security, the security of US allies, and US worldwide interests is the Soviet Union. Thus, for the United States, one primary objective throughout the strategic arms control process has been to establish and maintain a balance of US and Soviet strategic capabilities. In his report to Congress in 1972, President Nixon spoke of the need to establish an equivalence of US-Soviet capabilities that would yield "no unilateral advantage and would contribute to a more stable strategic environment."[23] Concerned that the SALT I agreement had conceded some numerical advantages to the Soviet Union, both houses of Congress, in their approval of the SALT I treaty, signaled their commitment to nothing less than a balance of US-Soviet strategic arms by urging the President to "seek a future treaty that . . .

would not limit the United States to levels of intercontinental strategic forces inferior to limits provided for the Soviet Union."[24]

During the SALT II process, then Secretary of Defense Harold Brown defined what he meant by balance, or "essential equivalence" as he called it, and underscored the importance of US-Soviet equivalence as an objective. He said that by "essential equivalence" he meant:

> ... any advantage in force characteristics enjoyed by the Soviets are offset by other US advantages. Although we must avoid a resort to one-for-one matching of individual indices of capability, our strategic nuclear posture must not be, and must not seem to be, inferior in performance to the capabilities of the Soviet Union.[25]

He went on to note that equivalence serves several major political and military purposes:

> It helps to ensure that political perceptions are in accord with military realities, and it minimizes the probability that opposing strategic forces will be used to seek diplomatic advantage over us. It reduces the chance that one side or the other will become vulnerable to charges of a bomber or missile gap and contributes thereby to strategic stability. It enhances stability in a crisis by reducing incentives for either side to strike first or preempt.[26]

Similarly, President Reagan has spoken of the need to achieve a stabilizing balance with the Soviet Union.[27] Indeed, the belief that it is essential that the United States accept nothing less than parity with the Soviet Union has been a central tenet of US strategic arms control policy.

The Soviet Union, on the other hand, has never sought through the SALT process an "essential equivalence" or a specific "balance" with the United States. Rather, Moscow has stressed the need to achieve "equal security" through an agreement which insures that neither side, "directly or indirectly" is afforded a "one-sided advantage."[28] This theme has been stressed by the USSR throughout the SALT/START process and has become a central issue in the negotiations on limiting intermediate-range nuclear forces (INF) in Geneva. It is rooted in a perception of threat which differs substantially from that held by the United States. From the Soviet point of view, of the five powers which possess "strategic" nuclear weapons, four must be considered potentially hostile. Thus, in the Soviet planner's view the strategic forces of Britain, France, and China, as well as those of the United States, must be considered in calculations concerning balance, if the Soviet Union is to achieve a sense of security equal to that of the United States.

While the nuclear capabilities of Britain, France, and China are dwarfed by the strategic might of the Soviet Union and the United States, the composite of those capabilities is sufficient to destroy every city and town in the Soviet Union with a population greater than 100,000.[29] Thus, while Washington has been compelled to seek an agreement with the Soviet Union that prohibits Moscow from achieving a real or perceived superiority of strategic forces, Soviet leaders have been concerned that they not be placed at an overall strategic disadvantage as a result of capabilities which they see as potentially additive to US strategic might.

At the close of the SALT I negotiatons, the Soviet Union registered its apprehensions over non-US strategic forces. In a unilateral statement issued on May 24, 1972 and repeated on May 26 (the day of the signing of the US-Soviet "Interim Agreement"), the Soviet Union declared that for the period of the agreement should US allies in NATO increase the number of their modern ballistic missile submarines, which they had operational or under construction at that time, the Soviet Union had the right to a corresponding increase in ballistic missile submarines. The United States rejected this attempt by the Soviet Union to include the forces of third parties in bilateral strategic arms control agreements.[30] Undoubtedly, the US rejection was founded on its own perceived need to maintain nothing less than a balance with the Soviet Union for military as well as psycho-political reasons. Almost certainly, the rejection was also based on two other factors. First, the nuclear forces of the British and French as well as those of the Chinese were already offset by Soviet immediate- and medium-range nuclear capabilities. And, second, no long-term effort to control and limit strategic armaments could be sustained if parties to the negotiations demanded to have strategic forces equal to those of all possible combinations of potential opponents.

During the later stages of SALT II, Moscow again demonstrated an evident concern over non-US strategic forces, especially as the United States and China moved toward rapprochement. No doubt, the Kremlin continues to have misgivings about the status of British, French, and Chinese forces; witness Soviet efforts to include British and French forces in the current INF negotiations.

No long-term solution, however, to the treatment of third party strategic nuclear forces has yet been found. Thus, the problem of threat comparability remains, as the Soviet Union and the United States seek an equitable balance of strategic armaments through arms control negotiations.

Definition. The problem of definition is related to the question of threat comparability in that it affects both Soviet and American perceptions of what constitutes "equal security" or "balance" at the strategic level. The problem of definition focuses on *which* forces of the two superpowers should be considerd in strategic arms control negotiations and why.

Are forces "strategic" because they are of a range sufficient to strike targets at great distances? Or are they "strategic" because they can strike the territory of the other superpower? The *SALT Lexicon,* produced by the US Arms Control and Disarmament Agency, defines "strategic" broadly, contending that strategic "relates to a nation's military, economic, and/or political power and its ability to control the course of military/political events."[31] The *Lexicon,* however, fails to define strategic forces. Are strategic forces those that can strike strategic targets? Is an attack on Washington, whether it be by ICBMs stationed at distant points in the Soviet heartland, by sea-launched cruise missiles SLCMs stationed on ships 200 or 300 miles off shore, or by aircraft forward-based in Cuba, a strategic attack? If so, should all such weapon systems be considered strategic and, hence, included in negotiations on strategic armaments? Or are certain armaments more threatening or potentially more destabilizing in crisis situations and thus, more strategic in some sense than other armaments? While both previous SALT agreements frequently have relied on range as qualifying criterion for inclusion of a weapon system under the agreement,[32] the issue is far from settled.

On November 26, 1969, shortly after the opening of SALT I, Deputy Foreign Minister Vladimir S. Semenov, head of the Soviet delegation, raised what perhaps has proven to be the thorniest of issues—the forward-based systems (FBS) question. Agreements based on equal security, he asserted, have to cover all nuclear delivery systems which could hit targets in the other country regardless of whether their owners called them strategic or tactical. The US response to this attempt to define strategic armaments so broadly was that to do so would "ensnarl the conference in extraneous political and military problems that would block any SALT agreement."[33] Thus, from the US perspective, the exigencies of attempting to achieve some form of agreement, which would constrain the growth of strategic forces, however limited the agreement might be, played a role in determining what forces should be considered "strategic" for SALT negotiating purposes. Nevertheless, the Soviet Union continued to raise the FBS issue throughout the SALT I negotiations.

According to Ambassador Gerard Smith, the head of the US delegation to SALT I, the failure to settle the FBS question blocked a comprehensive SALT I treaty limiting offensive arms. Even the interim offensive freeze of 1972—a device Smith contends was used to get around the FBS issue—to some extent, apparently reflected FBS considerations. Indeed, Henry Kissinger, President Nixon's National Security Advisor and architect of the freeze, justified permitting the Soviet Union a superior number of missile launchers, in part, by emphasizing the US advantage in FBS. According to Smith, in a briefing to congressional leaders on the SALT I agreements Kissinger said:

> It was decided to exclude from the freeze bombers and so-called forward-based systems. To exclude, that is, the weapons in which this country holds an advantage . . . . We urge the Congress to keep this fact in mind when assessing the numerical ratios of weapons which are subject to the offensive freeze.[34]

The FBS issue continued to figure prominently during the SALT II process. The Soviet Union dropped its demands that FBS be included in strategic force calculations at the Vladivostok meeting between President Ford and Secretary Brezhnev in November 1974 in exchange for US concessions to include heavy bombers in the SALT II ceiling on strategic forces and not to pursue a cutback in Soviet heavy missiles.[35] However, when President Carter's new proposal for deep cuts was presented by Secretary of State Vance in Moscow in March 1977, Brezhnev once again sounded the FBS alarm. Already irritated over the Carter human rights campaign, the stagnation of SALT, and the apparent rejection of the Vladivostok accord by the Carter Administration, Brezhnev, categorically, rejected the US proposal. He argued, among other things, that all the US talk about the Triad was, in a way, deceptive; the United States had a fourth threat to use against the

Soviet Union—its forward-based forces in Western Europe.[36] Thus, the FBS issue was never far from the surface in SALT II. When the aggregate levels of strategic ICBM, SLBM, and bomber forces being proposed fell below a certain threshold, the Soviet negotiators would then argue that they would be vulnerable to US FBS. Similarly, when the United States pressed to exempt conventionally armed cruise missiles (believed by some US and Western Europeans to be needed to bolster conventional defenses in Europe) from consideration under the Protocol, Soviet negotiators made it clear that if the United States persisted in its attempt to use SALT to bolster NATO's theater forces, the Kremlin would dredge up the FBS question.[37]

With the opening of the INF negotiations in Geneva in November 1981, the forum for negotiations on FBS shifted somewhat. Nonetheless, the problem of definition remains. At the INF talks, the US proposals have focused on intermediate-range Soviet and US forward-based missiles—a category of weaponry it considers completely out of balance in the European theater today. The Soviet Union has attempted to include US forward-based aircraft—a category of weaponry in which it could be argued that balance already exists.[38] At the START negotiations, the United States, in addition to seeking significant reductions in missiles and warheads, has called for an equal ceiling on heavy bombers below the US level in SALT II and certain constraints on cruise missiles. The Soviet proposal has also called for limitations on missiles and bombers as well as cruise missiles. Yet, the question of what constitutes a strategic bomber or strategic cruise missile remains to be settled.

SALT II limited the long-range Soviet Bear and Bison aircraft and US B-52 and B-l aircraft. Thus, unrefueled range appears to have been a major factor in determining which bombers were to be considered strategic. But does unrefueled range really matter? Today, with aerial refueling, forward staging and/or recovery at forward bases, a number of aircraft with less range which are currently in the superpower inventories would be capable of conducting intercontinental missions. These have been major points made by those who argue that the Soviet Backfire bomber should be considered as a strategic system. Rather than range, perhaps the assigned mission of the aircraft should be the controlling factor. The Soviet Bears and Bisons and US B-52s have recognized intercontinental missions. This is also the case with the US B-1. On the other hand, Soviet leaders have argued that Backfire bombers are assigned theater not intercontinental missions and that the current basing of these aircraft supports this contention. But missions can change and aircraft can be moved to forward staging bases. Should that be taken into account? And if so, how?

Similarly, the question of what constitutes a strategic cruise missile will continue to plague strategic negotiations. Should cruise missiles on submarines or surface ships, or aircraft be considered strategic? Should they only be considered strategic if they have ranges in excess of some set distance? What should the distance be? Why? What underlying rationale should be selected?

Force Comparability. The problem of force comparability focuses on what strategic capabilities should be constrained and how. It addresses the issues of how "balance" or essentially equal force aggregates can be achieved when the forces of the two superpowers are dissimilar in compositon and upon which measures of capabilities agreements should be based. Should only the most threatening forces, such as quick reacting ICBM and SLBM forces, be counted and should bombers be included? Should agreements be based on the total number of missile launchers and bombers? Or should the throw-weight[39] or numbers of warheads a missile can carry be considered, as well as the size of the bomb load of bombers? Or are the real concerns (and therefore factors that need to be constrained if balance is to be achieved) such things as aggregate deliverable megatonnage, equivalent megatonnage (EMT) or hard target kill capability?[40]

Because of differences in geography, technology, military strategy, and historic experience, the strategic forces of the United States and the Soviet Union have evolved in distinct ways. With its great land mass, restricted access to the seas, and few bomber recovery bases on the periphery of the United States, the Soviet Union has generally placed a relatively greater emphasis on the development of its land-based missile forces. Today, the Soviet Union has 350 more ICBM launchers than does the United States. Its ICBM forces also have a greater throw-weight than do those of the United States. Furthermore, Soviet "cold launch" techniques permit the rapid reloading of many of Moscow's ICBM silos.[41] The Soviet Union also has a greater number of SLBM launchers than does the United States (950+ to 568).[42] However, despite Soviet modernization of its sea-based ballistic missile forces, relatively few Soviet SLBMs include MIRV and Soviet nuclear missile carrying submarines are reported currently to have lower operational in-commission rates and to be noisier than those of the United States.

On the other hand, the United States has fewer ICBMs and less throw-weight, but its ICBMs are generally held in a higher state of readiness. The United States also has MIRVs on all its SLBMs, is developing a family of sea- and air-launched cruise missiles potentially capable of high accuracy, and has more intercontinental bombers than the USSR.[43] Moreover, bombers constitute a reusable force which, theoretically, can be recycled for follow-on retaliatory strikes after the missiles of both sides have been expended. Such differences of Soviet and American capabilities has led one observer to remark that "to compare American and Russian systems . . . is to talk apples and oranges."[44]

Achieving comparability in force aggregates is also complicated by the scenario dependence of comparability calculations. For example, advantages in day-to-day alert and in-commission rates are less relevant if conflict occurs after both sides have made extensive preparations. Similarly, advantages in accuracy and throw-weight are more relevant in a no warning attack on ICBM silos in which the defender fails to launch-on-warning (LOW) or launch-through-attack (LTA). If the defender decides to launch-on-warning or launch-through-attack, most of the attackers highly accurate missiles will fall on empty silos.

In order to avoid the difficult tasks of deciding what constitutes equivalent capabilities in each general category of strategic weaponry, the "freedom-to-mix" concept has frequently guided past negotiations. Thus, to some extent each side has been allowed to choose for itself what systems provide balance at the strategic level. This concept was first set forth in the early days of SALT I when the American delegation tabled, as a series of talking points, an agreed aggregate number of launchers for fixed or mobile land-based ICBMs and for sea-based strategic offensive ballistic missiles, with the freedom for each side to vary the combination of these types of launchers as it chose.[45] The concept was embodied in subsequent proposals and was included, in one form or another, in the final SALT I and II agreements.[46]

The problem of force comparability, however, has not been resolved by such an approach. Differences in force composition have continued to spark long and heated debates in Washington, Geneva, and, most probably, Moscow over what forces should be constrained and how. For its part, the United States remains concerned that the Soviet advantage in heavy throw-weight ICBMs with MIRVs, which when coupled with improvements in accuracy, now provide Moscow with, as a minimum, the theoretical capability to destory a significant portion of the US land-based strategic retaliatory force. From the US perspective, failure to achieve limits at START on such forces would permit a dangerous, and potentially destabilizing, asymmetry in the US-Soviet strategic relationship. Hence, the United States seeks specific subceilings on what it considers to be the most threatening class of Soviet missiles: SS-l7, SS-l8, and SS-l9 ICBMs. The United States also seeks to set limits on the total number of strategic nuclear warheads each side is permitted, the number of warheads that can be mounted on individual missiles, and the total number of heavy bombers and cruise missiles that can be carried by bombers.[47]

Moscow, on the other hand, seems less inclined to restrictions on throw-weight and, thus, on their large ICBMs which they contend would force them to restructure their strategic forces. The Soviet Union, however, is seeking limits on the total number of systems with MIRVs, including bombers, as well as limits on the aggregate number of nuclear charges (by which they mean missile warheads and bomber weapons). They are also seeking to limit cruise missiles and a ban on cruise missiles with ranges in excess of 600 kilometers.[48]

Despite what would appear to be areas of agreement between the United States and the USSR, however, American and Soviet negotiators are likely to have to labor long and hard before a balance of essentially dissimilar strategic structures can be achieved through START.

Vulnerabilities. The problem of vulnerabilities is linked directly to calculations of force comparability. It focuses on the queston of which side is more vulnerable to first and follow-on strikes and what kinds, if any, of qualitative and quantitative adjustments should be permitted in arms agreements in order to assure the existence of "balance" or "equal security."

In this regard, the United States has only a limited air defense capability. It has only a relatively limited capability to protect its civilian populace from nuclear attack through civil defense measures. Furthermore, the United States currently has no program for the protection or relocation of key industries.[49] Many of the US urban, industrial, and communication centers are located near the coasts and, hence, are vulnerable to attack by SLBMs or sea-launched cruise missiles (SLCMs), which offer little warning time when used for attack on coastal targets. Furthermore, the open nature of US society makes it almost impossible to guard against well-orchestrated attacks on the communication nodes used for strategic command and control during nuclear war.[50] However, the education and training of its people, multiple redundancies of communication and transportation capabilities, and a strong resources base may make the United States more capable of organizing and conducting local and national efforts in a post-attack environment.

On the other hand, the Soviet Union has a well-developed and highly regarded air defense network. It has undertaken extensive civil defense efforts to protect party and government leadership, workers, and essential industrial installations in the event of nuclear war.[51] Its economic system, however, is not nearly as strong or likely to be as resilient as that of the United States. The Soviet transportation system is woefully inadequate. As a result, basic supplies and food stuffs are likely to be in short supply for a considerable length of time following any strategic nuclear exchange. Furthermore, centrifugal ethnic and national forces within the Soviet Union may hinder Soviet recovery efforts following a nuclear war with the United States.[52]

How should such asymmetries be reconciled? Should the United States be permitted some additional number of bombers as offset Soviet air defense capabilities? Should certain strategic force imbalances be permitted in order to account for Soviet vulnerabilities? Or, are these vulnerabilities offset by a more favorable civil defense posture? Are such asymmetries too complex to judge and, thus, do they only serve to make an arms agreement impossible to achieve if such factors were considered?

Technological Change. One of the "banes" of the strategic arms negotiations, as Strobe Talbott noted in his analysis of SALT II, has been that new technologies frequently render arms control measures obsolete or inadequate.[53]

The problem of technological change focuses on the potential *impact* of future changes in capabilities which are likely to occur as a result of technological advances. Such issues arise as: what are the probable effects on strategic stability and on the balance of intercontinental forces of advances in missile guidance technologies—not only in a theoretical sense, but in terms of actual operational capabilities should strategic war occur? What kinds of missile guidance improvements can be anticipated over the course of the agreement? Is there an upper limit on the operational accuracies likely to be obtained by inertial guidance systems because of inherent systemic errors? Will terminal or stellar guidance technologies overcome or reduce systemic errors? What will be the impact on cruise missile capabilities of continued improvements in component miniaturization, in small engine technologies, in heavy hydrocarbon fuels, or in terrain mapping or radar correlation techniques? Will there be a breakthrough in submarine detection and tracking or in antimissile defense? Within what timeframe are such advances likely? And what specific provisions should be included in arms control proposals to limit the potentially adverse impacts of such advances?

Both SALT I and SALT II attempted to impede the advance of technology. SALT I, however, is of course best known for its failure to constrain the advance of MIRV technologies. This failure has contributed to a marked increase in the strategic capabilities and vulnerabilities of both superpowers—not only by permitting a dramatic increase in the numbers of warheads that Soviet and American missiles can deliver, but also by providing either side the opportunity to strike the other's missile forces with a relatively small number of its own strategic missiles. Nevertheless, SALT I did constrain the advance of antiballistic missile (ABM) and, to a much lesser extent, ICBM technologies.[54] However, the "Interim Agreement" on strategic offensive forces can perhaps better be understood in terms of the reluctance of either party to constrain itself in areas where technological advance seemed to offer some potential for future improvements in capabilities. On the other hand, SALT II did attempt to constrain a variety of technologies through prohibitions in development and testing. For example, both the United States and the USSR were prohibited from developing, testing, or deploying: (1) systems for the rapid reload of ICBM launchers; (2) ballistic missiles capable of ranges in excess of 600 kilometers for installation on waterborne vehicles other than submarines; (3) fixed ballistic or cruise missiles for employment on the ocean floor, on the seabed and so forth; and (4) mobile launchers for heavy ICBMs.

The problem of technological change was perhaps best summed up by Christoph Bertram, the former director of the International Institute for Strategic Studies.

> The trouble is that, because of technological change . . . it has become almost impossible for arms-control negotiators to produce treaties which will be unequivocally fair and equitable. A bargain struck on the basis of the technological characteristics of specific weapons existing at the time of agreement will become inequitable as one side or the other introduces qualitative improvements which have not been ruled out, or deploys alternative weapons systems which bypass the restrictions agreed upon.[55]

Verification. Perhaps no other strategic arms control issue has been so widely and heatedly discussed as has been the verification issue. Gerard Smith wrote that the first question that came to mind when SALT I limitations were considered was: "Can it be verified?"[56]

Verificaton is the process of identifying compliance or noncompliance with the provisions of the agreement. Once defense planners have determined what forces should be compared and how, and what limitations meet the requirements for balance and essential equivalence, they must then address the issue of how compliance with such force limitations can be verified. This is, of course, frequently an interactive process in which the ability to verify compliance ultimately affects which forces are to be constrained and how. Thus, the question of what forces *should* be limited to improve crisis stability and cap the arms race frequently yields to the question of what limitations *can* be verified. This deference to verification, however, is also grounded in a desire for stability. For if an arms agreement cannot be verified, then neither party can be certain that the other is adhering to its terms. As a minimum, confidence in one's security might well erode with consequent adverse impact on the political relations between the parties to the negotiation. Ultimately, the very objective of arms race and crisis stability may be threatened as each side attempts to hedge against what they may suspect may be covert attempts by the other side to improve its relative strategic position.

Emphasizing the importance of verification, George Seignious, while serving as director of the US Arms Control and Disarmament Agency, said in a statement before Congress:

> In SALT we don't rely on trust. Trust is not a basis for natonal survival. We verify Soviet compliance with the provisions of the agreement by using our diverse, powerful, and sophisticated intelligence capabilities. Taken together, these capabilities provide us with a substantial amount of detailed, accurate, up-to-date information on those Soviet forces and activities limited by SALT.[57]

Such National Technical Means (NTM), as the vehicles of verification have become known in both SALT I and SALT II, have been the fundamental basis upon which verification of strategic arms accords has rested. Article V of the SALT I "Interim Agreement" and Article XV of the SALT II accord permitted each party to use NTM to verify compliance consistent with the recognized principles of international law. Both SALT I and II also prohibited each party from interfering with the NTM of the other party and from using deliberate concealment measures to impede verification by NTM. Presumably, any new strategic arms agreement, as a minimum, will include similar provisions.

Despite the SALT I and II agreements on the use of NTM for verification and the considerable capabilities available to both the United States and the Soviet Union to observe each other's forces, verificaton remains a major problem for stategic arms negotiators. The rapid pace of technological advance has made it necessary to move beyond simple counts of missile launchers and bombers to achieve balance and stability at the strategic level. MIRV technology has multiplied the potential number of warheads a missile can carry and, thus, the number of targets it can strike. Advances in fuels technologies, small engine design, and warhead miniaturization have now made it possible to produce and deploy a new family of cruise missiles which can be used for strategic as well as tactical purposes. Advances on missile launch facilities and guidance technologies make it possible to deploy highly accurate mobile missiles. The potential development of common warhead designs and strap-on missile stages suggests a future ability to alter quickly the capabilities of one's strategic missile forces by adding to the warheads of the missile force or by converting medium-range systems to strategic systems.[58] All such developments seriously compound the problem of verifying compliance with any future agreement.

For example, if the number of missiles were limited instead of the number of missile launchers, as has been the case in the past, how could one side be certain that the other side wasn't building and hiding missiles which could be emplaced rapidly in silos after the first wave of ICBMs had been fired? Or, if the number of warheads to be placed on a specific family of ICBMs was limited, how could one side be certain that the other was adhering to the limits specified in the agreement? For instance, could the Soviet military be confident about the ability of a missile to release, say, twenty warheads even if they had only tested the release of up to ten in compliance with the specifics of an agreement?

Furthermore, if an agreement were reached to limit the number and ranges of strategic cruise missiles, how could one be certain that cruise missiles did not exceed the ranges specified in the agreement? Since range is, in part, a function of payload, could a signatory, through advances in miniaturization or accuracy, reduce the size of the warhead and increase the amount of fuel, thereby extending the range of its cruise missile force? Perhaps more importantly, how would one detect the deployment of cruise missiles and how could one determine if the missiles deployed were conventional or nuclear? Their small size allows them to be concealed easily aboard ships in numbers that might seriously affect the balance of strategic forces. Moreover, in the absence of intrusive inspection, would it be possible to determine if a specific family of cruise missiles were armed with conventional or nuclear warheads?

Finally, if technological advance coupled with increasing concerns over the vulnerability of fixed-site ICBM forces is leading both the United States and the Soviet Union in the direction of mobile missiles, how will either side determine if the specifics of an agreement are being observed? Mobile missiles depend for survival on confusing the opponent as to the specific location of the missiles. But if they cannot be seen, how can they be counted? Even if an opponent has multiple fixed sites, as was proposed under the MX multiple aim point (MAP) program, how does the other side determine how many missiles are actually in the fixed sites[59] and how can it be sure that additional missiles have not been secreted away to be placed in position during a severe crisis?

The problem of verification has been further complicated by Soviet efforts to encode telemetric information during missile tests. US officials have long considered access to Soviet missile telemetry important. By monitoring the signals transmitted by Soviet missiles to ground stations in the USSR, the United States can estimate such features as the size, number, and type of warheads and, thus, keep track of some of the information needed to verify compliance with the specifics of agreements. The increasing use of encoded telemetry now threatens to reduce the value to NTM, just at a time when agreements are becoming more complex, and confidence in being able to verify compliance will require more rather than less information.[60]

Sanctions and Ambiguity. The problem of sanctions addresses two issues: what should be done if a violation of an arms agreement is suspected and what should be done if one is confirmed? The solution to the first question is complicated by several factors. Neither side may wish to disrupt the climate of cooperation at the strategic level by pursuing suspected violations too vigorously, especially where evidence is scanty, suspicions may prove unwarranted or violations may be unintended and minor. Also, raising an issue may compromise intelligence sources. On the other hand, both sides are likely to wish to remain confident that mechanisms exist for challenging potential violations.

Perhaps one of the least publicized outcomes of the SALT I process was the establishment of the Standing Consultative Commission (SCC).[61] Article XIII of the ABM Treaty established the SCC to consider, among other things, questions concerning treaty compliance and unintended interference with NTM and to provide information on a voluntary basis to assure confidence in compliance. The SCC has functioned as one of the principal means of raising concerns over suspected violations of both the SALT I or SALT II agreements. For example, in 1973 the United States observed that the Soviet Union was building silos of a different design than had been seen before. If those silos were intended to serve as ICBM launchers they would constitute a violation of the SALT I Interim Agreement which prohibited construction of additional fixed land-based ICBM launchers after July 1, 1972. Washington brought the question to the SCC and a bilateral review panel was established. The issue was resolved when Moscow responded that the silos were not for ICBM launchers but for hardened command and control facilities. Subsequently, that explanation was confirmed.[62]

Similarly, the ABM Treaty prohibited the conversion of antiaircraft installations into antimissile defenses. In 1973 and 1974, US intelligence noticed that the Soviet Union was conducting tests using air defense surface-to-air missile (SAM) radars to track their ballistic missiles during test flights. The Soviet leaders said that they were using the radars to track the navigaton system of the ballistic missiles, not in an attempt to upgrade their SAMs for ABM use. The issue was taken before the SCC for resolution. A short time after the United States raised the issue in the SCC, the Soviet Union stopped using the radars for missile tests.

The Soviet Union has also used the SCC. For example, in 1973, the Air Force installed prefabricated shelters over minuteman silos at Malmstrom Air Force Base to protect workmen from the winter snows of Montana. The workman were hardening the silo covers so that as the accuracy and throw-weight of Soviet missiles increased, the US missiles would stand a better chance of surviving near-direct hits. The Soviet Union charged that the shelters violated Article V of the Interim Agreement forbidding measures which deliberately impede verification by NTM. The USSR contended that since the shelters were four times larger than those used during the contruction and modernization of Minuteman silos from 1962 to 1972, this was a deliberate impediment. The issue was considered as phony by some in Washington who argued that because of the open nature of US society the Soviet Union knew perfectly well that the shelters were not being used to conceal the substitution of heavy ICBMs for Minuteman IIs. Nevertheless, the ambiguity of what constituted "deliberate" remained. Finally, the Ford administration agreed to reduce the size of the shelters and, by 1977, the Carter administration actually reduced them by one-half.[63]

One observer has written:

> SALT verification is charged with proving a negative, that is, that the activities prohibited by treaty are not, in fact, taking place. That means that considerable exactitude must be used in drafting the treaty so as to remove any doubt about what activities actually constitute a violation.[64]

Eliminating ambiguity, however, has not always been easy. Indeed, a little ambiguity has frequently been the price of agreement at the negotiating table. For example, SALT I specifically prohibited the conversion of "light" ICBMs into heavy ICBMs. However, the Soviet Union refused to define what they mean by "heavy" missile launchers. Subsequently, the USSR deployed the SS-19 missile which it described as a "light" missile even though it had a volume 50 percent greater than the missile it was replacing. Thus, while the United States could detect deployment of the new missile, it was impossible to substantiate any explicit violation of the SALT I accord. Nevertheless, it was argued that deployment of this missile violated the intent of the accord and undercut unilateral US statements concerning maximum size of allowed missiles.

More recently, the Soviet Union is reported to have tested a new mobile ICBM with ten MIRV warheads in October 1982. While there is apparently some evidence to suggest that the missile tested may be a "heavy" rather than a "light" one,[65] nonetheless, Article IV of SALT II does permit each party to test and deploy one new type of "light" ICBM. In February 1983 the Soviet Union is reported to have tested another "light" ICBM which is mobile. The SALT II agreement does permit each side to test modernized versions of existing missiles. Since no existing Soviet "light" missiles are mobile, the February 1983 test would appear to be the second test of a new ICBM and thus constitute a violation of the SALT II accords. Nevertheless, despite attempts to eliminate ambiguity through a series of "Agreed Statements" and "Common Understandings" which are an integral part of the SALT II agreement, some ambiguity as to exactly what constitutes modernization remains.

It has also been reported that the Soviet Union is constructing a "massive new" radar in central Siberia near several ICBM sites. The new radar is aimed at the Pacific Coast facing Alaska not at China to the south.[66] Some defense specialists apparently believe that the Soviet Union intends to use the radar in conjunction with a missile defense system to protect ICBMs. This, again, would be a clear violation of the ABM Treaty. Whether and how the SCC might be used to resolve the issue has yet to be determined. However, the problem may well turn out to be one of the more difficult issues yet confronted in the strategic arms control process.

Its outcome could well affect the future of arms control agreements.

Finally, there is considerable ambiguity as to what constitutes a legitimate use of encryption of telemetry and, thus, is permitted by the SALT II agreement, and what use of encryption impedes verificaton and, thus, is prohibited by the treaty. Such ambiguities make it difficult to determine whether the Soviet Union is violating the specific provisions on encoding in the Common Understandings of the SALT II agreement. They also make it difficult to verify the other provisions of the accord through observations of Soviet telemetric data.

The second question addresses the issue of what is to be done if a violation is confirmed. Perhaps more importantly, what constitutes confirmation? Is a deliberate violation a statement of national intent? Should violations of different provisions of strategic arms accords be treated equally? Can sanctions be imposed which would enhance the strategic arms control process and the continued maintenance of strategic stability? Or should a clear violation be considered a unilateral abrogation on the entire treaty? Such are the questions which strategic arms control negotiators must confront if sanctions are to be considered.

THE FUTURE

The aforementioned complexities suggest that no easy solutions to the problem of achieving "balance" or "equal security" are likely to be forthcoming. Achieving agreement on limiting strategic armaments, however, is as much a political act as it is a function of the many technical complexities which must be overcome. Despite the Kremlin's decision to suspend START negotiations, as well as INF talks, in response to the NATO deployment of Pershing II and cruise missiles in Europe, a number of the concerns which drove US and Soviet leaders to sign the SALT I and SALT II accords remain. Both Washington and Moscow continue to share the nagging fear of nuclear holocaust. Both remain interested in avoiding strategic instabilities which might lead to nuclear war. Both are likely to be concerned over the growing vulnerability of some of their strategic systems. Both are apparently interested in creating an equilibrium in which their countries can be secure.

In Moscow, there is a renewed concern over the nature and extent of Washington's strategic force modernization program and the potential impact on US-Soviet strategic relationships of America's technological edge if American technology is left unconstrained by a START agreement. Likewise, there is, no doubt, a renewed concern over the economic implications of an expanded arms race. During his brief tenure, former Soviet President Yuri Andropov had signaled his interest in improving the Soviet economy.[67] The new Soviet leader Konstantin U. Chernenko is also known to be interested in improving the economy. According to Western estimates, however, the Soviet Union has been spending between 10 and 15 percent of its Gross National Product on defense. It also channels a large portion of its skilled manpower into defense and defense related industries. This tends to restrain civil oriented technological progress. Thus, there is reason to suspect that any arms agreement which capped expenditures on strategic forces would be welcomed in some quarters in the Kremlin, especially since more recently the United States has signaled its intent to match continued Soviet strategic force buildups. Indeed, even Defense Minister Ustinov, while underscoring that the Soviet Union is prepared to continue the arms race and, if necessary, deploy a new class of ICBMs, seems to have indicated a preference for a strategic arms agreement.[68]

Another, perhaps less obvious, factor may also serve as incentive for a strategic arms agreement. While it is likely that the selection of Chernenko had the support of the security ministries, the staying power of the new Soviet leader may well depend not only on his being able to improve the economy, but also on his ability to portray himself as a world leader and man of peace and, thus, enhance the image of the Soviet Union as a superpower. In this regard securing a strategic arms agreement with the United States might strengthen even further his position within the Soviet hierarchy among those interested in economic growth as well as those who believe that it is important for the Soviet Union to be seen as in the forefront of international arms control efforts. During Andropov's long illness in late 1983 the military appeared to be in the ascendance. Nevertheless, the collective Soviet leadership has long demonstrated a firm belief in Party dominance over the military. Thus, one should not dismiss the strength of those who believe that attention be paid to a wide spectrum of concerns which includes, but is not limited to, the buildup of military forces.

Likewise, in the United States, the growing antinuclear movement, although now somewhat muted, and public concerns over a continuing upward spiraling arms race and rising defense expenditures add to pressures to seek a strategic arms agreement. Moreover, election pressures may nudge US leaders in the direction of an agreement. Already there apparently has been an attempt by advisors to the President (as two observers of the Washington scene have put it) to "remove the Ghengis Khan cloak draped over Reagan's shoulders in the 1980 campaign and replace it with the olive branch."[69] Although at this writing it seems only a remote possibility, summit politics played in mid-1984 with Reagan and Chernenko at center stage and strong indications that a new strategic accord is forthcoming would virtually guarantee President Reagan's reelection in November, barring, of course, any unforeseen serious domestic economic downturn.

One is cautioned against over-optimism. The aforementioned technical obstacles still must be overcome. Furthermore, relations between Washington and Moscow remain strained. Years of distrust and misapprehensions, compounded by more recent events such as Afghanistan, Poland, Korean Airlines 007, Grenada, and missile deployments in Europe cloud the future. Nevertheless, one should not be overly pessimistic concerning the possibilities of reaching an agreement with the Soviet Union on strategic arms reductions, if not within the next year, within the next few years.

Whether reductions in strategic forces achieved through such an agreement would, in fact, contribute significantly to a curbing of the arms race and improved stability at the strategic level is quite another question. In large measure, that will depend on how well each of the principal problems confronting the negotiating parties is dealt with and whether the positions taken by the United States and the Soviet Union in dealing with these problems are framed from a coherent set of guidelines which attempts to address short-term concerns in the context of the long-term objectives of balance and stability. In short, the success of the current negotiations in Geneva depends heavily on whether START is addressed as a discrete event by the superpowers or viewed as part of a long-term strategy. In this regard, strategic arms control efforts, although not a zero sum game, in many ways, are similar to the game of chess.

Each movement is a statement of policy to which the opponent must respond. It is also an attempt to structure the behavior of the opponent in a small way so that the aggregate of moves secures for the player his long-term objectives. Each move demands reassessment of one's own as well as the opponent's capabilities and a reappraisal of the opponent's short- and long-term objectives. The game, of course, must be played in constant anticipation of contingencies which may arise from the misassessments or altered objectives of either side. However, the outcome depends on how well the player has structured his game plan and on how many moves in advance he is thinking when he touches a piece. This is called strategy. It takes into consideration the opponent's capabilities and intentions. It focuses on the near and the far, but never loses sight of the final objectives. It is an exercise in behavioral modificaton. It is the logical link between one's capabilities and the objectives one hopes to secure.

Unfortunately, both SALT I and SALT II, by and large, were treated as discrete events by the United States and possibly as such by the Soviet Union, rather than as a continuing process to achieve strategic arms limitations. To be sure, in the minds of those in Washington and Moscow, SALT II was a natural extension of SALT I and many of the concerns raised in SALT II were an outgrowth of the uncertainties which remained in the wake of the SALT I experience. No doubt, negotiators and national leaders had longer-term objectives in mind. However, there is little evidence to suggest that these negotiations were designed as part of a longer-term process, that the goals set for SALT I and SALT II were framed as part of a grand strategy aimed at security balance and stability at the strategic level—perhaps only imperfectly through these early negotiations, but incrementally achieving a high degree of stability at the strategic level by say SALT X.

Indeed, the nature of the strategic arms limitations process in the past has suggested that for both the Soviet Union and the United States, the defense planning cycle has been dominated primarily by procurement planning considerations rather than by political-military strategies which view arms control and force structure as integral parts of the same coherent whole carefully designed to improve the security of each nation.

By and large, the United States has not had a clear set of well-defined long-term objectives for strategic arms talks to serve. As a result, there was no way of measuring the contribution of SALT I or SALT II to the overall short- and long-term US security interests. Nor did US negotiators know precisely where they should go following the collapse of SALT II if such interests were to be served in the future. Yet, the price of indecision was borne by the American citizens who continued to pay the defense bill while receiving little in the way of an increased sense of security.

While there was general agreement in Washington on the broad objectives of strategic arms negotiations—preserving deterrence, increasing stability, and improving security at reduced cost—such objectives were too abstract to be useful. In contrast, no general consensus seemed to emerge on the more meaningful objectives of strategic arms talks. Similarly, there has been no general consensus on the direction of defense planning. What should be the long-term objectives of strategic arms reduction efforts? How should these objectives relate to the other defense objectives and to the more general desire to enhance deterrence and increase stability at the strategic level?

Parity or essential equivalence had become a guiding principal of strategic arms talks. Yet questions remained as to whether equivalence was desirable and how parity was to be measured. President Reagan, like the presidents before him, has underscored the need for balance. Others within the defense community and in academia frequently betray a certain nostalgia for the days of unquestioned US strategic superiority. Should parity be a fundamental basis for strategic arms talks and thus for defense planning with respect to the strategic weapons procurement process? Or should START and procurement planning be guided by renewed efforts to reestablish US strategic superiority? Some analysts have argued that the Soviet Union is already on the edge of mobilization for war, spending 40 percent more than the United States does for arms, from a GNP roughly half that of the United States. Thus, they contend that, the Soviet Union is near its weapons peak right now, while the United States has been resting on a lower plateau—suggesting that the United States could easily outspend and outarm the Soviet Union. Yet the question remains, can a meaningful strategic superiority be achieved in the nuclear age? McGeorge Bundy in his speech at Villars, Switzerland, at the 1979 annual conference of the International Institute for Strategic Studies, noted that despite the large difference in the strategic capabilities of the Soviet Union and United States in the late 1950's and early 1960's, it was his view and that of President Kennedy that parity existed from the moment the Soviet Union possessed a significant number of intercontinental missiles.[70] Moreover, if the success of American foreign policy in securing US interests abroad during the 1960's was any indication of the political utility of strategic superiority, then one might argue that it clearly was of little value. This suggests that even with a wide margin of superior capabilities the United States might not achieve a meaningful superiority. However, even if superiority could be achieved, the question remains as to whether America's sense of security would be enhanced. Or would continued attempts by the Soviet Union to match American capabilities lead to ever increasing levels of tensions and instabilities at the strategic level?

Perhaps the adoption of parity as a guiding principle for the SALT I and SALT II negotiations masked the original purpose of strategic arms control talks—to bring stability to the Great Power equation. Parity or essential equivalence was originally conceived as a negotiating objective that might form the basis for an easing of tensions and a Soviet-American understanding on measures to improve crisis and arms race stability. However, parity conceived in terms of quantitative limitations in weapons does not seem to have served well in this regard. The task now confronting the United States is to determine just what strategic environment is desired over the next 30 to 50 years and to fashion strategies that join arms control and defense procurement in an effort to secure that environment.

We must now ask ourselves, where do we wish to go? And how are we to get there? Are we to be captive of technology? Or, can technology be made to serve strategy? Must we insure that strategic arms control negotiations do not interfer with US defense programs? Or would it be more appropriate to ask that START and defense programs both serve the ends of a national strategy designed to improve deterrence and stability at the strategic level. If we are increasingly concerned that the continued improvement in Soviet quick reacting hard-target kill capability forecasts an increase in strategic instabilities and if we are convinced that deterrence depends on each side having a truly survivable second strike capability, should we now begin to seek the eventual elimination of all forces capable of quick reaction, such as ICBMs and SLBMs? Is this a feasible long-term objective? Can it be negotiated? Must it be pursued in conjunction with efforts to reduce active and passive defenses which might make effective retaliation a less credible deterrent threat? Or, should we begin to move toward truly mobile forces which could well be capable of defying real-time target intelligence? Can this be done in the absence of START? The MX basing mode debate suggested that strategic arms control talks were the key to the survivability of mobile systems—for without warhead limitations, the Soviet Union could simply multiply the number of warheads until they are able to cover the additional potential targets. Are there other systems that might serve better? Should the United States and Soviet Union move to sea? Is President Reagan's "build-down" strategic arms proposal[71] the first real attempt to restructure strategic forces for survivability and, thus, for strategic stability? If so, will the future survivability of sea forces be dependent on a further set of agreements which set aside certain areas of the seas as sanctuaries? Are such agreements already being considered for START II or START III or IV as part of as US long-term arms control strategy? What is the probability of an imminent beakthrough in satellite reconnaissance which might furnish real-time target intelligence on submarine locations? Can START assist in reducing vulnerabilities and how? In the interim can the United States justify the acquisition of counterforce capabilities to strike certain hardened targets in retaliation or as part of its limited nuclear options while chiding the Soviet Union for improvements in accuracy? These are some of the questions which must be answered if the United States is to develop effective national security strategies which include strategic arms negotiations as an integral part. Until then we will continue to be captive of an ill defined parity as the fundamental guiding principal of short-term approaches and we will continue to be disappointed with the results.

ENDNOTES

1. For a thorough discussion of the beginnings of SALT I, see John Newhouse, *Cold Dawn,* New York: Holt, Rinehart and Winston, 1973.
2. *Ibid.,* p. 103.
3. *Ibid.,* p. 5.
4. On the ABM issue, Newhouse contends that "in a bureaucratic sense, the ABM issue may have been the toughest McNamara ever dealt with." Almost everyone in the Pentagon was for the ABM. The Joint Chiefs estimated that a thick system capable of defending US cities against Soviet missiles would cost about $10 billion. McNamara believed that $40 billion would be closer. He also believed the system could be easily overcome by the Soviet Union. Both the State Department and the Arms Control and Disarmament Agency (ACDA) feared an ABM deployment would increase strategic instabilities. Their views, however, were apparently little heard and less heeded. Congressional powers close to the President, namely Richard Russell (then chairman of the Senate Armed Services Committee), Senator John Stennis, and Congressman George H. Mahan all favored deployment of an ABM system. To avert total defeat on the ABM issue, McNamara suggested a compromise to which the President agreed. The Administration would not spend the initial $375 million that had been restored to the budget for initial ABM procurement. The Administration would also delay making a final decision on whether the ABM system would be a thick system or a thin system capable of protecting against accidents and limited Chinese capabilities until the State Department had explored the idea of talks on limiting strategic arms, especially ABMs. Thus, in one sense Washington was driven to SALT by clearly bureaucratic and institutional factors related to the ABM debate in the US defense community. See *Ibid.,* pp. 77-86.
5. *Ibid.,* p. 101.
6. The greater-than-expected threat came into the defense lexicon in the mid-1960's. It signified enemy capabilities that exceeded the high end of the range of threats projected by the National Intelligence Estimates (NIEs). In an age of growing Soviet strategic capabilities, conservative force planning suggested the need to hedge against just such threats.
7. Richard Nixon, *US Foreign Policy for the 1970's: A New Strategy for Peace,* Washington: US Government Printing Office, February 18, 1970, p. 143.
8. For a further discussion of these points see J. I. Coffey, "SALT Under the Carter Administraton," *Naval War College Review,* Winter 1979; Helmut Sonnenfeldt and William G. Hyland, "Soviet Perspectives on Security," *Adelphi Papers,* No. 150, Spring 1979; William D. Jackson, "Policy Assessment at the Crossroads: the Soviets and SALT," *The Bulletin of the Atomic Scientists,* April 1979; and Newhouse, p. 107.
9. Lawrence T. Caldwell, "Soviet Attitudes to SALT," *Adelphi Papers,* No. 75, February 1971, p. 2.
10. *Ibid.,* p. 3. In the author's view it would be a mistake to overdraw the role of the "modernists." Soviet leadership has long been interested in further economic advancement. However, it has shown no unwillingness to delay economic expansion when funds were perceived as necessary to meet defense needs. Efforts by Soviet leadership to prepare their citizens for a new round of belt-tightening to meet defense needs in the wake of Grenada and missile deployments in Europe should be seen in this light.

11. *Pravda,* March 15, 1954.

12. *Pravda,* December 22, 1952, cited in William D. Jackson, "The Soviets and Strategic Arms: Toward an Evaluation of the Record," *Political Science Quarterly,* Summer 1979, p. 249.

13. Raymond L. Garthoff, "Mutual Deterrence and Strategic Arms Limitations in Soviet Policy," *International Security,* Summer 1978, pp. 114-125.

14. For example see *Pravda,* April 8, 1978, p. 1.

15. Ambassador Gerard C. Smith, *SALT: The First Strategic Arms Negotiation,* as reported in Raymond Garthoff, "Mutual Deterrence and Srategic Arms Limitations in Soviet Poicy," *International Security,* Summer 1978, pp. 113-125.

16. See *The New York Times,* March 5, 1979, p. A5.

17. *The Washington Post,* March 5, 1979, p. A5.

18. See US Congress, Senate, *The SALT II Treaty Hearings before the Committee on Foreign Relations,* 96th Congress, 1st Sess., Part 1, Washington: US Government Printing Office, p. 435.

19. *Ibid.,* p. 539.

20. Colin S. Gray, "SALT II: The Real Debate," *Policy Review,* Fall 1979, pp. 16 and 19.

21 See *The New York Times,* February 3, 1981, p. A1.

22. Richard Burt, "The Evolution of the US START Approach," *NATO Review,* September 1982, pp. 1-2. Also see President Ronald Reagan's speech at Eureka College on "East-West Relations," *Vital Speeches of the Day,* June 1, 1982, pp. 482-485 and his November 18, 1982 speech before the National Press Club in Washington, "US Program for Peace and Arms Control," *Current Policy No. 346,* Washington: US Department of State, Bureau of Public Affairs, November 18, 1981.

23. Richard Nixon, *US Foreign Policy for the 1970's: The Emerging Structure of Peace,* Washington: US Government Printing Office, February 9, 1972, pp. 172-173.

24. *The SALT Process,* Washington: US Department of State, June 1978, p. 9.

25, Harold Brown, Secretary of Defense, *Department of Defense Annual Report: Fiscal Year 1979,* Washington: Department of Defense, February 2, 1978, p. 56.

26. *Ibid.,* pp. 56-57.

27. See, for example, President Reagan, "US Program for Peace and Arms Control," speech before the Natonal Press Club in Washington, on November 18, 1981, *Current Policy No. 346,* p. 4; President Reagan's speech at Eureka College, *Vital Speeches,* p. 485; President Reagan's speech before the second UN General Assembly Special Session on Disarmament, New York, June 17, 1982, "Agenda for Peace," *Current Policy No. 405,* Washington: US Department of State, Bureau of Public Affairs, p. 3; and President Reagan's address before the Los Angeles World Council, March 31, 1983, "Reducing the Danger of Nuclear Weapons," *Current Policy No. 473,* p. 3. In September 1982, Richard Burt outlined the four key objectives of the arms control policy of the Reagan Administration—security, militarily significant reductions, equality, and verifiability. Concerning equality, he wrote: "Equality is fundamental to balanced arms control, deterrence, and stability and to a US-Soviet relationship based on mutual restraint and reciprocity." See Burt, *NATO Review,* p. 3.

28. For example, see *Pravda,* January 19, 1977; February 23, 1977; and April 26, 1978.

29. According to the International Institute for Strategic Studies, at present the British have 64 strategic nuclear missiles in place on 4 nuclear submarines. In addition, they have 48 Vulcan and 50 Buccaneer strike aircraft capable of delivering nuclear weapons on targets in the Soviet Union. The French have about 18 land-based intermediate range ballistic missiles (IRBMs) and 80 sea-launched ballistic missiles (SLBMs) capable of striking the Soviet Union with plans to increase the size of their nuclear powered ballistic missile fleet by two additional submarines in the 1980's, and, thus, add an additional 32 missiles to their stategic forces. The French also have 34 MIRAGE IVA strategic bombers. While estimates of Chinese strategic nuclear capabilities vary widely, it is reported that the Chinese have deployed approximately 50 medium range ballistic missiles (MRBMs) and between 60-85 IRBMs. Both these systems are capable of reaching targets in the Eastern USSR. They also may have begun to deploy a limited number of multistaged ICBMs (CSS-3s) with a range sufficient to strike targets in the European USSR (excluding Moscow), as well as a full range ICBM (the CSS-X-4) capable of striking targets anywhere in the Soviet Union. In addition to their ballistic missiles, the Chinese have about 90 TU-16 medium bombers with a range of about 3000 km. They also have begun to deploy a nuclear powered submarine with 12 missile tubes. *The Military Balance 1983-1984,* London: The International Institute for Strategic Studies, 1983, pp. 82-84. Also see Ronald T. Pretty, ed., *Jane's Weapon Systems,* London: Jane's Publishing Co., Ltd., 1982, pp. 1-2.

30. See unilateral statements made at the close of SALT I in Smith, pp. 514-515.

31. *SALT Lexicon,* Washington: US Arms Control and Disarmament Agency, 1974, p. 16.

32. Both SALT I and SALT II frequently relied on range as the qualifying criterion for the inclusion of a weapon system under the agreements. For the purpose of the SALT I agreement, ICBM launchers capable of launching ballistic missiles with ranges in excess of the shortest distance between the northeastern border of the continental United States and the northwestern border of the continental USSR were considered strategic. SALT II further clarified the definition of ICBMs by setting the range between these two points at 5500 km. Range, although not specifically mentioned, also seemed to be an underlying qualifying criteria for "heavy bombers" in the SALT II agreement. The Soviet Bear and Bison aircraft and the US B-52 and B-l type aircraft are all capable of what could be considered intercontinental ranges. However, aircraft such as the US FB-111 and the Soviet Backfire bomber were not included in the SALT II agreement. Likewise, the Protocol to the SALT II Treaty set limits on SLCMs based on range. See Smith, p. 509 and *SALT II Agreement,* Washington: US Department of State, Bureau of Public Affairs, Selected Documents No. 12A, June 18, 1979, pp. 27-28.

33. See Smith, pp. 90-91.

34 *Ibid.,* p. 93.

35. Strobe Talbott, *Endgame: The Inside Story of SALT II,* New York: Harper and Row Publishers, 1979, p. 33.

36. *Ibid.,* p. 72.

37. *Ibid.,* pp. 148 and 189.

38. For example, see Robert Kennedy, "Soviet Theater Nuclear Capabilities: The European Nuclear Balance in Transition" in *Defense of the West: Strategic and European Security Issues Reappraised,* edited by Robert Kennedy and John M. Weinstein, Boulder: Westview Press, 1984.

39. Throw-weight has been defined as "... the maximum useful weight which has been flight tested on the boost stages of the missile. The useful weight includes weight of the reentry vehicles, penetration aids, dispensing and release mechanisms, reentry shrouds, covers, buses and propulsion devices with their propellants (but not the final boost stages) which are present at the end of the boost phase." See *SALT Lexicon,* p. 18.

40. Equivalent megatonnage (EMT) is a measure used to compare the destructive potential of differing combinations of nuclear warhead yields against relatively soft countervalue targets. EMT is a computed function of yield (in megatons) which compensates to a degree for the fact that blast damage resulting from a nuclear detonation does not increase linearly with an increase in yield. Thus, if the destruction of a soft target is desired, it may be more effective to use two weapons each of small yield than a single weapon of a higher total yield even if its yield was much higher than the total yield of the two small weapons. Hard target kill capability is a function of both the accuracy of the weapons system and the yield of the warhead. Accuracy, however, is the predominant factor.

41. Cold launch is the technique of ejecting a missile from a silo before full ignition of the main engine. This technique leaves the missile silo essentially undamaged and available for reload. How much time it would take to actually reload a silo would depend on th locaton of the space missile and other factors related to the silo preparation and the physical loading of the missile. Estimates vary. Some contend that the Soviet Union would be ready to fire a second missile within 6 hours.

42. See *Soviet Military Power 1983,* Washington; US Government Printing Office, March 1983, p. 14; and Caspar Weinberger, *Annual Report to the Congress Fiscal Year 1984,* Washington: US Government Printing Office, February 1, 1983, p. 333.

43. The bomber balance has been a seriously disputed issue. The SALT II agreement only included B-52, B-l, Bear, and Bison type aircraft in the counts of US and Soviet strategic bomber forces. Today, according to US Department of Defense estimates, the Soviet Union has about 145 long-range Bear and Bison aircraft. The Bear has an unrefueled combat radius of 8300 km. The Bison's range is slightly less. The United States has about 241 operational B-52s which have a combat radius of about 8000 km. Thus, the United States has approximately 100 more operational strategic bombers than does the Soviet Union. However, the Soviet Union also has deployed over 200 Backfire bombers to perform conventional, maritime, and nuclear strike missions. The Backfire has a combat radius of 5500 km. If deployed to Arctic staging bases or refueled in flight, the Backfire can attack targets anywhere in the United States. The United States deploys 56 FB-111 medium-range bombers which would rely on inflight refueling and forward basing for intercontinental attack. If Backfires and FB-111s are added to the counts of strategic forces, the USSR would have about 50 more operational strategic bombers than does the United States. See *Soviet Military Power,* pp. 14, 13, and 25; Weinberger, *Annual Report,* p. 333; and *SALT II Agreement,* Washington; US Department of State, Bureau of Public Affairs, June 18, 1979, pp. 28-29.

46. See Smith, pp. 504-507 and *SALT II Agreement,* p. 32.

47. Michael Getler, "US Arms Reducton Plan Contains More Missile Cuts Than Announced," *The Washington Post,* April 13, 1983, p. Al.

48. *Security and Arms Control,* p. 25; and Michael Getler, "Soviets Advance Revised Proposal on Arms Limits," *The Washington Post,* July 13, 1983, A1.

49. Both President Carter, with the signing of Presidential Directive 41 (PD-41) and President Reagan, with National Security Decision Directive 26 (NSDD-26), have taken steps to improve America's Civil Defense posture. The three elements of the current US Civil Defense program now being administered by the Federal Emergency Management Agency (FEMA) are population protection, industrial protection, and blast sheltering. See S. Norris, "President Reagan's Civil Defense Program," *The Defense Monitor,* Vol. XI, 1982. For a thorough analysis of Soviet and American civil defense efforts see John M. Weinstein, "The Strategic Implications of Civil Defense," in *The Defense of the West.*

50. Direct up and down links between the national command authorities (NCA) in Washington and missile sites and bomber bases are not likely to be very vulnerable to well-orchestrated attacks except those resulting from nuclear bursts designed specifically to impede such communications. However, the multitude of other communications which rely on relay stations and ground networks are likely to be very vulnerable to such attacks.

51. See Weinstein "The Strategic Implications of Civil Defense."

52. For a wide-ranging examination of Soviet vulnerabilities see John M. Weinstein, "All Features Grate and Stall: Soviet Strategic Vulnerabilities and the Future of Deterrence," in *The Defense of the West.*

53. Talbott, p. 157.

54. Article V of the ABM Treaty specifically prohibited the development and testing as well as deployment of sea, air, space, or mobile land-based ABM systems and components. It also prohibited both parties from developing and testing ABM launchers capable of launching more than one ABM interceptor missile or capable of rapid reload. Article VI of the treaty was designed to constrain the advance of associated radar, missile, and launcher technologies which might be converted from non-ABM use to use as part of an antiballistic missile system. It could be argued that Article II of the "interim agreement" on strategic offensive forces also limited to some degree the rate of technological advance by prohibiting the conversion of ICBMs of older types deployed prior to 1964 into land-based launchers for heavy ICBMs of types deployed after that time. However, Article II was more a reflection of American concerns over the vulnerabilities to US Minuteman ICBM missile forces which were developing as a result of the Soviet deployment of its heavy throw-weight SS-9 missiles, than it was a reflection of a specific attempt to control technological advance.

55. Christopher Bertram, "The Future of Arms Control: Part II—Arms Control and Technological Changes: Elements of a New Approach," *Adelphi Papers,* No. 146, Summer 1978, p. 2.

56. Smith, p. 99. John Newhouse noted that perhaps no problem had focused more analysis and internal debate in Washington than had the problem of verification. Similarly Strobe Talbott contended that verification was the "single biggest concern of the Congress" in its deliberations on the SALT II Treaty; see Newhouse, p. 14 and Talbott, p. 96.

57. ACDA Director George M. Seignious, "Statement before the Committee on Foreign Relations of the US Senate, July 10, 1979," in *SALT II Senate Testimony, Current Policy No. 72A,* Washington: US Department of State, Bureau of Public Affairs, July 9-11, 1979, p. 24.

58. One of the many concerns during the SALT II negotiations was the so-called SS-20/SS-16 conversion problem. The Soviet Union had tested a mobile ICBM labeled by the West as the SS-16. It then deployed the SS-20, an intermediate-range ballistic missile—essentially, the SS-16 minus its third propulsion stage. Thus, a number of strategic force analysts were concerned that the Soviet Union might be able to store the third stage of this missile and, in a crisis, quickly convert its SS-20s to ICBMs.

59. One solution to this problem was that at a specified time the United States would uncover all its map shelters so that Soviet satellites could verify the numbers of missiles the United States actually was shuffling between sites. The Soviet Union never indicated whether such an arrangement would be satisfactory. Had the United States, however, adopted a deep trench mobile basing mode for its missiles, the problem might haved been more complex.

60. For a further discussion of some of the problems of verification, see Les Aspin, "The Verification of the SALT II Agreement," *Scientific American,* February 1979, pp. 38-45; Robert Perry, *The Faces of Verification: Strategic Arms Control for the 1980's,* Santa Monica: The Rand Corporation, August 1977; Amron H. Katz, *Verification and SALT: The State of the Art and the Art of the State,* Washington: The Heritage Foundation, 1979; Paul H. Nitze, James E. Dougherty, and Francis X. Kane, *The Fateful Ends and Shades of SALT,* New York: Crane, Russak and Company, 1979; Seymour Weiss, "SALT Verification" in John F. Lehman and Seymour Weiss, eds., *Beyond the SALT II Failure,* New York: Praeger Publishers, 1981, pp. 67-81; and Stockholm International Peace Research Institute, *Strategic Disarmament, Verification and National Security,* New York: Crane, Russak and Company, Inc., 1977.

61. For a detailed discussion of the SCC, see Colonel E. Asa Bates, Jr., USAF (Ret.), "The SALT Standing Consultative Commission: An American Analyses," *Millenium,* Volume 4, 1975, pp. 132-145.

62. Talbott, *Endgame,* p. 143.

63. *Ibid.,* pp. 114-117.

64. John F. Lehman, Jr., "Verification Concerns," in *Beyond the SALT II Failure,* p. 25.

65. See Rowland Evans and Robert Novak, "SALT Loophole," *The Washington Post,* February 23, 1983, p. A17.

66. Evans and Novak, "A Smoking Gun in Siberia?"

67. For example, see Dusko Doder, "Soviet Leader Calls for Economic Reform," *The Washington Post,* August 16, 1983, p. A12.

68. Dusko Doder, "Soviets Seem Near Arms Escalation," *The Washington Post,* December 8,. 1982, p. Al.

69. Evans and Novak, "A Smoking Gun in Siberia?"

70. McGeorge Bundy, "Strategic Deterrence Thirty Years Later: What Has Changed?" in *The Future of Strategic Deterrence: Part I, Adelphi Papers,* No. 160, London: The International Institute for Strategic Studies, Autumn 1980.

71. Details of the "build-down" proposal remain sketchy at this writing. However in general the proposal calls for a minimum reduction in strategic forces of 5 percent per year. Thus, for each new system added older systems would have to be retired. The American proposal appears to be designed to retire the more vulnerable systems quickly. Thus, for each new ICBM with MIRV, such as the MX, two older systems with MIRV would have to be retired. However, for each three new SLBMs added, only two older systems would have to be retired.

PART 2
EUROPEAN SECURITY ISSUES

The Soviet Union's substantial advances in the number and lethality of its strategic nuclear weapons and its achievement of strategic parity with the United States propel to the fore questions about the status of the military balance in Europe. In the section's opening essay, Robert Kennedy traces the rapid growth of the Soviet Union's theater nuclear capabilities during the last two decades. The proliferation of the mobile SS-20 with MIRVs, the improvement of theater aviation, and the development of several new missiles have reversed the theater superiority once enjoyed by NATO. Kennedy refutes the major Soviet justifications of their massive theater deployments and argues persuasively that NATO must address this increasing imbalance, especially in long-range theater assets. Kennedy's concern with the theater nuclear balance reflects traditional NATO wisdom that its theater and strategic nuclear forces are the ultimate guarantors against Warsaw Pact conventional aggression in Europe.

Otto Chaney, drawing on a career of direct observation of and interaction with the armed forces of the Warsaw Pact, brings a critical eye to the argument that the Russians are ten feet tall. While outlining the impressive Soviet materiel acquisitions, technological improvements, and doctrinal modifications, Chaney identifies the numerous vulnerabilities, uncertainties, and mitigating factors which apparently moderate the calculations of Soviet military planners. Chaney concludes that while NATO cannot afford to be complacent and while many of the current and proposed NATO initiatives are necessary, the dire predictions of some pundits are unwarranted.

Chemical weapons occupy the hazy region between conventional and nuclear military operations. John Weinstein and Henry Gole examine the potential role of these weapons as well as the arguments of those who favor and oppose US chemical rearmament. They demonstrate that a compelling case can be made for the production of short- and long-range binary weapons although European political sensibilities make such a move unlikely in the near term.

The conventional military issues outlined above must be addressed from two perspectives. The first, outlined by Edward Corcoran, involves military strategy, doctrine, and equipment. Corcoran criticizes NATO's current forward defense attrition strategy and suggests a highly mobile, fluid and echeloned defense alternative exploiting the vulnerabilities of Soviet strategy, armor, and equipment/logistics dependencies.

The challenges of maintaining a stable deterrence are not met by military initiatives alone. Arms control is the necessary political complement to the quest for security. William Boyd's analysis of the various arms control negotiations in Europe illustrates why this quest is often frustrating. Mutual antagonisms, different force structures with different sets of missions, technological problems concerning verification and divergent conceptions of security are among the many factors that often slow the pace of arms control to a crawl.

Differences concerning the nature of security and the most effective means of stabilizing the deterrent balance do not lie exclusively between East and West. NATO has not been spared frequent strains. These strains, most recently demonstrated by the opposition of many Europeans to the deployment of NATO's Pershing II and ground launched cruise missiles, are due to the members' divergent views regarding the nature of the threat and the most effective way of dealing with it as well as their different historical experiences and perspectives. In the book's concluding chapter, Henry Gole examines these sources of stress "through European eyes" and provides an optimistic and realistic prescription for continuing NATO strength and resolve.

7

SOVIET THEATER NUCLEAR CAPABILITIES: THE EUROPEAN NUCLEAR BALANCE IN TRANSITION

Robert Kennedy

PHASES IN WESTERN DEFENSE

Since World War II, the principal focus of Western defense policies has centered on efforts designed to offset what has been perceived generally as a preponderance of Soviet conventional power on the European continent.[1] To this end, Western defense policies can be viewed as having passed through three phases and are currently in the fourth.

The American Nuclear Monopoly. Phase I began immediately after the close of the war, lasted until the early 1950's, and was characterized by America's nuclear monopoly. Shortly after VE Day, the United States, Britain, and Canada withdrew most of their forces from Europe. Within a year, the combined strength of their forces, which had approached five million men at the close of the war, had dwindled to about 880,000.[2] The Western nations were left with about 12 or so understrength divisions confronting 175 Soviet divisions, the great majority of which were then believed to be at battle strength.[3]

In addition, the Soviet Union appeared to be sustaining its armaments production at wartime levels and maintaining its military forces on a wartime footing. Soviet expansion, which was already well underway before the war's end—outright annexation of Latvia, Lithuania, Estonia, and areas of Finland, Poland, Romania, and eastern Czechoslovakia—continued. Moreover, the presence of the Soviet army in the heart of Europe had compelled Albania, Bulgaria, Romania, Eastern Germany, Poland, and Hungary to fall under the Kremlin's domination. Furthermore, the failure of the Moscow Conference (March and April 1947) to reach a settlement of the differences between the Kremlin and the West over Germany; the actions of the Soviet Union in Iran, Turkey, and Greece; Moscow's clandestine support of the Italian and French strikes; and finally, the events surrounding the "coup" in Czechoslovakia compounded Western anxieties over Soviet intentions.

In response, Western states forged a trans-Atlantic partnership which, above all, tied US strategic nuclear forces to the defense of Europe. While there may have been little fear of the massive Soviet invasion,[4] Western European states were concerned that the vastly superior Soviet forces would prove to be a useful psychological tool in effecting the political infiltration, subversion, and the ultimate takeover of Western Europe. On this point, Lord Ismay, the first Secretary-General of the North Atlantic Treaty Organization, noted:

> The situation all over the world was going from bad to worse. It was proving impossible to reach agreement with the Soviets on any international issue . . . . From behind the Iron Curtain came nothing but slander and bullying.[5]

Europeans had already begun to move toward increased defense cooperation. In March 1947, the British and French had signed the Dunkirk Treaty, establishing a basis for collaboration between their two countries. One year later, Belgium, France, Luxembourg, the Netherlands, and the United Kingdom joined in signing the Treaty of Brussels and, thus, committed themselves to a joint defensive system, as well as to a strengthening of economic and cultural ties. In the aftermath of an exhaustive war and in light of the immediacy of economic recovery, few Europeans believed, however, that Europe could muster the forces necessary to offset Soviet conventional military power. So, in April of 1949, through the formation of the North Atlantic Treaty Organization, the US Strategic Air Command (SAC) was tied to the deterrence of Soviet aggression in Europe. The US monopoly of strategic nuclear power was seen generally as a sufficient deterrent to overt Soviet aggression. Furthermore, under such a protective umbrella, it was believed that European states would be freed from the psychological constraints imposed by the huge Soviet army and, thus, would be able to devote their resources and energies to the pursuit of the economic recovery necessary for their long-term stability.

Developing Soviet Strategic Power. Phase II began early in the 1950's, lasted until sometime in the early 1960's, and was characterized by the Soviet development of strategic nuclear weaponry. The explosion of an atomic device by the Soviet Union in late 1949 did little to change Western faith in the deterrent value of US strategic weapons. Most knowledgeable observers concluded that for deterrence to be effective the United States simply had to maintain its nuclear superiority.[6] With the outbreak of the Korean War, however, new perceptions of the Soviet threat began to emerge. Some defense specialists were concerned that the North Korean attack on South Korea might be a prelude to a Soviet aggression on Europe.[7] A number of Europeans and Americans were becoming increasingly uncertain as to whether America's nuclear weapons were sufficient to deter the Soviet Union. Some Western analysts reasoned that the Soviet possession of nuclear weapons might deter America's punitive use of such weapons, except in response to a nuclear attack on the United States or on Western Europe.[8] What, then, would deter Soviet conventional aggression?

In response, Western leaders met in Lisbon, and in February 1952 agreed to improve substantially their collective conventional capabilities. By the end of 1952, NATO's member states were to contribute to the joint defense a total of 50 divisions, 4,000 aircraft, and "strong naval forces," and provisionally 75 divisions and 6,500 aircraft by 1953 and 96 divisions and 9,000 aircraft by the end of 1954.[9] Despite considerable progress in improving NATO's conventional capability, however, it was becoming evident by mid-1953 that the alliance was either unwilling or unable to meet the force goals set at Lisbon and that a serious imbalance would remain between Soviet and NATO conventional capabilities.

Once again, NATO turned to its technological superiority in nuclear weapons—this time in the form of tactical atomic munitions. By 1953, the United States had successfully tested low-yield, battlefield atomic devices. Later that same year, President

Eisenhower authorized the deployment of tactical nuclear weapons to Europe. Reactions in Europe to the NATO decision to deploy tactical atomic munitions were mixed, reflecting an uneasy balance between apprehension and hope[10] (perhaps presaging things to come). On the one hand, Western Europeans were clearly concerned over the potential impact of atomic weapons used in the defense of Europe. Such concerns were exacerbated by the Supreme Headquarters Allied Powers Europe (SHAPE) wargame "Carte Blanche" held in Western Germany, the Lowlands, and northern France in June 1955. The simulated dropping of 355 atomic bombs on military targets resulted in an estimated 1.7 million killed and 3.5 million wounded—a vivid suggestion of the magnitude of the immediate destruction that could be anticipated if tactical nuclear weapons were actually used in the defense of Europe.[11] On the other hand, Western Europeans could reason that at a time when the Soviet Union possessed neither tactical atomic weapons nor a credible strategic second strike capability, the deployment of tactical nuclear weapons appeared to provide NATO with an effective deterrent to Soviet conventional aggression which was of a tolerable cost in terms of men and money. After all, wouldn't Soviet leaders, contemplating aggression in Western Europe, be deterred by the potential for the annihilation of their forces by these battlefield devices?

Impending Strategic Parity. Phase III began in the early 1960's and lasted until the mid-1970's. This phase was characterized by an impending US-Soviet strategic balance and expanding Soviet theater nuclear capabilities. Soviet advances in medium range and intermediate range ballistic missiles (MR/IRBMs), the launching of two earth satellites, their successes with intercontinental ballistic missiles (ICBMs), and the growing availability of tactical nuclear munitions to Soviet ground forces served notice that a NATO first use of tactical nuclear weapons might be met by a Soviet response in kind. Writing in 1960, Liddell Hart expressed his pessimism concerning the fundamental question underlying Western defense plans—namely, can Europe be defended? His reply:

> For defense in a real sense of the word, as defined in dictionaries, means to 'preserve, protect, keep safe, by resisting attack.' At present, if nuclear weapons . . . are actually used no country can hope to keep safe, or even to avoid fatal destruction.[12]

In response, NATO once again focused its efforts on improving Western conventional defenses. By 1967, NATO had adopted the concept of *flexible response* and signaled its intent to respond effectively regardless of the level of aggression. Many Europeans, however, were never completely satisfied with the concept of *flexible response*. For economic reasons, Europeans generally were spontaneously hostile to improvements in conventional capabilities of a magnitude likely to be sufficient to offset Soviet conventional forces.[13] For some Europeans, *flexible response* and its emphasis on conventional force improvements seemed to decouple the defense of Europe from the American strategic deterrent, thus making a prolonged conflict in Europe more likely.[14]

Nevertheless, NATO did make some significant gains in improving its conventional capabilities. Moreover, those who argued for increased conventional capability were encouraged by the effective use of precision-guided conventional munitions in both the latter days of the Vietnam conflict and during the 1973 Arab-Israeli War.[15] Nevertheless, by the mid-1970's most nations of Western Europe, suffering from a crisis in energy and economics and confronted with multiple competing demands in the domestic sectors of their economies, were reluctant to consider matching the conventional capabilities of the Warsaw Pact. Detente further complicated the problem of allocating resources for military forces since Western publics were unconvinced of the need for additional military expenditures in the absence of a clear or present danger.[16] Thus, NATO continued to rely principally on the threat of nuclear escalation to offset the continued preponderance of Soviet conventional power and to deter the Soviet Union not only from conventional aggression, but also from the use of chemical[17] and nuclear munitions. After all, Western leaders could still reason that senior Soviet leadership would be deterred from an aggression that might reach a level of conflict at which Soviet forces were still at some *relative* disadvantage.

The Changing Theater Nuclear Balance. The latest phase began in the mid-1970's. It has been characterized by an approximate balance of US and Soviet capabilities at the strategic level and by what appears to be a Soviet attempt to achieve superiority at the theater nuclear level. In a landmark speech delivered at the International Institute for Strategic Studies in London in 1977, Helmut Schmidt expressed his concern over the changing conditions which were now confronting the alliance. According to the Federal German Chancellor, the Strategic Arms Limitation Talks (SALT) had codified the Soviet-American strategic nuclear balance, thus neutralizing the strategic nuclear capabilities of the superpowers. As a result, he cautioned, the significance of the East-West balance of tactical nuclear and conventional weapons had been magnified.[18]

Since Western Europeans and Americans had long been aware of what has generally been perceived as a clear Soviet conventional advantage in Europe, Schmidt's remarks focused public attention on a series of issues which were already commanding high level NATO interest and, thus, sparked an intensification of the debate over the nature of the Soviet theater nuclear buildup, over the implications of that buildup for deterrence and defense, and over appropriate NATO responses.

SOVIET THEATER NUCLEAR FORCE IMPROVEMENTS[19]

Over the last decade and a half, the Soviet Union has methodically improved its theater nuclear forces at all levels. In short-range systems (systems with ranges of 160 km or less), NATO once possessed an overwhelming superiority that in some quarters was perceived as one of the primary pillars of the Western deterrent. Today, the Warsaw Pact has over 600 FROG and SCUD A missile launchers readily available to the central front. Over 400 of these can be considered to have a nuclear mission. Moreover, they are now replacing these older FROG rockets with the SS-21. While little information is currently available on the SS-21, it is reported to be more accurate and have almost twice the range of the FROG missiles, and presumedly has incorporated improvements in reaction time, missile reliability, and handling characteristics. NATO, on the other hand, has about 100 short-range nuclear-tipped Lance and Honest John tactical missile launchers.[20] Even when French systems are included, the West only has about 140 short-range launchers. As a result, the Soviet Union and its Warsaw Pact allies now have a three to one advantage over the West in short-range tactical missile systems.

The Soviet Union is also now deploying dual-capable, self-propelled 152 mm, 203 mm and 240 mm artillery. Today, the Soviet military has about 450 nuclear-capable artillery tubes; NATO has about 1050. Until recently, it was thought that Soviet nuclear artillery was deployed only in the western military districts of the Soviet Union. According to the US Department of Defense, however, the Soviet Union has now begun deploying these systems with their forces in Eastern Europe.[21]

While NATO still retains a relative overall advantage in short-range systems as a result of its substantial deployment of nuclear artillery, it should be noted that these weapons, whose warheads fall on the territory of the defender, are least usable in the eyes of the Europeans for the reasons described above by Hart. In any event, the gap between NATO and Warsaw Pact battlefield capabilities has narrowed considerably over the past decade and a half and the overwhelming superiority once enjoyed by NATO has disappeared (see Table I).

The Soviet Union also has been upgrading its intermediate-range nuclear forces (INF). In shorter range INF systems (forces with ranges from 161-900 km), the Soviet forces have currently deployed approximately 600 SCUD B and SS-12 (SCALEBOARD) missile launchers and a large number of tactical aircraft, of which about 350 can be presumed to have a nuclear mission.* Today, Moscow is capable of delivering nearly 1,000 warheads with these systems not counting refires. Furthermore, they are now replacing their older SCUD B and SCALEBOARD missiles with SS-23s, and are rapidly improving the nuclear strike capabilities of their tactical aircraft. The addition of later versions of FITTER (SU-17) and MiG-21 aircraft with improved avionics and generally greater ranges than the older Soviet fighters suggests an improved capacity for low altitude penetration and attack.[22]

In comparison, NATO fields 180 Pershing 1a missiles and about 350 tactical aircraft.* Additionally, the French have about 100 aircraft in this category which are likely to be reserved for nuclear

---

*While both the Warsaw Pact and NATO have a number of additional aircraft (e.g., FENCERS, FLOGGERS, F-4s, F-111s) that can be employed against medium-range targets, because of the longer maximum operational ranges of such aircraft, they have been considered in the comparisons of the longer range intermediate-range nuclear forces (LR/INF).

TABLE I
SHORT RANGE NUCLEAR SYSTEMS*

	Deployed	PNM	Rx
Warsaw Pact			
Artillery			
152mm	—	150	—
203mm ⎫	—	300††	—
240mm ⎭			
TOTAL		450	
Tactical missiles			
Frog/SS-21	492	328	70/120†
Scud-A	150	100	70
TOTAL	642	428	
NATO			
Artillery			
155mm	1706	853	14
203mm	431	215	29
TOTAL	2137	1068	
Tactical missiles			
Lance ⎫	100††	100	110
Honest John ⎭			40
TOTAL	100††	100	
French-Pluton	42	42	120

*Short-range nuclear systems are those systems having a range ≤ 160 km. Warsaw Pact systems are all systems in Eastern Europe, including those in the western military districts of the Soviet Union; NATO systems are all systems assigned to the European theater. French forces, which are not a part of NATO, have been included for illustrative purposes only. With respect to Warsaw Pact nuclear capable artillery, NATO has estimated that the Soviet Union has deployed a total of 300 203mm guns and 240mm mortars. The US Secretary of Defense in the 1983 version of *Soviet Military Power* has confirmed that the Soviet Union has now deployed nuclear capable 203mm guns and the 240mm mortars, as well as the 152mm guns to Eastern Europe. It is reasonable to assume that at least 150 152mm guns haved a nuclear mission. PNM = probable number of artillery systems/missile launchers with a nuclear mission. Rx = approximate maximum range in kilometers.

SOURCES: †Department of Defense, *Soviet Military Power*, Washington, DC: US Government Printing Office, March 1983; ††*NATO and the Warsaw Pact Force Comparisons*, Brussels: North Atlantic Treaty Organization, n.d.; and *The Military Balance 1982-1983*, London: The International Institute for Strategic Studies, 1982.

missions. Such differences suggest a stark imbalance in shorter-range INF systems in favor of the Warsaw Pact (see Table II).

Perhaps of most concern on both sides of the Atlantic has been the slow but methodical change that has taken place in the balance of capabilities of the longer range intermediate-range nuclear forces (LR/INF), the *Eurostrategic* or grey area forces as they once were called. In the middle to late 1960's, the West was perceived to have a clear advantage in such systems. US Polaris submarines committed to NATO, US intermediate-range strike aircraft deployed on the continent or offshore on carriers, the British bomber and Polaris submarine fleets, and the French Mirage IVA strike aircraft and their expanding ballistic missile submarine fleet were seen as a more than adequate match for Soviet medium bombers and the over 600 or so medium and intermediate-range ballistic missiles (MR/IRBMs) the Soviet Union had deployed to support long-range nuclear operations in Europe.

During the last decade and a half, however, the Soviet Union has made what appears to be a determined effort to achieve a superiority in intermediate-range nuclear forces.[23] With the introduction of the FENCER (SU-19/24) and the FLOGGER (MiG-27) aircraft, the Soviet Union has substantially improved the range, payload, avionics, and electronic countermeasure capabilities of its European nuclear strike air arm.

According to the Secretary of Defense, the FENCER and FLOGGER:

> ...have had a particularly profound impact on Soviet offensive capabilities. The Fencer with its all weather, low-altitude penetration capability manifestly increases Soviet ability to carry out deep strikes into NATO territory with little advanced warning.[24]

Coupled with improvements in its nuclear-capable fighter aircraft, the Soviet Union has also been deploying a new generation of variable geometry supersonic bomber, the BACKFIRE. A product of the Tupolev design bureau, the BACKFIRE is reported to have a maximum speed at high altitude of Mach 2.0 and a low altitude supersonic capability. It can carry a full range of free fall/gravity weapons, as well as the most technically advanced air-to-surface nuclear cruise missiles available in the Soviet inventory. To date, the Soviet Union has deployed approximately 75

TABLE II
SHORTER RANGE INTERMEDIATE NUCLEAR FORCES*
(SR/INF)

	Deployed	PNM	Rx
Warsaw Pact			
Missiles			
SCUD-B/SSX-23			3-500†
SS-12/SS-22	623	623	900†
TOTAL	623	623	
Tactical aircraft			
Su-7 (Fitter-A)	198	66	400
Su-17 (Fitter-C/D/H)	516	172	700†
Su-20 (Fitter-C)	35	12	600
MIG-21 (Fishbed J-N)	—	100	400
TOTAL	—	350	
NATO			
Missiles			
Pershing-I	180	180	740
TOTAL	180	180	
Tactical aircraft			
F-104	209	97	800
Jaguar	72	35	600
F-16	68	23	900
TOTAL	349	155	
French			
Jaguar	—	45	600
Sup Etendard	36	18	560
Mirage IIIE	105	30	600

*Shorter range intermediate nuclear forces are those having a range of 161-900 km. (See Table I for definitions of PNM and Rx). It was assumed that one-third of all tactical aircraft, approximately one-half of the Jaguar and Super Extendards would be retained in a nuclear role. Ranges for tactical aircraft assume a hi-lo-hi combat mission profile.

SOURCES: †*Soviet Military Power, 1983, NATO and the Warsaw Pact Force Comparisons, Jane's All the World's Aircraft 1982-1983*, and *The Military Balance 1982-1983*.

BACKFIRE bombers to the European theater and an additional 75 in a maritime role. Production continues at the rate of 30 aircraft per year, with an expected total deployment including those for maritime uses of 250-400 aircraft.[25]

The system that has caused the most concern in the West has been the introduction of the SS-20 IRBM. The SS-20 is a solid-fueled, two-staged, mobile missile with multiple independently targetable reentry vehicles (MIRVs). It is currently replacing or augmenting the older, less accurate SS-4s and SS-5s. One expert, formerly a senior Department of Defense civilian official now writing under the name of Justin Galen, has contended that the reliability, accuracy, reload, and retargeting capability of the SS-20 could permit its use in a mass strike "against virtually every NATO air base, weapons storage site, C^3 (command, control, and communications) site and fixed missile site with negligible warning."[26] A more poignant illustration of the concern raised by the SS-20 is to be found in the remarks of French strategist Pierre Gallois. Gallois contends that with the addition of the SS-20 the Soviet Union can now destroy NATO's entire inventory of nuclear weapons in 10 minutes.[27]

Today, while there is an approximate parity in long-range INF aircraft with a dedicated nuclear mission and when SS-20 missiles available as reloads to SS-20 missile launchers are counted, the Soviet Union fields about 770 MR/IRBMs (SS-4s, SS-5s, SS-N-5s, and SS-20s) with over 1,700 warheads. NATO, on the other hand, does not field any land-based LR/INF missile systems and only about 160 SLBMs when British and French forces are counted. Thus, Soviet missile deployments outnumber the West by well over 4 to 1. Even when the 40 US Poseidon missiles already included in SALT counts, but supposedly dedicated to SACEUR for theater use, are included, the Soviet Union still has almost a 4 to 1 advantage in missiles (see Table III) and about a 3 to 1 advantage in warheads.

The inherent "softness" of the data available on Soviet and Western nuclear capabilities prohibits precise calculations of the balances of theater nuclear capabilities. We are captive of the many assumptions that must be made, especially with respect to aircraft.[28] Nevertheless, given the data available, the composite of theater-nuclear capabilities now available to the Soviet Union suggests that the NATO/Warsaw Pact balance of nuclear forces has shifted over the past decade from one that favored the West to

TABLE III
LONGER RANGE INTERMEDIATE NUCLEAR FORCES*
(LR/INF)

	Deployed	PNM	Rx
Warsaw Pact			
Missiles			
SS-4 (Sandal)	248†	248	2000†
SS-5 (Skean)			4100†
SS-20	243	486	5000†
SS-N-5 (Serb)	39	39	1400
TOTAL	530	773	
Aircraft			
SU-24 (Fencer)	412	137	1800†
MiG-23/27 (Flogger)	412	137	1200†
TU-16 (Badger)	232	116	2800
TU-22 (Blinder)	94	47	3100
TU-26 (Backfire)	75	38	5500†
TOTAL	1225	475	
NATO			
Missiles			
Polaris	64	64	4000
French			
SSBS-S3	18	18	3000
MSBS-M20	80	80	3000
Strategic			
Poseidon	40	40	4600
Aircraft			
Vulcan-B2	48	48	2800
Buccaneer	50	25	950
F-111	156	78	1900
F-4	424	141	1000
A-6	20	10	1600
A-7	48	24	950
TOTAL	746	326	
French Mirage-IVA	34	34	1600
Aggregate LR/INF Capabilities			
Warsaw Pact	1755	1248	—
NATO	810	390	—
NATO (Incl French & US StrategicSystems)	982	562	

*Longer Range Intermediate Nuclear Systems are those systems having a maximum range of 901-4800+ km. (See Table I for definitions of NATO, Warsaw Pact, PNM, and Rx). French forces which are not a part of NATO forces have been included for illustrative purposes only, as have been US Poseidon missiles which are counted under SALT as strategic. It is assumed that 243 SS-20 missile launchers are deployed within range to strike targets in Central Europe and that one reload is available per launcher.

SOURCES: †*Soviet Military Power, 1983, The Military Balance 1982-1983,* and *Jane's All the World's Aircraft 1982-1983.*

one that now favors the Soviet Union and its Warsaw Pact allies. While the West may retain an advantage in short-range systems, the Soviet Union is certainly ahead in intermediate-range forces. On this point, the prestigious International Institute for Strategic Studies has concluded that "the balance is distinctly unfavorable to NATO and is becoming more so."[29]

SOVIET DOCTRINE

For those concerned about Soviet theater nuclear force improvements, an understanding of Soviet doctrine has compounded the anxieties. Since the days of Nikita Khrushchev, Soviet military writers have rejected Stalin's World War II idea of adopting the strategic defensive during the early phases of conflict.[30] Today, Soviet doctrine extols surprise, rapid offensive, high-tempo operations. Surprise is seen as one of the most important principles of the military art. As a result, "the desire for surprise has begun to permeate all decisions for the conduct of operations and battles."[31] Indeed, Colonel A. A. Sidorenko, in a work listed as recommended reading in "The Officer's Library" and intended for reading "by officers of the Soviet Army, students in higher military schools and reserve officers" has argued that the history of conflict itself has emphasized the value of surprise. "Extremely often the absence of surprise turned out to be the reason for the failure of an operation at its very beginning."[32]

Equally stressed by Soviet military theorists is the importance of rapid offensive combat operations. Soviet military science considers the offensive as the foremost type of military combat action. V. Ye. Savkin writes: "the offensive is the basic form of combat actions, since only by a decisive offensive conducted at a high tempo and to a great depth is total defeat of the enemy achieved."[33] Similarly, in his seminal work on offensive warfare, Sidorenko stressed the need for "swift development of the breakthrough," the value of a rapid "offensive in depth" and, in general, the importance of maneuver and shock action on the modern battlefield.[34] Likewise, Division Commander Colonel Lobachev has argued that "a high tempo is not a goal in itself, but a means to achieving victory in combat. The speed of movement of the attackers denies the enemy the opportunity to freely maneuver with his forces and equipment, to utilize the reserve . . . and it neutralizes many of the strengths of the enemy defense."[35]

What is disconcerting, however, is that Soviet military theorists have consistently contended that nuclear weapons—indeed all weapons of mass destruction, nuclear, chemical, and biological—enhance the element of surprise and rapid offensive operations. Likewise, surprise and rapid offense increase the value of nuclear weapons in securing victory. Describing the relationship between nuclear warfare and Soviet doctrine and defense planning, Soviet writers have proclaimed the nuclear weapon to be the "most important element of the battle,"[36] "the basic means of destruction."[37]

They contend that "the side which employs nuclear weapons with surprise can predetermine the outcome of battle in his favor."[38] They further argue that the combat qualities of highly mobile shock forces permit rapid exploitation of "the results of the employment of nuclear and other means of mass destruction most effectively, overcoming the enemy's defense at a high rate, breaking through into his deep rear swiftly, advancing over any terrain including that contaminated with radio-active substances, and inflicting powerful blows on the enemy."[39] Moreover, "nuclear strikes can destroy the strongest centers and strongpoints in the enemy defense, his reserves, means of mass destruction, and other important objectives." Consequently, Soviet military writers have concluded that through "the stunning effect of surprise attacks by nuclear and conventional weapons and decisive offensive operations by troops, the enemy's capabilities are sharply lowered, . . . the correlation of forces changes immediately . . . . He may panic and his morale will be crushed."[40]

Thus, a number of defense analysts on both sides of the Atlantic are not only concerned about Soviet theater nuclear force improvements but also about the harmony that exists between those force improvements and current Soviet doctrine.

IMPLICATIONS FOR NATO

A Devalued Deterrent. As Klaas de Vries, former chairman of the Dutch Defense Committee, has argued, Soviet theater nuclear force improvements have not neutralized the ability of the West to deter conflict in Europe.[41] Moscow is likely to harbor few illusions about the destructive potential of the West's nuclear arsenal—which by any standards remains formidable. Soviet leaders are not likely to set out deliberately on a course which they believe might lead to a nuclear war.

Nevertheless, in a broader sense, Soviet theater nuclear force improvements have resulted in a depreciation of the deterrent value of the West's nuclear arsenal. From a Western perspective, the deterrence once provided by Western nuclear superiority was simply never limited to the notion of deterring the deliberate initiation of conflict. Rather, an effective deterrent was also viewed as one which served to limit Soviet policy options in time of crisis and, thus, reduce the potential for a slow slide to nuclear war based on mutual miscalculation. In theory, while Soviet leaders could be expected to test Western resolve in any number of ways, ultimately they would be deterred not only from the deliberate initiation of conflict, but also from specific actions which might lead to conflict and an ensuing escalation to levels at which they were at a relative disadvantage.

Today, in an age of strategic parity, Soviet INF superiorities are likely to provide Moscow with a sense of increased room for political maneuver. While Soviet leaders are basically conservative in outlook and well aware of their own limitations as well as of the probable consequences of conflict in Europe,[42] they are also keenly aware of Western European concerns about the potentially devastating effect of a nuclear war in Europe. In light of such concerns, Soviet leaders now are likely to believe that "sober" assessments by the West of the new balance of nuclear capabilities on the continent of Europe further reduce the risk of war erupting from serious disputes. Thus, in a crisis with the West, Soviet leaders are likely to feel somewhat more confident today that they can successfully engage in political coercion, crises bargaining, and bluff than they felt, say in the early 1960's. Unfortunately, coercive bargaining and bluff on the part of Soviet leadership during a crisis are likely to increase the possibility of miscalculation and confrontation and, thus, the potential for the very conflict all sides seek to avoid.

A Decline in Western Self-Confidence. Perhaps as significant as the potential for Soviet miscalculation during crises is the debilitating effect knowledge of that potential and of Soviet military capabilities has on Western elites during peacetime. As the balance of nuclear capabilities moves increasingly in favor of the Soviet Union, Western confidence in its ability to provide an effective deterrent declines. Few, if any, believe the Soviet Union is likely to attack Western Europe in the foreseeable future. The West is uncomfortable, nevertheless, with Soviet conventional, chemical, and nuclear might. Today, we in the West are uncertain what current imbalances mean in light of detente as amended by events in Afghanistan, Poland, Africa, and Latin America and by continued Soviet arms acquisitions. We are uncertain about the nature of security provided through the NATO link. Under such circumstances, consensus for action diminishes. Confidence and determination are replaced by confusion, anxiety, hesitation, and political fragmentation—the resulting combined effects further weaken our ability to achieve consensus within and among the member states of NATO.[43]

The bottom line is that the Kremlin knows full well the potential political impact of superior military power. According to Thomas W. Wolfe, long-time Soviet specialist for the Rand Corporation, civilian and military elements of the Soviet leadership elite appear to share similar attitudes toward military power, ascribing to it a more positive value than is generally the case in the West. Wolfe notes that among the values ascribed to military power are its utility for gaining political objectives, for supporting an ambitious foreign policy, and for opening opportunities to advance communism in the world.[44]

In short, the Soviet elite believes military strength pays dividends beyond deterrence, that superior military power is a useful peacetime psychological tool, with a subconscious component that can serve in subtle ways to secure Soviet interests in Europe. As Josef Joffe, senior editor of the German weekly *Die Zeit,* has noted while speaking on a related subject: A kind of "psychological setting" can be created "where arm twisting becomes superfluous." Power—real power—"is when you don't have to threaten."[45]

Increased Vulnerabilities. In 1971, the late Minister of Defense Marshal Grechko detailed Soviet targeting priorities for their longer-range theater nuclear forces. Top on the priority list were US Pershing missile bases, nuclear-capable NATO air force units, tanker bases, British and French nuclear submarines, tactical nuclear weapons storage sites and US aircraft carriers. Such targets were then followed by major ports, military bases and barracks, nuclear reactors, command and control centers, and the transportation and supply nets.[46] Thus, the West's nuclear forces and critical command, control, and supply nodes have been principal candidates for Soviet attack for over a decade. However, the addition of the SS-20 and the continued deployment of new generation tactical fighter/bomber aircraft such as the FENCER and BACKFIRE has significantly increased the vulnerability of Western forces.

The high accuracy of the SS-20 has reduced the number of warheads required to assure the destruction of a specific target, while the warhead with MIRV has increased the potential number of targets that can be struck by a single missile by threefold. In the past, it would have been necessary for the Soviet Union to launch two, perhaps three, of their older SS-4 or SS-5 missiles in order to have a high confidence of destroying a specific target—rapidly exhausting their capabilities. Today, with the SS-20 and MIRV, it is theoretically possible for Soviet forces to destroy with slightly over 100 SS-20 missiles the same number of targets it would have taken their entire force of SS-4s and SS-5s to destroy. Likewise, older generation aircraft frequently lacked the avionics, electronic countermeasures, range, and payload characteristics which make the new generation fighter bombers and BACKFIRE-like aircraft a serious threat to NATO's deep rear.

THE NATO RESPONSE

In December 1979, NATO Foreign and Defense Ministers agreed in Brussels to modernize NATO's nuclear forces by deploying US land-based intermediate-range missile systems in Europe. At the same time, in what became known as the dual-track decision, the ministers agreed to seek negotiations with the Soviet Union to limit INF and announced that NATO's INF requirements would be examined in light of the results achieved through negotiations.[47]

Both decisions were the product of extensive alliance consultations on the impact of Soviet nuclear force improvements. By 1977, Western defense specialists were becoming increasingly concerned that while the Soviet SS-20 would not be included in SALT II limitations, the protocol to the SALT II Agreement would ban both ground and sea-launched US cruise missiles with ranges in excess of 600 km. Perhaps even more important, through a series of further SALT restrictions on technology transfers, Moscow was seeking to make certain that none of America's European allies would be able to compensate for continued Soviet SS-20 developments with their own deployments of cruise missiles. Thus, when NATO heads of government met in May of 1977, they agreed, as a part of NATO's Long-Term Defense Program, to examine ways of modernizing the Alliance's theater nuclear forces (TNF). The following October, NATO's Nuclear Planning Group (NPG), the alliance forum for nuclear policy consultation, created the High Level Group (HLG). Its task was to establish a comprehensive framework for an assessment of NATO's long-term needs for theater nuclear forces. The HLG met three times in late 1977 and early 1978 and concluded that an "evolutionary adjustment" in NATO's theater nuclear forces that provided somewhat more long-range capability was needed. The initial findings of the HLG were noted at the NPG Ministerial meeting in Fredrikshavn, Denmark, in April 1978. NATO ministers agreed then that the issue needed careful attention because of the growing threat from the East and the potential political implications and cost considerations that would attend any move to improve NATO long-range nuclear forces.[48] The position of the United States, however, remained somewhat ambivalent on whether any upward adjustment of NATO's TNF was necessary. While some elements within the US national security community were prepared to accept the HLG conclusions, others were concerned that any theater nuclear force improvements would further complicate SALT and contribute to potential divisive discussions within NATO touching basic alliance nuclear doctrine and practice.[49] Moreover, there was a belief in some quarters that European concerns over growing Soviet power could be offset by some further commitment of US sea-based nuclear forces. By 1979, however, any ambivalence in the US position had disappeared as the United States lined up firmly behind the HLG consensus view.[50]

Western reactions to the NATO 1979 "double decision" have been mixed. Much of the popular opposition to any deployment of Pershing II or cruise missiles has been founded on a general emotional reaction to what has been wrongfully perceived as further additions[51] to the world's already immense nuclear arsenals and to the understandable concerns over the implications for Europe, indeed for mankind, should deterrence fail. Misunderstandings of the fundamental objectives of President Carter's countervailing strategy and concerns over early policies and pronouncements of the Reagan Administration, both exacerbated by a well-organized Soviet disinformation campaign, have further contributed to public anxieties, added impetus to nuclear freeze and no first use of nuclear weapons movements, and dotted the landscape of Europe with antinuclear protest marches.

Beyond the emotional level, however, alliance deployment of Pershing II cruise missiles has been opposed for three fundamental reasons. First, some have argued that a balance exists, that any further deployments will only provoke the Soviet Union unnecessarily into further missile deployments in an unending pattern of deployments and counterdeployments, and that the alliance would be better served by accepting the Soviet offer to limit its European SS-20 missile deployments to a number equal to the British and French long-range missile deployments. Second, some observers contend that cruise missiles and, especially, Pershing II, threaten the Soviet Union with a potential first strike. However, because these missiles are vulnerable, they invite Soviet preemption and, thus, contribute to crisis instability rather than stability. Finally, it has been argued that Pershing II and cruise missiles do little to enhance NATO's deterrent posture. Each of these substantive concerns warrants further examination.[52]

The Balance and Britain and France. In November 1977, Leonid Brezhnev declared that the Soviet Union wished to preserve the approximate equilibrium that existed between East and West in Central Europe.[53] At that time, the Soviet Union had deployed about a dozen SS-20s. Since then, Moscow has deployed over 230 additional SS-20 launchers within striking distance of all of Western Europe. Thus, despite Soviet propaganda—which has gone to great lengths in its attempts to portray a balance in Central Europe by excluding from data counts many of its own nuclear-capable aircraft and by grossly inflating the numbers of American aircraft based in Western Europe or on aircraft carriers off Europe,[54] available evidence clearly indicates that the balance of intermediate-range nuclear capabilities has shifted in favor of the Soviet Union. Today, the United States deploys no LR/INF missiles. Even when British and French sea and land-based long-range nuclear forces are included, the Soviet Union has nearly a 5 to 1 advantage in missiles. Likewise, the Soviet Union enjoys an advantage in the numbers of nuclear-capable tactical aircraft (see Table III). With the current imbalance in Soviet and American capabilities in mind and after close consultations with America's NATO partners, the United States informed the Soviet Union in November 1981 that it was willing to cancel the deployment of Pershing II ballistic missiles and ground-launched cruise missiles (BGM-109G) if the Soviet Union would dismantle its SS-20, SS-4, and SS-5 missiles. President Reagan's initiative—the so-called "zero option"—was widely welcomed in the West as an important first step in attempts to reduce the overall number of nuclear weapons in Europe. Moreover, the initiative was designed to address directly the growing imbalance of intermediate-range nuclear forces where it exists—in intermediate-range missiles.

Moscow responded by first promising a moratorium on INF deployments for the duration of the negotiations and then with proposals which included British and French forces.[55] Moscow's logic for including the British and French forces in its calculations is the demand for "equal security" in Europe.[56] The USSR contended that:

> Making the number of Soviet medium-range missiles in Europe equal to that of the member-countries of the North Atlantic Alliance would conform to the principle of equality and equal security . . . . It is obvious that NATO is represented in the balance of medium-range nuclear weapons in Europe by the United States, Britain and France, while the Warsaw Treaty Organization is represented only by the Soviet Union, since there are no other nuclear powers in the latter alliance. All those Western weapons—and not only those of the United States—are targeted against the Soviet Union and its allies.[57]

On the surface, such an argument appears to have a compelling simplicity; however, a number of factors should be considered before conceding to Soviet demands. First, British and French forces are national strategic forces. While British forces are assigned to NATO, they are also reserved for independent strategic deterrent needs. French forces are not even under NATO control. In terms of roles and missions, British and French forces do not differ from the strategic SLBM and ICBM forces of the Soviet Union or the United States. Their fundamental mission is to provide Britain and France minimum deterrent protection from strategic attack.

Perhaps a case could be made for the inclusion of such forces in talks on strategic force limitations. However, one must remember that as minimum essential deterrent forces, the sum total of British and French forces is small compared to those of the Soviet Union and the United States and that numerical advantage conceded to the Soviet Union in both SALT I and SALT II have more than compensated for British and French strategic capabilities.[58] In any case, because of their strategic characteristics, inclusion of British and French forces in the current INF negotiating forum would appear to be inappropriate.

Second, the INF negotiations in Geneva are bilateral negotiations between the United States and the Soviet Union. Neither the United States nor the Soviet Union have any authority to speak for Britain or France. Nor can either dictate the size of British or French strategic forces. Furthermore, both the British and French have stated explicitly that they oppose having their forces included in current INF negotiations. If Moscow wishes to include British and French forces, it must take the unpopular step of terminating current bilateral talks with the United States and call for multilateral INF talks which include Britain and France. Another, potentially more rational, alternative might be to call for multilateral START negotiations and deal with independent strategic forces in a proper strategic context.

Third, the Soviet demand to include British and French forces in INF negotiations under the guise of "equal security" is tantamount to a call for "absolute security" underwritten by "absolute superiority." What Moscow, in essence, is seeking through arms control is a recognition that it should be permitted to maintain forces equal in number to the nuclear weapons of all the other nuclear powers combined. They have already indicated that their SS-20 missile forces facing China and Japan (both already threatened by Soviet strategic forces) are sacrosanct. Now they demand to have additional forces to offset those of Britain and France as well as those of the United States. In theory, if every country demanded to have nuclear forces equal to those of all other possible combinations of adversaries, arms control would be impossible. Indeed, there would be a rapid spiraling of the nuclear arms race.

Finally, it is the potential for the involvement of US theater nuclear and, ultimately, US strategic forces that serves as the principal deterrent to Soviet conventional or nuclear aggression in

Europe. On this point Lawrence Eagleburger, Under Secretary of State for Political Affairs, has commented:

> Stability (in Europe) depends on a clear American commitment to the security of our allies. Only when it is plain to everybody, especially the Soviet Union, that the full weight of American military might stands ready to defend Western Europe can the Europeans be free from the threat of Soviet intimidation. American nuclear weapons are deployed on the continent to protect our allies, whether or not they have nuclear weapons of their own. Only American weapons can perform this task because only the United States can match the size and strength of the Soviet nuclear arsenal. There is no substitute, strategically or politically.[59]

Since the individual nations of NATO cannot be certain that either the British or the French would actually be willing to use their minimum deterrent nuclear forces in response to a Soviet attack on, say, West Germany, rather than hold them in reserve to deter a direct Soviet attack on their own countries, the only forces that are actually a deterrent counterbalance to Soviet INF deployments are US INF forces. Furthermore, from the Soviet perspective a Soviet planner is likely to reason that the probable link to US strategic forces and a strategic exchange is far stronger if US INF forces are involved in a conflict in Europe than if British and French forces are.

Vulnerability and Crisis Stability. It also has been argued by some that the highly accurate[60] and quick reacting Pershing II missile force will be able to strike high value Soviet targets—Soviet political and military leadership, command and control facilities, and hardened military installations—in a matter of minutes. Thus, these weapons threaten the Soviet Union with "decapitation."[61] It is further argued that since these weapons are relatively vulnerable they invite Soviet preemption and hence, contribute to instability. Indeed, one observer has stated, "more than any other weapon in NATO's inventory, the Pershing II threatens crisis stability."[62] Moreover, Moscow contends that like the Pershing II, cruise missiles with their capacity to fly at low altitudes, elude discovery, and strike targets with pinpoint accuracy also are capable of such a "decapitating" first strike.[63]

This form of crisis instability—preemptive instability or, in this case, the inclination of the Soviet Union to resort to a preemptive first strike in a severe crisis to avoid having its own nuclear capabilities and command and control nets destroyed by a first strike by US INF systems,[64] however, is more a function of the potential vulnerability of US INF systems than of any first strike capabilities the Soviet Union may perceive these systems to have. That is to say, Soviet leadership is not likely to initiate a nuclear war through preemption if the probability of destroying US INF systems is low despite any notions they might have about US INF first strike capabilities.

Nonetheless, once deployed in Europe, NATO's Pershing II and cruise missile forces will be neither capable of decapitation nor inherently vulnerable to a Soviet preemptive attack. First, the size of the deployment is too small to offer high probabilities of success in such a strike, given the defenses, redundancy, and hardening of Soviet facilities. Second, only the Pershing II ballistic missile can strike targets quickly and its range (1800 km)[65] is insufficient to strike Moscow. Third, despite its potential accuracy, the NATO ground-launched cruise missile force must traverse Eastern European countries and parts of the Soviet Union before striking its targets, thus providing hours of warning.

Concerning potential vulnerabilities, while it is true that in their peacetime locations in Western Europe US INF systems would be vulnerable to a surprise attack, a "bolt out of the blue" attack is simply unlikely. What is, of course, of concern is that warning signals will be misinterpreted or that political warning will not be translated into operational military warning for any of a variety of reasons.[66] In either case, however, a conflict in Europe initiated by Soviet forces with direct deep nuclear and conventional attacks on Western missile forces and command and control facilities would involve such enormous destruction in densely populated Western Europe that it would be of enormous psychological and political consequence in the West. To take such a nuclear initiative in Europe, as Francois de Rose, former French Ambassador to NATO has said: "The leaders in Moscow would have to believe that it would not entail the risk of a major confrontation with the United States;" an assumption which is very unlikely to mark the rationale of Soviet policy.[67] On the other hand, if Soviet planners were to assume the more likely, that such an attack might well invite a US/NATO strategic retaliatory nuclear response, then they would be wise to advise Soviet leadership of the necessity to begin hostilities with a full strategic preemptive attack on America's retaliatory force in an attempt to limit damage to the Soviet Union. It is difficult, however, to envisage any initial Soviet objectives in Western Europe which would be worth initiating a US-Soviet strategic nuclear war.

Notwithstanding, with a modicum of warning the inherent mobility of Pershing II and cruise missiles makes these weapons largely invulnerable to a Soviet preemptive attack. It has been argued that once these missiles are removed from their storage depots there will be no hardening to protect them, and, although they are mobile, they will not move swiftly nor be easily concealed on the crowded highways of West Germany. Thus, if Soviet overhead reconnaissance cannot keep track of them, Soviet agents on the ground will.[68] However, these missiles when moved will be protected by Western forces. They will be able to be dispersed to a large number of sites. Presumedly, there will always be a portion of the force on the move to new locations. Under such circumstances one should not underestimate the complexity of the problem posed to the Soviet Union in any attempts to target such a force. Even if it received information from its agents or from satellite photography concerning the specific location of some of the dispersed missiles, by the time that information was processed and targets assigned to firing units, what confidence would the Soviet leadership have that all the information was accurate and that the missiles were still in their original location? Indeed, John Erickson, a well-known specialist on the Soviet military, has noted that one point which has not been lost on the Soviet command is that a "high confidence first-strike capability" is an elusive animal.[69] There is little question that the USSR might be successful in targeting some of NATO's Pershing II and cruise missile forces. Once dispersed, however, these systems will be clearly less vulnerable than much of NATO's current nuclear forces. Thus, Pershing II and cruise missiles will reduce, rather than increase, the temptation of the Soviet Union to preempt during a severe crisis or conventional conflict. As a result, there should be a relatively greater incentive to seek solutions to crises or terminate a conventional conflict early before nuclear weapons become involved.

Some observers have argued that NATO would be better served to deploy these forces at sea since Pershing II and cruise missiles deployed in land-basing modes will not be perfectly invulnerable to attack. Under such circumstances, however, from a Soviet perspective these forces would be virtually indistinguishable from US/NATO's strategic retaliatory forces. Thus, an intermediate option which strengthens the linkage between conflict in Europe and US strategic forces would be lost. Furthermore, while the Soviet Union has already deployed cruise missiles at sea and the United States, for the near term, also is planning to deploy sea-launched cruise missiles with nuclear warheads on attack submarines and surface ships,[70] it may still be possible to limit through arms control such deployments. The problem will be further complicated if NATO moves its Pershing II and cruise missiles forces to sea.

Deterrence in the Age of Strategic Parity. Deterrence depends on the credible threat of pain. It is the expectation of violence, as well as the potential level of violence that might be anticipated in response to one's actions that influences decisions. During the era of US strategic superiority, the linkage between the threat of aggression and the threat of pain was clear. The linkage was forged of a logic that suggested that the side possessing an overwhelming nuclear advantage (the US/NATO) was likely to use that advantage, if necessary (i.e., deliberately escalate a conflict), to assure a favorable outcome should an adversary (the USSR/Warsaw Pact) initiate a major aggression in Europe. Thus, deterrence seemed assured. No adversary would commit national suicide.

Today, that logic, and thus the linkage, is less certain. In the age of US-Soviet strategic parity, deterrence depends less on the concept of "deliberate escalation" and more on the maintenance of capabilities which suggest to a potential aggressor a high probability that the flow of events in a conflict might ultimately result in a strategic nuclear exchange and a concomitant level of pain and horror never before experienced throughout the history of conflict—not because the United States or NATO would deliberately choose such a response in the first instance, but because NATO's capabilities underscore the potential for an interaction, should the Soviet Union attack, which is likely to result sooner or later in an exchange of strategic nuclear forces.

Thus, deterrence in Europe today depends on a balance between certainty and uncertainty. Soviet leaders must be certain that the West has the capacity to respond to any level of aggression Moscow may choose. At the same time, Soviet leadership must remain uncertain as to just *how* the West will respond, what impact the force of events will have on the potential for escalation, and, hence, what the risks and costs of an aggression would be. This suggests the need for the West to maintain a number of options across the spectrum of capabilities. Indeed, such options forge the conceptual link between Soviet conventional aggression in Europe and US/NATO strategic retaliatory forces and are the bulwark of the Western deterrent in the age of strategic parity.[71] Pershing II and cruise missiles will fill an already existing gap between NATO and Soviet/Warsaw Pact capabilities.

The Soviet Union has argued that Pershing II and cruise missiles are strategic weapons. They can strike the Soviet Union, while SS-20s, indeed the entire panoply of Soviet theater weapons, can only reach into Western Europe. What the Soviet leadership must be made to understand is that from the perspective of the North Atlantic Alliance, including the United States, a nuclear strike on Paris, Bonn, or Bremen is as strategic as a strike on the United States. Thus, if the Soviet Union is unwilling to negotiate serious reductions of its SS-4s, SS-5s, and SS-20s, the deployment of Pershing II and cruise missiles will offer additional options which enhance the ability of the West not only to deter Soviet conventional aggression, but also a Soviet nuclear aggression—including the use of its SS-20s and other intermediate-range nuclear forces. NATO need not match one for one Soviet deployments to accomplish this task. However, a rough balance should be maintained for psychological as well as military purposes. Moreover, to the extent that Pershing II and cruise missiles represent a shift in emphasis from short-range systems which threaten Western Europe with destruction if used to longer-range systems which threaten Eastern Europe, including the Western USSR, there should be a corresponding further improvement in the deterrent effect of the Western nuclear arsenal and an increase in Western self-confidence.[72] Correspondingly, failure to fill the gap in theater nuclear capabilities created by the extensive Soviet deployments of the SS-20 IRBM will further erode the West's capacity to deter aggression in Europe.

A strong criticism of providing additional nuclear options to decisionmakers is that while such options may improve deterrence, they are likely to lower the nuclear threshold. Moreover, from a European perspective, options below the US-Soviet strategic level might result in a nuclear war confined only to Europe. The common line of argumentation is that US and Soviet leaders might be more inclined to use theater nuclear options than to engage each other's strategic forces with cataclysmic consequence. This, in fact, is the great dilemma of deterrence in the age of parity. Credible deterrence requires options which clearly appear more useable to a potential adversary than the threat of mutual annihilation. Yet, those very options suggest an increased probability that nuclear weapons *will* be used in something less than a full strategic exchange should war actually occur. Here I would suggest that while contemporary wisdom on this issue is correct, at least in theory, in practice the availability of options below a total strategic exchange is not likely to lower the nuclear threshold very much if at all. This is so because of the propensity, especially in a nuclear environment with an eminent potential for total annihilation, for worst case planning on both sides. Thus, for the Soviet leaders' part, they are likely to assume that should their forces succeed in breaking through Western defenses in an attack on Central Europe, the West, driven by bureaucratic momentum, established procedures, and an impetus to use rather than lose its nuclear weapons,[73] would be likely to resort to those weapons to avoid being overrun. On the other hand, the American President and other Western leaders, despite bureaucratic momentum, and so forth, are likely to reason that any use of nuclear weapons would result in a Soviet nuclear response. Hence, nuclear options below the strategic level greatly reduce the probability of a conflict of any kind occurring in Europe without, in practice, measurably altering the nuclear threshold.

CONCLUSION

It is necessary to keep in mind that a relative balance of nuclear capabilities is important for deterrence. There need not be an absolute equality in all categories of weapon systems. In the age of rough nuclear parity, however, the overall balance, as well as the balance in any major category of potential options, should not be allowed to get too far out of line if an effective deterrent to aggression is to be maintained. Soviet theater nuclear improvements over the past decade and a half have succeeded in shifting the balance of nuclear capabilities in favor of the Soviet

Union. This is especially true of both shorter and longer-range INF systems. The effect on NATO of that shift has been a devaluation of deterrence, a decline in Western self-confidence, and an increase in NATO vulnerabilities.

If the Soviet Union is unwilling to negotiate a significant reduction in the INF systems which now pose a serious threat to the West, the NATO deployment of Pershing II and cruise missiles will not only help to restore balance to the NATO/Warsaw Pact nuclear equation, but will also enhance deterrence, reduce NATO vulnerabilities, and thus, contribute to crisis stability in Europe.

While it is important to examine alternatives for improving NATO's conventional capabilities as a means of raising the nuclear threshold, it is even more important to assure a rough balance of NATO-Warsaw Pact nuclear capabilities exists and the linkage to US strategic retaliatory forces is preserved—for as one European statesman has observed: while Europe has been at peace there have been more than 140 wars in the rest of the world. And it has been "precisely nuclear weapons, with their tremendous powers of devastation, that have forced the great powers to the green table and made the amicable settlement of disputes the only acceptable form of political agreement."[74]

ENDNOTES

1. Whether Western fears of Soviet capabilities or intentions were justified or rather served to produce policies which evoked a Soviet reaction and thus contributed to setting the "Cold War" in motion (as a number of alternative explanations of post-World War II history might suggest) is not material to the discussion. The fact is that for the most part the fears were genuine and the policy responses were a natural outgrowth of those fears. For a review of revisionist literature on the origins of the "Cold War" see Robert James Maddox, *The New Left and the Origins of the Cold War*, Princeton: Princeton University Press, 1973; J. L. Richardson, "Cold-War Revisionism: A Critique," *World Politics*, July 1972, pp. 579-612; and Robert W. Tucker, *The Radical Left and American Foreign Policy*, Baltimore: The Johns Hopkins Press, 1971. See also Matthew A. Evangelista, "Stalin's Postwar Army Reappraised," *International Security*, Winter 1982/1983, pp. 110-138.

2. See Lord Ismay, *NATO: The First Five Years 1949-1954*, Netherlands: Bosch-Utrecht, n.d., p. 4.

3. Writing in 1962, Robert E. Osgood in his seminal work on NATO noted that the Soviet Union maintained 25 fully armed divisions in Central Europe and, overall, at least 140 of 175 divisions at battle strength. He did not define what he meant by battle strength, however. See his *NATO: The Entangling Alliance*, Chicago: The University of Chicago Press, 1962, p. 29. By the late 1950's and early 1960's it was becoming more apparent that actual manpower levels of Soviet divisions differed, based on their location, with the more forward divisions more fully manned. See Evangelista, pp. 111-112.

4. Osgood, p. 30.

5. Ismay, p. 6.

6. Osgood, pp. 52-53.

7. For example see President Truman's "Statement, June 17, 1950," *Department of State Bulletin*, July 3, 1950, p. 5 and statement by Secretary of Defense Johnson before the US Congress, Senate, Committee on Appropriations, *Supplemental Appropriations for 1951*, Hearings before the Senate Committee on Appropriations, 81st Cong., 2d Sess., p. 272. Also see Roger Hilsman, "NATO: The Developing Strategic Contest," in *NATO and American Security*, edited by Klaus Knorr, Princeton: Princeton University Press, 1959, p. 18.

8. For example see Andre Beaufre, *NATO and Europe*, New York: Alfred A. Knopf, 1966, pp. 57-58 or Denis Healey, "Britain and NATO," in *NATO and American Security*, p. 210.

9. Osgood, p. 87.

10. For a thorough discussion of some of the factors which contributed to allied uneasiness as the Alliance came to rely increasingly on tactical nuclear weapons for defense see Hilsman, pp. 24-29.

11. See Osgood, p. 127. For an analysis of the impact of "Carte Blanche" on German opinion see Hans Speier, *German Rearmament and Atomic War*, White Plains, New York: Row, Peterson & Co., 1957, especially Chapters X and XI. See also Karl W. Deutsch and Lewis J. Edinger, *Germany Rejoins the Powers*, Stanford, California: Stanford University Press, 1959, p. 27.

12. B. H. Liddell Hart, *Deterrent or Defense*, New York: Frederick A. Praeger, 1960, p. 47.

13. Raymond Aron, *The Great Debate*, Garden City: Doubleday and Company, Inc., 1965, p. 69.

14. See Alain C. Enthovin and Wayne K. Smith, *How Much is Enough?*, New York: Harper & Row, Publisher, 1971, p. 117.

15. For example see Amos A. Jordan, "Introduction: New Technologies and U.S. Defense: Planning for Non-member Conflict," in *The Other Arms Race*, eds. Geoffrey Kemp, Robert L. Pfaltzgraff, Jr., and Uri Ra'anan, Lexington, Massachusetts: D. C. Heath and Company, 1975; Brigadier General John E. Ralph, "Tactical Air Systems and the New Technologies," in *The Other Arms Race*, John T. Burk, "The Changing Nature of Modern Warfare," *Army*, March 1974; and James F. Digby, *Precision Guided Munitions: Capabilities and Consequences*, Santa Monica, California: The Rand Corporation, June 1974.

16. Ronald Wakeford and James Dornan, Jr. in their study on Western European perceptions of NATO contended that "The most crucial dilemma faced . . . by Western Europeans, especially their respective Defense Ministers (was) how to reconcile the need for defense and security with an atmosphere of detente with the Soviet Union." See Wakeford and Dornan, *West European Perceptions of NATO*, Arlington, Virginia: Stanford Research Institute, Strategic Studies Center, November 1975, p. 7. For a further discussion of the effects on Western Europe of the dual Soviet policies of detente and arms improvements see Robert Kennedy, "Nonconsonant Detente and NATO," in *National Security and Detente*, New York: Thomas J. Crowell Co., 1976, pp. 117-129.

17. For an explanation of Soviet chemical capabilities, see John M. Weinstein and Henry Gole, "Chemical Weapons Rearmament and the Security of Europe: Can Support be Mustered?," *The Defense of the West: Strategic and European Security Issues Reappraised*, Boulder: Westview Press, 1984.

18. Helmut Schmidt, "The 1977 Alastair Buchan Memorial Lecture," *Survival*, January-February 1978, pp. 2-10.

19. The following three sections borrow heavily and expand on the ideas presented in an earlier work by the author. See Robert Kennedy, "Soviet Theater-Nuclear Forces: Implications for NATO Defense," *ORBIS*, Summer 1981, pp. 331-344.

20. Department of Defense, *Soviet Military Power*, Washington, DC: US Government Printing Office, March 1983, pp. 37-38 and *NATO and the Warsaw Pact Force Comparisons*, Brussels: North Atlantic Treaty Organization, May 1982, p. 46.

21. *Soviet Military Power*, p. 40. NATO believes the Soviet Union has deployed approximately 300 203 mm and 240 mm nuclear artillery pieces. The Soviet Union, currently, has in excess of 1800 152 mm guns in Eastern Europe and the three Western military districts of the Soviet Union. It is reasonable to assume that as a very minimum about 150 are now nuclear capable.

22. *Ibid.*, pp. 38, 42-43.

23. A wide variety of less than ominous reasons have been offered for the current buildup in Soviet nuclear capabilities. For example see Raymond L. Garthoff, "Moscow's Less Than Ominous Reasons for Deploying SS-20s," *The New York Times*, May 13, 1983, p. 30. However, at a time of continued economic difficulty at home the extensive nature of Soviet "modernization" efforts suggests a more impelling political-strategic rationale.

24. *Ibid.*, p. 42.

25. John W. R. Taylor, ed., *Jane's All the World's Aircraft 1982-83*, London: Jane's Publishing Company, Ltd., 1982, p. 232 and *Soviet Military Power*, p. 24.

26. Justin Galen, "The Nuclear Balance, Part One: Recent Force Trends and Improvements," *Armed Forces Journal International*, December 1977, p. 30.

27. See Joseph Fitchett, "NATO Arms Talks Test US-Europe Ties," *International Herald Tribune*, April 30, 1979, p. 1.

28. This is one reason why the United States to date has sought to exclude aircraft from the INF arms control talks.

29. *The Military Balance 1982-1983*, p. 135.

30. See Thomas W. Wolfe, *Soviet Military Power and Europe, 1949-1970*, Baltimore: The Johns Hopkins University Press, 1979, p. 199.

31. See V. Ye. Savkin, *Operational Art and Tactics*, Moscow: Military Publishing House, 1972, pp. 90, 230, and 234.

32. A. A. Sidorenko, *The Offensive*, Moscow: Military Publishing House, 1970, pp. vi and 30.

33. Savkin, p. 248.

34. See Sidorenko, pp. 11-39.

35. Colonel Lobachev, "A High Tempo of Attack - The Indispensable Condition for Victory," *Voyenni Vestnik [Military Herald]*, February 1977, p. 44, as quoted in Colonel Frederich E. Turner, *Comments on FM 100-5 From a Soviet Point of View*, Carlisle Barracks, PA: US Army War College, 1978, p. 19.

36. Sidorenko, p. 40.

37. Colonel General N. A. Lomov, ed., *Scientific - Technical Progress and the Revolution in Military Affairs*, Moscow: Military Publishing House, 1973, p. 40.

38. Sidorenko, p. 112.

39. *Ibid.*, p. 46.

40. See for example, Sidorenko, pp. 40-70, 109-124; Savkin, pp. 232-233; and Lomov, pp. 40-41, 143-156.

41. Klaus G. de Vries, "Responding to the SS-20: An Alternative Approach," *Survival*, November-December 1979, p. 253.

42. For an excellent view of the uncertainties which would confront Soviet leadership in a time of crisis, see Benjamin S. Lambeth, "Uncertainties for the Soviet War Planner," *International Security*, Winter 1982/1983, pp. 139-166. For a wide-ranging examination of Soviet vulnerabilities see John M. Weinstein, "All Features Grate and Stall: Soviet Strategic Vulnerabilities and the Future of Deterrence," in *The Defense of the West*.

43. Strong American rhetoric, a less than skillful choice of words by some senior American officials concerning NATO strategy, and the skillful manipulation of both of these factors by the Soviet Union certainly have contributed to cross-Atlantic misunderstandings. Nevertheless, the change in the nature of the nuclear balance in Europe—coupled with the politics of detente as currently pursued by the Soviet Union with Western publics—has contributed immeasurably to the malaise which now confronts the Alliance. For a further discussion of the current problem, see Kennedy, "Nonconsonant Detente and NATO."

44. Thomas W. Wolfe, *The Military Dimension in the Making of Soviet Foreign and Defense Policy*, Santa Monica, CA: The Rand Corporation, 1977, p. 38. Similarly, Dimitri K. Simes, former member of Moscow's Institute of World International Relations (IMEMO) and executive director of the Soviet and East European research program at Johns Hopkins School of Advanced International

Studies contends that the Kremlin believes that a shift in the strategic balance of power in its favor provides greater room for political maneuver. See his "Moscow: Ready to Wage Unwinnable War," *International Herald Tribune,* November 12, 1981, p. 4. It should be noted, however, that while perceptions of Soviet military capabilities and Moscow's capability and willingness to sell modern armaments on the cheap have increased Moscow's room for maneuver in the international community, the Kremlin, so far, has had little success in advancing international communism.

45. See Josef Joffe, "Europe and America: The Politics of Resentment (Con't)," *Foreign Affairs,* Vol. 61, 1983, p. 571.

46. Marshal A. A. Grechko, *On Guard for Peace and the Building of Communism* as cited by Hubertus Hoffman, "SS-20 Multiplies USSR's Nuclear Superiority," *NATO's Fifteen Nations,* December 1978-January 1979, p. 44.

47. See the "Communique of the Special Meeting of Foreign and Defense Ministers" republished in *NATO Review,* February 1980, pp. 25-26.

48. See Stephen R. Hanmer, Jr., "NATO's Long-Range Theater Nuclear Forces: Modernization in Parallel With Arms Control," *NATO Review,* February 1980, p. 4. Also see Gregory F. Treverton, "Managing NATO's Nuclear Dilemma," *International Security,* Spring 1983, pp. 109-110.

49. See Treverton, pp. 109-110.

50. Treverton notes that this shifting of view was as much "a sign of the seriousness of the United States in addressing allied concerns as an indication of clear US preference." *Ibid.,* p. 110.

51. NATO made clear its intent to reduce the overall numbers of warheads in Europe as an integral part of the TNF modernization decision. One thousand warheads were to be withdrawn as soon as feasible. Further, the NATO ministers decided that the 572 Pershing II and cruise missile warheads would be accommodated within the reduced level. See the "Communique of the Special Meeting of Foreign and Defense Ministers," p. 25.

52. For one thorough review of these and other concerns that have been raised, see Eckhard Lubkemeier *PD 59 and LRINF-Modernization: Military Strategic and Security Implications of Extended Deterrence for the Federal Republic of Germany,* Bonn: Friedrick-Ebert-Stiftung, December 1981.

53. Vice President Bush, "Peace and Security in Europe," Current Policy N. 47, Washington, DC: US Department of State, Bureau of Public Affairs, January 31, 1983, p. 3.

54. See for example, *How to Avert the Threat to Europe,* Moscow: Progress Publishers, 1983, pp. 28-29.

55. For greater detail on proposals and counterproposals, see *US Arms Control and Disarmament Agency 1982 Annual Report,* Washington, DC: US Government Printing Office, 1983, pp. 8-12.

56. For another interpretation of the issue of "equal security," see Lawrence S. Eagleburger, "Why We Don't Count the French and British Missiles," *The Washington Post,* May 8, 1983, p. B8. For an expanded discussion of the problem of "threat comparability," see Robert Kennedy, "The Problems and Prospects of START," *The Defense of the West.*

57. *How to Avert the Threat to Europe,* pp. 51-52.

58. Article III of the SALT II Agreement limited both parties to an overall aggregate of 2250 strategic systems. In the "Memorandum of Understanding" between the United States and the Soviet Union, the United States indicated it had 2284 systems. This included 574 heavy bombers which, as defined by the Treaty included B-52 and B-1 types. In fact, only by counting B-52s in the "bone yard" at Davis-Monthen Air Force Base in Arizona and thus no longer in service, could the United States be considered to have 574 heavy bombers. In fact, the United States possessed between 316 and 386 operational heavy bombers at the time. Today, while the Soviet Union retains strategic systems well in excess of 2400, the United States has about 1900 ICBMs, SSBNs, and heavy bombers. See *SALT II Agreement*, Washington, DC: US Department of State, Bureau of Public Affairs, Selected Documents No. 12A, 1979, pp. 32 and 49; Caspar W. Weinberger, Secretary of Defense, *Annual Report to the Congress Fiscal Year 1984*, Washington, DC: US Government Printing Office, February 1, 1983, p. 333; *The Military Balance 1979-1980*, p. 88; and *Soviet Military Power*, p. 14.

59. Lawrence S. Eagleburger, "How We Count European Missiles," *The New York Times*, February 7, 1983, p. A19.

60. According to information provided to Congress, "The Pershing II system employs radar area correlation to achieve pinpoint accuracy. Radar 'pictures' of the target area, in cassette form, are inserted in the missile prior to launch. As the reentry vehicle approaches the general target area, it takes its own radar 'pictures' of the terrain, comparing them to the original. By making course corrections until the two pictures coincide, the missile can achieve surgical accuracy." See *Hearings Before the Committee on Armed Services*, US Congress, Senate, 97th Cong., 1st Sess., p. 1365.

61. For example, see Ullman, p. 46. Also see *How to Avert the Threat to Europe*, p. 34.

62. Ullman, p. 47.

63. *How to Avert the Threat to Europe*, p. 34.

64. See Rene Herrman, *Zum Verhaltnis zwischen strategischer Politik and Entspannung*, Ebenhausen: Stiftung Wissenschaft und Politik, January 1974, quoted in Lubkemeier, p. 53.

65. *Soviet Military Power*, p. 35.

66. For an excellent discussion of this form of "surprise attack," see Richard K. Betts, "Surprise Attack: NATO's Political Vulnerability," *International Security*, Spring 1981, pp. 117-149.

67. Francois de Rose, "Inflexible Response," *Foreign Affairs*, Fall 1982, p. 141.

68. Ullman, pp. 46-47.

69. John Erickson, "The Soviet View of Deterrence: A General Survey," *Survival*, November/December 1982, p. 248.

70. *Annual Report to Congress Fiscal Year 1984*, p. 222.

71. On this point Manfred Worner, the West German Defense Minister, has stated that "the best guarantee against . . . conflict is balanced forces at every level and our ability to respond flexibly, fittingly, and incalculably." See "Speech by Defence Minister Manfred Worner (excerpts) 20 October 1982," *Survival*, January/February 1983, p. 37. Moreover, the Soviet Union has further helped to strengthen the linkage between conflict in Europe and a US-Soviet strategic exchange by continuing to argue that nuclear war once begun will inevitably become all-out warfare. See Leslie H. Gelb, "Moscow Angrily Settles Back to Await End of

Reagan," *The New York Times,* March 30, 1983, p. A1; Dusko Doder, "Warsaw Pact Official Warns of 'War Danger'," *The Washington Post,* April 7, 1983, p. A1; and Leslie H. Gelb, "Soviet Marshal Warns U.S. on its Missiles," *The New York Times,* March 18, 1983, p. A1.

72. For a further amplification of this view, see Kennedy, "Soviet Theater Nuclear Forces," pp. 346-350. Also see Treverton, pp. 97-102.

73. This is, in fact, the rationale which, according to one observer, would lead to a US decision to use nuclear weapons. See Richard H. Ullman, "Out of the Euromissile Mire," *Foreign Policy,* Spring 1983, p. 45.

74. Worner, p. 37.

8

THE SOVIET THREAT TO EUROPE: PROSPECTS FOR THE 1980's

Otto P. Chaney

> I repeat again and again: We do not seek military superiority. We have never intended and do not now intend to threaten any state or group of states. Our strategic doctrine is a purely defensive one. Allegations that the Soviet Union is building up its military might on the European Continent on a scale not called for by its defense requirements have nothing to do with reality. This is deliberate deception of the public at large.
>
> Leonid I. Brezhnev, October 1979[1]

In a rare admission during the "battle of the booklets," the Soviet authors of *Whence the Threat to Peace* (published in response to US Secretary of Defense Caspar Weinberger's late 1981 *Soviet Military Power*) wrote: "True, the USSR has more divisions in its ground forces than the USA." "But," they explained, "this is quite natural because owing to its geographical and strategic position the Soviet Union has to maintain the balance of forces not only in Europe but also in other regions adjoining its borders." They also admitted with some qualifications, that "the Warsaw Treaty countries have a somewhat greater number of combat aircraft" and "more tanks" than NATO. Nevertheless, they concluded that the Soviets are threatening no one and that "unrestrained intimidation of peoples with the spurious 'Soviet military threat' is no longer effective."[2]

Despite such denials of aggressive intent, the Soviet Union not only has maintained, since the close of World War II, a significant quantitative superiority of conventional forces on the continent of Europe, but has, in recent years, steadily expanded and upgraded its conventional and nuclear forces. As a result, most Westerners remain concerned over the nature of the Soviet threat and the implications of the continued buildup for Western defense. (Indeed, 18 months after the publication of Mr. Weinberger's booklet, many of his key figures on Soviet deployments were already out of date, prompting a second edition in March 1983.) Moreover, the recent introduction of air assault brigades at the *front* level, the rapid proliferation of the mobile and highly accurate SS-20 missile, and the tripling of artillery in many motorized rifle regiments,[3] when coupled with a doctrine that stresses surprise, shock effect, and high tempo operations, suggest the Soviets are deliberately fielding forces opposite NATO capable of rapid offensive warfare. While it may be argued that the Soviet Union does not plan to attack NATO, that given the experience of World War II against a numerically inferior German army and the continued need to keep their East European Allies in line, the Soviet buildup is purely defensive in nature. Some will argue that the Soviet Union's weapons buildup in Europe (and in the USSR itself) is only a response to our own weapons deployments.[4] These arguments notwithstanding, the recent improvements in Soviet forces have given rise to concerns in the West that if NATO fails to redress the balance, the Soviets will gain psychopolitical leverage in peacetime and a significant advantage during crises or war in Europe.

This paper will examine the nature of the Soviet military threat to Western Europe for the remainder of the decade. It will focus on quantitative as well as qualitative factors in an attempt to understand the likely prospects for and consequences of a Soviet-initiated conflict in Europe.

SOVIET/WARSAW PACT CAPABILITIES

Organization and Combat Strength. The Soviet army in Eastern Europe, or the "forward area," is organized into four groups of forces: the largest and most important is the Group of Soviet Forces, Germany (GSFG) with 19 divisions and a supporting artillery division;[5] the Northern Group of Forces (NGF), with two divisions, located in western Poland; the Central Group of Forces (CGF) with five divisions on Czechoslovak soil; and the Southern Group of Forces (SGF) in Hungary, with its four divisions. All 30 Soviet maneuver divisions and GSFG's artillery division are classified by NATO as Category I, meaning that they are combat ready, between three-quarters and full strength, with all of their authorized equipment.[6]

These Groups of Forces are supported by tactical air forces (frontal aviation) consisting of fighters, fighter-bombers, transports, helicopters, reconnaissance units, and miscellaneous support units. With the tactical air units of the East European nations, these forces number over 3,000 combat aircraft in the central region, with another 1,000 deployed on the flanks.[7]

Each of the Warsaw Pact countries is tied closely to Moscow, not only by the 1955 Warsaw Treaty which obligates the signatory nations to act jointly "in the event of armed attack in Europe," but also by a system of bilateral treaties which require assistance to the USSR but with no geographic limitations.[8] The headquarters of the "Staff of the United Armed Forces" is in Moscow. The Soviets always occupy the posts of commander in chief and chief of staff of the Warsaw Pact forces. Additionally, the Soviet Ministry of Defense provides general officer "representatives" to the armed forces of each Warsaw Pact country. In wartime, these individuals and their staffs would probably serve as Stavka (General Headquarters of the Supreme High Command) representatives to Pact members.[9]

Current non-Soviet Warsaw Pact divisional strength is 56 (60 percent of which are Category I) (see Table 1).[10]

When the military forces of the Soviet Union and those of their East European Allies are combined, the Warsaw Pact is superior to NATO in almost every traditional quantitative measure of military capability. On the ground, NATO, with 69 divisions, is confronted by 164 Soviet and non-Soviet Warsaw Pact equivalents.

Thus, while NATO and the Warsaw Pact are roughly comparable in total available air and ground force manpower, NATO finds itself outnumbered in combat formations by over two to one (see Table 2). In the past, differences in the numerical count of formations have been discounted, since Soviet divisions have generally been smaller than those of the West. However, in recent years, the average Soviet division has increased not only in size but

	Motorized Rifle/ Mechanized	Tank	Other
Bulgaria	8		
Czechoslovakia	5	5	1 artillery
GDR	4	2	
Hungary	5	1	
Poland	8	5	1 airborne 1 amphibious assault
Romania	8	2	
TOTALS	38	15	3

SOURCE: Based on author's calculations of data presented in *The Military Balance, 1982-1983*, London: The International Institute for Strategic Studies, 1982.

Table 1. Non-Soviet Warsaw Pact Divisional Strength

	Northern and Central Europe[a]		Southern Europe[b]		Total	
	NATO	Warsaw Pact	NATO	Warsaw Pact	NATO	Warsaw Pact
Divisions						
Armor	12 1/3	42	4 1/3	4	16 2/3	46
Infantry Mechanized & Airborne	15 2/3	71	36 2/3	47	52 1/3	118
TOTAL	28	113	41	51	69	164

SOURCE: Based on author's calculations of data presented in *The Military Balance, 1982-1983*, London: The International Institute for Strategic Studies, 1982.

NOTES:
[a]Includes, on the NATO side, the US, British, and Canadian forces in Germany and the forces of Belgium, Denmark, the Federal Republic of Germany, Luxembourg, the Netherlands, and Norway. On the Warsaw Pact side it includes the forces of the German Democratic Republic, Czechoslovakia, and Poland, and those forces of the USSR stationed in those three countries or stationed in the Western military districts and likely to be committed to the Baltic or Norwegian area operations and as follow-on echelons for combat in the central region.

[b]Includes, on the NATO side, the Italian, Greek, and Turkish land forces. On the Warsaw Pact side, it includes the ground forces of Bulgaria, Hungary, and Romania, and the Soviet forces stationed in Hungary and the southwestern USSR.

Table 2. Ground Forces Available in Peacetime

also in available firepower (see Table 3). Hence, today NATO is outnumbered not only in total available combat formation, but also in tanks by almost two to one, and in aircraft by over two to one (see Table 4). In fact, the prestigious International Institute for Strategic Studies concludes:

> The numerical balance over the last twenty years has slowly but steadily moved in favour of the East. At the same time the West has largely lost the technological edge which allowed NATO to believe that quality could substitute for numbers. One cannot necessarily conclude from this that NATO would suffer defeat in war, but one can conclude that there has been sufficient danger in the trend to require remedies.[11]

Force Modernization and Improvements. While NATO—since the late 1960's—has increased its manpower and the numbers of combat formations, tactical aircraft, and tanks in the northern and central regions of Europe, it continues to fall behind in those critical items which have given modern armies their mobility and shock power. During the same period, the Warsaw Pact has substantially increased the number of tanks and aircraft available for combat in these regions. Indeed, since the mid-1960's, the Soviets have been carrying out a vigorous program of modernizing and upgrading their forces. This comprehensive program has vastly improved their mobility, firepower, command and control, obstacle-crossing capability, air defense, electronic warfare, logistical support, and thus their capacity for shock action. Among the many improvements benefitting the ground forces were the introduction of T-64 and T-72 tanks and the continued development and fielding of a new tank, the T-80, which incorporates major advances in armor protection, mobility, and fire control. The Soviets have replaced many older towed guns with self-propelled 122 and 152mm weapons and are deploying nuclear-capable heavy artillery brigades equipped with 203mm howitzers and 240mm mortars. They are currently introducing more accurate, longer-range SS-21, SS-22, and SS-23 tactical surface-to-surface missiles as replacements for the FROG, SCUD, and SCALEBOARD missiles. A new 16-tube 220mm multiple rocket launcher has been deployed opposite NATO since 1978. The Soviets are improving their communications equipment, including the introduction of tropospheric scatter and communications satellite equipment to enhance command and control. They have begun deploying air assault brigades at the *front* (army group)

| | Armored | | Mechanized | | Airborne |
Countries	Men	Tanks	Men	Tanks	Men
United States	18,000	324	18,500	216	16,800
Soviet Union	11,000	335	14,000	266	7,000
Britain	8,500	148	–	–	–
West Germany	17.000	300	17,500	250	8-9,000

SOURCE: Based on data presented in The Military Balance, 1982-1983, p. vii.

Table 3. Comparative Divisional Compositions

	Division Equivalents[a]	Tanks	Combat Aircraft
NATO			
Belgium	2 2/3	359	164
Canada	1/3	59	42
Germany	12	3,938	473
Netherlands	2	1,811	172
United Kingdom	4	840	194
United States	4 2/3	3,000	306
TOTAL	25 2/3	10,007	1,351
Warsaw Pact			
Czechoslovakia	10 1/3	3,400	471
Germany	6 1/3	1,500	359
Poland	16	3,060	705
USSR	26	9,300	1,730[b]
TOTAL	58 2/3	17,260	3,165

SOURCE: Based on author's calculations from data presented in The Military Balance, 1982-1983.

NOTES:
[a]Includes all divisions, brigades, and other formations aggregated on the basis of three brigades to a division. Supporting artillery battalions are not included.

[b]The Military Balance (p. 17) estimates 2,000 tactical aircraft in Eastern Europe. Since the Soviet Southern Group of Forces in Hungary is not listed here, by extrapolation the figure has been reduced to 270. In addition, all Warsaw Pact countries have paramilitary forces, some of which are sizable. For example, the paramilitary forces of the German Democratic Republic number over 70 thousand, 45 thousand of which are well-armed border guards organized into 27 regiments.[12] In the event of hostilities, these paramilitary forces would be employed to complement regular military forces and missions.

Table 4. The Central European Balance

level, and the total attack force opposite NATO has grown from 400 helicopters in 1978 to a current level of 800. They have continued to maintain a significant lead in air defense with the development of a variety of new surface-to-air missiles, including a new SAM with enhanced low-altitude capabilities and with the potential to defend against tactical ballistic missiles. The Soviets also are making important qualitative improvements in their tactical air forces with the introduction of FENCER, FITTER, FOXBAT, and FLOGGER aircraft. (The FROGFOOT ground attack aircraft, currently being used in Afghanistan, may eventually be deployed in Europe.) The Tactical Air Forces have been converted from a basic defensively-oriented force once dominated by interceptor type aircraft to one with greatly increased offensive capabilities for theater warfare. These new aircraft carry bombs, rockets, and guided munitions. Furthermore, new armaments, now under development, will greatly increase effectiveness of sorties against hardened ground targets.[13]

Highlighting improvements in Soviet tactical airpower, General Charles A. Gabriel, who at the time of the interview was Commander in Chief, US Air Force in Europe and Commander of Allied Air Forces Central Europe, stated:

> The quality/quantity argument is familiar to everybody: we stand short on numbers, but not on quality.
>
> We've always said that we'd make up the difference with our technology. *That's wearing a little thin now. That gap has closed considerably* with the new generation of Soviet Floggers, Fencers, Fitters, Foxbats, Backfires, and the long-range Soviet theater nuclear force. *All have come on recently and very fast, so the technology gap is closing.* (Emphasis added)[14]

Simultaneously with force modernization and improvement, the Soviets have been expanding the size of their divisions and have been adding to the divisional equipment. They have added an artillery battalion to their tank regiments; have expanded the motorized rifle company to a battalion within tank regiments of tank divisions; increased from 31 to 40 the number of medium tanks in the tank battalion of each motorized rifle regiment (MRR); have added medium tanks to their reconnaissance battalions; equipped one MRR in each tank and motorized rifle division (MRD) with the BMP armored personnel carrier; and added a road/bridge construction company to divisional engineer battalion.

Such improvements have been designed to enhance the shock action, mobility, and firepower of Soviet forces.[15] The net effect of these improvements has been a significant increase in the Soviet capacity for offensive warfare which, when coupled with Soviet doctrine, has raised serious concerns in the West.

Soviet Doctrine and Tactics. The impressive quantitative and qualitative improvements in Soviet forces now underway are the outgrowth of a long, serious study of military doctrine, operational art, and tactics, especially as these applied to fighting in Central Europe. In the late 1960's, Soviet military planners and strategists concluded that if a war broke out "it was clearly in the interests of the Soviet Union to be able to win it *before* the Western Alliance could reach a decision to use nuclear weapons."[16] In the early 1970's, emphasis gradually shifted in Moscow from a study of the nuclear battlefield to examination of conventional operations, although the Soviets recognized that in a major conflict nuclear weapons might be used at any time.[17]

As Christopher Donnelly observes,

> Whether any war which began in Europe would remain purely conventional or would involve nuclear weapons, the Russian victory, the Soviets believe, would only be certain if the war could be won quickly.
>
> Forced to meet the political requirement that the Soviet army be able not only to fight and win a war with conventional weapons, but to do so *very quickly indeed* so as to lessen the dangers of escalation to global holocaust, it must have rapidly become clear to the Soviet general staff that both the tactics and equipment were not adequate to the task. Equipment was available in insufficient quantity and was often of an unsuitable type. Tactical doctrine for conventional war was weak, and the army was poorly practiced in it.[18]

Having identified these various shortcomings, the Soviet military leaders encouraged debate on tactical issues which eventually centered on two areas of concern. One related to tactical practice and viability of combat and logistical units on the modern battlefield (use of the BMP, deployment of artillery, flexibility of command and control, coordination problems of a high-speed offensive). The other concern involved the ability of the officer himself to cope with tactical problems and to develop qualities which would improve the training, motivation, and morale of his soldiers.[19]

At the same time that these questions were being discussed, the Soviets reexamined their principles of military art in light of sweeping changes in weapons capabilities, troop mobility, and the "scientific-technological revolution."[20] One Soviet theoretician, Colonel Vasiliy Savkin, listed the important principles of military art: mobility, high rates of combat operations, surprise, and concentration, all of which reflect the clear Soviet preference for bold offensive operations.[21] While contending that the defensive form of warfare will undoubtedly be employed in a future war, "victory over the enemy (will be) achieved only by resolute attack."[22]

The importance of the offensive as the principal manifestation of Soviet doctrine cannot be overemphasized. Soviet writings are replete with praise for such principles as surprise, maneuver, the breakthrough, high tempo operations, mobility and offensive combat in the enemy's rear.

Surprise is seen as one of the most important principles of military art. Savkin writes, "Use of surprise brings success in a battle or operation."[23]

> As a result of the stunning effects of surprise . . . and decisive offensive operations by Soviet troops, the enemy's capabilities are sharply lowered and the correlation of forces changes immediately. He may panic and his morale may be crushed.[24]

Moreover, Savkin contends that "The desire for surprise has begun to permeate all decisions for the conduct of operations and battles."[25]

Surprise is closely related to mobility and activeness. (Savkin contends success is achieved by that side which, with all else equal, is more active and resolute, takes the initiative, and holds it firmly.[26]) Mobility and maneuver not only permit the amassing of shock forces for surprise, but also provide the means for the rapid development of the offensive. Savkin writes that the development of mobility and high tempos of combat operations is "the most important principle of operational art and tactics . . . ."[27] A high degree of mobility permits the massing of superior forces in a timely manner at the required location in order to achieve surprise and a successful breakthrough.

For the Soviets, then, surprise is absolutely essential. According to one of their military publications,

> Surprise is achieved by the use of various ways . . . by leading the enemy into error concerning one's own intentions, by preserving in secret the plan of

battle, by speed and decisiveness of action, by hidden artificial maneuvers, by the *unexpected use of the nuclear weapon* and other new combat means . . . .[28] (Emphasis added)

A number of Western statesmen and defense specialists have concluded that Soviet forces are, indeed, capable of doing just what their doctrine dictates: that war in Europe would be characterized by a little or no warning massive armored blitzkrieg-type offensive. But NATO, though outgunned and outmanned, is still a powerful force capable of a credible forward defense. The Warsaw Pact can weight certain axes to give itself superiority in a particular sector, thus facilitating a breakthrough. NATO's operational strategy of active defense has been designed to permit the maximum of flexibility. Thus, NATO should be able to shift forces quickly to meet this threat.

A Warsaw Pact study which describes active defense as combining both positional and mobile defense states that it is intended to compel the attacker to make repeated attempts to break the defensive line, so that the attacker should expend forces and time without gaining momentum.[29] Thus, while the Soviet high command might prefer a quick blitzkrieg drive to the English Channel, it cannot count on a quick and decisive victory.[30] To cope with NATO's innovative defenses, the Soviets are taking deliberate steps to improve their offensive posture. They have revived a World War II exploitation force, the mobile group (podvizhnaya grupa). Mobile groups, or Operational Maneuver Groups (OMG's), as they are now known as, are large tank and mechanized formations principally designed to *complete* a breakthrough of the enemy's defenses already begun by forward forces.[31] While little is available in current Soviet literature on the subject, it appears that the Soviets also will use their OMG's to attack the defenses which have been weakened by relocation of NATO reserves to a threatened sector. OMG's also will be tasked with penetrating deep into NATO's rear to operate for a limited period, destroying nuclear missile sites, command posts, electronic warfare equipment, and antiaircraft defense weapons. They also will be used to prevent withdrawal of NATO troops, to impede NATO's ability to reposition reserves, to interdict supplies, and to seize and hold important areas and objectives until the approach of the main forces.[32] As one Warsaw Pact journal noted:

> The aim of deploying an army's Operational Maneuver Group is to switch the focus of the fighting into the rear of the enemy formation; to destroy important objectives which cannot be destroyed by other means; to achieve chaos and disorganization; and to limit the freedom of maneuver and the effectiveness of enemy action . . . .[33]

Thus, the Warsaw Pact is probably changing its operational strategy to deal with NATO's effective active defense.

ATTACK SCENARIOS

In the event of war, the Soviets would probably divide Europe into theaters of military operations (teatry voyennykh deistvii or TVD), a Soviet term describing a major portion of a continent, including adjacent seas and airspace above, where military forces are deployed for strategic-level warfare. While the Soviets do not discuss their own TVD's on the European Continent, they do delineate NATO's theaters, which may suggest their own military division of Europe. The northern European TVD embraces the territories of Norway, Denmark, part of the Federal Republic of Germany, and the water area around these nations. It stretches almost 2,200 kilometers from Hamburg to Nordkapp. The Central European TVD includes the remainder of the FRG, the Netherlands, Belgium, Luxembourg, and France, and stretches 1,100 kilometers from north to south. The Southern European TVD encompasses Italy, Turkey, the Mediterranean, and the southern part of the Black Sea. From north to south, this theater stretches about 1,500 kilometers.[34] Forces allocated to a TVD might consist of one to six *fronts,* one or more air armies and fleets, one or more airborne divisions, and long-range aviation, military transport aviation, troops of air defense, and strategic rocket forces, as required.[35]

The Central Region. There are a number of avenues of approach into NATO's central sector, and the Warsaw Pact could choose any combination of them. (See map.)

One of the potentially more threatening scenarios for an offensive against Western Europe is a fixing attack along the south German front (two German corps and the US V and VII Corps) which would occupy the bulk of NATO forces, followed by main thrusts toward Hamburg and across the North German Plains. Such an attack, if executed with shortened warning, might catch the forces of NATO's Northern Army Group (NORTHAG) far

LIKELY WARSAW PACT AXES OF ADVANCE IN AN ATTACK AGAINST NATO

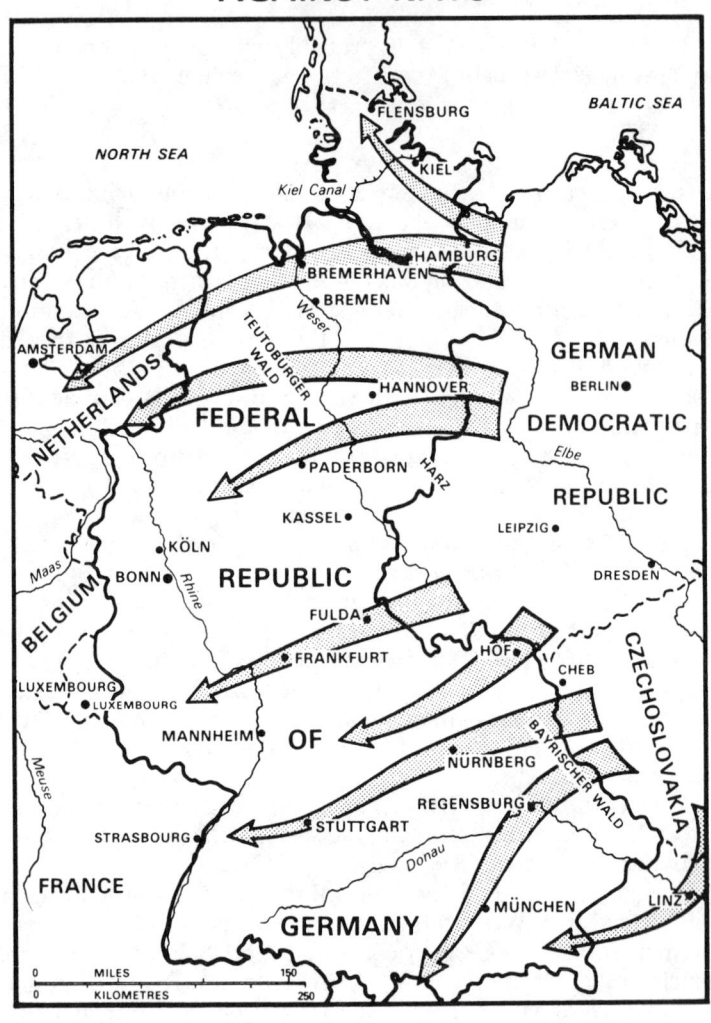

from their defensive positions. NORTHAG contains four corps—Dutch, German, British, and Belgian from north to south—but the divisions and separate brigades comprising these corps are not normally deployed near their wartime defensive positions along the potential front. One US brigade moved from southern Germany to NORTHAG in 1978 in order to enhance the peacetime deployments and wartime readiness of NORTHAG. Other needed redeployments have not been carried out.[36]

Soviet, Polish, and east German formations augmented by airborne units and helicopter forces to facilitate rapid forward movement might quickly capture or control Hamburg, Bremen, Bremerhaven, Kiel, Rotterdam, Antwerp, and Brussels, effectively cutting the north-south supply lines to the bulk of the NATO defenders.[37] Airborne and "spetsnaz" (special operations) forces would attempt to seize or destroy crucial bridges, airbases, nuclear storage sites, and nuclear delivery systems, as well as large storage areas, POL tank farms, and US POMCUS (prepositioned overseas materiel configured in unit sets) sites. Concerning the potential impact of "spetsnaz" and heliborne forces on NATO air assets, General Charles Gabriel stated: "The Soviets have the capability to come into the rear areas, damage our airbases and delay or stop sortie generation. With the Army committed to the front lines and unable to dedicate forces for airbase ground defense, we must take this threat seriously."[38]

The Northern Flank. Simultaneously with an attack against Central Europe, the Warsaw Pact would probably also strike NATO's northern and southern flanks. The Soviets have considerable interest in the Northwestern Region, that area encompassing the Kola Peninsula; the White Sea; the countries of Finland, Sweden, and Norway; and the surrounding waters of the Barents Sea, Greenland Sea, Norwegian Sea, North Sea, Danish Straits, Baltic Sea, Gulf of Bothnia, and Gulf of Finland.[39] They are well aware that this region contains naval chokepoints which, if controlled by NATO, could deny them access to their critical operating areas in the North Atlantic. Thus, it is likely that they would want to secure early the Northwestern Region in order to: (1) control the airfields, harbors, and strategic geography of Scandinavia; (2) prevent NATO's aircraft carrier forces from entering the Norwegian Sea and threatening targets in the Kola Peninsula; (3) intercept vessels resupplying NATO forces in Europe; (4) establish a springboard for amphibious operations to other area; (5) prevent NATO from using Scandinavian countries as forward bases; and (6) increase Soviet strategic ballistic missile offensive capabilities by controlling Northeast Atlantic submarine missile launch areas.[40]

To accomplish its missions against the Northern Flank, the Soviets would use naval forces from the Baltic and Northern Fleets, possibly a naval infantry regiment, airborne forces, and eight motorized rifle divisions and an artillery division from the Leningrad Military District,[41] supported by fighters and bombers from tactical aviation and the Navy. East German and Polish units might also participate. Soviet amphibious and airborne forces could be used in an attempt to eliminate NATO's superior geographical position along the strategic Greenland-Iceland-United Kingdom (GIUK) Gap. The Soviets might try to secure both ends of the Gap, control of which would provide them excellent base locations for gaining quick access to many vital sea lines of communications. Iceland, key to this control, would have to be seized and occupied.[42]

The Southern Flank. In the south, NATO's southern flank (Turkey, Greece, and Italy) faces the combined forces of Bulgaria, Romania, Hungary, and those positioned in the three Southern Soviet Military Districts (North Caucasus, Trans-Caucasus, and Turkestan). Historic animosities between Greece and Turkey resulting from conflicting territorial and nonterritorial interests in the Aegean have weakened the NATO Alliance. Greece actually withdrew its forces in 1974 but has now rejoined it. The Warsaw Pact has had its own reverses in the area. Albania withdrew officially from the organization on September 13, 1968 and shows no inclination to rejoin. Romania has been somewhat of a maverick.

The Soviet Union, and Russia before it, has long had an interest in the Mediterranean. "Imperial Russia," writes John C. Campbell, "devoted over a century of effort—never really successful—to breaking out of the Black Sea and becoming a Mediterranean power. Thus the impulse remains and continues to move the leaders of the Imperial Soviet Union."[43] The USSR has long been frustrated by Turkey's ownership of the strategic straits of the Bosporus and Dardanelles which, according to the Montreux Convention, can be transited by foreign warships only after specific request made eight days in advance. The Soviets also feel hemmed in by the need to file for permission to overfly Turkey. In the past, that permission has not always been granted.[44]

For many years, the Kremlin leaders have looked on the straits as part of the USSR's security zone, and in the fall of 1940, it will be recalled, Stalin demanded that Hitler sanction the establishment of Soviet land and naval bases "within range of the Bosporus and the Dardanelles."[45] With the growth of its naval power over the past decade, with its expanding global mission and preoccupation with power projection, the Soviets attach far greater significance to the straits than they did in 1940 when their demands infuriated Hitler. Thus, in the opening hours of a general war, one would expect the Soviets to attempt to seize the Turkish straits and destroy Turkish airbases in order to avoid having its Black Sea fleet bottled up and destroyed and to insure its uninterrupted access to the Mediterranean Sea.

Current Soviet interest in the Mediterranean can be measured by the growing presence of its naval vessels there. In mid-1964, the Soviets established a continual presence in the Mediterranean, and an average of five Navy ships were maintained on station in the Mediterranean that year. Subsequently, an average of at least 40 to 50 ships have been maintained on station (although the number rises sharply in periods of crisis—70 ships in June 1967, 96 in November 1973).[46] Moscow also continues to seek base facilities on the Mediterranean littoral, preferring more permanent arrangements for bases with greater facilities than presently available (limited support facilities are currently available in Tartus, Syria; overhaul and repair facilities are available on a contract basis in Yugoslavia, Tunisia, and Greece).[47]

PROBLEMS FOR THE PACT

Despite significant improvements in their military forces and Soviet interests in Central Europe and on the flanks, the Soviets face a number of operational problems which would serve to limit Soviet chances for quick success on the battlefield in Europe and then to discourage Soviet leadership from engaging in military adventurism in Western Europe in the near future. While some of the problems are individually manageable, many are not clearly defined and when taken together they are likely to be of serious concern to Kremlin hawks.

Warning Time and Topography. As noted above, Soviet doctrine calls for speed and surprise to enhance shock effect. Nevertheless, no matter how carefully and covertly they plan their operations, Soviet planners must assume that NATO will have some warning time in which to move their forces out of garrisons to wartime positions. Once NATO forces are in these defensive positions, a rush to the Rhine by Soviet forces will be no easy task. Thus, Soviet planners must ensure that sufficient forces are brought to bear and that these forces are backed by adequate logistics. However, the greater the degree of mobilization the more likely the probability that surprise will be lost.

Further, Soviet military planners know that their rush to the Rhine will not be so simple because the urbanized terrain in Western Europe will no longer permit open terrain tactics. "Terrain that once contained ample maneuver space between urban areas," writes Lieutenant Colonel John W. Burbery, Jr., "is now virtually covered by man-made structures such as buildings, roads, and canals." To illustrate this problem, Burbery notes that "studies show that the average brigade sector in Western Europe encompasses 25 towns with populations up to 3,000. This does not include the larger towns and cities found in brigade sectors." Where sizable man-made structures do not exist, Burbery notes, "much of the ground is covered with forests and steep hills, topographical features that also tend to be severely restrictive in terms of tactical movement."[48] If nuclear and chemical weapons were used, rubble and contamination in these built-up areas would slow the attackers even to a greater degree.

Former Commander in Chief of the US Army in Europe, General James H. Polk, claims that a Warsaw Pact attack across the North German Plain would not be without difficulties, especially in wet weather, which is fairly common in this area. At this time, "all travel is roadbound," he writes, and "cross-country transit can be said to be good only in the dead of winter, when the terrain is frozen hard. The North German Plain, while indeed flat, does not in any considerable degree favor the attacker." On the other hand, General Polk points out, south of the Plain, "the going is fairly good for the attacker in places," and that once he has crossed the Weser River and passed through the Teutoburger hills into the plains around Paderborn, there are few obstacles to his movement except for the many small villages and towns. "Once into this area in force, some 100 kilometers inside the Federal Republic of Germany," writes General Polk, "the Ruhr is at risk and the armies of Central Europe are split down the middle."[49]

Logistics. Long considered the Achilles' heel of the Soviet army, logistical support has been greatly improved. Smaller cargo trucks are being replaced by much larger ones with double and triple carrying capacity; POL trucks, trailers, and pipelines have increased in number; some 2,000 tank transporters organized in heavy lift regiments reduce dependence on rail. Stocks have been significantly increased, and GSFG now has ammunition for at least 37 days and fuel for 16. GSFG's river-crossing assets have been augmented with at least four ponton bridge battalions, while the organic battalions have been reinforced with heavy amphibious vehicles and GSP ferries.[50]

Nevertheless, the Soviet logistics system remains vulnerable. The large pipelines which run from the oil-producing areas of the Soviet Union (Oktyabrski and Kuibyshev) to the large refineries at Bratislava, Czechoslovakia, and Schwerin, East Germany, and the pipeline, still under construction from Tyumen to Szczecin, Poland, would probably not survive the first few days of a war in Europe. The railroad container service between Riga-Rostock-Prague, Moscow-Warsaw-East Berlin, and Rostock-East Berlin-Prague-Budapest-Belgrade-Sofia also would very likely be disrupted or halted in such a war.[51] Further, all cargo moving on rail from the USSR must be offloaded from Russian trains (which operate on a different gage than European trains) and reloaded onto East European trains. These transloading points along Western borders of the USSR, which are essential to east-west traffic, would be vulnerable. Thus, despite the extensive stockpiling of combat and strategic materiel (tanks, bridging, fuels, munitions, etc.) in the forward area wartime resupply is likely to be a critical problem for the Soviets.

Moreover, with the expansion, reequipping, and modernization of Soviet divisions, logistics problems have grown in magnitude and complexity. Tracked self-propelled howitzers are more difficult to maintain than the towed artillery piece they replace. The BMP personnel carrier is more complicated to maintain than the wheeled APC. Surface-to-air missiles and their associated fire control systems are far more complex than antiaircraft guns. In fast-moving, hard-charging combat, such systems—especially tracked vehicles—would soon require time-consuming maintenance and even replacement.

Nevertheless, Warsaw Pact equipment is, for the most part, standardized which facilitates resupply. Several East European countries manufacture their own versions of Soviet military equipment, including armored personnel carriers and tanks. Warsaw Pact air forces also benefit from standardized aircraft servicing and handling facilities.[52]

Moscow's pressure on its Warsaw Pact Allies to buy Soviet-designed equipment certainly has caused hardships on already-strained economies in Eastern Europe. As prices of high technology weaponry rise, the high commands of the various Pact countries must make hard decisions: to make do with older, out-of-date equipment for a little longer or to purchase the expensive new items which their economies can ill afford. It appears that some countries have compromised by retaining old equipment and buying some new items. The Czechoslovak air force, for example, has acquired the versatile FLOGGER, while still flying the antiquated MIG-15—which is older than most of the pilots flying them.[53]

Certainly then, logistics, although improving over the last decade, remains a problem for Soviet military planners. Logistical difficulties often account for the bulk of critical articles in the official army newspaper, *Krasnaya Zvezda (Red Star)*. In the month of September 1982, for example, 4 percent of the newspaper's space allocated to all Soviet military topics was critical or negative in tone in regard to individual or unit performance. Eleven percent of the space about Soviet military discipline and morale was critical, but a not-so-surprising 17 percent of the space allocated to the subject of military logistics was critical in tone.[54] Such an emphasis on logistics difficulties cannot but leave the Soviets with some nagging doubts about their ability to carry out and sustain prolonged offensive warfare.

RELIABILITY AND EFFECTIVENESS OF SOVIET ALLIES

How reliable are the Soviets' Warsaw Pact Allies? How well will they cooperate during wartime? Will they fight? More importantly, would they fight an offensive war, beyond their own territory, or would their forces hold together in a campaign in which they were being defeated? There are no certain answers for these questions.

In the current Polish crisis there were those who predicted that the Army would side with the people and would never participate in crushing solidarity. Not surprisingly, Deputy Prime Minister Mieczyslaw Rakowski, in an interview with Oriana Fallaci, in the wake of the initial Polish government success in defeating solidarity activists, declared that,

> the extremists of Solidarity had convinced themselves that, when things would boil until the use of force, the Army and the militia would side with them. They counted, I guess, on the fact that many soldiers belong to Solidarity. What naivete . . . . The point is that naivete wasn't limited to the frontiers of Poland: The West too was very naive.[55]

Certainly, the efficiency and firmness of the Army surprised a number of people, some of whom had predicted bloody widespread revolt. Nevertheless, one does not have to travel extensively in Poland to realize that for many of the Polish people, the Soviets are among the most despised neighbors of Poland. Thus, the Polish army's value to the Warsaw Pact, especially in an offensive operation, is still a matter of question.

The Czechoslovaks, whose reliability is also given low marks by some,[56] probably feel trapped by history and geography and, therefore, see no other choice but to do the Soviets' bidding, at least in peacetime. They will quickly tell you that the events of 1938, 1948, and again in 1968 proved that help from the West was never seriously considered. They will tell you, too, that wedged between Germany and the Soviet Union they have had to choose their friends carefully. Finally, as do other East European countries, they look to the USSR as the principal source of raw materials for their industry[57] and see no way out of this situation. However, it is likely that the Soviets harbor some uncertainties concerning the wartime performance of the Czechoslovak military. Would they stand and fight? Would their performance be scenario-dependent?

Soviet perceptions of Hungarian reliability undoubtedly have been affected by the events of World War II—when Budapest sided with the Germans—and the 1956 uprising, which was put down with much bloodshed. As for the Romanians, Moscow chafes at their semi-independence and maverick behavior and probably holds Romania's armed forces in low regard and expects little support in time of conflict. There is no ambivalence in the

Kremlin's attitude toward the Bulgarian military, who often give the impression of being more Soviet than the Soviets.

How reliable would the East German army be in a war in which they would immediately see hard action and where they would be facing fellow Germans? One would certainly expect some defections, especially if the battle were going against them, but otherwise the East Germans could prove to be some of the staunchest, most disciplined fighters. Western military liaison officers who have observed the National Volksarmee at close range have been impressed with its order, thoroughness, and increasing confidence in itself.[58] Man for man, the East Germans in many ways outshine their Soviet "guests," especially in appearance, military bearing, and overall care of their facilities. Nevertheless, one must ask, as has one author, "Why are the military forces of the GDR, particularly the ground forces, kept at relatively small numbers in spite of the fact that the GDR economy and population size would support a significantly larger force?"[59] The Soviet High Command may have some lingering fears about the use of Germans to fight Germans. Christopher Donnelly concluded the GDR military forces "are the most trustworthy and least trusted of the military forces in East Europe."[60]

Historic national and ethnic enmity also is likely to contribute to frictions which reduce the effectiveness of the Warsaw Pact in time of conflict. Poles make no secret of their dislike for Germans and Czechs as well as Russians. Invaded by East Germans, Poles, Hungarians, and Bulgarians in 1968, the Czechoslovaks would probably like to return the favor, if the opportunity ever presented itself. The East Germans have no love for Poles or Soviets. The Hungarians would list Romanians, Russians, and Czechs as some of their least favorites. Romanians feel animosity toward Hungarians, Russians, Bulgarians, while their neighbor to the south, Bulgaria, dislikes Romanians (and Yugoslavs, Greeks, and Turks).[61] In gatherings of Warsaw Pact officers, the East Germans sometimes find themselves the "odd man out," especially when the subject of the Great Patriotic War (World War II) is brought up. Despite their rewriting of history, the Soviets have not yet been able to convince anyone that all the fascists and Nazis resided in what is now the Federal Republic.

Frederick Turner, who served for 5½ years as a member and as Chief of the US Military Liaison Mission in GSFG, wrote about the Soviet soldier:

> In East Germany, he finds himself in a foreign land, an enemy land. In general, Germans are still hated and feared, although Soviet propaganda does try to distinguish, without much success, between the East (good) Germans and the West (reactionary, revanchist) Germans.[62]

For the remainder of the 1980's, the probability of renewed tensions in Eastern Europe is likely to add to Soviet uncertainties about the wartime allegiances of their allies. Poland's economy, in serious trouble, will probably worsen, as debts mount with little possibility of repayment. Since crucial supply routes and reinforcements must cross Poland, the Soviets are particularly sensitive to turmoil in what constitutes GSFG's rear. Past Polish labor problems have drawn quick reaction by the Soviets, including, in some cases, the military establishment, such as in October 1956. If the Soviet Union fails to fulfill the goals of its eleventh (1981-85) and twelfth (1986-90) Five-Year Plan, the effects will be felt throughout the bloc, and further labor unrest may erupt. East Europe is especially dependent on the Soviet Union for oil, and the Soviets have served notice that there will be no further increases in oil deliveries, which may force these countries to buy on the world market. With shortages of hard currency, East European countries will soon feel the pinch. Some of them might seek financing in the West, which would offer only temporary relief. The experience of Poland's debt servicing problems may make Western financing less obtainable, and West European economic difficulties may also play a role (for example, the FRG may reduce its annual generous interest-free loans to the GDR if its own economic problems continue). Such problems could further destabilize the situation in Eastern Europe and will almost certainly have an impact on the Warsaw Pact's warmaking capability.

To add to their woes, the Soviet leaders must realize that their Marxist-Leninist ideology is bankrupt and Communist revolutionary enthusiasm is fast disappearing. Noting the Yugoslav defection in 1948, Albania's "political meanderings," Romania's independent foreign policy, and various East European uprisings, Stanford Professor Wayne Vucinich concludes that,

> Marxist-Leninist ideology has been made the servant of realpolitik and thereby reduced to the level of theoretical discussion. To be sure, discussion continues as to the relevance and irrelevance of ideology in Eastern Europe, and various views have been expressed by men of prominence . . . . But, in general, ideology appears to consist of little more than the observance of

informalities. It has been reduced to hollow ritualism, and the revitalization of Marxist-Leninism as a viable ideology is not likely.[63]

The populations which have lived under Soviet domination are disillusioned, disappointed, and apathetic. Their productivity is best expressed by a joke popular in East Europe: "They (the regime) pretend to pay us and we pretend to work!"

In sum, from the Soviet perspective, the reliability of East European forces cannot be taken for granted. There may be unforeseen factors affecting reliability over which the Soviet Union has little or no control.[64] While Western analysts do not seem to be able to agree on the issue of reliability of Moscow's Warsaw Pact allies, one can safely assume that the Soviet leadership has its own doubts and misgivings about its military partners, all of whom, except Czechoslovakia, were enemies in World War II, and most of whom, including Czechoslovakia, have been bullied by Soviet intervention forces since the war.

In an attempt to improve reliability and at the same time tighten control, the Soviets bring promising East European officers to the USSR for training. A number of officers study at the famed Frunze Military Academy in Moscow which provides a 3-year course concentrating on preparing officers for combined arms warfare. Higher ranking officers may attend the Voroshilov Military Academy of the General Staff, also located in Moscow, and graduates are often destined for senior positions. In 1978, all ministers of defense of the Warsaw Pact countries were graduates of this academy.[65]

The Kremlin has other means for enhancing the reliability and dependability of their Warsaw Pact Allies. The Soviet Union controls many of the key interests of the East European military, including the level of spending and the modernization of the armed services. In addition, notes Condoleezza Rice,

> Soviet policy toward the East European elites is aimed at forging strong identification with the Soviet Union. There are even appeals to pan-Slavism and, in some cases, identification with the old Russian empire. Classes in the Russian language, history, and culture attempt to encourage a greater appreciation among the satellite elites of the Soviet Union. Working class heritage is no longer the primary requirement for mobility through the officer ranks. Study in the Soviet Union's military or military-political academies is also an important factor. Moreover, numerous awards, citations, and special projects are intended to ensure that East European officers remember to whom they owe their prestige and level of advancement.[66]

Very senior officers of the Warsaw Pact countries are aware that they occupy their key posts, as a minimum, because of Soviet sufferance, and some leaders owe their jobs to the Soviet stamp of approval. One such individual is General Martin Dzur, the Czechoslovak defense minister who first supported Dubcek, then pressured Dubcek to accept Marshal Grechko's post-invasion ultimatum to take radical steps to restore order in Czechoslovakia. His reward for siding with the Soviet defense minister was keeping his job when Gustav Husak replaced Dubcek—a job he still occupies in 1983.[67]

At the same time that they call for closer cooperation among the Warsaw Pact partners, the Soviets make it absolutely clear that they will play the dominant role in the alliance. Former Defense Minister Grechko, in his *The Armed Forces of the Soviet State,* discussed how the alliance could be strengthened. He called for unanimity of views on fundamental problems of theory and practice of military development; for joint troop and command and staff exercises; exchange of experience in combat and operational training; technical cooperation; mutual assistance in training cadres; and a number of other endeavors. In all these efforts, Grechko wrote, the USSR would play the leading role: "The existence of a very comprehensive combat experience in the Soviet Armed Forces, a first-rate material-technical base, and a well-trained military cadre ensures Soviet military scholars a vanguard role in the resolution of problems of military science."[68]

The use of a common language also contributes to the improvement of working relationships between forces of the Warsaw Pact. A great number of the East European officers speak Russian, which naturally facilitates communication among Warsaw Pact units and enhances professional and social contacts. In Czechoslovakia, for example, Soviet and Czechoslovak units sometimes train together, and the winter exercise is launched when engineers of the two armies build a pontoon bridge, named for the occasion "most druzhby," meaning "bridge of friendship" in both languages.

What are the Soviets doing to improve reliability and dependability of the rank-and-file of East European armies? Grechko claimed that Soviet soldiers who are to serve abroad are acquainted "with the traditions, state system, laws and customs of the friendly socialist country . . . where they will perform service."[69] But in this area the Soviets must receive low marks, since their young soldiers are allowed almost no contact with the local populace in East Europe. He is not permitted to date the girls of the "host" country, and his rare visits to sightseeing attractions, museums, and other cultural spots are made toward the end of his stay as part of an officer-supervised group. Thus, propaganda extolling Soviet virtues would reach the East European soldier from political sessions conducted by his own officers, rather than from personal contacts with Soviet soldiers stationed nearby.

Quality of Forces. The image of the semiliterate *muzhik* serviceman bereft of any creative initiative and lacking in basic mechanical skills should have disappeared years ago. Today's Soviet soldier is most likely a high school graduate who began his military training in the ninth and tenth grades.[70] He may have been active in the DOSAAF (the Voluntary Society for Cooperation with the Army, Aviation, and the Fleet), where he probably learned to shoot, and may well have learned to drive, operate a radio, fly, and parachute. Thus, former Secretary of Defense Harold Brown said, "the traditional argument that we are able to offset pact numerical superiority with fewer, higher quality forces, is no longer persuasive by itself."[71]

Nevertheless, the Soviet army in Eastern Europe is beset with some of the same problems facing other armies serving abroad. There is insufficient space for training, especially in East Germany and Czechoslovakia; many of their hosts would prefer their being back in the USSR; and the majority of Soviets would rather be home ("zdes' khorosho, no doma luchshe"—"Here it's OK, but it's better at home," they will quickly tell you). Criminal acts against the local populace, maneuver damage, traffic accidents, competition for scarce goods in the marketplace do not endear Soviet soldiers to their fraternal hosts.

Discipline problems, though downplayed, do exist. Former KGB Captain Aleksei Myagkov has described some in his book.[72] He wrote of drunken fights among officers, womanizing, thefts of government property, illegal financial transactions, black marketeering and other serious breaches of discipline. The rank-and-file soldiers were subjected to mistreatment by "old" soldiers (those whose term of service is nearing an end) or career soldiers, and sometimes young men died from beatings. Suicides are not uncommon, and in the 20th Guards Army (around Berlin), 24 men killed themselves in 1972, 33 in 1973. Desertions also are not isolated incidents, Myagkov writes, and many of these desertions end in crimes of robbery, rape, and murder. Some young soldiers have made off not only with automatic rifles but occasionally also with armored personnel carriers and even tanks, events which ended in tragic loss of life.

Kirill Podrabinek, who served in the Soviet army, confirms these stories of maltreatment of young soldiers, especially the beatings and verbal abuse. "A weakling (first-year conscript) is not beaten every day, of course," writes Podrabinek, "but kicks are a daily occurrence. They don't take someone to the hospital with broken ribs every day, but bruises are commonplace. It's not every day they ship a soldier's corpse home to his parents in a zinc coffin, but the weakling is humiliated constantly."[73]

Richard Anderson observes:

> Podrabinek's testimony puts the lie to the fearsome image of the Soviet Army. Western scholars have established that the effectiveness of soldiers depends on the cohesion of small units. Men fight on the battlefield primarily because they want to maintain the respect of their fellow soldiers. When this motive is absent . . . , soldiers will at best fight indifferently and at worst refuse to fight at all. No army so constituted that half the enlisted men maltreat the other half with the knowing complicity of their officers will fight hard, as the performance of the Soviet army in Afghanistan attests.[74]

The discipline problems described by Myagkov and Podrabinek are not confined to ground combat units but appear to be common throughout the Soviet armed forces.

Lieutenant Viktor Belenko, the Soviet MiG-25 pilot who defected to Japan in September 1976, described the same problems of drunkenness, brawls among soldiers, suicides, desertions, mutinies, and murders. In his supposedly elite air defense unit, men lived in filth, with no place to wash themselves and with 180-200 men jammed into barracks marginally adequate for 40. When Belenko pleaded with a visiting political officer to help solve these problems, he was told:

> You ask the Party to give, give, give, give me utopia, now. You show that you lack the imagination to grasp the magnitude of the problem, much less the difficulty of solving it. *You do not understand that our country cannot build complex aircraft, modern airfields and barracks all at the same time.* (Emphasis added)[75]

The Soviet army newspaper constantly exhorts its officer readers to improve discipline, to take their job seriously, to stop abusing their positions, to report violations, and to respect regulations. Young officers are warned not to be too hasty in marriage, since it is difficult to find quarters and divorce rates are high. Training failures are attributed to poor leadership, poor organization of training, lack of strict daily routine, unwise use of time, disunity of officers, and a lack of competitive spirit. Dishonesty and cheating are criticized, and officers are cited for resorting to unscrupulous tactics for the sake of winning. Published letters to the editors reflect widespread abuses, such as thefts of aircraft de-icing fluids for drinking. Poor management and leadership, morale problems, sloppy maintenance, and disregard for safety are regular themes in *Krasnaya Zvezda*.[76] One must assume that all of these problems are serious, even epidemic, to be described continually in the open press.

Quoting Richard Anderson again,

> The accounts we have of Soviet soldiers' behavior suggest desperation. Who but a man at the end of his rope would drink de-icing fluid from an airplane or antifreeze from a truck? Who else would paint a piece of bread with shoe polish, place it in the sun to dry, scrape off the residue of wax and eat the bread for its alcohol content? Who else would desert from the Soviet army in the certain knowledge that escape is all but impossible and that a prison term or sentence to the disciplinary battalions is the best he can hope for? Soviet soldiers do desert. A fair number cross the border from East to West Germany, and they desert even inside the USSR.[77]

Soviet troops in the forward area find life especially difficult. As already mentioned, they are not allowed social contacts with the local populace, except for rare occasions when groups sponsored by the German-Soviet Friendship Society, for example, are brought to the bases for a cultural event. The young trainees receive the equivalent of about $6 a month, and to supplement these miserable wages many men smuggle auto parts, grease, gasoline, rope, boots, and overcoats off base to nearby villages where they sell or barter these goods for alcohol. Army food for these troops is unappetizing: cabbage, potatoes, macaroni, *kasha* (buckwheat porridge), bread, fish, tea, and a little meat make up the soldier's diet.[78] Rather than making him a tough, determined soldier, these hardships serve to make him want to terminate his military service as soon as possible.

Training is also a problem. The Soviet soldiers train long and hard. There are a number of things, such as river crossings and airborne operations, they have come to do very well during training exercises. They, however, perennially do not perform well in march discipline, camouflage, night driving, and map readings. Concerning map reading, Frederick Turner has noted: "Since maps are classified materials that only officers are allowed to handle, in most cases the soldier has no idea where he is or of any master plan for movement."[79] Field sanitation and realism in training are also serious shortcomings. One would expect training weaknesses to be exacerbated in a real war situation.

Unfortunately for the Soviet army (and this must be an embarrassment), its combat experience since the end of World War II has been confined to fighting so-called friends—East Germany (1953), Hungary (1956), Czechoslovakia (1968), and Afghanistan (since December 1979). (The Soviets and the Poles were very near to a shooting war in October 1956, but Khrushchev backed down and withdrew his invasion force after a bitter confrontation with Gomulka.[80]) Fighting unarmed workers or bullying hapless Czechs—or even doing combat with illiterate Afghan partisans—has provided few lessons for fighting West Germans, Britons, Americans, or any of the NATO partners.

For the remainder of the 1980's and into the 1990's, the quality of Warsaw Pact forces will also be affected, albeit only moderately, by manpower shortages, economic problems, leadership changes, pacifism, and the continuing conflict in Afghanistan.

It has been estimated that over the next decade the draft pool in the USSR (and East Europe has similar problems) will decline by some 20 percent from its 1979 peak, and simultaneously, the proportion of ethnic minorities in the pool will rise substantially.[81] While the Soviet economy will be competing for a greater share of the manpower pool, there is little doubt that military demands will prevail, not, however, without some adjustments here and there. For example, some of the units not immediately earmarked for reinforcement of Soviet groups of forces in East Europe or the Sino-Soviet border area might not be manned beyond cadre strength. The ethnic problem may not be so easy to resolve. The Soviet's 1979 census confirmed an extremely low rate of growth of Slavs (who are dominant in three republics: RSFSR, Ukraine, and Belorussia). Large increases were recorded in the predominantly Muslim republics of Azerbaidzhan, Kazakhstan, Kirgizia, Tadzhikistan, Turkmenistan, and Uzbekistan.[82] The percentage of

Muslim nationalities in the draft-age pool is expected almost to double from the 1970 percentage of 13.1 to 24.1 in 1985.[83] And the percentage will continue to grow thereafter.

The Soviet military leadership is very concerned about the expected increase in non-Russians in the armed forces and regards the language problem serious enough to comment on in official writings. Marshal Nikolai Ogarkov, First Deputy Minister of Defense and Chief of the General Staff, recently discussed the requirement for Soviet soldiers to speak the Russian language. In his 1982 book, *Always Ready for Defense of the Motherland,* he wrote:

> Considering the question of preparing youth for military service, one especially ought to point out the importance to them of a good knowledge of the Russian language. Regrettably, a number of young people still come into the army today with a *weak knowledge of the Russian language, which seriously hinders their military training.* In the armed forces, as is known, all regulations, instructions, training aids, technical and weapons manuals are in the Russian language. Orders, directives, and commands also are rendered in the Russian language. It is completely understandable that, if young people have a weak grasp of the Russian language, it will be more difficult to master weapons and technology entrusted to them; coordination of crews, teams will take place much more slowly; and all this in some degree will impact negatively on the level of combat readiness of subunits. (Emphasis added)[84]

Thus, Soviet military leaders, at least, perceive a problem with their conscripts who lack a fluency in the Russian language.

In their study of the ethnic factor in the Soviet armed forces, Wimbush and Alexiev found that Slavs and non-Slavs are isolated into their ethnic groups and that there is intense racial discrimination against Central Asians and other dark-skinned non-Slavs. "Ethnic awareness," they report, "is heightened, not reduced in a close-quarter military environment. The conflict level between Slavs, and especially Central Asians and other Turkic or Muslim servicemen, is pronounced, often resulting in armed clashes of various intensity."[85]

Former KGB Captain Myagkov describes a young soldier, Dzhavadze, in the 20th Guards Army, Group of Soviet Forces in Germany, who was a Georgian by nationality. He spoke Russian badly, which led to unending jokes by other soldiers in his regiment and humiliations by the other soldiers. Even the officers often called him an insulting name. Finally, unable to take it any longer,

Dzhavadze cut his throat, but survived and remained an invalid for the rest of his life.[86]

In addition to manpower problems, the economy will continue to plague the Soviets, despite an ambitious eleventh Five-Year Plan. The military, long pampered by a generous Politburo, may find competition for scarce resources increasing, as overall economic growth slows. Marshal Ogarkov, writing in *Kommunist* in July 1981 (and repeating himself the next year in *Vsegda v Gotovnosti k Zaschite Otechestva*), appeared to be making "a rather blatant pitch to protect his budget," probably fearing that "economic stringencies would impinge on defense's share of the country's resources."[87] Rather than give up any resources, the Soviet military is laying claim to even more. Ogarkov reminded his readers that modern weapons change every 10-12 years, implying, therefore, that future cuts would be dangerous.[88]

> This military claim [writes William Hyland] is even more significant when we consider that for most of 1979 and 1980, Brezhnev was warning the heavy industry clique that they had to make a greater contribution to consumer goods production, and that defense industries in particular had to help out. Hence, Ogarkov may be answering Brezhnev.
>
> In any case, the stage is set for a struggle over defense policy after Brezhnev. It could not really be otherwise if we consider that defense claims 12-15 percent of the Soviet national economic product.[89]

As with demands on the manpower pool, so it is with the slice of the economic pie: something has to give, but will it be the spoiled military? Brezhnev was especially kind to the military, far kinder than his predecessor, Khrushchev. Now that Brezhnev has left the scene, Andropov may not give the military everything it asks for. Will Andropov and the new leadership lose patience with an Ogarkov who tells them costly weapons systems must be replaced every 10-12 years? Or will they eagerly seek some accommodation with Western leaders to reduce armaments? Surely, neither side wants an all-out arms race for the remainder of the decade. Nevertheless, the evidence is disquieting: the Soviet military leadership appears to be closing ranks behind Ogarkov, who seems prepared to press for major military expenditures for the indefinite future. He may even be challenging some of the Party's moderates when he urges the Party to explain to all of the people *"in a more profound and better reasoned form* the truth about the existing danger of war."[90] (Emphasis added)

The second most powerful man in the new government appears to be Dmitri Ustinov, the Defense Minister, who, following Andropov, delivered the second eulogy at Brezhnev's funeral. The two men serve on the Defense Council, the Politburo's dominant committee and "the real, as opposed to the official, supreme center of power in the Soviet Union."[91] Until recently, Andropov, as head of the KGB, was responsible for political and military-strategic intelligence, while Ustinov was—and still is—the Defense Council member responsible for military-strategic intelligence produced by the GRU.[92] With the loss of key Defense Council members in 1982 (Suslov, Brezhnev, and Kirilenko), the power, influence, and prestige of Andropov and Ustinov have increased.[93] Thus, the military, for a while at least, may continue to receive priority on scarce resources, including manpower.[94]

As the Soviets look to the future, they must also wonder about their costly commitment in Afghanistan, a war already 3 years old and one in which they keep pouring in ever-increasing numbers of men. By now, the Soviet people must know that their own government is lying to them, that their young men are not simply providing humanitarian assistance and technical support to the Afghan army against "bandits," "gangsters," and "mercenaries."[95] As the number of Soviet dead and wounded continues to climb, the truth will emerge, despite secret burials by military authorities or sending wounded and disfigured soldiers to East Germany for treatment.[96]

If he can be believed, Vladimir Kuzichkin, a former KGB major who defected to the British in June 1982, said that Brezhnev himself overruled repeated advice from Yuri Andropov's KGB not to turn Afghanistan into a Soviet satellite.[97] Now that Brezhnev has left the scene, Andropov would be well-advised for economic, as well as political reasons, to take steps to extricate the USSR from its quagmire.

Another problem which faces the Soviets and their Warsaw Pact allies in the 1980's is the antiwar sentiment among the youth. In his 1982 book, Ogarkov discusses this matter, saying that where elements of pacifism appear they must be decisively dealt with.[98] In East Germany, for example, authorities recently refused to allow young people to wear badges and armbands advocating disarmament, claiming that their symbol, a sword beaten into a plowshare, undermined military service.[99] And at the same time that demonstrators in America were calling for a ban on nuclear weapons, the Soviets detained seven West Europeans in Moscow's Red Square as they attempted to unfurl a hand-lettered banner which read, "Bread, Life, Disarmament." "The police action," John F. Burns reported, "contrasted with Soviet support for Western European groups that have demonstrated against military spending by the United States and its plans to deploy a new generation of medium-range nuclear missiles in Europe."[100] But, as Ogarkov made plain, Soviet young people must not display pacifist sentiments, no matter how sincere they may be.

CONCLUSIONS

The Kremlin, given the current quantitative and qualitative balance of forces in Europe, cannot now launch a *blitzkrieg* against Europe which would lead to a quick and decisive victory. NATO appears to have the capability to deny the Soviets early victory and then turn the conflict into a protracted struggle which the Soviets do not want.[101]

Nevertheless, one must warn the reader that the delicate scheme of things could change. A very real danger is that the Soviets could continue their force buildup, without an adequate response from the NATO side. "NATO must provide for the continuation of ongoing improvements in its force structure," John J. Mearsheimer writes. "There is no evidence that the Soviet effort to modernize her forces in Central Europe is slowing down. Therefore, NATO must continue to make improvements if it is to maintain the present balance."[102]

Not only will the Soviets be constantly examining the balance of forces, but they also will be looking for exploitable weaknesses in the NATO military edifice. They will be especially alert to maldeployments and soft, vulnerable spots in NATO's forward defenses. They will put high priority on evaluating NATO's strategic warning capability, which is essential for timely mobilization and deployment of forces to wartime positions. But most of all, they will be continuously assessing NATO's political cohesiveness, searching for a fissure which they can take advantage of, such as disagreements over Olympic boycotts and sale of components for the Siberian gas pipeline. These tensions among major NATO partners probably give the Soviet leadership considerable satisfaction. At the same time, they must realize that some future threatening gesture from their side would have a great unifying effect on NATO.

The question that Moscow must ask itself is whether unleashing a war in Europe, even after getting the jump on NATO in mobilization, is worth the risk to its national survival. Despite tough talk by their military chieftains, such as Chief of the General Staff Nikolai Ogarkov, the leaders are not reckless men. Even in military operations, they tend to be extremely cautious: witness, for example, the huge force they assembled to overwhelm the Hungarians (some 2,000 tanks), or the docile Czechs (the equivalent of 29 divisions),[103] or the more than 105,000 soldiers now in Afghanistan. The Kremlin leaders also see opportunities for mischief-making and power projection in other parts of the world which are far less risky than aggression in Europe.

Several months ago, Milovan Djilas was interviewed in his Belgrade apartment. Asked about the future of the USSR, he declared: "I think the Soviet system is in a state of rotting. But this may be prolonged, because the ruling class in the Soviet Union is relatively stable." But, he warned, "to avoid internal problems, they may go for expansion." And what can the West do? "The West must be strong if it wants to save peace and stop Soviet expansionism. If it is stopped, the process of rotting will go faster. In some ways, the West is damned to be strong."[104]

The remainder of the 1980's will be an uneasy period for both sides, as the Kremlin tests the strength of the NATO Alliance and continues to project the image of its awesome military might in Europe and elsewhere. At the moment, the Alliance is fairly strong[105] and the Soviet leadership dares not take it on. But this is not the time for complacency; indeed, that is a luxury which never will be afforded us. NATO must continue to strengthen its shield in a spirit of friendly cooperation, determined not to be bullied by a power which specializes in military aggression. The future will not be calm and easy—but when has it been?

ENDNOTES

1. *Pravda,* October 7, 1979, cited in Vernon V. Aspaturian, "Soviet Global Power and the Correlation of Forces," *Problems of Communism,* May-June 1980, p. 6.

2. *Whence the Threat to Peace,* Moscow: Military Publishing House of the Ministry of Defense, 1982, pp. 69-78. The Russian language version is *Otkuda Iskhodit Ugroza Miru.* This booklet was quickly compiled in response to Caspar Weinberger's *Soviet Military Power,* Washington: Department of Defense, 1981.

3. *Soviet Military Power,* pp. 2, 25, 29; and Harold Brown, *Report of Secretary of Defense to the Congress on the FY 1982 Budget,* Washington: Department of Defense, 1981, p. 69. The second edition of *Soviet Military Power* was released in March 1983. (Hereafter, these editions will be referred to as SMP II.)

4. See the excellent editorial, "Giving Europe a Defense," in *The Wall Street Journal,* January 14, 1983, p. 22. Describing a United States Strategic Institute study authored by Donald R. Cotter, James Hansen, and Kirk McConnell, the editorial notes:

> The authors put to rest the myth that the Soviet Union's weapons buildup in Europe, as well as the whole arms race, is only a response to our own weapons deployments. Their analysis of Soviet nuclear weapons deployment in Europe reveals an integrated air and ground *offensive* military system. The types and numbers of Soviet weapons, along with their military doctrine, training, and rate of acquisition, 'describe a Soviet theater nuclear force capability that is far in excess of anything that could conceivably be characterized as counterdeterrent to NATO nuclear capabilities.' In other work, the Soviet forces deployed against Western Europe are designed for attack.

5. The 6th Guards Tank Division was withdrawn from East Germany after Brezhnev's unilateral pledge of October 6, 1979 to withdraw up to 20,000 personnel and 1,000 tanks, although there are reports that the withdrawal of this division was more than offset by reassignment of smaller tank units to other East European-based divisions. Daniel S. Papp, "From the Crest All Directions Are Down: The Soviet Union Views the 1980s," *Naval War College Review,* July-August 1982, p. 67. See US Joint Chiefs of Staff, *United States Military Posture,* supplement to overview by General David C. Jones, USAF, for FY 82, p. 104; for a listing of GSFG divisions see Friedrich Wiener, *The Warsaw Pact Armies,* Vienna: Carl Ueberreuter Publishers, 1981, pp. 62-63. Of the 30 Soviet maneuver divisions in Eastern Europe, 15 are tank, 15 are motorized rifle. See the International Institute for Strategic Studies (hereafter IISS), *The Military Balance, 1982-1983,* London: IISS, 1982, p. 14. The importance the Soviets attach to their largest group, GSFG, is shown by the title of its senior officer (currently General of the Army M. M. Zaytsev who succeeded Ye. F. Ivanovskiy in December 1980), who is designated "commander in chief," one of eight such positions in the Soviet military structure. See Harriet Fast Scott and William F. Scott, *The Armed Forces of the USSR,* Boulder: Westview Press, 1979, p. 206. Also, "Glavnokomanduyushchiy" in *Sovetskaya Voyennaya Entsiklopediya,* Vol. 2, Moscow: Military Publishing House of the Ministry of Defense, 1976, p. 564.

6. *The Military Balance, 1982-1983,* p. 15. For more information on Soviet and East European order of battle, see the outstanding work by William J. Lewis, *The Warsaw Pact: Arms, Doctrine, and Strategy,* McGraw Hill Publications, 1982.

7. Brown, p. 69.

8. Dietrich Frenzke, "New Czech-Soviet Alliance Treaty," *Aussen Politik,* English edition, March 1970, pp. 328-329. See also Avigdor Hasselkorn, "The Expanding Soviet Collective Security Network," *Strategic Review,* Summer 1978, p. 64. As pointed out by Hasselkorn, "In all such treaties concluded since 1967, the obligations of mutual assistance of the signatory nations have been extended to include attacks upon the USSR outside Europe."

9. Scott and Scott, pp. 203-205.

10. *The Military Balance, 1982-1983,* pp. 20-23; *SMP I,* p. 6.

11. *The Military Balance, 1982-1983,* p. 131.

12. *Ibid.,* p. 22.

13. *SMP I,* pp. 28-29, 32-34; *SMP II,* pp. 38, 40. Also, David C. Jones, *United States Military Posture for 1983,* Washington: The Organization of the Joint Chiefs of Staff, 1982, p. 111.

14. Benjamin F. Schemmer (interview with General Charles A. Gabriel, USAF), "We Can Count on *Our* Allies. I'm Not Sure the Warsaw Pact Can Count on Theirs," *Armed Forces Journal International,* January 1982, p. 25.

15. Harold Brown, p. 69, and David C. Jones, p. 104.

16. C. N. Donnelly, "Recent Debates in the Soviet Military Press," *Military Review,* June 1979, p. 19. Mr. Donnelly's article appeared earlier in *International Defense Review,* Vol. 11, No. 9, 1978. Emphasis in the original.

17. *Ibid.*

18. *Ibid.* Emphasis is Mr. Donnelly's.

19. *Ibid.,* pp. 19-20.

20. Appreciation is acknowledged for Robert Kennedy's bringing some of the following materiel to my attention. See his "Advanced Technology and NATO Defense," Unpublished Ph.D. Dissertation, Georgetown University, 1978, pp. 76-82.

21. V. Ye. Savkin, *The Basic Principles of Operational Art and Tactics (Soviet View),* translated under the auspices of the US Air Force, Washington: US Government Printing Office, 1972, pp. 52-122.

22. *Ibid.,* p. 242.

23. *Ibid.,* p. 230.

24. *Ibid.,* pp. 232-233.

25. *Ibid.,* p. 234.

26. *Ibid.*

27. *Ibid.,* p. 168.

28. *Explanatory Dictionary of Military Terms,* p. 75, cited in Joseph D. Douglass, Jr., *The Soviet Theater Nuclear Offensive,* Washington: US Government Printing Office, 1976, p. 26.

29. C. N. Donnelly, "The Soviet Operational Maneuver Group: A New Challenge for NATO," *International Defense Review,* No. 9, 1982, p. 1180. Mr. Donnelly is a senior analyst at the Soviet Studies Centre, Royal Military Academy, Sandhurst.

30. For an interesting and useful discussion of the Soviets' prospects for carrying out a *blitzkrieg* against NATO, see John J. Mearsheimer's "Why the

Soviets Can't Win Quickly in Central Europe," *International Security,* Summer 1982, pp. 3-39.

31. V. A. Smirnov, "Podvizhnaya Grupa," *Sovetskaya Voyennaya Entsiklopediya,* Moscow: Publishing House of the Ministry of Defense, 1978, Vol. 6, p. 373.

32. Donnelly, pp. 1181-1182.

33. *Ibid.,* p. 1182, citing Polish Colonels Lachiewicz and Rajmanski, "Helicopter Reconnaissance and Fire Missions in Support of Land Operations at Night," *Air Force and Air Defense Review,* June 1981.

34. "Teatr Voyennykh Deistviy (TVD), *Sovetskaya Voyennaya Entsiklopediya,* Moscow: Military Press of the Ministry of Defense of the USSR, 1980, Vol. 8, pp. 8-9.

35. Department of the Army, *Soviet Army Operations,* Washington: US Government Printing Office, 1978, pp. 2-5, 2-6. A Soviet *front* is not a fixed organization, but is tailored for the situation and mission. A *front* would consist of several armies and varying numbers of surface-to-surface missile brigades, artillery divisions or brigades, multiple rocket launcher brigades or regiments, antitank brigades or regiments, surface-to-air missile brigades or regiments, signal brigades or regiments, combat engineer brigades or regiments, ponton regiments, and chemical brigades. *Ibid.,* pp. 2-6, 2-7.

36. See John M. Collins, *US-Soviet Military Balance: Concepts and Capabilities,* Washington: McGraw Hill Publications, 1980, p. 313, and Sir John Hackett, *et. al., The Third World War,* New York: Macmillan Publishing Co., Inc., 1978, p. 162.

37. Clayton A. Pratt, "The Benelux and Northern German Plains Avenue of Approach," *Military Review,* June 1978, pp. 2-8.

38. Interview in Schemmer, p. 27. General Gabriel went on to describe how the airbases will be defended—with security police, wartime augmentation forces, and host-nation forces.

39. William K. Sullivan, "Soviet Strategy and NATO's Northern Flank," *Naval War College Review,* July-August 1979, p. 26.

40. *Ibid.,* p. 29.

41. *The Military Balance, 1982-1983,* p. 15.

42. Sullivan, p. 31.

43. John C. Campbell, "Communist Strategies in the Mediterranean," *Problems of Communism,* May-June 1979, p. 3.

44. Lawrence J. Whetten, "Turkey and NATO's Second Front," *Strategic Review,* Summer 1981, p. 60.

45. George F. Kennan, *Soviet Foreign Policy, 1917-1941,* Princeton: D. Van Nostrand Co., Inc., 1960, pp. 111, 183.

46. Norman Polmar, ed., *Soviet Naval Developments,* Annapolis: The Nautical and Aviation Publishing Company of America, 1979, pp. 5-6.

47. Department of the Navy, Office of the Chief of Naval Operations, *Understanding Soviet Naval Developments,* Fourth Edition, Washington: US Government Printing Office, 1981, pp. 17-18.

48. John W. Burbery, Jr., "Urbanized Terrain: Perspective and Patterns," *Military Review,* March 1978, pp. 3-4.

49. James H. Polk, "The North German Plain Attack Scenario: Threat or Illusion?," *Strategic Review,* Summer 1980, pp. 61-62.

50. John Erickson, "Trends in the Soviet Combined Arms Concept," *Strategic Review,* Winter 1977, p. 44. As the Soviets attempt to resupply their forces in the forward area, they will experience some rail delays among their Western frontiers because of the requirement to change gage (5 feet to 4 feet 8 inches) as they move west. They have sought to overcome this problem somewhat by the creation of eight heavy-lift regiments. Each regiment reportedly can transport simultaneously almost all the tanks of a division, covering a distance of 500-600 kilometers in 24 hours. The Soviets and their Warsaw Pact Allies will also rely heavily on mobilization of transport resources from the civilian economy to meet wartime needs. An extensive network of quasimilitary transport units in the USSR, known as avtokolonny, which are manned by reservists, can be mobilized quickly to supplement regular units. *United States Military Posture for 1980,* pp. 54, 88; and Friedrick Wiener and William J. Lewis, *The Warsaw Pact Armies,* Vienna: Carl Ueberreuter Publishers, 1977, p. 67.

51. Jacquelyn K. Davis and Robert L. Pfaltzgraff, Jr., *Soviet Theater Strategy: Implications for NATO* (USSI Report 78-1), Washington: United States Strategic Institute, 1978, pp. 44-45.

52. *The Military Balance, 1982-1983,* p. 131. See also Lewis A. Frank, *The Arms Trade in International Relations,* New York: Frederick A. Praeger Publishers, 1969, pp. 55-57. Some specialists argue persuasively that the Warsaw Pact lacks standardization, citing the variety of armor vehicles, artillery pieces, diesel and gasoline vehicles, and the older, obsolescent equipment in the non-Soviet Warsaw Pact armies. See Keith Dunn, *Soviet Military Weaknesses and Vulnerabilities: A Critique of the Short War Advocates,* Carlisle Barracks, Pennsylvania: Strategic Studies Institute, 1979, pp. 17-18. Consider, for example, the problems posed by the variety of tank ammunition: the T54/55's gun is 100mm; the T-62, 115mm smoothbore; the T-64, T-72, and T-80, 125mm smoothbore.

53. *The Military Balance, 1982-1983,* p. 21. See also *IISS, Strategic Survey, 1979,* London: IISS, 1980, pp. 104-105.

54. *Krasnaya Zvezda Soviet News and Propaganda Analysis,* Vol. 2, No. 9, 1982, p. 31.

55. Oriana Fallaci, "Even an Angel Can Become a Whore," *The Washington Post,* February 21, 1982, p. D1. Some readers may insist that the ZOMO's, or riot police, rather than the Polish Army, enforced martial law. The Army was also largely responsible, manning roadblocks, rushing in tanks and armored personnel carriers, and in other ways supporting the military rule of General Jaruzelski. "The most open supporters of the regime are, of course, the ZOMO's (the riot police), and at least a part of the Army, who are pampered, fed, given special bonuses, and kept sufficiently isolated from the rest of society not to become 'contaminated' by public unrest," writes a young Polish social scientist under the pseudonym Casimir Garnysz in "Holding a Bear by the Tail," *Encounter,* September-October 1982, p. 77.

56. See, for example, the article by Dale R. Herspring and Ivan Volgyes, "Political Reliability in the Eastern European Warsaw Pact Armies," *Armed Forces and Society,* Vol. 6, Winter 1980, p. 289.

57. To quote again Polish Deputy Prime Minister Rakowski,

> I am a very convinced advocate of strict ties with the Soviet Union. I firmly believe that our place is on the side of the Soviet Union. Of course, I have my national pride, I want to be independent and to be treated as an equal, but I

say that Poland should stay very close to the Soviet Union. I say it as a realist, not only as a Communist. The Russians are Slavonic people, they are rich, they represent a tremendous market. We need them. Where else would we get the raw material we get from the Soviet Union?
Fallaci, p. D4.

With the deductions in Western aid, Poland will be even more dependent on the Soviet Union and East European neighbors. See Tad Szulc's interview with Wojciech Jaruzelski, "Can Poland Be Free?," *Parada,* July 18, 1982, pp. 4-6.

58. R. L. Giles, "Die Nationale Volksarmee aus der Sicht Eines Britischen Offiziers," lecture given at the joint conference of the "Arbeitskreis fuer Wehrforschung," the "Clausewitz Gesellschaft" and the "Deutsche Gesellschaft fuer Wehrtechnik" in Bonn, November 14-15, 1979. Lieutenant Colonel Giles served 4½ years as Russian interpreter and liaison officer with the British Military Liaison Mission to the Group of Soviet Forces in East Germany. For a most useful discussion of the reliability of the Polish East German, and Czechoslovak armed forces, see A. Ross Johnson, Robert W. Dean, and Alexander Alexiev, *East European Military Establishments: The Warsaw Pact Northern Tier,* Santa Monica, California: Rand, 1980.

59. Thomas O. Cason, "The Warsaw Pact Today: The East European Military Forces," in *The Warsaw Pact: Political Purpose and Military Means,* edited by Robert W. Clawson and Lawrence S. Kaplan, Wilmington, Delaware: Scholarly Resources, Inc., 1982, p. 151.

60. Cited in *Ibid.,* p. 152.

61. Herspring and Volgyes, p. 280. See, too, George Gibian, "The Way the Czechs View the Crisis in Poland," *The Wall Street Journal,* September 21, 1982, p. 34. Professor Gibian, during a recent visit to Czechoslovakia, found that "negative reactions to Poland far outweighed anti-Communist, anti-Soviet feelings of partnership and sympathy with the Poles."

62. Frederick C. Turner, "The Soviet GI," *Air Force Magazine,* March 1977, p. 83.

63. Wayne S. Vucinich, "Major Trends in Eastern Europe," in *Eastern Europe in the 1980s,* ed. by Stephen Fischer-Galati, Boulder, Colorado: Westview Press, 1981, p. 25.

64. Dale R. Herspring, "The Warsaw Pact at 25," *Problems of Communism,* September-October 1980, p. 11.

65. Scott and Scott, pp. 354, 356.

66. Condoleezza Rice, "The Problem of Military Elite Cohesion in Eastern Europe: The Case of Czechoslovakia," *Air University Review,* January-February 1982, pp. 66-67.

67. Michel Tatu, "Intervention in Eastern Europe," in *Diplomacy of Power: Soviet Armed Forces as a Political Instrument,* ed. by Stephen S. Kaplan, Washington: The Brookings Institution, 1981, p. 255.

68. A. A. Grechko (Marshal of the Soviet Union), *The Armed Forces of the Soviet State,* Moscow: Military Publishing House of the Ministry of Defense, 1975, translated and published under the auspices of the US Air Force, Washington: US Government Printing Office, pp. 340-343.

69. *Ibid.,* p. 343.

70. Scott and Scott, p. 316.

71. Harold Brown, *Department of Defense Annual Report for Fiscal Year 1982,* Washington: Department of Defense, 1981, p. 69.

72. Aleksei Myagkov, *Inside the KGB,* New Rochelle, New York: Arlington House Publishers, 1976, pp. 86-112. See also Richard A. Gabriel, *The New Red Legions: An Attitudinal Portrait of the Soviet Soldier,* Westport, Connecticut: Greenwood Press, 1980, pp. 151-182.

73. Kirill Podrabinek, "An Inside Look at Life in the Soviet Army," *Russia,* No. 3, 1981, p. 11. An editorial in the May 1982 issue of *Voyenno-meditsinskiy Zhurnal* revealed that the Soviet armed forces are suffering from dysentery and hepatitis, and that the diseases are related to poor living conditions: overcrowded, dirty barracks, lack of sewage systems, contaminated water supply, food poisoning, and lack of personal hygiene. See "Hard—and Dirty Life for Soviet Soldiers," *Soviet World Outlook,* August 15, 1982, p. 6.

74. Podrabinek, p. 12, Richard Anderson's afterword.

75. John Barron, *MIG Pilot: The Final Escape of Lieutenant Belenko,* New York: Reader's Digest Press, 1980, pp. 95-103.

76. The Special Operations Division of the Organization of the Joint Chiefs of Staff publishes a monthly *Krasnaya Zvezda Soviet News and Propaganda Analysis.* See, for example, Vol. 1, No. 11, 1981, pp. 24-29; Vol. 1, No. 12, 1981, pp. 23-26; and Vol. 2, No. 2, 1982, pp. 30-34.

77. Anderson's afterword to Podrabinek, p. 12.

78. "Moscow's Military Machine," *Time,* June 23, 1980, p. 27.

79. Turner, p. 83.

80. Otto Preston Chaney, Jr., *Zhukov,* Norman: University of Oklahoma Press, 1971, pp. 372-376.

81. Ellen Jones, "Soviet Military Manpower: Prospects in the 1980s," *Strategic Review,* Fall 1981, p. 65.

82. Murray Feshbach, "Between the Lines of the 1979 Soviet Census," *Problems of Communism,* January-February 1982, pp. 29, 33.

83. Jones, p. 71.

84. Nikolai Vasiliyevich Ogarkov (Marshal of the Soviet Union), *Vsegda v Gotovnosti k Zashchite Otechestva,* Moscow: Military Press of the Ministry of Defense of the USSR, 1982, p. 64. (Author's translation.)

85. S. Enders Wimbush and Alex Alexiev, *The Ethnic Factor in the Soviet Armed Forces: Preliminary Findings,* Santa Monica, California: The Rand Corporation, May 1980, p. vi. This interesting study is based on indepth interviews with former Soviet servicemen.

86. Myagkov, p. 110.

87. William G. Hyland, "Kto Kogo in the Kremlin," *Problems of Communism,* January-February 1982, p. 24. Hyland cites Ogarkov's article, "Defending Peaceful Endeavor," *Kommunist,* No. 10, July 1981, pp. 80-91. Ogarkov repeats himself in *Vsegda v Gotovnosti k Zashchite Otechestva,* p. 31, declaring that "realizing this dialectic process is especially important in the present time when on the basis of scientific-technical progress major weapons systems are to be renewed after every 10-12 years." (Author's translation.)

88. *Ibid.*

89. *Ibid.*

90. Ogarkov in *Kommunist,* cited by Hyland, p. 24.

91. Michael Sadykiewicz, "Soviet Military Politics," *Survey,* Winter 1982, p. 180.

92. *Ibid.*, p. 193.

93. Brezhnev was described as Chairman of the Defense Council in *Sovetskaya Voyennaya Entsiklopediya,* Vol. 1, p. 588, sent to the typesetters in September 1974. The Supreme Defense Council was created in 1958 to unify the leadership of the war departments and Nikita Khrushchev was appointed chairman. See Roy Medveder, *Khrushchev,* Garden City, New York: Anchor Press/Doubleday, 1983, p. 128.

94. Some months before Brezhnev's passing, Rand Senior Economist Abraham S. Beck wrote that "all that we have learned about the political context of Soviet decisionmaking suggests that the idea of drastic defense cuts would be abhorrent to the political-military leadership waiting in the wings . . . . The most attractive option for Mr. Brezhnev's successors, as it has been for Mr. Brezhnev, may be the decision to change nothing." Becker, "Guns, Butter and the Brezhnev Succession," *Wall Street Journal,* June 21, 1982, p. 16.

95. David Satter, "What Russia Tells Russians About Afghanistan," *The Wall Street Journal,* November 11, 1982, p. 30. Six men who were described as Soviet deserters from their military units in Afghanistan said in a February 17, 1983 interview on the ABC News Program "20-20" that they had been misled into believing that they would be fighting foreign mercenaries. See Stephen Kinzer, "Soviet Deserters, on TV, Say They Joined Afghan Rebels," *The New York Times,* February 18, 1983, p. A3.

96. Satter, p. 30.

97. "Coups and Killings in Kabul," *Time,* November 22, 1982, pp. 33-34. Kuzichkin provides an interesting accounting of the storming of the presidential palace the day after Christmas 1979 by a few hundred Soviet *spetsnaz* troops, plus a specially trained assault group of KGB officers. After killing a number of Afghan troops, the Soviets, who were wearing Afghan uniforms and using vehicles with Afghan markings, killed President Amin. The Soviet in charge, Colonel Bayerenov, head of the KGB's terrorist training school, was shot and killed by his own men in the confusion of the attack.

98. Ogarkov, *Always Ready . . . ,* pp. 65-66.

99. "East German Pastors Protest Ban on Pacifist Badges," *The New York Times,* April 12, 1982, p. A3.

100. John F. Burns, "Seven West Europeans Detained in Soviet," *The New York Times,* April 20, 1982, p. A12.

101. Mearsheimer, pp. 3-4.

102. *Ibid.,* pp. 36-37. According to Mearsheimer,

> It is absolutely essential . . . that deployment of the American corps in NORTHAG be completed. It is also imperative that the Belgians, the British, and the Dutch continue to modernize and upgrade their conventional forces. More specifically, these forces, especially the British, must increase the firepower of their individual brigades. The Germans, for their part, must maintain their commitment to developing a formidable Territorial Army.

103. According to British writer Adam Roberts, about 400,000 Polish, Hungarian, East German, Bulgarian, and Soviet troops invaded Czechoslovakia. Cited in Michel Tatu, p. 230.

104. Thomas J. Bray, "A Conversation With Yugoslavia's Milovan Djilas," *The Wall Street Journal,* October 20, 1982, p. 33.

105. Much remains to be done. See Sam Nunn (Senator), "NATO: Can the Alliance Be Saved?," *The Atlantic Community Quarterly,* Summer 1982, pp. 126-138.

9

CHEMICAL WEAPONS REARMAMENT AND THE SECURITY OF EUROPE: CAN SUPPORT BE MUSTERED?

John M. Weinstein and Henry G. Gole

Among the most vexing policy issues confronting American and Western European military planners today concerns the scope and direction of the West's chemical warfare doctrine and capability. This issue has arisen in response to a number of developments on the military and political scenes, both at home and abroad.

The continuing expansion of the Soviet Union's strategic and theater arsenals has stimulated considerable debate regarding the balance of conventional and tactical nuclear forces in Europe. In the past, NATO's strategy to deter Soviet/Warsaw Pact aggression relied upon the former's tactical and theater nuclear superiority to counterbalance the latter's conventional might. If NATO's nuclear edge has disappeared, as is argued by numerous military and civilian analysts,[1] this development is disturbing indeed. The alleged erosion of NATO's military capabilities *vis-a-vis* those of the Soviet Union and the Warsaw Pact raises critical questions for military planners and politicians on both sides of the Atlantic. Foremost among these questions are "how much is enough?" and "what intentions underlie the Soviets' force developments?" As one might expect from an alliance composed of members from different hemispheres and different historical experiences, the NATO response has not been unanimous. Generally, the United States, especially under the current administration, has urged a rapid military buildup to deter the Soviet Union and to signal US renewed determination to conduct East-West relations from a position of strength. On the other hand, many Europeans continue to eschew military emphasis as the primary policy tool.[2] They have emphasized the role of interlocking and mutually beneficial political and economic relations between East and West to obviate the need for the extensive military buildup urged so forcibly by Washington.

The divergence between European and American perceptions of the nature of the threat, as well as the most expedient and efficacious response, has been demonstrated repeatedly and spectacularly in the intra-alliance debates on the need for such weapons and systems as the enhanced radiation warhead (neutron bomb), ground-launched cruise missile, the Pershing II intermediate range ballistic missile, and a no-first-use of nuclear weapons policy.

Additional strains upon the increasingly fragile Atlantic alliance[3] arise from uncertainty about the course of the Soviet Union in the post-Brezhnev period. It remains to be seen whether the myriad economic, social, and demographic problems which are currently tearing at the fabric of the last of the great international empires will turn the Soviet Union inward toward a less threatening orientation or cause it to resolve its internal contradictions through aggression. Related to this uncertainty is the question of where such aggressive behavior would be directed if it did in fact occur. Would it be directed against Western Europe, especially if NATO had been emasculated by internal dissention, inertia in its force development programs, or a no-first-use nuclear weapons policy? Or might the Soviets decide to employ their expanding abilities to project their force and strike at vital US interests in the Third World? Since few military planners believe that the United States can achieve the global omnipresence and unquestioned economic and military ascendancy enjoyed in the fifties and sixties, the anticipation of the timing and direction of the Soviet threat is a matter of some moment. It will play a large role in determining whether the United States opts for a new maritime/rapid deployment strategy or continues to emphasize the continental strategy upon which we have relied in the postwar period.[4]

It is within this complex web of issues that US and NATO chemical warfare (CW) capabilities and strategies must be evaluated. The chemical warfare issue, important in its own right, takes on broader significance because it affects the overall military doctrine and posture of the United States, our relations with the Soviet Union, the essence of deterrence, and the very fabric of the NATO alliance. Because of the importance of the chemical warfare issue, it is not surprising that discussions of CW have taken on the quality of a religious debate in which convictions rather than evidence often dominate discourse.

The United States currently is considering the future of our chemical warfare arsenal. Proponents of expanded US/NATO chemical capabilities cite the growing imbalance of NATO-Warsaw Pact (WP) military capabilities in general and CW capabilities in particular. Noting that Soviet and Pact CW capabilities are greatly in excess of those needed for defense or retaliation against NATO's allegedly small and rapidly diminishing stocks,[5] they counsel a rapid improvement of our offensive and defensive CW capabilities as a prudent and necessary means of deterring the Soviets from using chemical weapons against us. Should deterrence fail, they argue, NATO should be able to respond in kind to Soviet use of chemical weapons as a deterrent to continued Soviet use and as a means of avoiding the no-win choice between surrender and resort to nuclear weapons.[6]

Numerous military and civilian analysts take quite a different view of the CW issue. In general, these CW opponents make one or more of the following arguments: assessments of the Soviet chemical threat rely on questionable data about Soviet CW offensive capabilities and tenuous interpretations of Soviet intentions; given the alliance's defensive posture, NATO's CW arsenal is large enough to deter the Soviets from resorting to their CW capabilities; CW modernization and expansion will deflect monies and interests away from more urgently needed improvements for our conventional and theater nuclear arsenals; and an American initiative for an enhanced CW capability may push an already fragile NATO beyond its breaking point or sour the Europeans to the extent that other more necessary yet controversial programs, such as the deployment of the long-range theater nuclear forces, are not implemented.[7]

The Reagan Administration has accepted the recommendations of those who advocate an expansion of America's CW capability.

Late in 1981, a divided Congress approved $20 million to install production equipment for the new nerve gas agents at the Pine Bluff, Arkansas arsenal. Current plans to initiate the production of binary weapons and upgrade existing offensive and defensive capabilities will require significant budget increases.[8] These increases have drawn strong criticism from those who question the need for an enhanced CW capability and those who propose, in these days of increasing scrutiny of the defense budget, that defense funds be spent on other weapons and systems.

The battle is joined and the dust has not settled. Let us examine some of the central issues from the points of view of the CW advocates and critics in an attempt to see our way through the haze to a realistic and prudent CW posture.

THE CASE FOR CHEMICAL WEAPONS

> Whether or not gas will be employed in future wars is a matter of conjecture, but the effect is so deadly to the unprepared that we can never afford to neglect the question.
>
> General Pershing
> Annual Report to the Congress, 1919

General Pershing's admonition to Congress in 1919 occurred long before the development of the supertoxic nerve gases such as Tabun, Sarin, Soman, and VX which now constitute the bulk of the superpowers' chemical arsenals. Nevertheless, such a warning is still appropriate today and coincides with the most compelling argument made by contemporary Western advocates for chemical weapons.

In general, analysts advocating chemical weapons rearmament argue that (l) the Soviet/Warsaw Pact CW capability is much larger, more effective, and at a higher state of readiness than its US/NATO counterpart; (2) most of the factors that traditionally have discouraged the use of chemical weapons are absent from Soviet considerations; (3) the potency and flexibility of the Soviet CW arsenal would give decided advantages to the Warsaw Pact in both conventional and tactical nuclear war with NATO; (4) the essentially passive CW defensive posture of NATO is neither sufficient for the protection of our troops, nor does it constitute an adequate deterrent; and (5) the rather modest price tag associated with chemical modernization and enhanced preparedness relative to the improvement in deterrence and the protection they will provide to NATO troops make improved CW capabilities cost-effective and prudent. Let us consider these arguments in turn.

East-West[9] Chemical Warfare Arsenals Compared. Most succinctly stated, the offensive chemical forces of the Soviet Union/Warsaw Pact are reputed by some to exceed those of the United States by *two to three orders of magnitude.*[10] In an overview entered into the *Congressional Record* for September 16, 1980, it was noted that the

> Soviet Union outnumbers the United States 35 to 1 in chemical units, 14 to 1 in production facilities, and outnumbers [the US] also in chemical personnel, decontamination equipment, chemical munitions, and ground-based delivery systems.[11]

There is, however, little agreement within the defense community on the exact size and nature of the Soviet Union's CW arsenal and production.[12] Estimates of the Soviet chemical arsenal range from 20,000 to as much as 700,000 agent tons[13] and that 5 to 30 percent (the latter figure is probably closer to reality) of the massive conventional ammunition stockpile of the Soviet Union consists of chemical munitions.[14] Nevertheless, even the lower range of the estimates of the Soviets' CW arsenal suggests a potent capability.

According to unclassified sources, Soviet chemical troops constitute a separate combat arm of the military forces. The peacetime strength of the CW troops is estimated to be from 50,000 to 100,000 men with a sizable surge reserve available for crises.[15] These troops, classified as "specialists," undergo extensive preparation and training under battlefield conditions with live agents. Chemical units are located throughout the Soviet armed forces to provide CBR (Chemical-Biological-Radiological) defense down to regimental and company levels.[16] These troops operate a host of automatic warning units and decontamination units (vehicles, steam units, boilers), provide reconnaissance operations, and are trained in the treatment of battlefield CW casualties.

John Erickson, an authority on Soviet military affairs, argues that:

> There is abundant and incontrovertible evidence that the Soviet high command has now fully integrated chemical warfare into the structure, training, and equipment of all branches of the Soviet armed forces, including ground, air, and naval elements.[17]

To proponents, this assertion seems valid since: (a) CW is one of the most lethal means of destroying an enemy and a highly effective means of incapacitating him under combat conditions; (b) Soviet artillery units are normally provided CW shells;[18] (c) chemical munitions are considered weapons to be routinely available;[19] (d) Soviet tanks and personnel carriers are equipped with overpressure ventilation systems that would facilitate operations in a chemical environment; (e) chemical munitions would be an important means of neutralizing an enemy's nuclear installations; and (f) Soviet military doctrine insists that only the mass use of any weapon can be decisive.[20] Moreover, the Soviets apparently maintain multiple options for delivering chemical weapons including 122mm, 130mm and 152mm guns, multiple rocket launchers, free rockets (FROG), guided missiles (SCUD), land mines, aircraft fragmentation bombs, aircraft spray tanks, and possibly cruise missiles.[21]

Juxtaposed against this awesome capability are the "very limited chemical warfare capabilities" of the NATO alliance.[22] While the *minimum* estimate of the Soviet chemical arsenal is 20,000 agent tons, the total US retaliatory capability is identified between 30,000 and 40,000 agent tons: 20,000 tons of nerve agents manufactured between 1953 and 1967 and 10,000 to 20,000 tons of mustard agent[23] in munitions or in bulk form.[24]

However, even the 40,000-ton estimate of the US chemical arsenal is misleading for several reasons. In the first place, mustard gas freezes at 57°F which means that much of NATO's retaliatory CW arsenal might present operational problems if war were to break out during late fall or winter.[25] Second, much of our chemical stockpile may not be in projectiles.[26] Therefore, the chemical agents available in bulk form probably would not be ready for use in the event of hostilities. Consequently, the state of the 20,000 tons of nerve agents takes on crucial importance. This brings us to a third problem which detracts from the credibility of the US CW deterrent: approximately 5,000 of the estimated 30-40,000 agent tons have been decommissioned in the demilitarization of obsolete munitions.[27] Finally, it is probable that some quantities of nerve agents in our 15-30-year-old arsenals are no longer reliable, raising the ugly prospect that some NATO crews may be victims of their own chemical munitions.[28] When one considers the collective effects of these problems, it is possible that the entire operational US CW arsenal consists of less than 10,000-12,000 agent tons in increasingly obsolete munitions.[29]

Perhaps even more disturbing is the fact that only a small percent of our total CW arsenal is deployed.[30] The bulk of these munitions would permit only limited NATO CW retaliatory operations,[31] assuming that the stockpiles were not destroyed by Soviet preemptive strikes. To respond in kind to the Soviets' purported ability to conduct month-long CW operations 500km into enemy territory[32] would require the movement of massive quantities of chemical munitions from the United States. This situation would pose numerous problems for American and European military planners. First, CW munitions would be one among many important items that would have to compete for scarce cargo space in a time of crisis. Space taken up by CW munitions would replace other critical war materiel needed in Europe. Second, if hostilities had commenced, it is not certain that CW munitions would get through at all or in time.[33] Finally, major legal and logistical obstacles would have to be overcome to get CW munitions to troops in battle, especially if the battle is fast moving and mobile as anticipated by the AirLand battle concept under consideration by Pentagon planners.[34] In other words, speed and wide dispersion of tactical forces, both operational virtues relied upon by NATO tacticians, pose logistical nightmares for the employment of CW by NATO.

According to proponents, additional problems bedevil US and NATO CW planners. The Western Alliance has neither the numbers of weapons and personnel nor the extensive training of its eastern adversaries.[35] Indicative of the asymmetry that exists across a broad range of capabilities is the West's decontamination capability at the division level which is, *at best,* 25 percent of that of the Soviets. Above the division level, the US decontamination capability is virtually nonexistent.[36]

Another serious problem concerns the readiness of Western forces to operate in a CW environment. Distribution of protective equipment and the training to use it effectively have been spotty, leading General Jones to comment that:

> Current overall protective capability [of US forces] must still be rated as marginal to limited, primarily because of insufficient supplies of protective clothing, protective shelters, decontaminating equipment, and the lack of adequate forward area warning systems.[37]

The disturbing preponderance of the Soviets' CW capability becomes even more ominous in light of General Jones' warning that "their offensive and defensive chemical operations beyond a level required for deterrence leads one to suspect that the Soviets plan to use their CW stocks primarily in an offensive posture."[38]

The Absence of Constraints to Soviet Use of CW. Some analysts concede that the Soviets have a significant CW capability but take strong exception to the view that they will use their chemical weapons in an offensive mode. They cite, for instance, that during World War II, Nazi Germany refrained from using chemical weapons despite its overwhelming qualitative lead over its adversaries in this area.[39] Nazi CW restraint during World War II is particularly important because its overwhelming lead is comparable to that of the Soviet Union today. Also, there are few illusions about the willingness of the Nazi leadership to employ barbarous measures against their fellow man. If the Nazis had the means and were not restrained by moral scruples, why did they not employ their significant CW capability? More importantly, is it possible that the same restraints that prevented the Germans from taking advantage of their unique position also apply to the Soviet Union today? Let us examine the restraints that prevented German use of CW.

In the first place, Adolph Hitler had political and personal motives for not using chemical weapons. As a soldier in 1918, he suffered considerably as a wounded survivor of a British mustard gas attack.

> I, too, was seized with pain which grew worse with every quarter hour and at seven in the morning I stumbled and tottered back with burning eyes . . . . my eyes had turned into glowing coals: it had grown dark around me.[40]

Most likely this experience influenced his judgment in later years. Furthermore, Hitler had to be concerned with domestic and world opinion. His concealment of the nature and extent of the "Final Solution" demonstrated his concessions to both. Hitler, the consummate propagandist, was likely to place considerable stock in the revulsion and propaganda reverses that would accompany the use of chemical agents.

A second restraint upon the Germans, which affected Hitler and certainly became real toward the end of the war as the Luftwaffe lost control of German air space, was the fear of retaliation.

German intelligence had grossly overestimated the Allies' CW capability and the fear which Albert Speer expressed in 1943 summarized German attitudes at the time:

> ... all sensible army people turned gas warfare down as being utterly insane, since, in view of America's superiority in the air, it would not be long before it would bring down the most terrible catastrophe upon German cities.[41]

A third restraint was German unpreparedness, in spite of their possession of nerve agents. The super-efficient lethality of the nerve agents led German political and military planners to anticipate the use of the weapon against population centers and to underestimate its tactical applications.[42] As a result of their countervalue views, the Germans packaged a large proportion of their chemical agents in bombs rather than in the artillery shells or spray tanks which were preferable for tactical deployment.[43] Not only were the Germans unable to employ sizable tactical chemical stocks, they were unable to deliver what munitions they had as the Luftwaffe lost control of the German air space and concentrated on the production of fighters to defend the homeland rather than bombers for offensive operations.

Finally, the German Officer Corps maintained an antipathy toward CW in spite of the fact that it was first to employ it during World War I.

> The German General Staff and the German general officers, with few exceptions, were not interested in chemical warfare. The lack of interest was not based on a lack of faith or on disbelief of its promises of success; the reason was simply that ... chemical warfare was not understood, nor did the majority of German generals try to understand it.[44]

In addition to this antipathy and aversion, German general officers were concerned particularly about "logistical strain," "unpredictability," and "extra coordination between units." In summary, then, it might be said that the Germans lacked the means, the understanding, the appropriate stocks, and the dedication to employ what might have been a most formidable weapon.

Proponents of improving NATO's CW capability, however, see no similar restraints functioning today on Soviet leadership. As noted above, proponents assert that Soviet military forces have sufficient quantity of agents, types of munitions, and trained manpower. The Soviet military has emphasized CW in its writings on military doctrine. More importantly, the limited ability of the West to respond in kind to Soviet CW use (given the inadequacy of NATO's CW stocks and CW training, political dissention on CW, and doctrine which, unlike the Soviets', fails to address comprehensively the integrated use of conventional, chemical, and nuclear munitions) may moderate the Pact's fear of a NATO CW response, while presenting perceived opportunities and advantages which could undermine deterrence.

Incentives for the Soviet Use of CW. Apart from the absence of serious restraints upon Soviet use of CW against Europe, proponents contend that there are numerous incentives for its use. First, chemical weapons are capable of providing great tactical flexibility which would contribute significantly to the achievement of quick success upon the battlefield before the West's economic and technical superiority could be brought into play. Peter Vigor describes the quick success scenario as one of the three "war winning" factors, any one of which, should it become operative, could persuade the normally cautious Soviets to abandon their pessimistic view of confrontation with the West and entice them into launching an attack.[45]

Chemical weapons could afford the Soviet military planner great flexibility in a number of operational scenarios and situations. Certain chemical agents, such as hydrogen cyanide (Agent AC), lend themselves to achieving successful tactical breakthroughs which require speed, surprise, and shock. Agent AC, which attacks oxygen in the blood, is fast acting (it is effective in less than 30 seconds); it is difficult to detect by mechanical means in the early stages (the element of surprise); and it would generate many casualties within a short period of time (the element of shock). Furthermore, it dissipates in 7 to 10 minutes after the attack. Advancing troops could launch their attack against adversaries unable to respond in kind and unsure of when the next CW round would be fired. Therefore, the defenders (unlike the attackers) would be required to don cumbersome protective suits.[46]

Area denial is another quick success scenario that would invite the use of chemical agents. Highly persistent blister agents, such as mustard, cause casualties when the vapors are inhaled or when the liquid comes in contact with the skin.[47] Its oily consistency allows it to cling to protective clothing and equipment, thereby making imperative time-consuming decontamination of men and machines passing through the area. Area denial may range from several days to several weeks depending upon weather conditions, the type of agent(s) employed, and the concentration of the attack.[48] Successful area denial would reduce the mobility of the enemy and channel its movement through areas well-prepared by the Soviets as killing zones. Such Warsaw Pact capabilities would hinder NATO's ability to resupply troops in the field and to reinforce besieged positions, thereby undermining the integrity of NATO's forward defense strategy.

Other agents such as thickened Soman (GD) which combine high toxicity, persistence, rapid effectiveness, and incapacitation would be well-suited for the interdiction of Western air and command, control, and communication (C^3) facilities.[49] In short, the contribution of chemical munitions to surprise, shock, and speed in these as well as other scenarios makes them very expedient weapons.

A second incentive that would encourage the Soviets to use CW is their specificity. Chemical munitions only attack living organisms. Therefore, collateral damage to equipment and installations is negligible. If the Soviets were to attack Western Europe, undoubtedly they would wish to preserve as much of its existing infrastructure as possible for postwar reconstruction. Chemical weapons would serve this end.

A third set of incentives focuses on the ability of chemical munitions to reduce the efficiency of enemy forces. Operation in a CW environment requires respirators and heavy protective equipment. Even troops fortunate enough to don their protective equipment in time (disregarding problems arising from defective equipment and inadequate training) face numerous physical and psychological problems that degrade their efficiency by as much as 50 percent.[50] For instance, the protective gloves issued to US forces result in a loss of tactile sense and suffer a loss of protective capability when they come in contact with petroleum products such as diesel fuel. Any loss of manual dexterity would severely degrade the efficiency of those assigned C^3, maintenance, refueling, targeting, and similar operations. Furthermore, Soviet employment of chemical agents would necessitate the reassignment of significant numbers of Western personnel to purely defensive tasks such as chemical reconnaissance, decontamination, and casualty handling. Western training and capabilities for such operations are marginal. This is especially true for civilians responsible for logistic support in the rear areas.

A final incentive that would encourage the Soviets to use their CW capability in a conflict with NATO would be the stakes at hand. If war between East and West were to break out, the Soviets would be fighting for the survival of socialism, as well as the survival of their political system and empire.[51] The outcome of such a conflict would be all important and one can only expect that the Soviets would pursue victory with every means at their disposal. Not to use their chemical munitions would be to forfeit a substantial advantage. It is unlikely that the Soviets would exhibit much restraint in such a cataclysmic conflict. The following statement by Marshal V. D. Sokolovsky, one of the Soviet's most influential military strategists, supports this contention.

> A war must be conducted decisively, using the necessary forces and means to achieve political and military goals. The need for success is incompatible with the requirements for limiting the scale of combat operations.[52]

Additional support for this Soviet view is provided by V. Ye Savkin:

> The degree of influence of new means of warfare on methods of conducting combat operations is directly related to the number and quality of those means. New forms of weapons and military technology employed in small numbers cannot have a substantial influence on the character of combat operations.[53]

In sum, it can be said that Soviet use of chemical weapons would degrade the West's combat capability seriously, and further contribute to the already adverse balance of conventional power in Europe. The benefits that might accrue to the Soviets from their use of CW without the threat of a NATO significant retaliation in kind has prompted many Western planners to prescribe the rapid revitalization of NATO's chemical arsenal in addition to a commitment to "accelerate antichemical warfare measures."[54]

Deterrence and the Shortcomings of a Passive Defense. The advocates of CW rearmament point out that NATO's capability to wage CW is so miniscule relative to the CW capability of the Warsaw Pact that the Western Alliance would be left without an adequate response to Pact employment of this effective weapon short of a nuclear response. Is the threat of such a response credible to the Soviets and their allies?

The credibility of a NATO nuclear response to a successful Soviet attack with chemical weapons is predicated upon numerous complex and uncertain considerations. It will depend upon the allies having the political will and the technical abilities to deliver nuclear weapons. Furthermore, there must be consistency between the severity of the threat and the response evoked for the latter to be viewed as credible.

According to proponents, a persuasive case can be made that these considerations diminish the credibility of the US/NATO protective nuclear umbrella. In the first place, some evidence supports the contention that the United States—as well as its NATO allies—lack the will to employ such weapons. In the late 1950's, Charles de Gaulle maintained that the United States would not risk the existence of New York or Washington to save Paris or Bonn from a Soviet onslaught. More recently, former Secretary of State Henry Kissinger stunned NATO members when he noted:

> it is absurd to base the strategy of the West on the threat of mutual suicide. [NATO should not rely too strongly on] strategic assurances that [America] cannot possibly mean, or if we do mean, we shouldn't want to execute, because if we do execute then we risk the destruction of our civilization.[55]

Comments such as these—as well as the increasing frequency of calls by influential Americans to (a) adopt a no-first-use policy governing NATO nuclear weapons,[56] (b) withdraw some US troops from Europe,[57] (c) adopt a maritime strategy,[58] and (d) rely increasingly on a light and highly mobile rapid deployment force—do little to reassure the European allies that the United States views its national security as coincident with that of Western Europe.[59]

Undoubtedly, the Europeans believed that the Soviet Union was deterred from attacking conventionally when the US theater nuclear arsenal was superior. However, the credibility that NATO's theater nuclear arsenal would be employed against a Soviet conventional attack is mitigated by a number of factors: the achievement, according to numerous Reagan Administration analysts, of Soviet theater nuclear superiority;[60] the expectation that the Soviets, who ridicule as unrealistic Western limited warfighting scenarios, would respond massively against Europe and the United States to any first use of nuclear weapons;[61] and the

West Europeans' well-publicized hesitancy to bet their survival upon the deployment of additional nuclear weapons whose deployment many view as counterproductive to peace and stability.

Even if one assumes away the substantial technological and political[62] obstacles standing in the way of efficacious employment of theater weapons, the credibility of the threat to use these weapons is rendered uncertain by possible problematic relationships between the Soviet threat and the NATO nuclear response. In light of the massive and incomprehensible destruction that would be visited upon both sides in a conflict which escalated to nuclear conflagration, are the Soviets likely to find credible the threat of a NATO nuclear response as an automatic consequence of their tactical use of *limited* quantities of mustard or nerve gas? A NATO nuclear response, totally out of proportion to the severity of the threat, may be characterized as *mismatched deterrence*. In his widely acclaimed *Strategy of Conflict,* Schelling illustrated such a condition:

> Automatic destruction for small misdemeanors, like expensive incarceration for overtime parking, would be superfluous but not exorbitant *unless the threatened person considered it too awful to be real and ignored it.* (Emphasis added)[63]

Clearly, the credibility of NATO's theater deterrent would be strained severely under certain limited CW scenarios, especially in light of the Soviet Union's impressive and growing nuclear capabilities. The proponents of CW modernization argue that NATO must be able to respond swiftly and decisively to a Soviet CW attack *in kind* since the threat of an escalation to nuclear war is not credible. Hence, they argue, NATO's current posture is insufficient and, ultimately, dangerously destabilizing.

The Costs of CW Modernization. Relative to certain conventional and strategic programs with price tags running into the scores of billions of dollars, the proponents of CW modernization and expansion note that the costs involved are quite modest. The production of chemical agents offers few technical or financial obstacles to a country with the political will and even meager funds. The production of phosgene, mustard, and hydrogen cyanide is easily within the capability of most underdeveloped countries, hence the reference to chemical weapons as the "poor man's atom bomb." After World War II, the Soviets took advantage of captured German scientists, the low production expenses, and the potential lethality of nerve agents to produce a sizable chemical stockpile to provide a counterbalance to the US atomic monopoly.

Even the production of the more sophisticated nerve agents holds few technical obstacles inasmuch as their chemical properties are extensively described in the open literature.[64] A 1974 development and production estimate for 155mm and 8-inch binary projectiles (with these binary weapons as the most expensive of all chemical systems) was $191 million: $23 million for R&D, $10 million for the production base, $117 million for 155mm procurement, and $40 million for 8-inch procurement.[65] Adjusting these figures for inflation still does not put CW production beyond the means of the scores of countries with defense budgets running into the billions of dollars.[66] Chemical rearmament advocates note that, given the flexibility and lethality of chemical weapons, an investment of $7-14 billion during this decade is prudent and wise. Funds spent for an offensive capability will provide credibility to NATO's deterrent posture, and monies spent for defensive capabilities will increase the likelihood of survival for US and West European forces should war occur.

Furthermore, the demonstration of American resolve by opting for chemical rearmament might benefit chemical arms control negotiations with the Soviets which have been pursued vigorously since 1977, but with disappointingly little success. Apart from problems of verification which have hindered arms control success, it has been argued that the Soviets have no incentive to negotiate away their potent arsenal in the absence of an equal American capability. Just as the Soviets have argued that the United States did not become seriously interested in strategic arms control until the Soviet Union attained strategic parity, it can be argued now that the West cannot hope seriously to interest the Soviets in chemical weapons arms control until we improve our CW arsenal. If, by taking steps now to reduce the asymmetry between the Soviet and US chemical forces, we increase the chance for arms control in the future, then our policies are wise indeed.[68]

The actual and projected US expenditures for chemical weapons and programs which appear below demonstrate the Reagan Administration's resolve to strengthen the country's CW capabilities.[69]

Year	Expenditure (in $ Millions)	Percent Increase
1978	111	
1979	123	9.8
1980	157	21.7
1981	262	40.0
1982	455	42.4
1983	810	43.8
1984	1400	42.1

The United States has committed or is planning to commit these funds to a number of ambitious projects over the next 5 years. These projects include:[70]

• Plans to produce two chemical binary weapons: the 155mm GB projectile and the BIGEYE VX bomb. "Consideration of other systems, to include more effective agents and longer range delivery systems, are currently under review."

• The reestablishment of the Army Chemical School at Fort McClellan, Alabama. This school will provide training, including detoxification training with live agents.

• The activation of a Nuclear, Biological, Chemical (NBC) Company in each division, separate brigade, and corps, in addition to placing an NBC qualified noncommissioned officer in every company and a lieutenant and noncommissioned officer in every combat arms battalion.

• In the Army, the 7,400 chemical personnel will increase to 11,200 by the end of FY 87 with a target strength of over 21,000.

• The Marine Corps is creating NBC defense units at Marine Division, Marine Aircraft Wing, and Force Service Support Group levels.

• NBC warrant officers will be assigned throughout the Marine Corps structure down to the regimental level.

• The Air Force will increase its force structure by placing 800 chemical defense specialists at bases in the high threat areas in FY 83 and FY 84. A total of 707 additional life support technicians will be placed to maintain aircrew protective equipment.

• Over 630,000 unserviceable, unrepairable munitions have been identified for immediate demilitarization. An R&D program ($13 million) is planned for FY 83 to continue development of safe, efficient, and cost-effective technology to replace the current energy intensive and costly methods of disposal.

As might be expected, the breadth and scope of such ambitious CW plans have generated significant criticism from numerous military and civilian national security analysts. Their arguments touch on elements as diverse as Soviet intentions, the reliability and validity of national intelligence estimates, the nature of deterrence, ethics, and intra-alliance politics. Proponents, however, absolutely are convinced that modernization and increased US offensive capability is necessary.

THE CASE AGAINST CHEMICAL WEAPONS.

One suspects that the opponents of an ambitious US chemical weapons modernization program are motivated by a profound moral aversion to an inhumane instrument designed to destroy human life. Producing and contemplating the use of poison gas clashes with convictions that the United States has a noble purpose that would be tainted and somehow diminished by association with so odious a means of killing. However, it has been argued by some that killing with chemical munitions is not any worse than killing with nuclear weapons. Yet, NATO is willing to deploy the latter, but not the former. Therefore, there must be a difference between the two which does not rely solely upon moral arguments. This difference, and the heart of the case against chemical weapons, focuses on six policy considerations: (1) a lack of unambiguous evidence regarding the quantities of chemical agents the Soviets produce, where they store them, and where they are deployed; we cannot be sure whether the primary Soviet CW effort is offensive or defensive; (2) while the politically significant aversion to CW in Western democracies, often underestimated by Western CW proponents, has no visible counterpart in the Soviet Union, practical inhibitions to Soviet CW use against NATO do exist; (3) the West has enough chemical munitions, and NATO defensive measures—combined with maintaining existing stocks and non-CW military capabilities—are sufficient to deter Soviet CW use; (4) even if used first by the WP, a large-scale NATO response in kind would have only marginal military effects; (5) assets planned for the binary weapons program would be better invested in other Western military systems; and (6) political costs outweigh the military advantages of a vigorous US chemical weapons modernization effort.

Interpretation of the Threat: The Hard Evidence. CW advocates typically cast the Soviet CW threat in words like these:

> The USSR represents the most serious threat to the United States and its allies. The Soviets' massive CW defensive preparation, extensive training and awesome offensive delivery capability leave little doubt as to their capability to conduct CW operations. The WP forces are better equipped, structured, and trained than any other in the world for fighting in a chemical environment. Moreover, their capabilities continue to improve and the CW disparity between the WP and NATO countries continues to increase. It is apparent that the Soviets are prepared for the possibility that chemicals would be used in a European conflict.[71]

According to CW opponents, to make an offensive threat of this carefully worded statement requires the linking of extensive Soviet CW defensive preparations, which can be proved, to the "awesome offensive delivery capability," which raises more questions than it answers.

Certainly, opponents argue, both the United States and the USSR are *capable* of delivering conventional, chemical, and nuclear weapons anywhere in the world. The Soviets could point to US artillery, missiles, and aircraft and rightfully assert that we are *capable* of using them to deliver lethal chemical agents. Further, reference to continuing Soviet CW improvements can be applied across-the-board to Soviet efforts to catch and pass the United States in virtually all military areas.[72] Our renewed interest in CW, it is argued, whether measured in defensive terms, official Army Field Manuals (such as FM 3-10) which instruct on target selection and attack procedures (with tables to determine the number of chemical weapons that need to be fired into a target area to obtain the desired level and types of casualties), or by plans to build the Pine Bluff binary production facility, allows the Soviets to see us as we see them. In the statement cited above: we are improving our offensive and defensive CW capabilities, and we have a limited but deployed delivery capability. Hence, in all likelihood, the Soviets see us as a threat. This is hardly surprising, considering the profound suspicion each of the superpowers exhibits toward the other. Consequently, Soviet and American strategic planners view each other's moves with the presumption of hostile and sinister intent, despite the claims of each that CW preparation is designed for deterrence, defense, and retaliation to the other side's first use.

Worst case planning results, with each side subscribing to what it sees as the exigencies of prudence. In such situations, planners may overestimate their adversary's capabilities and underestimate their own. Speculation and circumstantial evidence are viewed too often as hard intelligence. Those who question the validity and reliability of the data on Soviet capability are seen as naive and, therefore, to be heeded only at the risk of national unpreparedness. They are told that there can be no compromise with the devil whose language is duplicity and currency is force.[73]

However, according to opponents, the theoretical capability to do something does not necessarily indicate a willingness to do it. This raises the issue of intent, consideration of which leads to assumptions regarding Soviet willingness to engage in first use of CW in violation of treaties to which the USSR is signatory.[74] Opponents of the binary modernization program seek evidence of Soviet capability and indicators that the Soviet Union is willing to take the risks inherent in using CW against a superpower.

Substantial evidence suggests that the Soviet Union is concerned deeply with defending its soldiers against the effects of chemical warfare. Opponents concede that the Soviets have protective masks and suits, many of their fighting vehicles are secure from the effects of chemical agents, and they have gone to great effort and expense to field decontamination equipment. We also know that Soviet troops are trained to operate on a CW battlefield and that chemical units are found at every level of the Soviet armed forces.[75] Thus, according to opponents, the issue is not Soviet concern for CW, but rather whether their concern is for defense or offense. That isn't easy to sort out.

Soviet doctrine is not particularly helpful in this connection. While one can interpret Soviet doctrine as being compatible with the offensive use of CW,[76] no clear statement of Soviet intent to use CW in a "conventional" attack can be found. A case could be made by selectively citing Soviet literature to show that CW fits nicely into Soviet offensive doctrine. But the case remains circumstantial and speculative in the absence of evidence, giving rise to numerous and often contradictory interpretations. Thus, opponents of increased NATO CW capabilities contend that Soviet defensive preparations may be just that: defensive. They believe that this view is quite plausible since, in World War I, the Russian armies suffered more than 60 percent of the total fatalities and 35 percent of the casualties produced by CW.[77]

World War I Chemical Warfare Casualties/Fatalities

Country	Fatalities (000)	Casualties (000)
United States	1.5	73
Russia	56	475
Italy	4.6	60
Austria-Hungary	3	100
Britain	8.1	189
France	8	190
Germany	9	200
TOTAL	90.2	1,284

To allay Soviet concerns, opponents contend, it is not enough for us to say that the President—or even a treaty—rejects first use of chemical agents by the United States.[78] The Soviets are no more inclined to trust us than we are to trust them. Thus, General Pershing's admonition, cited earlier, remains valid today: prudent planners in all armies—including the United States and Soviet armies—are well-advised to protect their soldiers against the possible use of lethal chemical agents.

Opponents contend that the United States has made great efforts to connect alleged use of lethal BW or CW agents in Afghanistan, Laos, and Kampuchea to the USSR, but thus far much of the world remains unconvinced. However, they note that attempts to find the smoking gun in the hand of the Soviet Union have not been crowned with success despite a mass of circumstantial evidence suggesting that someone has been using CW in these Third World countries.[79] Reports of CW use are frequent, and a sample from Southeast Asia has been produced. The reaction around the world has been decidedly unenthusiastic, although fewer remain unconvinced. One suspects that the world chooses to view charges and countercharges by the superpowers as manifestations of their competition, a propaganda war in which each attempts to demonize the other. There seems to be just enough evidence to allow proponents and debunkers to maintain their positions. The US Government tacitly admitted as much when it circulated a thick compilation of news stories and reports in the UN suggesting Soviet CW use in Afghanistan, Laos, and Kampuchea.[80] The following disclaimer appears on page 2 of the document:

> This document responds to requests made by other governments, international organizations and individuals for a collection of reports of the use of chemical weapons in Afghanistan, Laos, and Kampuchea which have come to the attention of the US Department of State. This information is from multiple sources and therefore reflects varying degrees of knowledge of the events. This document also contains denials that these weapons have been used. Much of the text is based upon verbatim testimony. The reports for each country are in chronological order—from earliest to most recent.

The cover sheet carried only the title and no date appeared. The document was provided to UN delegations before debate on alleged CW use, but it was not formally entered as evidence. This is not the way a government normally presents its brief to an international forum when hard evidence is available. The document insinuates and alleges, but it does not prove. Presumably the US Government recognized that the document was less than conclusive proof and behaved as it did to raise the issue without investing prestige in a weak case. Reasonable doubt seems to characterize the attitudes of the nations of the world as they observe what probably appears to many to be yet still another propaganda battle between the Soviet Union and the United States. We seem to expect that benefit of the doubt should work to our advantage, but the moral ascendency the United States once enjoyed no longer can be assumed. Increasingly, the world views both the United States and the USSR as powerful and potentially dangerous troublemakers lacking restraint. The November 1981 "Report of the Group of Experts to Investigate Reports on the Alleged Use of Chemical Weapons," directed by the UN General Assembly, was inconclusive. The group of experts "found itself unable to reach a final conclusion as to whether or not chemical warfare agents had been used"[81] because their access to the region was constrained.

Thus, opponents contend US efforts based on circumstantial evidence may be counterproductive. They note that the Soviets are quite capable of turning US allegations to Soviet advantage by charging the United States with waging a campaign to smear the USSR in order to cover the US decision to go ahead with a large CW effort. One needn't be an inspired propagandist to point out that, while US charges of Soviet CW use in Afghanistan and Southeast Asia are unproved, US efforts to fund a CW production facility in Pine Bluff are real.

Aside from the propaganda aspect of alleged Soviet CW use in the Third World, important as that may be, opponents contend that the question of what even proven use there would mean to war in Europe remains. It is one thing to use CW against poorly armed tribesmen in remote areas and another to use CW against foes equipped with a chemical retaliatory capability and nuclear weapons. Mussolini used CW in Ethiopia, but not against the British and Americans who assaulted his homeland. The Japanese made limited use of CW against the Chinese, but not against the Americans, even when the Japanese faced imminent defeat in 1945. The fact is that, since World War I, CW use has been restricted to use against victims who not only lacked the capability to respond in kind but against those incapable of effectively responding in any significant manner. Such is not the case as the Soviets contemplate CW use against the United States and NATO. It is not clear that in kind retaliation is the only or the best deterrent of a foe capable of using chemical weapons.

In the years after World War II when the United States enjoyed first a nuclear monopoly and later unquestioned nuclear superiority, the Soviets may well have emphasized CW as the poor man's weapon of mass destruction. The Soviets are notoriously loathe to discard old weapons systems.[82] It may be that their CW stocks consist largely of munitions similar to those US stocks that proponents of CW modernization consider old and deteriorating. Since such matters are closely guarded secrets, it is exceedingly difficult to collect hard intelligence, but to convince opponents of CW modernization and to mobilize allies, proponents of CW modernization must:

- Produce evidence that the Soviets stock chemical munitions. It is certainly difficult to do so, but plausible information regarding amounts and locations of Soviet CW stocks would help the proponents' case.
- Produce more than circumstantial evidence that Soviet doctrine includes plans to incorporate CW routinely.
- Produce more than general statements of Soviet capability and still photographs of Soviet soldiers in protective suits if allegations of Soviet offensive first use of CW are to be credible.

Raising the question of evidence irritates the proponents of CW. They complain that the evidence demanded of them regarding Soviet production and storage of chemical agents isn't demanded of those who assert that the Soviets have menacing capabilities in their conventional and nuclear forces. While it is true that unambiguous evidence of Soviet CW production, storage, and deployment has not been produced, Western intelligence agencies have been far more successful in accounting for Soviet tanks, artillery, manpower, and nuclear weapons. CW advocates are frustrated by the fact that it is almost impossible to determine the amount of chemical agents the Soviets produce and the locations of their stockpiles. Clearly these are well-guarded secrets. National technical means of detection cannot produce answers.[83] At best, they produce data that fit into a larger mosaic which requires interpretation. Skeptics of the alleged Soviet superiority in CW are all too well aware that the fictitious bomber, missile, and ABM gaps that frightened American security analysts periodically since World War II were the results of circumstantial evidence filtered through the prism of worst case analysis.

In sum, opponents of CW argue that the Soviet CW threat is exaggerated, in part to justify US modernization plans, and continue to press for evidence that as of yet is apparently unavailable. They maintain that attempts by the US Government to lay charges of CW use in Afghanistan, Laos, and Kampuchea at Moscow's feet haven't gotten the reaction hoped for either at home or abroad and are irrelevant to the CW debate in Europe.

Constraints. Quite aside from producing evidence proving the precise nature of the Soviet CW threat, opponents argue that tactical, technical, and strategic constraints deserve the attention of those who advocate US CW initiatives. The general repugnance of chemical agents pushed the CW issue to philosophical discourse and political debate. Without denigrating the ethical and moral aversion to CW—inherently important and policy relevant in the popular democracies of NATO—and without underestimating the resistance and fears of ordinary Americans and Europeans to the very idea of using chemical weapons, opponents contend that the constraints often are overlooked in what is clearly an emotionally charged subject.

Meteorological conditions, civilian population density and human fallibility play a much greater role in the effective use of chemical agents than they do in the use of most conventional weapons. Gordon Burck notes that the effects of chemical weapons depend on wind speed and direction, atmospheric stability, humidity, temperature gradients, sunlight, and the type of terrain. If there is little vertical air movement, the lethal cloud from an intense attack could drift as much as 60 miles, affecting friendly as well as hostile troops.[84]

Opponents note that the accident in the vicinity of Dugway Proving Ground in March 1968 illustrates the possibility of a human catastrophe when invisible gas is used even under carefully controlled conditions by experts. Some 6,400 sheep died in a 200-square mile area at an average distance of 27-30 miles from the intended target during a test. Whatever the exact cause, equipment failure or human error, the accident has a chilling effect as one considers what might have happened had the incident occurred in densely populated Europe instead of in sparsely populated Utah. One observer noted: "... two hundred square miles of West Germany may be expected to contain *about 128,395* citizens . . . ."[85] Even if lethal agents are transported and stored in relatively safe binary munitions, their use as a weapon after they have been combined into a lethal agent cannot rule out human error or equipment failure. Since the United States hasn't used CW in anger since 1918, no claim to great experience in their employment can be made. One needn't be a pacifist to express grave concern for the safety of civilians and troops who might be victims of their own side's use of CW. East and West Europeans who live where the NATO-WP battles are likely to be fought can be expected to be more dubious than the superpowers about chemical storage in peacetime and use in war.

Opponents argue that uncertainties and constraints abound on both sides. Among the inhibitions to Soviet enthusiasm for CW are: the deficiency of particularly cumbersome Soviet protective suits which quickly exhaust soldiers wearing them;[86] fear in Eastern Europe and in the Soviet Union that Soviet CW use might result in terrible retribution by NATO, whatever form such retribution might take; increased Soviet dependence upon Central Asian Muslims and Transcaucasian infantrymen, many of whom do not speak Russian well, are poorly trained to operate efficiently in a CW environment, and generally are regarded as less than enthusiastic Soviet soldiers;[87] and the terrible losses in both World War I and II inflicted upon Russians by Western armies, largely the consequence of historic Western technological superiority.[88] These considerations suggest that the Soviets may not be eager to promote CW, and their concerns may be more defensive than offensive.

The West, opponents contend, suffers from many similar constraints. Moreover, they argue the political relevance of moral and emotional aversion among Europeans and Americans, concern for accelerating a CW arms race, further damage to US claims of moral ascendency *vis-a-vis* the Soviet Union, additional strains to the NATO Alliance which is already burdened with internal disputes, and various logistic problems associated with CW combine to suggest that it might be unwise to venture beyond the CW capabilities we already possess. Most opponents of increases in NATO offensive capability, however, recognize that these restraints do not suggest any less need for prudent defensive measures.

Both sides would find CW proliferation dangerous, and both must consider the probability that use of CW would take a higher toll among unprotected civilians than among trained and protected soldiers. Neither side welcomes the logistical burden, the security precautions required, or the risk that terrorists and third countries could complicate superpower calculations by emulating the superpower CW efforts.[89]

Deterrence. Any Soviet consideration of the exclusive use of chemical agents against NATO must take nuclear response, current US chemical capabilities, and some very deadly conventional weapons into account. While it is true that nuclear response by NATO to Soviet CW use would cause much soul-searching in Western capitals, there is no way for the Soviets to know what the outcome would be. Chemical warfare opponents contend that it would be out of character for the normally cautious Soviets to initiate CW use in the hope that NATO's response would not be nuclear. Prudent Soviet planners are not likely to take that chance. The momentous decision to risk Armageddon would probably dictate initial use of all the means at the Soviets' disposal—conventional, chemical, and nuclear—to take maximum advantage of shock and bring the war to its most rapid conclusion. In such a case, a Western CW response would be of marginal value, if not irrelevant, whether based upon current capabilities or on a modern binary system.

Keeping the possibility of cataclysmic nuclear war uppermost in the minds of Soviet planners is the strategic preference in Europe, as well as among those in the United States who oppose further expansion of US/NATO CW capabilities, since it links US nuclear retaliation to possible defeat of NATO's conventional forces, irrespective of how that defeat may occur. That is, the Soviet planner must take very seriously the need to smash US troops in any Soviet offensive in Western Europe. US troop presence makes that necessary, and it is for Soviet leadership to contemplate the possible consequences of a major blow to the US forces in Europe. The fundamental element of deterrence in Europe is the link between what the Soviets might be able to do—charge to the Channel—and the consequent question posed: what then? The starkness of the proposition is what appeals to European strategists, because the Soviets cannot be certain of the US response. According to opponents, the introduction of what generally is seen as an intermediate level of war (chemical warfare is generally regarded as more than conventional and less than nuclear) undermines this application of the theory of deterrence because it lengthens and makes less automatic the leap from conventional to nuclear war and, therefore, contemplates superpower war limited to European soil. In other words, it suggests to all Europeans that war might be limited to that theater. Furthermore, it suggests to West Europeans that the US nuclear umbrella might be uncoupled from the defense of NATO, amounting to a radical revision of the alliance's strategy. Through the eyes of the Europeans, this weakens the alliance, undermines deterrence, and ultimately endangers their very existence.

Often overlooked, opponents further argue, in the doomsaying that makes a Soviet charge to the English Channel a simple technical task[90] is how that act would affect Soviet security as it is seen from Moscow. To get to the Channel, the Red Army would need to defeat hundreds of thousands of American citizens and soldiers who would be killed, wounded, interned, or simply stranded in Europe. Under such dangerous and unpredictable circumstances, could the normally conservative Soviet decisionmakers be certain that the Soviet Union would be more secure on the Channel than at the Elbe? Even if the Soviets were to control West European territory, they would confront a number of serious problems. The English and French SLBM forces, invulnerable to the Soviets' antisubmarine warfare capability, would be capable of dreadful retaliation even if the United States and the People's Republic of China were not to become involved. However, the USSR could hardly count upon such a passive response from its eastern neighbor or its principal adversary. Even rapid Soviet "success" in Western Europe would leave both the

PRC and the US homelands unscathed, hostile, and capable of terrible counterblows. Further, it is one thing to conquer and another to control, as recent events in Poland and Afghanistan demonstrate. Control of all of Europe and exploitation to Soviet advantage are no simple tasks. Finally, opponents of increased NATO CW capabilities argue that potentially lethal risk-taking by the Soviets makes little sense when patient and consistent political pressure, applied in the context of US-West European differences on numerous issues such as the pipeline and INF deployment, seems safer and equally effective. It makes little sense for the Soviets to climb out on slender branches when it may be merely a matter of time for the breezes of Western dissention to shake the fruit from the tree. In brief, the usefulness of war itself is questionable as a means of pursuing a particular policy. The role of Soviet military power is to deter the West from attempting to reverse by force what they see as the inevitable flow of history.[91] It makes no sense to risk the gains of two-thirds of a century on a single cosmic roll of the dice, especially if the dice were loaded with a CW capability which might well kill more European civilians than NATO soldiers.

Thus, opponents argue, Soviet use of CW in a nonnuclear war is theoretically possible, but unlikely, because it would reserve for the West the all-important decision of choosing the time and place for the first use of nuclear weapons. In the event of a Soviet nibble or testing of the water in, for example, Berlin or Spitzbergen, the use of CW by the Soviets would seem to be provocative out of all proportion to the test—the purpose of which, presumably, would be to demonstrate a lack of coherent and determined NATO response. Should NATO's response be firm and decisive, the Soviets—one must suppose—would like to allow a means to back off, an option possibly precluded by the use of CW. It might appear that Soviet use of CW means that they have accepted the risk of a NATO nuclear response. If the Soviet CW attack is limited, we have enough for a limited CW response. Massive Soviet use of CW clearly risks a NATO nuclear response, especially if Soviet planners believe that NATO lacks a massive CW retaliatory capability. It is difficult to imagine the combination of circumstances that would justify such high risk-taking by the Soviets. In brief, according to opponents, NATO's nuclear power deters massive Soviet CW use, and NATO's CW capability is sufficient to answer limited Soviet CW probes.[92] In unlimited war in Europe, NATO's CW capability quickly becomes irrelevant.[93]

Some Military Problems of CW. The military advantages to the West of a modern CW retaliatory capability are not the only issues affecting modernization plans. Western possession of numerous chemical weapons might deter the Pact from resorting to CW by threatening retaliation in kind. Furthermore, NATO use of chemical munitions would certainly threaten to degrade Pact operation performance by obliging its soldiers to fight in cumbersome protective suits. Finally, the production of a massive chemical arsenal by the West would demonstrate resolve in peace and determination if used in war.

In spite of the plausibility of these contentions, numerous military arguments against increased Western reliance upon chemical munitions hinge upon the fact that most Army officers are unenthusiastic about CW. Major General Frederic J. Brown, Deputy Chief of Staff for Training, US Army Training and Doctrine Command, in *Chemical Warfare, A Study in Restraints,* makes a telling point when he says that CW was never assimilated by the US Army.[94] Soldiers understandably feel more comfortable with familiar weapons and tried concepts than with the new, especially when the consequences could be both unpredictable and catastrophic. This uncertainty is not difficult to understand. Artillery officers would prefer to carry basic loads of munitions which *would* be used in combat rather than munitions that *might* be used. Quartermaster, Ordnance, and Transportation Corps officers would not welcome the transportation, storage, and security problems associated with lethal gas, even in a binary form. Aviators are not enthusiastic about delivering poison gas, particularly the delivery of invisible and odorless substances by spray tank. Logisticians are concerned that the sheer bulk of chemical munitions might reduce their capability to insure the continuous flow of nonchemical weapons and equipment from North America to Europe in time of need.[95] Planners, on the purely technical level, must ask how proficient staff officers are to plan, target, and conduct CW operations, a somewhat arcane and neglected art in which error could be serious indeed. In brief, a renaissance of interest in CW in the US forces would constitute far more than the introduction of a new weapons system. It may not be an exaggeration to call it a revolution affecting everyone in uniform, from the Army's Chief of Staff to the private in the foxhole. This explains why it has been so long since the US Army has given anything more than lip service to CW.

A second major problem confronting CW advocates concerns stationing. If Europe won't store additional stocks of chemical munitions, and that is probable as we shall see below, chemical stocks would presumably be maintained in the United States for deployment in time of tension or war. There is no way to forecast whether shipment of chemical weapons to Europe in time of crisis will heighten or reduce the crisis. Furthermore, no one has indicated what might be displaced by chemical agents, as both sea and airlift, already strained to the breaking point, would require the specification of clear priorities among troops, weapons, munitions, fuel, equipment, and chemical agents. Getting large quantities of CW to possible users in time of war will be very difficult, even if all but one cannister per munition is deployed at the outbreak of hostilities. Matthew Meselson, the Harvard biochemist who has been following the chemical warfare issue for 20 years, "calculates that to bring 5,000 tons would require the full-time services of 2,000 C141-B transport planes (of which the United States has 234) and 3,000 semitrailer trucks for 12 days."[96]

Given present moods in Europe, getting Europeans to station larger CW stockpiles in Europe in peacetime is unlikely. Senator Gary Hart (D-Colorado) cautions that asking NATO allies to accept deployment of binary weapons, in addition to the weapons already on hand, "would only create an intense and divisive debate on the issue and endanger the deployment in Europe of our existing stocks."[97] The obvious question becomes: if we can't store chemical munitions where we want them in peace and can't transport them there in war, why produce them? It has been suggested that the binary weapons might be more acceptable to the Germans and other Europeans because they are safer to handle than older unitary CW stocks, but it is uncertain to CW opponents that these arguments will be decisive. While some German officers on the NATO military staff may agree with the assessments concerning the safety and potential use of chemical weapons, members of the Social Democratic Party—the party of former Chancellor Helmut Schmidt—have insisted that the party press for the removal of existing CW stocks currently stored in the Federal Republic.[98] It is unclear whether this initiative is another manifestation of the antinuclear mood in the FRG or a direct reaction to announced US plans to build a plant for the production of binary chemical weapons. It is doubtful that any FRG government would welcome a US push for additional chemical weapons while it is still trying to muster support in Europe for the deployment of the Pershing II and cruise missiles.

Despite the laudatory claims made by the proponents of binary weapons, opponents cite an additional reason to approach them cautiously. The military effectiveness of the binary weapons has been challenged because they haven't been field-tested. Major General Niles J. Fulwyler, Director of the Nuclear and Chemical Directorate, Department of the Army, said in an interview with *The New York Times*: ". . . we do not need live testing because we can do all the necessary testing in a laboratory environment with modern technology."[99] On the other hand, Saul Horvats, a former executive in the development laboratories at Edgewood Arsenal, who was in charge of developing, testing, and producing the weapons now stocked, is less optimistic. He anticipates a failure rate of 20-30 percent in artillery rounds and 50 percent in the BIGEYE bombs if only simulant and computer tests are performed. Furthermore, due to the vagaries of the mixing process, binary rounds may not be as efficient as unitary loads. In contrast, he says that less than 1 percent of existing weapons, which wouldn't experience mixing problems, would fail.[100] Senator Hart and Professor Meselson also lament the lack of field-testing.[101] The General was probably taking political realities into account and making virtue of necessity. Since we can't field-test, we'll have to accept laboratory testing.

Irrespective of the hypothesized superiority of binary munitions, the choice of weapons to deliver them provides little or no military advantage. The first production priority at Pine Bluffs is chemical agent fill for 155mm artillery rounds.[102] The characteristics of the gun mean that the binary munitions will be fired at the same range as the old (unitary) 155mm CW round. They will not reach out to Soviet second echelon targets. Assuming that they would be fired from positions in the FRG, they would land 16-24km from where fired—in the FRG. The bombs planned for later production could be delivered against deeper targets, but manned aircraft sorties would be much in demand for the delivery of other munitions in either close air support or interdiction missions. As in the case of strategic mobility, hard decisions need to be made regarding priorities for limited delivery assets.[103] Missile or rocket delivery of CW is still in the concept phase. Priorities for binary production as of 1982 remain 155mm munitions and bombs to be delivered by manned aircraft.

Cost. Opponents argue that CW modernization will divert funds from other military requirements and is likely to stimulate interservice rivalry. The cost estimates for the administration's modernization plans vary from $7 to $14 billion in the decade of the 1980's.[104] By Department of Defense spending standards, these costs are neither prohibitive nor the most serious obstacle to binary production. Those amounts, however, would purchase a lot of strategic lift, conventional artillery, tanks, reserve stocks of munitions, precision-guided missiles, additional quality manpower, or any number of other items on the DOD shopping list. Presumably, the Navy and the Air Force could recommend some interesting ways to spend an extra $7 to $14 billion. As the Congress demonstrated in its postponement of the Administration's CW initiatives, the proponents of CW will find it more difficult to compete with those seeking increasingly scarce funds for the equipment noted above, all of which are *certain* to be needed during a war. Requests for unprecedented levels of funding in support of CW will result in fierce budget battles between bureaucratic leviathans.

The Political Dimension. According to CW opponents, the really tough nut for chemical warfare proponents is the political resistance to US CW initiatives. Psychological and moral aversion to CW is the background to specific objections. Calling such opponents emotional and naive doesn't make them go away. Thus, despite the merits of refutations of specific objections to CW, the fact is that the Western World simply doesn't like the stuff. Of course, neither does the West (nor the East for that matter) like nuclear weapons. Herein lies the peculiar nature of the debate that often confounds CW proponents who make military arguments to support their case. They may wonder, if dead is dead, what difference does it make whether the means of dispatch are nuclear or chemical? In fact, it might even be argued that, inasmuch as chemical weapons do not destroy property, they are less destructive than nuclear weapons and present fewer obstacles to the postwar efforts of survivors to resume their lives. The problem is that, with the exception of two isolated incidents in far away places, nuclear weapons have not been used and nobody in Europe has experienced their terror. The threat of being atomized is almost surreal and beyond comprehension. On the other hand, the very mention of chemical warfare evokes memories in many Europeans of terrible personal experiences that resulted from the use of these odious weapons. It elicits the imagery of Remarque's *All Quiet on the Western Front:* trenches, writhing flesh in agony, low-hanging, noxious clouds, and the very lunacy of wasting hundreds of thousands of lives for temporary possession of a few square kilometers of barren land. The point is that opposition to CW will not be overcome by military logic or political exhortation. The proponents of CW are bedeviled by the proposition that an ounce of image is worth much more than a pound of substance.

The general aversion to lethal chemicals has been a constant since World War I, and the grass roots demand for a nuclear freeze in Europe and the United States promises a similar response as the publics on both continents become aware of US plans for renewed attention to another weapon of mass destruction. An administration already depicted by its critics as inclined to confrontation is certain to be cast in the villain's role as the CW story unfolds. The United States continues to see itself as the hero wearing the white hat, but the world has clearer memories of our involvement in Indochina and the Watergate affair than of Wilson's Fourteen Points, the Marshall Plan, and the Berlin airlift. To many non-Americans, the land of the free and the home of the brave is just another self-seeker in a world bereft of nobility. Thus, opponents contend, our advocacy of CW will do nothing to enhance our self-image as the chosen people.[105]

CW response in kind has a certain *sui generis* appeal to those who find comfort in symmetry and believe that deterrence is based upon a rigid system for system equality rather than on an overall parity of forces.[106] There is a danger, however, that exclusive reliance upon a technical solution to a military problem might demonstrate a convincing internal logic that fails to take into account crucial but indeterminate external factors that might result in political costs out of all proportion to those military gains. Strong CW initiatives taken by the United States violate Clausewitz' most basic assertion regarding military purpose. Moreover, these initiatives are likely to do serious harm to the Alliance which is already seriously strained.

It is distasteful and often incomprehensible for Americans concerned with national security to understand that our friends might see us, rather than the Soviet Union, as the disturbers of the peace. The unrelenting growth of the Soviet military has been so consistent that this growth is regarded as a constant in political life, something akin to fog in London. On the other hand, US efforts have been so inconsistent that periodic American efforts to redress a military imbalance which favors the Soviets appear bellicose and frightening to our allies. Western European fears, heightened when American military efforts are coupled with confrontational rhetoric, were illustrated recently by the German parliamentarian who said: "... the Poles want their superpower to stop telling them how to live and we want ours to stop telling us how to die."[107] This can be seen as a lament marking the death of detente, a death attributed by some more to Washington than to Moscow. There is no reason to believe that US chemical warfare initiatives will be seen differently. They will appear to be further evidence of the US preference for confrontation, while Europe prefers detente.[108]

As is the case with intermediate nuclear forces (INF), Europe remains to be persuaded that CW is good for it. Recent evidence of European aversion to chemical weapons was provided by the governments of Norway and Holland which stated they would not allow the deployment of such weapons on their territory. Moreover, the stated policy of the FRG is not to allow the training of its troops in the use of chemicals "now or in the future."[109] Even if a convincing CW threat can be established, Europe can be expected to continue to resist both stationing in time of peace and use in time of war—for good political reasons.[110]

NATO's defensive strategy virtually insures that combat in the Central Region, should it occur, will be conducted in the Federal Republic of Germany. Soviet attacks into the FRG would be unable to bypass population centers thereby placing Western leaders in the untenable position of knowing that their tactical use of chemicals would kill more friendly civilians than enemy soldiers, a serious inhibition to NATO use of CW on European territory. Hence, opponents suggest that we recognize the political circumstances confronting the leaders of our democratic allies. Political exigencies are more urgent and tangible than military contingencies which are perceived as unlikely to occur. We cannot divorce military hardware and strategy from their political purposes lest we violate Clausewitz' most elementary dictum regarding their inseparability and thus risk undermining the integrity of NATO.

The current mood in Europe can be characterized in a word: unsettled. The popular reaction to both INF and the enhanced radiation warhead (neutron bomb) suggests that a Europe accused of being neutralist, pacifist, and anti-American will be unenthusiastic should we attempt to impose improved lethal chemical weapons on our allies. Such pressure could undermine US attempts to persuade the Europeans to increase their military budgets and proceed on schedule with the deployment of the Pershing II and ground-launched cruise missiles. There is reason to believe that the already strained relations between the United States and NATO Europe might be stretched to the breaking point by such pressure. Stationing additional chemical munitions in Europe, in whatever form, is simply not in the cards for the foreseeable future.

Nor does the problem reside wholly with the Europeans. Those who would convince Western Europe of the need to modernize and deploy chemical weapons shouldn't take American willingness to do so for granted.[111] The wave of grass roots resistance to nuclear armament felt in the United States seems to be an echo of what had been described earlier as European "neutralism, pacifism, and anti-Americanism." The movement to "freeze" the levels of weapons of mass destruction is strong on both sides of the Atlantic. Obviously, "anti-Americanism" does not apply on this side of the Atlantic, and it probably isn't a very accurate description of what is happening on the other side. A general feeling of unease is manifest in the West, and it cannot be ascribed wholly to European leftists or American campus radicals. Church organizations, former defense officials, citizens of Western and Eastern Europe and American small towns assemble to express concern for what they fear is a superpower nuclear race to the precipice. The climate is not congenial for initiatives which frighten Americans, our allies, and our adversaries. The production of new or additional chemical weapons has met resistance in the United States and the deployment of such weapons will not be supported by our allies.

CONCLUSIONS AND RECOMMENDATIONS

So what does all this mean?

We have presented the arguments for and against a US chemical weapons modernization program. The essence of the proponents' case for the binary system can be summed up as "better safe than sorry." The case against an ambitious US effort to produce binary weapons essentially considers what we know about US and Soviet CW capabilities and concludes that the existing US capability is adequate when seen in the context of overall US and Soviet military capabilities;[112] the marginal CW improvement of our security posture is not worth political costs.

There is merit in the arguments of both sides. The evidence discussed in this essay leads one to the following conclusions.

- The Soviets and the Warsaw Pact have a potent CW force, although precise estimates of the nature and extent of the threat are unattainable.
- In spite of Soviet CW strength, uncertainties (due to weather, terrain, etc.) attending the use of chemical agents, as well as the scope and severity of a NATO response, make an assured and rapid victory far from certain for the Soviets and may therefore deter their employment of chemical agents more than is commonly acknowledged.
- The size and potential lethality of the US/NATO chemical arsenal may be understated. The West's chemical arsenal is probably adequate to deter the Soviet use of chemical weapons in any limited conflict scenario, Soviet chemical munition quantitative advantages notwithstanding [because of (a) the degradation of performance due to deficiencies of Soviet protective gear, (b) the collapse of morale and paralysis of will which would accompany a successful NATO counterstrike with chemical weapons, (c) the difficulty of exercising command and control in a chemical environment (all of which pose serious obstacles to the Soviets' quick victory doctrine and goals,[113] and (d) the fact that the Soviets could not be sure that an unsuccessful NATO limited CW response might not hasten the use of nuclear weapons[114]].
- In an all-out offensive employing nuclear and chemical munitions, it is unclear that the West would accrue any significant advantages by pursuing a massive chemical munitions buildup.

The policymaker is confronted with the difficult task of reconciling conflicting claims to truth and wisdom and devising a policy that is militarily prudent, yet mindful of the political exigencies inherent in a multilateral alliance such as NATO. Our analysis of available evidence leads us to the following recommendations which might be useful to those who make decisions affecting the security of the United States and Western Europe.

• The search for a military equalizer should not be allowed to blur the national interest, nor should it so focus on a single tree that we forget we are deep in a forest. Risking the continued existence of NATO for a marginal increase in military capability is like buying new tires for an automobile whose engine and transmission may burn out if they are driven much further. Thus far, we have sought to play the CW tune in a relatively low key, because we do not want to jeopardize the fragile INF dual decision. However the INF issue works itself out, there is no indication that Western Europe is prepared to welcome additional chemical weapons on the continent. Another acrimonious debate between Europe and the United States would do further damage to NATO as the Soviet Union is fully prepared and able to exploit transatlantic differences. We should not attempt to force our allies to do things they will not do. Many do not want to store or use additional chemical weapons.

• The inclination of some US defense analysts to stare fixedly at Soviet capabilities tends to result in efforts to match them in kind, an inclination that too often causes us to study a single part while forgetting the integrated whole. In other words, overemphasizing the chemical balance may cause us to underestimate the impact of weapons such as PGM's and fragmentation cluster bombs which are highly efficient means of thwarting an attack by armor and infantry in a CW environment. The criterion against which contemplated policy must be measured is, ultimately, what deters war. Prudent military measures designed for fighting wars must be fitted into the higher priority of what prevents wars. Paradoxically, military measures to make marginal improvements to warfighting ability can do harm to deterrence should the military measures undermine alliance cohesion. Deterrence is, in fact, an amalgam of military capability and political will. Both are necessary. Military capability must be seen in its entirety as it appears to the adversary. The task for the United States is to elicit cautious behavior by the Soviets without frightening our allies. Emphasis on a single component of our broad military capability, particularly one unacceptable to allies, is not in the West's best interests.

• Improving NATO's defensive CW posture is imperative. Therefore, training, distribution of protective equipment and research should continue.[115] Protecting our soldiers against chemical weapons makes good sense to even the most passionate opponent of CW. It gives a clear signal of concern and places the adversary in the villain's role, which is precisely where we want him. Further, by reducing the efficiency of Soviet chemical weapons against military targets, it becomes clear that civilians are the likely victims of Soviet CW use. The conquest of territory inhabited by the survivors of CW is unlikely to win their hearts and minds, thus deterring Soviet use on the basis of both limited efficiency against NATO forces and alienation of a population presumably to be governed by the Soviets in the postwar period.

- A two-part declaratory policy by the United States is needed. It should state that: (1) use of "weapons of mass destruction" against NATO will find a NATO response using "weapons of mass destruction at the appropriate level," and (2) NATO regards chemical, biological, and nuclear weapons as weapons of mass destruction. This declaratory policy links the US nuclear weapons to Europe without inviting the political debate that would accompany US proposals to alter CW policy significantly, and it is sufficiently ambiguous to increase the problems and risks for Soviet planners as they consider possible CW use. Chris Donnelly, a noted analyst of Soviet military policy, supports this option when he notes:

> If the Soviets believe that their initial and widespread use of lethal chemical agents during a conventional phase might induce NATO to retaliate with nuclear weapons, or might substantially bring forward in time a NATO decision to permit nuclear release, it is certain that, in Russian eyes, this would render the use of chemical weapons completely counterproductive.[116]

- A low key upgrading of the US chemical arsenal, on a unilateral basis and without drawing Europe into a debate, is desirable. Pending the resolution of technical deficiencies and consultation with our NATO allies, the one-for-one *replacement* of existing US military stocks with binary weapons is recommended to (1) keep our hand in the state of the art, (2) address the safety concerns of the Europeans while not asking them to accept additional CW munitions, and (3) improve the readiness and effectiveness of our CW arsenal. The objective of the retaliatory component of the US program is to maintain the smallest, safest stockpile that denies a significant military advantage to any initiator of chemical warfare. We need not, and should not, plan to match the Soviets in agent/munition quantities and types. Further, our allies have been informed that no decisions have been made regarding deployment of chemical weapons. Should it ever be determined that overseas deployment is desirable, there must be full consultation with the allies involved prior to making any decision. This seems a prudent route and follows our low key approach.[117]

- However, the delivery means should not be conventional artillery, as is now planned. The reason for ruling out conventional artillery is basic: chemical munitions fired from artillery tubes almost certainly land on friendly territory because of the limited range of the delivery system. Even if this territory is occupied by Warsaw Pact forces, the prospect still frightens our European allies. Furthermore, the logistical problems associated with CW munitions make it unlikely that they would arrive on the battlefield due to competing demands for transportation of people and equipment that would certainly be used in combat. Long-range delivery means circumvent doctrinal problems of use, psychological and political problems of storage in Europe, and logistical problems associated with getting chemical munitions to where they might be required. Aerial spray tanks allow for rapid movement and employment for admittedly limited strikes designed more as evidence of political will than military effectiveness. The point here is to give a political signal to Moscow *in extremis* without alarming European NATO in time of peace. Long-range delivery insures that the victims, if CW is ever used, would not be friendly civilians.[118]

- Some improvement of CW capabilities by the United States is probably necessary if the Soviets are to be expected to negotiate reductions of their capability—whatever it is. Negotiations to eliminate or reduce CW capabilities on both sides are absolutely necessary even if a successful outcome is in doubt due to such intractable problems such as verification. Our allies expect us to make that effort, and failure to do so would assist the Soviets in dividing NATO. Maintaining and rehabilitating existing stocks of CW, while continuing research in laboratories with a goal of replacing rather than augmenting existing stocks, is less provocative and more in the spirit of arms control than the creation of a massive CW arsenal with limited military utility and enormous political costs.

ENDNOTES

1. See McGeorge Bundy, George Kennan, Robert McNamara and Gerald Smith, "Nuclear Weapons and the Atlantic Alliance," *Foreign Affairs,* Spring 1982, pp. 753-768.

2. Henry Gole, "Through European Eyes," *Parameters,* December 1981, pp. 14-23.

3. S. M. Shaffer, "West European Public Opinion on Key Security Issues, 1981-1982," Washington: International Communications Agency, Office of Research (European Branch), June 1982.

4. See Robert W. Komer, "Maritime Strategy vs. Coalition Defense," *Foreign Affairs,* Summer 1982, pp. 1124-1144.

5. P. Graveley, "Defense or Deterrence? The Case for Chemical Weapons," *RUSI Journal,* December 1981, pp. 13-20; Association of the United States Army (AUSA) Special Report, "A Chink in Our Arms—The Urgent Need for Chemical Weapons," Arlington: no date; C. J. Dick, "Soviet Chemical Warfare Capabilities," *International Defense Review,* January 1981, pp. 31-38; John Erickson, "The Soviet Union's Growing Arsenal of Chemical Warfare," *Strategic Review,* Fall 1979, pp. 63-71; Senator John Tower (R-Texas), "The Politics of Chemical Deterrence," *The Washington Quarterly,* Spring 1982, pp. 25-37; Major Adrian P. Bambini, Jr., "Chemical Warfare and the NATO Alliance," *Military Review,* April 1981, pp. 28-33. Also, see note 38.

6. R. L. Wagner and T. S. Gold, "Why We Can't Avoid Developing Chemical Weapons," *Defense 82,* Arlington: American Forces Information Services, July 1982, pp. 3-11; C. J. Dick.

7. For instance, see M. Meselman, "A Biochemist's Case Against the New Nerve Gas," *Christian Science Monitor,* May 17, 1982; Senator Gary Hart (D-Colorado), Letter to the Editor, *The Wall Street Journal,* February 4, 1982, p. 31; G. Burck, "Old Fears, New Weapons: Brewing a Chemical Arms Race," *The Defense Monitor,* Vol. IX, No. 9, Washington: Center for Defense Information, 1980, pp. 1-8; and J. P. Perry Robinson, "Chemical Warfare Capabilities of the Warsaw and North Atlantic Treaty Organizations: An Overview from Open Sources," in *Chemical Weapons: Destruction and Conversion* by Stockholm International Peace Research Institute, London: Taylor and Francis, Ltd., 1980, pp. 9-56.

8. Wagner and Gold. Also Tower (p. 31) notes:

> The most controversial element of the President's request [for chemical rearmament] is likely to be the roughly $50 billion for procurement of long-lead items needed to produce 155mm binary artillery shells and BIGEYE aircraft-deliverable bombs.

9. The comparisons and figures cited in this paper exclude the chemical warfare stockpiles and capabilities of France. For a discussion of France's "not negligible" CW capability and doctrine, see Dick, January 1981, p. 35; Robinson, pp. 28, 39; and J. Pergent, "Services des Poudres," *Forces Aeriennes Francaises, 24,* 1970, pp. 89-102.

10. A. Hoeber and J. Douglas, "The Neglected Threat of Chemical Warfare," *International Security,* Summer 1978, pp. 55-82.

11. Entered into *Congressional Record,* September 16, 1980. Cited in AUSA, p. 17.

12. Robinson, pp. 10-12; Graveley, pp. 13, 17; AUSA, pp. 17, 20; Dick, p. 31; and Tower, p. 3. Robinson notes (p. 10) that the last serving Soviet official who spoke or wrote openly about CW did so in 1938.

13. Tower, pp. 27-28; C. N. Donnelly ("Winning the NBC War: Soviet Army Theory and Practice," *International Defense Review,* August 1981, pp. 989-996) explains the substantial variation in Western estimates of the Soviet CW arsenal (p. 990).

> Nor is the difference of opinion over what is chemical, and what is not, confined solely to toxins. The Soviets consider smoke to be a chemical weapon; this fact alone may be enough to account for the wide differences in Western estimates of Soviet stocks of chemical munitions. The Soviets also consider all nonlethal and incendiary agents (e.g., napalm) to be chemical weapons.

14. Dick, p. 36; John Erickson, (p. 65) credits the Soviet Union with giving "as much as 50 percent of all filled munitions for missiles and bombs stockpiled by Warsaw Pact forces in Central Europe." However, John Tower (p. 27) cites US intelligence estimates as correct that "approximately one-third of the Soviet shells, rocket warheads, and bombs are stored in Eastern Europe."

15. Wagner and Gold, p. 6; Dick, p. 32; and Burck, p. 5.

16. John Erickson.

17. *Ibid.,* p. 65; Tower, p. 27.

18. Tower, p. 28; and AUSA, p. 20. Both sources rely upon the sensational, though unsubstantiated, (Oleg) Penkovsky papers which are based upon the revelations of a Soviet intelligence officer who defected to the West almost two decades ago. Also, see Brown.

19. *Ibid.,* Tower, AUSA, and Brown.

20. Dick, pp. 36-37. Also, see endnotes 52 and 53.

21. Wagner and Gold, p. 7; AUSA, pp. 18-19; Dick, pp. 33, 35-36.

22. Cited AUSA, p. 20. Also, see Tower and Erickson.

23. AUSA, p. 20; Burck, p. 3.

24. According to Tower (p. 27), it may take "several years" to load chemical agents in bulk form into projectiles.

25. AUSA, p. 21; Wagner and Gold, p. 6 (these authors note that mustard freezes at 58°F).

26. AUSA, p. 21.

27. *Ibid.*

28. Wagner and Gold, p. 7.

29. AUSA, p. 21.

30. Dick (p. 35) cites 50 percent of the US supply of chemical weapons is in Europe. Robinson (p. 38) puts this figure at a much lower (less than 10 percent) level.

31. In this context, "limited" operations refer to those lasting two weeks or less. See Burton (p. 27) who notes, "Those CW weapons which are deployed in the Federal Republic of Germany . . . would last for about two weeks of widespread operations."

32. Burton, p. 25.

33. Bambini, pp. 31-33. See endnote 90.

34. Bambini (p. 32) cites legal obstacles that inhibit or prevent storage or transit of CW munitions in certain European countries. For instance,

> ... Norway and Holland have recently stated that they would not allow their forces to use chemical weapons or permit chemical weapons deployment on their territory. The stated policy of the Federal Republic of Germany is not to train its troops in the use of chemicals 'now or in the future.'

Furthermore, Italy has foresworn the right to chemical retaliation.

35. Wagner and Gold, p. 6. For instance, the Soviets provide their troops 100-400 hours per year of formal CW training compared to 16-100 hours for US forces. Furthermore, the Soviets maintain 19 CW training battalions to our one. Also, see Erickson, AUSA, Bambini, Tower, and Donnelly.

36. See AUSA, pp. 17, 22.

37. Cited Graveley, p. 18.

38. General David Jones, *Military Posture for FY 1980,* Washington: Joint Chiefs of Staff.

39. This question is explored expertly by A. F. Graveley, "Defense or Deterrence? The Case for Chemical Weapons," *RUSI Journal,* December 1981, pp. 13-20. Also see F. J. Brown, *Chemical Warfare—A Study in Restraints,* Princeton: Princeton University Press, 1968.

40. Cited *Ibid.,* p. 16.

41. Albert Speer, *Inside the Third Reich.* Cited Graveley, p. 15.

42. J. H. Rothschild, *Tomorrow's Weapons: Chemical and Biological,* New York: McGraw-Hill, 1964.

43. Brown. See also Graveley, p. 15.

44. Rothschild.

45. Peter Vigor, *The Soviet View of War, Peace and Neutrality,* London: Routledge and Kegan Paul, 1975. The other two scenarios (besides the quick victory) which Vigor identifies as independent "preconditions" for a Soviet attack against the West are (1) overwhelming Soviet strategic superiority and (2) political discord within the West so divisive as to allow the Soviets to defeat the various nations one at a time.

46. Graveley, p. 14; Dick, pp. 36-37.

47. Adapted from Dick, *Chemical and Biological Weapons,* p. 230. (See chart on next page.)

48. *Ibid.* (See chart on next page.)

49. Dick, pp. 37-38.

50. Wagner and Gold, p. 4. Also, see Dick, pp. 24-35.

51. See A. Ross Johnson, R. Dean and A. Alexiev, "The Armies of the Warsaw Pact Northern Tier," *Survival,* July/August 1981, pp. 174-182.

52. V. D. Sokolovsky, *Soviet Military Strategy* (translated by Harriet Fast Scott, *et al.*), New York: Crane, Russak & Co., 1975, pp. 68-69.

53. V. Ye. Savkin, *Osnovi Printsipi Overativnogo Iskusstva Taktiki,* Moscow: 1972 (translated by US Air Force as *The Basic Principles of Operational Art and Tactics,* p. 107).

54. Extracted from NATO Communique reported in *The London Daily Telegraph,* May 15, 1980. Cited Graveley, p. 18.

ESTIMATED POTENCIES OF SELECTED CW AGENTS

Agent Aerosolized or Vaporized Over Target

	To Incapacitate		To Kill		
	Respiratory ID-50[1] mg-min/m^3	Time to Effect	Respiratory LD-50[2] mg-min/m^3	Percutaneous LD-50[2] mg-min/m^3	Time to Effect
Phosgene (CG)[3]	1,600	3-12 hrs	3,200	NA	3-24 hrs
Mustard (HD)	200[4]	4-6 hrs	1,500	10,000	4-24 hrs
Hydrogen Cyanide (AC)	NA	NA	5,000	NA	½-15 min
Tabun (GA)	100	1-10 min	400	40,000	10-15 min
Sarin (GB)	55	1-10 min	100	12,000	2-15 min
Soman (GD)	25	1-10 min	70	10,000	1-15 min
Agent VX[6]	5	1-10 min	36	1,000	4-10 min

[1] Dosage estimated to incapacitate half those exposed to it.
[2] Dosage estimated to kill half those exposed to it.
[3] As gases, Hydrogen Cyanide and Phosgene only are effective through the respiratory system. They disperse downwind and cannot contaminate ground.
[4] For eye injury.
[5] Sarin vapor disperses so rapidly that, save in very cold conditions, it is not suitable as a ground contaminant; that is, it is effectively nonpersistent.
[6] The performance of agent VR-55 may be roughly similar.
NA = nonapplicable.

PERSISTENCY OF SELECTED LIQUID CW AGENTS[1, 2]

Agent	Weather Conditions		
	Sunny, Around 20°C, Light Breeze	Wet and Windy, Around 10°C	Calm, Sunny, Lying Snow, Around -10°C
Mustard (HD)	2-7 days	1½ days	2-8 weeks
Tabun (GA)	1-4 days	3 hours	1 day-2 weeks
Sarin (GB)	¼-4 hours	½ hour	1-2 days
Soman (GD)	2½-5 days	20 hours	1-6 weeks
Agent VX	3-21 days	6 hours	1-16 weeks

[1] The length of time for which contaminated ground/equipment may present a potential contact hazard.
[2] Single figures are average estimates.

55. Henry Kissinger, "The Future of NATO," *The Washington Quarterly,* Vol. 2, Autumn 1979, pp. 6-7.

56. Bundy, *et al.*; Tower, pp. 36-37.

57. For instance, see Stansfield Turner, "A New Strategy for NATO," *The New York Times Magazine,* December 13, 1981, p. 42, and David Broder, "Rising Isolationism," *The Washington Post,* January 13, 1982, p. 23.

58. Turner; for a thorough discussion of the advantages and disadvantages of the maritime strategy, see Robert W. Komer, "Maritime Strategy vs. Coalition Defense," *Foreign Affairs,* Summer 1982, pp. 1124-1144. Also, see John Weinstein, "US Defense Abroad: Sea Power Is Not Enough," *The New York Times,* July 29, 1982, p. 22.

59. See Kissinger; Gole; Turner; Erik v. Kuehnelt-Leddihn, "Shaky Alliance," *National Review,* March 5, 1982, p. 234; Neil Ulman, "US Army in Europe: 'Warfighting' vs. 'Deterrence'," *The Wall Street Journal,* April 28, 1982; "Focus on: The Mood of a Nation," published by *The German Information Agency,* April 1982.

60. Wagner and Gold, p. 4; Bundy, *et al.*; Dick, pp. 34-36; Turner, pp. 36-37; Bambini, pp. 28-29.

61. Donnelly, p. 990; also, see D. Doder, "Kremlin Defense Official Warns of Policy Shift to Quicken Nuclear Response," *The Wall Street Journal,* July 13, 1982; John Collins, *US-Soviet Military Balance 1960-1980,* New York: McGraw-Hill, 1980, p. 118; and Robert Kennedy, "The Strategic Balance in Transition," in *Soviet Armed Forces Review Annual,* edited by David Jones, Gulf Breeze, Florida: Academic International Press, 1980, pp. 356-357.

62. For instance, see S. Gilbert, "Italy Begins Cruise Missile Base Despite Left's Protest," *The Washington Post,* April 18, 1982, p. A37.

63. Thomas Schelling, *The Strategy of Conflict,* Cambridge, Massachusetts: Harvard University Press, 1960.

64. Beckett, "Chemical Warfare Available to Terrorists," *New Scientist,* October 12, 1978.

65. House Defense Appropriations Subcommittee Hearings, April 25, 1974.

66. As of 1979, 42 countries had defense budgets (in current dollars) in excess of $1 billion. *Compiled From World Military Expenditures and Arms Transfers, 1970-1979,* Washington: Arms Control and Disarmament Agency, March 1982.

67. For instance, Wagner and Gold (p. 10) cite a $6-7 billion investment required between FY 1983-87.

68. Bambini, p. 29 and Burton, p. 28. Donnelly (p. 996) argues that the Soviets have incentives to negotiate with us when he states that the Soviets

> are becoming aware of their own special vulnerability to any surprise mass use by NATO of toxic chemical agents . . . . The Soviets are now coming to perceive a serious danger of NATO actually arming itself with an effective chemical warfare capability. They will take all possible measures to try and (sic) prevent this . . . . At the same time, they will strive to improve their own chemical and nuclear delivery and protective systems, just in case.

Also, see Tower, p. 2; Weinberger, III-143.

69. Richard Halloran, "US Plan Reported on New Nerve Gas," *The New York Times,* January 15, 1982. Much of these expenditures are allocated to the demilitarization of obsolete weapons.

70. Casper Weinberger, *Annual Report to Congress, Fiscal Year 1982,* Washington: US Government Printing Office, February 8, 1982.

71. *NATO Chemical Warfare Policy,* Study Brief, Carlisle Barracks: Strategic Studies Institute, August 3, 1981, p. 2.

72. For comprehensive analyses of the shift in the military balance, see: John M. Collins, *US-Soviet Military Balance, Concepts and Capabilities, 1960-1980,* New York: McGraw-Hill, 1980; *Annual Report to the Congress, FY 1983,* Caspar W. Weinberger, Secretary of Defense, Washington: US Government Printing Office; Kennedy.

73. For an extensive analysis of the problems in dealing with Soviet intelligence estimates, see John Prados, *The Soviet Estimate,* New York: Dial Press, 1982.

74. All members of NATO and the Warsaw Pact, including the Soviets, are parties to the 1925 Geneva Protocol, which outlaws at least the first use of poison gas. See J. P. Perry Robinson, "Chemical Weapons and Europe," *Survival,* January-February 1982, pp. 9-18, for a thoughtful analysis of the significance of renewed US interest in CW.

75. See Caspar W. Weinberger, pp. III-143 to III-148 for a recent restatement of the DOD position and appreciation of Soviet capability in CW.

76. This is usually hedged as follows:

> Although available data on the Soviet CW stockpile are limited, *it is assumed* that the stockpile is adequate to meet the combat tasks foreseen by Soviet planners, that production and storage capabilities would not limit the Soviet CW posture, that chemical munitions are sufficient to support sustained, high-intensity chemical conflict, and that the Soviet units are prepared for immediate resort to CW on both an offensive and a defensive basis. (Emphasis added)

Of course, if one assumes all of that, it saves the need for evidence. *Evaluation of Chemical Warfare Alternatives 1980-1990,* Carpenter, *et al.,* Menlo Park, California: Stanford Research Institute, December 1976, p. 5 (a government contract).

77. AUSA, p. 15; Donnelly (p. 996) notes that recently renewed Soviet interest in CW may be the *result* of renewed US interest and initiatives.

78. The US Senate ratified the 1925 Geneva Protocol on December 16, 1974. The President signed it into law on January 22, 1975. *Evaluation of Chemical Warfare Alternatives 1980-1990,* Carpenter, *et al.,* Menlo Park, California: Stanford Research Institute, December 1976, p. 24.

79. "Moscow's Toxin 'Truths'," *The Wall Street Journal,* July 7, 1982, p. 20, begins:

> Even though the administration presented compelling evidence last year of the use of deadly toxin warfare agents in Southeast Asia and Afghanistan by the Soviet Union and its allies, there has been some scientific skepticism.

Compelling to whom? This is a suggestion that we haven't digested an important lesson in the past 15 years: we do not enjoy automatic respect any more. The world is as suspicious of us as it is of the Soviet Union. These suspicions are aggravated by exchanges such as the following, cited by Burck, p. 3:

> The following comments appeared in a hearing before the House Foreign Affairs Committee on February 8, 1980. Rep. Lagomarsino questioned Dr. Edward M. Collins, Vice Director for Foreign Intelligence in the Defense Intelligence Agency, and Bruce C. Clarke, Director of the National Foreign Assessment Center of the Central Intelligence Agency.
>
> Q: Do we have any information on the use of chemical warfare in Afghanistan other than just rumors?
>
> DIA: There is no confirmation at all that they have used chemical weapons.

Q: . . . the common perception is that the Russians are using it there because there have been a lot of rumors in the papers.

DIA: I don't see anything wrong with letting that rumor run.

It is also interesting to note that the Soviet Union, which views napalm as a chemical weapon, evaluates our use of the substance in Vietnam as evidence of our disposition to use chemical weapons.

The most recent comprehensive and compelling evidence was released November 1982 by the US Department of State. See George P. Shultz, *Chemical Warfare in Southeast Asia and Afghanistan: An Update,* Special Report No. 104, Washington, DC. However, as we see below, willingness to accept the evidence and its impact in the policy arena is limited.

80. *Reports of the Use of Chemical Weapons in Afghanistan, Laos, and Kampuchea,* no date, no credit line. Also see Department of State Special Report No. 98, dated March 22, 1982, "Chemical Weapons in Southeast Asia and Afghanistan."

81. *Report of the Group of Experts to Investigate Reports on the Alleged Use of Chemical Weapons,* General Assembly, United Nations, November 20, 1981, p. 34. The experts consisted of representatives from Egypt, Kenya, the Philippines, and Peru.

82. Tanks illustrate the point. According to *Organization and Equipment of the Soviet Army,* HB 550-2, Fort Leavenworth, Kansas: Threats Office, Combined Arms Combat Development Activity, July 15, 1980, pp. 4-8 and 5-50 through 5-58, the Soviet Army maintains the following medium tanks in its inventory: T-55, T-62, T-64, T-72 and T-80. The T-55 was introduced in 1958, but, in fact, it is a product of continual refinement of the T-54 introduced in 1949. Later models build on previous models in the Soviet system, and old models are retained. So it is with other military equipment; so it may be with CW as is argued by Burton (p. 2). Much of it may be quite old. Also, see Dick, *Chemical and Biological Warfare,* p. 221.

83. The production of lethal agents is exceedingly difficult to detect without on-site inspection. Chemical plans producing harmless substances could hide CW production among other activities. This state of affairs led former Secretary of Defense Harold Brown to testify that "There is no decent estimate" of the Soviet chemical weapons stockpile. (Cited Burton, p. 4.)

84. Burck, p. 3.

85. Based upon a population density of 247 people per square kilometer, the figure published by the Press and Information Office of the Government of the Federal Republic of Germany, the arithmetic comes to 127,946 Germans. But the point is clear: an accident in the FRG like the one in Utah would be a catastrophe. Gene Lyons, "Invisible Wars," *Harper's,* December 1981, p. 40.

86. Major General Niles J. Fulwyler states that US troops wearing protective suits in tanks had to get out of them in 40 minutes ". . . or risk a health hazard . . . ." "Would War With Gas Mean Holocaust?," *The New York Times,* May 2, 1982, p. E5. The Soviet suits are generally regarded as inferior to US protective suits. Burck (p. 4) notes that Soviet protective clothing can be worn only 45 minutes at 70°F in the field and 3 hours at temperatures below 59°F. Also, see Constance Holden, "Binary Nerve Gas Production Plans Debated," *Science,* Vol. 216, April 30, 1982, p. 496; Donnelly, p. 992; Burton, p. 24.

87. Kirill Podrabinek, "An Inside Look at Life in the Soviet Army," *Russia,* No. 3, 1981. Ethnic problems, alcoholism and physical abuse are not unusual in the Soviet Army. The relative decline of European ethnic Great Russians relative to its Muslim population may cause the Soviets to rely more upon their Eastern European allies. To the extent that the non-Soviet Pact members are unenthusiastic about the use of such weapons may reduce the likelihood of their employment.

88. Soviet specialists constantly remind us that since the time of Peter the Great, Russia has felt inferior to the West in technical matters. Despite its many technical achievements, especially in space, the Soviets still turn westward for assistance in building a gas pipeline and for high technology.

89. Some of the moral and political problems attending a renewed US emphasis upon chemical munitions were pointed out by Rep. Clement Zablocki, Chairman of the House Foreign Affairs Committee, on September 10, 1980:

> Perhaps most ominous [effect] is the globally destabilizing effect the inclusion of this $3.15 million program will have for the short term as well as the future. It would be interpreted by the American people and the rest of the world as an abandonment of America's deeply held commitment and efforts to a complete and effective ban on the use in war of lethal chemical weapons, to consider producing them. It would remove another deterrent to the usage of lethal chemical weapons by terrorist groups worldwide. At best, it would make our longstanding foreign policy efforts to ban lethal chemical warfare a sham and at worst a potential human tragedy.

Also, see Rone Tempset, "Nerve Gas: A Stockpile of Secrets," *The Los Angeles Times,* March 10, 1982.

90. For an excellent refutation of the view that a quick conventional victory of the Soviets against NATO is assured, see John Mearsheimer, "Why the Soviets Cannot Win Quickly in Central Europe," *International Security,* Summer 1982, pp. 3-39.

91. See John Weinstein, "Soviet Civil Defense and the US Deterrent," *Parameters,* March 1982, pp. 70-83 (see p. 78); Matthew Meselson, Professor of Biochemistry at Harvard University, calculates that the ratio of civilian to military deaths could be on the order of 20:1 in chemical warfare. *The New York Times,* May 2, 1982, p. E5.

92. Senator Carl Levin, member of the Senate Armed Services Committee, supported the continued credibility of NATO's CW deterrent on September 16, 1980, when he stated:

> Contrary to the overly pessimistic description of our present chemical weapons stockpile . . . Secretary of Defense Brown testified to our committee just two weeks ago that these present stocks of chemical munitions still are a "credible" deterrent and they could cause "tremendous" damage if actually used against Soviet troops.

Also, see Robinson, p. 39.

93. Donnelly, pp. 993-996, provides an excellent discussion of Soviet operational problems resulting from a NATO nuclear response.

94. Brown, pp. 293-296. There is no reason to believe that this argument is less valid in 1982.

95. Burck (p. 3) notes:

> An attack may catch men who are ill-trained, too surprised to dress in time, or with defective equipment, but this cannot be counted on. For average weather conditions in open terrain at a distance of 6 miles, it would require more than 1300 155mm GB shells to cause 30 percent casualties among a prepared platoon. That quantity of shells weighs about 70 tons.

96. Holden, *Science,* p. 497. See note 95. Also, despite Army estimates that it would require 2 million tons of war supplies in the first 60 days of war in Europe, as recently as 1978, Pentagon planners acknowledged that airlift could only deliver 115,000 tons (one mechanized infantry division) in the first 19 days. See W. Flannery, "US Ground Forces: Inappropriate Objectives, Unacceptable Costs," Washington, DC: Center for Defense Information, November 1978.

97. Lois R. Ember, "Senate Votes Funds for Binary Chemical Weapons," *Chemical and Engineering News,* May 31, 1982, p. 27. See also the essence of Senator Hart's views on CW production in his letter in *The Wall Street Journal,* February 4, 1982, p. 31.

98. Ember, p. 29. Julian Perry Robinson, a senior fellow at the science policy research unit of the University of Sussex, England, has studied chemical warfare for over 15 years. He offers no encouragement to those who would expect Western Europe to welcome the storage of CW.

99. *The New York Times,* May 2, 1982, p. 3.

100. Ember, p. 28.

101. *The New York Times,* May 2, 1982, p. 3.

102. Weinberger, p. III-146, and *Military Posture for FY 1982,* David C. Jones, Chairman, JCS, Washington, DC: US Government Printing Office, p. 79.

103. Strategic mobility, by air or sea, is a problem currently being addressed, but it will require consistent support and funding if US worldwide commitments are to be met. The alternative to strategic mobility is forward-basing, a solution accompanied by diplomatic hurdles. See Weinberger, especially pp. III-91 to III-110 for programs addressing the mobility issue.

104. Frank Greve, "Chemical-Weaponry Tab Could be $14 Billion for Decade," *The Philadelphia Inquirer,* March 7, 1982, p. 6.

105. See note 89.

106. In this vein, it can be argued that precision-guided missiles against tankers and fragmentation cluster bombs (each equivalent to 600 mortar rounds) against troops on foot are more effective killing instruments than chemical munitions.

107. Flora Lewis, *The New York Times,* January 11, 1982, p. A19, citing a remark made by a German deputy during Brezhnev's November 1982 visit to Bonn.

108. In addition to the record of NATO governments on security issues, it is useful to note the public opinions in Europe in the last several years for clues to possible reactions to US chemical warfare initiatives. The CW issue has not been addressed in USICA polls, but responses regarding the superpowers, military balance, the threat, support for NATO, support for INF, and opposition to neutron weapons tells us what might be expected should we press Europe to store modern CW stocks. See "West European Public Opinion on Key Security Issues, 1981-82," prepared by Stephen M. Shaffer, European Branch, Office of Research, International Communications Agency, USA, June 1982. For some explicit negative

European reaction to CW, see *Der Spiegel,* February 22, 1982. The cover story is "Todeswolken uber Europa" (Death Clouds Over Europe), pp 32-52. For a British reaction, see: Paul Aaron, "Many Britons Concerned Over US Chemical Weapons," *Boston Globe,* January 11, 1982, p. 6. Danish and Norwegian refusal to store nuclear weapons on their soil promises a similar response to CW. Increasingly, the Soviets are finding their Eastern allies resistive across a wide range of defense policies. For instance, see John Tagliabue, "4000 East Germans Dispute Official Defense Policy," *The New York Times,* February 15, 1982, p. A3.

109. M. Meselman. Also, see note 114.

110. It is important that one not overestimate the attraction of the safety factor to the European allies. Their opposition to chemical munitions runs deeper than their fear of accidents involving these weapons. Their opposition to these weapons shares certain similarities to their opposition to the Pershing II and cruise missiles: (a) that they are likely to antagonize the Soviets and heighten the arms race; (b) that they allow the United States to plan for a nonnuclear war fought solely on European soil; (c) that they are political liabilities for the party that permits their deployment; (d) that they may result in the uncoupling of the US nuclear umbrella from Europe, etc.

111. On July 22, 1982, the House provided the binary program a setback by voting 251-159 against the retaliatory capability sought by the Administration while approving the funds for defensive measures. Richard Halloran, "The House Rejects Funds to Produce Chemical Weapon," *The New York Times,* July 23, 1982, p. A1.

112. See note 92. Also, despite the argument that America's CW arsenal is dangerously obsolete, there is some evidence that the extent of the problem has been overstated by advocates of binary production in order to support their case. For instance, in a September 1977 Report to Congress (*Stockpile of Lethal Chemical Munitions and Agents—Better Management Needed,* Study LCD-77-205), the Comptroller General of the US General Accounting Office concluded (pp. i-iii):

> Department of Defense officials have testified in congressional hearings that the stockpile is deteriorating and that much of it is unserviceable. They said that the stockpile was inadequate in quantity and quality; consequently, they requested funds to prepare to produce a new chemical munition known as a binary.
>
> *The true condition of the stockpile is unknown. Its serviceability may have been greatly understated. For example, many of the unserviceable classifications are a result of minor nonfunctional defects, such as container rust, which do not affect usability.* Also, inspection samples are neither random nor representative, block storage hampers access during inspection, entire production lots are classified unserviceable for a few defects . . . . (Emphasis added.)
>
> Little has been done to maintain the stockpile in a serviceable condition or to restore the unserviceable portions. *Using anticipated approval of the binary program as a reason for not maintaining the stockpile is inconsistent with sound management.* Lack of maintenance could seriously compromise US retaliatory capabilities. (Emphasis added.)

Furthermore, the GAO advised the Army to stop classifying entire production lots as unserviceable because of a few defects when reporting on the stockpile's condition; and stop disposing of usable stocks until stockpile requirements have been defined.

113. See Mearsheimer.

114. Donnelly, pp. 993-996.

115. See Wagner and Gold. The Reagan Administration's CW budget allocates more than 70 percent of projected expenditures to defense purposes.

116. Donnelly, p. 996.

117. See Warner and Gold, pp. 8, 10.

118. Due to force-to-space ratio constraints, a Soviet advance against NATO positions would necessitate the stacking of Soviet brigades in second and third echelon positions. NATO planners increasingly have looked to means of destroying these reserve forces since their destruction would limit supplies and reinforcements to first echelon troops, thereby taking the steam out of a potential Soviet blitzkrieg. (See Mearsheimer.) The long-range delivery of chemical agents against rear echelon troops, C^3 installations, rail and other transshipment points, etc., would help to limit Soviet prospects of a quick victory, thereby reducing the likelihood of war in Europe.

10

IMPROVING EUROPE'S CONVENTIONAL DEFENSES

Edward A. Corcoran

Since the 1950's, nuclear weapons have been the rock upon which the entire NATO defense edifice was built. This initial emphasis on nuclear weapons was a conscious decision by countries tired of war and anxious to get on with the long and costly task of rebuilding their shattered economies. Instead of developing sturdy armies to counter those of the Soviet bloc, the United States and its West European allies chose a less expensive option—an apparently solid defense relying on a relatively small number of overwhelmingly powerful US nuclear weapons. For several decades this nuclear approach served the Alliance well. Its members prospered in evident security. Now the decision has come back to haunt NATO.[1] The West's emphasis on nuclear weapons has skewed the resulting arms buildup in that direction. Through the decades, the Soviets have matched the US nuclear arsenal while the numbers of weapons on both sides have grown dramatically. The path of nuclear defense, which earlier seemed so beguilingly attractive, now threatens to lead into a blind alley of nuclear standoff. At best, the nuclear stalemate reemphasizes the conventional arsenals, in which the East traditionally has enjoyed superiority. At worst, the dependence on nuclear weapons may lead to cataclysm. More and more insistently the question is raised: Is there another path?

By the early 1980's, the emotional rejection of the old path by small groups of antinuclear activists had mushroomed to rallies of dramatic size and broadened to include support from prominent religious, civilian, and military figures.

Much of the opposition expressed before the 1980's had voiced concern over the increasing levels of nuclear weapons on both sides, but offered few alternatives. Reacting to this void in defense planning, a number of analysts are beginning to explore new options. For example, four prominent American statesmen have examined with dismay the profusion of nuclear weapons and the "total impossibility for either side of any guarantee against unlimited escalation." They call for NATO to reverse its current military strategy and to adopt a no-first-use policy backed by "an effective conventional defense."[2]

And there's the rub. Calls for an emphasis on conventional forces are not new. Writing a decade earlier in the same journal, Michael Howard stressed the need for stronger conventional forces "not to act according to traditional concepts as if nuclear weapons did not exist, but to operate so as to minimize the possibility of the adversary using his nuclear forces at all." But Howard then added the additional requirement "to maximize the credibility of the nuclear threat of their own government."[3] Similarly, a German response to the no-first-use proposal stressed the importance of the nuclear option as a deterrent in the face of Soviet conventional superiority, and expressed deep skepticism about the feasibility of a conventional balance.[4] Do the economic pressures on NATO military budgets, the decided Pact conventional superiority, and the disturbing evidence of Pact chemical and biological warfare activities[5] make a NATO conventional defense essentially unrealizable?

CONVENTIONAL FORCE PROBLEMS

The conventional force imbalance is exacerbated by a number of factors which favor the Warsaw Pact. For example, NATO concedes the initiative to the Pact, even though NATO decisionmaking requires time-consuming multilateral consultations. But the most sweeping NATO problems concern three operational issues: forward defense, rear area security, and reinforcement.

NATO's forward defense, necessitated by political considerations and by the lack of strategic depth in Central Europe,[6] leaves the defense vulnerable to massed breakthroughs. The Pact's military doctrine and its large armor forces are ideally suited to this vulnerability. Furthermore, a number of major NATO units are stationed far from their frontline positions. In a crisis, even with warning of a Pact mobilization, a NATO concern not to appear provocative could easily inhibit a decision to deploy units forward. As a result, many NATO forward defense positions might not even be manned at the outbreak of hostilities.

Emphasis on forward defense also has inhibited planning for operations within NATO territory, particularly in urban areas. In the immediate postwar period, the US nuclear umbrella protected European cities, while US strategic superiority insured that the risk was also low for US cities. Furthermore, if deterrence failed, Warsaw Pact doctrine stressed bypassing population centers and fighting in the relatively open countryside. Consequently, NATO did not develop urban defense forces which could have relied on cities as strongpoints of the allied defense. But 30 years of urban sprawl have totally obliterated any prospects of defending cities by fighting in the countryside. At the same time, NATO's arsenal has come to include such a diverse stock of theater nuclear weapons that its very fighting capability threatens widespread urban destruction, particularly if Pact units stay close to urban areas as a means of discouraging NATO use of nuclear options.[7] Further, the widespread lack of planning for systematic fighting within NATO territory can make an attack more attractive to the Warsaw Pact by easing its problem of consolidating control over any seized territory and simplifying security within its tactical rear area.

A second major NATO problem is rear area security. Few NATO installations are hardened. Headquarters elements, telecommunications sites, support units, port facilities, and storage depots (including fuel, ammunition, and equipment reserves) are at lightly defended locations well known to the Warsaw Pact. It is also clear that the Pact plans to capitalize on these NATO vulnerabilities. Hundreds of Pact agents are either in place in Western Europe or could be infiltrated easily prior to hostilities. Added to this are the Pact's own deep strike weapons and its sizable airmobile forces and operational maneuver groups which are specifically trained for disruption of the NATO rear area.[8] By simply promoting confusion and panic among the NATO civilian population, the Pact might be able to hopelessly clog the NATO transportation net in some critical sectors.

A particularly troublesome aspect of rear area security is the high percentage of support troops and their modest preparations for combat operations. In a US infantry division, about half of the division base is headquarters or support troops. They are typically required to fight as infantrymen when necessary, but this is usually taken to mean fighting as riflemen in perimeter security roles or against small raiding parties. There is no combat organization and little training in the use of machine guns, antiarmor weapons, mines or explosives, particularly among the growing percentage of women soldiers. This means that tens of thousands of US troops can have only a minimal impact in direct combat.[9]

A third NATO operational problem is reinforcement. The bulk of NATO reinforcements comes from the United States. But other contingencies (say Korea, Cuba, or the Middle East) could easily disrupt the flow of these reinforcements by reducing the strategic lift or the forces available for Europe. Also, projected US deployment times to Central Europe compare poorly with those of massive Soviet reinforcements.[10] And, as with the forward movement of units currently stationed in Europe, reinforcement early in a crisis could be hampered by a concern not to appear provocative—a concern the Soviets would undoubtedly work hard to manipulate and intensify. Moreover, is reinforcement feasible once Western Europe is under attack? What would be the effects of sabotage on the ports? Commando strikes on key reception facilities or transportation nodes? Conventional or chemical strikes on equipment depots, including materials prepositioned to support early arriving units? Contested airspace over major airfields? Streams of refugees blocking highways? Hostile submarine activity on the sea lanes? Such questions highlight the military risks of relying on a cumbersome system of long-distance reinforcement.

Any new NATO defense approaches must address these problems. Western Europe must better capitalize on advantages available to the defender—prepared positions, interior lines, and operation on familiar territory. It must also better exploit the high lethality of modern weapons and the Pact's own vulnerabilities: the questionable reliability of both the East European forces and Soviet ethnic minorities, the Pact overemphasis on armor, and the

Soviets' uncertain and potentially vulnerable lines of reinforcement.

THE EAST-WEST POLITICAL SETTING

Militarily, East European cooperation would be critical for the success of any Soviet attack on NATO Europe—about half of the immediately available Pact divisions in Central Europe are East European. The Soviets have clearly demonstrated, perhaps with the exception of Rumania, that they can coerce their Pact allies into adopting desired internal policies and generally into supporting Soviet foreign policy. But it is questionable whether they could coerce them into war, and the fighting reliability of East European forces remains quite suspect.[11] It is patently clear that the same Soviet troops cannot be used simultaneously to attack NATO and to coerce Eastern Europe. East European recalcitrance could even frustrate Soviet attempts to mount an attack on NATO—withholding forces would reduce both the troops available to the Pact command and the Soviet ability to insure control of its lines of communication. Except for clear prospects of a quick victory, it is hard to project motives which would induce East European political elites to support a Pact military thrust. For them, this would involve high risks of domestic destruction with little expectation of gain, particularly as NATO builds its capabilities to conduct military operations in Warsaw Pact territory.

And so, East European attitudes have a direct impact on the European military balance. NATO strategy must be sensitive to these concerns by reducing as much as possible any potential incentives for Eastern Europe to support a Soviet military thrust.

This raises the question of the extent to which the offensive aspects of the NATO posture can be viewed as a credible threat to Eastern Europe. In the early 1950's, despite the purely defensive aims expressed in the NATO charter, there were widespread hopes that some day, somehow, an opportunity might arise for the free world to "roll back" the Soviet occupation of East Europe.[12] NATO forces were compatible with these vague hopes. Although smaller than the Pact forces, they had a significant technological advantage, were backed by a considerable US nuclear superiority, and were clearly capable of offensive as well as defensive operations should an opportunity arise. Tank divisions, fighter wings, artillery batteries, and infantry battalions can all fight offensively and, indeed, prefer to do so. Khrushchev himself has said that the often paranoid Stalin "lived in terror of an enemy attack."[13]

The events in Hungary in 1956 forced NATO to confront these vague aspirations and to conclude that the prospects for a military solution to European security were negligible. Talk of "rollback" ceased. Now, with the continued rise of Soviet military strength, the very thought of a NATO military move eastward has become an absurdity. An absurdity, that is, to NATO. But not necessarily to the East. NATO's fighting elements still retain an inherent offensive capability, a capability which current attention to deep strike operations would expand. Unceasing Pact propaganda on the horrors of World War II keeps alive the specter of a German menace. On a propaganda level, where ideological preconceptions are combined with the ogre of "German revanchism," the threat can strike a responsive chord in Eastern Europe and justify Soviet pressures to maintain excessively large defense establishments. To the extent that the NATO military posture can be pictured as offensive, it helps to penetrate such justifications.

The more clearly defensive the NATO military posture, the harder it is for the Soviets to justify to their allies (and to their own population) the burdensome levels of high Pact military expenditures. East European resistance, especially by the Poles and Rumanians, to preferred Soviet spending levels has been a source of contention within the Warsaw Pact in the past. NATO must show enough strength, cohesion, and durability without posing an excessive threat so that the Soviets ultimately conclude the benefits from their military programs are so marginal that they cannot justify current levels of military spending.[14]

But ultimately is a long time away. For NATO, there will be no ultimate solutions if the short-term military strategy fails. The military strategy is—in effect—a holding strategy, expending assets as necessary for defense while political, economic, and psychological actions remove incentives for military solutions and encourage the Soviets and East Europeans to shift resources into developmental programs and eventual peaceful social competition.

CONVENTIONAL DEFENSE REQUIREMENTS

Wars have a way of ending differently from what their initiators planned. For this reason alone, the Soviet leaders, both conscious of history and cautious in their initiatives, are unlikely to start a war if they are not confident of a quick victory.[15] But this is not the only reason. The Soviets are also well aware of the West's superior resources and of the potential for the Soviet empire to unravel. As a result, they have little incentive to strike against a prepared adversary. Therefore, NATO's conventional defense must appear credible enough so that in a crisis the Soviets are not tempted into adventurism by an apparently weak opponent. The NATO posture must also be as resistant as possible to neutralization by nuclear, chemical, or biological attack. Moreover, if such a force were clearly defensive in nature, it would lend support to NATO's political efforts. Such a conventional defense must focus on the Pact armor forces—the linchpin of the Pact structure for deep, fast penetration and quick victory. However, fashioning an effective defense against armor formations is no easy task.

Armored formations represent a relatively small number of discrete targets—an entire tank regiment, representing a quarter of a division's maneuver forces and covering a front several kilometers wide, has only about 150 major targets. Nevertheless, they are tough targets. Even in good visibility, aircraft are hard-pressed to engage tanks, particularly in the face of formidable Pact mobile air defense capabilities. With their mobility and hardness, tanks also are very difficult targets for artillery. A typical battlefield nuclear weapon striking a normally dispersed tank company may kill only a few of its tanks.

Pact armored formations, supported by massed artillery fire and operating under the cover of poor visibility or smoke (each Soviet tank has its own smoke generating system), can concentrate enormous firepower to shatter even a well-prepared defense.

However, Pact armor forces are not without their vulnerabilities. One prime vulnerability is their rigid command and control system. Pact tanks typically have one radio and are tightly controlled by commanders at each echelon. Maps are tightly controlled also, and are normally held only by these same commanders. The destruction of a handful of a regiment's tanks—those of its unit commanders—can cripple its operations. And these tanks are readily identified by position and external equipment, particularly multiple radio antennas.[16]

By choosing tactics of rapid penetration instead of area control, the Soviets set the stage for defenders to engage their main forces and flanks with the carefully measured feints, leverages, and thrusts of a karate defense. Even more than most other tanks, Soviet tanks stress frontal armor at the expense of side and top protection. The Soviets take the classic gamble—that shock action can overwhelm a defender before he can take advantage of the attacker's exposed flanks and overextended logistic lines, or can bring his own military and psychological resources to bear.[17] The Soviets cannot have their cake and eat it, striking deep yet retaining flank security. A moving tank column cannot afford to sweep its flanks every time a shot is fired from the side, but such shots have the potential to destroy its effectiveness by killing its commanders and neutralizing its minesweeping and air defense assets.[18] Modern weapons enable defenders to engage tank-sized targets selectively from standoff distances up to three kilometers, by both direct and indirect fire weapons.[19] Mortars firing antiarmor munitions with infrared or millimeter-wave homing sensors can wreak havoc on passing armor columns. Laser-guided weapons, smart bombs, and scatterable mines can provide significant augmentation firepower even to personnel operating behind enemy lines. Cluster bomblets and flechette ammunition are extremely effective against personnel in the open, including combat personnel at refueling or mess stops.

A tank screened by darkness, fog, rain, or smoke makes a very difficult target. But it also becomes very difficult for the crew, buttoned up in the protective armor of its vehicle, to follow what is happening outside, particularly to identify and engage flank targets. Under these conditions, tanks become very vulnerable to mines. Even simple systems of pulling mines across their route of movement can be very effective against tanks moving across hostile territory. Night or poor visibility also aids the defenders who can use radio warning nets and their superior knowledge of local terrain to choose vantage points for standoff attack. Presently, available munitions could also be specifically adapted to attack armor from the flanks. Short-range antiarmor missiles, for example, could be developed into a simple roadside-emplaced, command-detonated mine which could engage selected targets with a relatively high degree of safety for the defender. Even the standard dual-purpose 40mm round, now used with a variety of grenade launchers, could be adapted to such a role with a small firing tube. Its 2-inch armor penetration capability would make it a deadly weapon against all Pact lightly armored vehicles—personnel carriers, self-propelled artillery, tracked air defense systems, light tanks, and command vehicles. High velocity weapons in the 30mm range could also be effective against tanks, particularly from the sides. Sniper and light weapons fire can insure that armored vehicles remain buttoned up, and also preclude use of external fuel tanks.

While the Soviets possess substantial artillery assets for softening prepared NATO defenses and increasingly acknowledge the protective role of dismounted infantry in an environment of handheld precision munitions, such actions are executed at the cost of rapid offensive maneuver, the paramount element of Soviet doctrine.

Armored vehicles rely heavily on resupply of ammunition and fuel. Soviet practice has supply columns following behind armor thrusts, preferably moving at night or under conditions of poor visibility. Needless to say, such columns are extremely vulnerable to ambush. Machine guns, mortars, or artillery firing incendiary munitions could create spectacular detonations hardly conducive to improving the morale of supply convoy personnel or sustaining Soviet combat operations.

Pact operations also rely on many lightly armed signal elements, messengers, and other small support elements operating freely in their tactical rear area. FROG and SCUD missile launch platoons also disperse throughout the countryside—certainly risky since the capabilities of an entire launch section could be destroyed by one well-placed sniper shot into electronic guidance equipment or liquid-fueled SCUD missiles.

The NATO defense must also be prepared to exploit the vulnerabilities of the Pact's strategic rear area. Soviet lines of communication cross 500 miles of Poland, East Germany, and Czechoslovakia, and are vulnerable to interdiction both by disaffected elements of the local populations and by deep NATO strikes.

TWO APPROACHES

John Mearsheimer contends that NATO is in such good shape conventionally that the Soviets cannot hope to win quickly. His argument is based largely on the sterile arithmetic of frontages and force densities, and generally slights the significance of follow-on echelons and chemical capabilities. But it provides some necessary balance by underscoring the Pact's own serious problems.[20] The most serious fault in Mearsheimer's argument is his assumption that NATO responds adequately to strategic warning of an impending attack. Mearsheimer himself is acutely sensitive to the tenuous nature of this assumption. First of all, he clearly underscores this assumption in his introduction, and references Richard Betts's detailed analysis of NATO's political vulnerability in just such a situation.[21] He then stresses simultaneous mobilization throughout the body of the paper. Finally, in his closing paragraph, he reemphasizes the criticality of a prompt NATO response to warning of any Pact mobilization. Stressing the importance of prompt and concerted NATO action, however, does not make the problem disappear. In fact, even pessimistic analysts would probably agree that NATO has a reasonable chance of holding if . . . *if* warning is available and used, *if* US reinforcement is not seriously impeded, *if* chemicals are not used, *if* NATO interdictions is effective, and *if* Soviet potential problems do materialize. Because he assumes all these if's, Mearsheimer's conclusions are simply too iffy.

Another approach to the pressure for improved conventional force posture is the US Army's new concept for defense known as the AirLand Battle, and the parallel NATO emphasis on deep strike options.[22] Emphasizing precision-guided munitions and focusing on interdiction of Pact reinforcements, these efforts seek to redress many of the shortcomings of NATO's conventional defense posture.

Unfortunately, the ability of NATO to implement these initiatives is problematic. For those seeking a new security blanket, a magic technological shield is offered as a means of reducing NATO's current reliance on the nuclear umbrella. However, the success of the AirLand Battle depends heavily on NATO interdiction efforts. NATO's capability for shallow interdiction through the use of its conventional artillery, although not expansive, is likely to be adequate. But deep interdiction will depend primarily on NATO's air forces[23] and, hence, on a favorable outcome of the air battle. This prospect is uncertain in the face of a better than 2:1 Pact superiority in tactical aircraft and substantial Pact air defense assets. The Army manual which describes the AirLand Battle tersely acknowledges that "long-range weapons will be scarce."[24] Moreover, many of the deep strike weapons are still in development and will not be fielded for years to come. In addition, deep strike relies heavily on intelligence collection assets, including electronic warfare units, reconnaissance aircraft, and national technical systems.[25] In other words, it depends heavily on signal intelligence and overhead coverage. Overhead coverage is severely constrained by the darkness and poor weather, which may be normal operating conditions for days on end. Signal intelligence suffers from a general inability to pinpoint targets. It must penetrate strict Soviet radio discipline and is obviously vulnerable to deception. Data analysis relies largely on templates which, at best, direct attention to specific areas on the assumption that the enemy is following his normal procedures.[26] One is thus forced to agree with Trevor Dupuy's conclusion that target acquisition problems cast doubt on the whole concept.[27] Furthermore, in the US Army doctrine at least, deep strike emphasizes the particular effectiveness of nuclear weapons.[28] Certainly NATO would have to expect answering strikes on its own territory. Such a renewed emphasis on nuclear weapons can only reinforce Soviet claims that Eastern Europe must rely on the USSR for its security. Although the deep strike concept may offer some promise for attrition of Soviet rear echelon forces, it could easily degenerate into the "empty shell" envisioned by one European analyst—a Western strategy to which everyone pays lip service, but which fails to find genuine solutions to the challenges it faces.[29]

SEEKING AN ALTERNATIVE

Despite the shortcomings of these approaches, the premise of this paper is that it is feasible to construct an effective conventional defense which also would provide inducements for long-term positive change within the Soviet bloc. Militarily, NATO seeks, in the words of its charter, "to restore and maintain the security of the North Atlantic area" in the event of an armed attack against a member state. But the fundamental goal of the NATO states is much broader: "to safeguard the freedom, common heritage and civilization of their peoples founded on the principles of democracy, individual liberty and the rule of law." Thus, NATO seeks to develop a durable structure of international relationships, inhibiting the causes of war and promoting long-term East-West accord through the implementation of such principles as those expressed in the Helsinki Final Act: elimination of tensions and the increase of confidence between European states, economic and humanitarian cooperation, and freer circulation of information. Developing social, political, and economic approaches which will promote such change is beyond the scope of this paper. But the military means which check the Soviet threat should support, or at least not impede, the development of nonmilitary instruments of policy. The ultimate deterrent to conflict is not NATO's military posture, but the entire mosaic of political, military, social, and psychological factors which jointly inhibit the Warsaw Pact political leadership from seeking military solutions to East-West differences.

Unfortunately, because of the threat of nuclear blackmail, substantial NATO nuclear capabilities remain necessary. But *using* these capabilities to stem a Pact conventional invasion is no longer an attractive option. Only by strengthening its conventional capabilities can NATO improve its deterrent posture, while avoiding the psychological dilemma of having to choose between surrender or nuclear annihilation.[30] Furthermore, the development of a stronger but clearly defensive conventional posture could decrease Pact incentives to maintain large military forces and so improve the long-term prospects for European arms reduction.

With a population matching the Warsaw Pact's and an economic output several times as large, Western Europe clearly has the financial resources to construct its own defense. Nevertheless, West European political fragmentation, traditional economic priorities, and constrained geographic position have thwarted realization of this potential. The Pact has been able to translate its relatively modest resources into an impressive and threatening military presence considerably superior in conventional military forces.[31] But convincing the NATO members that major shifts in strategic approaches are needed is no easy task. Deterrence has worked for almost 40 years. Why expend scarce resources now to strengthen war fighting capabilities which may simply lead to widespread devastation? Europe endured such devastation in the early 1940's and does not easily suffer the prospect of facing it again. Thanks to the US nuclear guarantee, it was long able to avoid such messy questions as how to conduct a fighting withdrawal through Nurnberg or a meeting engagement on the plains of Lower Saxony.

But when the nuclear balance shifted, doubts rose in Europe. Would the United States really risk Boston for Bremen? In the past, there had been one final hope—if the unthinkable happened, perhaps the superpowers would annihilate each other and Europe would survive even the holocaust. But now that hope was lost with a new worry—nuclear war might be fought not over the heads of the Europeans, but under the feet of the superpowers. Europe might become the nuclear battlefield and the superpowers might emerge unscathed. Yet, if reducing the risk of nuclear devastation meant raising the risk of conventional devastation, the prospect was hardly an appealing one. In the final analysis, Soviet attainment of nuclear parity is forcing NATO Europe to prepare to fight if it wants to deter, to address such messy questions as Nurnberg and Lower Saxony. Yet, even serious war fighting preparations unfortunately cannot guarantee deterrence, for deterrence is ultimately based not on NATO's posture but on Soviet perceptions.[32] No one can state exactly what has deterred the Soviets to this point. Against the background of a changed military balance, what will deter the emerging Soviet leadership of the 1980's remains an unanswerable question. Nevertheless, the construction of a militarily credible *and* politically feasible defense posture, consistent with apparent European preferences for a strong and reasonably low-cost yet nonthreatening deterrent, is possible.

THE FOUR-PART DEFENSE

Now that discussions of nuclear war fighting have raised the question of potential destruction so vividly, the emotional reaction of many Europeans to the West's current nuclear strategy is easily understandable. The conventional wisdom that a nonnuclear defense of Europe is infeasible makes any reassessment all the more painful. Yet, if Europe is to deter the Soviets while reducing the risk of nuclear war, the potential for improving conventional capabilities must be examined more thoroughly. Military planners need to focus research, development, and planning on how best to do this. While NATO's emphasis on forward defense reflects the relatively confined space available for defensive maneuver, the Alliance cannot hope to stop the Pact dead at the border.[33] Hence, NATO must address the question of how to fight on its own territory with the highest probability of success. By exploiting the advantages of the defense, the lethality of modern weapons and the vulnerabilities of the Soviet military posture, NATO could build a staunch conventional defense from four fighting elements: regular combat units, Area Combat Troops (ACT's), support troops, and penetration forces.

These four elements would form a forward defense zone, a neutralization zone, and a rear defense zone. The forward defense zone would not be a wall designed to repel an invader, but rather a thicket designed to disorganize and cripple him. It would insure that penetration comes slowly at a heavy cost and that territory is not relinquished simply because Pact forces have transited it. The forward defense zone would include extensively-prepared obstacles defended by regular forces and ACT's capable of being reinforced rapidly.[34]

Regular combat units provide the primary conventional means of destroying Pact units. Initially, they would play the primary role in the forward defense zone, actively opposing initial Pact intrusions and then gradually withdrawing to conduct mobile operations in the neutralization zone. Combat engineer elements would set obstacles and minefields, supplemented by air and artillery-delivered scatterable mines[35] and area munitions. The large Pact numerical superiority means that NATO must strike a very difficult balance in the deployment of its own forces. It must have sizable regular combat units of its own, but reliance on long-distance US reinforcement must be decreased. For this reason, better liaison with French forces and contingency agreements for their employment are important.[36] NATO combat-ready maneuver units must not be placed so far forward nor tied so strongly to specific terrain that they are unable to react flexibly. Yet, NATO cannot adopt a maneuver defense which simply throws away the advantages of the defense. The overall NATO defense must be constructed so that its maneuver elements can depend on engaging Pact units under clearly favorable conditions.[37]

The responsibility for developing such favorable conditions will rest heavily on the second element of the four-part defense—the ACT's. These would be strong territorial forces, largely reservists, with two major missions: rear area security behind NATO lines, and active combat operations within overrun or penetrated areas.

They would assume primary combat responsibilities as regular combat forces were pushed out of forward areas or as battle lines blurred into vaguely defined contested zones. They would emphasize ambushes and standoff engagement of critical Pact elements, contributing to the continuous attrition and disruption of Warsaw Pact capabilities. Their own antiarmor weapons, mines, and mortars could be supplemented by artillery and close air support which, in turn, the ACT's could assist with beacon or laser designators. These efforts would concentrate on command, air defense, and mine-clearing vehicles. Area Combat Troops would neutralize Pact stragglers and make Pact efforts to establish flank security, a source of heavy Pact losses. Pact ammunition or fuel resupply and any operations involving exposed personnel would become high-risk activities.

Continuous attrition of Pact forces in the forward defense zone would greatly benefit NATO combat maneuver units. Area Combat Troops would also provide direct assistance within the neutralization zone by continuous disruption and intelligence operations.[38] At the same time, the ACT's would destroy Pact reconnaissance parties, throttling the Pact's own information-gathering capability. By exploiting the intelligence supplied by the ACT's and their disruption of Pact combat elements, NATO maneuver units could initiate controlled meeting engagements which did not sacrifice the inherent advantages of the defender.

Area Combat Troops would also destroy or contaminate supplies likely to be seized and used by Pact forces, encourage Pact desertions by providing haven to deserters, and incorporate any bypassed NATO units or personnel. In short, they would make the countryside as hostile as possible to Pact elements and as friendly as possible to NATO forces. Applying their detailed knowledge of the local region, ACT's would exploit relatively safe areas. By using prepared, well-hidden positions, they could retain at least a reporting capability for an extended period, as well as a capability to strike high value targets of opportunity. Their organization, equipment, and training would reflect the peculiarities of their operational zones, such as urban, forest, or mountain areas. By drawing on local resources and husbanding their initial ammunition supplies, they could operate for extended periods with little resupply. Where appropriate, they could also plan for wartime use of local government vehicles and other assets.[39]

By emphasizing dispersion and standoff engagements, area combat operations would decrease Pact incentives to use weapons of mass destruction. Operating elusively and having their own individual protective equipment, ACT's would make extremely poor targets for nuclear weapons and would be relatively safe from chemical or biological attack. They could also operate very effectively at night and in poor weather or on difficult terrain, conditions which can significantly hamper many other NATO elements. As a result of their ability to operate in small units and in a highly mobile and decentralized manner, they also are ideally suited for operations in urban areas.[40]

Furthermore, being reserve forces closely tied to operations within their own country, ACT's would pose a minimal external threat and so provide maximum support to NATO peacetime political and diplomatic efforts. Since they would generally operate in their own home regions, they could be mobilized on short notice. Most ACT's could have their basic equipment at home and be familiar with designated emergency rally points.

Another major consideration which makes area combat forces especially attractive is the sheer volume of military manpower which could be involved. If NATO countries in the central region followed the Norwegian example and mobilized all available current and former, active and reserve manpower resources, there would be an additional seven million troops in this critical area. West Germany, in fact, already has two million men in its General Reserve, which the International Institute for Strategic Studies does not even count in its military manpower figures because they have no concrete defense assignments.[41] It also has a Territorial Army, composed largely of reservists, which could expand to more than two hundred thousand troops within a few days of mobilization. These forces are basically area security forces, although they include six maneuver units—Home Defense Brigades—capable of reinforcing forward defense elements. The current wartime mission of the German Territorial Army calls for it to operate in the rear combat zone to maintain the operational freedom and logistic support of NATO forces. While its combat capabilities have been expanding steadily, there are no general plans for its incorporation into the NATO command structure or its employment in the forward defense zone (with the possible exception of the six Home Defense Brigades) or in overrun or contested areas.[42] Because of these reservations, the Territorial Army now fills only a relatively small portion of its potential area combat role.

A number of other European countries, including Norway, Switzerland, and Yugoslavia, have strong territorial combat forces.[43] Such forces have also been proposed for West Germany a number of times. Immediately after the war, British Air Marshal Sir John Slessor strongly advocated such a defense by supplementing active divisions with a

> highly trained semistatic Home Guard armed primarily with antitank guns with light automatics as the personal weapon. The Federal Republic . . . should be covered with a network of these units composed of local men, knowing every inch of the ground, every coppice and stream, land and side street, responsible for the defence of their own Kreis and town or village and inspired by the knowledge that they are protecting their own homes and their own kith and kin. They would be responsible for the storage and protection of landmines in peace and of laying the minefields when so directed . . . . Their job would be to block every road and destroy every tank moving across country in their zone.[44]

Similarly, George Kennan—in his 1958 Reith Lectures over the British Broadcasting Corporation—stressed territorial forces as constituting the core of resistance in overrun areas; for this he was ridiculed by Willy Brandt in the German Parliament.[45]

The question naturally arises as to why the Germans have been so wary of the concept, particularly since irregular forces in World War II tied up dozens of German divisions. Germany, of all countries, should be aware of the potential of such forces, yet has emphatically rejected their use except in rear areas. The rejection is undoubtedly tied to considerations for forward defense. The development of territorial forces implies preparations for extensive and prolonged fighting on one's own territory. The French, who have also developed strong territorial forces, try to avoid this implication by unequivocally emphasizing that their territorial forces are intended strictly for rear area security and not to repel invaders.[46] Germany, with Pact forces poised on its borders, cannot separate the two missions easily.

Territorial forces have also been faulted for their inability to conduct decisive operations against enemy forces. World War II German divisions were not defeated by irregular forces, and no one expects that territorial forces in Norway, Switzerland, or Yugoslavia would be able to repel an invasion of their countries. However, in Central Europe, territorial forces would be fighting in conjunction with sizable combat maneuver forces. As such, they would provide a greater capability than the tenacious, but essentially harassing, role performed by partisans in the past. For this reason, this paper has termed them Area Combat Troops to stress that their primary task is neither to defend territory, nor to provide a basis for long-term resistance in occupied areas. Rather, it is to conduct active combat operations.

Within the NATO rear defense zone, ACT's would have the primary responsibility for security and for guaranteeing the mobility of NATO regular combat forces. Their pervasive operational net would make it difficult for Pact diversionary elements to operate efficiently, and would provide a local combat reaction capability against penetrations or airborne/heliborne raids. Using the same tactics as in the other two zones—subjecting hostile combat elements to constant attrition and continually reporting their position—they would prepare larger Pact penetration for neutralization by NATO maneuver or combat air elements. They could also provide for local defense of critical positions.

The third major combat element of the four-part defense is support troops. These troops would maintain close liaison with ACT's, and be prepared to conduct active combat operations in conjunction with them if the tactical situation required.

In fact, support troops should be an important combat force. When drawn into active combat, every support unit should be prepared to break down into an effective infantry organization, not just rifle teams. Selected individuals should be trained in the use of the wide range of weapons available to such units, and the command group should be prepared to implement standard combat procedures, such as requesting artillery support, reporting enemy movements, and coordinating activities with adjacent units; most importantly with the ACT's. Basically, NATO support units should be prepared to exert an active presence similar to and in conjunction with the ACT's in each of the various defense zones.[47] NATO cannot afford to have large numbers of troops unable to fight effectively against Pact units.

The final NATO combat element should be penetration forces intended to strike within Pact territory, interdicting Pact reinforcements, and taking the battle to enemy territory in order to avoid the self-deterrent effect of being prepared to fight only on NATO territory. The air, missile, and artillery strikes envisioned by AirLand Battle and NATO deep strike preparations have the potential to seriously disrupt Pact combat unit movements, transportation nets, airfields, logistics, and command and control.[48] At the same time, NATO Long Range Reconnaissance Patrols and light infantry elements can create maximum confusion in Pact tactical rear areas.[49] They are also needed to collect the intelligence which deep strikes require and which signal intelligence and overhead coverage cannot adequately provide. These units should be prepared for insertion immediately upon the outbreak of hostilities. Operating within Pact territory, their activities would certainly be more restricted than those of the ACT's, but they would exploit the same Pact vulnerabilities—rigidly centralized command and control, vulnerable resupply columns, and dispersed small elements. By disrupting and reporting on Pact operations beyond the NATO border, they would aid the NATO military efforts significantly.

Within the Pact strategic rear area, NATO Special Forces would operate in conjunction with psychological appeals to disaffected elements of the indigenous populations. Regular combat forces could also be used to execute raids and diversionary attacks throughout Pact territory. By increasing the potential for internal disorder, they could provide additional disincentives for Pact operations against NATO and add an important dimension to NATO military capabilities. They would show that, even under nonnuclear conditions, any Pact initiation of hostilities would result in fighting and destruction on Pact territory.

Since such elements add an inherently offensive capability to the NATO posture, their type and size must be carefully measured. They must be strong enough to add imponderables into any Warsaw Pact assessment, yet should not be so strong that they pose a significant threat in their own right. For this reason, deep strike options cannot be the mainstay of the NATO defense—they run counter to the long-term thrust of NATO policy, and certainly against the grain of NATO Europe's search for improved relations with the East.

There is no military solution to this dilemma which is, after all, not a military dilemma. Military strategy cannot be fitted into a larger political strategy when the latter is only vaguely articulated. NATO's political strategy has to emphasize political solutions to East-West problems, but at the same time stress that a Pact attack will inevitably result in devastation within Eastern Europe. In the 1980's, the security of Western Europe will depend increasingly on the capitals of Eastern Europe, on NATO's ability to discourage their support of any Soviet plans for military action.

REBUILDING NATO DEFENSE

The concepts sketched above outline an approach to a tough conventional defense which emphasizes the interaction of regular combat maneuver forces and Area Combat Troops within NATO territory and the broadening of NATO capabilities to strike into Pact territory. Regular combat units would be able to conduct a much more efficient maneuver defense because they would be engaging Pact units which already suffered attrition and disruption by ACT's and possibly by NATO penetration elements. Furthermore, continued improvement in NATO-French military cooperation could ease the requirement for rapid US reinforcement. NATO support troops must also improve their capability for active combat so that they can fight effectively in conjunction with ACT's against Pact airborne and airmobile forces or armor penetrations. Finally, NATO penetration elements should provide a capability to direct combat operations into the Pact's own territory to exploit significant Pact vulnerabilities.

One should not conclude that Area Combat Troops will be a panacea for European defense.[50] Significant resources invested in regular forces and careful planning will remain necessary if NATO is to fashion effective defenses.

While Area Combat Troops do not provide a simple answer, they do offer NATO forces in Central Europe a means of achieving a tough conventional defense using available resources. Furthermore, their essentially defensive posture would not threaten Eastern Europe or the Soviet Union. The area combat approach would also reduce the pressure for early resort to nuclear weapons and could free more US forces for engagements elsewhere, including flank reinforcement or penetration missions into Pact territory.

Evolution in this direction could build on a number of developments already in progress. First, the role of the German Territorial Army could be broadened to include closer liaison with NATO units and a gradual assumption of territorial combat responsibilities, perhaps initially in difficult terrain or in particularly critical urban areas. Second, continued development of antiarmor weapons and the adaptation of these weapons to what is likely to be a more dispersed and fast-moving battlefield environment would contribute significantly to a general improvement in the overall military posture of NATO. Third, growing Franco-German military cooperation[51] could ease the pressure for rapid US reinforcement. Finally, the United States has activated two Ranger battalions and, in conjunction with AirLand Battle concepts, is giving more thought to the use of these forces in the Pact rear area or on difficult NATO terrain.[52]

The forward defense belt of NATO needs to be stiffened by more prepared obstacles, more dispersed gun positions, and more extensive mine warfare preparations. On a larger scale, the Alliance must develop a comprehensive East European policy which is in harmony with the evolution of the NATO defense posture. An essential goal of this policy should be to reduce East European incentives to join in a Soviet move westward. It is time to reverse the train of thought which concedes all the advantages to the Warsaw Pact. Rather, NATO should be prepared to exploit its potential to destroy a conventional attack by conventional means.

Taken as a whole, the NATO military posture should add as many imponderables as possible into Soviet assessments of military operations in Central Europe.[53] Invading forces should expect constant attrition of critical elements, uncertain resupply and an ever-present potential for sudden direct engagement on unfavorable terms.

Few developments could advance long-term prospects for stability in Europe as much as turning the Soviet armor goliath into a white elephant, a mammoth but unusable millstone around the neck of Pact economic and social development. Paired with an essentially defensive NATO posture, this would undermine the Pact justification for excessive standing military forces and discourage the current high levels of Soviet direct military expenditures in the European theater. By disabusing the Soviets of any notion of military or even political utility of high force levels in Europe,[54] a credible NATO conventional defense could be combined with the carrots of economic and social exchanges to institutionalize a Soviet shift to peaceful social competition and eventual cooperation in addressing the wider problems confronting Europe. In the final analysis, an effective defense policy must be combined with political, military, economic, and psychological factors into a comprehensive allied strategy. Otherwise, not only will problems of cohesion continue to plague NATO, but clear criteria for evaluating defense programs will remain out of reach.[55]

ENDNOTES

1. Earl Ravenal in "Counterforce and Alliance," *International Security,* Spring 1982, p. 27, offers a thoughtful discussion of the intertwined concerns of deterrence, cost, and credibility. Concern over the implications of an emphasis on nuclear weapons was already being expressed in the 1940's, but it was simply ignored (Eugene Rabinowitch, "Forewarned—But Not Forearmed," in *The Atomic Age,* ed. by Morton Grodzins and Eugene Rabinowitch, New York: Simon & Schuster, 1965, pp. 137-143). For a current European view on nuclear weapons as "a cheap way out," see Pierre Lellouche, "Does NATO Have a Future?," *The Washington Quarterly,* Summer 1982, p. 47. See also Sam Nunn, "Saving the Alliance," *The Washington Quarterly,* Summer 1982, p. 21.

2. McGeorge Bundy, *et al.,* "Nuclear Weapons and the Atlantic Alliance," *Foreign Affairs,* Spring 1982, pp. 757 and 765.

3. Michael Howard, "The Relevance of Traditional Strategy," *Foreign Affairs,* January 1973, p. 261.

4. Karl Kaiser, *et al.,* "Nuclear Weapons and the Preservation of Peace," *Foreign Affairs,* Summer 1982, pp. 1157-1170.

5. Gary Eifried, "Russian CW: Our Achilles' Heel, Europe," *Army,* December 1979, pp. 24-28; Matthew Meselson and Julian Perry Robinson, "Chemical Warfare and Chemical Disarmament," *Scientific American,* April 1980, p. 38; "Aspin Reports on Sverdlovsk Blast," *Defense Week,* June 30, 1980, p. 1; and US Department of State, "Chemical Warfare in Southeast Asia and Afghanistan: An Update," Special Report No. 104, November 1982.

6. For a detailed discussion of the strategic imperatives of the forward defense, see Colin S. Gray, *Defending NATO Europe,* Hudson Institute Report DNA-4567F, November 1977, pp. 8-16.

7. Gary L. Guertner, "Nuclear War in Suburbia," *Orbis,* Spring 1982, pp. 49-70, and Paul Bracken, "Urban Sprawl and the NATO Defense," *Survival,* November/December 1976, pp. 254-260.

8. "Soviet Airborne Forces," *Aerospace International,* March-April 1973, p. 13; David C. Schlachter and Fred J. Stubbs, "Special Operations Forces: Not Applicable?," *Military Review,* February 1978, pp. 23-24; Robert Close, *Europe Without Defense?*, New York: Pergamon Press 1979, pp. 183-184; C. N. Donnelly, "Operations in the Enemy Rear," *International Defense Review,* No. 1, 1980, pp. 35-41; and C. N. Donnelly, "The Soviet Operational Maneuver Group: A New Challenge for NATO," *Military Review,* March 1983, pp. 43-60.

9. For example, the current Army manual (FM 29-77, June 20, 1980) on the Supply and Transportation Company in a separate combat brigade does not even mention fighting armor. This is slowly being changed, as in the present training and evaluation program for the Support Battalion Headquarters and Headquarters Company in separate brigades (ARTEP 29-156, April 7, 1982) which addresses defense against light armor vehicles and the need for liaison with artillery and combat air support units—certainly steps in the right direction.

10. Of the 17 combat-ready divisions potentially available for NATO reinforcement, 13 are from the United States (and 3 others are French); some smaller units are also available. See John M. Collins and Anthony H. Cordesman, *Imbalance of Power,* San Rafael, California: Praesidio Press, 1978, pp. 284-287. For analysis of the problems in moving these US reinforcements and the need for

their rapid support, see D. M. O. Miller, "Strategic Factors Affecting a Soviet Conventional Attack in Western Europe," *International Defense Review*, No. 6, 1978, pp. 858-859; "US Ground Forces: Already Too Large to Fight," *The Defense Monitor*, November 1978, pp. 4-6; Robert Lucas Fischer, *Defending the Central Front: The Balance of Forces*, Adelphi Papers No. 127, Autumn 1976, pp. 18-25; John Fialka, "Ill-Equipped, Undermanned US Army is Decimated in 'Nifty Nugget' Exercise," *The Washington Star*, November 2, 1979, pp. 1, 2; and Daniel Gans, "'Fight Outnumbered and Win' . . . Against What Odds?," *Military Review*, December 1980, pp. 31-46.

11. Short of war, there can be no definitive determination of this point, but assessments give little basis for Soviet confidence. See Dale R. Herspring and Ivan Volgyes, "Political Reliability in the Eastern European Warsaw Pact Armies," *Armed Forces and Society*, Winter 1980, pp. 270-296.

12. See, for example, George Kennan's comments in *Memoirs: 1950-1963*, Boston: Little, Brown and Company, 1972, pp. 97-100, on agitation within the United States for support of intervention in East Europe.

13. Strobe Talbott, ed. and trans., *Khrushchev Remembers*, London: Little, Brown and Company, 1970, p. 393; see also pp. 361-364.

14. For a current view on offensive versus defensive orientations, see Jonathan Alford, "NATO's Conventional Forces and the Soviet Mobilization Potential," *NATO Review*, June 1980, pp. 18-22. For commentary on East European views, see Jack E. Owen, Jr., *Political and Strategic Assessment of the US Military Commitment to NATO*, Annapolis: US Naval Academy, May 21, 1973, pp. 92-96.

15. See Benjamin S. Lambeth, "Uncertainties for the Soviet War Planner," *International Security*, Vol. 7, Winter 1982/1983, pp. 139-166.

16. US Defense Intelligence Agency, *Soviet Tank Battalion Tactics*, Report DDB-1120-10-80, November 1980, pp. 3-5. The commanders' tanks are critical nodes in the radio nets, and these are the only tanks that do not move in groups.

17. John Keegan, "Soviet Blitzkrieg: Who Wins?," *Harper's*, May 1982, pp. 46-53; Guertner, pp. 61-62; "Quick Europe War Called Soviet Aim," *The New York Times*, October 10, 1982.

18. The Soviets are clearly aware of the difficulty and have emphasized increasingly the role of dismounted infantry in a combined arms attack. Dismounting, however, slows the attack.

19. George H. Heilmeier, "NATO Defense Technology Outlines," *Aviation Week and Space Technology*, July 17, 1978, pp. 64-66; Palmer Osborn and William Bowen, "How to Defend Western Europe," *Fortune*, October 9, 1978, pp. 152-153; antitank capabilities are critical, and this is an area of high technological emphasis. See Robert Kennedy, "Precision ATGMs and NATO Defense," *Orbis*, Winter 1979, pp. 897-927; John J. Mearsheimer, "Precision-Guided Munitions and Conventional Deterrence," *Survival*, March/April 1979, pp. 69-71; John Marriott, "Anti-Tank Warfare," *NATO's Fifteen Nations*, May 1979, pp. 61-68; Seymour Deitchman, *New Technology and Military Power*, Boulder: Westview Press, 1979; Paul F. Walker, "Precision-Guided Weapons," *Scientific American*, August 1981, pp. 37-45; and Benjamin Schemmer, "NATO's New Strategy: Defend Forward But STRIKE DEEP!," *Armed Forces Journal International*, November 1982, p. 65.

20. John J. Mearsheimer, "Why the Soviets Can't Win Quickly in Central Europe," *International Security*, Summer 1982, pp. 3-39.

21. Richard K. Betts, "Surprise Attack: NATO's Political Vulnerability," Spring 1981, pp. 117-149.

22. US Department of the Army, *Operations, FM 100-5,* August 20, 1982, Chapter 7, Schemmer, pp. 50-68.

23. *Operations,* p. 7-13.

24. *Ibid.,* p. 7-14.

25. *Ibid.,* p. 6-4.

26. *Ibid.,* pp. 6-7, 6-8.

27. Trevor N. Dupuy, "Why Deep Strike *Won't* Work," *Armed Forces Journal International,* January 1983, p. 57.

28. *Operations,* p. 7-15.

29. Lellouche, p. 51.

30. Francois de Rose, "Inflexible Response," *Foreign Affairs,* Fall 1982, pp. 141-142.

31. A stark assessment of the growing Warsaw Pact relative strength is in Justin Galen, "Restoring the NATO-Warsaw Pact Balance: 'The Art of the Impossible'," *Armed Forces Journal International,* September 1978, pp. 32-33. See also William Schneider, Jr., "Soviet General Purpose Forces," *Orbis,* Spring 1977, pp. 99-105; Leslie H. Gelb, "Questions and Answers on the Military Balance in Europe," *The New York Times,* April 11, 1982, p. E-3.

32. Robert Jarvis, "Deterrence and Perception," *International Security,* Winter 1982/1983, pp. 3-30; see also Ravenal, p. 36.

33. See T. N. Dupuy, "The Nondebate Over How Army Should Fight," *Army,* June 1982, pp. 34-45.

34. The use of fortified positions has been neglected by NATO, partly because the Maginot Line misleadingly serves as a symbol of their uselessness and partly due to a reluctance to emphasize the East-West border. For discussions of the potential security gains from fortifications, see Keegan, pp. 52-53; Joshua M. Epstein, "On Conventional Deterrence in Europe: Questions of Soviet Confidence," *Orbis,* Spring 1982, pp. 85-86; Waldo D. Freeman, Jr., *NATO Central Region Forward Defense,* National Security Affairs Issue Paper No. 81-3, Washington: National Defense University, 1981, pp. 7-8, 11-14; William O. Staudenmaier, "Some Strategic Implications of Fighting Outnumbered on the NATO Battlefield," *Military Review,* May 1980, pp. 45-46; Raymond E. Bell, Jr., "Fighting From Fortified Battle Positions," *Army,* July 1979, pp. 34-39; and Robert Komer, "Is Conventional Defense of Europe Feasible?," *Naval War College Review,* September-October 1982, p. 83.

35. Mine warfare also has been a badly neglected component of the NATO posture. Recent developments have significantly increased its potential for slowing any Pact attack. See Michael A. Andrews, "Tank Delivered Scatterable Mines," *Military Review,* December 1978, pp. 34-39, and Martin B. Chase, "Scatterable Mines," *Army Research, Development and Acquisition Magazine,* March-April 1980, pp. 6-9.

36. Komer (page 84), among others, stressed the importance of cooperation with the French. Such cooperation is consistent with current French defense policy. See Peter J. Barger, "The Course of French Defense Policy," *Parameters,* September 1982, pp. 19-26.

37. See John J. Mearsheimer, "Maneuver, Mobile Defense, and the NATO Central Front," *International Security,* Winter 1981/1982, pp. 104-122, for a detailed discussion of the dangers of adopting a traditional mobile defense.

38. Although ACT's would play only a secondary role in the forward defense zone, they could have primary responsibility for sectors with more difficult terrain, urban belts, critical strongpoints, and dug-in artillery or air defense positions. In those areas where maneuver elements were conducting active operations, ACT's would provide liaison teams and assist with the detailed knowledge of the local area.

39. Such a development of Area Combat Troops would be compatible with the "forest infantry" and "blocking divisions" advocated by Steven Canby in "Mutual Force Reductions: A Military Perspective," *International Security,* Winter 1978, p. 130. See also his other articles: "Dumping Nuclear Counterforce Incentives: Correcting NATO's Inferiority in Conventional Military Strength," *Orbis,* Spring 1975, pp. 54-55; and "Territorial Defense in Europe," *Armed Forces and Society,* Fall 1980, pp. 51-67; William E. Simons, *Some Thoughts on Future European Defense,* Rand Report P.6188, August 1978, pp. 25-26; William O. Staudenmaier, "Territorial Defense: An Ace in the Hole for NATO," *Army,* February 1978, pp. 35-38 (with comments by Daniel D. Plant in *Army,* May 1978, p. 2, stressing the usefulness of these forces, particularly in the enemy rear area); Close, p. 219 (stressing their use in forested or urban area); Walter Stutzle, "The Impact of New Conventional Weapon Technology on NATO Military Doctrine and Organization," *New Conventional Weapons and East-West Security, Part 1,* Adelphi Paper No. 144, Spring 1978, pp. 26-27; and Frederick Sowery, "An Unconventional Approach to Defense Resources," *Survival,* November/December 1982, pp. 252-259.

40. For analysis of urban warfare under current conditions, see Bracken. Also: P. H. Vigor, "Fighting in Built-Up Areas: A Soviet View—Part I," *Journal of the Royal United Services Institute,* June 1977, pp. 331-347; C. N. Donnelly, "Fighting in Built-Up Areas: A Soviet View—Part II," *Journal of the Royal United Services Institute,* September 1977, pp. 63-67; "Soviet Techniques for Combat in Built-Up Areas," *International Defense Review,* No. 2/77, pp. 238-242; and US Army Science Board, Final Report, *Ad Hoc Group on Military Operations in Built-Up Areas (MOBA),* Washington, 1978.

41. See *The Military Balance 1979-1980,* p. 25, and Rudolph Woller, ed., *Reservists-Partners at Home and Abroad,* Bonn: Wehr and Wissen, 1978, p. 8. The assessment that NATO Europe could or should improve its reserve utilization is a very common one: see Kenneth Hunt, *The Alliance and Europe: Part III: Defense With Fewer Men,* Adelphi Paper No. 98, Summer 1973, pp. 31-32; Close, pp. 195, 219; Fischer, pp. 35-40; and Rudolph Woller, *Warsaw Pact Reserve Systems,* Munchen: Bernard and Graefe Verlag, 1978, pp. 20-21.

42. *White Paper 1979,* Bonn: Federal Minister of Defense, September 4, 1979, pp. 154-156. For one approach to expanding the capabilities of West Germany's Territorial Army, see Robert Kennedy, "NATO Defense Posture in an Environment of Strategic Parity and Precision Weaponry," in *Strategies, Alliances and Military Power: Changing Roles,* Leyden, The Netherlands: A. W. Sijthoff, 1977.

43. For descriptions of these forces, see Adam Roberts, *Nations in Arms,* New York: Praeger Publishers, 1976, Chapters 3, 6, and 7.

44. Cited in Horst Menderhausen, *Territorial Defense in NATO and non-NATO Europe,* Rand Report R-1184-ISA, February 1973, p. 37. See also: Udo Philipp, "NATO Strategy Under Discussion in Bonn," *International Defense Review,* No. 9, 1980, pp. 1367-1371.

45. *Encounters With Kennan,* Totowa, New Jersey: Frank Cass and Co., Ltd., 1979, pp. 24, 66.

46. Pierre Michel, "La Nouvelle Orientation de la Defense Operationnelle du Territoire," *Defense Nationale,* January 1978, p. 42.

47. Edward A. Corcoran, "Support Troops in Combat Operations," *Army Logistician,* January-February 1978, pp. 18-23.

48. The Warsaw Pact logistics infrastructure is assessed as an area of potentially disastrous shortcomings. See Jacquelyn K. Davis and Robert L. Pfaltzgraff, Jr., *Soviet Theater Strategy: Implications for NATO,* United States Strategic Institute Report 78-1, p. 44. See also C. N. Donnelly, "Rear Support for the Soviet Ground Forces," *International Defense Review,* No. 3, 1979, pp. 345-349; and "Tactical Problems Facing the Soviet Army," *International Defense Review,* No. 9, 1978, p. 1410; Graham H. Turbiville, "Soviet Logistic Support for Ground Operations," *Military Review,* July 1976, pp. 34-38; and Richard P. Clayberg, *The Problem of Soviet Vulnerabilities,* Carlisle Barracks, Pennsylvania: Strategic Studies Institute, December 30, 1977.

49. Henry G. Gole, "Bring Back the LRRP," *Military Review,* October 1981, pp. 2-10.

50. Training is a constant problem in all the countries with large territorial reserve forces. Although this problem can be eased by relatively simple-to-operate weapons and by a high degree of individual specialization, constant work is needed to maintain the proficiency of territorial reservists. Supply would also require careful planning as Area Combat Troops may well have to rely on their initial supplies and caches for an extended period.

51. "Paris-Bonn Military Ties: A Time for Reappraisal," *The New York Times,* October 20, 1982.

52. See "The Employment of Non-Mechanized Infantry," *Journal of the Royal United Services Institute,* December 1980, pp. 56-69.

53. The importance of uncertainties to a deterrent posture can hardly be overstressed. See Stanley Sienkiewicz, "Observations on the Impact of Uncertainty in Strategic Analysis," *World Politics,* October 1979, pp. 90-110; Daniel O. Graham, *A New Strategy for the West,* Washington: The Heritage Foundation, 1977, pp. 49-50.

54. The political use of Soviet forces is often seen as more threatening than their actual military use. See Robert Art's commentary, "To What Ends Military Power?," *International Security,* Spring 1980, pp. 3-35, on the "swaggering" use of military force.

55. Edward Heath, "10 Precepts for a Strategy," *The New York Times,* March 19, 1980, p. A27; Wolfgang W. E. Samuel, "The Impossible Task—Defense Without Relevant Strategy," *Air University Review,* March-April 1980, pp. 15-25; Michael Howard, "The Forgotten Dimensions of Strategy," *Foreign Affairs,* Summer 1979, pp. 975-986.

11

THE ONCE AND FUTURE QUEST: EUROPEAN ARMS CONTROL—ISSUES AND PROSPECTS

William P. Boyd

INTRODUCTION

"And they shall beat their swords into plowshares and their spears into pruning hooks . . . ." This quote from the Biblical scriptures reflects a quest for disarmament as old as Isaiah. Despite various false starts and frustrations in this quest, the goal continues to capture man's imagination.

The current initiatives in East-West arms control have their genesis in the late 1960's with the beginning of the Strategic Arms Limitations Talks (SALT), the latest initiative in a movement that began in the mid-19th century which has been concerned with the growth of the destructive power of weapons. The several Geneva Conventions, beginning in 1864; the Hague Conventions; the League of Nations Covenant and the UN Charter, as well as the 1925 Geneva Protocol on chemical and biological warfare; the 1922 and 1930 Naval Treaties of London; and other efforts were all designed, in part, to curtail the development and the use of weapons so as to decrease the likelihood of war, and to increase the possibility of restraint and humanitarian conduct should war occur.

By the late 1960's, the proliferation of Soviet and American nuclear forces and the continued confrontation of NATO and Warsaw Pact forces in Europe sparked a new recognition by statesmen of the need for negotiations directed toward a peaceful resolution of issues between the superpowers. Actually, the recognition of this need had been developing for over a decade. It started with the Antarctic Treaty of 1959 and was followed by the "Hot Line" and Partial Test Ban Treaties of 1963, the Outer Space Treaty of 1967, and the Nonproliferation Treaty of 1968. The continuing efforts toward peaceful resolutions by more direct and specific negotiations are the basis for the analyses of this paper.

We will examine the factors that encourage continued efforts at arms control and the reduction of tensions as well as those which serve as impediments to the successful conclusion of arms agreements in Europe. We will also review and analyze what could be called the three major efforts toward this end, namely: the Conference on Security and Cooperation in Europe (CSCE); the conference on the Mutual Reduction of Forces and Armaments and Associated Measures in Central Europe; and the talks on Intermediate-Range Nuclear Forces (INF) currently underway in Geneva.

FACTORS ENCOURAGING ARMS CONTROL

A number of factors compel the United States, the nations of Europe, and the Soviet Union to seek agreements on limiting armaments in Europe.

Historical Conditioning. Henry Kissinger, addressing the impact of historical experiences on nation-states, once noted:

> The more elementary the experience, the more profound its impact on a nation's interpretation of the present in light of the past. It is even possible for a nation to undergo an experience so shattering that it becomes the prisoner of its past.[1]

In some ways much of the impetus for arms control in Western Europe today is driven by ghosts of the past. From the wars of

Louis XIV through the Napoleonic expansion, to the terrible carnage of the conflicts of this century, the horrors of war have conditioned the people of Europe. The invention and prolific deployment of the nuclear weapon, however, has added a new and awesome dimension to modern warfare. The potential for "Armageddon" is now a reality and has greatly reinforced the Western hope of establishing a mechanism that would preclude the possibility of another war, incredibly more devastating, in Europe. As a result, stability in crises as well as control of the arms race have become important objectives to be sought through the mechanism of limitations on armaments.

The Soviet attitude toward arms control, conditioned by militant and revolutionary ideology along with an aggregate of complex emotions—zenophobia, suspicion, fear of internal upheavals, and so forth—also has been influenced by the destructive experiences of history.[2] Military invasions from the time of Genghis Khan and the Mongols to Hitler's Germany not only have affected the Soviet view of the world but also have colored Soviet judgment on defense needs and the potential utility of compromise and accommodation.

In the East, the Soviet leadership traditionally has seen the Chinese as a threat. China and the USSR share a 4,500 mile border (a significant portion of which is in dispute), along which the Soviet Union now has stationed 47 divisions.[3] Therefore, it is not surprising that at a time when Soviet-Chinese political and ideological differences were approaching their zenith, the Soviet Union was actively pursuing detente with the West. Indeed, concern over the possibility of confronting adversaries on two fronts may well have driven the USSR to seek arms agreements with the West, if for no other reason than to free troops for deployment to the Far East.

In the West, heavy losses to the Germans during the First World War and the swift march to Moscow by numerically inferior Nazi forces during the Second Word War have undoubtedly left their indelible imprint on the Soviet psyche. Thus, it is likely that Soviet leaders have become conditioned to an uncertainty over how much is enough military force and continue to remain concerned over any resurgence of German military power.

Soviet leaders also seem to be aware of the potentially catastrophic consequences of nuclear war. Indeed, as early as 1961 Khrushchev warned that "within 60 days of an atomic attack 500 million to 750 million people could perish." Departing from the Stalinist inevitability of war between capitalism and communism, he concluded that "sober calculation of the inevitable consequence of nuclear war is an indispensable requirement for pursuing a consistent policy of preventing war."[4] Since Khrushchev's statement in 1961, one apparent and clearly understandable principal aim of Soviet policy has been the avoidance of nuclear war.[5]

While certain identifiable common threads run between European (East and West) and Soviet views of the role of European armament—particularly nuclear weapons—and the political exigencies of East-West relations, certain clearly divergent perspectives characterize the American view. The impacts of the markedly different historical experiences and geographic locations must be understood if one is to appreciate the areas of contention between the United States and its European allies. On one hand, the allies' search for national identity—stretching back as much as a millenium and fashioned by their participation in and recovery from numerous wars and their experiences with numerous hegemonic states, Spain in the past, the Soviet Union today—has developed into a long-term and cosmic view of the vagaries of history and their place within it. In short, the Europeans appreciate and are reconciled to the undeniable importance of politics and the indeterminancy of national life. They recognize that technological innovations such as exotic weapons may affect national developments but do not necessarily convey permanent advantages. The roles of politics, economics, law and social convention are viewed as primary dimensions of international politics that coexist with national military power.

On the other hand, the geographical isolation of the United States, its relatively brief history yet rapid economic development and its industrial might are among the factors that have fostered a short-term perspective that places great confidence in the efficacy of technological solutions to the problems of states. Moreover, the United States has strong beliefs in the notion that politics is an anathema that is counterproductive to progress and in the assurance that virtue as well as the prerogative of leadership reside on the US side of the Atlantic. Hence, it should not come as a surprise that the United States places primary emphasis upon defense rather than deterrence (as emphasized by the Europeans) and becomes easily exasperated with its recalcitrant allies who refuse to defer to its automatic leadership, who resist US exhortations to increase their defense budgets, and who take ambivalent positions on their 1979 decision to deploy the 572 INF missiles if arms control progress with the Soviet Union is not forthcoming at Geneva.[6]

Another interesting issue between the United States and its allies is their differing perspectives on the role of nuclear weapons. Because of asymmetry of conventional forces favoring the Warsaw Pact (WP), the Western allies desire to retain a relatively low nuclear threshold as a threat to WP aggression. Notwithstanding, there has been growing sentiment in the United States that the United States and its allies must augment and modernize their conventional military assets in this age of theater and strategic parity to maintain the credibility of NATO's flexible response doctrine and *raise* the nuclear threshold so as to avoid nuclear holocaust.

This leads to a concern on the part of some in Western Europe about whether, and under what circumstances, the United States would use nuclear weapons in the defense of Europe. The ability of the United States to provide Western Europe with a nuclear umbrella and its willingness to use nuclear weapons for the defense of Europe were from the beginning the cornerstone of the Western Alliance. By the early 1960's, the Soviet Union, however, had gained a second strike capability, at which point the credibility of the US deterrent became questionable.[7] Would the United States risk losing its cities if it launched a nuclear strike in response to a Soviet conventional attack on NATO? Accordingly, Europeans worried that since the USSR had gained strategic nuclear parity, the United States would be less likely to use its nuclear weapons to defend Western Europe against a WP attack should the need arise.[8]
This also drew Western European attention to the distorted balance in theater forces.[9] By the mid-1970's, the Soviet Union was fielding the SS-20, and the Backfire bomber had long been a concern to NATO defense planners. The NATO response was the "dual-track" decision in December 1979 to deploy in Western Europe ground-launched cruise missiles (GLCM) and Pershing II, both capable of striking the USSR. While this decision was hailed as evidence of NATO solidarity, it reinforced concern in some quarters of Western European public opinion about the decoupling

of US strategic interests from those of its European allies.[10] This concern was not new. SALT I and II had raised the issue of reducing the US Forward Based System (FBS) (missiles, land- and sea-based aircraft, and missile-carrying submarines in Scotland and Spain). While the FBS never became a part of SALT, the discussions had raised fears among Europeans that the United States might be trying to detach its nuclear deterrent forces in Western Europe from the US strategic nuclear deterrence on which Western Europe still depended for its ultimate security.[11] The point here seems to be that any change in nuclear deterrence stands the chance of causing a fear in Western Europeans of decoupling and raising the nuclear threshold.

Western Europeans, aware that any large-scale conventional conflict on the continent would result in great devastation, have long since pressed for a policy of pure nuclear deterrence. Under this concept, every WP act of aggression would be met with strategic retaliation. The United States, conscious of the risks such a strategy implies (i.e., for US cities and population), has sought a more flexible approach.[12] The United States clearly is concerned about escalation control. If deterrence fails, conflict should be contained at the lowest possible level and response should be designed to meet aggression with equal force. Western Europe has accepted the concept of flexible response in politics, but it is not comfortable with it. While Western Europe is also concerned about escalation control, it sees the best deterrence to be the threat of strategic retaliation against the USSR. And so, within the Western alliance there are different opinions between the United States and its European allies on nuclear strategy and how best to defend Western Europe. These opinions, however, generally have been kept below the political surface. There has been encouragement for negotiations to reduce arms and, thereby, reduce tension and, hopefully, the probability that NATO would be confronted with a decision on nuclear escalation.

The existence of different interpretations of the Soviet threat, deterrence, the efficacy of detente, and other difficult issues within NATO should not lead one to conclude that the United States and its allies do not retain powerful cultural and economic bonds and share mutual interests in the perpetuation of a Western community. Nor should one infer that NATO does not share with the Soviet

Union and its Warsaw Pact allies an all too recent and vivid recollection of the horrors of war, a desire to limit financial costs of defense, and attempts to bring some calculability to their respective force planning efforts to hedge against one side's technical breakthrough as well as to reduce perceived weaknesses that could trigger nuclear conflict. Also, the strength of nuclear-freeze and peace movements in the United States, Western Europe, and increasingly in Eastern Europe,[13] as well as European interests in continuing to enjoy the economic, cultural and social fruits of detente, make the control and limitation of European armaments, particularly nuclear systems, quite an attractive goal for all parties.

Force Asymmetries. From the Western perspective, the first and, perhaps, overriding factor encouraging the pursuit of arms negotiations has been the perception of most Western defense planners of a persistent and potentially destabilizing imbalance of forces in Europe. Since the early days of the Atlantic alliance, Western defense planners have struggled with attempts to offset what they saw as a preponderance of Soviet conventional forces on the continent of Europe. This was accomplished first through a reliance on the clearly superior US strategic arsenal and later through a reliance on Western superiority of theater nuclear forces. These forces were not only capable of destroying Soviet conventional military formations, but also posed a threat of escalation to a still somewhat superior US strategic force.[14] The advent of strategic parity and the continued growth of Soviet theater nuclear capabilities, however, has altered the deterrent equation and heightened concern over the stability of the current balance of forces in Europe should a serious crisis occur. As a result, the West has sought through arms control negotiations to reduce the Warsaw Pact advantage in conventional forces as well as prevent a further shift in the balance of theater nuclear and strategic forces.

Defense Costs. Another factor encouraging arms control in Europe is the cost of defense. Generally, Europeans as well as Americans have been loath to spend large sums of money on defense. In fact, it could be argued that the prime reason for the long-standing imbalance of conventional forces has been the cost associated with any real attempt at matching those of the Soviet Union and Warsaw Pact. In the immediate post-World War II era, the demands of recovery and reconstruction seemed to preclude the kinds of expenditures demanded by the Lisbon decision of the North Atlantic Council in February 1952, i.e., to improve NATO conventional capability significantly. Nuclear weapons seemed to offer "more bang for the buck" and, thus, appeared to provide a cost-effective deterrent at a time when Europe was hard pressed to expand economically.[15]

By the early 1960's, however, Soviet advances in medium-, intermediate-, and intercontinental-range ballistic missiles (MRBM/IRBM/ICBM) seemed to presage an era of declining US nuclear superiority. In Washington, recognition of an impending nuclear parity was marked by a reemphasis on the need to shore-up NATO conventional defenses. The doctrine which issued from a number of studies and pronouncements during the Kennedy Administration became known as the doctrine of *flexible response.* While this doctrine was designed to contain a conflict at the lowest possible level, it nevertheless became a euphemism for conventional improvements.

European reaction to this new doctrine was mixed. A number of Europeans were concerned that the new doctrine might be the first step of a subtle US attempt to reduce the risk of involving the American mainland in the devastation that might accompany a full-scale nuclear war in defense of Europe, i.e., a decoupling of US strategic interests from those of its European allies. Most Europeans, however, as Raymond Aaron has noted, were "spontaneously hostile" for economic reasons to increases in the size of the NATO conventional forces.[16]

Thus, while NATO formally accepted the new doctrine, Europeans continued to oppose, as they had in the past, efforts designed to produce conventional forces to match those of the Warsaw Pact. Indeed, even in the United States the cost of European defense remained an issue and was a driving force behind the Mansfield "Sense-of-the-Senate" Resolution in 1971 to reduce US forces in Europe.[17]

By the early to mid-1970's, with the clear emergence of parity at the strategic level and an impending theater nuclear parity, European and American defense establishments, once again, began to focus on ways of improving the NATO conventional defenses.[18] To many Western defense specialists the absence of an adequate conventional defense in an age of strategic and theater parity appeared to leave NATO without a credible deterrent to conventional attack. Nevertheless, the crisis in energy and national economics along with the multiple demands of competing domestic sectors of European as well as the American economies constrained the growth of Western conventional and nuclear forces and continued to add impetus to efforts to achieve a balance of military capabilities in Europe.

Unlike democratic societies which do not always have the option, totalitarian societies will make whatever sacrifice they can to provide themselves with defense forces of their choosing. Even so, the huge cost of defense, undoubtedly, has had an effect on the Soviet Union. Moscow spends a considerably greater percentage of its Gross National Product (GNP) on defense than does the United States or its European allies. Ascertaining the weight of defense as a component of Soviet GNP is one of the more difficult tasks in any study of the Soviet Union. The Soviet defense budget is not open for inspection as is that of the United States. The declared defense budget, which in 1981 amounted to 17.05 billion rubles or only about 2.8 percent of the Soviet GNP, is thought to exclude a number of elements such as military research and development, stockpiling, and civil defense. Indeed, some analysts contend that the declared budget covers only the operating and military construction costs of the armed forces.[19] Most Western estimates fix Soviet expenditures on defense over the past decade at between 10 and 15 percent of their GNP.[20]

In addition to such large financial outlays for defense, the Soviet Union channels a large portion of its skilled manpower into defense and defense-related industries. This channeling of trained manpower to the arms effort has tended to restrain civil-oriented technological progress and, in general, inhibit economic growth.

In 1964, Nikita Khrushchev pointed explicitly to the adverse impact of military expenditures on the Soviet economy. Writing in *Kommunist* he said:

> Doesn't the need to support the defense might of the USSR at the present-day level hinder raising the well-being of the people. With all straightforwardness I reply: Yes, it hinders it. Rockets and cannons—these are not meat, not milk, not butter, not bread, and not *Kasha*. If it were not necessary constantly to strengthen the might of the Soviet armed forces, we could sharply raise the living standards of our people . . . .[21]

Other Soviet leaders, including Leonid Brezhnev, have lamented the conflicting demands between the military and consumer parts of the economy.[22] In recent years, the rate of growth of the Soviet GNP has declined. In the 1970's, it averaged about 4 percent; in 1981, it dipped below 2 percent.[23] Sensitive to the glowing prospects for renewed economic growth and capital separation, Yuri Andropov also emphasized the need for improving the Soviet economy. Thus, the constant tug-of-war between defense needs and economic development and expansion, although not as apparent in a totalitarian society as in a democracy, probably has and continues to impel Soviet leadership in the direction of detente and arms control in Europe. Moreover, the Soviet Bloc's prospects for attaining required Western credit, trade, and technology to increase the pace of its economic development are well served by a reduction in tensions brought about through detente and arms control.

Detente. The slow move toward detente, or *peaceful coexistence* as it has been called by Soviet leaders, began sometime in the mid to late 1950's. An increasing concern over the potential catastrophic consequences and risk of nuclear war gave rise to efforts to reduce tensions between East and West and to bring stability to an otherwise potentially unstable nuclear environment. By the mid-1950's, Secretary Khrushchev had become increasingly uncertain over the potential utility of weapons of mass destruction as instruments in the class struggle. While the Lenin doctrine espoused the inevitability of war between rival factions, the possibility of mutual devastation from a nuclear conflict caused Khrushchev to modify this doctrine at the 20th Party Congress in 1956 where he advocated the policy of *peaceful coexistence.*[24] This was a necessary doctrinal change for laying the ideological foundations for arms control.

Likewise, concerns over the potential impact of a nuclear war with the Soviet Union were being voiced in the United States as well as in Europe. These concerns came to a focus during the Kennedy Administration as it fought to shift away from the nuclear strategy of *massive retaliation* to what was thought to be a more balanced strategy that emphasized a graduated response which, at least in theory, would raise the nuclear threshold. By 1963, the Soviet Union and the United States had agreed to establish a "hot line" between the two capitals to assure quick and reliable communication directly between the heads of state to reduce the danger of an accident or miscalculation triggering a nuclear war.

Over the next decade, the United States and the Soviet Union were signatories to a host of agreements designed to defuse crises and moderate the arms race.

Prior to 1969, the Christian Democrats who governed West Germany had maintained a confrontational approach toward the East. The Social Democrats who came to power under Willie Brandt in 1969 believed that the old approach had gained them very little, particularly with regard to some sort of reconciliation with East Germany, and so the new Chancellor initiated *Ostpolitic* (or his opening toward the East). The limitation of arms in Central Europe fitted well into this concept. Arms control would contribute to the lessening of tension, thereby enhancing detente.

Today, the continued desire to avoid an increase in tensions or a return to the cold war helps fuel the drive for arms control negotiations which are seen as a way of sustaining detente. This is particularly true in Western Europe. Western Europeans recognize the Soviet military threat, of course, but they must live within the shadow of the threat and, therefore, perceive a need for political reconciliation—a need for focusing on ways and means of alleviating the consequences of the division of Europe as well as the potential consequences of another war. Thus, they see arms control and detente as a political venture to achieve political objectives.

Many in the United States view arms control in more military and technical terms. They see arms limitations as a means of reducing the risks caused by the technical capabilities of the weapons themselves and seek ironclad verification procedures to ensure that the lowest possible risk is achieved. They do not see arms control as an element embedded in a larger political strategy to the extent that many Western Europeans do. Nevertheless, even in the United States, the desire in a number of quarters to continue Soviet-American cooperative efforts to increase stability in the nuclear age, albeit under a superpower relationship amended by the realism of Afghanistan, Poland, and what many consider an unrelenting Soviet drive for military superiority, has sustained interest in arms control negotiations.

The Soviet Union, since Khrushchev's open gambit on *peaceful coexistence,* also has been moved to the arms control conference table. While Soviet strategy and, thus, motives may be questioned,[25] they frequently have expressed their concern publicly over crisis stability and on the potential adverse effects of the arms race.[26]

The Peace Movement. Both Western and Eastern Europe as well as the United States have seen the rise of peace movements. They have become a common factor on the political landscapes of most Western European states since World War II. In recent years, however, they have grown in size and significance. As Western Europeans have become increasingly concerned about the continued growth of the nuclear arsenals of the superpowers and their deployment of nuclear weapons in Eastern and Western Europe, there has been a corresponding growth in the size of the peace movement. Today, in Western Europe and in the United States, citizens concerned over what they perceive to be a growing potential for nuclear war have become active participants in national debates over arms and arms control and have become, in some instances, a major force impelling governments to pursue arms control as an alternative to weapons deployments and as part of a broader, national security strategy.

Even the governments of Eastern Europe have not gone untouched by efforts of private citizens to affect the direction of government in the nuclear age. In 1982, evidence of a peace movement in Eastern Europe began to surface. A handful of independent peace activists has been known to exist in Hungary and the USSR for some time. What has been surprising, has been the peace movement in East Germany—one of the most rigid and outwardly loyal of the Soviet satellites. The church is also involved, but the movement seems to extend beyond the church. Groups as large as 5,000 people have gathered to protest armaments buildup. An estimated several hundred East German youths are serving jail terms for refusing to serve in the armed forces.[27] In a closed society, it is impossible to calculate what percentage of the population supports such a movement. Nevertheless, there is an apparent public pressure in the East as well as the West for arms control.

IMPEDIMENTS TO ARMS CONTROL

While a number of factors impel both East and West toward arms control negotiations and suggest some promise for achieving agreements to limit arms in Europe, the negotiations themselves are hampered by a host of impediments.

Trust. The common denominator of arms control agreements is trust. In spite of the fact that, in theory, it can be argued that both sides stand to gain through effective arms limitations, each side fears that the other may attempt to achieve unilateral advantage and undermine the arms control efforts. Such fears are inherent in a nation-state system where each sovereign state ultimately is responsible for its own security and where history stands as evidence that increments to the security of a state are often realized at the expense of others. Concern over the motives of others at the negotiating table is further compounded by the differing historical experiences, perceptions, and capabilities each side brings to the negotiating table as well as an inclination not to divulge, for security reasons, any more information than is necessary to further one's own negotiating objectives.

In the absence of trust, states have sought to establish, during the course of negotiations, those procedures necessary to verify treaty compliance. However, verification is only a weak sister of mutual trust. Even in the presence of procedures which might provide an unambiguous verification capability (and none apparently have been devised), lack of trust can still undermine the basis for an agreement even after it has been reached—which was, in part, the case with SALT II—or to undermine the process before an agreement can be reached—which may now be the case with the current strategic arms reduction talks (START) or the negotiations on intermediate-range nuclear forces.

Comparability of Forces. The attainment or maintenance of parity has been the primary motive behind the West's arms control negotiations of the last two and one-half decades. The West generally has seen parity as a key to stability. While Soviet leaders apparently accept parity as a negotiating objective, it is not clear to US leaders and analysts just what the concept of parity *really* means to Soviet leaders and analysts. However, even if one assumes the Soviet Union and its East European allies are seeking a true balance of capabilities with the West, agreement among negotiating parties on what constitutes a parity of forces with weapons and force structures that differ in fundamental ways can be a major obstacle to successful negotiations.

The SALT I interim treaty on offensive weapons resulted in Soviet superiority in numbers of ICBM launchers in exchange for a lesser number of launchers but more warheads for the United States, whose systems were considered to be of a superior quality (partially the result of an advantage in multiple independently-targeted reentry vehicles [MIRV] and improved guidance technologies). The United States learned immediately after SALT I of a problem in trading quantity for quality. By permitting unequal quantitative aggregates, without a corresponding restraint on qualitative improvements, the Soviet Union was free to improve its systems, add warheads with MIRV to their missiles, and thus quickly alter the perceived strategic balance within the parameters achieved through negotiation.

At the Mutual and Balanced Force Reduction talks in Vienna, it took three years of negotiating before the East finally agreed to the principle of conventional force parity. While the West's concern all along was parity of ground forces in Central Europe, the East took the position that the forces considered should include nuclear forces and other US forward based systems (FBS). Again, the problem of attempting to compare dissimilar forces impeded progress in achieving a negotiated arms control agreement. Likewise, French forces were of concern to the East. The West, despite continued French opposition, agreed to make allowances for French forces in Germany in any reduction agreement. France, however, was not an MBFR participant nor are French forces a part of NATO's integrated military commands. Therefore, it was generally agreed that French forces in France would not be a part of any parity agreement. It is true that for their part, Soviet leaders had evaded having their forces in Hungary and the indigenous Hungarian forces included. Since the Soviet Union believes it needs forces positioned in Central Europe to maintain order in the bloc, it is likely that Soviet leaders considered the overall weight in numbers not as great as it appeared on the surface to Western observers. The East also has been concerned over the quickly mobilizable West German Territorial Army reserves which have not been included in the forces count. There is a total in all services of 750,000 troops, about 600,000 of which are presumed to be Army.[28] For the West, one of the greatest difficulties to overcome in attempting to ensure a comparability of forces in Europe after a negotiated settlement was the result of geographical realities. US forces would have to pull back some 10,000 km across an ocean, whereas reduced Soviet forces would only have to pull back 1,000 km across land. Such differences have made it impossible to agree on what would constitute parity. Yet, such issues cannot be ignored.

Data Base. The data base is inextricably linked to estimates of parity. Even if the difficult questions pertaining to force mission and comparability can be reconciled, there is no basis for discussing tradeoffs—which are the heart and soul of negotiated attempts to achieve an acceptable balance of forces—without a mutually acceptable data base. While the data base has never been a major issue in SALT, it has virtually dominated MBFR. Not only has the type of forces to be counted been an issue, but also at issue has been the number of troops in place—troops being the one type of force both sides could agree to count. For the first three years of MBFR, the East would not reveal the number of troops it had in Central Europe. Finally, in mid-1976, it presented a figure. While the East agreed with the West's data on western forces, the West felt that the East's data on eastern forces fell short by about 150,000 troops. Whether or not the East is deliberately trying to deceive, one cannot say. Nevertheless, it remains certain that a mutually acceptable data base is essential as a point of departure if negotiations are to be successful. Unfortunately, it is more difficult, although not impossible, to get a fairly close count of troops and divide their missions than it is to do the same with ICBMs, bombers, or submarines.

The INF negotiations offer a potential for similar problems over data base. At the present time the problem at INF talks has been more over what to count than the numbers of systems in each of these categories. However, if nuclear capable tactical aircraft are ultimately included, one can be sure there will be serious disagreements over what constitutes a nuclear capable aircraft.

Verification. Verification clearly has been a major issue in the West. In both the SALT I and II agreements, the United States and the Soviet Union agreed to rely on the national technical means (NTM) of verification at their disposal to assure treaty compliance.[29] They also agreed not to interfere with each other's NTM. In the provisions of SALT II, though unratified by the US Senate but generally observed by the superpowers, they went even further and agreed to prohibit deliberate concealment measures which might impede verification by NTM of the provisions of the agreement.

As long as agreements focus on missile launchers in sites, surface launched ballistic missiles (SLBM) and bombers, verification of compliance with limitations on strategic systems can be reasonably

Proposed by United States and NATO	Proposed by Soviet Union and Warsaw Pact	Comments Differences In Proposals:

Fall, 1973
US and Soviet Reductions:
. 29,000 US troops
. 1 Soviet tank army
  -68,000 troops
  -1,700 tanks
	3 Stage Reductions (Total c. 17%):
	. reductions by all forces in Europe.
	. reductions based on % contribution to alliance's ground forces.
	. reduced foreign (US, USSR) troops returned to homeland.
	. reduced indigenous forces must be disbanded.
		. West reductions limited to ground forces vs. East desire to include all forces (including nuclear forward based systems-FBS).
		. West reductions aimed at collective alliance ceilings of 700,000. East proposed national sub-ceilings so that Benelux could not absorb FRG's reduction requirements.
		. US proposal would reduce US presence relative to USSR and Western allies. Soviet proposal would maintain US presence as stabilizing factor while limiting European forces, especially those of FRG.

December 1975 In return for reduction of 68,000 man Soviet tank army and the acceptance of collective ceilings on each bloc's force levels (i.e., no demand for specific European sub-ceilings), the West offered to include some FBS in their withdrawals. . 1,000 tactical nuclear warheads . 54 nuclear capable F-4 aircraft . 36 Pershing I nuclear missiles	February 1976, 2 Stage Reduction Plan: I: Equal US and USSR Reductions . 2-3% air and ground troop strength . 1 Corps HQ (with combat support and supply units) . 300 tanks each . 54 nuclear capable F-4 and SU 17/20 . 36 Pershing I and Scud B missiles II: 1978 reduction by all parties to equal 15%	. Western goal was to get East to accept principle of asymmetric reductions. According to West, the number of Pact forces was 965,000 rather than East's 805,000 figure. . Western proposal came to be known as OPTION III. . 300 tanks were 4% of NATO's tank strength and 15% of US tank strength but only 2% of Soviet tank strength. This reduction would increase Pact advantage in this crucial weapon. . Pact continued to insist on national sub-ceilings. . Pact refused to acknowledge asymmetrical reductions.
April 1978 . 700,000 troops on each side should be final force levels. . NATO would agree to some specificity on national sub-ceilings on national sub-ceilings if Pact would agree to 700,000 man ceilings	2 Stage Reduction Plan: I: US withdraw 14,000 men; 1,000 nuclear warheads, 54 nuclear capable aircraft and 36 Pershing I missiles . . . . USSR withdraw 20,000 men, 1,000 tanks, and 250 combat vehicles. II: Further reductions by each bloc to 700,000 men.	. Soviet reductions demanded by NATO did not have to be an integrated tank army. . Soviets dropped rigid sub-ceiling requirement and seemed to accept West concepts of unequal reductions (i.e., Soviet armor for US nuclear assets). . Soviets insisted that no state could constitute more than 50% of alliance's members (i.e., Benelux should not obviate need for FRG to reduce forces.

SUMMARY OF MBFR PROPOSALS, 1973 – 1983

Proposal	Comments
5 October 1979 • Unilateral Soviet withdrawal of 20,000 men and 1,000 tanks from DDR.	• Soviets presented this reduction as part of Phase I of their 1978 proposal. • NATO noted that the numbers of troops and tanks withdrawn from DDR equalled the difference between NATO and Warsaw Pact estimates of force strength in DDR. However, Soviet reductions were not verifiable.
December 1979 2 Stage Reduction Plan I: 13,000 US/30,000 Soviet troops reduced AFTER both sides agreed on a mutually verifiable data base and on instituted confidence building/associated measures such as those accepted in 1975 in Helsinki (e.g., notification of troop movements). II. Specific Western European pean reductions. • US announced withdrawal of 1,000 of 7,000 US tactical nuclear warheads but dropped other FBS elements of Option III.	
July 1980 • 13,000 US troops • 20,000 Soviet troops (in addition to 20,000 already withdrawn from DDR). • no country can comprise more than 50% of alliance's ground forces.	• Soviets labelled as excessive US demand for USSR withdrawal of 30,000 troops in light of its 1979 withdrawals. • Soviets angered that other nuclear elements of Option III were withdrawn. • Associated measures (8 elements) not made public. These measures are likely to include the identification of specific passage points for troop movements and disengagements of certain military formations from chosen areas (e.g., no tank formations within specified ranged from inter-German border).
February 1982 • Soviet proposal recapitulated proposals of last 9 years.	• Soviet proposal failed to address data base validity of verification.
July 1982, FRG Proposal 4 Stage Reductions Over 7 years: • Withdrawal of 13,000 US/ 30,000 USSR troops to their respective countries. • Each phase is to be fully verified on basis of agreed data before start of next phase. • Eventual collective ceilings for each bloc of 900,000 forces (700,000 of which are ground troops). • "Associated Measures" must be included in agreement.	
18 February 1983 • Withdrawal of 13,000/20,000 troops to respective homelands. • Pact suggested 900,000 ceiling be reached without further debate on current numbers.	• Soviets agree on effective ceiling of 900,000/ 700,000 forces as proposed by NATO. • Small difference between US and USSR reductions as proposed by Soviet Union implies force asymmetries are not as great as NATO contends. • Soviets still refuse to offer a means of verifying pull-out of their forces.

assured through NTM. Agreements which focus on mobile launchers, missiles instead of launchers, or on size of warheads or throw-weight are likely to complicate seriously the verification problem since NTM are not likely to be effective in determining such less easily identified factors. Moreover, the US problem of determining whether the Soviet Union is complying with agreed missile and warhead limits will be compounded if the Soviet military continues to encode its telemetry during missile tests, as it has in recent years.[30] This is a treaty violation about which the United States has not always protested since it might reveal US intelligence gathering capabilities.

The problem of verification is likely to be even more complex once one moves away from the strategic level. For instance, it may be difficult to determine if a cruise missile has a nuclear or conventional warhead; or whether certain tactical aircraft are capable of nuclear missions; or, since range is a function of payload, whether a certain class of cruise missiles is exceeding the agreed range limitations. INF talks can easily become bogged down over these issues. Likewise, verification at MBFR talks poses formidable problems. Determining gross manpower levels or explicit or implied ceilings on other conventional forces would be difficult at best. John Keliher has noted MBFR verification is a three-tier challenge. First, each side must determine that the agreed upon reductions have taken place. Second, the West must be able to identify promptly any massive reintroduction of Soviet forces and/or a mobilization of East European forces. Finally, and perhaps the most difficult problem, the West must be able to monitor small changes of forces which over time might lead incrementally to an alteration of the agreed upon balance.[31] To such ends, the West has proposed, as part of the MBFR "associated measures," a periodic exchange of data and information on the forces in the area after the treaty becomes effective, ground inspections, and declared MBFR entry and exit points at which each party has the right to place inspectors.

The East apparently considers such measures as too intrusive and refuses to agree to them. The Soviet passion for secrecy is well known, and so their aversion to the type of verification the West believes it must have may well be genuine. They also understand the advantages a closed society has in competing with an open society for information. Without the means upon which the West is insisting, verification of an MBFR treaty will be much more difficult for the West than the East. The East can complement its NTM with a fill array of information from the West's comprehensive public debates on military plans and weapons and from an abundance of published western documents. The West, on the other hand, can only guess at missions of weapons systems it observes through NTM and make only tentative estimates of ranges and payloads of missiles.[32] Another advantage the East has is that the West is virtually proscribed from cheating by an active and alert media and ever watchful political opposition parties.

Under such circumstances, the East's position on verification measures is not surprising. Nevertheless, from a Western perspective, effective verification remains the *sine qua non* for arms control. As Edward Luttwak has noted, arms control without a high confidence of verification is a contradiction of terms. In the absence of adequate verificaton procedures, arms control may increase rather than reduce incentives for force building and the risk of conflict.[33]

Technological Improvements. Technological improvements impinge on both the parity and verification issues. First, during arms control negotiations, how does one compensate for current disparities in the levels of technology of the forces considered? Second, how does one verify changes in technological capabilities after the conclusion of an agreement? Finally, how does one compensate for technological change?

There is also a psychological dimension to the problem of technology which undoubtedly affects the way the Soviet leaders think about arms control. Despite recent Soviet advances in technology, the Soviet Union harbors a long-standing fear of Western technological achievements and remains concerned over the capacity of the West, through rapid technological advance, to alter suddenly the balance of power. From the Soviet perspective, almost every innovation in the technology race has been Western. For example, the West has been first to have: U-2 spy planes, spy satellites, nuclear submarines, missile-launching submarines, a man on the moon, the space shuttle, cruise missiles, computer technology, stealth technology, MIRV, and so on. There are good reasons to believe the Soviet leaders are seriously concerned about the technologies associated with the MX and the cruise missiles, Pershing II and Trident, modern US tactical fighters, and other

US advances and their consequent impact on the future balance of power. For example, during the 1982 war in Lebanon, the US-supplied Israeli Air Force shot the Soviet-supplied Syrian Air Force out of the sky while successfully avoiding Soviet built antiaircraft missiles. While the Syrians were not equipped with the most advanced Soviet equipment and the ability of the Syrians to employ efficiently their weapons may be called into question, such encounters are likely to increase Soviet uncertainty about the potential impact of what they see as a clear Western edge in technology.

Stability. The desire for stability may draw both East and West to the conference table, each side seeking to attain or retain a stable balance of forces and, thus, gain or maintain a position of relative security. Agreeing on what balance of forces and weapons systems will result in a stable environment, however, is not an easy task. Two aspects of stability have been of primary concern among Western elites. First, during noncrisis situations, the balance of forces is such that neither side is driven to major arms acquisitions which may ultimately result in a spiraling arms race. Second, during a crisis, the balance of forces is dynamically stabilizing; that is, no incentives exist which would encourage the preemptive use of force or a mobilization of forces which could result in a military confrontation. Rather, positive incentives exist for parties to the crisis to reduce tensions.

From a Western perspective, the current asymmetry of ground forces in Central Europe has long been a destabilizing force. Moreover, a number of Western defense analysts now consider the Soviet theater nuclear buildup as potentially destabilizing. Both the long-standing imbalance of conventional forces and the growing imbalance in favor of the Soviet Union at the theater nuclear level have sparked incentives for a Western arms buildup in reply to reduce the number of potential advantages in peacetime as well as during crises that Soviet leaders may believe are exploitable.

Notwithstanding, the East contends that an overall balance exists. As a minimum, the Soviet Union and other Warsaw Pact states apparently are relatively secure with the current balance and are loathe to alter it in any clearly asymmetrical way. Thus, while the West has sought greater reductions in the conventional forces of the Warsaw Pact than those of NATO and the United States seeks to reduce both the US and Soviet intermediate-range nuclear forces to zero, Soviet leaders have generally preferred equal reductions which affect all the forces of both alliances. Moreover, while the ever increasing power of forces in the East seems destabilizing to the West, the threat of ever expanding and improving Western technology may seem destabilizing to the East. "O wad some power the giftie gie us, To see oursel's as ethers see us."[34] If opposing sides could, they might be able to agree on what constitutes stability.

Consensus Achievement. The European arms control negotiating process is complex. It is dealing with an array of different types of force systems—both conventional and nuclear. It must wrestle with force levels and deployment patterns, with the asymmetries in force structures, and with diverging military missions and options. It is a multilateral process in which many countries are involved, creating a requirement for continuous consultation, at least on the NATO side (not a great deal is known about what goes on inside the WP). The interests of the various parties within and between the states involved are multifaceted and frequently divergent and stakes and risks are often too high for bold initiatives or clever proposals to emerge. As a result, initiatives as well as agreements in many instances reflect the lowest common denominator.[35]

Linkage. Perhaps one of the more perplexing problems confronting those who have sought to pursue arms control efforts over the last few years has been the problem of linkage. Linkage refers to the deliberate or nondeliberate linking of events outside of the arms control arena to efforts of arms control. It is a psychological phenomenon, especially in democracies where the consent of the governed is an important part of the political process, as much as it is an act of deliberate political choice. As a psychological phenomenon, it is linked to trust and involves calculations about the intentions of the other party and about the relative merits of proceeding with arms control efforts. Thus, for example, whatever merits of the SALT II treaty, in the wake of the Soviet invasion of Afghanistan it was unlikely that the treaty would have received the necessary support in the US Senate for ratification. Likewise, Soviet actions in Poland, Latin America, Africa, and elsewhere have complicated efforts to move toward negotiations on arms control issues in Europe. On the question of linkage, former Secretary of State Alexander Haig noted:

... we seek arms control bearing in mind the whole context of Soviet conduct worldwide.

Such 'linkage' is not a creation of US policy; it is a fact of life. A policy of pretending that there is no linkage promotes reverse leverage. It ends up by saying that in order to preserve arms control, we have to tolerate Soviet aggression.[16]

CONFERENCE ON SECURITY AND COOPERATION IN EUROPE

The Conference on Security and Cooperation in Europe (CSCE) was not an arms control conference in the specific sense of the word, in that it did not address a particular weapon system or type of weapon. Nevertheless, to understand European arms control efforts and negotiations, one must have an appreciation of CSCE, how it came about, and what it has accomplished. CSCE can be seen as a treaty settlement of outstanding European issues unresolved since World War II. Rather than focusing on specific weapons' systems, the idea was to create an atmosphere conducive to the resolution of specific issues separating East from West. In a sense, it was a broad umbrella under which assurances given would allow concerned parties to later address particular cases.

Motives. For reasons explained here, the Soviet leadership was the driving force behind CSCE. The vulnerability of European Russia to invading armies is a security concern that has occupied every Russian ruler since the earliest days of the Kievian and Muscovy city-states. The importance of the lands adjacent to Soviet territory as jumping off points for brutal invasions have been lost neither to the Csars or Commissars. As a result, rebellions in East Germany (1953), Hungary (1956), and Czechoslovakia (1968) against Soviet occupation; the rearmament of West Germany and entry into NATO in 1955; and continued Western rhetoric during the 1950's promising to roll back Soviet influence from Eastern Europe produced what appeared to be genuine fears among Soviet leaders and national security analysts. Although failure by the West to aid the Hungarian and Czech bids for freedom proved that Western rhetoric had been hollow, the prospects for continued unrest in Eastern Europe and the potential for Western interference caused the Soviet leaders to push for Western recognition of a divided Germany and a Soviet sphere of influence in Eastern Europe, without which "fraternal assistance," *à la* the Brezhnev Doctrine, could be interpreted as aggression. The

Soviet leaders had justified their intervention in Czechoslovakia as a "socialist duty." They claimed they had a legal right to intervene based on ideology. That was essentially what the Brezhnev Doctrine was all about. While recognition of the Soviet sphere of influence was the political impetus behind CSCE, there were military considerations as well. Warsaw Pact mobilization under the auspices of the Brezhnev Doctrine could be misinterpreted by NATO and viewed as a threat to Western Europe. While the West might disapprove of such mobilization, the mobilization would stand less of a chance of being misinterpreted if the West had acquiesced to the Brezhnev Doctrine by agreeing to spheres of influence.

The Soviet leaders, however, had other concerns. A primary one was the deteriorating Sino-Soviet relationship which culminated in the 1969 clash along the border on the Ussuri River. This raised the spectre of having to support two widely dispersed armies. Their push for CSCE was an attempt to bring more equanimity to the situation in the West, so they could direct their attention to the East.

Another Soviet concern was the West German Army, the Bundeswehr. During the 1950's, the Soviet-led East proposed a series of European arms control packages, which were designed to forestall the rearmament of West Germany and obtain Western recognition of the division of Germany. The West refused to give serious attention to the proposals, and in 1955, West Germany joined NATO. Even with this, the East did not give up hopes of bringing about some sort of neutralized Germany. However, by the mid-1960's, Soviet leaders had to face up to the fact that they had failed to curb the development of the Bundeswehr. Without a World War II peace treaty, without formal recognition of the international boundaries in Central Europe, and without formal recognition of the two Germanies, the Bundeswehr stood as an instrument for turning back the clock 25 years. This, to the Soviet leaders and analysts, created a destabilizing situation.

The United States and Western Europe were also concerned about stability in Central Europe, but they viewed the problem from a different perspective than did the Soviet Union. The West's greatest concern was the continuing expansion and modernization of the Soviet forces. By 1968, both blocs had proposed conferences to negotiate stability in Central Europe. However, the respective proposals reflected different points of view. The East discussed security from the standpoint of recognition of the status quo and the West discussed it from the standpoint of force reductions. This disjointed dialogue continued for several years. The East wanted a politically oriented conference that would settle the issues left unresolved in the absence of a peace treaty. The West wanted a conference that dealt with the technical aspects of arms reductions. Neither side was initially interested in the other's pursuit. NATO, however, finally recognized some merit in the East's proposal in that a stable situation could not exist in Europe without a solution to the German question. NATO recognized that a lack of stability and uncertainty brought about by the irresolution of this problem precluded a balanced reduction of opposing military forces. Some Western states saw CSCE as supporting detente. And while it might give some recognition to the Soviet hold over Eastern Europe, that situation was in any event a *fait accompli* which, as demonstrated as recently as 1968 in Czechoslovakia, was not about to be unsettled by active Western intervention. So recognition of Soviet hegemony over Eastern Europe might not be all that important if the West could get something in exchange. But an enhancement of detente was not the primary reason the West agreed to CSCE. The West wanted MBFR and an agreement on access routes to Berlin. That would be the *quid pro quo* for CSCE. Initially, Soviet leaders showed no interest in a conference on arms reduction, because presumably they judged the weaker West would attempt to negotiate for parity.[37] After the intervention in Czechoslovakia and its staining of detente, Soviet leaders apparently came to realize that if they were to get the West to agree to a security conference, the Soviet Union would have to agree to force reduction negotiations and make concessions on the Berlin access question.

In 1970, however, it appeared that the Soviet leaders would get much of what they wanted from CSCE without a conference. Under his policy of Ostpolitik, Willy Brandt concluded two treaties with the East. On August 12, West Germany signed a treaty with the USSR recognizing the frontiers of all states in Europe as being inviolable including the Oder-Neisse line between East Germany and Poland and the frontier between the Federal Republic of Germany and the German Democratic Republic. On November 18, West Germany signed a treaty with Poland recognizing the Oder-Neisse line.[38] This whole process added up to nothing less than *de facto* recognition by all parties that the Federal Republic was the real Germany—which meant that East Germany was separated from West Germany,[39] a realization that may have caused the West German Parliament's delay in ratification. These treaties were not ratified until May 1972. On June 3, the USSR signed the Four Power Agreement on Berlin which had been negotiated in September 1971. The USSR had withheld its signature until the 1970 treaties had been ratifed.[40] (It should be noted that a third treaty was signed between East and West Germany on December 21, 1972, formally confirming the existence of two German states—the FRG formulation was two states, one nation.) Through one concession on the Berlin access routes, the Soviet leaders had already gained much of what they wanted from a security conference. Why then would they continue to push for CSCE? One typically Western view was that they wanted a broader spectrum of recognition of their hegemony over Eastern Europe than the German treaties gave them.[41] As a result they ultimately agreed to the MBFR talks in exchange for CSCE.

The Conference. CSCE opened in Helsinki on July 3, 1973, continued in Geneva from September 18, 1973, to July 21, 1975, and was concluded in Helsinki on August 1, 1975. The declaration signed in Helsinki was divided into categories called baskets. These are summarized as follows:

• Basket 1 called for refraining from use of force, plus respect for sovereignty, the inviolability of existing borders and advance notice of military maneuvers.

• Basket 2 expressed the resolve to expand cooperation in trade, industry, scientific and technological areas and environmental problems, and in promotion of tourism.

• Basket 3 emphasized "free movement and contacts, individually and collectively," between countries, including help in uniting families, nonhinderance to marriages between citizens of different countries, wider dissemination of printed, filmed and broadcast information, and acceleration of cultural and educational experience exchanges. (This is the human rights basket which has been an issue between East and West ever since Helsinki.)

• Basket 4 provided for follow-up measures to check on how agreements negotiated are being carried out.[42]

The provisions of the Helsinki final act have important implications for European arms control. The confidence-building measures (CBM) of Basket 1 relate most directly. There was an agreement that notification would be given 21 days in advance of maneuvers exceeding 25,000 troops. Prior notification of smaller maneuvers and of major military movements and the exchange of observers for maneuvers were encouraged.[43] Thus, CSCE recognized the threat posed by opposing forces and the need for precluding misunderstanding regarding their dispositions.

The follow-up measures provided for by Basket 4 have resulted in two subsequent conferences, one in Belgrade from October 1977 to March 1978, and one in Madrid, which began in October 1980. There was disappointment on the part of many of the Western states with the meager results of the Belgrade Conference. This has made security issues loom larger for Madrid, where expanding the CBM in the Helsinki final act was to be a primary objective.[44] However, the air in Madrid has been so heated from recriminations over the Soviet invasion of Afghanistan and martial law in Poland that little of a substantive nature has been accomplished.

The Contributions of CSCE. What has CSCE contributed to arms control? As has been pointed out, it was a major factor in getting MBFR started. It established CBM which, as we have already seen, is an issue in MBFR. In MBFR, the West considers CBM as part and parcel of any arms reduction agreements. In his January 1980 testimony to the US Congress, Matthew Nimetz, State Department Counselor, stated that "in the area of security . . .

CSCE has established a means of creating a regime of confidence-building measures which has the long-term potential for enhancing warning time of a surprise attack. . . ."[45] Mr. Nimetz may have overstated the case. However, a concept had been agreed upon that could be important in reading subsequent agreements to any freezing or reducing of arms. It had the implication of eventually being extended to MBFR and expanded to include verification.

MUTUAL AND BALANCED FORCE REDUCTION TALKS (MBFR)

The previous section described how the MBFR talks were linked to the motives and strategies pursued by each bloc in the CSCE negotiations. However, the MBFR agenda, which focuses specifically upon the number of troops and conventional weapons systems in Central Europe, is much more complex than that considered in CSCE. Whereas, CSCE was concerned largely with principles and political stability to which all can agree in theory, the focus of MBFR has been quantitative, and agreement becomes largely a matter of definition and accounting. Since the forces of East and West emphasize and perform different missions, the establishment of mutually acceptable balance has proven elusive.

Motives. Many of the motives underlying the CSCE negotiating objectives of the East and West exist in MBFR as well. Both sides appear to be dedicated to the moderation of what they see as a potentially dangerous situation, and to the relaxation of East-West tension which could foster the expansion of economic and cultural ties between blocs. In MBFR, both see an apportunity for a reduction of manpower and economic national defense burdens at a time of declining numbers of 17-19 year old youth in the United States, the Soviet Union, and Europe. Increased demands for consumer spending in both blocs and opposition by increasingly vocal peace movements to military expenditures, particularly in the West, also create pressures for MBFR. Within the East, desires to achieve troop reductions are heightened by general economic malaise.[46]

In MBFR, the West has sought to reduce the asymmetry of conventional forces which favors the Warsaw Pact. These NATO efforts became particularly pronounced in the middle of the last decade with the disappearance of the West's tactical and theater nuclear superiority.[47] In spite of this conventional asymmetry, there was a threat of a unilateral withdrawal of US ground forces from Europe,[48] the fear of which may have been the driving force behind the initiation of MBFR. The West saw a need to use these forces as a bargaining chip, therefore unilateral force reductions (UFR) would have removed Soviet incentives to negotiate. The Allies also feared a US withdrawal would be perceived by the East as a reduction of the US commitment to Europe and thereby cause a destabilizing effect on the West's deterrence. There are opinions that the Mansfield "Sense of the Senate" resolution in 1971 on unilateral US troop reductions in Europe may have also pushed the Soviet Union into agreeing to MBFR. Soviet leadership may have concluded that a unilateral US withdrawal might result in stepped up efforts for Western European political unity and common defense. They may have also feared it would cause Western Europe to assume a more militaristic posture. It is doubtful that the Soviet leaders wanted US withdrawal without constraints on West

Germany (FRG).[49] This may be one reason why the Soviet Union was willing to enter MBFR even after the Ostpolitik treaties with West Germany had given the East much of what it wanted from CSCE.

Issues and Prospects. MBFR talks have been in progress since 1973. In spite of numerous proposals and counterproposals by both sides (see chart), the extent of agreement has been one in principle to a first phase US-USSR troop reduction followed by reduction of forces of other nations stationed in the area. There are still major areas of disagreement on both sides.

An issue of major importance to the East is the establishment of national ceilings as a means of putting a legal ceiling on the Bundeswehr. The East remains opposed to a collective ceiling within which national ceilings can fluctuate. While the West, especially the FRG, does not want to give the Soviets veto power through negotiations over the size of their national forces, there has been some interest in the Eastern proposal to set limits so that no single national force will exceed 50 percent of the troops of the bloc. However, any reduction formula must be considered carefully. Reductions and limitations, particularly for the West, tend to have a finality about them that must foster a very cautious approach to ensure that security will not be jeopardized. Consider the following. The Bundeswehr constitutes the bulk of the NATO ground forces in the area, whereas the Soviet forces constitute the bulk of those of the Warsaw Pact. Each side views those forces on the other side as the major threat. But consider the difference in reducing those threats. A Soviet reduction constitutes a withdrawal but those troops could be reintroduced quickly from Western Soviet military districts in the event of hostilities; a Bundeswehr reduction entails deactivation of units—a considerable difference with broad security implications. Further, the withdrawal of US forces to the continental United States would reduce their utility to Europe in any scenario other than a very protracted conventional war.

While the East agreed early to the West's data on Western forces, Eastern data on its own forces was judged by western intelligence to understate the actual force levels by about 150,000 men. This has been an intractable issue since mid-1975. While the East has agreed to a common ceiling of 700,000 ground force personnel for either side, the agreement is contingent upon the use of eastern data. Based on their data, the East rejects asymmetric reductions of

Warsaw Pact manpower of the magnitude demanded by the West. There is little indication the East will ever agree to such reductions in the future, since the West demands an Eastern reduction of a magnitude unacceptable in relation to the political and military objectives of the USSR.[50]

Another major issue is verification. The East's fundamental approach is to agree to limitations first and verification means later. The West's position is that it is essential to accomplish these concurrently. To the West, this is a fundamental confidence-building measure. Soon after the much publicized departure of the first of the 20,000 Soviet troops from East Germany, under the Soviet unilateral reduction announcement of October 1979, suggestions were made in the press that the USSR was filtering men back to increase the strength of Soviet units in Eastern Europe. Whether true or not, the fact is that without reliable verification means, neither side can have confidence in the other.[51] National Technical Means are the only methods the Soviet leaders have accepted for verification. These, however, are limited to monitoring troop movements and to determining the number of troops.

The apparent Warsaw Pact objective is to maintain its advantage in manpower and armor and to reduce and place limits on the Bundeswehr's size. Any Warsaw Pact advantage in manpower and other ground forces is clearly incompatible with the West's idea of stability in Central Europe in an age of theater and strategic nuclear parity. Some have argued, however, that given the Soviets' experiences in past wars they may not consider themselves at an advantage despite the unequal manpower levels. Nevertheless, the Western approach to MBFR has sought to reduce the threat of a surprise attack from the East. This goal would be accomplished through "associated measures" which would establish specified and monitored passage points for troop exercises and movements, and through the disengagement of certain military formations (e.g., tanks) in certain areas (e.g., a specified distance from the inter-German border). The West also seeks a large reduction of Warsaw Pact forces since such a reduction would require the Pact to effect a large buildup of forces which the West could detect long before the actual attack. To date, however, the West has been unsuccessful in these initiatives because of its lack of sufficient bargaining strength. The West's principal concern is Soviet troops and tanks. The Soviet Union, which has little reason to fear massive conventional rearmament by the NATO European allies, has little incentive to reduce its strong capabilities in the absence of an appropriate Western *quid pro quo*.

There is little by way of tangible results to show for the thousands of manhours and words expended in Vienna. The two sides have not been able to agree on an arms control scheme congruent with one another's political objectives and security concerns. For instance, the Soviet Union is not anxious to undertake large troop withdrawals from Eastern Europe given the volatile situation in Poland. Another contributing factor has been the heightened US distrust of Soviet intentions due to the shadow thrown over detente by Soviet strategic and conventional arms acquisition and modernization, its policies in Afghanistan, its alleged use of chemical warfare in Asia, and its increasing presence throughout the Third World. The persistence of the problems resulting in the inability of the negotiators to reach an agreement has caused critics to label the MBFR talks as failures.

While MBFR talks have not resulted in significant negotiated arms reduction, they have succeeded in preventing US unilateral reductions that would have jeopardized the solidarity and military capability of Western Europe and the stability of Central Europe. Also, the conference serves as a *de facto* multilateral standing consultative committee within and between alliances to exchange information and query suspicious deployments. Thus, it may have virtue in its potential to defuse destabilizing situations. The MBFR talks well may become a forum for providing reassurances about East and West force deployments in Central Europe.[52]

INTERMEDIATE-RANGE NUCLEAR FORCES/THEATER NUCLEAR FORCES REDUCTIONS

Of the three sets of European arms control negotiations explicitly addressed in this essay, those pertaining to intermediate-range nuclear/theater nuclear forces (INF/TNF) have been the most widely debated and the most publicized. Such exposure is hardly surprising given the catastrophic consequences that would result from a nuclear war in Europe and the rapidity with which these consequences could occur.

Viewed through the prism of their mutual economic, social and political vulnerabilities which reflect their complex societies' interdependences, the Europeans contend with genuine and understandable zeal that the distinctions between limited and total war, spasmotic and protracted war, theater and strategic war and, ultimately, winning and losing, are more apparent than real. Yet, despite the Europeans' certain abhorrence of the consequences of nuclear weapons, the NATO allies maintain that their very horror and the uncertainty attending their use are the best deterrents of war.[53] Consequently, the Western European governments, while pursuing efforts to improve conventional defense capabilities, generally have eschewed a massive conventional rearmament and no first-use initiatives that would raise the nuclear threshold and contribute to the belief that war in Europe might remain conventional. They fear that under certain scenarios, the Soviet Union might become inclined to exploit conventional superiority to achieve certain political or economic objectives, especially if Soviet leaders thought that a war would not escalate to a nuclear exchange with the Americans and that only European territory would be destroyed. In short, many Europeans, while unhappy living in the shadow of nuclear obliteration, believe that the Soviet people harbor similar fears, and, thus, a low nuclear threshold remains the best deterrent to Armageddon. West European confidence in this proposition is supported further by their general belief that war in Europe is neither inevitable nor imminent.[54]

The Soviet Union and their East European Pact allies part company with NATO regarding the utility of American nuclear weapons in maintaining a credible deterrent and peace in Europe. Because Soviet leaders see little difference in the effects of American missiles deployed from the continental United States or from European territory, they contend that the "theater/strategic" labels the United States uses to categorize much of its arsenal are not relevant. It is not surprising that the Warsaw Pact and the Western Europeans have named such European based systems as "gray area" or "Eurostrategic" weapons. In fact, long before the current INF/TNF debates regarding the deployment of Soviet Backfire bombers and mobile Soviet SS-20 with MIRV, and the proposed NATO deployment of ground-launched cruise missiles (GLCM) and Pershing IIs, "gray area" aircraft and missile systems were already at the center of the East-West debate. Arguing that the NATO Forward Based Systems (FBS) such as its shorter range Pershing I missile, its nuclear capable F-4 and F-ll aircraft and its submarine launched ballistic missiles were destabilizing and deadly additions to the US strategic arsenal in every sense except in name, the Soviet leaders attempted to incorporate these weapons first into the SALT I negotiations and later into the MBFR talks and then into SALT II. The United States refused to include these weapons in the above negotiations, however, maintaining that apart from supporting the NATO general nuclear strategy, these weapons balanced Soviet/Warsaw Pact systems such as the SU 17-20 aircraft and the SS-4 and SS-5 missiles.

While the goals of INF/TNF arms control are attractive, they have proven elusive. In general, the US positions are that (1) any agreement incorporate equal ceilings and be verifiable, (2) the SS-20 and Backfire systems constitute an unwarranted buildup against US FBS, designed only to counter Pact conventional superiority, (3) US dual purpose aircraft not be counted in the agreement lest the Soviet advantage in aircraft be increased further, and (4) the modernization of NATO's nuclear arsenal should proceed at the end of 1983 if progress in the US-USSR INF/TNF talks (which convened October 16, 1980 in Geneva) is not forthcoming.[55] The Soviet Union counters that theater nuclear parity now exists[56] and that as a result the "zero option" proposed by the United States on November 18, 1981, for attaining equal ceilings is unacceptable. It further argues that the US/NATO FBS constitute a strategic threat and, therefore, should be negotiable, as should be the 162 British and French nuclear tipped missiles. The Soviet leaders have made various offers for a moratorium on deployments, one being no additional Soviet deployments for no US deployments of the 572 cruise and Pershing II missiles. This is unacceptable to the West because it leaves the Soviet Union at an advantage in INF/TNF deployment. Soviet leaders have also made an offer to withdraw their 350 plus SS-20s east of the Ural Mountains. This, too, is unacceptable because the missiles could still hit Western Europe; could be reintroduced, because of their mobility, during a time of crisis; and, from their eastern position, would increase the threat to the Peoples Republic of China and US Asian allies.

Different definitions of security, divergent classifications of weapons, the unwillingness of each bloc to trust the other or take at face value its adversary's stated peaceful intentions, and contention within the West about the "zero option" all have mitigated against the conclusion of a successful treaty. The March 1983 election of

Chancellor Kohl and the willingness of the Reagan Administration, first expressed publicly in the Spring of 1983, to opt for a partial deployment of GLCM and Pershing II missiles in return for a partial reduction of SS-20 targeted against Europe[57] may be the two ingredients necessary to breathe new life into the realization of Western arms control objectives. These show greater Western European determination to support the 572 missile deployment decision and greater American flexibility to seek the middle ground. Until early 1983, the positions were reversed. The United States was determined and inflexible in its insistence upon the zero-option, while Western Europe was ambiguous in its support. As such, intra-NATO consensus and, consequently, inter bloc agreement were rendered highly unlikely.

A CONCLUDING NOTE

While, in theory, an alliance's military strategy should drive the members' conventional and nuclear development and deployments, the casual link between strategy and forces in-being is not always so unambiguous. Current forces in-being set limits to the strategy one can pursue and the goals that can be achieved. For instance, the unwillingness of NATO to maintain conventional forces in-being to match those of the Warsaw Pact forced the former to adopt a nuclear strategy that promised early use and rapid escalation in the use of nuclear weapons in the event of conventional hostilities.

Sovereign states bring different perceptions, experiences and goals to the matters of arms control and national security. The US pursuit is to reduce risk; it sees reduced relative quantities of forces and weapon systems as being a key to this. Its European allies, however, perceive the problem more as one of reducing tension, thereby alleviating the consequences of the division of Europe. While relative quantities of forces play a role in this, the quality of the political environment is probably more important. The Soviet perception of the Bundeswehr as a threat and the implementing of the Brezhnev Doctrine as a requirement not to be impeded are the forces driving the Soviet arms control negotiations. What this amounts to is that all are interested in stability, but all view it from a different background. Herein lies a major reason why the establishment of consensus within and between alliances on issues pertaining to survival, the most fundamental requirement of national policy, has been and will remain so difficult to achieve.

Another observation which can be drawn from the analysis above is that distinctions between strategic and theater nuclear systems and therefore regional and global security interests of the United States and the Soviet Union are more artificial than real. Such an acknowledgment is consistent with the assertion that the world is shrinking in the economic and political senses and that the course of "Spaceship Earth" is crucial to us all. To the extent that such linkage exists in the area of arms control, it means that CSCE, MBFR, and INF/TNF are integrally linked to other regional arms control (e.g., chemical disarmament) and superpower strategic (e.g., START) efforts. Indeed, President Reagan's "Berlin initiative" of June 1982 contains linkage elements which embrace START, INF/TNF, and MBFR aspects and, as such, suggests that only one East-West military balance exists. Inasmuch as such an interpretation of the nature of arms control is realistic, it does, however, complicate the procedure and potentially retards the quest for progress. It presents negotiators with more parameters than they can readily handle and impedes efforts to divide problems into subcomponents so as to deal first with those most amenable to resolution.

What can be concluded from these observations? Certainly one should not expect that the military and political issues dividing the East and West in general, and the USSR and the United States in particular, will be solved easily or quickly. We have seen the thorny obstacles to man's efforts to beat his swords into plowshares and should not be surprised that these efforts, though well-intended in many instances, have not taken root. Therefore, prudent leaders are well advised to maintain credible defenses consistent with the threats to their national interests.

Nevertheless, the elusiveness of progress in arms control does not render it a goal unworthy of pursuit. In addition to the previously described motives of the superpowers and the Europeans to realize such progress, one should understand that arms control and limitations contribute elements of certainty and calculability to the strategic calculus of the players. It has been noted earlier that to retain confidence in the survivability of the MX missile in *any* mode will remain impossible in the absence of any constraints upon Soviet missile development and deployment.[58] As such, arms control is correctly viewed as the "fourth leg" of the US strategic triad and is destined to remain a future quest.

ENDNOTES

1. Henry Kissinger, *A World Restored,* quoted in John Newhouse, *Cold Dawn,* New York: Holt, Rinehardt and Winston, 1973, pp. 56-57.
2. See James E. Dougherty, *How to Think About Arms Control and Disarmament,* New York: Crane, Russak and Company, 1973, p. 64.
3. *The Military Balance 1982-1983,* London: The International Institute for Strategic Studies, Autumn 1982, p. 15.
4. *Pravda,* January 25, 1961, p. 2, quoted in William D. Jackson, "The Soviets and Strategic Arms," *Political Science Quarterly,* Summer 1979, p. 247.
5. For example see Michael McGuire, "Soviet Strategic Weapons Policy, 1955-70," in *Soviet Naval Policy: Objectives and Constraints,* ed. by Michael McGuire, Ken Booth, and John McDonnell, New York: Praeger Publishers, 1976, p. 488. Also see Robert Legvold, "Strategic 'Doctrine' and SALT: Soviet and American Views," *Survival,* January/February 1979, pp. 8-13, and Robert Kennedy, "The Strategic Balance in Transition: Interpreting Changes in US/USSR Weapons Levels," *Soviet Armed Forces Review Annual,* ed. by David R. Jones, Gulf Breeze: Academic International Press, 1980, p. 356.
6. Henry G. Gole, "Through European Eyes," *Parameters,* Vol. 11, No. 4, December 1981, pp. 14-23.
7. This point is discussed by many authors who have written about arms control. For instance see John H. Barton, *The Politics of Peace, An Evaluation of Arms Control,* Stanford University Press, 1981, p. 177.
8. See John Newhouse, *Cold Dawn,* p. 4; and Thomas W. Wolfe, *The SALT Experience,* Cambridge, Mass: Ballington Publishing Company, 1979, p. 15.
9. An issue raised by Chancellor Helmut Schmidt in his Alister Buchan Memorial Lecture at the London International Institute for Strategic Studies (IISS) on October 28, 1977.
10. Theodor H. Winkler, "Arms Control and the Politics of European Security," *Adelphi Papers 177,* London: International Institute for Strategic Studies, 1982, p. 4.
11. Robin Ranger, *Arms and Politics 1958-1978,* Toronto, Ontario: The Macmillan Company of Canada Limited, 1979, p. 193.
12. Winkler, p. 4.
13. John Togliabue, "400 East Germans Dispute Official Defense Policy," *The New York Times,* February 15, 1982, p. A3.
14. In early 1952, the Allies set about the task of fashioning conventional forces to offset Soviet conventional capabilities in Central Europe. The final alliance decision announced in Lisbon in February 1952 by the North Atlantic Council set forth an ambitious set of conventional force goals for NATO. Member states agreed to contribute to the joint defense a total of 50 divisions, 40,000 aircraft, and "strong naval forces" by the end of 1952 and, provisionally, 75 divisions and 6,500 aircraft by 1953, and 96 divisions and 9,000 aircraft by the end of 1954. Despite considerable progress in improving the NATO conventional capability, however, the alliance was either unwilling or unable to meet the force goals set at Lisbon and continued to rely on the superior US strategic and theater arsenal to deter conflict in Europe. For a sampling of the European debate on defense expenditures during this period see Leon D. Epstein, *Britain - Uneasy Ally,* Chicago: The University of Chicago Press, 1954, pp. 240-241; and Robert Osgood, *NATO: The Entangling Alliance,* Chicago:

The University Press, 1962, pp. 81-84. Also see C. L. Sulzberger, "Military Revival in France a Vital Factor in US Policy," *The New York Times*, May 17, 1951, p. 12, and "Stikker Cautions on Economic Peril," *The New York Times*, September 19, 1951, p. 6.

15. For a thorough review of some of the factors which contributed to allied uneasiness over the deployment of tactical nuclear weapons to Europe see Robert Hilsman, "NATO: The Developing Strategic Context" in *NATO and American Security*, ed. by Klaus Knorr, Princeton: Princeton University Press, 1959, pp. 24-29.

16. See Raymond Aron, *The Great Debate*, Garden City: Doubleday and Company, Inc., 1965, p. 69.

17. Ranger, p. 191.

18. Growing interest in improving the NATO conventional defenses was clearly evident in a number of official statements, communiques, and defense memoranda of the period. For example see NATO, Defense Planning Committee, "Ministerial Guidance - 1975," in *Texts of Final Communiques 1975*, Brussels: NATO Information Service, 1976, p. 15; Netherlands, Ministry of Defense, *Our Very Existence at Stake: The Defense Policy in the Years 1974-1983*, The Netherlands: Ministry of Defense Memorandum, July 9, 1974, p. 16; Great Britain, Ministry of Defense, *Statement on the Defense Estimates 1976*, London: Her Majesty's Stationery Office, March 1976, pp. 9-10; and Donald H. Rumsfeld, *Annual Defense Department Report FY 1978*, Washington: US Government Printing Office, January 17, 1977, p. 85.

19. *The Military Balance 1982-1983*, p. 12.

20. See for example, *ibid.*, p. 15. Also see William T. Lee, *Soviet Defense Expenditures in an Era of SALT*, Washington: United States Strategic Institute, 1979, p. 7; Great Britain Ministry of Defense, *Statement of Defense Estimates 1981*, London: Her Majesty's Stationery Office, April 1981, p. 4; and *Soviet and US Defense Activites 1970-79: A Dollar Cost Comparison*, Washington: Central Intelligence Agency, January 1980.

21. N. S. Khrushchev, "O miri i miron sosuchcheslvovanii," *Kommunist*, May 1964, quoted in Lincoln P. Bloomfield, Cambridge, Massachusetts: The M.I.T. Press, 1966, p. 228.

22. Leonid Brezhnev, "Speech to Central Committee," October 25, 1976.

23. Central Intelligence Agency, *Handbook of Economic Statistics*, Washington: September 1982, pp. 26-27.

24. For a discussion of the ideological debate concerning the relationship of war to revolution and politics, see Thomas W. Wolfe, "The Communist Theory of War," in *Marxism, Communism, and Western Society: A Comparative Encyclopedia*, edited by C. O. Kernig, Vol. VIII, pp. 307-318.

25. While the Soviet Union posed as a leading advocate for disarmament from 1955 to the early 1960's, some have argued that its advocacy was merely a device to manipulate world opinion. For example, see Dougherty, pp. 69-71. Others contend that today the Soviet Union is merely using arms control to divide the West.

26. For example, see *Disarmament: Soviet Initiatives*, Moscow: Novosti Press Agency Publishing House, 1977, and L. I. Brezhnev, *Our Course: Peace and Socialism*, Moscow: Novosti Press Agency Publishing House, 1977.

27. Adam Hochschild, "East German Dissent," *The New York Times*, September 29, 1982, p. A27.

28. *The Military Balance, 1982-1983*, p. 38.

29. See *SALT II Agreement,* Selected Documents No. 12A, Washington: US Government Printing Office, June 1979, p. 21.

30. See for example Richard Halloran, "US Aides Uneasy on Soviet Coding," *The New York Times,* January 4, 1983, p. A3.

31. John G. Keliher, *The Negotiations on Mutual and Balanced Forced Reductions,* New York: Pergamm Press, 1980, p. 131.

32. See Edward N. Luttwak, "Why Arms Control Has Failed," *Commentary,* January 1978, p. 24.

33. *Ibid.,* p. 24.

34. From "To A Louse," a poem by Robert Burns.

35. Winkler, pp. 2 and 8.

36. "Excerpts From Haig's Speech on Administration's Policy on Arms Control," *The New York Times,* July 15, 1981, p. A10.

37. There are good background discussions on the East and West agreeing to CSCE and MBFR by Ranger, pp. 187-192; Barton, p. 178; and by Keliher, pp. 16-33.

38. Keliher, p. 24.

39. This was not the FRG's view at the time. Ospolitik was seen as a way of developing closer ties with the GDR and ultimately loosening Soviet-GDR economic ties and, over many years, political ties.

40. *Strategic Survey 1972,* London: International Institute for Strategic Studies, pp. 23-25.

41. Keliher, p. 145.

42. "At European Summit, Russia Will Achieve A Major Goal," *US News and World Report,* July 28, 1975, pp. 17-18.

43. Matthew Nimitz, "CSCE and East-West Relations," *Department of State Bulletin,* April 1980, p. 44.

44. *Strategic Survey 1979,* London: International Institute for Strategic Studies, p. 119.

45. Nimetz, p. 44.

46. Brezhnev's commitment to detente with the West was a means of easing Soviet ecnomic woes.

47. This has been a NATO policy since 1967. For a view of the changing theater nuclear balance see Robert Kennedy, "Soviet Theater-Nuclear Forces: Implication for NATO Defense," *Orbis,* Vol. 25, Summer 1981, pp. 331-350.

48. Reasons for Mansfield (1971) and Nunn (1982) resolutions: reduce defense burden; force Europeans to do more; RDJTF: Asia first/maritime strategy.

49. Keliher, p. 41.

50. Keliher, pp. 147-148.

51. *Strategic Survey 1980-1981,* London: International Institute for Strategic Studies, p. 111.

52. *Ibid.*

53. See "Europes Fear of Frying," *The New York Times,* October 25, 1981, p. 18E.

54. Gole, pp. 14-23.

55. Keliher, pp. 104-105.

56. "The Threat to Europe," *Progress Publishers,* Moscow: 1981, pp. 5-15, as cited in *Soviet Press: Selected Translations,* US Air Force Intelligence Directorate of

Soviet Affairs, January 1982, pp. 23-28. Note the Soviet leaders were arguing that parity existed even before they deployed their 350 plus SS-20 missiles.

57. Michael Getler, "Moscow Rejects Reagan Missile Proposal," *The Washington Post,* April 3, 1983, p. 1.

58. Robert Kennedy, "START: Problems and Prospects," in *The Defense of the West: Strategic and European Security Issues Reappraised,* ed. by Robert Kennedy and John Weinstein, Boulder, Colorado: Westview Press, 1984.

12

NATO DEFENSE THROUGH EUROPEAN EYES

Henry G. Gole

America's security arrangement with Europe is based upon a rather common sense deduction from both the short and long-term consequences of history.[1] In this century, the US involvement in two great European wars suggests a connection binding the fates of Europe and the United States. A longer view of the historical relationship reveals that America's political institutions, languages, and culture—measured by what we eat, how we dress, and the aesthetic pleasures derived from art—share much with what is generically described as the Western experience. Despite non-European cultural influences and what, until recently, was a geographical remoteness leaving us out of Europe's mainstream, we are a child of Europe. Well before the age of rapid communications, the tie was maintained by regular waves of immigrants whose arrival insured a flow of correspondence across the Atlantic, visits back to the "old country," and a sense of connection between Europe and the United States. The same connection to Europe can be found among the French-English neighbors to our north or the Spanish-Portuguese neighbors to our south, but in the 20th century the United States cast a long shadow and found it impossible to be unobtrusive. What we did or failed to do mattered outside of our national frontiers. The child of Europe had grown and become the head of the household.

In the years after the 1939-45 war, it seemed prudent for the United States to shape events in Europe rather than entering and exiting *in extremis* much as the local fire department makes its presence felt. Fire prevention seemed to be preferable to fire fighting, if one had a choice. We did have a choice. We determined that it was in our national interest to maintain a military presence there, to set aside George Washington's admonition about avoiding "entangling alliances," and to resist that part of our national character that tended to isolationism. But a pluralistic society is capable of nurturing many impulses simultaneously. It is fair to say that there was a certain pride—even arrogance—among the American people as the United States was regarded almost universally as a superpower and one spoke of a *Pax Americana*. Our contribution in 1917-18 was equally decisive, but impatience with European intractability and a preference for cultivating our own garden took us from center stage. After World War II, it was clear that we could not withdraw to the wings, but it wasn't clear whether we could set things right and return to our garden after some short involvement or if the involvement would be lasting.

The responsibilities of power seemed to draw the United States frequently and deeply into the affairs of others in even the remotest corners of the world. Most Americans had to be told where Pearl Harbor, Korea, and Vietnam were after American lives had been lost in those places. Power in Washington, however, was not matched by sophistication in the American heartland. Our citizens understood the Great Crusade from 1941-45, and the clear outcome was gratifying, but since then both clarity and gratification have been denied us. Impatience with ambiguity characterizes the American popular mood of the early 1980's, and strategists are almost as confused as the people while the sorting out of priorities takes place. One of the issues requiring hard thought is the place of our security arrangement with Europe and how it fits into an emerging global strategy.

THE HERE AND NOW

Squabbles between the Western European members of NATO and the United States are not a recent development. What is alarming in the early 1980's is the frequency with which one hears that this time it is different.[2] The more sanguine view, that transatlantic differences are the normal state of affairs, is being drowned out by concern for a new divergence in the way that NATO Europe and the United States see their respective interests. Perhaps, according to the more pessimistic interpretation, differences are so great that they will spell the end of NATO. Whether alarmist or a correct forecast of things to come, concern for the demise of NATO—an institution that has served so long, so well—suggests that responsible Americans might attempt to see things through European eyes and take steps to insure the survival of NATO and prove the events of the early 1980's just another rough spot in the road to NATO cooperation. One would hope that Europe would reciprocate by attempting to see the world through American eyes.

Strategy, indeed security itself, may not be the most important issue dividing the United States and Europe, though the military is a frequent target because uniforms draw attention and weapons frighten rational citizens. Bread and butter economic issues may be the chief stumbling block to a close and continued relationship between us; economic issues directly affect our peoples while security concerns are normally abstractions left to high officials hired to worry about such things. Wars and near-war crises attract public attention from time to time, but inflation and unemployment, prices and career opportunities are a part of daily life. However, one has the impression that fear has brought together both a generalized concern for war in Europe and personal concerns for individual futures as Europeans, particularly the young, contemplate the direction of events in the early 1980's.

Students of European and American security are asking if the current NATO strategy dating from 1967 is out of step with new realities, and American strategic thinkers seem to be most concerned.[3] The "realities" since 1967 can be reduced to two: increased Soviet military capability has probably altered the "correlation of forces" so that the US advantage has disappeared; Western Europe no longer marches to American commands. These two developments influence the way we look at strategy and tell us much about essential differences between Americans and Europeans as they study the same facts and come to different conclusions.

The European challenge is to keep the Americans in Western Europe in order to keep the Soviets out, to do enough to placate the Americans but not enough to enrage the Soviets. The American strategic task is to maintain peace and stability in Europe while being prepared for contingencies around the world. Clearly the more the Europeans do, the more likely the success of the American strategy. Differences derive from estimates of what is enough and of the utility of military and nonmilitary means.

NATO Europe emphasizes the nonmilitary elements of strategy and seems to be generally satisfied that the current strategy is successful in its main purpose. America stresses the military aspect of strategy and is clearly dissatisfied at what it chooses to see as European apathy.[4] It would be too simple and incorrect to attribute differences exclusively to transient moods. An effort needs to be made to understand why Europeans behave the way they do and how the United States might serve its best interests by meeting Europeans halfway. Too often differences on various issues are addressed without taking into account fundamental differences in European and American world views.

EUROPEANS ARE DIFFERENT

The United States, by its very location, starts from a position of relative security simply unattainable for Europe. Broad oceans and weak neighbors, vast space and abundant resources, a large population and—perhaps the key to the European-American difference—a unique point of view distinguishes the way Americans see the world: the notion that we can disengage from an ungrateful world and its problems at will. We can fix any problem; if others fail to recognize that, we can simply withdraw to our continent in the security provided by nature.

The European experience has produced a very different point of view. Despite the profound influence of Europe in shaping the world we find around us in the 1980's, Europe is a small, crowded, diverse continent dependent upon raw materials not indigenous to it, a collection, in fact, of intermediate powers which, since the devolution of colonial empires, have not yet decided upon a role in the world outside of Europe. Europeans have been bumping into one another for centuries. From time to time, various states have made a bid for hegemony: Spain, France, Germany, and since

World War II, the USSR. The Habsburgs, Bourbons, Napoleon, and Hitler are gone, but Switzerland, Italy, and the others survived these bids for hegemony and are still there, alive and well. Denmark was conquered in 4 hours on a day in April 1940 during the last German bid for European hegemony. Danes lived as well as their conquerors and better than most Europeans during World War II. Copenhagen was hardly damaged.[5] In 1945 the conquerors went away, not as a result of Danish actions but because the Great Powers made it happen. Rotterdam, on the other hand, was the target of terror bombing because the Dutch resisted. There is a lesson in this: the smaller states of Europe are like corks in a heavy sea subject to winds and tides beyond their control.

Over the centuries, the options available to the lesser powers of Europe have been there. The most attractive is to stay out of harm's way, a Swiss solution since Napoleon's time and a solution for Sweden during the world wars in this century. Albania has accomplished a miracle: it is invisible. Geography and immediate circumstances dictate the terms of this arrangement. Those states astride the Great North European Plain, which stretches from the Urals to the French Altantic Coast, have been unable to hide. The unhappy history of Poland can be understood by noting the absence of natural frontiers in the East and West and the presence of powerful neighbors in those directions. The militaristic history of Prussia can be explained by the determination of that kingdom to survive as a great power despite modest means and a geographical reality that continues to locate the two Germanies of the 1980's between East and West. The lowlands have represented a convenient doorway used by stronger powers with some frequency. Some nations can avoid confrontation, some cannot.

If it is impossible to stay out of harm's way, it is sometimes possible to band together with others to thwart the strength of a great power bent on extending its influence or frontiers. Coalitions, alliances, and defensive treaties fill the pages of European history. The weak have had to join forces to bring down the powerful France of Napoleon or the powerful Germany of Hitler. Strength external to the continent was often required to restore what came to be known as the balance of power. Britain intervened often over the centuries, generally throwing its weight on the side of a coalition resisting the state attempting to rise above the others. The United States played and is playing a similar role in our century, first against the Germans and now against the Russians. Alliances among the European states, it should be clear, are legal arrangements made to address specific circumstances, not marriages binding the contracting parties until death do they part, which seems to be the American understanding of alliance.

When unable to avoid danger or to constitute a coalition powerful enough to resist the most recent troublemaker, another alternative is available to the relatively weak: accommodation. The very thought of bowing to another state is odious to Americans, but to Europeans this historically has been viewed as a valuable alternative. On the crowded continent there is a sense of *deja vu* as the personalities change, but the game continues to be played by rules made permanent due to unchanging geopolitical realities. This appreciation of the need to take the world as it is has settled in the bones of Europeans who, since the dissolution of colonial empires, have few illusions about altering the human condition or remaking the world. Their inclination is to adjust rather than to remake. If Americans wish to ignore this lesson Europeans take from their history with a derogatory slogan, accusing Europe of a better red than dead defeatism, so be it, but it seems unwise to set aside the centuries-long evolution of a culture with a shrug of the shoulders—if we truly want to understand Europe.

Sometimes a vignette out of one's personal experience makes a point more effectively than reading a number of books. In the summer of 1973, a young German of modest circumstances showed his new house built in a small Bavarian village to his American friend for whom the house plan had been scratched in dust on the actual building site four years earlier. It is a marvelous house: as solid as a bunker, spacious and up-to-date. The house tour ended in the cellar. The oil tank is twice the size of what one would expect in an American home; the furnace has a mysterious second compartment. When asked about the second compartment, the unsophisticated German explained in a most matter-of-fact manner without change of expression, "That's a wood furnace for when the bad times come."

Not *if* but ". . . *when* the bad times come." It is difficult to formulate a clearer expression to characterize the essentially different points of view of Europeans and Americans. This scene took place before the energy crisis was visible to any but insiders and specialists. There are simply good times and bad times. One muddles through. One has no control over certain forces; one endures.

Perhaps the difference suggested partially explains an anomaly: how Europe, so close to "the threat," manages to be more dispassionate about it than America, so far from it. Those who live next to the railroad tracks become accustomed to the sound of passing trains; visitors are distracted by the noise. Indignant, even incredulous, American voices have been asking why the United States should be more concerned with European security than Europeans seem to be.[6] The question misses the point on two counts: first, we aren't: we're concerned with US security; second, Europeans are concerned but can't do much more about their security position without risking the transformation of the very natures of their societies or possibly making the problem worse by enraging the bear. An unkind European might mention that he sleeps about as well in the Soviet shadow as Mexicans and Canadians sleep in the shadow of American power. One accommodates to things that cannot be changed.

All of this bears on how Americans and Europeans think about NATO strategy. Looking at the same words in the NATO documents agreed to by all members, it seems that we draw different conclusions just as one fellow sees the glass half empty and the other sees it half full. Europe sees the glass half full and concludes that the strategy, in this less than perfect world, is not all bad.

With the exceptions of France and the United Kingdom, due to their still-fresh memories of Empire, Western Europe foresees the use of its military force as being limited to the continent and then only when survival itself is threatened. This general appreciation of military power and its use promises to dominate European thought to the end of this century. It is a purely defensive feeling, an approach suitable to a gentleman in ripe middle age more concerned with the pleasures of life in retirement than with making a great career. It spurns adventure and prefers low risk-taking. It buys locks and pays policemen; it does not take karate lessons or keep loaded pistols near the bed.

This essentially conservative approach to the role of the military in security policy takes into account that there are rascals out there in the world, but it prefers to deal with them primarily by means other than military. It recognizes that a good business deal is not a quick buck realized by establishing one party as a winner and the other a loser; two winners is the object of a truly good business deal. Two winners insure continued business to mutual benefit and congenial long-range relationships. The establishment of ties that profit both parties diminish the attractiveness of any sharp departure from profitable business as usual. Mutual profit does not require affection or even agreement among the parties involved. It tends to relegate to the background anything that might disturb the reason for the relationship: mutual advantage. Europe has also become accustomed to "security on the cheap" by being protected from the outside.[7]

Further, while the United States continues to debate seriously the relative importance of spending for social welfare as compared to spending for defense, this issue was settled a century ago in Europe. Sacrificing social welfare for defense spending in any situation short of war itself simply lacks a European constituency. Social welfare is fully integrated into what Western Europe understands liberal democracy to mean. It is as much a part of the European landscape as the Alps and the Rhine.

Europe may prefer the United States, but Western Europe wants and needs the USSR and Eastern Europe—as well as other world regions, including North America—for reasons of economics, politics, and security. The interruption of normal relations among the states of Central Europe since World War II is often considered a rather permanent fact of political life by Americans. Not so in Europe. Trade patterns, travel, and cultural bonds characterized relations in the center of Europe from time immemorial, and a yearning to resume them exists on both sides of the political dividing line which evolved out of the last European war. These considerations, as well as political expediency, are the foundation of Ostpolitik and detente.[8]

The conclusion to be drawn from these observations is that Europe is disinterested in high drama and much prefers a predictable world based upon diverse ties with both those it likes and those it dislikes. Security is not an object to be grabbed, but rather the by-product of decidedly nonmartial activities, activities so attractive to all concerned that only an actual threat to self-preservation—not a theoretical threat based upon hostile "capabilities"—would put business as usual at risk.

It would be in the American interest to recognize this European attitude toward security and to consider it when military policy initiatives are contemplated. Men have been known to leave nagging wives, even beautiful nagging wives. NATO—or something like it—will survive the year 2000 unless its utility is put in question. Only four developments are likely to put into serious question the utility of NATO: the end of a feeling of threat from the East; the general feeling that unreasonable burdens are being placed upon European NATO by a nagging United States; concern that an immature America is increasing the risk of war; a US determination that Europe must be left to its own devices as America realigns its strategic interests. All are possible, but the first is less in our control than the latter three. As we deal with Western Europe we must understand that Europe has regularly faced various bids at hegemony resulting in bloody wars over the centuries. The desire in Europe at the end of the 20th century is to avoid bloody war; to attain security by the establishment of various binding ties, even with political adversaries; to blur differences rather than to highlight them; and to negotiate disarmament. A continual state of heightened tension should not be forced upon NATO Europe by the United States if the Alliance is to survive. The European notion that security is based upon something other than the accumulation of guns and tanks needs to be taken into account by US policymakers if Western Europe and the United States are to share in the preservation of a security arrangement.

There are two general appreciations of the current state of the North American connection with Western Europe. One says that we've been there before, that crises have come and gone, that the Alliance remains vital despite a permanent low grade fever. The other says that current problems are different, more serious, deeper rooted and threatening to a relationship that has served European and American interests well for a long time. Regardless of which appreciation proves to be correct, the Alliance doesn't need strains on it that could be avoided. This should mean to America that the attainable good should be preferred to the unattainable perfect, that a less-than-perfect NATO is better than no NATO. The Soviet Union, a Eurasian power, has partially shared the European experience and understands the indeterminacy of politics better than the Americans. This has policy implications.

INTERPRETATIONS OF NATO STRATEGY

A reading of the North Atlantic Treaty reveals that the signatories wanted to keep the Russians out of the NATO area. They still want that. The strategy since 1967 has been to preserve peace and to provide for the security of the area *primarily* by a credible deterrence. Should deterrence fail, NATO will attempt to preserve or restore the integrity and security of the area.

Instead of leaping to military capabilities and counting tanks, guns, and soldiers, let us take a look at some of the nonmilitary considerations in the agreed strategy, those which Europeans stress.

The NATO strategic concept assumes that Soviet policy will continue to be based on:
- Economic means
- Political means
- Propaganda
- Subversion
- Military power

in the order listed.

Warsaw Pact capabilities range from major aggression possibly supported by tactical nuclear and chemical weapons to limited aggression, harassment or blockade of Berlin, covert actions, incursions or infiltrations and actions in peripheral areas outside the NATO area. The more probable actions appear to be those at the lower end of the spectrum, such as creating tension by harassment, or blockading Berlin, or other political bullying on the flanks of Europe. This is clearly an appreciation of Soviet intentions, for Soviet capabilities do not limit options to the lower end of the spectrum. Such an appreciation by Europeans is in part self-serving since it produces a threat at a level commensurate with European willingness to address it. On the other hand, it also attempts to see NATO through Russian eyes.

If the only Soviet concern were NATO, the Alliance would have cause for even more anxiety than one finds in Europe today. A case could be made that, given the choice of Soviet or American problems, a reasonable person would prefer the latter. Despite overwhelming Soviet military superiority on its Eastern frontier, Soviet leadership is deeply concerned with China. The fragility of the Warsaw Pact in peace must gnaw at the Soviet military planner as he considers his landlines of communication to the West in time of war. Afghanistan provides yet another illustration of a great power finding it very difficult to accomplish a relatively modest political purpose through the use of military force. Ukrainians, Estonians, Muslims, and a host of other Soviet citizens are unenthusiastic about central direction from Moscow. Economic problems abound in the very system that regards economics as the first cause in understanding the nature and destiny of man. It must be discouraging to Soviet officials to recognize that, despite achievements in space, military preparedness, and great power status, their system faces an array of problems begging for solution.

Marshall I. Goldman contends ". . . there is no doubt that Kremlin leaders are facing the most severe economic problems since the 1940's. Moreover, the long-run prospects for fundamental improvements are bleak." He cites chronic agricultural inefficiencies that have contributed to three successive bad harvests in the USSR, forcing the country into the hard currency markets for grain and beef; the cost in hard currency of financing its empire in Afghanistan, Poland, and Cuba; falling prices for petroleum and gold, the export of which earns the Soviet Union more than 60 percent of its hard currency; an equally depressing situation in industry; and the reinstitution of food rationing in nearly a dozen cities. All of this affects citizen morale, worker discipline, and confidence both in leadership and in the future.[9]

According to this general estimate of Soviet concerns, NATO probably appears far less feeble and fractious to Moscow than it might appear in Western capitals. It is one thing to see a project fail or to suffer a setback and quite another to lose one's religion. Communist theology promises true believers that abundant internal contradictions will bring about the collapse of the West. Cracks in the capitalist system have been studied in Moscow dating from the German revolution in 1918 through the Great Depression to contemporary Western European antinuclear movements. They are scrutinized by Communists for signs of the beginning of the end, but we muddle through; the resilience of the West and its ability to manage without central direction probably causes some dismay in the Soviet Union. Despite highly publicized squabbles that are literally routine in the Alliance, it holds together and Spain has joined NATO. These may be viewed as minor achievements in the West, but it is quite likely that concerned Russians attach more importance to them than we do. This interpretation suggests that NATO strategy is adequate in its first purpose: to deter.

The Soviets see five power centers in the world—the USSR, the USA, Western Europe, China, and Japan—and conclude that four of them are anti-Soviet. Such a conviction—and the need for numerous internal security forces, a need foreign to the American mind—might explain the Soviet sense of being surrounded by enemies and a defensive requirement for large armed forces. We see those armed forces as an offensive threat directed at Western Europe. Clearly, it would be irresponsible for Western political leaders to rule out Soviet aggressive intent. The Russian history of invasions from all directions could produce a paranoia explaining Soviet emphasis on military strength, but Russian expansion over the centuries and Communist rhetoric is to be disregarded at our peril. The point is merely that domination of Western Europe is not the sole reason for Soviet armed forces nor are Western armed forces the only source of Western strength.

NATO's current strategic concept and the measures to implement it emphasize the need to demonstrate the cohesion and determination of the Alliance. Certainly in a strategy designed to defend Europe against possible Russian aggression, military means and instruments are important, but Europeans prefer to stress the nonmilitary thrust of the strategy. This is a reflection of the broader European concept of deterrence which contrasts sharply with the American inclination to spring immediately to a discussion of military means, means which are, after all, just one instrument in the statesman's bag of tricks.

Michael Howard, hardly an innocent, says it another way, a way which speaks for many Europeans.

> We may accept therefore that there is at present [1979] little in the nature of Soviet society or Soviet political intentions to justify the ringing of alarm bells in the West, the evocation of the militaristic elements in our society, and the conversion of the nations of Western Europe into garrison states. Indeed, to do anything of the kind could easily make the situation more dangerous, rather than less. The Soviet leadership is no more prone than we are ourselves to accept that the military preparations of its neighbors are purely defensive, and to refrain from responding in kind.[10]

But it isn't purely a matter of refusal to transform Western societies into garrison states that affects European strategic thinking. They also see the threat to their well-being differently.

Howard goes on to say:

> We [West Europe] are not a prey to be devoured. We are a potential threat which might have to be neutralized, reluctantly and *in extremis,* in full consciousness of all the social, political, as well as military costs involved, and only if all else fails . . . . The attack would be improbable unless the Soviet military could promise rapid success without nuclear escalation, and the alternative appeared to be the disintegration of the Soviet empire.[11]

If Howard is right and if this interpretation of Europe's reading of the NATO documents is correct, the 1967 strategy applies quite well to NATO's situation today and into the 1980's. We seek to deter war. Failing that, our flexible response promises direct defense, deliberate escalation, and general nuclear response. These were and are appropriate measures designed to make it impossible for the Soviet military to promise Soviet political authorities rapid success without a risk of nuclear escalation. A mistaken estimate of Western intentions could have such frightening consequences that inherently conservative Soviet officials can be expected to err on the side of caution. Recollections of US willingness to fight in Korea and Vietnam might give pause to Russians considering the use of force in Europe, particularly since their own military couldn't deliver even on the small problem of Afghanistan.

Bernard P. Kiernan, presumably in response to the general thrust of the Reagan Administration's evolving security policies, makes an impassioned plea for restraint in "The Myth of Peace Through Strength" by suggesting that policies simply saying "more" are dangerous. "Faith in peace through strength requires a kind of magical thinking, a tunnel perspective in which our own power deters everyone else, but no one tries to use *their* power to deter us."[12] In brief, the arms race is frightening not just because it increases the potential levels of violence in conflict, but also because it conditions attitudes so that war is made to appear inevitable. There may be a way to hold down the levels of arms even in the absence of successful negotiations by some tacit signalling to the other side.

This way of devising means to address a threat is essentially European, an approach that can be called a "minimalist strategy."[13] Ken Booth's "Security Makes Strange Bedfellows: NATO's Problems From a Minimalist Perspective" is the most lucid and convincing statement of the minimalist position. In his conclusion he warns that the greatest threat to NATO is the different expectations on the different sides of the Atlantic. The implication is that when NATO comes to an end it will be because Washington's impatience caused its demise: "There is no doubt that the integrity of the Alliance as we have known it has more to fear from the political puritanism and maximalist expectations of some of its supporters than from any Warsaw Pact blitzkrieg . . . . Despite its problems, NATO can be regarded as not falling far short of an optimum Alliance posture after a long period during which the conditions in which it was created have markedly evolved." It emphasizes the appearance of Alliance coherence and determination. The United States certainly takes the appearance of Alliance coherence and determination into account but prefers to emphasize military capability. American military thinkers believe that, under conditions of strategic parity, the best deterrent is one that denies a potential aggressor any possibility of success on the battlefield. It underlines the inclination to leap to military means to solve what American leaders see as a military problem, an engineering solution to a clouded political problem, a craving for a quick fix.

Few soldiers could be happy with NATO's current military strategy, and few American soldiers are happy with the minimalist solution. But military strategy is what soldiers do or plan to do with the means provided by the societies they serve. NATO strategy is specifically designed to handle an admittedly more powerful adversary; it implies risk. Military means are but one element of the total strategy. With the tools provided by our politicians, current NATO strategy recognizes what Bismarck called the art of the possible. While we might prefer the strategy suitable to the sledgehammer we don't have, NATO strategy suits the more modest military tools we have. It says to the Russians: you can't expect a cheap victory; you must go all out; you must expect very serious consequences; you cannot be sure of the outcome. We sometimes forget that current strategy was, after all, an American design as we moved from massive retaliation to flexible response.

Further, for the Russians even a quick victory in Europe isn't winning the war. It only alienates and mobilizes their most dreaded foe, who presumably has just lost a quarter of a million men, has a million American citizens stranded in Europe, and all of its nuclear weapons stationed in Europe in Russian hands—unless they've been fired, an even less attractive prospect considering the likely target. It's not the end of the Russian security problem, but only the middle and offers no obvious or inevitable settlement in their long-run advantage. An angry and unpredictable America is still out there. An even more suspicious China, if that is possible, is still there. Japan might decide that its honeymoon is over. A drive to the Channel starts a process, the outcome of which is no more certain than it would be before the attack. Even if Soviet leaders believe that they enjoy marginal military advantages, they are unlikely to charge West. Their problem at the Channel is more or less what it was at the Elbe. It is most likely that Soviet military might exists to blackmail the West.

This is not to suggest that conventional force levels are unimportant. In time of war the size and effectiveness of NATO's conventional force would certainly influence the timing of decisions that could bear on early defeat or early nuclear escalation. More effective conventional forces would provide a degree of flexibility allowing allied military leaders to fix Soviet forces and political leaders time to face the possible course to the use of nuclear weapons. In this connection, force levels and force development bear directly on the efficacy of the strategy, but military strategy remains, above all, a political question. Military strategy must be fitted into the national strategy it serves. This is the basic message one takes from a reading of Clausewitz.

Our current strategy works in its primary purpose, to deter. Its ability to preserve and restore the integrity and security of the NATO area would obviously be improved if its physical military components—conventional, theater nuclear and strategic forces— were stronger. Absolute superiority, if attainable, is always more assuring. The much-lamented demise of American ascendancy in the strategic balance, the tactical nuclear edge now enjoyed by the Soviet Union, and the longstanding advantage of the Warsaw Pact over NATO in sheer numbers of conventional forces are clearly matters of serious concern to the West, but we have strengths. America and Europe do virtually everything better than the USSR—with the exception of maintaining in-being military power, and that is the consequence of Western societies making choices in priorities. The central question is whether the recognized deficiencies in all three legs of the military strategy cause the total strategy to unravel. That is what must be thought through in connection with the instruments of military strategy, the *what* of that strategy. Related, but something different, is the *how* of the strategy: the concept of flexible response based upon forward defense, reinforcement of the thinly manned forward defense, and the believability of graduated escalation. Simply posed, the question is: do we need a new NATO strategy or should we keep the one we have and implement it better—if only in marginal ways? Need we replace the tool or maintain it?

A NEW STRATEGY FOR NATO?

What is it in NATO strategy that should be changed? To suggest that one rejects deterrence is to express a preference for war. Certainly deterrence has no enemies within the Alliance. Should deterrence fail, NATO declares its intention to defend itself. It would be defeatist to say otherwise. Flexible response forces the aggressor to anticipate resistance at all levels of combat, and graduated escalation means that the aggressor cannot know where it will all end. Perhaps the most frequent target of NATO strategy is forward defense—for good reason.

Professional soldiers shudder at the thought of an enemy breakthrough piercing the thin forward shell, rolling up the flanks, and putting the forward defenders in a sack before external reinforcement arrives on the battlefield. Defense in depth and more mobile reserves would be the prudent military means to prevent such a catastrophe, but both depth for maneuver and mobile reserves are denied NATO field commanders whose forces are deployed in the Federal Republic of Germany.

German insistence upon forward defense is understandable. The prospect of attack from the East, withdrawal from the homeland leaving families to Soviet mercy, and counterattack from the Rhine, English Channel or Pyrenees is singularly unattractive to German statesmen and soldiers whose nation provides the very backbone of NATO's ground forces. The *White Paper 1979* can hardly be accused of equivocating on this subject:

> For the Federal Republic of Germany there can be no alternative to forward defense; in view of her geostrategic situation, her population density near the border to the Warsaw Pact, and the structure of her economy, any conceptual model of defense involving the surrender of territory is

unacceptable. Thirty percent of the population live in a 100 kilometer-wide zone this side of the intra-German border, and twenty-five percent of our industrial capacity is located in that zone. These geographic circumstances rule out any defensive operations conducted flexibly in the depth of the area and accepting the loss of territory . . . . [14]

At times it appears that we are analyzing two strategies: the one the Europeans emphasize is the strategy in place before a shot is fired in anger; the other, the one Americans emphasize, plays its role after that shot. Neither denies the other, but emphasis does matter. It matters in a way very unhelpful to the Alliance. Phony distinctions are made and debated: posing the issue as one of deterrence *or* defense (warfighting capability). Somehow a soldier with a rifle becomes a warfighter, and a strategic weapon system, a Polaris for example, becomes a deterrent. Both can fight wars; both deter. The tough talk of the Americans in the early 1980's tends to emphasize differences when there is a need for emphasis on shared interests and values. Regarding Europe as a "theater" of American global interests and the use of rhetoric-like "warfighting" and "shots across the bow" does not fill Europe with confidence in America's sense of responsibility and is particularly damaging as the sensitive INF issue works itself out. Production of enhanced radiation weapons and construction of a chemical warfare facility in Arkansas adds still more fuel to the transatlantic debate.

Perhaps at root it is the European minimalist approach to NATO strategy that exasperates American leaders and causes them to charge Europe with attempting to get a free ride, but Europe would strenuously object to that contention and point out that the European allies contribute 90 percent of the land forces and 80 percent of the combat aircraft fielded by NATO.[15] Perhaps it is that we wonder why a prosperous Europe cannot provide for its own security 38 years after World War II, but without US leadership Western Europe might well regress to the fractiousness which brought the United States into World Wars I and II. Perhaps it is their idea that we are in Europe to protect Europeans from Russians, but we are in Europe to protect our interests. In any event, these nagging doubts distract us from what is more basic: the European emphasis on the nonmilitary elements of the strategy has never been fully accepted by Americans, and the American emphasis on military means is suspect in a Europe which increasingly regards both Russians and Americans as reckless.

Americans may resent the recent European tendency to see both us and the Russians as irresponsible gamecocks ready to test themselves in Europe's barnyard, but there is an unscientific and unsatisfying explanation for this perception. Soviet behavior has been impressively consistent in its emphasis on increasing its military power. It is about as remarkable as aging as the years pass or the movement from summer to fall. Striking, however, is American behavior which regularly shifts to leave Europeans blinking in surprise. The parliamentary systems softens surprises as one knows in general outline what might be expected of the opposition should it come to power. Little in the European political process prepares Europe for a change of government that goes to philosophical roots. What the Americans accepted as the orderly transfer of power from Mr. Carter to Mr. Reagan is virtually impossible in Europe without a revolution. The willingness of Americans to change course so dramatically is generally disconcerting to Europe. The return of confrontation and the suggestion that detente be sacrificed at the altar of military readiness is unacceptable.

Those most disappointed with NATO are those who expect too much of it, those who feel uncomfortable with anything less than total assurance.[16] They are typically American. Those generally satisfied with NATO are the Europeans, to whom the notion of total assurance is foreign, even laughable given the history of Europe. Here is precisely where the difference in point of view matters. Europeans, as well as Americans, could sleep better if we had, for example, 12 to 15 more NATO divisions in the Central Region, but Europe realizes that such an increase in allied strength is not going to happen, indeed, may be counterproductive to the vitality of the West and its long-term competition with the Soviet Union. The renewed American interest in defense is not matched in Europe where the preference is for a more relaxed international scene. The mainstream of European public opinion in the early 1980's can be summarized as follows: we need the United States; we need NATO; the Soviets represent a threat; we prefer not to station nuclear weapons in our homeland; we choose not to pay more for defense. One might add: we are not interested in adventures around the world; we are interested in living well now and in our old age, and laying a foundation of peace for future generations.[17]

America does not welcome this report from Europe and doesn't want to live with it, but we are not discussing a failed strategy.[18] We want an improved military capability while Europe is telling us that the appearance of Alliance cohesion and determination makes the current balance acceptable to Western Europe, Eastern Europe, and the Soviet Union. It should be acceptable to the United States for it means stability. It would be most useful to the Alliance to shift the discussion from doubts about strategy to means of improving capability at acceptable costs while employing nonmilitary means to civilize the semibarbarians to the East. The strategy serves the Alliance well.

CONCLUSIONS

The European minimalist theory of deterrence may be wishful thinking, more a convenient rationale for doing less than an accurate appraisal of the East-West power relationship, but it seems to be the way Europeans understand NATO and deterrence. Since we see things differently, several courses of action are open to us.

• Continue to press Europe to do more for its security in Europe and for "defense of the West" in selected regions around the globe. This seems to be what the Reagan Administration will do while beefing up both our military means and our tough guy vocabulary. It will produce an incessant series of nagging debates between the United States and Western Europe on a case-by-case basis within the context of a generally deteriorating NATO. That is, raising contentious issues will insure the continuance of acrimonious debate. Differences will fill the pages of newspapers and periodicals, enjoy coverage on the nightly TV news, and generally undermine the appearance of cohesion and determination in the Alliance, all of this at a time when the US pro-defense mood promises to collide with European anxieties and fear while feeding Soviet propaganda designed to make the United States appear to be the disturber of the peace.

• Withdraw to Fortress America seething with resentment directed at those Europeans who refused to be educated by us and rejected US leadership, an option which receives impetus from Senator Ted Stevens and others who argue for reduction in Europe. It is reflected in the harsh language used in security debates to describe unfair burdensharing. American withdrawal from Europe

would also provide us with even less control over Europeans than we have now, thereby further complicating our security calculations.
- Reduce our presence in Europe allowing us to address problems outside the NATO area as European NATO takes up the military slack created by a reduced US presence in Europe. This is an exceedingly dangerous option for it could have the appearance of withdrawal under pressure, seeming evidence that the Soviets are prepared to stay the course while we are not. Unfortunately, this option is attractive to those who see areas outside of Europe as deserving the main US effort in the 1980's. The psychological reaction almost certain to accompany a hasty drawdown in American forces in Europe could cause irreparable damage there and around the world. Europe might cross that nebulous line that separates minimalist deterrence from accommodation and make us an unattractive ally in most corners of the world. One fears that the Soviet Union is well-equipped to exploit such a course of action by calling desertion that which US planners would call a rational reallocation of assets.[19] Before withdrawing US troops from Europe, certain minimal political and military conditions must be met. Among the political conditions: a relatively low state of tension in Europe and around the world, particularly as it applies to the United States and the Soviet Union; willingness on the part of Western Europe to defend itself; the appearance of a rational reorientation of policy rather than the appearance of ignominious defeat. Among the military considerations: readiness of Western Europe to substitute European soldiers for American soldiers; the creation of an internal reinforcement capability, one probably based upon European reservists, the products of conscript systems; resolution of the problems associated with European control of European nuclear weapons. Perhaps most important is the question of who, in the absence of the United States, would lead a European defense or just how Europe would cooperate to defend itself. Whether US troops leave in the 1980's, 1990's, or in the next century, these minimal considerations must be addressed.
- Take into account the European minimalist theory as we proceed in a low-keyed way to improve the West's security stance. This can be undertaken through a combination of arms control

measures as well as through improvements in military forces. Differences should not be exploited for domestic political purposes to the extent that they undermine confidence in the Alliance. Improvements in the NATO area will be marginal, but physical improvements on the military side are less important than influencing the mind of the Soviet planner who must be convinced that NATO is a coherent and determined force.

It is likely that we will continue to press Europe to do more while entertaining plans to reduce US forces in Europe. If the Alliance is to be preserved and strengthened, the preferred course of action is to take Europe's minimalist approach into account while working toward modest increases in readiness and sustainability and to avoid public haggling with our allies which undermines the appearance of cohesion and determination in the Alliance. We should follow a strict policy of no surprises by insuring that US initiatives are thoroughly discussed with allies in private, stressing fundamental shared interests served by the initiatives. Differences will certainly arise, but trade-offs are possible at the highest levels before interest groups on both sides of the Atlantic become involved and complicate already sensitive issues. Planning for the midterm future removes issues from the passion of today.

The "no first use" of nuclear weapons policy proposed by four distinguished Americans experienced in policy formulation bears on this point.[20] The policy recommended appeals to this writer, but even suggestions for gross adjustments in the delicate balance can be dangerous no matter how sound they may be. Arguments similar to those used to resist precipitous US troop withdrawal from Europe seem to apply. That is, there is an equilibrium in Europe that has somehow allowed two inimical systems to avoid armed conflict despite a gut feeling that a clash between East and West is inevitable. The equilibrium is difficult to quantify, but the bits and pieces on both sides seem to balance out and should be adjusted only with great care. One can estimate outcomes of redistribution of the weights, but one cannot be sure that balance could be maintained in the process of adjustment. Detailed consultation and quiet discussion must precede change. Bold action and colorful rhetoric aimed at domestic constituencies should not lead to hasty or careless swipes at the balanced scale.

ENDNOTES

1. The author is aware of the differences in culture, geopolitical factors, and economic conditions that make use of the word "Europe " a sometimes dangerous generalization. Life is filled with risks, so he'll accept this one with his eyes wide open.

2. *Western Security: What Has Changed? What Should Be Done?*, Karl Kaiser, Winston Lord, Thierry de Montbrial, and David Watt, simultaneously published in French by the Insitut Francais Des Relations Internationales under the title, *La Securite De L'Occident: Bilan Et Orientations* and in German by the Forschungsinstitut Der Deutschen Gessellschaft Fur Auswartige Politik under the title *Die Sicherheit Des Westens: Neue Dimensionen Und Aufgaben.* The English title is published by the Council on Foreign Relations, Inc., 58 East 68 Street, New York, NY l0021 and the Royal Institute of International Affairs, 10 St. James's Square, London SWIY 4Le, England, pp. 8-9. "To be sure, tensions or even disagreements are scarcely new in the Western Alliance . . . . Nonetheless, the current transatlantic crisis cannot be considered as just one of a series of short-term episodes. It is more far-reaching . . . ." The authors go on to point out that current differences between Europeans and Americans involve all the Europeans and not only the French as was the case in the 1960's, that divergencies bear not on a single issue but on a whole spectrum of issues, and that the amount of public disagreement has contributed to increasing mutual suspicions and misunderstandings. This crisis, they conclude, is worse than others. Indeed, the authors call the current differences in the Alliance "formidable" because ". . . a key characteristic of the current international situation is precisely that the West is undergoing a phase of strain and dissension at the very time when it also has to deal with a crisis in the East, crisis in the Third World, and a prolonged economic and energy crisis on a global scale," p. 8. See also *Foreign Affairs,* Spring 1981, "European-American Relations: The Enduring Crisis," Josef Joffe, pp. 835-851. Joffe contends that the situation in 1981 ". . . turns the many disputes of the past into minor family squabbles," p. 835. For a sample of deep concern regarding the Alliance, see also: Stephen S. Rosenfeld, "Where Is The Alliance Going?," *The Washington Post,* January 8, 1982; *Time,* November 30, 1981, p. 39, cites Helmut Sonnenfeldt: "You're not just dealing with differences among governments. You're dealing with differences that run deeply into the body politic;" Morton M. Kondracke, "Talking Ourselves Into Breaking Up the Alliance?," *The Wall Street Journal,* January 7, 1982, p. 21; Stephen Haseler and Werner Kaltefleiter, *NATO and Neutralism,* The Heritage Lectures, No. 8, The Heritage Foundation, Washington, DC, 1981; *The Times,* (London), February 15-18, 1982, comments on the Alliance by James Calloghan, Zbigniew Brzezinski, Willy Brandt and Mairice Couve de Murville; *Time,* "Perils and Promise," cites George Ball: "Unease in Europe over American leadership 'is greater than any time I recall since the end of World War II.'" "The Alliance at a Crossroad," Current Policy No. 350, US Department of State, Washington, DC; Ronald C. Nairn, "Why NATO Doesn't Work," *The Wall Street Journal,* March 26, 1982; Hodding Carter, "A 'Great Debate' on the Atlantic Alliance," *The Wall Street Journal,* March 11, 1982.

3. Alexander Haig, while Supreme Allied Commander, Europe, addressed NATO's strategic doctrine in a speech made on October 13, 1976 to the Association of the United States Army. (See *Survival,* January/February 1977, pp. 33-35 for

excerpts from text.) He welcomed the concern for a review of NATO strategy, but generally cautioned against precipitous change in NATO's strategy. He stressed deterrence and seemed to be generally sympathetic to European sensitivities and the European view of our common strategy. Part of the misunderstanding might be the word strategy itself. It might be that Americans generally infer "military" strategy from the word while Europeans normally mean "national" or "total" strategy. See also Waldo D. Freeman, Jr., "NATO Central Region Forward Defense: Correcting the Strategy/Force Mismatch," National Security Affairs Issue Paper No. 81-3, National Defense University, Fort NcNair, Washington, DC 20319; George W. Ball, "How to Frighten Europe Even More," *The Washington Post,* January 26, 1982, p. 19; Drew Middleton, "NATO's Strategy: Major Debate Developing," *The New York Times,* March 4, 1982.

4. Concern for European apathy, pacifism, and neutralism and the general state of the Alliance is reflected in a recent outpouring of articles in the popular press and in scholarly journals. A small sample includes: Leslie H. Gelb, "NATO Is Facing Paralysis of Will, Experts Contend," *The New York Times,* July 12, 1981, pp. 1 and 14; David S. Broder, "Fading Memories Threaten the West," *The Washington Post,* July 12, 1981, pp. C1 and C5; Irving Kristol, "NATO at a Dead End," *The Wall Street Journal,* July 15, 1981; William Greider, "Let's Tell Our Allies Uncle Sucker Is Dead," *The Washington Post,* July 12, 1981, pp. C1 and C5; Simon Serfaty, "The United States and Europe," *The Washington Quarterly,* Winter 1981, pp. 70-86; John Vinocur, "Anti-Americanism in West Germany Appears in Many Guises," *The New York Times,* July 12, 1981; Uwe Nerlich, "Change in Europe: A Secular Trend," *Daedalus,* Winter 1981, pp. 71-103; Theodore Draper, "The Western Misalliance," *The Washington Quarterly,* Winter 1981, pp. 13-69; "Anti-Americanism in Germany," *US News and World Report,* an interview with US Ambassador Arthur F. Burns, April 19, 1982, pp. 63-64; Gerald Frost, "A Last Chance to Save the Western Alliance," *The Wall Street Journal,* February 24, 1982; Flora Lewis, "Confidence in the West," *The New York Times,* March 4, 1982, p. A23; Bernard Gwertzman, "Some Congressmen Suggest Bringing the Boys Back Home," *The New York Times,* March 14, 1982.

5. Richard Petrow, *The Bitter Years,* New York: William Morrow & Co., Inc., 1974. Petrow reports that the Danish Army lost 13 dead and 23 wounded; 20 Germans were killed or wounded, p. 49.

6. George Ott, "The Case Against NATO," *The Washington Monthly,* December 1980, pp. 34-36. Other voices could be cited, but this one is so shrill that it makes the point in very clear terms.

7. *Western Security,* p. 13.

8. See Helmutt Schmidt, "A Policy of Reliable Partnership," *Foreign Affairs,* Spring 1981, pp. 746 and 753-755, for a recent utterance about East-West relations within the context of the Western partnership. See also *Western Security,* p. 23.

Detente policy in general is seen in Europe as having had positive results; while it literally affected millions of Europeans—Germans in particular—detente did not affect the average American and has therefore been generally perceived as a failure.

9. Marshall I. Goldman, "Let's Exploit Moscow's Weakness," *The New York Times,* April 4, 1982, p. E19.

10. Michael Howard, "Social Change and the Defense of the West," *The Washington Quarterly*, Vol. 2, No. 4, Autumn 1979, p. 28.

11. *Ibid.*, p. 29.

12. Bernard P. Kiernan, "The Myth of Peace Through Strength," *The Virginia Quarterly Review*, Vol. 57, No. 2, Spring 1981, pp. 193-209. It would seem that Kiernan was on the leading edge of what has become a popular nuclear "freeze" movement in this country. Whether we are witnessing the export of deep concern for an arms race from Europe to the United States or an almost simultaneous expression of a feeling on both sides of the Atlantic that governments have lost control of events is unclear. In any event, the following excerpt from the Kiernan piece in the spring of 1981 has its echo in the daily press in the spring of 1982:

> Our willingness to accept for so long the risks of nuclear escalation, in the search for military superiority, is now bearing the bitter fruit of greatly increased danger of mutual nuclear annihilation, a precarious impasse created by the illusion that we could achieve absolute security only through absolute military power.

13. Ken Booth, "Security Makes Strange Bedfellows: NATO's Problems From a Minimalist Perspective," *Journal of the Royal United Services Institute for Defense Studies*, December 1975, pp. 3-14.

14. *White Paper 1979: The Security of the Federal Republic of Germany and the Development of the Federal Armed Forces*, published by the Federal Minister of Defense on behalf of the Federal Government, p. 126.

15. *Ibid.*, pp. 23-24.

16. Booth, p. 3.

17. Any number of polls and public opinion surveys would bear out the conclusion arrived at in the text, but see the following "Briefing Papers" produced by the Office of Research, US International Communications Agency, Washington, DC 20547: "West European Public Opinion Deems NATO Essential But Gives Limited Support to Increased Defense Spending," December 3, 1980; "Many West Europeans Oppose Stationing New Nuclear Missiles on Their Soil," November 6, 1980; "West German Views on Security Issues," November 13, 1980; "Norwegians Inclined Against TNF Modernization, But Strongly Supportive of NATO, in Late 1979 Polls," February 13, 1980; "Italians Predominantly Support NATO . . .," February 5, 1981; "Alliances Study: Widespread Support for NATO Continues Among West European Publics, But Few Favor Greater Defense Spending," May 11, 1981.

18. For a sample of American petulance regarding the European "minimalist" perspective, see Ott, pp. 34-36 and William Safire, *The New York Times*, December 11, 1980, p. A35. For a more understanding appreciation of the European security dilemma, see Walter Laqueur, *The New York Times*, January 27, 1981, p. A19; Walter F. Hahn, "Does NATO Have a Future?," *International Security Review*, Summer 1980, pp. 151-172; Laqueur, "Euro-Neutralism," *Commentary*, June 1980, pp. 21-27; Jeffrey Record, "The Western Alliance, Japan and International Security Threats," in *Rethinking US Security Policy for the 1980s*, National Defense University Press, Fort McNair, Washington, DC, 1980; and Edward A. Kolodziej, "European Perspectives on Europe's Roles in the World: The Partial Partner," also in *Rethinking US Security Policy for the 1980s*.

19. Henry G. Gole, "Siren Call to Disaster: The Emerging Campaign for US Troop Reductions in Europe," *Parameters,* Vol. XI, No. 3, September 1981, pp. 22-30. This article develops the point made in the text.

20. "Nuclear Weapons and the Atlantic Alliance," McGeorge Bundy, George F. Kennan, Robert S. McNamara and Gerard Smith, *Foreign Affairs,* Spring 1982, pp. 753-768. Despite passionate reactions to this carefully worded article, it should be emphasized that it calls for the study of ways to strengthen and restructure conventional forces before we relinquish the "first use" option. Edward Corcoran addresses this problem in his "Building a NATO Conventional Defense" in this text.

EPILOGUE

A number of important observations come together in this book. The first is that the relationship between strategic and theater defense issues may be inextricable. Moreover, the complexity of the dynamic interactions between these issues is likely to become more pronounced in the foreseeable future. The implications of the decreasing distinctions between strategic and theater defense issues are enormous. In the arms control area, a strong case can be made for combining the START and INF talks if we aren't disuaded by the utter complexity of it all. Naturally, such a combination would provide increased maneuver room for both sides to include issues for tradeoffs and compromise. However, additional actors and the proliferation of issues would make the achievement of concensus a difficult, lengthy, and uncertain proposition. Also, the ever increasing complexity of defense issues will make it more difficult for US civilian and military national security officials to plan for the future and to explain decisions to concerned publics. Greater lethality and the longer lead times required to develop and field weapon systems combine to make procrastination or miscalculation potentially disastrous.

The second set of crucial points concerns the difficulty of calculating the military balance between the United States and the Soviet Union. The actual state of the balance is less important than each superpower's perceptions of the other's intentions and capabilities. Perceptions, in turn, are based upon cultural dictates deriving from the respective historical experiences and domestic characteristics of the superpowers. NATO allies also bring divergent perceptions of the balance to current political-military developments. Hence, all estimates of the East-West strategic and theater military balance are uncertain and highly dependent upon perspectives and assumptions. It is hardly surprising, then, that estimates placing sole reliance on static measures—numbers of missiles and warheads and total megatonnage—ignore factors that tend to animate human beings.

A third theme, which flows from the first two, concerns the current and projected states of the US-USSR balance. The Soviet Union's rapidly increasing military capabilities create serious problems for the western democracies. It follows that the current US force modernization initiatives appear to be the most direct means of maintaining a credible deterrence of war between the superpowers. However, US civilian and military national security planners are well-advised not to overreact to: the threat; maintenance of empire; demographic trends; questions about future leadership; the Soviet military's vulnerabilities; and the potency residing in the US military forces—all of which are uncertainties that must bedevil Soviet warplanners. Ironically, facile and consistent overstatements of Soviet strength may result in lessened credibility of the nature of the threat. Such overstatements may also stimulate domestic opposition to military programs as well as create doubts in the minds of our friends and adversaries about the vitality of the US deterrent and the willingness of the United States to defend its most crucial interests.

Some of the weapons we will have on hand at the turn of the century are in a conceptual state, some are being developed, and most all are being debated today. Yet, weapons acquisition cannot be undertaken in a policy vacuum. We must ask ourselves in the 1980's where we want to be at the turn of the century. The debate about where we want to go and how we are to get there requires, at a minimum, some concept of the global role and strategy the United States envisions for itself. Moreover, this concept of the future will depend on a thorough understanding and integration of political, economic, and military realities, as well as the cultural dictates of the societies concerned. Certainly questions remain: How do we persuade the US and European publics that nuclear weapons in their backyards are good for them? How do we obtain bipartisan concensus for long-term strategies, when such a concensus seems to surface only in times of clear and present danger? The answer to these questions and others as well as the formulation of US foreign and national security policy increasingly will necessitate comprehensive public debate and, in all likelihood, demand the evolution of bipartisan approaches to these complex and highly integrated problems. *The Defense of the West* takes an important step in this direction.

                              KEITH A. BARLOW
                              Colonel, Infantry
                              Director, Strategic Studies Institute

CONTRIBUTORS

KEITH A. BARLOW, Colonel, US Army, has been Director of the Strategic Studies Institute since June 1981. An Infantryman of over 27 years' service, he is a Ranger and a Master Parachutist. Colonel Barlow saw combat as an advisor to the Vietnamese Airborne and as an Infantry Battalion Commander. During the atomic tests in the 1950's, he was a pathfinder evaluator. Additionally, he has served in numerous staff assignments including Special Assistant to the Army Chief of Staff. He served three years in Iran before, during, and after the 1979 revolution. He has lectured widely and appeared on National Television in regard to the Middle East. Colonel Barlow graduated from the US Military Academy and earned his master's degree at the University of Pennsylvania.

WILLIAM P. BOYD, Colonel, US Army, has been assigned to the Strategic Studies Institute since the summer of 1980. He is a graduate of West Point and holds a master's degree in nuclear physics from Tulane University. Colonel Boyd served in Vietnam where he commanded a field artillery battalion. He has served on the Department of the Army Staff as Military Assistant to the Chief Scientist, and on the staff of Headquarters US Army Europe and 7th Army, Heidelberg, West Germany, where he was Chief of Manpower.

OTTO P. CHANEY, Ph.D., is a consultant on defense matters. Prior to his retirement from the Army, he was an analyst with the Strategic Studies Institute, US Army War College. He joined the Institute after serving as Deputy Chief of Staff, Intelligence, US Command, Berlin. He is a graduate of the Army's Foreign Area Officer Program, specializing in the USSR and East Europe, and has earned a doctorate in Russian Area Studies from American University. He has served twice on the Soviet missile desk in the Office of the Assistant Chief of Staff, Department of the Army, and Defense Intelligence Agency; two tours with the US Military Liaison Mission, East Germany; as Army Attache, Czechoslovakia; and with the Office of National Estimates, CIA.

EDWARD A. CORCORAN, Ph.D., works as a private consultant in Soviet affairs. In addition to a doctorate in political science from Columbia University, he holds a certificate from Columbia's Russian Institute and has had extensive Soviet area experience as a member of the US Army's Foreign Area Officer Program. His Army assignments included service in the Office of the Deputy Chief of Staff for Intelligence in Headquarters, US Army Europe, a tour as a liaison officer to the Soviet Commander-in-Chief in East Germany, and four years' experience as a strategic analyst and study manager at the Strategic Studies Institute of the US Army War College.

HENRY G. GOLE, Colonel, US Army, is a Strategic Research Analyst with the Strategic Studies Institute, US Army War College. He is a graduate of Hofstra University and holds master's degrees in education from Hofstra; in history and politics from the Fletcher School of Law and Diplomacy, Tufts University; and in German history from Stanford University. Colonel Gole was the Assistant Army Attache in Bonn from 1973 to 1977, and he subsequently taught European history for three years at the US Military Academy. Colonel Gole's career has also included three previous tours in Germany, two tours in Vietnam, and enlisted service in Korea during the Korean War.

ROBERT KENNEDY, Ph.D., is currently the Professor of Military Strategy in the Department of National Security at the US Army War College. A graduate of the US Air Force Academy, Dr. Kennedy completed his graduate work in political science at Georgetown University. Dr. Kennedy served on active duty briefly with the Army and then with the Air Force from 1958 to 1971 and is currently a reserve officer. Prior to his present position, he was a senior researcher at the Strategic Studies Institute.

DANIEL S. PAPP, Ph.D., is Professor of International Affairs and the Director of the School of Social Sciences at Georgia Institute of Technology and was formerly a Research Professor at the Strategic Studies Institute of the US Army War College. A graduate of Dartmouth College, he received his doctorate in international affairs at the University of Miami's Center for Advanced International Studies. During the academic year 1983-1984, Professor Papp has served as a Senior Research Fellow at the Airpower Research Institute of the Air University. He has published and lectured widely on international affairs.

TODD R. STARBUCK, Lieutenant Colonel, US Army, is a Political-military Analyst assigned to US Army Japan/IX Corps. He previously served as a research analyst with the Strategic Studies Institute from 1980 to 1983, following an assignment in Singapore. A China Foreign Area Officer and a specialist in Asian security matters, he holds master's degrees from the Naval Postgraduate School (national security affairs) and the US Army Command and General Staff College (military art and science). He has also served in a variety of armored cavalry command and staff assignments in the United States and Vietnam.

JOHN M. WEINSTEIN, Ph.D., author of numerous articles on Soviet and American strategic matters, is a Strategic Nuclear Forces Analyst on the Army General Staff. After receiving a Ph.D. in international politics from the University of Florida, Dr. Weinstein taught at several colleges and universities and served as a Visiting Research Professor at the US Army War College's Strategic Studies Institute. He has attended courses on weapons effects and employment at the Interservice Nuclear Weapons School and the US Army Chemical School.

INDEX

Aaron, Raymond, 382
ABM. See Antiballistic missile systems
ABM Treaty, 159, 175, 176, 207, 208, 209, 221(n54)
Accommodation, defined, 155(n58)
ACDA. See Arms Control and Disarmament Agency
ACTs. See Area Combat Troops
Adelman, Kenneth L., 114(n68)
Advanced Technology Bomber (ATB), 28
Afghanistan, 117, 123, 129, 131, 132, 140, 142, 240, 288, 297(n95), 297(n97), 400, 404, 423
Air defenses. See Antiballistic missile systems; Ballistic missile defense; Bomber forces; Tactical Air Forces
AirLand Battle, 60, 65, 358-359, 369
Air Launched Miniature Vehicle (ALMV), 160
Albania, 279, 417
Alexiev, Alex, 286
Alliance, defined, 155(n58)
All Quiet on the Western Front, 330
ALMV. See Air Launched Miniature Vehicle
Altunin, A., 93
Always Ready for Defense of the Motherland, 286
Amalrik, Andrei, 63
Amin, Hafizullah, 297(n97)
Anderson, Richard, 283, 284
Andropov, Yuri, 44, 45, 55, 211, 287, 288, 384
Antarctic Treaty, 376
Antiballistic missile systems (ABM), 30, 172
  SALT and, 188, 203
  Soviet, 27, 263
  U.S., 158, 159, 189-190, 217(n4)
  See also entries for individual weapons systems
Antisatellite (ASAT) capabilities, 158-159, 169
  Soviet, 160-161, 184(n35)
  U.S., 160, 162, 168
Antisubmarine warfare (ASW), 18, 22. See also Submarines
Area Combat Troops (ACTs), 362-364, 366, 367, 368, 373(n38), 373(n39), 374(n50)
Armed Forces of the Soviet State, The, 281
Armor forces, 343(n82), 355-357, 370(n9)
Arms control, 31, 66, 185-186, 375-412, 439
  ambiguity, 209-210
  definition problems, 196-199
  force comparability and, 199-201
  "freedom-to-mix" concept, 200

historical incentives, 376-381
impediments to, 386-396
MBFR proposals, 390-391
NATO and, 195, 256(n51)
objectives, 213-214
PRC and, 191, 195
range and, 219(n32)
sanctions, 207-210
technological advance and, 202-204, 205-206, 393-394
threat comparability and, 189, 193-196, 217(n6)
See also ABM Treaty; Mutual and Balanced Force Reduction; Strategic Arms Limitation Talks; Strategic Arms Reduction Talks
Arms Control and Disarmament Agency (ACDA), 85, 217(n4)
ASAT. *See* Antisatellite capabilities
ASEAN. *See* Association of Southeast Asian Nations
Association of Southeast Asian Nations (ASEAN), 121, 122, 123, 130
ASW. *See* Antisubmarine warfare
ATB. *See* Advanced Technology Bomber
Atlantic Richfield Company, 124
Australia, 151(n54)
Automobiles, 70(n27), 82, 111(n29)

BACKFIRE bombers, 14, 220(n43), 233, 235, 241, 406
Baikal-Amur Mainline (BAM), 128-129
Ballistic missile defense (BMD), 157-184. *See also* Antiballistic missile systems
BAM. *See* Baikal-Amur Mainline
Bayerenov, 297(n97)
Bear bomber, 198-199, 220(n43)
Beck, Abraham S., 299(n94)
Belenko, Viktor, 283
Bertram, Christoph, 204
Betts, Richard, 41, 358
B-52 bomber, 28, 198-199, 220(n43)
Binary weapons. *See* Chemical weapons
Bison bomber, 198-199, 220(n43)
BMD. *See* Ballistic missile defense
Bomber forces
  Soviet, 14, 28, 198-199, 220(n43), 233, 235, 241
  U.S., 26-28, 188, 198-199, 200, 220(n43), 257(n58), 270(n43)

445

Bond, Daniel, 70(n19)
B-1 bomber, 28, 198–199, 220(n43)
Booth, Ken, 425
Bosporus, 272–273
Brandt, Willy, 365, 385, 398
Brezhnev, Leonid, 118, 125, 130, 191, 197, 243, 259, 287, 288, 291(n5), 297(n93), 297(n94), 383
Brezhnev Doctrine, 396–397, 407
Brinton, Crane, 49
Britain, 178, 185, 219(n29), 417, 419
 arms control and, 195
 strategic balance and, 244–246
Brown, Frederic J., 326
Brown, Harold, 12, 194, 343(n83), 344(n92)
Brzezinski, Zbigniew, 5
"Build-down" proposal, 222(n71)
Bulgaria, 278
Bundy, McGeorge, 214
Burbery, John W., Jr., 274
Burck, Gordon, 321
Burke, Kelley, 184(n35)
Burns, John F., 71(n32), 289
Burt, Richard, 193, 218(n27)
Buzdalov, I. N., 48

Caldwell, Lawrence, 190
Campbell, John C., 272
Canada, 151(n4)
"Carte Blanche," 228
Carter, Jimmy, 5, 6, 160, 430
 arms control and, 197, 208
 BMD policy, 183(n24)
 civil defense policy, 95, 96, 107, 221(n49)
 European defense and, 242
 PRC policy, 121
 Presidential Directive 41, 80, 95, 107, 111(n15)
 SALT and, 191
 Soviet Union policy, 120
Central Asian republics, 51
Central Group of Forces (CGF), 261
CGF. *See* Central Group of Forces
Chaney, Otto P., 61
Chemical Warfare, A Study in Restraint, 326
Chemical weapons, 299–347
 cost of, 312–315, 329, 337(n8)
 defense against, 343(n86)
 delivery systems, 336, 345(n106)
 as deterrents, 335
 effectiveness of, 308–310, 339–340(n54)
 NATO, 304, 333
 Soviet, 303–304, 306, 316–317, 338(n13), 342(n76), 343(n83), 344(n87), 404
 U.S., 304–305, 314–316, 338(n30), 346–347(n111)
 use constraints, 306–308, 321–323, 326–329, 329–332, 344(n89), 345(n95), 345–346(n108), 346(n110)
 use history, 306–307, 317–321, 342–343(n79)
 use training, 339(n35)
Chernenko, Konstantin U., 211, 212
China, 117–118. *See also* People's Republic of China
Civil defense
 crisis stability and, 95–96, 98–99
 deterrence and, 79, 95–96, 98
 Soviet, 20–21, 78–95, 106–107, 108–109, 112(n34), 202
 U.S., 80, 95–106, 107–109, 202, 221(n49)
Clark, William P., 151(n2)
Clarke, Bruce C., 342(n79)

Clausewitz, Karl von, 8, 9, 330, 332
Clayberg, Richard, 61
Cold Dawn, 187
Cold launch, 220(n41)
Cold War, 253(n1)
Collins, Edward M., 342(n79)
Command, control, communications and intelligence (C³I)
 armor forces and, 355
 civil defense and, 109
 recovery and, 90, 92–93
 Soviet, 62, 81
 U.S., 29, 221(n50)
Committee on the Present Danger, 7
Communist Party of the Soviet Union (CPSU), 56
Conference on Security and Cooperation in Europe (CSCE), 57, 396–401, 402, 408
Conventional forces
 FRG, 428–429
 cost of, 381
 NATO, 60, 229, 261, 262(table), 263, 264(table), 349–374, 382–383, 397, 402, 409(n14), 410(n18), 427, 428, 437(n20)
 Soviet, 60, 155–156(n67), 259–261, 262(tables), 263, 264(tables), 265–266, 343(n82), 371(n18), 374(n54), 403–404
 Warsaw Pact, 60, 260–261, 262(table), 263, 264(table), 294(n52), 351–352, 353, 355–357, 403, 427
Conventional war, 269, 270(fig.), 271–276, 324–325, 331, 339(n45), 347(n118), 351–352, 362–364, 366–367, 372(n34), 373(n38), 380, 422, 426–427, 428
Corcoran, Edward, 61
Counterforce options, 36(n38)
CPSU. *See* Communist Party of the Soviet Union
CR. *See* Crisis relocation
Crisis relocation (CR), 101–106, 115(n90), 116(n93). *See also* Civil defense
Crisis stability, 9, 26, 30, 31, 246–249
 BMD and, 173–175
 civil defense and, 95–96, 98–99
Cruise missiles
 in Europe, 66, 242, 247, 248, 250, 252, 256(n51), 379
 U.S., 29
CSCE. *See* Conference on Security and Cooperation in Europe
C³I. *See* Command, control, communications and intelligence
Cuba, 423
Czechoslovakia, 277, 278, 280, 295(n61)
 invasion of, 133, 186, 281, 297(n103), 397, 398
 rebellion, 396

Dardanelles, 272–273
Data base, 389. *See also* Verification
Defense Civil Preparedness Agency, 96
Defense spending
 NATO, 381–382
 Soviet, 77, 383–384
 U.S., 163(fig.), 164, 383
Defense Technologies Study Team, 164
DeGaulle, Charles, 40, 111(n12), 311
Democratic centralism, 72(n72)
Deng Xiaoping, 134, 135, 137, 138
Denmark, 417
de Rose, Francois, 247
DET. *See* Directed energy transfer weapons

Detente, 384–385, 420
  defined, 155(n58)
  European view, 435(n8)
Deterrence, 35(n30), 64, 374(n53)
  BMD and, 173, 174, 176–177
  of chemical warfare, 310–312, 323–326, 344(n92)
  chemical weapons and, 335
  civil defense and, 79, 95–96, 98
  credibility, 35–36(n37), 238–240, 249, 251, 311–312, 360, 379, 380
  escalation and, 11, 30–31
  in Europe, 244, 245–246, 249–251, 323–326, 405
  European concept of, 424
  extended conflict and, 61
  launch-on-warning policy, 65, 200
  NATO and, 240, 360
  nonmilitary adjustments, 41–42
  Soviet view, 8, 10–13
  strategic balance and, 250, 251–252, 257(n71), 381, 382–383
de Vries, Klaas, 238
Directed energy transfer (DET) weapons, 157–158, 162–164, 165, 166, 168–169, 171–172, 180, 181
Disarmament, 410(n25)
Djilas, Milovan, 290
Donnelly, Christopher, 266, 278, 292, 335
Dornan, James, Jr., 254(n16)
Downey, Thomas J., 26
Dubček, Alexander, 281
Dulles, John Foster, 35(n37)
Dunkirk Treaty, 226
Dupuy, Trevor, 359
Dzur, Martin, 281

Eagleburger, Lawrence, 64, 68, 246
East Germany. *See* German Democratic Republic
Economic and Social Consequences of Nuclear Attack on the United States, 105
Eisenhower, Dwight D., 228
Electromagnetic pulse (EMP), 15
Ember, Lois R., 345(n97)
EMP. *See* Electromagnetic pulse
EMT. *See* Equivalent megatonnage
Entente, defined, 155(n58)
"Equal security," 244–245
Equivalent megatonnage (EMT), 199, 220(n40)
Erickson, John, 10, 248, 303
Ermarth, Fritz, 9
Escalation, 266, 405, 425, 428
  control, 93, 114(n68), 380
  deterrence and, 11, 30–31
  dominance, 13, 16, 30
Europe
  conventional war in, 269, 270(fig.), 271–276, 324–325, 339(n45), 347(n118), 351–352, 362–364, 366–367, 372(n34), 373(n38), 380, 422, 426–427, 428
  defense of, 39–40, 69(n1), 111(n12), 226–258, 259–297, 349–374, 413–437
  economy, 415, 419
  occupation of, 225–226, 253(n3)
  PRC and, 137, 140
  Soviet trade with, 67, 76(n124)
  world view, 416–421, 429–431
Eurostrategic forces, 233, 405
Exxon Corporation, 124

Fallaci, Oriana, 277

FB-111 bomber, 270(n43)
FBS. *See* Forward-based systems
Federal Emergency Management Agency (FEMA), 96, 221(n49)
Federal Republic of Germany (FRG), 339(n34), 417
  arms control and, 385
  Bundeswehr, 397, 402, 403, 407
  conventional forces, 428–429
  conventional war in, 331
  GDR and, 398–399, 411(n39)
  MBFR and, 388
  Territorial Army, 364–365, 388
FEMA. *See* Federal Emergency Management Agency
FENCER, 233, 241
Feshbach, Murray, 50, 72(n62)
First-strike capability, 81, 85
  Soviet, 15, 19–20, 22, 57, 77, 93, 248
  U.S., 24
Flexible response, 229, 380, 382, 425, 428
FLOGGER, 233
Footprint, 37(n63)
Force comparability, 199–201
Force expansion
  Soviet, 40–41, 44, 57, 58, 155–156(n67), 227–228, 254(n21), 254(n23), 260, 440
  U.S., 291(n4)
Force modernization, 23–29, 289
  deterrence and, 64
  NATO, 241–243, 297(n102)
  Soviet, 78, 230–237, 287, 296(n87)
  U.S., 440
  Warsaw Pact, 263, 265–266
Force quality
  Soviet, 296(n73), 344
  Warsaw Pact, 282–289
Ford, Gerald R., 5, 33(n11), 197, 208
Forward-based systems (FBS), 196–198
  NATO, 405–406
  U.S., 380
Four Power Agreement on Berlin, 399
France, 419
  arms control and, 195
  MBFR and, 388
  military capabilities, 219(n29)
  NATO and, 372(n36)
  strategic balance and, 244–246
  territorial forces, 365
Fratricide, 19
Freeze movement, 436(n12)
FRG. *See* Federal Republic of Germany
Fronts, 293(n35)
Frunze Military Academy, 280
Fulwyler, Niles J., 328

Gabriel, Charles A., 265, 271
Gaither Report, 34(n12)
Galen, Justin, 235
Gallois, Pierre, 235
Gandhi, Indira, 123, 131
Garnysz, Casimir, 294(n55)
Garwin, Richard, 86
Gelman, Harry, 126
Geneva Conventions, 375
Geneva Protocol, 342(n74), 375
German Democratic Republic (GDR), 278, 291(n5), 417
  FRG and, 398–399, 411(n39)
  peace movement in, 386
  rebellion, 396

447

recognition of, 397–399
German-Soviet Friendship Society, 284
Germany. *See* Federal Republic of Germany; German Democratic Republic
Gibian, George, 295(n61)
Giles, R. L., 295(n58)
Goldman, I., 423
Gomulka, Wladyslaw, 285
Goure, Leon, 82
Graham, Daniel O., 170–171
Gray, Colin, 9, 65
"Greater-than-expected" threat, 189, 217(n6)
Grechko, Andrei Antonovich, 240, 281
Group of Soviet Forces-Germany (GSFG), 60, 260–261, 275
GSFG. *See* Group of Soviet Forces-Germany
Guertner, Gary, 90

Hague Conventions, 375
Haig, Alexander, 143, 395, 434–435(n3)
Hallovan, Richard, 163, 164
Harker, R. A., 101
Hart, Liddell, 228, 231
Hasselkorn, Avigdor, 292
Hatfield, Mark, 191
Hegemony, Soviet, 225–226, 227, 424
Hitler, Adolf, 273, 306, 377, 417
HLG. *See* North Atlantic Treaty Organization, High Level Group
Holland, 339(n34)
Hong Kong, 151(n4)
Horvats, Saul, 328
"Hot line," 376, 384
Howard, Michael, 350, 424–425
Hua Guofeng, 133
Huang Hua, 143
Human rights, 68
Hungary, 277, 278, 359
 MBFR and, 388
 peace movement in, 386
 rebellion, 396
Husak, Gustav, 281
Hu Yaobang, 133, 134
Hyland, William, 287

ICBMs. *See* Intercontinental Ballistic Missiles
India, 131
Indonesia, 130
Industry vulnerability, 96, 107–108
 Soviet, 84–88, 87(fig.), 91(fig.), 112(n32), 112(n48), 202
 U.S., 105–106, 202
INF. *See* Intermediate-range nuclear forces
Intercontinental Ballistic Missiles (ICBMs), 180, 188
 basing, 15, 17–18, 24, 78
 BMD and, 175
 guidance systems, 16, 17, 22
 missile hardness, 171–172
 reentry reliability, 16
 SALT and, 203, 387
 Soviet, 13–14, 16, 39, 78, 188, 199–200, 201
 U.S., 14–15, 24, 188, 200
 warhead yield, 17–18
Intermediate range ballistic missiles (IRBMs), 235
Intermediate-range nuclear forces (INF), 246
 control of, 194, 195, 198, 210, 241, 245, 389, 404–407, 408, 439. *See also* Arms control
 deterrence and, 252
 in Europe, 241, 243, 244

NATO, 231, 233, 234(table), 235, 236(table)
 Soviet, 231, 233, 234(table), 239
 U.S., 247
International Institute for Strategic Studies, 62
Iran, 131, 153(n38), 160
IRBMs. *See* Intermediate range ballistic missiles
Islam, in Soviet Union, 72(n70)
Ismay, Lord, 226
Israel, 154(n48)

Jackson, Henry, 5–6
Japan, 121, 122, 127, 129, 131, 140, 142, 146, 151(n4), 424, 427
 BMD and, 177, 178, 179
 Soviet relations, 245
 trade relations, 153(n38)
Jaruzelski, Wojciech, 294(n55)
Joffe, Josef, 240
Johnson, Lyndon B., 186, 190
Jones, David, 305–306
Jones, T. K., 81, 85, 86, 88, 89, 93, 112(n30)

Kampuchea, 122, 130, 132, 140, 142
Katz, Arthur, 105
Keegan, George J., Jr., 6–7, 33(n11)
Keliher, John, 392
Kemp, Geoffrey, 86
Kennan, George, 365
Kennedy, John F., 23, 215, 384
Kennedy, Robert, 58
Khrushchev, Nikita, 9, 45, 55, 67, 132, 140, 190, 237, 285, 287, 297(n93), 354, 377–378, 383, 384, 385
Kiernan, Bernard P., 436(n12), 425
Kim Il-sung, 122, 130
Kirilenko, Andrei, 288
Kissinger, Henry, 111(n12), 197, 311, 376
Kohl, Helmut, 407
Korean War, 227
Kosygin, Alexei, 55, 186
Kuzichkin, Vladimir, 288, 297(n97)
Kuznetsov, V. V., 186

Lagomarsino, Robert John, 342(n79)
Lambeth, Benjamin S., 11, 35(n30), 58–59, 61
Laser weapons. *See* Directed energy transfer weapons
Launch-on warning (LOW), 65, 200
Launch-through-attack (LTA), 200
Laurino, R. K., 101
Lawson, Eugene, 155(n61)
League of Nations, 375
"Legends of the Strategic Arms Race," 7
Legvold, Robert, 10
Leibermanism, 55
Lenin, V. I., 9, 11, 48, 55
Levin, Carl, 344(n92)
Levine, Herbert, 70(n19)
Lifton, Robert J., 89
Linkage, 30, 249, 257(n71), 395–396, 408
Lobachev, G., 237
Logistics
 in chemical warfare, 326–327, 339(n34), 345(n96), 345(n98), 345(n103)
 Soviet, 275–276, 294(n50)
LOW. *See* Launch-on-warning
LTA. *See* Launch-through-attack
Luttwak, Edward, 393

McGovern, George, 191

McNamara, Robert, 188, 217(n4)
Maginot Line, 372(n34)
Mahan, George H., 217(n4)
Malaysia, 130
Malenkov, Georgiy, 9, 190
Maneuverable reentry vehicles (MaRVs), 172
Mansfield Resolution, 382, 401
Mao Zedong, 118, 132, 133, 135
MaRVs. *See* Maneuverable reentry vehicles
Marxism-Leninism, 73(n74)
MBFR. *See* Mutual and Balanced Force Reduction
Mearsheimer, John, 60–61, 289, 297(n102), 357–358
Mediterranean Sea, 272–273
Meselson, Matthew, 344(n91)
Microwave weapons. *See* Directed energy transfer weapons
Midgetman missiles, 25
Military doctrine
 chemical weapons and, 317–318
 Soviet, 9, 237–238, 266–269
Military spending. *See* Defense spending
Military training, 374(n50)
 for chemical warfare, 339(n35)
 Soviet, 61
 U.S., 67
 Warsaw Pact, 284–285
Miller, C. F., 101
Mine warfare, 372(n35). *See also* Space mines
Minimalist strategy, 425–426, 429, 431, 432–433
Minuteman missiles, 24–25
MIRVs. *See* Multiple Independently Targetable Reentry Vehicles
Mobile missiles, 206–207
 in Europe, 248
 Soviet, 209, 222(n58), 235
 U.S., 25
MPS. *See* Multiple protective shelter
Multiple Independently Targetable Reentry Vehicles (MIRVs), 180, 183(n29), 205
 control of, 203, 387–388
 deterrence and, 177
 SALT and, 387–388
 Soviet, 14, 15, 39, 78, 200, 201, 235, 241
 U.S., 189–190, 200
Multiple protective shelter (MPS), 24
Mussolini, Benito, 320
Mutual and Balanced Force Reduction (MBFR), 66, 388–393, 398, 399, 400–404, 406, 408. *See also* Arms control
MX system, 24–25, 206, 216, 408
Myagkov, Aleksei, 282, 283, 286
"Myth of Peace Through Strength, The," 425

Napoleon I, 417
National Command Authority (NCA), 15
National Intelligence Estimate (NIE), 6–7
Nationalism, Soviet, 50–51
National security, 119–120
 PRC, 133, 136
 Soviet, 73(n82), 125–132, 146–147, 152(n22)
 U.S., 120–125, 151(n2)
National Technical Means (NTM), 205, 206
NATO. *See* North Atlantic Treaty Organization
Naval Treaties (1922 and 1930), 375
NCA. *See* National Command Authority
Newhouse, John, 187, 217(n4), 221(n56)
NGF. *See* Northern Group of Forces
NIE. *See* National Intelligence Estimate
Nimetz, Matthew, 400

Nitze, Paul H., 6, 7, 33(n8), 33–34(n12), 192
Nixon, Richard, 197
 arms control and, 189, 193
 defense policy, 112(n32)
 PRC and, 117
 SALT and, 189
No first use policy, 433, 437(n20)
Nonproliferation treaty, 187, 376. *See also* Arms control
Normalization, defined, 155(n58)
NORTHAG. *See* Northern Army Group
North Atlantic Treaty Organization (NATO), 142, 145, 226
 arms control and, 195, 256(n51)
 BMD and, 177–179
 cohesiveness, 79, 255(n43), 289, 290, 300, 332, 380, 414–415, 421, 423, 424, 426, 431, 433, 434(n2)
 defenses, 39, 40, 60, 227, 230–237. *See also* Europe, defense of
 dual-track decision, 241, 242–243, 379
 German partition and, 397–399
 High Level Group (HLG), 242
 Long-Term Defense Program, 242
 missile installations, 66, 210, 242–243, 244, 246, 247, 248, 250, 252, 256(n51), 379
 Nuclear Planning Group (NPG), 242
 objectives, 359–360
 PRC and, 137
 Special Forces, 367
 strategy, 419, 422–431, 435(n3)
Northern Army Group (NORTHAG), 269, 270, 297(n102)
Northern Group of Forces (NGF), 260–261
North Korea, 121, 122, 130
Norway, 339(n34), 364, 365
NPG. *See* North Atlantic Treaty Organization, Nuclear Planning Group
NSC-68, 33–34(n12)
NTM. *See* National Technical Means
Nuclear exchange
 casualties, 88–89, 94, 114(n72)
 effects of, 88–90, 92, 113(n59)
Nuclear free zones, 187

Obasanjo, Olusegun, 76(n123)
Occidental Petroleum Corporation, 124
Oder-Neisse line, 398
Ogarkov, Nikolai, 286, 287, 290, 296(n87)
OMGs. *See* Operational Maneuver Groups
Operational Maneuver Groups (OMGs), 268–269
Osgood, Robert E., 253(n3)
Ostpolitic, 385, 398, 402, 411(n39), 420
Outer Space Treaty, 160, 175–176, 376

Pakistan, 123, 131
Parity. *See* Strategic balance
Partial Test Ban Treaties, 376. *See also* Arms control
Particle beam weapons. *See* Directed energy transfer weapons
Peace movement, 381
 in Europe, 332
 in U.S., 212
 in Warsaw Pact nations, 288–289, 386
Penetration forces, 366–367
Penkovsky, Oleg, 338(n18)
People's Liberation Army (PLA), 137, 138, 155(n65), 156(n67)
People's Republic of China (PRC), 117–156, 406, 424, 427

arms control and, 191, 195
ASEAN nations and, 123
Cultural Revolution, 118
economy, 138, 139, 147
Europe and, 137, 140
Japan and, 139
military capabilities, 138–139, 147–150, 219(n29)
modernization, 133–135, 137, 154(n35)
security interests, 133, 136
Soviet relations, 117, 118–119, 125–132, 136–137, 140–142, 145–147, 245, 377, 422
Thailand and, 151(n9)
Third World and, 118, 119, 135–136, 142–143
U.S. relations, 117, 118, 119, 120–125, 127, 133, 136, 137, 142–144, 145, 154(n48), 155(n61)
Perle, Richard, 97, 99, 104
Pershing, John Joseph, 302, 318
Pershing II missiles
 basing, 248–249
 in Europe, 66, 210, 242–243, 244, 246, 247, 250, 252, 256(n51), 379
 guidance, 257(n60)
Philippines, 130
Pike, Alan, 162
Pipes, Richard, 7–8, 10, 33(n8)
PLA. *See* People's Liberation Army
Podrabinek, Kirill, 283
Poland, 129, 240, 277, 278, 279, 294(n55), 294–295(n57), 295(n61), 398, 400, 404, 417, 423
Politburo, 55
Polk, James H., 274
Population vulnerability, 79
 Soviet, 80–84, 112(n31), 202
 U.S., 96, 97, 202
 See also Civil defense
PRC. *See* People's Republic of China
President's Commission on Strategic Forces. *See* Scowcroft Commission
Proxmire, William, 191–192

Rakowski, Mieczyslaw, 277
Rapprochement, defined, 155(n58)
Reagan, Ronald, 5, 6, 41, 77, 184(n35), 430, 431
 arms control and, 192–193, 212, 214, 216, 218(n27), 222(n71), 244, 406, 407, 408
 Berlin initiative, 408
 BMD policy, 157–158, 161–164, 165, 166, 174–175, 176, 184(n35)
 chemical weapons and, 301, 313–314, 337(n8)
 civil defense and, 80, 96–98, 107, 221(n49)
 defense priorities, 109, 425
 European defense and, 243
 Security Decision Directive Number 26, 96, 98, 107
 Soviet Union policy, 120, 126
 zero option proposal, 244, 406
Recovery
 C³I and, 90, 92–93
 Soviet capability, 88–93
 U.S. capability, 100–106, 107, 115(n88), 115(n89)
Reentry vehicles (RVs), 172
Rice, Condoleezza, 280
Romanians, 277, 278, 279
Ross, Dennis, 10
Rowny, Edward, 192
Rumsfeld, Donald H., 107
Rush-Bagot agreement, 185
Russell, Richard, 217(n4)
RVs. *See* Reentry vehicles
Rybkin, Ye., 66

SAC. *See* Strategic Air Command
Sagan, Carl, 21
SALT. *See* Strategic Arms Limitation Talks
Salt Lexicon, 196
Sanctions. *See under* Arms control
Savkin, Vasiliy Ye., 237, 267, 310
SCC. *See* Standing Consultative Commission
Schelling, Thomas, 312
Schlesinger, James R., 5, 112(n32)
Schmidt, Helmut, 229–230, 327
Scowcroft Commission, 18, 24, 29, 73(n81), 112(n42), 180
"Security Makes Strange Bedfellows," 425–426
Seignious, George, 205
Semenov, Vladimir S., 196
SGF. *See* Southern Group of Forces
SHAPE. *See* Supreme Headquarters Allied Powers Europe
Short range systems, 232(table)
Sidorenko, A. A., 237
Silo hardness
 uncertainties of, 17–18, 24
 verification and, 208
Simes, Dimitri K., 255(n44)
Singapore, 130
Single Integrated Operational Plan (SIOP), 12
Sino-Japanese Treaty of Peace and Friendship, 129
SIOP. *See* Single Integrated Operational Plan
SLBMs. *See* Submarine-launched ballistic missiles
SLCMs. *See* Cruise missiles
Slessor, John, 365
Smith, Gerard, 197, 204
Sokolovsky, V. D., 310
Southern Group of Forces (SGF), 261
South Korea, 146, 151(n4)
Soviet Military Power, 57, 77, 259
Soviet Union
 agriculture, 47–49, 71(n37)
 demographics, 47, 50–53, 72(n62), 72(n66)
 economy, 43–50, 70(n19), 70(n23), 128–129, 190, 202, 217(n10), 279, 383–384, 423
 ethnic tensions in, 50–53, 344(n87), 423
 military doctrine, 9, 237–238, 266–269
 national debt, 71(n43)
 political vulnerabilities, 53–57
 stability of, 202
 workforce, 47, 71(n31), 71(n32), 72(n62)
Space-based defenses, 157–184
Space Laser Office, 161
Space mines, 169. *See also* Antisatellite capabilities; Mine warfare
Space Shuttle, 161
Space Technology Center, 162
Spain, 423
Speer, Albert, 307
SRF. *See* Strategic Rocket Forces
SS-20 missiles, 235, 241, 245, 250, 260, 406
Stability, 394–395, 431
 in Europe, 397–398
 of Soviet Union, 63, 65
Stalin, Joseph, 11, 47, 55, 56, 61, 237, 273, 354
Standing Consultative Commission (SCC), 207–208, 209
START. *See* Strategic Arms Reduction Talks
Stealth bomber, 28
Stennis, John, 217(n4)
Strategic Air Command (SAC), 226

450

Strategic Arms Limitation Talks (SALT)
  Europe and, 230
  impediments to, 193–210
  negotiation of, 191–192, 213–214, 219(n32), 222(n58), 242, 406
  objectives, 214, 215
  origins of, 186–191, 217(n4), 375
  resistance to, 7, 395
  terms of, 222(n58), 241, 245, 257(n58), 380, 387–388, 406
  verification and, 387, 389
  See also Arms control
Strategic Arms Reduction Talks (START), 193–222, 245, 387, 408, 439
Strategic balance, 5–37, 193–196, 199–201, 214, 215, 229–230, 239, 256(n44), 427, 440
  arms control and, 381
  chemical weapons and, 301, 334
  deterrence and, 250, 251–252, 257(n71), 381, 382–383
  Europe and, 243–246, 289
  NATO and, 401
  PRC and, 144–150
  stability and, 394
Strategic Rocket Forces (SRF), 77, 78
Strategic vulnerabilities, 73(n83), 201–202
  NATO, 240–241, 246–249
  Soviet, 57–76, 82, 112–113(n49), 246–247, 341(n68)
  U.S., 15–16, 18, 22, 23–30, 73(n81), 112(n42), 178, 221(n50)
Strategy of Conflict, 312
Submarine-launched ballistic missiles (SLBMs)
  BMD and, 69
  Soviet, 199–200
  U.S., 25–26, 29, 188
Submarines
  Soviet, 14
  U.S., 18, 25, 26
Support troops, 366, 373(n41)
Supreme Headquarters Allied Powers Europe (SHAPE), 228
Survivors, psychology of, 88–89
Suslov, Mikhail, 288
Sweden, 417
Switzerland, 364, 365, 417

Tactical Air Forces, 265
Taiwan, 118, 119, 123, 124, 136, 143–144, 151(n4)
Talbott, Strobe, 202
Tanks. *See* Armor forces
Taylor, Maxwell D., 42
Team B, 6–7, 33(n8), 33(n11)
Teatry voyennykh deistvii. *See* Theaters of military operations
Technology
  arms control and, 202–204, 205–206, 393–394
  Soviet doctrine and, 267
  transfer of, 67, 241, 344(n88)
Territorial forces, 364–366, 388
Thailand, 122, 130, 151(n9)
Theater Nuclear Forces (TNF), reductions, 404–407, 408
Theaters of military operations, 269
Third World
  influence in, 66–67, 76(n123)
  PRC and, 118, 119, 135–136, 142–143
Throw-weight, defined, 220(n39)

Tinsulanonda, Prem, 151(n9)
TNF. *See* Theater Nuclear Forces
Tomahawk missiles, 29
Training. *See* Military training
Trans-Siberian Railroad, 128, 131, 146
Treaty of Brussels, 226
Triad, 18, 23–28, 59
Trident missiles, 25
Trinkl, F., 101
Trofimenko, Henry, 73(n82)
Troxall, John, 108
Truman, Harry S, 33(n12)
Turco, Richard, 21
Turkey, 272–273
Turner, Frederick, 278, 285
TVD. *See* Theaters of military operations

Ulam, Adam, 92
United Nations, 375
United States
  Asian policy, 121
  Europe and, 413–415, 431–433. *See also* North Atlantic Treaty Organization
  nuclear monopoly, 225, 226–227
  trade relations, 151(n4)
Ustinov, Dmitri, 211, 288

Vance, Cyrus, 197
Van Cleve, William, 33(n8)
Verification, 204–207, 208, 222(n59), 385
  chemical weapons and, 343(n83)
  MBFR and, 392–393, 403
  SALT, 204, 205, 207, 221(n56), 387, 389
Vietnam, 122, 130, 131, 132, 136, 142, 151(n9), 155(n65)
Vigor, Peter, 308
Vogt, John, 33(n8)
Voroshilov Military Academy, 280
Vucinich, Wayne, 279

Wakeford, Ronald, 254(n16)
Warsaw Pact
  air defenses, 358–359
  cohesiveness, 276–289, 292(n8), 294–295(n57), 353, 422
  military capabilities, 230–237
  Soviet munitions and, 338(n14)
Warsaw Treaty, 261
Washington, George, 414
Weinberger, Caspar, 64, 77–78, 121, 161, 162, 163, 164, 259, 260
West Germany. *See* Federal Republic of Germany
Whence the Threat to Peace, 259
White Paper 1979, 428–429
Wimbush, S. Enders, 286
"Window of vulnerability," 5, 24, 33(n2)
Wohlstetter, Albert, 6–7
Wolfe, Thomas W., 33(n8), 240
Wolfowitz, Paul D., 33(n8)
Worner, Manfred, 257(n71)

Yugoslavia, 279, 364, 365

Zablocki, Clement, 344(n89)
Zero option proposal, 244, 406
Zhao Ziyang, 133, 134, 151(n9)
Zhou Enlai, 133
ZOMOs, 294(n55)

8282